THE PROMISE OF LEGALITY

This book assembles critical contributions on the work of TRS Allan, the Professor Emeritus of Jurisprudence and Public Law at the University of Cambridge, whose leading work in legal and constitutional theory spans almost 45 years.

Allan has charted a distinctive path for legal, political, and moral theory and practice and has become a highly significant figure in the UK and in common law/parliamentary systems around the world. His ideas challenge established opinions about constitutional law within these systems as well as established views about the rule of law from more abstract or philosophical perspectives.

Allan claims that law and morality find an inherent connection through the rule of law. He argues that there is a connection that flourishes in common law jurisdictions because although Parliament has sovereign legislative powers, its laws gain their full legal meaning only through an interpretive lens. This lens seeks to reconcile sovereign will with legality's basic moral ideals, especially the idea that law must be general and capable of guiding behaviour and thus respectful of the equality and dignity of its subjects.

Allan's scholarship is powerful yet controversial, and it has inspired 20 leading scholars from the UK, Canada, Australia and New Zealand to engage with the central themes of his work. By doing so, the contributors help to make that work accessible to a new generation of scholars and students. They also provide a timely framework for engaging in the most important challenges facing our democracies today: how our legal systems do, or do not, honour and respect democracy and therefore legislative sovereignty while at the same time honouring and respecting the rule of law, or the 'Promise of Legality'.

The Promise of Legality

Critical Reflections on the Work of TRS Allan

Edited by
Geneviève Cartier
and
Mark D Walters

•HART•
OXFORD • LONDON • NEW YORK • NEW DELHI • SYDNEY

HART PUBLISHING

Bloomsbury Publishing Plc

Kemp House, Chawley Park, Cumnor Hill, Oxford, OX2 9PH, UK

1385 Broadway, New York, NY 10018, USA

Bloomsbury Publishing Ireland Limited, 29 Earlsfort Terrace, Dublin 2, D02 AY28, Ireland

HART PUBLISHING, the Hart/Stag logo, BLOOMSBURY and the Diana logo are trademarks of Bloomsbury Publishing Plc

First published in Great Britain 2025

A catalogue record for this book is available from the British Library.

Library of Congress Cataloging-in-Publication data

Names: Cartier, Geneviève, editor. | Walters, Mark D., 1965- editor.

Title: The promise of legality : critical reflections on the work of TRS Allan / edited by Geneviève Cartier and Mark D. Walters.

Description: Oxford ; New York : Hart Publishing, 2025. | Includes bibliographical references and index. | Summary: "This book assembles critical contributions on the work of T.R.S. Allan, the Professor Emeritus of Jurisprudence and Public Law at the University of Cambridge whose leading work in legal and constitutional theory spans almost 45 years. Allan's scholarship is powerful yet controversial, and it inspired 20 leading scholars from the UK, Canada, Australia and New Zealand to engage with the central themes of his work. By doing so, the contributors help to make that work accessible to a new generation of scholars and students, and provide a timely framework for engaging in the most important challenges facing our democracies today"—Provided by publisher.

Identifiers: LCCN 2024057439 (print) | LCCN 2024057440 (ebook) | ISBN 9781509970957 (hardback) | ISBN 9781509970995 (paperback) | ISBN 9781509970964 (Epub) | ISBN 9781509970971 (pdf)

Subjects: LCSH: Allan, T. R. S. (Trevor R. S.) | Common law. | Public law. | Rule of law. | Constitutional law—Philosophy.

Classification: LCC K588 .P76 2025 (print) | LCC K588 (ebook) | DDC 340.5/7—dc23/eng/20241203

LC record available at https://lccn.loc.gov/2024057439

LC ebook record available at https://lccn.loc.gov/2024057440

ISBN: HB: 978-1-50997-095-7
ePDF: 978-1-50997-097-1
ePub: 978-1-50997-096-4

Typeset by Compuscript Ltd, Shannon

For product safety related questions contact productsafety@bloomsbury.com

To find out more about our authors and books visit www.hartpublishing.co.uk. Here you will find extracts, author information, details of forthcoming events and the option to sign up for our newsletters.

ACKNOWLEDGEMENTS

This volume is the result of a symposium held on 16 and 17 September 2022 in the province of Quebec in Canada, to mark the outstanding contribution of Professor TRS Allan to issues of constitutionalism and the rule of law. Under the theme 'The Promise of Legality: Critical Reflections on the Work of TRS Allan', the symposium brought together 22 academics from Canada, the United Kingdom, Australia and New Zealand. We thank them all for accepting our invitation, for the time they devoted to preparing and revising their texts, and for the fascinating and creative discussions these texts provoked on issues that are more relevant than ever.

The conference would not have been possible without the support of the Social Sciences and Humanities Research Council of Canada, from which we obtained a Connection Grant. Professor David Dyzenhaus and the Faculty of Law of the University of Toronto generously contributed to the funding of the event, as did Professor Evan Fox-Decent and the Canada Research Chair in Cosmopolitan Law and Justice at McGill University, and Professor Mark D Walters and the Faculty of Law of Queen's University. The Faculty of Law of the Université de Sherbrooke provided us with the logistical resources essential to the organisation of the event. We would especially like to thank Annie Bezeau, who supported us through the maze of financial arrangements for the event, as well as David Jobin and Marie-Luce Cheney, for their creative contribution to communications.

Montreal law firm Renno & Vathilakis provided financial support for the event. One of its founding partners, Mr Karim Renno, a graduate of the Sherbrooke and Queen's law faculties, has shown an interest for academic conferences for a number of years. We would like to express our gratitude to him and to all the members of his firm.

Hart Publishing was quick to show an interest in publishing this volume. We thank the publisher, Kate Whetter, for her advice and patience, and Verity Stuart, assistant editor, for her diligent support. Our research assistants, Charlotte Paniccia and Ariane Duguay provided substantial help in revising the footnotes.

The conference that led to this volume was held at an inn on Lake Massawippi in Quebec, and we wish to thank the Musée national des beaux-arts du Québec for giving us permission to use an image of John Lyman's painting, 'La cabane rouge au lac Massawippi' (1945), for the cover of the book.

Our deepest gratitude goes to our colleague and friend Trevor, for the remarkable and fascinating work he has built up over many years, for agreeing to take part in the symposium, and for leaving us a work that will generate discussion for years to come.

Geneviève Cartier
Mark D Walters

CONTENTS

LIST OF CONTRIBUTORS

Thomas Adams is Associate Professor of Law at the Faculty of Law and Tutorial Fellow at St Catherine's College, University of Oxford.

TRS Allan is Professor Emeritus of Jurisprudence and Public Law, University of Cambridge, and Fellow of Pembroke College, Cambridge.

Peter Cane is Emeritus Professor of Law at the Australian National University and Honorary Professor of Law at the University of Sydney.

Geneviève Cartier is Professor of Law at the Université de Sherbrooke.

Paul Craig is Emeritus Professor of English Law at St John's College, University of Oxford.

Paul Daly is University Research Chair in Administrative Law and Governance at the University of Ottawa.

Hasan Dindjer is Associate Professor of Law at the Faculty of Law and the Blanesburgh Fellow and Tutor in Law at Balliol College, University of Oxford.

David Dyzenhaus is University Professor of Law and Philosophy and Albert Abel Chair at the University of Toronto.

Michael Foran is Lecturer in Public Law at the School of Law of the University of Glasgow.

Evan Fox-Decent is Professor of Law and Canada Research Chair in Cosmopolitan Law and Justice at McGill University.

Jeffrey Goldsworthy is Emeritus Professor of Law at Monash University, Professorial Fellow at the University of Melbourne, and Adjunct Professor at the University of Adelaide.

Stuart Lakin is Associate Professor of Law at the School of Law of the University of Reading.

Joanna Langille is Assistant Professor at the Faculty of Law of the University of Western Ontario.

George Letsas is Professor of the Philosophy of Law at the Faculty of Laws of University College London.

Matthew Lewans is Professor of Law and TC Energy Chair in Administrative and Regulatory Law at the Faculty of Law of the University of Alberta.

Janet McLean is Professor of Law at the Law School of the University of Auckland.

Hillary Nye is Associate Professor of Law at the Faculty of Law of the University of Alberta.

Richard Stacey is Associate Professor of Law at the Faculty of Law of the University of Toronto.

Christine Sypnowich is Professor of Philosophy, cross-appointed to the Faculty of Law, and Queen's National Scholar at Queen's University.

Mark D Walters is Professor of Law at the Faculty of Law of Queen's University.

Jacob Weinrib is Associate Professor of Law at the Faculty of Law of Queen's University.

Alison L Young is the Sir David Williams Professor of Public Law at the Faculty of Law and Fellow of Robinson College, University of Cambridge.

Han-Ru Zhou is Associate Professor of Law at the Faculty of Law of the Université de Montréal, and Associate Research Fellow at the Institute of Commonwealth Studies, School of Advanced Study, University of London.

Introduction: The Promise and Spirit of Legality

GENEVIÈVE CARTIER AND MARK D WALTERS

1. Introduction

The chapters in this book critically examine the work of TRS Allan on the rule of law and constitutionalism. Trevor Allan has been writing on these topics for some 40 years, and for almost all of this time he has been based at the University of Cambridge in the United Kingdom. However, the essays in this volume were presented at a conference held in an inn located in Ayer's Cliff, a village at the south end of Lake Massawippi in the Eastern Townships of the province of Quebec in Canada. The cover of this book is a painting of Lake Massawippi by John Lyman.[1]

As organisers of this conference and editors of this volume, our objective was to bring Trevor into a conversation with scholars of varying backgrounds and perspectives who share with him a commitment to the ideals of legality and constitutionalism. We selected our home ground as the place for this conversation, but not only for self-interested reasons. We thought that de-centring the conversation about Trevor's work from its obvious British orientations was important in part because of Trevor's own scholarly ambitions.

Trevor's work explores general jurisprudence through examining the theory and practice of constitutionalism within the common law tradition wherever its legacy is felt. As he wrote in his 2001 book, *Constitutional Justice*, the commitment to the rule of law forms a 'natural unity' between common law jurisdictions, and, despite the different written constitutional instruments they may have adopted, these jurisdictions '*share* a common constitution.'[2] 'Beneath and beyond' constitutional enactments found in different countries, Trevor wrote in 2017, 'lies a *common law constitution* – a set of ideas and assumptions about the nature and conditions of legality, which, in turn, define the character of legitimate government.'[3] For Trevor, the common law tradition manifests

[1] J Lyman, 'La cabane rouge au lac Massawippi' (1945), Collection du Musée national des beaux-arts du Québec (1970.515).

[2] TRS Allan, *Constitutional Justice: A Liberal Theory of the Rule of Law* (Oxford, Oxford University Press, 2001) 4–5.

[3] TRS Allan, 'The Moral Unity of Public Law' (2017) 67 *University of Toronto Law Journal* 1, 1.

the rule of law in a particular way; however, he also thinks there is a broader unity of constitutionalism underlying all liberal democracies.[4]

Trevor's effort to link constitutional fundamentals across different peoples and places is controversial. Yet we think there is value in understanding constitutionalism as interpretive practices within a shared tradition. For example, in a leading Canadian case on the rule of law, *Roncarelli v Duplessis*, an action for damages against the prime minister of Quebec for abuse of discretion, Justice Ivan Rand can be seen to have interpreted statutory powers within what the famous British constitutional scholar, AV Dicey, called the 'spirit of legality' in a way that exemplifies common law constitutionalism – and this despite the fact that the action was brought under Quebec's civil code.[5] The case shows the broad interpretive horizon that Trevor's work imagines. We also note that papers examining *Roncarelli v Duplessis*, in which Trevor's work was duly cited, were presented in 2009 at a conference held in a village located at the north end of Lake Massawippi.[6] There is, it seems, something in the waters of this lake.

That Trevor would one day find himself confronted by admirers and critics on the shores of a Canadian lake in a French-speaking province would have been a surprise to him when he began his academic career. Trevor Robert Seaward Allan was educated at St. Albans School in Hertfordshire and he read law at Worcester College, Oxford, where he received a BA and a BCL. Although he was called to the Bar as a member of Middle Temple, Trevor Allan was and remains a legal scholar *par excellence*. He began his academic career as a lecturer in law at the University of Nottingham before moving to the University of Cambridge where he became a fellow of Pembroke College and was later appointed Professor of Jurisprudence and Public Law. In recognition of his achievements, he has been elected a Fellow of the British Academy and awarded an honorary LLD by the University of Cambridge.

Our objective in this Introduction is to provide a brief overview of Trevor Allan's distinctive approach to the rule of law and constitutionalism. This overview sets the stage for the chapters in this volume that explore Trevor's contributions in much greater detail. In the final chapter of this book, Trevor offers thoughtful responses to each contribution – a testament to his respect for the work of others but also to his enduring passion for a good argument.[7]

[4] eg, on Germany and German *Rechtsstaat*, TRS Allan, 'The Rule of Law' in D Dyzenhaus and M Thorburn (eds), *Philosophical Foundations of Constitutional Law* (Oxford, Oxford University Press, 2016) 204.

[5] *Roncarelli v Duplessis* [1959] SCR 121. Counsel for the plaintiff, the law professor FR Scott, later said that he simply delivered his law school lecture on Dicey to the court: S Djwa, *The Politics of the Imagination: A Life of FR Scott* (Toronto, McClelland & Stewart, 1987) 308, 311. On the 'spirit of legality', see AV Dicey, *Introduction to the Study of the Law of the Constitution*, 8th edn (London, Macmillan, 1915) 409.

[6] G Cartier (ed), 'Special Issue: The Legacy of Roncarelli v. Duplessis, 1959–2009' (2010) 55 *McGill Law Journal*.

[7] The chapters in this book were presented at a conference held on 16–17 September 2022 at Ayer's Cliff, Quebec, at which Trevor Allan had the opportunity to respond. Authors revised their papers for publication in light of the conference discussions. Trevor then read the revised papers in preparing the response that appears in this volume. We felt it was appropriate on this occasion to give Trevor the final word on the many debates arising from the original and revised papers.

2. Interpretive Form and Substance

We begin not with content but with style. There is something special about Trevor's style of writing. We give as an example a passage from his recent essay, 'Why the Law is What it Ought to Be':

> It is widely supposed by lawyers and legal theorists alike that the law, as it is understood and applied in practice, falls short of what it ought to be. It falls short in the sense of being morally deficient, failing to match the standards of justice or political morality by which it must be measured. If, however, we often disagree about what those standards require, at least in particular cases or contexts, the law may provide a legitimate basis for governance, capable of eliciting our support in spite of its many imperfections. When the necessary conditions are met, the law is in an important sense what it ought to be. The law's content may diverge from what each of us may in our private capacities consider that justice, ideally conceived, would ordain. But we should nonetheless accept the law's demands in our public capacities as members of the political community, allowing it to determine disputes between people whose moral and political disagreements extend far beyond the specific issues immediately in point. While we must not abandon our moral ideals, as external critics, we may nevertheless be morally required to obey the law as it is correctly interpreted – consistently with the principles that underpin its legitimacy. If, moreover, those principles determine the lawful exercise of official state power, defining basic rights of persons against improper coercive interference, the law is what it ought to be.[8]

In this passage, Trevor moves briskly from the reality that we often disagree about whether law is just or unjust to the conclusion that law is as it ought to be. The argument consists of efficient statements expressed with confidence, each of which Trevor assumes we will accept – and it is hard not to accept them. However, by the end of the paragraph we find ourselves agreeing with something with which we did not expect to agree, and we are then left wondering whether we really do agree. This is the magic of Trevor's method.

Trevor has said that he sometimes composes his work at an empty table on plain, lined paper using a sharp pencil. We picture him, books having been read and ideas having been formed, crafting crisp sentences in order, one by one, into paragraphs and then full and flowing narratives. But we imagine that the books – law reports, legal commentaries, works of jurisprudence and political theory – must still be close at hand. Trevor's writing engages with a vast range of sources. His treatment of the judges and scholars whose contributions have shaped the tradition of legality is careful and never rushed. Let's pause, Trevor seems to say, to consider, for example, Dicey or Hayek or Fuller; let's take time to explore, for example, the significance of the reasoning of the House of Lords in *Anisminic* or the Australian High Court in *Kable*. The pencil fills the page with methodical purpose, moving back and forth between practical examples and broader principles to build out a compelling story about governance and equal liberty under the rule of law.

A consideration of Trevor's work glides easily from form to substance because the two are for him inseparable. If his own work involves oscillating between specific examples

[8] TRS Allan, 'Why the Law is What it Ought to Be' (2020) 11 *Jurisprudence* 574, 574.

and larger theories in search of principled coherence, this is because in his view this is what the good common lawyer does and what the ideal of legality demands. The heart of Trevor's account of the rule of law and constitutionalism is a distinctive *interpretivist* theory of law. 'According to the interpretative account of law and legal practice I am defending,' he wrote in 2013, 'the rule of law is not merely an ideal or aspiration *external* to the law … It is a value internal to law itself'.[9] The task of interpreting law is a quest for a form of principled consistency in the interests of the constitutional equality of persons, one generated by the demands of legality itself rather than some higher law. Through adopting 'an interpretative or hermeneutic approach', he said in 2018, we recognise that law is always 'a matter of moral construction' and our moral obligation to obey the law arises because it represents 'our current collective understanding of justice – the scheme of justice implicit in our practice, grounded in a fundamental commitment to the equal dignity of all'.[10]

Trevor's rule of law promotes individual liberty and moral agency or 'freedom as independence'[11] and is thus a form of 'individualistic' or 'liberal constitutionalism'.[12] However, the rule of law, on Trevor's account, 'is compatible with many rival accounts of social justice' and 'with a variety of liberalisms'.[13] One wonders, though, whether certain forms of libertarianism are ruled out. The long passage quoted above assumes that individuals will participate in the interpretive tradition in their 'public' rather than 'private' capacities; Trevor's liberal constitutionalism builds upon the 'republican tradition of political thought'[14] and emphasises a thick sense of 'political community'[15] and 'common good'.[16]

Individuals in Trevor's view are not atomistic but civic-minded; they have rights against but also obligations to the community. Although Trevor's rule of law protects non-citizens,[17] it places a special accent on 'equal citizenship'.[18] The interpretivist project he contemplates requires 'collaboration' and 'moral dialogue' between participants in a shared tradition or practice,[19] and so it imagines forms of civic engagement that embrace broad notions of 'public reason' consistent with the values of 'deliberative democracy'.[20] For Trevor, the rule of law is a 'rule of reason',[21] and the reasons needed

[9] TRS Allan, *The Sovereignty of Law: Freedom, Constitution, and Common Law* (Oxford, Oxford University Press, 2013) 88.

[10] TRS Allan 'Principle, Practice, and Precedent: Vindicating Justice, According to Law' (2018) 77 *CLJ* 269, 275.

[11] Allan, *Sovereignty of Law* (n 9) 96.

[12] TRS Allan, 'Legislative Supremacy and the Rule of Law: Democracy and Constitutionalism' (1985) 44 *CLJ* 111, 119; TRS Allan, 'Citizenship and Obligation: Civil Disobedience and Civil Dissent' (1996) 55 *CLJ* 89, 91; TRS Allan, *Law, Liberty, and Justice: The Legal Foundations of British Constitutionalism* (Oxford, Clarendon Press, 1993) 3.

[13] TRS Allan, 'The Rule of Law as the Rule of Reason: Consent and Constitutionalism' (1999) 115 *LQR* 221, 224.

[14] Allan, *Sovereignty of Law* (n 9) 32. See also Allan, 'The Rule of Law' (n 4) 205.

[15] TRS Allan, 'Law as a Branch of Morality: The Unity of Practice and Principle' (2020) 65 *American Journal of Jurisprudence* 1, 5, 10.

[16] Allan, *Constitutional Justice* (n 2) 22.

[17] Allan, *Sovereignty of Law* (n 9) 93.

[18] Allan, 'The Rule of Law as the Rule of Reason' (n 13) 231; Allan, *Sovereignty of Law* (n 9) 32, 92.

[19] TRS Allan, 'Interpretation, Injustice, and Integrity' (2016) 36 *OJLS* 58, 82.

[20] Allan, *Constitutional Justice* (n 2) 287; TRS Allan, 'Text, Context, and Constitution: The Common Law as Public Reason' in DE Edlin (ed), *Common Law Theory* (Cambridge, Cambridge University Press, 2007) 201.

[21] Allan, 'The Rule of Law as the Rule of Reason' (n 13); Allan, *Constitutional Justice* (n 2) 2.

for any interpretation of law must make moral sense in light of the tradition or practice being interpreted, and especially the scheme of justice underlying the law; the duty to provide reasons that will make sense to other participants within the tradition falls not just upon judges or officials but each member of the community when advancing their own views of the law or deciding what legal obligations they confront in any given situation.

Trevor's legal interpretivism shares some key features of Ronald Dworkin's theory of 'law as integrity', including a commitment to the inherent link between law and morality through interpretation and a disdain for schools of legal positivism that deny this link.[22] Says Trevor, 'Ronald Dworkin's theory of law as "integrity" encapsulates the essential features of the rule of law, interpreted as a theory of constitutionalism'.[23]

However, we think that there are good reasons to believe that Trevor developed his basic approach to interpretation independently of Dworkin in the very early years of his academic career and that the work of Lon Fuller may have had a more profound impact on the development of his ideas. Furthermore, Trevor departs from – or rather corrects – Dworkin's theory of law as integrity in important ways. Indeed, an exploration of Trevor's critique of Dworkin is an effective way of bringing to the surface the principal features of Trevor Allan's theory of the rule of law – which we proceed to do in the next section.

3. Legality, Equality, and Integrity

The interpretive approach to legality is implicitly at work in Trevor's very first publication in 1983. In this article, Trevor argued that the positivist understanding of law as grounded in a foundational 'political fact', 'rule of recognition', or 'grundnorm', obscures how the legal principle of parliamentary sovereignty may evolve through 'interpretation' rather than 'revolution' to accommodate the supremacy of European Community law within the United Kingdom.[24] Trevor was reading Dworkin's work at this time, but had not yet invoked his theory of interpretation.[25] Two essays Trevor wrote in 1985, when he was still a young lecturer at Nottingham, show that the ideas he would defend during the next 40 years were formed early in his career, though details were still developing.

In 'Legislative Supremacy and the Rule of Law', Trevor cited Dworkin to identify a 'problem', the tension between human rights and democracy, but he did not invoke Dworkin when he laid out his solution to this problem.[26] At the time, arguments for a written bill of rights in Britain were mounting. Trevor argued that before this question could be considered, it was necessary to be clear about how the common law, properly interpreted, already protected rights. In developing this idea, Trevor introduced authors and arguments that he would return to time and again during the following decades.

[22] eg, R Dworkin, *Law's Empire* (Cambridge, Belknap Press, 1986).
[23] Allan, 'The Rule of Law as the Rule of Reason' (n 13) 232.
[24] TRS Allan, 'Parliamentary Sovereignty: Lord Denning's Dexterous Revolution' (1983) 3 *OJLS* 22.
[25] eg TRS Allan, 'A Right to Pornography' (1983) 3 *OJLS* 376.
[26] Allan, 'Legislative Supremacy' (n 12) 111, citing R Dworkin, *Taking Rights Seriously* (Cambridge, Harvard University Press, 1977).

AV Dicey takes centre stage, initially as both villain and hero – but in the end hero. Dicey's rule of law was resurrected to counterbalance his parliamentary sovereignty. 'Dicey's attempt to reconcile his two fundamental principles was', Trevor wrote, 'not as lame as has sometimes been asserted'.[27] The positivist reading of the rule of law as formal or procedural by Joseph Raz was denounced by Trevor in favour of a richer version of legality – a critique of Raz that Trevor would deepen over the years.[28] The relationship between law's generality on the one hand and the values of equality and freedom on the other was introduced though the work of FA Hayek.[29] There was the beginning of the idea that the rule of law implies a reciprocal relationship between ruler and subject requiring law's justification according to fundamental moral principles. Trevor would later invoke Fuller in making this idea central to his account of the rule of law.[30] But on this occasion he cited JR Lucas.[31]

Fuller was cited in the article, but for a different set of ideas. Fuller, not Dworkin, seems to have been an inspiration for the interpretive understanding of law. Referencing Fuller's 1968 book, *Anatomy of Law*, Trevor made a series of points about what he would soon call '*common law constitutionalism*'[32] (emphasis added) centered around the interpretive integration of legislative meaning and common law rights. Trevor would develop these ideas in the years to come, insisting that the British constitution 'is a multi-faceted creature of common law thought, rooted in fundamental moral values'.[33] His work would explore how 'the Rule of Law' and '(common law) constitutionalism' are, in effect, equivalents.[34]

The second 1985 article, 'Limits of Parliamentary Sovereignty', suggests that Trevor's ideas were evolving quickly.[35] In this article, Trevor linked legal interpretation to Dworkin's claim that 'community morality is the political morality presupposed by the laws and institutions of the community'.[36] He then argued that parliamentary sovereignty is a legal principle that presupposes a particular political morality that embraces not just democracy but the rule of law. Trevor returned to Dicey's account of the rule of law and now placed emphasis on his point about 'equality before the law', and, citing Dworkin, said that one of its consequences is 'a deeper conception of the equality of citizens' that forms the basis of democracy as well as civil and political liberties.[37] Trevor

[27] Allan, 'Legislative Supremacy' (n 12) 143.

[28] eg Allan, *Law, Liberty, and Justice* (n 12) 23; Allan, *Constitutional Justice* (n 2) 37–39; Allan, *Sovereignty of Law* (n 9) 110–11. Trevor's target is J Raz, 'The Rule of Law and its Virtue' (1977) 93 *LQR* 195.

[29] Allan, 'Legislative Supremacy' (n 12) 113, invoking FA Hayek, *The Constitution of Liberty* (Chicago, Chicago University Press, 1960) 153.

[30] eg Allan, *Constitutional Justice* (n 2) 52–59.

[31] Allan, 'Legislative Supremacy' (n 12) 125 invoking JR Lucas, *The Principles of Politics* (Oxford, Clarendon Press, 1966) 107.

[32] TRS Allan, 'Constitutional Rights and Common Law' (1991) 11 *OJLS* 453, 472, 478.

[33] Allan, *Sovereignty of Law* (n 9) 135.

[34] Allan, 'Constitutional Rights' (n 32) 478. For other examples of Trevor's discussions of common law constitutionalism, see Allan, *Law, Liberty, and Justice* (n 12) 4, 10–16; Allan, *Constitutional Justice* (n 2) 243–281; TRS Allan, 'Text, Context, and Constitution' (n 20) 185; TRS Allan, 'In Defense of the Common Law Constitution: Unwritten Rights as Fundamental Law' (2009) 22 *Canadian Journal of Law & Jurisprudence* 187; Allan, 'Moral Unity of Public Law' (n 3); TRS Allan, 'Constitutionalism at Common Law: The Rule of Law and Judicial Review' (2023) 82 *CLJ* 236.

[35] TRS Allan, 'The Limits of Parliamentary Sovereignty' [1985] *PL* 614.

[36] ibid 615 (citing Dworkin, *Taking Rights Seriously* (n 26) 126).

[37] ibid 629.

then concluded that, despite the superficial tension between parliamentary sovereignty and the rule of law, 'Dicey's account finally suggests the correct solution': 'The limits of the sovereignty of Parliament are to be discovered … in that deeper constitutional morality from which the rule of law derives its power and strength'; the more an Act of Parliament appears to invade this constitutional morality, the more 'interpretation' will blend into 'non-application' of the statute so that injustice is avoided.[38] In making these points, Trevor cited for the first time a set of ideas that would, in many ways, come to dominate his legal thought: Fuller's 'internal morality of the law'.[39]

Reading Dworkin's *Law's Empire*, published the following year, seems to have been a watershed moment for Trevor. Trevor was riveted by Dworkin's idea of 'integrity' – that integrity demands fidelity not just to rules but to the theories of fairness and justice which the rules presuppose. The link that Dworkin made between this idea and 'equality before the law' opened up for Trevor new ways of reading Dicey's classic account of the British constitution, leading him to conclude that both Dworkin and Dicey reject a 'merely procedural account of the Rule of Law'.[40] Trevor concluded that 'Dworkin's enterprise, though more sophisticated, is essentially similar to Dicey's', and that 'Law as Integrity offers a complex and sophisticated interpretation of the Rule of Law'.[41]

These early articles suggest that the interpretivist account of legality was understood by Trevor not as a theory imposed from outside but as inherent within common law method. Law's authority arises, on this view, through an interpretation of extant cases that show them to hold together in a coherent way in light of a theory of their animating principles of political morality that secures the equal dignity of each person. Wrote Trevor, 'The common law provides a model of the thorough-going rationality envisaged by the constitutional conception of the rule of law'.[42] 'I follow Dworkin,' he said, 'in making the common law the central focus of my general account of law'.[43] In our view, however, it was less the case that Trevor was following Dworkin and more that he and Dworkin were both following their own paths toward accounts of legality that build upon ideas largely implicit within the common law tradition.

Although the impact of Dworkin is clear, it is hard to imagine Trevor's theory of legalism and constitutionalism today without the influence of Fuller. Over the years, Trevor has woven into his interpretivist account of the rule of law Fuller's basic insights, exploring how the forms or inner morality of law – law's generality, intelligibility, prospectivity, consistency, etc. – ground a substantive vision of justice centered upon a reciprocal relationship between the lawgiver and the subject as a morally autonomous agent for whom laws are always capable of drawing moral allegiance. In this sense, the rule of law is a 'rule of reason' or 'discourse of reason' that builds moral legitimacy into law such that every law may be justified for every person as the pursuit of an understanding of the

[38] ibid 617.
[39] ibid 623, citing LL Fuller, 'Positivism and Fidelity to Law – A Reply to Professor Hart' (1958) 71 *Harvard Law Review* 630, 648–57 and LL Fuller, *The Morality of Law* (New Haven, Yale University Press, 1964).
[40] TRS Allan, 'Dworkin and Dicey: The Rule of Law as Integrity' (1988) 8 *OJLS* 266, 267.
[41] ibid 267, 276.
[42] Allan, 'The Rule of Law as the Rule of Reason' (n 13) 241.
[43] Allan, 'Interpretation, Injustice, and Integrity' (n 19) 60 fn 12.

common good consistent with their equal moral worth.[44] For Trevor, the final decision about what the law means is always a question of morality and never fact or fiat, and so there can be no final arbiter whose will determines what the law is; the responsibility to interpret law lies with each of us acting collaboratively in our public capacities within the shared practice that establishes the moral authority of law.[45]

As Trevor began to fill in these points about the rule of law, his initial enthusiasm for Dworkin's interpretivism gave way to a more critical perspective. Although Trevor commended Dworkin for his explication of integrity, he condemned him for failing to follow through on its true promise.[46] The problem for Trevor arises from 'Dworkin's *via media* between positivism and natural law'.[47] Said Trevor, '[Dworkin's] chosen path between legal positivism, on one side, and a more robust natural law stance, on the other, looks quite unstable'.[48] Dworkin ends up making 'concessions to legal positivism'[49] that are 'at war with his larger vision'.[50] In particular, Dworkin insisted that interpretation must, to ensure that it does not lapse into invention, have a dimension of both technical fit and moral justification: proposed interpretations that may commend themselves on grounds of morality will be ruled out by the 'brute facts of legal history' if they do not 'fit' extant sources of law.[51] Sometimes only wicked laws will survive integrity's requirement of fit.[52]

None of this makes sense to Trevor. In his view, the virtue of integrity, once accepted, can never be in conflict with a substantive theory of justice that grasps the fundamental equal moral worth of each person: 'Fundamental conflicts between law and justice are already ruled out by integrity itself: they are excluded by the basic requirement of equal concern'.[53] Dworkin had fallen back on legal positivism by permitting law as 'brute fact' to control the outer bounds of integrity's interpretive potential. This method of addressing the concern that interpretation may improperly become invention is, in Trevor's view, unnecessary. So long as the interpreter enters upon the task of interpretation with a sincere commitment to engage with the tradition or practice in good faith, then questions of fit and justification will blend together to be considered as a seamless part of the moral-legal analysis. From this perspective, an interpretation denying the status of 'law' to a gravely unjust statute can never be ruled out. This conclusion may not, at first

[44] See especially Allan, 'The Rule of Law as the Rule of Reason' (n 13) 235–236; Allan, *Constitutional Justice* (n 2) 2; Allan, *Sovereignty of Law* (n 9) 42, 110–112; and Allan, 'Constitutionalism at Common Law' (n 34) 239.

[45] Allan, 'Constitutionalism at Common Law' (n 34) 238.

[46] Arguments critical of Dworkin are found in: TRS Allan, 'Justice and Fairness in Law's Empire' (1993) 52 *CLJ* 64; Allan, *Law, Liberty, and Justice* (n 12) 130–134; TRS Allan, 'Law, Justice and Integrity: The Paradox of Wicked Laws' (2009) 29 *OJLS* 705; Allan, *Sovereignty of Law* (n 9) 162–166; Allan, 'Interpretation, Injustice, and Integrity' (n 19); Allan, 'Principle, Practice, and Precedent' (n 10) 271–277; Allan, 'Law as a Branch of Morality' (n 15) 11–12; Allan, 'Why the Law is What it Ought to Be' (n 8); TRS Allan, 'The Law in Quest of Integrity: Interpretation, Invention and Internal Critique' in T Bustamante and M Martin (eds), *New Essays on the Fish-Dworkin Debate* (Oxford, Hart Publishing, 2023) 119.

[47] Allan, 'Interpretation, Injustice, and Integrity' (n 19) 66.

[48] Allan, 'Law in Quest of Integrity' (n 46) 210.

[49] Allan, *Sovereignty of Law* (n 9) 162.

[50] Allan, 'Why the Law is What It Ought to Be' (n 8) 575.

[51] Dworkin, *Law's Empire* (n 22) 255.

[52] ibid 219.

[53] Allan, 'Paradox of Wicked Laws' (n 46) 712.

glance, fit with existing law in the British tradition when considered as a matter of fact; however, once 'the doctrine of legislative supremacy [is seen] as itself a rule of common law' capable of reinterpretation at its margins in the face of unusual or new circumstances, then, Trevor insists, the decision that an unjust statute is not a law will cohere with the rest of the law in just the way that integrity demands.[54]

Trevor's rule of law embraces a much richer conception of integrity than Dworkin's. What is the difference? Trevor includes within his theory of legality an insight that Dworkin either missed or misunderstood, namely, the Fullerian insight that equal concern and respect is not just a moral principle that guides legal interpretation, but it is integrated into the inner morality of law's essential formation or structure; the virtue of integrity is captured by the principles of legality (generality, prospectivity, intelligibility, etc.) that make law legally possible, and its negation in a purported law makes that law legally impossible.[55] Although he says that he wishes 'to rescue a "natural law" understanding of the common law from Dworkin's errors',[56] Trevor's natural law is internal and integral rather than external and separate from ordinary law and ordinary legal method. Perhaps one of Trevor's greatest contributions to legal philosophy, then, is to integrate Dworkinian and Fullerian insights into a morally rich theory of the rule of law.

4. Conclusion

Trevor concludes that Dworkin redeemed himself, at least in part, by insisting in his last major work, *Justice for Hedgehogs*, that law and morality form parts of a single, unified normative discourse.[57] In his own work over the course of the last 40 years, Trevor has never flinched from the view of law as fully integrated into the morality that animates human flourishing. Trevor does not simply say law and morality overlap or intertwine. Rather he says that as an interpretive discourse law is itself a moral discourse – that '[l]egal judgment is moral judgment in which doctrinal legal argument serves to focus the moral dialogue, making every question of law, in the final analysis, a matter of interpretation of the larger scheme of justice in which it arises'.[58]

From this position, Trevor has been able to offer distinctive contributions to debates about public law and theory within the common law world. Invariably his arguments reject artificial binaries that tend to dominate legal and jurisprudential debate. There is no divide, in Trevor's world, between legal theory and legal practice, between law's meaning and law's application. There is no divide between administrative law and

[54] Allan, 'Justice and Fairness in Law's Empire' (n 46) 86.

[55] On how Dworkin's approach to unjust laws fails because of his failure to accept Fuller's insight, see D Dyzenhaus, 'Dworkin and Unjust Law' in W Waluchow and S Sciaraffa (eds), *The Legacy of Ronald Dworkin* (Oxford, Oxford University Press, 2016) 131, 153–159; D Dyzenhaus, *The Long Arc of Legality: Hobbes, Kelsen, Hart* (Cambridge, Cambridge University Press, 2022) 17–19.

[56] Allan, 'Interpretation, Injustice, and Integrity' (n 19) 60.

[57] Allan, 'Law as a Branch of Morality' (n 15) 17. See R Dworkin, *Justice for Hedgehogs* (Cambridge, Harvard University Press, 2011). Yet Trevor remains concerned about Dworkin's treatment of unjust laws at *Justice for Hedgehogs*, 410–411; Allan, *Sovereignty of Law* (n 9) 164; Allan, 'Principle, Practice, and Precedent' (n 10) 272; Allan, 'Law in Quest of Integrity' (n 46) at 122.

[58] Allan, 'Moral Unity of Public Law' (n 3) 6.

constitutional law, and as a result the divide between the so-called ultra vires and common law schools of judicial review of administrative action is sterile and shallow. There is no real divide between common law systems that have and those that do not have written human rights guarantees, and so the distinction between striking down legislation as invalid and restrictive interpretation to avoid injustice is one of degree not kind. From Trevor's distinctive vantage point for legality, distinctive positions in relation to these and other hard legal questions emerge. The chapters in this volume explore examples in careful and critical detail.

We close by returning to a point that, in many ways, defines Trevor and his work: his insistence that moral and legal integrity must align with personal integrity, the personal integrity that all of us should seek to embrace in our lives. We believe that Trevor's work is compelling precisely because his pencil fills the page with a narrative premised upon a deep and abiding sense of personal integrity. Trevor's legal arguments would not be the same otherwise.

We know Trevor as someone who was passionate about theatre in his undergraduate days, as someone who continues to develop his skills as an accomplished pianist, and as someone who finds meaning in the beauty of the hills, valleys, rivers, and waterfalls of the British Isles. We see in his work a creative vision that celebrates the grandeur of law and the possibilities for the flourishing of individual and collective human good, someone who sees promise in the human condition in large part because he believes in the promise of legality. Indeed, there are few legal scholars who match his uncompromising faith in the rule of law and the capacity of people – everyone, all of us – to engage as active participants in the discourse of reason essential for liberty, equality, and public good. As we write today, the belief in the value of constitutionalism and the commitment to human decency it requires appear to be under threat in many parts of the world. Trevor's work demands our attention now more than ever.

PART I

Allan, Dworkin, Dicey

1

TRS Allan and the Common Law Tradition

PETER CANE

It is a great honour and an even greater pleasure to have been invited to join this celebration of the scholarship of our dear friend. I have known Trevor Allan for many years and have enjoyed more stimulating intellectual exchanges with him than I deserve or can count. Trevor is widely acknowledged as the leading theorist of what has come to be called 'the common law constitution'. Trevor's theory is multi-faceted, rich, and complex. The main aim of this chapter is to locate Trevor's distinctive vision within a larger context of thinking about the constitution in what is now sometimes referred to as 'the common law tradition'. Its surprising conclusion is that Trevor's vision owes little to traditional conceptions of the common law.

1. The Common Law Tradition

A tradition is a story we tell ourselves about the past. There is no one, correct way of telling the story of the common law tradition. My broad-brush telling will reveal four different strands in that tradition: the common law as a set of institutions and processes; the common law as a set of norms; the common law as the guardian of individuals' civil and political rights; and the common law as a method or mode of reasoning (as opposed to an assertion of will).

A. The Common Law as Institution and Process

The England that William successfully invaded in 1066 was probably the most highly centralised and governmentally sophisticated polity in Europe at that time. It possessed a dense network of local institutions, involved in keeping the peace and regulating social and economic life, the operation of which was underpinned by a set of norms – rules, principles, conventions, customs and so on, some of which might have been documented but many of which were not. Because the conquered were many and well-organised, and the conquerors were few and, initially, strongly resisted, the Normans made the wise decision to leave local institutions and norms largely untouched and to focus on those matters that were of most significance for their long-term success, notably creating and maintaining social order and stability, and regulating ownership and use of the most important form of wealth and source of power – real property.

Besides brute force and political manoeuvring, perhaps the most significant of the Normans' tools of government and polity-building was dispute settlement. Amongst local government institutions in pre-Conquest England were meetings in which powerful landowners exercised 'jurisdiction', which was conceptualised as a form of property right. Inevitably, exercises of local jurisdiction could be a cause of dissatisfaction. The Norman kings seized this opportunity by providing, effectively, a system of appeals underwritten by monarchical force and a royal claim to be the ultimate source of all property rights, including jurisdiction: the right and power to adjudicate was claimed as a royal prerogative over all subjects, from the least to the greatest. Royal justice was administered by the king personally or by royal officials, at first on an itinerant basis, moving around as part of the royal entourage. By the thirteenth century, itinerant royal justice was supplemented by courts permanently located at Westminster. This helped to secure for the justices a degree of day-to-day independence from the monarch. The royal courts became very popular, and gradually local justice was replaced, in many contexts, by central justice. The common law – a system of courts and adjudication covering ('common to') the whole realm – was born.

By this stage, jury trial was firmly established. At first, the basic task of the judge was to decide whether or not there was a case to be put to the jury; and, if so, what questions the jury had to answer. At first, too, the questions put to the jury would relate to both 'law' and 'fact', as we now call them. No sharp distinction was drawn between the two. The modern distinction developed gradually as a technique for withholding certain issues from the jury: issues for the judge to decide were classified as 'legal' and issues for the jury to decide as 'factual'. The use of juries, not judges, to decide cases in royal courts was underpinned by the idea that justice was an aspect of the life of the community of which members of the community were the best judges. Jurors would know the relevant facts from personal experience; and they would understand the local customary norms relevant to resolving the case.

By the mid-thirteenth century, then, two of the elements of the common law tradition were in place: a cadre of judges and a trial process managed by them. In other words, the common law existed as institution and process.

B. The Common Law as Norms

In addition to the exercise of jurisdiction through adjudication, the government toolbox also contained what we now call legislation – the making of general rules. Like adjudicating, legislating was claimed as a royal prerogative; and, at first, it was rarely exercised. In time, Parliament (the Lords Temporal and Spiritual, and the Commons as virtual representatives of the people) became involved in legislating by advising the monarch and giving or withholding consent to royal legislative proposals. Henry VIII was, perhaps, the first monarch seriously to exploit the potential of Parliamentary legislation as a device for legitimating royal policy. As a result of the upheavals of the seventeenth century, the royal prerogatives of both legislation and adjudication were greatly curtailed. One of the weapons used by opponents of royal power, especially Sir Edward Coke, against the royal prerogative of adjudication was the idea of 'ancient constitution' – 'constitution' here referring to the socio-political system, not to written documents.[1] Adjudication, it was argued, involved the resolution of individual cases according to the common law of the realm. This law was the product of centuries of social development stretching back before the Conquest. The idea of the common law as a set of norms may be associated with the development of the distinction between law and fact. Coke argued that rightful guardianship of this common law and of the ancient constitution belonged to the royal justices, not the monarch. Being unlearned in the law, the king could not understand its 'artificial reason' or discern its justice.[2] Coke, it seems, went even further claiming that legislation, like court decisions, was properly understood as an instantiation or expression of the inherited common law and that it fell to the courts, as guardians of the ancient constitution, to determine whether or not particular acts of legislation faithfully embodied the common law.[3]

By this time, then, the tradition of the common law as institution and process was supplemented by the concept of the common law as a set of norms. After his dismissal from the judiciary, Coke continued the fight against royal prerogative as a Member of Parliament. However, his view of the nature of legislation was drowned by the incoming tide of Parliamentary supremacy, which left the prerogative of legislation intact but transferred it from the Monarch to Parliament.

C. The Common Law as Protector of Rights

The triumph of Parliament in the Glorious Revolution in 1688–89 had profound effects on the constitutional position of the institutions of the common law – the royal courts. In the old dispensation, judges were servants of the monarchy and, in that capacity, effectively disabled from reviewing or controlling its activities. Their independence from the monarchical executive was guaranteed by the Act of Settlement of 1701,[4] which also effectively protected their tenure of office from political attack by their new master, Parliament. This laid the foundation for the growth of judicial review of executive action by central government (a process that is still ongoing). At the same time, however, the logic of the Revolution settlement and the transfer of legislative sovereignty to Parliament was that the judges, now beholden to Parliament rather than the monarch, could not review its legislative activity. On the other hand, (subject to section 9 of the Bill of Rights 1689[5]), they could review its non-legislative activity and, most notably, its claim to exercise the formerly royal prerogative of detention for reasons

[1] JGA Pocock, *The Ancient Constitution and the Feudal Law: A Study in English Historical Thought in the Seventeenth Century* (Cambridge, Cambridge University Press, 1956).

[2] *Prohibitions del Roy* (1607), 12 Co Rep 63.

[3] 8 Co Rep (preface); 4 Co Rep (preface); *Dr Bonham's Case* (1610) 8 Co Rep 113b; *Rowles v Mason* (1612) 2 Brownl & Golds 192.

[4] Act of Settlement (1701) 12 & 13 Will III, c 2.

[5] The Bill of Rights (1689) I Will & Mary, session 2, c 2, s 9.

of state. Initially in the context of judicial control of Parliament's use of its regulatory powers, the common law came to be associated with norms protective of individual, civil and political rights, especially personal liberty, freedom of speech and security of property. In this way, the common law became established as a bulwark for citizen's rights against government attack.

D. The Common Law as Judicial Reason(ing)

At first, the immunity of Parliamentary legislation from judicial control did not matter much because in the eighteenth century Parliament passed relatively little general (as opposed to special) legislation: many Acts were, effectively, individualised administrative orders. This started to change in the early nineteenth century and general legislation gradually became the main substantive business of Parliament. The development of general legislation as a major tool of governance, in turn, fundamentally affected the relationship between Parliament and the courts. Increasingly, judicial law-making involved application and interpretation of statutory norms rather than development of judge-made norms. Driven by the theory of parliamentary sovereignty, statutory interpretation came to focus on the text (understood to express Parliament's intention) and to depend less on judicial assessment of the statute's underlying principles and 'purpose'. The old idea that legislation (like judge-made law) was, in some sense, an expression of pre-existing norms gradually gave way to an understanding of law (including the common law) as a product of decision-making by governmental institutions. Blackstone's *Commentaries*[6] contain elements of both theories; but Bentham's onslaught on the common law led to the triumph, by the mid-nineteenth century, of what we now call 'legal positivism'. The older theory is often referred to by the term 'natural law'. However, this term is misleading. In fact, in the late-medieval and early-modern periods various views were held about the nature of the pre-legal norms of which positive law was an expression. Some looked to divine law, others to some concept of 'human nature' and yet others, like Coke, to social custom. If positivism is understood as the idea that law is a product of social practice, Coke's theory was positivist.

As a result of these shifts in thinking, the older idea that statute and common law were two varieties of the same species gave way to the view that they were two different species of law made by two different institutions following different processes and procedures. The common law became associated with judicial reasoning and reasons, while legislation was associated with the will and intention of the law maker rather than with its underlying purpose or rationale. Finally, the 'fairy-tale' that judges 'find' the common law gave way to the 'realistic' view that the common law was 'made' by them.[7] These changes had significant implications for the constitutional position of senior courts, especially when coupled with several other important legal developments including: the gradual abolition of the civil (and, to a lesser extent, the criminal) jury;

[6] Sir William Blackstone, *Commentaries on the Laws of England*, W Prest ed (Oxford, Oxford University Press, 2016 [1783]).

[7] Lord Reid, 'The Judge as Lawmaker' (1972–73) 12 *Journal of the Society of Public Teachers of Law (New series)* 22.

the gradual transfer of executive power from the monarch to government ministers; democratisation; and the post-World War II development of a culture of rights.

2. The Judiciary's Legitimacy Problem

Jury trial had initially relieved judges of the responsibility of resolving disputes by confining their role to identifying the issues that would be decided by the jury in its absolute discretion, without explanation or the possibility of challenge. Gradually, realisation of the weaknesses of jury trial led to the development of a distinction between legal issues, which the judge had the power and responsibility to decide, and factual issues, which were the province of the jury. Increasingly, judges gave reasons for their decisions on issues of law, and increasingly such reasons were reliably recorded and made widely available. By contrast, juries continued to provide no reasons for their decisions, which remained largely unchallengeable. As a result of the effective abolition of the civil jury, the full weight of responsibility, to decide issues of both law and fact and to give written reasons for those decisions, came to rest on the judge. Furthermore, their decisions and reasons became increasingly subject to scrutiny by appellate courts. As dispute-resolvers and law-makers, judges no longer had anywhere to hide. The advent of reliable and, eventually, official law reporting facilitated the shift away from thinking of common law as grounded in pre-legal norms to conceiving of it as a product of judicial practice.

The position of the judges became even more exposed with the development of the cabinet and ministerial government after the Glorious Revolution. Under the old dispensation, the judges, as royal servants, were largely disabled from reviewing or controlling the central executive. The gradual transfer of executive power from the monarch to ministers and the development of ministerial responsibility to Parliament encouraged increasing judicial control of executive action. That process is still ongoing, the latest episode in the saga being *R (on the application of Miller) v The Prime Minister*,[8] itself a consequence of the further constitutional marginalisation of the monarchy during the second Elizabethan era.

The judiciary was left high and dry by democratisation and, eventually, universal adult suffrage. Before the Glorious Revolution, the legitimacy of the judiciary was closely tied up with the legitimacy of the monarchy. Initially, the removal from the judiciary of the yoke of executive control and the establishment of its 'independence' seemed thoroughly desirable. However, this left the judiciary with no obvious source of legitimation. The judges could not piggy-back off Parliament's legitimacy because, unlike Parliament, they could make no claim even to be 'virtually' representative. To make matters worse, Parliament's representative credentials were progressively bolstered by the broadening of the franchise, which inevitably highlighted the unelected status of the judges. Then came the post-WWII rights revolution. In the 1990s, the House of Lords began to exploit the legitimising potential of the concept of universal, fundamental human rights by developing the concept of fundamental common law rights.[9] The Human Rights

[8] *R (on the application of Miller) v The Prime Minister* [2019] UKSC 41 (*Miller II*).
[9] M Elliott and K Hughes (eds), *Common Law Constitutional Rights* (Oxford, Hart Publishing, 2020).

Act 1998 stalled the development of this technique and has, ironically, also exposed its weakness as a source of legitimacy. As courts have become more and more interventionist in the name of rights, their lack of democratic credentials has exposed them to increasingly severe criticism, particularly from rights-sceptics.

The overall upshot of these various factors is that the constitutional position of senior courts and the common law has become increasingly precarious, presenting advocates of a 'common law constitution' with an obvious problem of legitimacy. Trevor Allan, as I read him, addresses the problem in two ways. First, he stresses the importance of individual rights as counterweights to social policy, and the 'traditional' role of the courts as their independent guardians against undue encroachment by the organs of government that can claim legitimacy by virtue of being representative. Second, he emphasises that if it is to be more than general words on the page, legislation must necessarily be interpreted and applied in specific cases. Courts are law-appliers and, since the Revolution, they have enjoyed a monopoly of authoritative interpretation of legislation. This division of labour between Parliament and the courts ensures proper separation of governmental powers and guards against authoritarianism. Neither of these points, of course, addresses the judiciary's lack of representative credentials. A common underlying assumption seems to be that judicial representativeness would be inimical to protection of rights and separation of the making of law from its application.

3. The Invention of the Written Constitution

Besides important shifts in understanding of the nature of the common law and the constitutional position of courts, the eighteenth century also witnessed the invention of the written, canonical, constitutional document. The United States Constitution is the paradigmatic, big-C Constitution. In earlier usage, 'constitution' variously referred, inter alia, to legislation (as in 'the Constitutions of Clarendon' made by Henry II in 1154), a system of government (as in 'the English constitution'), and, more broadly, the make-up of things (as in 'she has a strong constitution'). As a constitutional technology, writing spread widely in the nineteenth century and has become all but ubiquitous since the fall of the Berlin Wall in 1989.[10] Notoriously, the United Kingdom is almost alone in not having a large-C Constitution.

In *Marbury v Madison*[11] in 1803 the US Supreme Court decided, in effect, that the US Constitution was a legal document with the force of 'higher' law. Implicit in this holding was that the Court's prime function was to enforce the Constitution and (as the Constitution itself provided) laws and treaties made in accordance with its provisions, on behalf of the People in whose name it was made. In this way of thinking, 'ordinary' law is made by delegates of the People: Congress and the Executive. The Court is law-applier and law-enforcer in chief. Three aspects of this further shift in constitutional thinking deserve explicit mention. The first involves the concept and location of

[10] L Colley, *The Gun, the Ship, and the Pen: Warfare, Constitutions and the Making of the Modern World* (London, Profile Books, 2021).

[11] *Marbury v Madison* 5 US 137 (1803).

sovereignty. During the turmoil of the seventeenth century in England, various bids were made to move sovereignty from the monarchy to civil society – not from one location within government (the monarchy) to another (Parliament), but from government to 'the people'. Such an idea of popular sovereignty was later adopted as the founding myth of the US Constitution. It is a myth because the US Constitution was made by an élite fearful of populism and, in its original form, created government by an élite. Nor does universal suffrage install the voters as sovereign in any meaningful sense. Second, the shift radically legalised the system of government by locating the ultimate source of political authority in a legal document and installing the Court as its champion and protector. Third, the shift made possible a sharp distinction between constitutional law and non-constitutional law: constitutional law is the law *of* the Constitution while non-constitutional law is law *authorised by* the Constitution.

4. Influential Storytellers

The story of the common law (constitution) now moves to two theorists to whom Trevor acknowledges a substantial debt: AV Dicey and Ronald Dworkin.

Even though Britain did not adopt a large-C Constitution in the nineteenth century, the invention of the written Constitution had a profound effect on the way the English thought about 'the constitution'. The classic statement of the new way of thinking is Dicey's *Law of the Constitution*[12] first published in 1885. As the work's title implies, its author's aim was to identify constitutional *law*. But how was this to be done in the absence of a written Constitution? Dicey settled on court enforcement as constitutional law's identifying feature. This move created various problems. Importantly, whereas a written Constitution (in theory, anyway) sets the parameters of the law-enforcement role of the constitutional court, in Dicey's scheme the enforcement activities of the courts establish the legal content of the constitution. It follows inexorably that the courts have power not only to enforce constitutional law but also to make it. According to Dicey, under the English constitution, constitutional law is made in precisely the same way as non-constitutional law – that is, by Parliament and the courts. So, whereas under the US constitution the Court is, in theory, the servant of the Constitution and, through it, the People, in the English system the courts share authorship of the constitution with Parliament and its legislative delegates. This latter approach is consistent with Coke's. However, Coke argued that both common law and statute were instantiations of a pre-existing normative system, embedded in and emergent from the life of the community. In that sense, both Parliament and the courts were, in his view, mouthpieces of the ancient constitution in a similar way as the US Congress and Supreme Court are both bound by the written US Constitution. Similarly, like the US Supreme Court, as constructed in *Marbury v Madison*, Coke's royal courts were the ultimate guardians of the ancient constitution and had the power to protect it against the legislature as well as the executive. As we have seen, however, the theoretical foundations of Coke's approach

[12] AV Dicey, *Lectures Introductory to the Study of the Law of the Constitution*, JWF Allison ed (Oxford, Oxford University Press, 2013 [1885]).

were fatally undermined by the Glorious Revolution, which ushered in a new regime of parliamentary sovereignty founded on Parliament's credentials as representative of the people.

Faithfully reflecting the outcome of the Glorious Revolution, Dicey considered parliamentary sovereignty to be one of the pillars of the English constitution. But what of the courts? In the beginning, the justices were at the centre of government – officials of the royal court promoting royal policy through adjudication. The Revolution settlement relegated them to a sort of constitutional limbo. Locke had found no place for judicial power in his explanation and justification of the Revolution.[13] In his account of the Revolution settlement, Montesquieu imagined judges as crude mechanicals, explaining and justifying their independence in terms of the desideratum of separating the making of law from its application.[14] Blackstone, by contrast, considered judicial independence essential to the preservation of the rights of the English people.[15] Dicey developed Blackstone's emphasis on judicial power into a theory of the rule of law as a second pillar of the English constitution.

On this basis, Trevor claims Dicey, properly interpreted and understood, as an intellectual fellow-traveller.[16] This claim strikes me as implausible.[17] In framing his account of the rule of law, Dicey seems to have had two main preoccupations. One was his suspicion of any distinction between 'ordinary' courts and 'administrative' courts and, relatedly, of any formal distinction between public law and private law.[18] In his view, there should be only one regime of law that applies to governors as much as to the governed, administered by a single set of courts. Dicey's antipathy to dual systems of law and courts – public and private – has regularly been interpreted as an antipathy to judicial control of executive action. It is certainly true that his account of judicial review is highly selective, focusing heavily on the writ of *habeas corpus*. However, given the centrality of courts to his account and the ideological use that has subsequently been made of Dicey's concept of the rule of law, the general charge seems implausible. Dicey was a follower of Austin and thoroughly positivistic in outlook. Within that frame, 'ordinary' courts and their law constituted, for him, crucial institutional counterweights to Parliament and its law, as well as to executive power; and judicial independence was essential for their effectiveness.

Dicey's other preoccupation was a conviction that individual rights are better protected by judicial than by legislative – especially constitutional – means. It is a 'special attribute of English institutions' (he wrote) that rights 'are the result [by generalisation] of judicial decisions determining the rights of private persons in particular cases

[13] MJC Vile, *Constitutionalism and the Separation of Powers*, 2nd edn (Carmel, Liberty Fund, 1998) 64–65.

[14] AM Cohler, C Miller and HS Stone (eds), *Montesquieu, Spirit of the Laws* (Cambridge, Cambridge University Press, 1989) Book XI, ch 6.

[15] Blackstone, *Commentaries* (n 6) Book I, 173–74, 259–60.

[16] TRS Allan, *Constitutional Justice* (Oxford, Oxford University Press, 2010) 13–20, 214; TRS Allan, *The Sovereignty of Law* (Oxford, Oxford University Press, 2013) 10–11, 19, 23–25, 31–36, 51–52.

[17] Anyway, it is not clear to me why Trevor needs or wants to recruit Dicey to his cause or to free him from 'the shackles of the Hobbesian authoritarianism he learnt from Austin': TRS Allan, *Law, Liberty, and Justice: The Legal Foundations of British Constitutionalism* (Oxford, Clarendon Press, 1993) 2. Why not simply say that Dicey got the wrong end of the stick?

[18] Dicey, *Law of the Constitution* (n 12) 100–15.

brought before the Courts'.[19] By contrast, 'under many foreign constitutions the security (such as it is) given to the rights of individuals results, or appears to result, [deductively] from general principles of the constitution'.[20] At one level, Dicey conceded, '[t]his is … merely a formal difference' suggesting that what concerned him was not how rights are generated – whether by legislative or adjudicatory procedures, for instance – but rather their enforcement. First, he claimed that the English approach was preferable because it put more emphasis on effective remedies for interference with rights than the 'foreign' approach.[21] Second, the foreign approach (he said) was apt to generate a distinction between more important-and-secure 'constitutional' rights, and less important-and-secure 'non-constitutional' rights.[22] Third, Dicey claimed that foreign, constitutional rights were more likely to be 'suspended' than English rights.[23] He considered 'suspension' of the Habeas Corpus Act (in the context of security 'emergencies') to be less drastic because it only affected one of the citizen's rights (personal liberty) and only in limited respects; it did not, *ipso facto*, affect the availability of the (common law) writ of *habeas corpus*.

Much changed constitutionally between the time Dicey was writing, in the 1880s, and the publication of what has become the bible of modern legal positivism – HLA Hart's *The Concept of Law*.[24] Expectations of government, and the nature and practice of governance, had been transformed in response to two World Wars, a global pandemic, and the Great Depression. Universal adult suffrage was some 30 years old, and the welfare state was approaching its heyday. Britain had been heavily involved in promoting and drafting both the Universal Declaration of Human Rights[25] and the European Convention on Human Rights.[26] In the post-war environment of peace and relative prosperity, the first shoots were appearing of a revolution to come, in the 1960s, in the judicial stance towards review and control of central government. Although Hart claimed a degree of universality for his theory of law, his account is rooted in English soil. So, it is surprising that courts figure only marginally in *The Concept of Law*, which focuses on legislation and legislatures. Hart's discussion of judicial reasoning is more-or-less confined to interpretation of 'general rules'.[27] The idea that law itself might be customary and non-canonical seems to get lost in the transition from Hart's pre-legal world, in which social normativity is a matter of custom, to his legal world in which custom figures as a possible source of law but not as one of its forms.

[19] ibid 115.

[20] ibid. The words in square brackets in this and the previous quotation have been interpolated from a different formulation of the point: ibid 116.

[21] ibid 117.

[22] ibid 118.

[23] ibid.

[24] HLA Hart, *The Concept of Law* (Oxford, Clarendon Press, 1961).

[25] The Universal Declaration of Human Rights (Paris, 10 December 1948).

[26] The Convention for the Protection of Human Rights and Fundamental Freedoms (Rome, 4 November 1950).

[27] 'In any large group, general rules, standards and principles must be the main instrument of social control, and not particular directions given to each individual separately': Hart, *Concept of Law* (n 24) 124. Hart devotes only two paragraphs to what he calls law-making by 'precedent' which, he says, makes 'minimal use of general classifying words': ibid.

AWB Simpson responded to Hart by arguing that the common law, as contrasted with statute law, is best understood precisely as a form of custom – judicial custom.[28] For Simpson, this account of the common law was perfectly consistent with positivism, understood as the theses that law is a social practice and that legal norms are categorially different from pre-legal or extra-legal norms.[29] Ronald Dworkin's reaction[30] to the thinness of Hart's account of judicial law-making was quite different from Simpson's. Dworkin argued that Hart's theory of law could not account for judicial law-making because of its commitment to a categorial distinction between law-as-it-is and law-as-it-ought-to-be: the thesis of 'the separation/separability of law and morality'. The role of the judge, Dworkin argued, is to take account of all legal materials – constitutional provisions, legislation, court decisions and so on – relevant to the case at hand and to resolve the case in accordance with the judge's best assessment of the force of those materials in the light of the values inherent or implicit in them.[31] The law, for any particular case, consists of the judge's assessment, in the light of the facts, of the resolution that best fits those materials and the values that underlie them. Dworkin called this judicial process of identifying law 'interpretation'; and he argued that understanding law 'as interpretation'[32] was inconsistent with distinguishing sharply between law-as-it-is and law-as-it-ought-to-be. Law as interpretation is Dworkin's answer to the problem of how to legitimise judicial law-making in a democracy.

5. Trevor Enters the Story[33]

Trevor's account of the constitutional 'rule of law' departs from Dworkin's account of law in distinctive and significant respects. Shorn of its metaphysics, Dworkin's normative account of judicial reasoning and, hence, of the common law is descriptively plausible and attractive, as witnessed by its popularity amongst the senior English judiciary in the 1980s. Unlike Dworkin (and Hart), Trevor does not provide a theory of law but rather a descriptive and normative account of the way law figures in the reasoning of individuals about what they ought to do. Neither Hart nor Dworkin addresses this question or, at least, not directly. Hart's approach focuses on how to identify law, not how to incorporate law into reasoning about what one ought to do.[34] For Hart, the latter is a 'moral' rather than a legal issue. Dworkin purports to provide both a descriptive and a normative account of creative *judicial* reasoning and uses it to undermine the thesis about the

[28] AWB Simpson, 'The Common Law and Legal Theory' in AWB Simpson (ed), *Oxford Essays in Jurisprudence (Second Series)* (Oxford, Oxford University Press, 1973).

[29] Thus, positivism contrasts with the idea of law as an expression of pre-legal norms: GJ Postema, 'The British Tradition of Legal Positivism' in T Spaak and P Mindus (eds), *The Cambridge Companion to Legal Positivism* (Cambridge, Cambridge University Press, 2021).

[30] Expounded, most notably, in R Dworkin, *Law's Empire* (London, Fontana Press, 1986).

[31] This account is crucially different from the idea that law is an expression of pre-legal norms. Rather, in this telling, law consists of norms and their inherent values as 'best assessed' by the judge. So understood, Dworkin's is not a 'natural law' theory but a 'judges' law' theory.

[32] Or, in a different rendering, subscribing to a theory of 'law as integrity'.

[33] What follows is very much my 'interpretation' of (perhaps better, 'spin on') Trevor's large, complex and mercurial body of work.

[34] The idea of law as reasons for action was developed by Hart's leading pupil, Joseph Raz.

relationship between law-as-it-is and law-as-it-ought-to-be that he attributes to Hart; and, hence, to propose a competing theory of law.

By contrast, Trevor's preoccupation is not with how to identify the law or with what is required of judges as such, but rather with the general questions of what one ought to do and how one ought to behave. For Trevor, answering these questions involves and requires taking all relevant considerations into account. Amongst the relevant considerations are legal norms, both legislative and judicial; but other types of norms ('religious', 'moral', 'political' and so on) can also be relevant. These questions and their appropriate answers depend partly on the position occupied by the questioner. For instance, the answer to the question 'what should I, as judge, do?' may be different from the answer to the question 'what should I, as citizen, do?' Trevor adopts the Dworkinian concept of interpretation to describe the process of deciding what one ought to do in whatever position one happens to occupy. In my understanding of Trevor's account, it does not generate a theory of law.[35] Nor does it provide a theory of judicial reasoning or obligation. Rather (in my telling) it is a theory of practical reasoning, which Trevor conceives in holistic terms that embrace all relevant norms of any and every type. For Trevor, practical reasoning involves interpretation of all relevant reasons.

Pursuing a different agenda from either Hart or Dworkin, Trevor uses the concept of interpretation to undermine the 'doctrine' of parliamentary sovereignty. His argument is that, in practical reasoning, what a relevant statutory provision says is one consideration to be taken into account, but only one. This makes obvious sense; but the point does not undermine the doctrine of parliamentary sovereignty as a legal rule for resolving conflicts between statute and common law or between Parliament and the courts. On the one hand, it does not follow from the fact that statute prevails over common law that statute prevails over every other relevant consideration. On the other hand, as a legal rule for resolving conflicts between Parliament and the courts, it might carry greater weight in the practical reasoning of judges, for instance, than in the practical reasoning of citizens.

In recent work, Trevor describes those who consider parliamentary sovereignty to be a pillar of the English constitution as taking an 'external' approach to the constitution in contrast to the 'internal' perspective that Trevor himself adopts and recommends in the name of 'the rule of law'.[36] I do not find this contrast helpful. It was, of course, central to Hart's hermeneutical positivism.[37] The way I understand Hart's account is in terms of

[35] Some (perhaps including Trevor) will contest this. For example, Trevor talks about 'the legal reasoner whose interpretation of legal materials constitutes the law': Allan, *Sovereignty of Law* (n 16) 165; and claims that 'there is no intelligible gap between personal moral conviction as regards the requirements of justice in the particular case and the true content of the law': TRS Allan, 'Constitutional Rights, Moral Judgement and the Rule of Law' in J Goudkamp, M Lunney and L McDonald (eds), *Taking Law Seriously: Essays in Honour of Peter Cane* (Oxford, Hart Publishing, 2022) 103. Trevor says: 'Final responsibility for acting in accordance with the law, understood by reference to fundamental principles of liberty and justice, remains with each individual, whether judge, public official or private citizen': Allan, *Sovereignty of Law* (n 16) 36. Or again, '… common law rules … are generalisations from specific decisions, guided not only by judicial reasoning but also by our critical appraisal of such reasoning': Allan, 'Constitutional Rights' (n 35) 111. However, I hesitate to read such statements as implying that 'the law is what each individual considers to be fair and just'. Such an approach would disable law from performing its social function of managing disagreement.

[36] Allan, *Sovereignty of Law* (n 16) 133–67.

[37] Hart, *Concept of Law* (n 24) 89–91.

a distinction between action and reasons for action. An *extreme* external point of view detects only action (such as stopping at a red light) and not reasons for the action (such as that the law requires stopping at red lights). From the internal point of view, that the law requires stopping at red lights provides a reason to stop at a red light. Much human behaviour, but by no means all, consists of normatively driven responses to reasons. The extreme external point of view detects only behaviour regardless of whether it is normatively driven. However, there is also a *moderate* external point of view that distinguishes between behaviour that is, and behaviour that is not, normatively driven, but regardless of whether the relevant norms provide the observer personally (from the internal point of view) with a reason to behave as the norm requires. From this perspective, an observer may be able to describe how other people decide what they ought to do without internally adopting that approach themselves.

The distinction between the internal point of view and the *strictly* external point of view is irrelevant to the debates about the sovereignty of statute in the British constitution. Those on both sides can be read as providing *moderately* external accounts – albeit very different accounts – of the English constitution that see not only action but also reasons for action. On the other hand, both accounts – the parliamentary sovereignty account and the rule of law account – can be adopted internally. Both accounts can be assessed for their descriptive accuracy and both accounts are available for adoption as guides to practical reasoning.

Hart's theory was notoriously plagued by metaphysical questions. As we have seen, Hart argued that law-as-it-is and law-as-it-ought-to-be are two different things. Central to Hart's position was the claim that law-as-it-is is a product of human social practice and mental activity: it is both practice-dependent and mind-dependent. However, Hart also believed that it was unnecessary for the legal theorist to commit to whether or not law-as-it-ought-to-be (which he thought to be a matter of 'morality') was a matter of human social practice and mental activity or, by contrast, dependent on neither. Dworkin argued, against Hart, that abstention was not possible; and, as I understand him, Dworkin opted ultimately for a practice-dependent and system-specific ('local', not 'universal') concept of value to explain (and legitimate) the judicial process of interpretation.

Trevor's account is not confronted by this metaphysical conundrum. According to him, the best way to understand law is as one amongst the universe of considerations relevant to holistic assessment of what one ought to do. It is for each individual to decide what should be done; and, in this sense, what one ought to do is mind-dependent. However, for Trevor's purposes it is irrelevant whether, in the mind of the decision-maker, what they ought to do is dependent on social practice, or on their own personal judgment, or on some other factor such as 'morality'. Admittedly, Trevor seems often to load the term 'morality' with connotations of objective universality. However, I think that Trevor's most recent statements of his position[38] are (at least) consistent with a functional account of 'morality' according to which it refers to each individual's ultimate judgments of value (whatever their form, content or source) by which, in case of

[38] Especially in Allan, 'Constitutional Rights' (n 35).

conflict, each person protects their autonomy from the judgments, values and demands of society and other individuals.[39]

In this light, Trevor's most recent book, *The Sovereignty of Law*,[40] would better be titled something like *The Sovereignty of Reason*.[41] By his account, law is not sovereign because, at the end of the day, it provides only relevant considerations that every individual is entitled (and, perhaps, required) to take into account in deciding what they ought to do (or think), whatever the situation they are in at the relevant time. What Trevor offers – or so I would argue – is not a theory of law, or a theory of the British constitution, or even a theory of legal obligation, but rather an account of practical reason that explains the relevance of statute and common law, amongst other things, to each person's decision about what they ought to do in any given situation.

6. Trevor and the Common Law Tradition

Read in this way, how does Trevor's theory of the role of law in practical reasoning relate to the common law 'tradition' surveyed earlier? Remember the four elements of that tradition: common law as institution and process; common law as a set of (inherited) norms; common law as a protector of civil and political rights; and common law as a distinctive, reason(s)-based ('reasoned') mode of law-making. I would suggest that Trevor's theory has most affinity with the fourth of these traditions of the common law. In his worldview, the common law method is a form of practical reasoning apt to answer the question of what the judge, responsible for application and development of the law, should do in the individual case. Trevor takes the common law judicial method as a sort of model for the way any participant in the legal system – citizen, legal scholar and so on – does and should approach the law, understood as a set of institutions, processes and norms. In practical reasoning, legislation and judge-made law are essentially similar in that both feature as, and only as, relevant considerations. Also important to Trevor's account is the tradition of the common law as the guardian of individual rights. This strategy harnesses the powerful rhetoric of rights; but at the same time it invites accusations of judicial overreach. Ironically, however, the role of the common law as rights-protector has been significantly taken over by international conventions and domestic constitutions and statutes. Even so, the power of rights rhetoric also underpins Trevor's rejection of the supposedly external parliamentary-sovereignty account of the constitution in favour of his supposedly internal rule-of-law account. In this respect, much turns on the idea that general rules derive their force only from their application and interpretation in individual cases: the general is always subject to its application to the particular. There is some slippage in Trevor's use of the term 'interpretation' to describe both a judicial method and an approach to determining the meaning of a text. This ambiguity facilitates his apparent claim that statutory 'interpretation' is an instance of the holistic 'interpretation' involved in practical reasoning.

[39] P Cane, 'Morality, Law and Conflicting Reasons for Action' [2012] *CLJ* 59.
[40] Allan, *Sovereignty of Law* (n 16).
[41] 'Only reason is sovereign …': ibid 171.

Trevor's theory owes little to the other two common law traditions. He says nothing about the institutions or the processes of law-making, or about legislating and adjudicating as different modes of governance, or about the sources of the common law. In this last respect, it is true that Trevor often associates law with 'morality';[42] and in Hart's terms, he sometimes equates morality with the 'critical' as opposed to the 'positive' (or 'social') variety.[43] However, I doubt that Trevor needs or wants to adopt some form of moral realism about constitutional values.[44] For him (or so I argue) both law and morality are ultimately matters for individual judgment, regardless of the basis on which such judgments are made. On the other hand, nor does Trevor's commitment to the radical individuality of value commit him to moral relativity or subjectivity. A functional account of morality sidesteps the metaphysical issue.

7. The Sovereignty of Reason

In the final analysis, then, Trevor's theory owes relatively little to traditions of the common law. Nor has it much to do with traditional understandings of sovereignty, according to which it resides either within government or outside government in civil society. In Trevor's radically individualistic approach, if 'sovereignty' is anywhere to be seen, it resides in each individual, not in any institution or group. Such radical individualism is consistent with any system of government that the individual is prepared to accept. Radical individualism can easily accommodate either parliamentary sovereignty or the common law/rule of law constitution because, at the end of the day, it is up to the individual to decide how various considerations bear on their practical reasoning. Trevor's theory tells us nothing much about the British constitution, either as such or as compared with any other constitution.

Consider, in this context, Trevor's account of constitutional conventions and the distinction between law and convention. The US Supreme Court's decision in *Marbury v Madison*[45] associated the Constitution with law, and law with judicially enforceable norms. No surprise, then, that Dicey adopted judicial enforceability as the identifying feature of the law of the constitution. However, Dicey also realised that there was a substantial body of 'constitutional' norms that previous writers (such as Bagehot[46] and Hearn[47]) considered to be 'political', not legal. Such norms he calls 'conventions

[42] For instance, '… legal reasoning is essentially moral reasoning …': Allan, 'Constitutional Rights' (n 35) 97; '… law is itself a segment of morality …': ibid 105.

[43] See, eg, Allan, *Sovereignty of Law* (n 16) 63–64.

[44] Instead, the values that Trevor champions in the names of, for instance, the 'rule of law' and the 'common good' may be understood as those to which he personally subscribes and which he recommends to all others (legislators, judges, legal scholars and citizens) as the ultimate standard for determining the right basis of decision and course of action in constitutional matters.

[45] *Marbury* (n 11).

[46] W Bagehot, *The English Constitution*, Fontana Classics of History and Thought, intro from RHS Crossman (London, Fontana / Collins, 1963 [1867]).

[47] WE Hearn, *The Government of England, Its Structure and Its Development* (London, Longmans, Green & Co, 1867).

of the constitution'. Although Dicey accepted that conventions were not, as such, judicially enforceable, he argued that they were indirectly enforceable because a breach of convention would sooner or later lead to a breach of constitutional law. A different way of distinguishing constitutional law from constitutional convention refers to their respective sources: law is made by Parliament and its delegates, and by senior courts; conventions are made (and enforced) by 'political actors' who may include, but are not limited to, officials who also possess law-making power. Conventions may be documentary or non-documentary. Documentary conventions may witness non-documentary conventions which are, in turn, products of the normative practices of political actors; or they may establish norms of political practice. Constitutional conventions are customary norms – 'political custom', we might say. So understood, they have much in common with the modern, institutional understanding of the common law as 'judicial custom'. Parliament also has its own normative custom(s), as does the judiciary.[48]

Trevor notes the analogy between conventions and common law but rejects both these accounts of constitutional conventions. Instead, he treats conventions, like statute and common law, as considerations relevant to individual's practical reasoning. So understood, he argues, there is no clear distinction between conventions and law. Such a distinction, he claims, only appears from an external point of view, not from the internal point of view of the practical reasoner. From the internal point of view, reasons are reasons are reasons. It is only from an external perspective of the detached observer, as opposed to the internal perspective of the committed participant, that differences between various reasons, and their individual force and salience, are discernible. Even if this analysis is accepted, what it provides is a theory of practical reasoning, not a theory of the British constitution in any recognisable sense. Traditional theories of the common law and of the British constitution are theories about the institutional activities of courts and the sources of law. At this level, Trevor's theory owes little to any common law tradition.

8. The Common Law Constitution

Given the eccentricity of my spin on Trevor' theory, I should, finally, say something about the concept of the 'common law constitution', with which Trevor has become firmly identified. According to Trevor,

> In the absence of a higher 'constitutional law', proclaimed in a written constitution venerated as a source of unique legal authority', the rule of law serves in Britain as a form of constitution. It is in this fundamental sense that Britain has a *common law constitution*; the ideas and values of which the rule of law consists are reflected and embedded in the ordinary common law.[49]

Again: '… the doctrine of parliamentary sovereignty … is itself a creature of the common law … whose detailed contents and limits are therefore matters of judicial law-making'.[50]

[48] S Stephenson, 'Constitutional Conventions and the Judiciary' (2021) 41 *OJLS* 750.
[49] Allan, *Law, Liberty, and Justice* (n 17) 4.
[50] ibid 10–11.

And yet again: 'The ideal of the rule of law is most fully realised in the common law, which is the ultimate foundation of the authority of court decisions'.[51]

Taking the last quote first: in the story told earlier in this article, the authority of court decisions was originally derived from the authority of the monarch. The common law was developed by royal justices exercising adjudicatory power delegated to them by the monarch. The monarch's adjudicatory power was, in turn, based on a claim of radical title to all property in the realm and to all the rights and powers that went with that title, including the right and power to adjudicate. The root of the English common law was the success of the Conqueror. In theory, at least, the position today is essentially the same. Royal justices 'independently' exercise the formerly (and formally) monarchical 'prerogative' power of adjudication. In modern terms, that power is established not by law but as a matter of 'convention' – of normative, social and political practice.

At one point (in contrast to what he says in the second quote above), Trevor gets quite close to taking the same view about parliamentary sovereignty:

> The nature and limits of [parliamentary] sovereignty are constituted, just as conventions are constituted, by the political morality which underlies the legal order. In this sense, the legal doctrine of sovereignty is perhaps the most fundamental of our constitutional conventions.[52]

Such an approach resonates with the historical story told earlier. Legislative power, like judicial power, was originally understood to be an incident of monarchical power supported, as Trevor puts it, by 'political morality', not by law. The sovereignty of Parliament resulted from the success of Parliament in a battle for political power. I would go slightly further than Trevor and say that parliamentary sovereignty is not a legal doctrine but a constitutional convention, a normative social and political foundation of the legal system.

So, what of the common law constitution? As I argued earlier, Trevor's theory says little, if anything, about the British constitution as such. What it implies is that the constitution, like the legal system, rests on the foundation of the practical reasoning of individuals who internalise its norms. This is true of any and every constitution and legal system. In most systems, a large-C Constitution, which may be accorded the status of law, is interposed between this foundation and the governmental system. The nature and dynamics of systems that include a large-C Constitution clearly differ in significant respects from those very few of systems (such as the British) that do not. For instance, it is only in quite recent years that US scholars have begun amply to appreciate and systematically to investigate the conventional elements of the US, small-c constitution. However, both types of system share the fundamental characteristic that they are based ultimately on normative social practices of internalisation of norms.

9. Conclusion

As a theory of the ultimate foundations of legal and constitutional systems, Trevor's radical individualism appeals to me. There can be no constitutions and no legal

[51] Allan, *Sovereignty of Law* (n 16) 121.
[52] Allan, *Law, Liberty, and Justice* (n 17) 283.

systems without people who internalise their norms. However, it is less attractive as an account of the quotidian operation of legal systems and constitutions. Moreover, unlike Trevor, I think that the human behaviour on which legal systems and constitutions are founded can be described from the outside, externally, by people who do not participate internally in the system but who understand what it means to be a participant on the inside.

2

More Protestant than Luther or Dworkin? TRS Allan on Law and Morals

DAVID DYZENHAUS[1]

Ronald Dworkin's 'interpretivist' theory of law has at its heart the 'one right answer thesis'. In 'hard cases', judges must interpret the law by finding the answer supported by the principles implicit in relevant law that show the law in its 'best moral light'.[2] His relentless focus on judges distracted attention from his claim that access to the answer is not the preserve of judges. The subjects of a jural community – the community of individuals bound together by law – have equal standing to interpret the law.

Dworkin thus transposed to legal theory the thesis Martin Luther installed at the heart of the Protestant Reformation. There is no Pope or high caste of priests with authority over the bible's message. Rather, each member of the faith community has equal access to the truth of the holy text. How does such secular protestantism square with Dworkin's suggestion that it would be counterintuitive to suppose that 'most of the subjects of most of the political communities over history had no moral duty to obey the laws of their community'?[3] If subjects have a moral duty to obey the law of their community, that surely must be the law as it is, not as they interpret it. Dworkin must, then, accept in some form one central tenet of the legal positivist theory of law which he spent his career criticising: the proposition that subjects have something like what HLA Hart termed a 'content-independent' duty to obey the law, a duty to obey the law whatever its content.[4]

[1] This chapter is my latest attempt to provoke my friend Trevor Allan, attempts mainly made in many lunchtime conversations in his college – including one in June of the year preceding the conference at which this chapter was presented – during which my objections to his position dissolve in the face of his unfailingly courteous responses. It draws on my *The Long Arc of Legality: Hobbes, Kelsen, Hart* (Cambridge, Cambridge University Press, 2022).

[2] The full version of this theory was set out first in 'Hard Cases': see R Dworkin, *Taking Rights Seriously* (London, Duckworth, 1977, New Impression with a Reply to Critics) 81 and refined in R Dworkin, *Law's Empire* (London, Fontana, 1986).

[3] Quoted in S Sreedhar and C Delmas, 'State Legitimacy and Political Obligation in *Justice for Hedgehogs*: The Radical Potential of Dworkinian Dignity' (2010) 90 *Boston University Law Review* 737, 746.

[4] HLA Hart, *Essays on Bentham: Jurisprudence and Political Theory* (Oxford, Oxford University Press, 1982) 254.

The symmetry of Dworkin's position in these regards is manifested in his account of civil disobedience.[5] The disobedient is someone who decides to disobey the law when it violates in an extreme way the demands of individual conscience. But disobedients do not fall into one of the two traps Hart claimed inhere in natural law, the trap of anarchism in which subjects claim that law fails to be law just because its content is by their own lights immoral.[6] Rather, they recognise the law as valid, but choose to disobey it because of its content. Similarly, but only in his very last work *Justice for Hedgehogs*,[7] Dworkin came up with a theory of civil disobedience for judges. If judges are faced with the situation in which the law has a very unjust content, they must recognise the law as valid; but, since this is a moral emergency, they should refuse to apply it. He thus moved from his earlier position that judges' duty is always to apply the law as they find it to one that allows them in extreme cases openly to refuse to do so.[8]

Hardly noticed in legal theory is that this move echoes a similar one in Hart. In 1958, Hart argued that the positivist Separation Thesis – there is no necessary connection between law and morality – is helpful to subjects in coming to the conclusion that X is the law, but too evil to obey. But he did not at that time suppose that the Separation Thesis offered the same benefit to judges. Rather, in his discussion of the Grudge Informer Case, he implicitly supposed that judges are under a standing duty to apply the law as they find it. It was only three years later that, without announcing the move, Hart proclaimed the symmetry. The Thesis facilitates both subjects and judges in concluding that '[t]his is law; but it is too iniquitous to be applied or obeyed'.[9]

The echo is, however, faint since it may be misleading to suppose that Hart has a position on *civil* disobedience. Civil disobedients not only recognise the validity of the law they disobey, but also that the obligation is an all-things-considered obligation. They conclude that their moral obligation to obey the law is overridden by the obligations of conscience. But for the Separation Thesis there is no clash of obligations. At most, one can observe that there exists an obligation according to law and a moral obligation. Since the former is 'normatively inert',[10] it exerts no pull at all on subjects, let alone a moral pull that could enter into a contest with the obligations of conscience. Subjects will have to factor into their deliberation the costs of disobedience; and prudence might counsel them to act against conscience. But the same is true of the person who obeys the armed robber. Thus, in his response to Hart in 1958, Lon Fuller was correct in his diagnosis that Hart tried to articulate an account of the judicial obligation of 'fidelity to law' but failed because of his commitment to the Separation Thesis. Fuller remarked that the description offered by the Thesis has 'the verbal formulation of a problem, but the problem it states makes no sense'. The obligations, he continued, 'exist in wholly separate worlds'.[11]

[5] Dworkin, *Taking Rights Seriously* (n 2) ch 8 'Civil Disobedience'.

[6] HLA Hart, 'Positivism and the Separation of Law and Morals' in HLA Hart, *Essays in Jurisprudence and Philosophy* (Oxford, Clarendon Press, 1983) 49, 54.

[7] R Dworkin, *Justice for Hedgehogs* (Cambridge, Harvard University Press, 2011).

[8] ibid 411.

[9] HLA Hart, *The Concept of Law*, 2nd edn (Oxford, Clarendon Press, 1994) 208.

[10] This is John Gardner's useful and telling phrase: J Gardner, 'Legal Positivism: 5½ Myths' in J Gardner, *Law as a Leap of Faith – Essays on Law in General* (Oxford, Oxford University Press, 2012) 19, 23.

[11] LL Fuller, 'Positivism and Fidelity to Law: A Reply to Professor Hart' (1958) 71 *Harvard Law Review* 630, 656.

Both Fuller and Dworkin in rather different ways tried to show that the obligations do not exist in separate worlds, Dworkin more radically in that in *Justice for Hedgehogs* he argued that there is only one world. There is no need to build a bridge between the worlds of morality and law.[12] But most philosophers of law regard their attempts as a failure and Anglo-American philosophy of law today is dominated by Hartian legal positivism, as refined by Joseph Raz, Hart's most influential student.

That dominance has its price, as Fuller and Dworkin after him noted. While Hart and his followers claim that legal positivism helps both judges and subjects to navigate the moral complexity occasioned when deciding what to do in the face of an unjust law, their insistence that law is normatively inert leaves them unable to explain how law could make such situations *morally* complex.[13] Their dominance thus leaves unsolved the puzzle of legal authority, which Hart set in 1958 when he said, in criticism of the Bentham and Austin's reduction of law to coercion, 'law is surely not the gunman situation writ large'.[14]

In short, the puzzle is how law can be a matter of both right and might. I will argue that we can make progress towards solving this puzzle by taking seriously the position that both Hart and Dworkin abandoned – that civil disobedience may be an appropriate stance for subjects, but not for judges since they have an all-things-considered obligation to apply the law. The leading articulation of just this position is, in my view, to be found in TRS Allan's legal theory. But I will also argue that some amendments are required for it to solve the puzzle. Section 1 explores the puzzle and why it occurs in much the same way for legal positivists and leading critics such as Allan and Dworkin. Section 2 sets out Allan's particular take and Section 3 sketches a way forward.

1. The Puzzle of Legal Authority

Hart, in what Dworkin termed an 'uncharacteristically vehement' criticism of his interpretivism, argued that Dworkin's claim that judges are always able to come up with a moral interpretation of the law amounts to 'an idle but confusing decoration to the positivist simple conclusion' that a law may be valid but too unjust to be obeyed.[15] Hart would have been right if that idea were the only string to Dworkin's bow. There were, however, two more strings, though Dworkin never developed a full account of them, which left his philosophy of law highly vulnerable to the objection that in a wicked legal system, one in which law is the instrument of a repugnant ideology, the principles implicit in the law will be the principles of that ideology.

In brief, the second string is that the legal system may be so illegitimate that it can't be the ground of even weak moral obligations, in which case judges may simply ignore the artefact whose only claim on them is that it complies with the system's formal

[12] Dworkin, *Justice for Hedgehogs* (n 7) ch 19 'Law'.
[13] Dworkin, *Taking Rights Seriously* (n 2) 327; R Dworkin, 'A Reply' in M Cohen (ed), *Ronald Dworkin & Contemporary Jurisprudence* (London, Duckworth, 1984) 247, 259; Fuller, 'Positivism and Fidelity to Law' (n 11) 656.
[14] Hart, 'Positivism and the Separation of Law and Morals' (n 6) 59.
[15] Hart, *Essays on Bentham* (n 4) 152–53; Dworkin, 'A Reply' (n 13) 257.

criteria of validity.[16] Dworkin consigned the third string to a footnote response to the wicked legal system objection. In the text, he expressed some doubt that the situation of a judge starkly faced with a clearly unjust law would easily arise, while in the footnote he suggested that he needed to distinguish more sharply than he had in his earlier work between 'explanation' and 'justification'.[17] In his view, an explanation did not 'provide a justification of a series of political decisions if it presents, as justificatory principles, propositions that offend our ideas of what even a bad moral principle must be like'.[18] He also said that he has more confidence than he had in earlier work in what he called the 'screening power of the concept of a moral principle'. He claimed that the requirement his theory imposes on judges – that they provide an argument which shows the legal record in its best moral light – will tend to screen out or exclude morally unacceptable principles.[19]

I will suggest that all three strings are required for a convincing response to the wicked legal system objection and that the most important string is the second, the basis for the legitimacy of legal order. By this I mean a basis that is not coextensive with the moral code of a judge or a subject that might lead them to civil disobedience. Luther's famous 'Here I must stand, I can do no other' expresses in this context the stand of someone in a genuine dilemma, one in which each horn exerts a moral pull. And as Fuller and then Dworkin explained in criticising Hart, a genuine dilemma arises only if there is a legitimating basis for the law of this kind. I will explain the cost of doing without an account of the legitimating basis altogether through Allan's refinement of Dworkin's interpretivism, which fails to see that what makes interpretivism possible at all is the second string.

Interpretivism is firmly rooted in the common law tradition.[20] It thus attracts the same two charges of illegitimacy which Bentham levelled in his polemic against Blackstone.[21] It is politically suspect because it makes 'judge and co.', an unelected elite, into the arbiters of the compulsory public morality of a society in place of the democratically-elected representatives of the people. And it is morally suspect, as the 'co.' suggests, because of the content of their morality, opposed as judges were to the legislative reforms of a parliament minded to serve the greatest happiness of the greatest number against the narrow interests protected by the elites of the day. Bentham therefore advocated marginalising judges to the greatest extent possible by stripping their judgments of precedential force and making statute law into clear and comprehensive codes.

Dworkin's restatement of the basic tenets of the common law tradition changed the terms of the debate between it and its positivist critics. Against the second charge, he argued that if judges understood their task as protecting each individual's right to be treated by the state with equal concern and respect, one could answer the first charge

[16] Dworkin, 'A Reply' (n 13).
[17] ibid 299 fn 4.
[18] ibid.
[19] ibid.
[20] R Dworkin, 'Law's Ambitions for Itself' (1985) 71 *Virginia Law Review* 173 and Mark Walters' fine work, for example, M Walters 'Legal Humanism and Law as Integrity' (2008) 67 *CLJ* 352.
[21] J Bentham, *A Fragment on Government* (Cambridge, Cambridge University Press, 1988 [1776]).

and justify keeping the judiciary at centre stage. Judges would no longer get in the way of what we can think of as New Deal or welfarist legislative programs which redistribute resources to the less well-off. Indeed, the commitment to equality in the idea of equal concern and respect would support such efforts.

The only constraint on the state, whether in its legislative or its executive capacities, would be that its legislation respected individual rights, though not a fundamental right to liberty of the sort that animated the infamous judgment of the US Supreme Court in *Lochner*.[22] For as Dworkin argued in an influential paper, liberals should understand that there are only rights to particular liberties, those that flow from the commitment to equality.[23] Since that commitment is also fundamental to democrats, one could, he supposed, reconcile liberalism and democracy in one theory and so rebut the first challenge. So long as judges see themselves as the guardians of a constitutional right to equality, not liberty, they can be understood as the guardians of democracy against legislatures temporarily captured by populists.

In the era of Trump, Orbàn and Johnson, and when law professors in leading law schools are providing cover for their efforts to undermine both liberalism and democracy under the thin guise of serving the 'common good', a defence of Dworkin's position seems even more important than when he first set it out in the 1960s and 70s, a time when liberal democracy seemed on an unstoppable march, a point to which I return below. But it is important to address a tension in that position between the dimensions of 'fit' and 'justification' in interpretivist theory, one which also afflicts Allan's work.

It arises out of the feature of their protestantism that access to the truth of the texts of the legal record can't be limited to the legislature, the executive, or even judges. Equal concern and respect requires that every legal subject has equal standing to interpret the text. And it is best appreciated by setting Dworkin's position in the legal positivist as well as the common law tradition. In that light, one can see that the tension is not only ineliminable, but also productive. And my question for Allan is whether he goes too far along the path to eliminating it.

It may seem strange to set Dworkin in the positivist tradition. But we should recall that he was uneasy about thinking of himself as a natural lawyer, if we understand natural law to be the view that judges may invalidate laws by relying on moral principles that have no foothold in the legal record. Rather, as Dworkin set out in his discussions of the dimension of fit, interpretation is of '*the* law', with the actual legal record of a jural community; and a successful interpretation is one that fits as much of the relevant bits of the legal record as possible.[24] That's a rather large proviso and Dworkin from the start emphasised that the dimension of justification has priority, so that in cases in which a very important moral principle is at stake, fit could be sacrificed, though not altogether. He also suggested from early on that fit can't be characterised outside of a context of justification, so that ultimately contests over interpretation boil down to contests between the different political ideals that rival legal theories take the legal order to serve.

[22] *Lochner v New York* 198 US 45 (1905).
[23] Dworkin, *Taking Rights Seriously* (n 2) ch 12 'What Rights Do We Have?'.
[24] Dworkin, 'Hard Cases' (n 2).

Dworkin's interpretivism starkly diverges from Bentham's model for an ideal legal order in which utilitarian expertise is best located in the legislature, and the content of its decisions should be transmitted through legislation to subjects with unelected judges being given as little opportunity as possible to impose their views on the law. However, it does not differ so starkly from the model advanced by his successor John Austin. Austin distrusted democracy because he thought that the masses were ill-educated and that utilitarian expertise is rather to be found in elites such as the judicial elite. So he was content with giving judges a large role in deciding on the content of the law.[25] There is of course the difference that he, and Hart after him, thought that such judicial decisions are 'discretionary', so that there is not, as Dworkin in line with the common law tradition claimed, only one right answer to any question of law.

But this difference almost vanished when Hart insisted against his positivist predecessors that law can't be understood as operating exclusively in the register of coercion, commands backed by threats, since it also operates in the register of authority and obligation. On Hart's view, legal officials must accept the authority of the law if they are to do their jobs. They must take the 'internal point of view' in contrast to a subject who can take the 'external point of view', in which compliance with the law depends on a calculation of the likelihood and severity of sanctions.[26] In addition, in a rather neglected passage late in *The Concept of Law*, Hart set out a list of the 'characteristic judicial virtues', the components of the internal point of view of judges: 'impartiality and neutrality in surveying the alternatives; consideration for the interest of all who will be affected; and a concern to deploy some acceptable principle as a reasoned basis for decision'.[27]

Hart was, I think, deliberately coy about the status of these virtues within his general argument in this chapter about what he called the necessary 'minimum content of natural law', the extent to which every legal order must serve the basic interests in security of at least some proportion of the population.[28] But I assume that he saw these virtues as the characteristics of the role of a judge who wishes to be true to the judicial role, the role whereby judges understand themselves as operating in a system of authority rather than a gunman situation writ large, and understand their legal order as catering to the minimum content of natural law he sketched.

Now suppose that we understand Dworkin's one right answer thesis as no more than the claim that judges must take their good faith and best shot at showing how the answers they propose are fully supported by legal reasons, reasons that seek to make sense of as much as possible of relevant law. On this view, the difference between Hart's positivism and Dworkin's interpretivism on discretion more or less vanishes because for Hart, from the internal point of view of a judge, the answer to a question about what the law requires must be the judge's good faith and best shot at showing that the legal order

[25] J Austin, *Lectures on Jurisprudence or The Philosophy of Positive Law*, 5th edn (London, John Murray, 1885) 218–19.

[26] Hart, *The Concept of Law* (n 9) 116–17.

[27] ibid 205.

[28] In my view, his coyness is symptomatic of the kinds of issues about the rule of law and legality that arise in his challenges to Fuller, as depicted by J Waldron, 'Positivism and Legality: Hart's Equivocal Response to Fuller' (2008) 83 *New York University Law Review* 1135.

speaks with one voice on the question. However, I wish also to claim that for Hart as much as for Dworkin, the answer must be based on principles which justify it to those whom it affects.

While Dworkin is firmly committed to the latter claim, Hart would baulk at it for at least three reasons. First, he emphasised that a legal order required only its officials to have the internal point of view. Subjects might obey only because they feared sanctions, though this would, he said, be a highly unstable situation.[29] Second, he emphasised that the reasons the officials had for adopting the internal point of view need not be moral reasons. Judges need not, though they well might, regard the legal order as legitimate.[30]

These two reasons connect in the third – Hart's commitment to the Separation Thesis. For if an existence condition for legal order is that subjects as well as officials must take the internal point of view, and if, further, subjects will only have that point of view if officials can justify their decisions about what the law requires as being in their interests, the Separation Thesis can no longer hold. Hart would have to concede a necessary connection between law and morality and he would fall into the second of the traps he diagnosed for natural law of 'obsequious quietism', of supposing that because X is the law, X must have a moral quality such that it should be obeyed.[31]

In my view, Hart was hard pressed to maintain his commitment to the Separation Thesis because of his commitment to explaining law in the register of authority. Indeed, it is on his struggles in this regard that some of his followers base their curious claim that Hart never espoused the Thesis, not even in the 'The Separation of Law and Morals', when, as the title indicates, the essay is from start to finish a clear defence of Austin's insistence that '[t]he existence of law is one thing, its merit or demerit another'.[32] But in Austin's hands, the Thesis operates from what Hart was to call the external point of view. Austin, following Bentham, did without an account of law's authority and there is a certain virtue from the perspective of the Separation Thesis to understanding law, as Hart described their command theory, as the 'gunman situation writ large'. If judicial decision making is seen from the external point of view, judges will understand themselves as having a free choice between the candidates for a plausible answer in hard cases and can do without 'the childish fiction' that judges never make law.[33] Similarly, if law is seen from the external point of view by subjects as no more than commands equipped with sanctions for non-compliance, they can think of law as normatively inert, and so can decide to obey a law or not based on their evaluation of its moral merits.

Hart's attempt to explain why philosophy of law must understand law in the register of authority muddies this ground. To maintain the idea that judges have a discretion in hard cases, he requires of them that they move from the vantage point of the internal point of view to the external. They must extract themselves from the space of their legal order, whose authority they constitute by their acceptance of its norms, and perch

[29] Hart, *The Concept of Law* (n 9) 117.

[30] ibid 203.

[31] Hart, 'Positivism and the Separation of Law and Morals' (n 6) 54.

[32] ibid 52. For example, L Green, 'Positivism and the Inseparability of Law and Morals' (2008) 23 *New York University Law Review* 1035.

[33] Hart, 'Positivism and the Separation of Law and Morals' (n 6) 66, quoting Austin.

outside so that they can make moral evaluations of the candidates for legal answers. Hart has less trouble in a sense with subjects, since he does not regard their internal point of view as an existence condition of legal order. However, only in a sense. As I already suggested, Hart himself was not only troubled by the prospect of a legal order in which most subjects viewed law as the gunman situation writ large, but also thought that such a legal order would have a precarious existence.

Moreover, while Hart in 1958 argued that it was important for philosophy of law to move away from Bentham and Austin's command theory by understanding law in the register of authority, he did suggest that Bentham had contributed to an understanding of such authority in his 'simple' 'recipe' for 'life under a government of laws': '"*to obey punctually; to censure freely*"'.[34] Bentham himself called the recipe the 'motto of a good citizen',[35] and it is hardly, despite Hart's claim, 'simple'. It requires that subjects obey the law while maintaining their freedom to criticise it, which assumes that law has an authority to which the good citizen must accord weight.

Now Bentham clearly thought that the law deserves this kind of respect when and only when the government has managed with some success to have its laws live up to the 'fundamental axiom' of his utilitarian political philosophy that 'it is the greatest happiness of the greatest number that is the measure of right and wrong'.[36] Put differently, the authority law has is measured by its accordance with an external moral measure, in Bentham's case utility.[37] On that view, there is no puzzle of legal authority. Law can be understood, as the command theory suggests, as a matter of coercion because, if it is legitimate, its legitimacy is not internally generated. Put differently, the gunman writ large becomes legitimate when and only when his commands in fact benefit those subject to his coercive power. The puzzle of legal authority arises only when philosophers of law try to explain the authority law has just in being law.

Hart confessed in later work that he had failed to solve this puzzle and attributed his failure to his antipathy to resorting to any notion of a moral component to legal authority.[38] Raz tried to avoid this problem by arguing not that the law 'has' authority, but that it necessarily 'claims' legitimate authority.[39] That allowed him to leave ambiguous his position on the situation when law fails in that claim, as it must often do on his account if it fails to make better judgments for individuals than they would make for themselves. This is the situation that arises when what Raz termed the 'Normal Justification Thesis' is not satisfied; and it is not clear whether Raz supposed that here the law has de facto authority, authority in fact, but not de jure authority, legitimate authority, or whether it lacks any kind of authority at all, and, because it lacks what it necessarily claims, even fails to be law.[40]

[34] ibid 53.

[35] Bentham, *A Fragment on Government* (n 21) 10.

[36] ibid 3.

[37] Indeed, the label 'Separation Thesis' is retroactively bestowed on the distinction between law and morality which Hart referred to in 1958 as the 'utilitarian distinction': Hart, 'Positivism and the Separation of Law and Morals' (n 6) 78.

[38] Hart, *Essays on Bentham* (n 4) 153.

[39] J Raz, 'Authority, Law, and Morality' in J Raz, *Ethics in the Public Domain: Essays in the Morality of Law and Politics* (Oxford, Oxford University Press, 1994) 194.

[40] ibid 198.

In my view, what I will call the 'Razian ambiguity' bedevils contemporary Anglophone philosophy of law. Consider that we have, on the one hand, Frederick Schauer's *The Force of Law*,[41] which seeks to resurrect the command theory of law for legal philosophy by relying exclusively on the idea of force as coercive force, that is, not the force of authority. On the other hand, we have Mark Greenberg arguing that legal obligations are a subset of moral obligations, those that have a 'moral impact',[42] and Scott Hershovitz arguing that our legal practices do not generate obligations that are distinctively legal, but at best moral rights and obligations some of which we label legal.[43]

Both Greenberg and Hershovitz suggest they are the true heirs to Dworkinian interpretivism as only the complete triumph of the dimension of justification over that of fit can vindicate law's claim to have authority, which in their hands seems to amount to a claim that law must make if it is to be law at all. They do not, however, so much solve the puzzle of legal authority as eliminate it from philosophy of law. They fail to explain the authority law has just in being law since law for them both has authority and is law only when it is just.

There are two problems with their position, one moral and political, the other theoretical. The moral and political problem is that it amounts to the kind of natural law position which is, as Alf Ross famously charged, '[l]ike a harlot, … at the disposal of everyone'.[44] I mentioned earlier the law professors in leading law schools who are providing cover for the extreme right in the US and the UK and that a defence of Dworkin's position seems even more important now than when he first set it out. However, if interpretivism is best explained by Greenberg and Hershovitz, perversely Dworkin's position can be instrumentalised by liberalism's enemies.

Consider the leading exposition thus far, Harvard Law Professor Adrian Vermeule's *Common Good Constitutionalism*.[45] The book is at first sight puzzling as for the most part it channels in sophomoric fashion Dworkin's theory of liberal constitutionalism. But it turns out that Vermeule's frequent references to Catholic natural law theory in the footnotes are behind his argument, which is that justification is not in terms of fit with the law, but with a body of allegedly timeless and universal principles that animate right wing Catholics and Evangelicals in the US.[46] He thus uses Dworkin to sanitise the political agenda of the extreme right.

Ironically, Vermeule's dropping of the dimension of fit is of a piece with his critique of the usual interpretive method of the legal right in the US, the various 'originalist' methods which resist liberal constitutionalism by purporting to find illiberal content frozen in the law at a particular time. At least, the originalists claim to take law seriously,

[41] F Schauer, *The Force of Law* (Cambridge, Harvard University Press, 2014).

[42] M Greenberg, 'The Moral Impact Theory of Law' (2014) 123 *Yale Law Journal* 1289.

[43] S Hershovitz, 'The End of Jurisprudence' (2015) 124 *Yale Law Journal* 1160.

[44] A Ross, *On Law and Justice* (Oxford, Oxford University Press, 2019) 338.

[45] A Vermeule, *Common Good Constitutionalism – Recovering the Classical Legal Tradition* (Cambridge, Polity Press, 2022).

[46] For the assertion that Vermeule's Catholicism can be separated from his common good constitutionalism, see Foran's chapter in this volume. I disagree with Foran's assertion. For Vermeule's views in this regard, see eg A Vermeule, 'Integration from Within' (2018) *American Affairs Journal*, americanaffairsjournal.org/2018/02/integration-from-within/ and A Vermeule, 'Beyond Originalism' (*The Atlantic*, 2020), www.theatlantic.com/ideas/archive/2020/03/common-good-constitutionalism/609037/.

even if the only difference between them and Vermeule is that they see the principles as time-bound when they speak as judges in their decisions, whereas Vermeule sees them as timeless, and thus as principles to which judges may appeal directly.

The theoretical problem is closely related. If the dimension of fit disappears, the legal theory that remains is the kind of position that Hart took Gustav Radbruch's to be. As I have explained elsewhere, Hart understood Radbruch's position that extreme injustice is no law to be positivism with a minus sign: the law of a legal order is its positive law, as certified by the criteria of legal validity in its most fundamental rules, minus those positive laws that are extremely unjust by the standards of a moral position external to the law.[47]

If this were correct, Radbruch would differ from Hart only in that Hart says that subjects should disobey extremely unjust laws, and judges not apply them, while for Radbruch there is no issue of disobedience to law since there is no law to be disobeyed. Radbruch's position would in fact lead to the 'dire confusions' which Hart diagnosed and which can be avoided only if we 'speak plainly' and say 'that laws may be law but too evil to be obeyed'.[48] This kind of natural law position would leave positivism's theory of law intact, adding only what we saw Hart charge of Dworkin's interpretivism – 'an idle but confusing decoration' of the moral position that one wishes the law contained. This theoretical problem leads to the moral and political problem since one can inject any set of views into the moral position – the extreme views of the Christian right turned into legal form by Vermeule in the US or John Finnis in the UK,[49] or the liberal views of Radbruch or Dworkin – and suggest to judges that they are entitled to invalidate laws of which they fundamentally disapprove.

2. Allan's Interpretivism

In two powerful essays Allan has diagnosed something of the same set of problems for contemporary philosophy of law, namely, that it seems caught between an anaemic and unsatisfactory positivistic theory of legal authority as de facto authority and a too robust moralised theory of legal authority which obliterates the place of law.[50] On my understanding of Allan's solution to the puzzle of legal authority, it deals with the Razian ambiguity in the following way. He emphasises that the authority is of the law as it is, not merely what the law claims but may not have. But he denies that there are two steps involved in working out what Greenberg calls the moral impact of the law: first, one determines its content; second, one evaluates it from one's moral perspective to see whether it is in fact law.

[47] Dyzenhaus, *The Long Arc of Legality* (n 1) ch 2 'The Puzzle of Very Unjust Law I: Hart and Dworkin'.

[48] Hart, 'Positivism and the Separation of Law and Morals' (n 6) 77.

[49] See D Dyzenhaus, 'The Snake Charmers' (*Verfassungsblog*, 7 March 2022) verfassungsblog.de/os5-snake-charmers.

[50] TRS Allan, 'Why the Law is What it Ought to Be' (2020) 11 *Jurisprudence* 574 and TRS Allan, 'Law as a Branch of Morality: The Unity of Practice and Principle' (2020) 65 *American Journal of Law and Jurisprudence* 1.

The denial rests on Allan's sophisticated account of common law adjudication which has made him the foremost standard bearer of the common law tradition since Coke and Blackstone. According to this account, the 'is' of the law in which its authority inheres must be understood as the content of the law as determined by a process of interpretation in which the fundamental moral commitments of the interpreter are engaged from the start. On this account, one cannot prise apart the dimension of justification from the dimension of fit with the result that the former is deployed to evaluate the results of the latter. Rather, justification shapes the entire process in which fit is determined. The role of fit with relevant existing law is that it significantly shapes the content of the conclusions at which judges arrive, but the content cannot be one that violates the judges' fundamental justificatory commitments.

If this is right, Allan's interpretivism corresponds best to what we can think of as Dworkin's middle period. At the outset, in the essays in *Taking Rights Seriously*, particularly the influential 'Hard Cases', interpretation involved an interaction between the two distinct dimensions of fit and justification. In the middle period, in *Law's Empire*, Dworkin clarified that justification has priority, while in the final period, *Justice for Hedgehogs*, he suggested that in extreme situations the two dimensions could come apart.

But throughout his career Dworkin supposed that legal and moral duty can come apart in ways that give rise to the situation of civil disobedience, with the important rider that in that situation the legal component has some moral force to it. The situation of civil disobedience is, as both Fuller and Dworkin pointed out against Hart, morally complex only if there is morality on both sides of the dilemma. The difference in *Justice for Hedgehogs* is not, then, any major change of view, only that Dworkin in his last bid to save his theory from the wicked legal system objection resorted to an explicit theory of judicial civil disobedience. And it is precisely here that Allan departs from him. Allan's argument is that just as one cannot prise apart the dimension of justification from the dimension of fit, so it must be the case that civil disobedience cannot be part of an interpretivism true to its moral ambitions.

Allan's interpretivism thus excludes the possibility of civil disobedience, at least for judges. If judges cannot determine a content consistent with their deep moral commitments, they should, it seems, conclude that there is no law to enforce. I say 'at least' when it comes to judicial civil disobedience because I think that Allan supposes that if judges do their interpretive job properly, subjects will generally not be faced with the kind of conflict of obligations presupposed by the idea of civil disobedience. Judges will, that is, be able to come up with an interpretation that makes it possible for subjects to conclude that their obligation is to obey the law without being faced with the moral pull of a conflicting obligation.[51]

There is much to this position, if my description is correct. But in the next section I quibble with some of its features and present my own alternative, which I think preserves Allan's central insight. In my formulation: as long as judges are operating in a legal order, judicial interpretation will be possible such that subjects will be able to get

[51] See Allan, 'Why the Law is What it Ought to Be' (n 50) 593–96 and 'Law as a Branch of Morality' (n 50) 8–9, 17.

an adequate answer to the question 'But, how can that be law for me?' But I will argue that, while Allan is correct that this formulation precludes civil disobedience for judges, he is wrong in inferring that it also does so for subjects.

3. Bad and Good Contingency

Allan's legal theory is built out of cases in the common law tradition which permits him to take advantage of the tremendous capacity that those who are adept in that tradition have to avoid confronting the prospect of invalidating a statute because of its repugnant content. Consider that Coke is famous for the following claim in *Dr. Bonham's Case*: 'it appears in our books, that in many cases, the common law doth control Acts of Parliament, and sometimes adjudge them to be void; for when an act of Parliament is against Common right and reason, or repugnant, or impossible to be performed, the Common Law will control it, and adjudge such an Act to be void'.[52] But Coke did not in fact invalidate the statute in that case, nor in any other case. Rather, he ruled that the charter of the College of Physicians did not as a matter of statutory interpretation permit it to sanction Bonham – an unlicensed practitioner – in the ways that it had, and that more generally the College could not be a judge in its own cause.[53]

However, the strength of such a theory is also a weakness, in that it is too tied to a particular context to provide the basis for a theoretical challenge to legal positivism. The problem here can be stated more generally as methodological and it applies in my view to Dworkin and Allan, as well as to much of my own work. It has two parts to it, the first to do with case selection. If one builds one's general legal theory out of a theory of adjudication and, moreover, of the adjudication of cases in not only the common law tradition, but also the tradition as located in a liberal democratic jurisdiction, it is hardly surprising that one can argue both that the law is what it ought to be and that one does not have to move outside of the public record of the law to make that claim.[54]

The second part has to do with the level at which one makes the argument. Legal positivists argue that a theory of law succeeds as a general theory only if it is pitched at the level of legal order since there is much more to legal order than the activity of judges deciding hard cases. As Hart put this point in 1958, such cases 'rightly' form the 'daily diet' of law schools, but something goes wrong if the diet is the main preoccupation of philosophy of law.[55] Here is my own proposal, briefly stated. It attempts a solution to the

[52] S Sheppard (ed), *The Selected Writings and Speeches of Sir Edmund Coke*, vol 1 (Indianapolis, Liberty Fund, 2003) 275.

[53] Indeed, it was just this room for judicial maneuver in the tradition that made Bentham so hostile to it because, as he saw things, its adepts were proficient at undermining legislative intention, all the while pretending to uphold it.

[54] Allan says that 'when the law embodies a scheme or charter of justice that honours the equal dignity of persons, according to a coherent account of that basic value, its obligations are genuine moral obligations': Allan, 'Why the Law is as it Ought to Be' (n 50) 595. But positivists would rightly point out that they both agree and that everything turns on the contingency of the 'when'.

[55] Hart, 'Positivism and the Separation of Law and Morals' (n 6) 72.

puzzle of legal authority by uniting the three strings to Dworkin's bow listed earlier, and it locates its argument at the right level in showing how a commitment to legal order makes interpretivism possible.

On my account, a theory of law's authority has three elements. First, following Fuller, it explains authority as compliance with fundamental principles of legality – the right-giving basis of legal order. Second, it gives to officials a role in interpreting enacted law in the light of such principles. It thus offers a theory of the role of official interpretation of the law in maintaining legal order. Given the first and second elements, the principles make up a grammar of legality in that enacted laws which are not interpretable in the light of the principles have a dubious claim to authority. If enough dubious laws are enacted, the order begins to shift from one of legal right to one of unmediated coercive power. Thus, to be legal, to count as valid law, law must be interpretable in a way which respects the fundamental principles.

Third, the way in which these two elements combine in a single legal theory requires invoking what I call a 'constitutionalist idea'. This is the idea of an ongoing practice which constitutes legitimate authority of the sort early modern social theorists, notably Hobbes, set out in versions of the social contract. These theorists substituted for the divine right of the monarch a secular basis for the authority of the modern legal state, one produced by the voluntary interaction of the very individuals who are subject to that authority.

Interpretability is key. Laws which are not interpretable in light of fundamental principles of legality lose their claim to authority because they do not bear the marks of having been enacted with legal right. They are, following Radbruch, 'illegal laws', laws which lack the quality of legality or lawlikeness.[56] Conversely, when laws are interpretable in this way, legal officials will be able to justify to the legal subject their exercise of authority. They will be able to answer the question 'But, how can that be law for me?' For legality mediates the conversion of public policy into the enacted law applied by officials to legal subjects. This process of mediation, whereby political judgments are converted into legal content, brings these fundamental principles to bear on the determination of the law which the officials apply. In this way, the officials maintain the constitutionalist idea through a dynamic process of application and interpretation of law.

In many ways, this account draws on the same sources as Allan, notably, Radbruch, Fuller, and Dworkin, as well as more generally on the common law tradition, including Albert Dicey's constitutional theory. But it differs in the last respect in that common law constitutionalism is seen as just one example of how a legal order may design its legal framework, rather than as the basis for a general legal theory. More important is that the account effects a rapprochement with legal positivism though it takes as its primary sources in this regard two philosophers who do not figure in Allan's legal theory, Thomas Hobbes and Hans Kelsen, so not the Hartian tradition that stretches from Bentham through Austin and Hart to Raz. The Hartian tradition is not at all left out of the rapprochement. Rather I argue that it is flawed in that it is too tied, as is Allan's legal theory, to a particular context. Indeed, it is tied to the very same common law context, though it privileges parliamentary supremacy, the rule of parliament over the rule of judges.

[56] G Radbruch, 'Statutory Lawlessness and Supra-Statutory Law' (2006) 26 *OJLS* 1.

Hobbes and Kelsen figure more prominently because I take their legal theories to be more general accounts of the legal order of the modern state, with Kelsen updating Hobbes to take account of the fact that the modern state is located in international legal order. This location permits Kelsen to explain how international law delegates to states their authority not only to make law for their subjects, but also to design their legal orders. The latter includes the authority to design their constitutions, both the internal constitutional relationship between state institutions and subjects and the external relationship with the international legal order and thus with other states.

Notice that this theory is still highly contingent. It is not a theory of how all societies that have ever existed have developed a normative public order to govern peaceful and stable interaction between the individuals in the community. Rather, it is a theory of the post-Westphalian state, with its internal division of functions between the different state institutions and its external relationship with other states, as mediated by the binding norms of international law. But it is not contingent on whether such a state is democratic, or has a written constitution or an unwritten one, or, if it has a written constitution, on whether it contains a liberal charter of rights and freedoms with judges given the authority to declare invalid violations of the constitution, or on whether the tradition of the state is common law or civilian.

I have argued at considerable length elsewhere that such a theory can account for the commitments shared among the leading philosophers of law of the last century, notably, Kelsen, Hart, Fuller, Dworkin, Raz and Allan.[57] I take these commitments to be: first, to understanding law from the perspective of those who accept the authority of their legal order, and through such acceptance constituting its authority; second, to recognising both constitutional law and international law as valid and therefore binding law, that is, not law that binds only when a state consents to be bound; third, to supposing that law to be law must meet more or less the 'desiderata' Fuller set out in his eight principles of legality, a precursor of which is to be found in Hobbes's 'laws of nature'; fourth, as part of the third commitment, to accepting Fuller's eighth principle of 'congruence' of official action with the law,[58] which finds expression in Kelsen's idea that the basic norm regulates legal order such that officials can find that its norms make up a meaningful whole,[59] or Dworkin's idea of 'integrity', or Hart's invocation in his list of the judicial virtues of the requirement that judges 'deploy some acceptable principle as a reasoned basis for decision'.

On my argument, the major division in philosophy of law is not between legal positivists and natural lawyers, but, as Kelsen explained, between 'dynamic' and 'static' theories of law.[60] The former include the dynamic process of legal change within the scope of philosophy of law while static theories consign change to some extra-legal space, as is the case in the Hartian tradition. Once these shared commitments are located within a dynamic theory, one can see how the mere existence of legal order makes judicial

[57] I leave John Finnis off the list for the reason alluded to in the text above and elaborated in Appendix 3 of Dyzenhaus, *The Long Arc of Legality* (n 1).

[58] LL Fuller, *The Morality of Law*, rev edn (New Haven, Yale University Press, 1969) 39.

[59] H Kelsen, *Introduction to the Problems of Legal Theory*, B and S Paulson (trans) (Oxford, Clarendon Press, 1992 [1934]).

[60] H Kelsen, 'The Pure Theory of Law and Analytical Jurisprudence' (1941) 55 *Harvard Law Review* 44.

interpretation possible of the kind that permits adequate answers to be given to the subject who asks 'But how can that be law for me?' That accounts for the standing obligation for judges to apply the law as they find it, an all-things-considered obligation that rules out civil disobedience for judges.[61] That same set of considerations make it the case that subjects will find that the law exerts a pull on them which makes morally complex a situation in which the answer, while adequate, violates the demands of conscience to the extent that they should consider civil disobedience.

[61] That does not mean that judges can do nothing. Judges can still condemn the law within their judgments, an informal equivalent of the formal declaration of incompatibility that judges must make in terms of section 4 of the UK Human Rights Act (1998) when they are unable to find an interpretation of the statutory provision in issue that is compliant with the rights enumerated in the Act, which is their duty under section 3.

3

Dicey on Parliamentary Sovereignty and the Common Law

JEFFREY GOLDSWORTHY*

1. Introduction

Trevor Allan has spent much of his career attempting to discredit the doctrine of parliamentary sovereignty, which has required that AV Dicey's classic defence of it be either refuted, or heavily qualified through reinterpretation.[1] In his recent book on Dicey's legal and constitutional thought, Mark Walters comes to Allan's aid.[2] Like Allan, Walters disputes the orthodox view that for Dicey, 'sovereign power always prevails over ideals of legal justice or the rule of law':

> Dicey had a far subtler, more nuanced understanding of the relationship between sovereignty and legality … he seemed to see sovereign authority as itself containing a law of reason, that the exercise of parliamentary sovereignty is in some sense conditioned by ideals of legality internal to the very idea of legislative sovereignty.[3]

Extrapolating from Dicey's account of how the judicial interpretation of statutes is legitimately used to enhance their compatibility with the rule of law, Walters suggests that this might justify the kind of creative or strained interpretation that Allan advocates, which in extreme cases may render a statutory provision void, in terms of its practical effect, even if it remains formally valid.[4]

Walters adds that his reinterpretation of Dicey reinforces an approach to Dicey that TRS Allan has been developing for more than 30 years, and that despite differences in

* I thank John Allison and Mark Walters for helpful comments on an earlier version of this chapter.

[1] TRS Allan, *Law, Liberty, and Justice: The Legal Foundations of British Constitutionalism* (Oxford, Clarendon Press, 1993) esp 4–5, 10–11, 266–67, 282–84, 290; TRS Allan, *Constitutional Justice: A Liberal Theory of the Rule of Law* (Oxford, Oxford University Press, 2001) esp 13–14, 17, 19, 42–43, 214–15; TRS Allan, *The Sovereignty of Law: Freedom, Constitution, and Common Law* (Oxford, Oxford University Press, 2013) esp 10–11, 24–25, 31–36, 50–54, 133, 140–43, 171–72, 206–207.

[2] MD Walters, *AV Dicey and the Common Law Constitutional Tradition: A Legal Turn of Mind* (Cambridge, Cambridge University Press, 2020).

[3] ibid 6.

[4] ibid 294. He notes that Allan goes one step further, and advocates formal invalidity.

his and Allan's interpretive methodology, they 'have arrived at roughly the same place'.[5] It is therefore fitting that in this book, celebrating Allan's work, Walters' reinterpretation of Dicey be carefully scrutinised.

In effect, Walters attributes to Dicey a version of common law constitutionalism, quite similar to Allan's position, in which parliamentary sovereignty is both established and constrained by the common law.[6] Dicey's understanding of parliamentary sovereignty, according to Walters, is as follows:

1. rather than being an instance of Austinian sovereignty that stands above and creates the law, it is part of the ordinary law of the land;
2. that ordinary law is the common law;
3. the common law is a multi-layered body of rules and principles, including broad foundational principles that provide coherence and guide decision-making in novel cases, which are identified by induction from judicial decisions, a process involving evaluative rather than empirical judgments;
4. the common law 'determines and conditions' parliamentary sovereignty and its exercise, especially through the judicial interpretation of statutes, to enhance their compatibility with the rule of law;
5. this justifies creative or strained interpretations of statutes, which in extreme cases may legitimately render a statutory provision void, in terms of its practical effect, even if it remains formally valid.

I will examine each of these claims, to determine the plausibility of attributing them to Dicey.

2. Claim 1: Rather than Being an Instance of Austinian Sovereignty that Stands above and Creates the Law, Parliamentary Sovereignty is Part of the Ordinary Law of the Land

Walters is right that Dicey was not an Austinian legal positivist.[7] Dicey said that, rather than parliamentary sovereignty being derived from abstract theories of jurisprudence, Austin's theory of sovereignty was a generalisation inspired by his familiarity with a Parliament made sovereign by 'the peculiar history of English constitutional law'.[8] Walters has also revealed that Dicey denied Austin's thesis that in every state there is necessarily some person or body of persons who possesses legislative sovereignty.[9]

[5] ibid 360.
[6] ibid 6.
[7] eg ibid 61, 95, 138–42, 148–49, 151, 153–54, 158–59, 160–61, 162, 165, 166, 179–81, 206, 215, 262, 270, 285, 339.
[8] AV Dicey, *Introduction to the Study of the Law of the Constitution*, 8th edn (London, Macmillan, 1915) 69–70.
[9] Walters, *AV Dicey* (n 2) 339.

However, Dicey did not completely free himself from Austinian thinking. He praised Austin (and Holland) for explaining 'the nature of sovereignty' with 'brevity and clearness', and 'admirably' stating the 'difficulties of imposing any limits whatever on sovereignty'.[10] To show that Parliament could not limit its own sovereign power, he relied partly on the distinctive development of the English constitution, but also on the supposed 'logic' of sovereignty. He said that 'sovereignty or the possession of supreme power in a state, whether it be in the hands of a Czar or of a Parliament, is always one and the same quality,' and was such that limited sovereignty 'is in the case of a Parliamentary as of every other sovereign, a contradiction in terms'.[11] On the other hand, he insisted that any sovereign could abdicate his or its sovereignty: 'If the Czar can abdicate, so can a Parliament'.[12] These were inferences from 'the nature of sovereignty', although they did not contradict his assertion that parliamentary sovereignty in Britain was established by law. He seems to have thought that whenever genuine sovereignty is established by law, it necessarily has certain characteristics.

Dicey erred in retaining this Austinian element in his thinking. Logic alone does not require that a sovereign cannot limit its own power. If Parliament's sovereignty is a creature of British law, then the law could conceivably confer what HLA Hart called 'self-embracing' sovereignty which, unlike 'continuing' sovereignty, can be used to limit itself either temporarily or permanently.[13] In fact, British law rejects self-embracing sovereignty, but is not compelled by logic to do so. Dicey was equally in error in insisting that any sovereign can necessarily abdicate its sovereignty; again, logic by itself does not entail that conclusion, so the law could conceivably forbid abdication.[14]

But does Dicey's insight that parliamentary sovereignty is contingently grounded in British law establish that it is 'an ordinary legal concept', established by 'the ordinary law of England'?[15] He did say that the law of the constitution was composed of the same elements as the law on any other topic, namely, statute law and judge-made law; its exposition was therefore subject to the same difficulties as 'any attempt to explain our law of contract, our law of torts, or our law of real property'.[16] Nevertheless, he never said that parliamentary sovereignty was established by 'ordinary law'.[17] He used that term frequently in drawing two different distinctions between ordinary law and extraordinary law.

The first distinction focused on claims that executive officials possess unique powers or privileges that are not subject to ordinary law or the jurisdiction of ordinary courts, such as power to override ordinary law in emergencies with legal impunity. Dicey relied heavily on this distinction in four related contexts: in discussing the Rule of Law in general; in agreeing with seventeenth-century common lawyers who opposed claims that

[10] Dicey, *Introduction* (n 8) 58–59 especially n 3.
[11] ibid 66 fn 2.
[12] ibid.
[13] HLA Hart, *The Concept of Law*, 2nd edn (Oxford, Clarendon Press, 1994) 149–50.
[14] J Goldsworthy, *Parliamentary Sovereignty: Contemporary Debates* (Cambridge, Cambridge University Press, 2010) 118–22.
[15] Walters, *AV Dicey* (n 2) 178, 162; see also 262, 248–49.
[16] Dicey, *Introduction* (n 8) 31.
[17] Dicey did say that the constitution is 'a judge-made constitution' and 'the result of the ordinary law of the land': ibid 192, 199, 281. But Walters rightly concedes that 'Dicey, read in context, was only referring to the protection of private rights here, not the whole constitution': Walters, *AV Dicey* (n 2) 254 fn 107.

the King possessed 'absolute' (legally unchallengeable) prerogatives;[18] in criticising the French system of *droit administratif*;[19] and in denying that English law permitted the imposition of martial law, even in emergencies.[20] The law of England exemplified the Rule of Law, which demanded the supremacy of ordinary law as opposed to arbitrary power,[21] as well as equal treatment in the administration of ordinary law by ordinary courts.[22]

In none of these four contexts was parliamentary sovereignty directly implicated. Indeed, Dicey stated that 'the supremacy of the law of the land means in the last resort the right of the judges to control the *executive* government'.[23] He also affirmed that in extraordinary circumstances Parliament could legitimately grant executive officials exceptional powers, and legal immunity in relation to their use.[24] He frequently mentioned Acts of Indemnity, describing them as 'the legalisation of illegality' – 'an exercise of arbitrary sovereign power' that is 'the highest exertion and crowning proof of sovereign power'.[25] He considered that judicious uses of this power did not violate the rule of law.[26] Nevertheless, it is an extraordinary power to override ordinary law that is not subject to judicial supervision.

Much more relevant to whether Dicey regarded parliamentary sovereignty as a matter of ordinary law is his second distinction, between ordinary laws and fundamental laws. The latter are exemplified by written constitutions that possess one or more of the following characteristics:

(a) they are widely regarded as having been created, not by ordinary law-making processes or even in accordance with prior law, but by the sovereign constituent power of 'the people' or 'the nation';
(b) they cannot be amended or repealed by ordinary law-making processes, but only by some special, more difficult process;
(c) they are superior to ordinary laws, which the courts must hold invalid if there is any inconsistency between them.[27]

Dicey regarded the American Constitution as a fundamental rather than ordinary law because it possessed all three characteristics.[28] Yet he also considered American constitutionalism to be more like that of the British, rather than those of some continental countries, because the American Constitution was interpreted and enforced by ordinary courts using ordinary legal reasoning.[29] Walters infers that therefore,

[18] Walters, ibid 48–49; Dicey, ibid 61, 263–64, 364–68.

[19] Dicey, ibid xlvii–xlviii, 190–91, 198, 261, ch XII. Dicey noted a similarity between the views of the 17th century English advocates of absolute royal prerogatives, and the ideas underpinning droit administrative: ibid vii, 364–68.

[20] ibid 283, 289, 303–304, 543–44, 549–51. See also Walters, *AV Dicey* (n 2) 56–57, on Dicey's response to the Eyre crisis.

[21] Dicey, ibid 198; see also 189, 199, 466–67.

[22] ibid 198.

[23] ibid 467 (emphasis added).

[24] ibid 406–408, 418.

[25] ibid 233, 48; also 228–33, 408, 418, 547–49, 553–54.

[26] Walters, *AV Dicey* (n 2) 279–80.

[27] Dicey, *Introduction* (n 8) 84–85, 88, 91, 95–96, 105, 107–108, 118–20, 122, 140–41, 170–71.

[28] ibid 4–5, 139–43, 146, 154–55, 466–67.

[29] Walters, *AV Dicey* (n 2) 349–51, quoting Dicey, *Introduction* ibid 5. See also Walters, ibid 1 for a comparison of French and common law constitutionalism.

for Dicey, this was the paramount criterion for ordinary law: 'ordinary law is largely a matter of adopting an *ordinary legal method* or *perspective*.'[30] Walters even declares that in the common law tradition 'the idea of a constitution is a paradox', because 'the laws that are supposed to be foundational for the ordinary laws that govern everyday life turn out to be an integral part of those same ordinary laws'.[31] But this is not at all paradoxical. The American Constitution is a fundamental and not ordinary law according to Dicey's second distinction between those terms, because it satisfies criteria (a), (b) and (c), even though it is an ordinary law in another sense because it is interpreted and enforced by ordinary courts in accordance with ordinary legal reasoning.

Moreover, for Dicey, judicial enforcement of constitutional limits was essential to their deserving the label 'law'. The French and Belgian Constitutions in his day purported to impose elaborate limits on legislative and executive power, but did not provide for judicial enforcement. Dicey therefore described them as 'maxims of political morality' or of 'policy', 'secured by moral or political sanctions' including public opinion, and 'not in reality laws'.[32] For Dicey these limits were not really fundamental laws at all, whereas their counterparts in the US Constitution were 'in reality as well as name the supreme law of the land'.[33]

There is a tendency in Walters' theorising to flatten the law by reducing all kinds of law to one level: 'the ordinary law of the land, the common law'.[34] He sidelines the way that ordinary legal thinking itself recognises a hierarchy among different kinds of law. A written Constitution is usually superior to statute law and common law, because it overrides them when they are inconsistent with it, and statutes are superior to common law for the same reason.[35] Dicey was explicit about this:

> English judges do not claim or exercise any power to repeal a Statute, while Acts of Parliament may override and constantly do override the law of the judges. Judicial legislation is, in short, subordinate legislation, carried on with the assent and subject to the supervision of Parliament.[36]

Moreover, this hierarchy of laws reflected a hierarchy of institutional authority:

> All the power of the English state is concentrated in the Imperial Parliament, and all departments of government are legally subject to Parliamentary despotism. Our judges are independent, in the sense of … being raised above the direct influence of the Crown or the Ministry; but the judicial department does not pretend to stand on a level with Parliament; its functions might be modified at any time by an Act of Parliament; and such a statute would be no violation of the law.[37]

[30] Walters, ibid 5, 160.
[31] ibid 1. The word 'paradox' is also used at 350.
[32] Dicey, *Introduction* (n 8) 130–31, 153.
[33] ibid 154.
[34] Walters, *AV Dicey* (n 2) 175.
[35] On the subordination of common law to a written Constitution, see *Theophanous v Herald & Weekly Times Ltd* (1994) 182 CLR 104, 126 (Mason, Gaudron and Toohey JJ), and to statutes, see *R (Miller) v Secretary of State for Exiting the European Union* [2017] UKSC 5, para 42, per Lord Neuberger, Lady Hale, Lord Mance, Lord Kerr, Lord Clarke, Lord Wilson, Lord Sumption and Lord Hodge.
[36] Dicey, *Introduction* (n 8) 58.
[37] ibid 152.

Dicey was certainly aware that the doctrine of parliamentary sovereignty was a fundamental law. He described it as 'from a legal point of view, the dominant characteristic of our political institutions'; 'the very keystone of the law of the constitution', 'the fundamental doctrine of English constitutionalists', and '[t]he one fundamental dogma of English constitutional law'.[38] He did not regard the rule of law as a constitutional principle of equal status. It is '*a* fundamental principle of the constitution', whereas '*the* underlying principle of all modern constitutionalism' and '*the* one essential principle of the constitution is obedience by all persons … ultimately to the will of the nation as expressed through Parliament'.[39]

More importantly, Dicey denied that the doctrine could be changed by Parliament. This is despite his frequent claims that Britain had no truly fundamental laws, because there were no laws that Parliament could not change.[40] He regarded it as an essential attribute of parliamentary sovereignty that Parliament 'can change any law whatever. Being a "legislative" assembly it can make ordinary laws, being a "constituent" assembly it can make laws which shift the basis of the constitution.'[41] It can change 'each and every part' of the constitution, even 'fundamental … or so-called constitutional laws', in the same way that it can change other laws.[42] This led him to deny the existence of 'any distinction between constitutional and ordinary laws' under the English constitution, although in the preceding paragraph he referred more cautiously to the lack of any 'marked or clear distinction between laws which are not fundamental or constitutional and laws which are'.[43]

But in saying this, Dicey overlooked a crucial exception. He denied that Parliament could effectively disable itself from amending or repealing a statute in the future; it could not limit, although it could abdicate, its own sovereignty.[44] Presumably, if Parliament had enacted a provision purporting to limit its lawmaking power, Dicey would have regarded the courts as duty bound to refuse to enforce it, and thereby to treat it, for practical purposes, as void. Therefore, applying Dicey's own definition of parliamentary sovereignty, he accepted on the positive side a limit to Parliament's law-making power which, on the negative side, the courts would have been required to enforce by holding void any statutory provision exceeding the limit.[45]

Thus, Dicey believed there was one law that Parliament could not change, at least in its essentials: the law that conferred continuing sovereignty upon it. Applying criteria (b) and (c) above, that law was clearly, on his view, a fundamental rather than an ordinary law, even if it was an ordinary law in the alternative sense that it was interpreted and applied by ordinary courts using ordinary legal reasoning.

[38] ibid xviii (and also 37), 68, c, 141.

[39] ibid 198, 450–52 (emphasis added). See J Allison, *The English Historical Constitution* (Cambridge, Cambridge University Press, 2007) 162–163, 212. *Cf* Walters, *AV Dicey* (n 2) 226, 262–64.

[40] Dicey, *Introduction* (n 8) 38, 84–85, 87, 141.

[41] ibid 84.

[42] ibid 86, 84.

[43] ibid 85.

[44] ibid 62–68.

[45] ibid 37–38.

3. Claim 2: Ordinary Law is the Common Law

Whether or not the doctrine of parliamentary sovereignty is fundamental or ordinary law may not matter much. What does matter is whether or not we classify it as part of the common law, because in the modern era the common law is generally regarded as judge-made law, whose principles remain subject to judicial development or even over-ruling. Dicey often distinguished between statute law and 'judge-made law',[46] although he also described the common law as 'the mass of custom, tradition, or judge-made maxims', implying that there is more to it than just judge-made law.[47] (I will return to that possibility later.)

There are examples of what Walters would call 'ordinary law' that are clearly not common law, such as statutes and written constitutions. It can be difficult to distinguish clearly between enacted laws and common law, given that in interpreting enacted laws judges also legitimately develop them, by supplementing the meanings of vague or ambiguous provisions that would otherwise be insufficiently determinate to settle disputes, and occasionally adjusting those meanings to prevent the lawmakers' purposes being stymied.[48] Also, the principles that judges use to interpret statutes are often called 'common law principles', because they were developed over centuries by the judiciary in somewhat the same way as ordinary common law principles.[49] In both Canada and Australia, whose constitutions were originally statutes enacted by the U.K. Parliament, apex courts initially chose to apply traditional principles of statutory interpretation.[50]

But the label 'common law' should not mislead us. The vast bulk of the common law consists of substantive rules and principles, governing property, contracts, torts and so on, that have been made and developed by the judiciary over centuries. Judges are recognised as having authority unilaterally to alter these rules and principles, by extending, contracting or even over-ruling them. By contrast, principles of statutory and constitutional interpretation concern the interpretation of laws, created by other institutions possessing superior lawmaking authority, that the judges do not have authority to change (except in strictly limited ways to prevent the lawmakers' intentions or purposes being frustrated).[51] Judges do not possess the same extensive authority to change these interpretive principles according to their assessment of justice and the public interest, as they have to change ordinary common law. There is some scope for judicial modification, but not so as to subvert or usurp the authority of the original lawmakers or

[46] Walters, *AV Dicey* (n 8) 159, citing Dicey ibid 31.

[47] Dicey, ibid 23.

[48] See J Goldsworthy, 'The Meaning and Interpretation of Statutes in Anglo-American Legal Systems' in T Gizbert-Studnicki, F Poggi and I Skoczeń (eds), *Interpretivism and the Limits of Law* (Cheltenham, Edward Elgar, 2022) 43.

[49] See J Goldsworthy, 'In Defence of the Traditional Methodologies' in S Lakin and D Kyritsos (eds), *The Methodology of Constitutional Theory* (Oxford, Hart Publishing, 2022) 41, section 4.

[50] J Goldsworthy and G Huscroft, 'Originalism in Canada and Australia: Why the Divergence?' in R Albert and D Cameron (eds), *Canada in the World: Comparative Perspectives on the Canadian Constitution* (Cambridge, Cambridge University Press, 2018) 183.

[51] See text to n 48.

those with the legal power of amendment. As Sir Gerard Brennan said, shortly before he became Chief Justice of Australia,

> it is clear that judicial development of the common law is a function different from judicial interpretation of statutes and of the Constitution … The Court, owing its existence and its jurisdiction ultimately to the Constitution, can do no more than interpret and apply its text, uncovering implications where they exist …. The notion of 'developing' the law of the Constitution is inconsistent with the judicial power it confers. Clearly the Court cannot change the Constitution …[52]

The doctrine of parliamentary sovereignty exemplifies another kind of law – fundamental customary law – that is ordinary law in the sense that it is enforced by ordinary courts, but not a matter of common law in the modern sense of law that was made and may continue to be altered by the judiciary. It can plausibly be regarded as part of what HLA Hart called the rule of recognition of the British legal system.[53] As the ultimate source of the validity of statutes, such a rule is part of the legal foundation of the entire legal system. It is a customary rule constituted by its acceptance as binding by senior legal officials in general, and not just judges.[54] Since it can change only if the consensus among them changes, it is much harder to change than either statutes or judge-made common law.

Dicey lived long before Hart formulated the concept of rules of recognition. In 1902 John Salmond proposed a somewhat similar idea that influenced Hart,[55] but there is no reference to Salmond in Dicey's *Law of the Constitution*, and Walters has apparently not found any in Dicey's other writings. Walters often emphasises Dicey's predicament: deficiencies in the two main existing schools of jurisprudence – of Austin and Henry Maine – made them incapable of adequately explaining the foundations and structure of legal systems.[56] The question is then whether Dicey's thinking seems more consistent with Hartian positivism than with the Dworkinian common law constitutionalism that Walters and Allan favour.

As I have previously argued, there is ample evidence that Dicey did not attribute Parliament's authority to judge-made common law.[57]

First, many of his observations are inconsistent with that view. They include his statements, previously quoted, that judge-made common law is 'subordinate legislation … subject to the supervision of Parliament', made by the 'judicial department' that is on a lower level than Parliament and 'legally subject to [its] despotism'.[58] How could the power of the superior body be established by decisions of the inferior one? Similarly, he

[52] *Theophanous v Herald & Weekly Times Ltd* (1994) 182 CLR 104, 143–44.

[53] Hart, *Concept of Law* (n 13) 100–110.

[54] See J Gardner, 'Some Types of Law' in DE Edlin (ed), *Common Law Theory* (Cambridge, Cambridge University Press, 2007) 51, 61–66. Gardner errs by attributing the custom to law-applying officials only. See J Goldsworthy, *The Sovereignty of Parliament, History and Philosophy* (Oxford, Clarendon Press, 1999) 240–43.

[55] Hart, *Concept of Law* (n 13) 292 citing JW Salmond, *Jurisprudence*, 11th edn (London, Sweet and Maxwell, 1957) 137 and Appendix 1. Walters refers to Salmond at Walters, *AV Dicey* (n 2) 149.

[56] Walters, ibid 63, 90, 151–52, 338–39, 359.

[57] Goldsworthy, *Parliamentary Sovereignty* (n 14) 44.

[58] Dicey, *Introduction* (n 8) 58, 152, quoted above at text to nn 36 and 37.

said that parliamentary sovereignty is 'a legal fact which forms the basis of our whole legislative and judicial system'.[59] It is hard to see how judge-made common law could be the basis of parliamentary sovereignty if the latter is the basis of the judicial system. Dicey's statement that '[t]here is no power which, under the English constitution, can come into rivalry with the legislative sovereignty of Parliament' also seems inconsistent with the idea that Parliament's sovereignty derives from, and therefore could be limited by, the exercise of judicial power.[60]

Second, Dicey thrice said that parliamentary sovereignty was a 'legal fact', which he distinguished from a 'political fact',[61] which casts doubt on Walters attribution to him of the view that 'law is not a matter of fact but of a "discourse of reason"'.[62] It might be argued that by 'legal fact' Dicey meant some kind of non-empirical normative truth. But he asserted that Parliament's supreme legislative authority 'is shown historically in a large number of instances' – in other words, shown by historical facts.[63] These facts consisted of various extraordinary statutes that he took to provide 'a remarkable example of the exertion of Parliamentary authority' (the Acts of Union),[64] a 'supreme display of legislative authority' (the Septennial Act),[65] an 'unprecedented use of its powers … [that] is at once the result and the standing proof of such Parliamentary sovereignty' (the Septennial Act),[66] a 'striking exhibition of absolute power' (frequent interference with private rights),[67] and 'crowning proof of sovereign power (Acts of Indemnity).'[68] These various proofs amount to the fact that such extraordinary statutes had always been accepted as valid laws by the nation as a whole; no-one had even considered challenging their validity in the courts. Dicey's reliance on this long-standing acceptance of the legality of extraordinary statutes is consistent with relying on the consensus among senior legal officials, and acquiescence of the populace at large, that constitutes Hart's rule of recognition. (Incidentally, this answers Walters' and others' objection that Dicey did not provide sufficient judicial authority for parliamentary sovereignty, and that extraordinary statutes do not prove anything.[69] When it comes to rules of recognition, especially ones that are customary, explicit judicial authority may be unnecessary; facts like Dicey's can clearly indicate judicial acquiescence in a broader official consensus.)

Third, it is doubtful that Dicey regarded even the common law as entirely judge-made: he described it as a 'mass of custom, tradition, or judge-made maxims'.[70] It is possible that Dicey regarded Parliament's sovereignty as a matter of long-standing,

[59] ibid 73.
[60] ibid 68.
[61] ibid 37, 66, 73; for the distinction, see 71.
[62] Walters, *AV Dicey* (n 2) 3.
[63] Dicey, *Introduction* (n 8) 41.
[64] ibid 42.
[65] ibid 43.
[66] ibid 46.
[67] ibid 46.
[68] ibid 48.
[69] Walters, *AV Dicey* (n 2) 163–64.
[70] Dicey, *Introduction* (n 8) 23.

fundamental custom which is a kind of common law in a now outdated sense of that term, but not judge-made law, and is 'law' because the courts are both obligated and obliged to accept and enforce it.[71]

Fourth, there is Dicey's understanding of the historical development of the British constitution, mentioned several times in *Law of the Constitution*. He said that at least since the Norman conquest, England had been governed by an 'absolute legislator'. The legislative authority of the Crown was never curtailed, but transferred from the Crown acting alone to the Crown acting together with the Houses of Parliament, and eventually in subordination to them.[72] These transformations resulted from political conflicts, in which

> The leaders of the English people in their contests with Royal power never attempted, except in periods of revolutionary violence, to destroy or dissipate the authority of the Crown as head of the State. Their policy, continued through centuries, was to leave the power of the King untouched, but to bind down the action of the Crown to recognised modes of procedure which, if observed, would secure first the supremacy of the law, and ultimately the sovereignty of the nation.[73]

So Dicey regarded these transformations as achieved, not primarily by judicial decisions, but by 'the leaders of the English people in their contests with Royal power'. Admittedly, lawyers played prominent roles in these contests: the transformations were facilitated by 'the constant use of fictions' that were 'the invention of lawyers … Legal statesmanship bears everywhere the same character'.[74] As for judicial decisions, Dicey's attitude is revealed by his statement that

> Unintelligent students may infer that the law of the constitution is to be gathered only from famous judgments which embalm the results of grand constitutional or political conflicts.[75]

In other words, these judgments merely gave legal recognition, and legal shape or form, to the results of political conflicts that transformed the possession and exercise of legislative power.

Sometimes Walters' observations seem consistent with this:

> Dicey thus thought that the constitution in the common law tradition has no beginning but rather exists through a constantly evolving set of customs and practices and is given a legal existence through the same distinctive legal turn of mind that shapes ordinary legal discourse in ordinary law courts.[76]

So the constitution both 'exists through a constantly evolving set of customs and practices', and also has a 'legal existence' in ordinary legal discourse in ordinary law courts. But, surely the 'legal existence' of its most fundamental elements – their recognition as

[71] Goldsworthy, *Parliamentary Sovereignty* (n 14) 44.
[72] Dicey, *Introduction* (n 8) 67 fn; see also 179.
[73] ibid 465–66 fn 2.
[74] ibid 466 fn. See further text to n 91 below.
[75] ibid 33.
[76] Walters, *AV Dicey* (n 2) 349.

law by courts – is determined largely by their factual existence in custom and practice, which judges are compelled by political reality to accept.

Walters denies that, had Dicey become acquainted with Hart's idea that the doctrine of parliamentary sovereignty was part of the British rule of recognition, he would have embraced it. On his account, Dicey regarded the content of the doctrine as something to be settled not by facts about an official consensus, but by courts employing ordinary legal reasoning, which is inherently evaluative rather than empirical. Walters relies on Dicey's argument against the Gladstone government's proposed Government of Ireland Bill 1886 (known as the First Home Rule Bill). The Bill, had it been enacted, would have established a unicameral Irish legislature, and ended Irish representation within Parliament, subject to clause 39 which provided that the Act could not be altered except by a law passed by Parliament either (a) with the consent of the Irish legislature, or (b) after the Irish peers and half the elected members from the Irish legislature were recalled to vote as members of the House of Lords and House of Commons.

Dicey argued that the courts might be called upon to decide whether or not clause 39 was legally binding. The Bill's supporters, including James Bryce, denied both that it was, and that it was intended to be. Bryce likened the clause to a promise, which could impose a moral obligation on Parliament but not a legally binding one.[77] But Dicey suggested that clause 39 could be interpreted as an abdication by Parliament of its sovereignty in favour of a new legislator, composed of Parliament acting together with either the Irish legislature or half the Irish legislators recalled as members of Parliament. This ingenious but unorthodox argument anticipated modern speculation that Parliament could reconstitute itself for a special purpose. But for Walters, the important point is that, regardless of the merits of Dicey's suggestion, it shows that he regarded parliamentary sovereignty is 'an ordinary legal concept susceptible to ordinary legal interpretation by the ordinary courts'. The question 'Who or what is Parliament?' was 'a thoroughly legal question to be answered in the ordinary legal way'.[78]

But this is debatable. Dicey's suggestion was based almost entirely on his residual (and mistaken) Austinian conviction that while sovereignty is inherently incapable of self-limitation, it is capable of abdication in favour of another lawmaker.[79] He cited the Act of Union with Scotland as a historical example.[80]

On the same occasion, Dicey also expressed a more pragmatic opinion about the likely result of litigation:

> It is easy to anticipate what would be the practical result of that Bill's ambiguities if it passed into an Act. Irish judges would honestly take one view, English judges would as honestly take another .... No court in either country could satisfactorily terminate the dispute. Force would no doubt settle what law had left undecided, but to interpret a Constitution by power of arms is in reality to substitute revolutionary violence for forensic discussion.[81]

[77] J Bryce, *Speech to House of Commons*, 17 May 1886.
[78] Walters, *AV Dicey* (n 2) 178.
[79] See text to nn 12 and 14.
[80] AV Dicey, *England's Case Against Home Rule*, 3rd edn (London, John Murray,1887) 241–45.
[81] ibid 247–48.

In *Law of the Constitution*, Dicey was less disapproving and more accepting of the inevitability of superior strength prevailing.

> Let it be remembered that no constitutional arrangements or fictions could get rid of the fact that England would, after as before the establishment of Home Rule all round, continue, in virtue of her resources and her population, the predominant partner throughout the United Kingdom, and the partner on whom sovereignty had been conferred, not by the language of any statute or other document, but by the nature of things. It would be hard indeed to prevent the English Parliament sitting at Westminster from not only claiming but exercising sovereign authority ….[82]

This is reminiscent of some other statements of his, such as: 'When the sovereign power can easily enforce its will, it may trust to its own action for maintaining its rights ….'[83] In these passages, judicial deference to the factual possession of political sovereignty seems to be taken for granted.

Be that as it may, the possibility of a dispute about parliamentary sovereignty being litigated and settled by judicial decision does not disprove that it is part of a customary rule of recognition constituted by a long-standing consensus among the senior officials of all branches of government. Hart acknowledged that a rule of recognition, like other legal rules, can be under-determinate in that its settled content does not answer all disputes that may arise.[84] The fact that courts have been called upon to adjudicate on disputed questions relating to parliamentary sovereignty – matters not clearly settled by the core of the doctrine – might confirm that it is in one sense 'ordinary law'.[85] But as we have already seen, it does not follow that it is part of the common law in the usual sense of judge-made law. Courts also have to adjudicate on questions concerning the meaning and application of statutes and written constitutions, which are not matters of common law.

Nor would successful judicial determination of previously unsettled questions prove that the judges have authority to diminish or reject the long-established core of the doctrine. Again, the authority of courts to determine the meaning of a written constitution, when it is under-determinate, does not prove that they have authority to amend or repudiate it. In both cases, it may be acknowledged that the courts have authority to settle disputes and uncertainties about the content of a law that is superior to judge-made common law, but their authority remains subject to constraints imposed by the clear and indisputable content of that superior law.[86] Dicey observed that 'the Constitution of the United States, as it actually exists, rests to a very considerable extent on judge-made law.'[87] Yet as he also acknowledged, 'The American judge must in giving judgment obey the terms of the Constitution, just as his English brother must in giving judgment obey every Act of Parliament bearing on the case.'[88]

[82] Dicey, *Introduction* (n 8) xc–xci.
[83] ibid 166; see also 108, where Dicey sets aside as a 'matter of politics' the means by which the government maintains the political sovereignty of the United Kingdom.
[84] Hart, *Concept of Law* (n 13) 123, 148–54.
[85] See text to nn 29–30.
[86] Goldsworthy, *Sovereignty of Parliament* (n 54) 259 (footnotes omitted); see also ibid 241–42.
[87] Dicey, *Introduction* (n 8) 466 n 1.
[88] ibid 155.

4. Claim 3: The Common Law is a Multi-layered Body of Rules and Principles, Including Broad Foundational Principles that Provide Coherence and Guide Decision-making in Novel Cases, which are Identified by Induction from Judicial Decisions Involving Evaluative Rather than Empirical Judgments

By quoting from many of Dicey's writings, Walters shows that Dicey thought of what he called judge-made common law in this way.[89] That is unsurprising: it encapsulates the classical understanding of the common law, recently revived by Ronald Dworkin, but going back at least to the time of Sir Edward Coke.[90] But as previously explained, Dicey did not regard parliamentary sovereignty as a doctrine of judge-made common law.

Moreover, Dicey sometimes expressed a more pragmatic understanding of the contribution of common lawyers to the development of the constitution.

> The fictions of the Courts have in the hands of lawyers such as Coke served the cause both of justice and of freedom, and served it when it could have been defended by no other weapons. For there are social conditions under which legal fictions or subtleties afford the sole means of establishing that rule of equal and settled law which is the true basis of English civilisation. Nothing can be more pedantic, nothing more artificial, nothing more unhistorical, than the reasoning by which Coke induced or compelled James to forego the attempt to withdraw cases from the Courts for his Majesty's personal determination. But no achievement of sound argument, or stroke of enlightened statesmanship, ever established a rule more essential to the very existence of the constitution than the principle enforced by the obstinacy and the fallacies of the great Chief-Justice .... [N]o one has stated so forcibly as my friend Mr. Freeman himself the peculiarity of all English efforts to extend the liberties of the country, namely, that these attempts at innovation have always assumed the form of an appeal to pre-existing rights. But the appeal to precedent is in the law courts merely a useful fiction by which judicial decision conceals its transformation into judicial legislation ....[91]

5. Claim 4: The Common Law 'Determines and Conditions' Parliamentary Sovereignty and its Exercise, Especially Through the Judicial Interpretation of Statutes, to Enhance their Compatibility with the Rule of Law

Dicey famously attempted to reconcile parliamentary sovereignty with the rule of law in Chapter 13 of *Law of the Constitution*, whose final paragraph Walters deems 'perhaps the most important passage in his book.'[92]

[89] eg Walters, *AV Dicey* (n 2) 65, 81–2, 91, 151, 153–55, 158, 263, 328, 337.

[90] For Sir Edward Coke, see CM Gray, 'Reason, Authority and Imagination: The Jurisprudence of Sir Edward Coke' in P Zagorin (ed), *Culture and Politics From Puritanism to the Enlightenment* (Berkeley, University of California Press, 1980) 28–40 and 'Parliament, Liberty and the Law' in J H Hexter (ed), *Parliament and Liberty: From the Reign of Elizabeth to the English Civil War* (Stanford, Stanford University Press, 1992) 155, 158–64 esp 162–3.

[91] Dicey, *Introduction* (n 8) 18.

[92] Walters, *AV Dicey* (n 2) 282.

> Dicey's basic but brilliant insight … is that in common law regimes that have no written and entrenched constitution … the critical values of legality are implicitly or indirectly enforced through judicial interpretation – not as a higher law but as an integrated and implicit part of every ordinary law.[93]

Walters relies heavily on a frequently quoted portion of that final paragraph, where Dicey states that although Parliament is the supreme legislator,

> from the moment Parliament has uttered its will as lawgiver, that will becomes subject to the interpretation put upon it by the judges of the land, and the judges, who are influenced by the feelings of magistrates no less than by the general spirit of the common law, are disposed to construe statutory exceptions to common law principles in a mode which would not commend itself either to a body of officials, or to the Houses of Parliament, if the Houses were called upon to interpret their own enactments.[94]

One reason for this is that, as Dicey observed a few pages earlier, English judges 'have always refused, in principle at least, to interpret an Act of Parliament otherwise than by reference to the words of the enactment'.[95] This is an exaggeration, because the judges for centuries took judicial notice of well-known historical facts about the genesis of legislation and the mischief it was intended to cure.[96] But as Dicey said, they traditionally took no notice of the resolutions of either House, of anything said in parliamentary debate, or even of amendments made to a Bill as it proceeded to final enactment.[97]

The absence or scarcity of direct evidence of legislative intent was filled by presumptions. Earlier in the book, Dicey wrote:

> There is no legal basis for the theory that judges, as exponents of morality, may overrule Acts of Parliament. Language which might seem to imply this amounts in reality to nothing more than the assertion that the judges, when attempting to ascertain what is the meaning to be affixed to an Act of Parliament, will presume that Parliament did not intend to violate the ordinary rules of morality, or the principles of international law, and will therefore, whenever possible, give such an interpretation to a statutory enactment as may be consistent with the doctrines both of private and of international morality. A modern judge would never listen to a barrister who argued that an Act of Parliament was invalid because it was immoral, or because it went beyond the limits of Parliamentary authority.[98]

He also stated categorically that the suggestion that 'an Act of Parliament cannot … overrule the principles of the common law … has never received systematic judicial sanction and is now obsolete'.[99]

Statutory interpretation as described by Dicey therefore resembles that way that the 'principle of legality' is often applied today, when judges ignore extra-textual evidence of legislative intention, and interpret the text by presuming that Parliament did not intend

[93] ibid 296.
[94] Dicey, *Introduction* (n 8) 409.
[95] ibid 403.
[96] See Goldsworthy, *Parliamentary Sovereignty* (n 14) 248.
[97] Dicey, *Introduction* (n 8) 403.
[98] ibid 60.
[99] ibid 59 fn 1.

to impinge on 'fundamental rights'.[100] This resemblance is confirmed by Dicey's opinion of the majority judgment in *R v Halliday, ex parte Zadig*,[101] expressed in a personal letter helpfully uncovered by Walters. That case concerned an application for habeas corpus by one of many people detained during the First World War under broad but vague provisions in the *Defence of the Realm Act* 1914, which authorised the government to take steps necessary 'for securing the public safety and the defence of the realm'.

In upholding the legality of the detention, a majority of the House of Lords affirmed that the Act authorised the detention of British subjects, provided only that the government genuinely believed that they constituted a danger to the nation. Dicey objected to this:

> I think on the whole that the decision of the Court was right in that it gave to an Act of Parliament the effect which those who drafted it wished it to have though probably they rather desire[d] not to make too plain to the whole House of Commons the result of an Act which interfered much more with personal liberty than the suspension of the Habeas Corpus Acts which were common during the war with France … I regret that in Zadig's case the Court did not insist upon the dangers that may ensue from the habit of extending governmental authority by the use of vague terms which conceal from many persons the extent of the power which the Government demands. Legislation of this kind may in future years be used to conceal and favour the attempt of a partisan Government to obtain indirectly a power of interfering with personal rights which such Government does not like to ask for in plain language.[102]

Dicey's position was and remains entirely orthodox, although modern judges now allow themselves to consult much more extra-textual evidence of legislative intent.[103] If the sponsors of a Bill used vague language to obscure the effect they desired from other members of Parliament, it is entirely proper for a court to interpret the language narrowly. It does not infringe the sovereignty of Parliament to decline to interpret a statutory provision in a way that a majority in Parliament may have overlooked and not intended. Dicey's position is reminiscent of the much cited justification of the principle of legality proffered by Lord Hoffmann in *Simms*: 'Fundamental rights cannot be overridden by general or ambiguous words … because there is too great a risk that the full implications of their unqualified meaning may have passed unnoticed in the democratic process'.[104]

According to Walters,

> Dicey meant to say the Court was right insofar as it identified the true intent of drafters who preferred not to make their intent plain. Of course, this is precisely the kind of situation in which Dicey had insisted judges were to read statutes in line with the rule of law rather than legislators' intent.[105]

[100] Jason Varuhas notes that 'Despite a more general opening up of the sources courts consider in interpreting statutes, in applying the [principle of legality] courts have rarely used any aid beyond the text': J Varuhas, 'The Principle of Legality' (2020) 79 *CLJ* 578, 604–605. The resemblance noted in the text applies only to what Varuhas calls the 'classic' principle of legality, and not the 'augmented' or 'proactive' principle: ibid 590ff.

[101] [1917] AC 260.

[102] AV Dicey to John St Loe Strachey, 8 and 11 Feb. 1916, Strachey Papers, STR 5/7/16, quoted by Walters, *AV Dicey* (n 2) 288.

[103] But see n 100, above.

[104] *R v Secretary of State for the Home Department, ex parte Simms* [1999] UKHL 33, [2000] 2 AC 115, 131.

[105] Walters, *AV Dicey* (n 2) 288.

This is inexact and misleading, because Dicey referred to the intent of the drafters, which might differ from the general 'legislators' intent', and he did not elevate the rule of law above the latter. Walters adds that 'Lord Shaw's dissent [in *Zadig*] is a remarkable example of what Dicey had in mind in the final paragraph of chapter 13 [of *Law of the Constitution*]'.[106] That may be true, but Lord Shaw said that, by the vague language in the Defence of the Realm Act, 'Parliament never sanctioned … such a violent exercise of arbitrary power'.[107] So he too did not elevate the rule of law above his assessment of Parliament's likely intention in enacting the statute.

The principle of legality (to use the modern terminology), when applied in this way, is not inconsistent with parliamentary sovereignty, or with the interpretation of statutes guided by evidence of, or plausible presumptions about, Parliament's likely intentions. Nor does it demonstrate that parliamentary sovereignty is part of the common law, or that the political ideal known as the rule of law is somehow 'implicit' either in the concept of parliamentary sovereignty or in every statute enacted by Parliament.[108]

6. Claim 5: This Extends to the Kind of Creative or Strained Interpretation that Trevor Allan Advocates, which in Extreme Cases may Legitimately Render a Statutory Provision Void, in Terms of its Practical Effect, Even if it is Formally Valid

Walters repeatedly insists that Dicey should have considered more carefully, and not dismissed as obsolete, strands of common law thought in the sixteenth and seventeenth centuries that appeared to undermine his case for parliamentary sovereignty.[109] These strands are arguably exemplified in Sir Edward Coke's famous declaration in *Dr Bonham's* case that the common law 'controls' statutes, and may deem them to be 'utterly void' if they are 'against common right and reason, or repugnant, or impossible to be performed'.[110] Walters believes that had Dicey drawn on these 'rich insights', they 'might have reinforced the basic claim that he advanced about the relationship between parliamentary sovereignty and the rule of law – the claim that the ideal of the legality inheres within the very idea of legislative sovereignty'.[111] Although Dicey never explicitly acknowledged this, '[u]nderstood as a legal concept, sovereignty gains legal characteristics that condition its exercise. Not just any exercise of power can count as the exercise of *legal* power'.[112]

> [T]he old common law on the control of repugnancy in statutes … suggest[s] that once Parliament enacts a regime explicitly contrary to principles of legality, or itself enacts arbitrary

[106] ibid 289.
[107] *Zadig* (n 101) 276–277, quoted by Walters ibid.
[108] See text to nn 3 and 93 above, and to n 113 below.
[109] Walters, *AV Dicey* (n 2) 187–188, 198–200.
[110] 8 Co Rep 118a, 77 Eng Rep 652.
[111] Walters, *AV Dicey* (n 2) 285. See also 6, 189, 200, 202.
[112] ibid 187–88.

> measures targeting specific people or situations in a manner inconsistent with a regime of law, then the statute, although formally valid in law will be repugnant to the very principles of legality intrinsic to law and thus the statute will be inoperable or void in the sense of being empty [of] any practical legal effect.[113]

There are two problems with this argument. First, to extend Dicey's views this far makes them self-contradictory, given his explicit affirmation of 'the non-existence of any judicial or other authority having the right to nullify an Act of Parliament, or to treat it as void or unconstitutional'.[114] Walters says that Dicey's position must therefore be 'modified',[115] which surely concedes that his account of it has gone astray. Second, Walters' understanding of the sixteenth and seventeenth century approach to statutory interpretation, including the concept of 'voidness', is highly contestable. But that is a topic that must be left for another occasion.[116]

7. Conclusion

I have examined five claims about parliamentary sovereignty and the common law, listed in the Introduction, that Walters attributes to Dicey. We can now conclude that, according to Dicey:

1. Parliamentary sovereignty is part of the law, rather than an instance of Austinian sovereignty that stands above and creates the law. But it is a fundamental law, not an ordinary law, as Dicey understands those terms.
2. Parliamentary sovereignty is not a matter of common law, in the modern sense of judge-made law. It is a long-standing custom of governance accepted as fundamental law by senior officialdom on behalf of the nation as a whole.
3. The common law, insofar as it is judge-made, is a system of rules and principles underpinned by more general principles that help provide coherence and guide decision-making in novel cases. But common lawyers have often deployed fictions to hasten developments in the law, including constitutional law.
4. Judges, when interpreting statutes, properly apply common law interpretive principles that help protect the rule of law. But they should go no further than the modern 'principle of legality', which properly understood is consistent with parliamentary sovereignty.
5. Judges are not legally permitted to engage in radically creative or strained interpretations of statutes that in exceptional cases, according to Walters, might render a statutory provision void in terms of its practical effect.

I conclude by returning to Trevor Allan, who according to Walters adopts roughly the same interpretation of Dicey but by a different interpretive methodology.[117] I take

[113] ibid 294.
[114] Dicey, *Introduction* (n 8) 87. See also 98.
[115] Walters, *AV Dicey* (n 2) 218.
[116] See J Goldsworthy, 'What Really Happened in *Dr Bonham's* Case: Statutory Interpretation and "Voidness" Then, and Now' (2025) *PL* (forthcoming).
[117] Walters, *AV Dicey* (n 2) 360.

Walters to be attempting to clarify and elaborate on Dicey's own views, as expressed in his writings. Allan, on the other hand, is a Dworkinian interpretivist, who explicitly detaches Dicey's text from its author's understanding of it, and interprets the text (as Dworkin interprets the law) 'in light of the political values that could justify its continued authority', as part of a (supposed) British tradition of common law constitutionalism.[118]

Dworkin's interpretivism aims at finding the most coherent and morally justified understanding of the phenomena under investigation. This involves identifying deeper moral principles that best fit and justify the phenomena overall, which may require rejecting or qualifying as 'mistakes' particular aspects of the phenomena that are inconsistent with those principles. The criteria of fit and of justification, and the balance between them, all require moral judgment; Dworkin says that they represent 'different aspects of a single overall judgment of political morality'.[119]

Insufficient space remains for a substantial response to Allan's approach, which as applied to law, I have criticised elsewhere.[120] When applied to Dicey's text, it is even more problematic. My response to Walters, which I have just summarised, casts grave doubt on the possibility of Allan's interpretation of Dicey's text satisfying Dworkin's criterion of 'fit'. Dicey's repeated, emphatic advocacy of an almost absolute doctrine of parliamentary sovereignty, unqualified apart from Parliament's inability to bind itself, is far too prominent a feature of his text to be set aside or heavily qualified on the ground that it was a mistake, due to inconsistency with principles of political morality that provide the best overall justification of democracy and the rule of law.[121]

Another problem is that it is very doubtful that Dicey's text is incoherent in this sense. The interpretive goal of maximal moral justification requires evaluative judgments that are inherently subjective and contestable. In earlier work, I presented a defence of the doctrine of parliamentary sovereignty, and showed that it could easily be framed as a Dworkinian interpretation of the British constitution.[122] In broad outline it could just as easily be framed as a Dworkinian interpretation of Dicey's text, based on the close reading presented here, to rival Allan's interpretation. Plainly, the disagreement between the two interpretations would ultimately concern which conception of political morality is preferable, rather than what interpretation of Dicey's text is the most accurate.

This leads to a final objection to Allan's interpretive methodology in this context. It is unclear why Dicey's writings should be 'interpreted' so as to make them maximally coherent and morally justified from the point of view of an 'interpreter'. It may be, as Dworkin argued, that coherence in the formulation and application of legal norms is essential to the fulfilment of fundamental principles of political morality, including

[118] Allan, *Sovereignty of Law* (n 1) 54. See also 10–11, 32–33, 36, 50–54.
[119] R Dworkin, *Justice in Robes* (Cambridge, Belknap Press, 2006) 15.
[120] Goldsworthy, *Sovereignty of Parliament* (n 54) 246–272; Goldsworthy, 'In Defence of Traditional Methodologies' (n 49) 58–63.
[121] See also Allison, *English Historical Constitution* (n 39) 210–13.
[122] Goldsworthy, *Sovereignty of Parliament* (n 54) 246–72.

legal equality, the rule of law, governmental legitimacy and political obligation.[123] But there is no equivalent need to purge inconsistencies from the writings of legal scholars. To the contrary, if our objective is to truly understand a scholar's writings, inconsistencies should be acknowledged and not swept under the carpet. If there are inconsistencies among ideas expressed in a text, critics are free to endorse some of them and reject others. But there would be little point in attempting to depict the result as the best interpretation of the text itself. It would amount to revising rather than elucidating the text.

[123] R Dworkin, *Law's Empire* (Cambridge, Belknap Press, 1986) 186–224.

4

A Catholic View of Protestant Argument in Law

STUART LAKIN*

1. Introduction

For an interpretivist, the familiar rule of law injunction that officials may only act 'in accordance with law' takes on an unfamiliar shape. Law here does not simply mean what is 'found in our books' – the literal or intended meaning of statutory texts, and the clear rules and principles laid down by judges in statutes and judgments.[1] It means the scheme of moral values and principles that animate our books and our political practices. When the state exercises power in accordance with the rule of law, so understood, say interpretivists, it possesses legitimate political authority. The decisions of the legislature and courts are – or, perhaps, *usually* are – morally binding and worthy of obedience.[2]

In the course of elaborating his interpretative theory of law as integrity, Ronald Dworkin tells us that an interpreter must take a 'protestant attitude' to the question of *which* scheme of principle animates our books and political practices.[3] This is an attitude, he says, 'that makes each citizen responsible for imagining what his society's public commitments to principles are, and what these commitments require in new circumstances'.[4]

* I am very grateful to Dimitrios Kyritsis, Aleardo Zanghellini, and the two volume editors for their very helpful comments. I also benefited greatly from feedback and discussions at the Sherbrooke and Queen's University joint conference in honour of TRS Allan in September 2022.

[1] *Entick v Carrington* [1765] EWHC KB J98.

[2] For a very clear statement of interpretive theories of law, see N Stavropoulos, 'Legal Interpretivism' at plato.stanford.edu/entries/law-interpretivist/.

[3] 'According to law as integrity, propositions of law are true if they figure in or follow from the principles of justice, fairness, and procedural due process that provide the best constructive interpretation of the community's legal practice': R Dworkin, *Law's Empire* (London, Fontana Press, 1986) 225.

[4] ibid 413. Dworkin also writes: 'Political obligation is then not just a matter of obeying the discrete political decisions of the community one by one .... It becomes a more protestant idea: fidelity to a scheme of principle each citizen has a responsibility to identify, ultimately for himself, as his community's scheme': ibid 190.

We find encapsulated in this attitude a conundrum. On the one hand, it is for each citizen to bring their individual moral convictions to bear on their community's past political decisions without deference to the views of others.[5] The right answer to a question of law is not necessarily the one a judge gives; or a decision may not be correct for the reasons the judge gives. On the other hand, protestant argument has, as Postema puts it, an 'interactive, public character' such that the interpreter argues with, and in the name of, their community about its moral commitments.[6] They imagine that the 'government speaks with one voice', even in circumstances of deep disagreement about why or when the actions of the community are legitimate and its laws binding.[7]

My aim in this chapter is to reconcile these Janus facing responsibilities of the protestant interpreter: those of individual conviction and community. I shall argue that, as interpreters, we should adopt an *inclusive and conciliatory attitude* towards other interpreters or interpretations. Or, to deploy the clumsy (but I hope not incendiary) title of this chapter for the first and last time: we must be catholic in our protestantism. By inclusive and conciliatory, I do not mean to eviscerate any sense of individual conviction in legal and constitutional argument. It is not the case, for instance, that an interpreter must compromise on the full rigour of their preferred moral theory, or that they should rein in their aspirations for it.[8] Nor is it the case that one theory of legitimacy may not give an objectively better account of the practice than another. I mean that the interpreter must see their individual arguments of conviction together with those of others as part of the same endeavour. They must *engage morally* with other theories, rather than seek ways to disqualify them. This is a responsibility of *inclusion*, I shall argue, in that it means accommodating interpretations ranging across each dimension of political morality – justice, fairness and procedural due process. It is a responsibility of *conciliation* in that it extends to making moral sense of views even if presented as morally neutral, positivist claims, or if otherwise couched in positivist-sounding language.[9]

I shall advance this account of – what we may call – 'inclusive protestantism' by way of a critique of Trevor Allan's distinctive and powerful interpretative theory of the rule of law.[10] I shall argue that Allan's approach is exclusive rather than inclusive, in that he privileges one justice-centric, judge-centric theory of legitimacy, making only minor concessions to interpretations that do not fall squarely within that theory.[11] It is non-conciliatory rather than conciliatory in that he typically seeks to *disqualify* the arguments of others on methodological grounds, rather than engage with them as moral theories. Less extremely, he is quick to designate decisions at odds with his theory

[5] 'A citizen's allegiance is to the law, not to any particular person's view on what the law is': R Dworkin, *Taking Rights Seriously*, rev edn (London, Duckworth Books, 1977) 185.

[6] GJ Postema, 'Integrity: Justice in Workclothes' in J Burley (ed), *Dworkin and His Critics* (Malden, Wiley-Blackwell, 2004) 295.

[7] Dworkin, *Law's Empire* (n 3) 165.

[8] See Section 3 below.

[9] See Section 2(B) below.

[10] For a comprehensive statement see TRS Allan, *The Sovereignty of Law: Freedom, Constitution, and Common Law* (Oxford, Oxford University Press, 2013).

[11] For a similar charge against Ronald Dworkin, see Postema 'Justice in Workclothes' (n 6) 295. I present Dworkin's theory as a more inclusive one in this chapter.

as 'mistakes' or misapplications of the true law (or 'Law'), rather than as genuine contributions to a political community's moral record.[12]

In Section 2, I juxtapose the two accounts of protestant argument just outlined. I begin at the extreme end of legal and constitutional disagreement, the issue of wicked laws. Even in this troubling area, I make the case for inclusive and conciliatory terms of engagement. The larger claim arising out of this discussion is against Allan's assimilation of interpretative argument to his own justice-centric, judge-centric moral theory. I argue that the protestant interpreter must be free to draw their convictions from the full gamut of political morality. By way of illustration, I discuss Dimitrios Kyritsis's 'assurance' model of legitimacy, one that takes separation of powers rather than justice as the key to legitimacy.[13]

In Section 3, I consider the specific responsibilities of the inclusive protestant towards other interpreters; and I sketch how these responsibilities might bear upon our understanding of the British constitution. I argue that the inclusive interpretivist should respect a good faith, reasonable attempt to understand the law, even if they fundamentally disagree with that understanding. The by-product of this inclusive style of protestantism, I suggest, is an inclusive constitution in which multiple different theories of legitimacy may take root, each aspiring (through their advocates) for supremacy. It is a 'patchwork quilt' constitution that strives towards one-piece-duvet unity.[14]

2. Inclusive and Exclusive Interpretivism: Opening Up the Channels of Interpretative Debate

In a series of important articles, Trevor Allan criticises Ronald Dworkin's analysis of the Fugitive Slaves Act – a provision requiring citizens from one state to return escaped slaves to their slave owners in another state.[15] Dworkin reasons that

> the slaveholders had, in principle, a political right to regain their slaves on demand but … this right was trumped … by an emergency – in this case a moral emergency. We express that thought best by saying what most lawyers would say: that the Act was valid law but too unjust to enforce.[16]

In ways that we shall examine below, Dworkin presents this argument as an *interpretative* one. Allan replies, to the contrary, that Dworkin's argument is 'contradictory' and 'paradoxical' from the perspective of interpretivism and integrity. This is because

> all considerations of political morality (including justice) relevant to the question of obligation or obedience are also granted a role in the interpretative process by which the content of

[12] For the doctrine of 'mistake', see Dworkin, *Taking Rights Seriously* (n 5) 11–123. For Allan's most explicit alignment of the rule of law with natural law ('Law') in his work to date, see TRS Allan, 'Constitutionalism at Common Law: The Rule of Law and Judicial Review' (2023) 82 *CLJ* 236.

[13] See generally, D Kyritsis, *Shared Authority* (Oxford, Hart Publishing, 2015), D Kyritsis, *Where Our Protection Lies: Separation of Powers and Constitutional Review* (Oxford, Oxford University Press, 2017); D Kyritsis, 'Constitutional Law as Legitimacy Enhancer' in D Kyritsis and S Lakin (eds), *The Methodology of Constitutional Theory* (Oxford, Hart Publishing, 2022) ch 8.

[14] I borrow the metaphor of a patchwork quilt from Postema. See Postema 'Justice in Workclothes' (n 6) 313.

[15] I shall focus in particular on TRS Allan, 'Law, Justice and Integrity: The Paradox of Wicked Laws' (2009) 29 *OJLS* 705 and TRS Allan, 'Interpretation, Injustice, and Integrity' (2016) *OJLS* 36, 58–82.

[16] R Dworkin, *Justice for Hedgehogs* (Cambridge, Belknap Press, 2011) 411.

> the law is ascertained or constructed. It follows … that Dworkin's theory cannot consistently acknowledge the existence of wicked laws, which ought to be resisted on grounds of justice. Such statutes or decisions are either not truly laws at all, from the perspective of integrity, or their legal status, if affirmed, amounts to the complete repudiation of political obligation: the claims of integrity are inapplicable to the regime in question.[17]

We need to be clear about the structure of this argument, placing it within Allan's broader interpretative theory of the rule of law. Allan contends that a statute or judgment has no meaning independent of 'basic principles of justice', including the protection of fundamental rights.[18] Such principles are among the necessary *determinants* of the law. In this way, 'legal and moral obligation perfectly coincide'.[19] It follows that an interpretivist judge has two options when faced with a wicked law. Either he must read it consistently with fundamental rights and other basic principles of justice; or, if that is not possible, he must declare that it is not law.[20] In that case, the judge must 'succumb to scepticism' (i.e. decide that moralised, interpretative argument is not possible in that community) and decide that the practice as a whole, 'deserves repudiation rather than allegiance'.[21] There is, Allan says, 'no half-way house' between these two options.[22] The only way that Dworkin can claim that a law can be valid yet unjust is to abandon interpretivism altogether for 'brute fact' conventionalism.[23] He must assume, that is, that we can identify (at least some extreme) laws in a descriptive, morally detached way, independently of considerations of justice. But this is to adopt the very two-system positivist separation between law and morality that he attacks in the rest of his work.[24]

What are we to make of this analysis? From the point of view of the interpretative purist, Allan must be right to say that considerations of justice are necessarily among the determinants of the law, rather than standards external to it.[25] As Dworkin himself argued in his early critique of legal positivism, judges have a legal *duty* rather than a 'strong' discretion to bring *all* relevant moral principles to their judgments of law.[26] Nonetheless, I think this is a good example of where the inclusive, conciliatory protestant attitude I defend in this chapter should come into play. Take Dworkin's claim that Congress

> was sufficiently legitimate so that its enactments generally created political obligations. The structuring principles that make law a distinct part of political morality – principles about political authority, precedent, and reliance – gave the slaveholders' claims more moral force

[17] Allan, 'Paradox' (n 15) 707.

[18] 'Even when fundamental rights are not formally entrenched against legislative interference, the judge may treat them as implicit features of enacted rules or necessary limitations on executive powers': Allan, 'Interpretation' (n 15) 62.

[19] ibid 59.

[20] ibid 64.

[21] ibid.

[22] ibid 68. Allan does contemplate a third option in the quotation: namely that an interpreter refers to the provisions of the system he has rejected as 'law' in a 'pre-interpretive' or 'sociological' sense: a shadow of law.

[23] 'Conventionalism' is Dworkin's moralised recasting of legal positivism. See Dworkin, *Law's Empire* (n 3) ch 4.

[24] For Dworkin's early statement of this position, see Dworkin, *Taking Rights Seriously* (n 5) ch 2 'The Model of Rules I' and ch 4 'Hard Cases'.

[25] For particularly clear arguments to this effect, see M Greenberg, 'How Facts Make Law' in S Hershovitz (ed), *Exploring Law's Empire* (Oxford, Oxford University Press, 2008) and Stavropoulos, 'Legal Interpretivism' (n 2).

[26] Dworkin, *Taking Rights Seriously* (n 5) ch 2 'The Model of Rules I'.

> that they would otherwise have had. But their moral claims were nevertheless and undoubtedly undermined by a strong moral argument of human rights. So the law should not have been enforced.[27]

Putting to one side the question of whether Dworkin flouts the strict logic of interpretivism, these claims clearly tap into host of moral concerns – indeed *interpretative* concerns – about how best to interpret the unfolding narrative of US constitutional history and practice.[28] His position is not the parodied view of interpretivism attributed to him by many critics – that law is constituted by *whichever* set of 'principles', no matter how wicked, underlie the legal system.[29] It is a nuanced view about how true[30] principles of political legitimacy, including the federalist principles structuring the US Constitution, properly interact with substantive considerations of justice to determine the content of the law and the duties of judges.[31] On a more abstract level, he asks whether the 'circumstances of integrity' may obtain in situations where a wicked law is anomalous within the broader constitutional settlement, as opposed to one where wickedness is systematic and persistent.[32] Did the Act lie 'at the heart' of the settlement, draining it of any residual legitimacy?[33] Would integrity have been best served by isolating the Act and minimising its impact on other parts of the law, rather than rejecting the legal system as a whole?[34] Would repudiating a legal order on the basis of isolated wicked laws entail rejecting most legal systems around the world and through history as illegitimate?[35]

I list these questions and concerns as no more than an unruly brainstorm of the types of considerations underlying Dworkin's position. I shall make no attempt to organise them or engage with them here.[36] My point is simply this: the complex of moral and philosophical arguments underlying Dworkin's position in this debate is very far from the stark, brute fact, two-system analysis of Herbert Hart,[37] or even the

[27] Dworkin, *Justice for Hedgehogs* (n 16) 411.

[28] For Dworkin's chain novel metaphor see R Dworkin, *A Matter of Principle* (Cambridge, Harvard University Press, 1985) ch 6 'How Law is Like Literature'.

[29] See eg HLA Hart, *Essays on Bentham: Jurisprudence and Political Theory* (Oxford, Oxford University Press, 1982) 150.

[30] On the importance of true moral principles, see N Stavropoulos, 'Why Principles' at papers.ssrn.com/sol3/papers.cfm?abstract_id=1023758.

[31] Compare Dworkin's speculation (well before the decision in *Dobbs v Jackson Women's Health Organization*, No 19-1392 (2022)) about whether 'leaving the abortion issue to individual states to decide differently if they wish is coherent in principle with the rest of the American constitutional scheme'. See Dworkin, *Law's Empire* (n 3) 186. cf J Waldron, 'Denouncing Dobbs and Opposing Judicial Review' (June 10, 2022) NYU School of Law, Public Law Research Paper No. 22–39, at ssrn.com/abstract=4144889.

[32] For Dworkin's differentiation between the antebellum situation surrounding the Fugitive Slaves Act and the Nazi order, see Dworkin, *Justice for Hedgehogs* (n 16) 411. cf J Waldron, *Law and Disagreement* (Oxford, Clarendon Press, 1999) 192–24, arguing that the circumstances of integrity no longer obtained at the time of the Fugitive Slaves Act and slavery.

[33] Dworkin, *Law's Empire* (n 3) 203.

[34] See R Dworkin, 'Reply to Critics' in J Burley (ed), *Dworkin and His Critics* (Malden, Wiley-Blackwell, 2004) 386 (responding to Postema, 'Justice in Workclothes' (n 6)).

[35] See D Dyzenhaus, *The Long Arc of Legality: Hobbes, Kelsen, Hart* (Cambridge, Cambridge University Press, 2022). See also the chapter by Dyzenhaus in this volume.

[36] For an excellent discussion, see Dyzenhaus, *The Long Arc of Legality* (n 35) ch 1 'The Puzzle of Very Unjust Law 1'.

[37] HLA Hart, *Essays in Jurisprudence and Philosophy* (Oxford, Clarendon Press, 1983) essay 2 'Positivism and the Separation of Law and Morals'.

relatively shallow moral position of Fuller.[38] His is a thoroughly moral inquiry, one that potentially bridges the imperatives of fairness, settlement and clarity underlying positivist legal theory, with the considerations of justice underlying the natural law theory argued for by Allan and others.[39] In these respects, Allan is mistaken, I think, to focus in this debate and elsewhere on whether Dworkin's arguments are properly categorised as interpretivist or conventionalist, internal or external. This misses the more pressing responsibility on interpreters to understand and meet each other's views as good faith moral arguments.

A. Interpretation across the Whole Gamut of Political Morality

This brings me to a larger point to take from the preceding discussion of wicked laws. There is a sense in this discussion and elsewhere, I think, that Allan *assimilates* interpretative argument to his justice-centric, judge-centric theory of the rule of law. This forces him to characterise arguments of the type that Dworkin offers above as *ineligible* understandings of law and the constitution: as *non*-interpretations. Now, before I develop this criticism, it is important to stress that Allan is perfectly entitled to argue for his theory of legitimacy from his own protestant convictions. These are deeply humane views which very plausibly have a strong foothold in British and US constitutional practices. I take no position on whether Allan gives a more *morally* persuasive account of the Fugitive Slaves Act than Dworkin or others. My argument is simply that there is no basis on which he can *privilege* his justice-centric view as the only one available to interpretivists. In so far as Allan is guilty of this charge, I think he unduly restricts the scope of interpretative argument.

Let us now attempt to de-privilege justice and judges from Allan's arguments, and open up the possibility for a more inclusive style of protestant argument. As Allan himself often says, interpretative argument takes place in the situation of disagreement not just about justice (the content of the law) but also fairness (who should decide on questions of justice) and procedural due process (by what procedures should decision-makers make their decisions). This is a judgment that Dworkin's famously puts in terms of 'fit' and 'substance':[40]

> [C]onvictions about fit contest with and constrain judgments of substance, and how convictions about fairness and justice and procedural due process contest with one another. The interpretative judgment must … meld these dimensions into an overall opinion; about which interpretation, all things considered, makes the community's legal record the best it can be from the point of view of political morality.[41]

[38] LL Fuller, 'Positivism and Fidelity to Law: A Reply to Professor Hart' (1958) 71 *Harvard Law Review* 630. As Hart comments of Fuller's 'inner morality' of law, such principles were 'unfortunately compatible with very great iniquity'. HLA Hart, *The Concept of Law* 2nd edn (Oxford, Clarendon Press, 1994) 207.

[39] This bridging is characteristic of the work of Kyritsis. See, eg the discussion in Kyritsis, *Shared Authority* (n 13) ch 1.

[40] For a full statement of these different values, see Dworkin, *Law's Empire* (n 3) 164–65.

[41] ibid 410–411. See further, R Dworkin, *Justice in Robes* (Cambridge, Harvard University Press, 2006) 183–86.

Once we zoom out from Allan's justice-centric theory to the broader range of political values available to an interpreter, we see that there is no a priori reason why the law must specifically track justice, or indeed any other single dimension of political morality, less still any particular theory nestled in any particular value. Take the 'assurance' model of legitimacy argued for by Dimitrios Kyritsis.[42] In the circumstances of deep disagreement about justice, and the ever present risk of moral lapses on the part of the state, we do better to explain legitimacy in a 'systemic' way over time, rather than – as Allan contends – in retail terms of the justice of the law taken decision by decision.[43] The best way to secure people's long term allegiance, he argues, is in the assurance that the community will act according to a reliable model of the separation of powers, one that assigns the right decisions to the right institutions, according to the extant model of separation within that system.[44] With this assurance, Kyritsis argues, people will be likely to keep faith with their system 'warts and all'. As he puts it:

> Structural considerations [i.e. separation of powers considerations] … are meant to give an assurance that the agents of governance of a political society will on the whole tend to act justly and efficiently …. A government that is structured in the right way strengthens [the standing disposition to obey]. Even when it enacts a policy with which I disagree or inflicts an injustice on me (albeit one, for which it has a moral warrant for obedience), my faith is not undermined.[45]

I offer this theory as an intriguing illustration of how an interpretivist may 'meld' together the various dimensions of political morality in a very different way to Allan. Differences in emphasis abound. Kyritsis agrees with Allan that 'equal concern and respect are conditions of democratic legitimacy',[46] but he and Allan disagree about what this means for institutional rights protection. For Allan, democracy necessarily *entails* the judicial protection of fundamental rights. It cannot be the case, he says, that a legislature whose political authority depends on democracy may act undemocratically, whether by infringing fundamental rights or some lesser form of morally sub-optimal law.[47] For Kyritsis, by contrast, it is a contingent matter whether courts should have a power of constitutional review; and, as we have seen, treating people

[42] Kyritsis characterises his assurance approach as one of *legitimacy* rather than justice: '[considerations of legitimacy] have to do with the conditions under which an actual political regime has a moral warrant to bind those subject to it or exercise coercive power over them given its moral imperfection and the existence of pervasive and ineradicable disagreement about moral issues that it must contend with': D Kyritsis, 'Constitutional Law as Legitimacy Enhancer' in Kyritsis and Lakin (eds), *Methodology* (n 13) 217.

[43] On the 'systemic' character of legitimacy, see Kyritsis, *Shared Authority* (n 13) 104–105.

[44] ibid chs 3 and 4. See further D Kyritsis, *Where Our Protection Lies: Separation of Powers and Constitutional Review* (Oxford, Oxford University Press, 2017) *passim*.

[45] Kyritsis, *Shared Authority* (n 13) 109.

[46] Kyritsis, *Where Our Protection Lies* (n 44) 124–25.

[47] '[S]ince the ideal of the rule of law is fulfilled only in a democracy, whereby every citizen is empowered to participate in establishing those conditions of freedom, adapted to the needs of time and place, an elected legislature cannot lawfully repudiate its own democratic basis': Allan, *Sovereignty of Law* (n 10) 293. See further, Allan, 'Paradox' (n 15) 717 endorsing Ronald Dworkin's constitutional conception of democracy. See R Dworkin, *Freedom's Law: The Moral Reading of the American Constitution* (Oxford, Oxford University Press, 1996).

with equal concern may still allow for moral lapses on the part of the government, provided that a political community adopts *some* stable form of separation of powers over time.[48]

Allan has an arsenal of powerful responses ready to counter such opposing views. He often says, for instance, that to reject a judicial power to ensure justice in the law is a failure to appreciate that 'legal theory is deeply and resolutely interpretative, in the manner of law as integrity',[49] or a failure adequately to mine the 'rich resources of the common law and constitution',[50] or a failure to take the 'internal, interpretative viewpoint … closer to the attitude of the judge',[51] or the 'perspective of any conscientious lawyer'.[52] But each of these and other such strategies beg the question against theorists who, like Kyritsis and Dworkin, advance different, bona fide theories of legitimacy. Dworkin's analysis of the Fugitive Slaves Act is 'resolutely interpretative' but in a way that argues for an interplay between fairness and justice that Allan rejects.[53] Neither Allan nor Kyritsis may say that the other has misunderstood the *true meaning* of equal concern and respect, or the *true meaning* of democracy,[54] or that '*any* eligible interpretation of law must reflect [the] constraints [for which they argue]'.[55] (emphasis added) To the contrary, it is a matter of substantive moral disagreement which is the better view. Similarly, how far a judge should 'mine' the common law depends on the theory in question. For some theorists, the value of integrity itself demands that a political community must face up to imperfect laws, rather than view them in the light of rigid common law principles of justice.[56] Finally, in answer to Allan's oft used device of the judicial perspective, we must reply that the perspective of judge or lawyer is that of one voice of conviction among many in a community deeply divided on its moral commitments. It is not the perspective of a single moral theory. Or at least that is the position I am defending in this chapter.

Does Kyritsis's claim that his account of legitimacy 'resonates better with political reality'[57] and with the circumstances of 'actual political regimes' than the natural-law style of interpretative theory offered by Allan undermine his interpretivist credentials? As we shall see below, Allan is deeply suspicious of any resort to the descriptive reality of what happens in practice. He rejects such manoeuvres as being 'external' to the

[48] Kyritsis, *Where Our Protection Lies* (n 44) 124. Kyritsis notes here that Dworkin is not committed by his constitutional conception of democracy to constitutional review. As Dworkin says: 'I do not mean that there is no democracy unless judges have the power to set aside what a majority thinks is right and just. Many institutional arrangements are compatible with the moral reading, including some that do not give judges the power they have in the American structure. But none of these varied arrangements is in principle more democratic than others. Democracy does not insist on judges having the last word, but it does not insist that they may not have it': Dworkin, *Freedom's Law* (n 47) 7.

[49] Allan, 'Paradox' (n 15) 706.

[50] Allan, 'Interpretation' (n 15) 77.

[51] ibid 58.

[52] Allan, 'Paradox' (n 15) 713.

[53] '[T]he political judgment [of an interpreter] is … complex and will sometimes set one department of political morality against another: his decision will reflect not only his opinions about justice and fairness but his higher-order convictions about how these ideals should be compromised when they compete': Dworkin, *Law's Empire* (n 3) 256.

[54] Allan, 'Interpretation' (n 15) 77.

[55] ibid 65.

[56] See Postema, 'Justice in Workclothes' (n 6) 296.

[57] Kyritsis, 'Constitutional Law as Legitimacy Enhancer' (n 42) 213.

practice.[58] Importantly, for the purposes of this discussion, this criticism does not sting Kyritsis. His theory, he says, is

> a thoroughly moral inquiry, but one that directs us to pay attention and give effect to political decisions that defined the institutional fundamentals of the regime in question. [Interpretivism] thereby bridges the moral force of the constitution and its contingent character as a political settlement.[59]

This is the right order of analysis. Moral values determine the relevance of empirical facts, not the other way round.[60] Of course, Kyritsis cannot (and does not) beg the question against Allan by arguing that Allan's justice-centric theory pays no attention, or insufficient attention, to actual practice.[61] As both Kyritsis and Allan are at pains to emphasise, the practice is what one's moral theory makes it. There are no brute facts which any eligible theory must fit.[62]

B. Collaborative Interpretation and British Constitutional Orthodoxy

I have argued above that Allan wrongly privileges his justice-centric, judge-centric moral theory in his account of interpretivism, leaving no space for rival theories of legitimacy. Perhaps I have got this wrong. A recurrent theme in Allan's work is the idea of 'collaborative' interpretation.[63] As he puts it:

> The courage of one's moral convictions must be tempered by respect for those other interpreters, equally charged to strive for harmony between private conscience and public practice. There is an important *collaborative* dimension to interpretation, requiring arguments to be framed and presented in the manner most likely to elicit a favourable response from other practice-participants.[64]

On its face, this is precisely the inclusive form of protestantism for which I argue in this chapter. Seeking harmony between the 'private conscience' and 'public practice' chimes with my attempt to reconcile the responsibility of an interpreter to their own convictions, with their responsibility to argue with, and on behalf of, their community. How does Allan propose that we square the circle? He says:

> While a protestant interpreter may challenge even a firmly entrenched paradigm, if necessary to sustain her own commitment to a morally acceptable practice, she should not do so when

[58] See section B below.

[59] Kyritsis, 'Constitutional Law as Legitimacy Enhancer' (n 42) 212.

[60] For a robust argument against theories that purport to be anti-positivist, but violate this order of analysis, see TRS Allan, 'Law as a Branch of Morality: The Unity of Practice and Principle' (2020) 65 *American Journal of Jurisprudence* 1.

[61] For arguments to the contrary, see the chapters by Peter Cane and Paul Craig in this volume.

[62] 'A threshold test of fit … mainly serves to distinguish a morally decent legal order, susceptible to the interpretive demands of integrity, from a wicked legal system resistant to integrity's embrace': Allan, 'Interpretation' (n 15) 69. See further the discussion in Kyritsis, *Shared Authority* (n 13) ch 3.

[63] For Allan's theory of constructive interpretation in statutory interpretation, see generally Allan, *Sovereignty of Law* (n 10) ch 5.

[64] Allan, 'Interpretation' (n 15) 17–18, citing GJ Postema '"Protestant" Interpretation and Social Practices' (1987) 6 *Law & Philosophy* 283.

> it is unnecessary – when a more orthodox interpretation is consistent with her convictions about the fundamental demands of justice.[65]

I am afraid that this way of unpacking the idea of collaboration does no more than pay lip service to practice-participant harmony. It suggests that an interpreter should only tolerate rival interpretations of a practice, including settled orthodoxy, in so far as they align with their individual view of justice. As I shall argue in the next part of the chapter, achieving harmony between interpreters requires much more than this. An interpreter must respect – if not embrace – moral theories of their practice even if fundamentally at odds with their own convictions.

Other parts of Allan's work tend to support my doubts about his collaborative instincts. In his sustained assault on standard textbook accounts of the British constitution, Allan finds it 'necessary' to challenge just about every established paradigm and orthodox interpretation one can think of. For instance, he charges those who defend parliamentary sovereignty as a Hartian Rule of Recognition as 'taking refuge in a bland sociological notion of law'.[66] He describes the grounds of review in administrative law as 'empty vessels' with no content.[67] He rejects the distinction between 'weak' and 'strong' review, appeal and review, substance and procedure, *Wednesbury* unreasonableness and proportionality, and a host of other bread and butter concepts and distinctions for English public lawyers.[68]

Take the grounds of judicial review. Allan offers a rich account of how a single value of 'due process' accounts for the full panoply of orthodox grounds and sub-grounds of judicial review enumerated in administrative law textbooks.[69] But why challenge orthodoxy here? We need not understand the invocation of heads of review as 'empty vessels' in the manner of an exclusionary rule. To the contrary, they may function as useful shorthands for a cluster of moral concerns common to both views. Allan himself seems to support this conclusion when he says:

> Even if common law rules, in particular, are only summary generalisations concerning the balance of moral principle in certain types of case, they are entitled to the respect of any lawyer who values the tradition in which she works … such rules should not be too readily modified or overridden.[70]

Furthermore, if, as Craig has argued, Allan's understanding does not lead to significant differences in reasoning or outcome to the orthodox understanding, then one might again wonder whether it is necessary to challenge it.[71]

Consider instead the doctrine of deference. Allan insists that there is no space for an independent *doctrine* of deference (or indeed doctrines of any kind).[72] But he

[65] Allan, 'Interpretation' (n 15) 65.

[66] Allan, *Sovereignty of Law* (n 10) 38.

[67] See TRS Allan, 'Doctrine and Theory in Administrative Law: An Elusive Quest for the Limits of Jurisdiction' [2003] *PL* 429 and TRS Allan, 'Constitutional Dialogue and the Justification of Judicial Review' (2003) 23 *OJLS* 563. See, generally Allan, *Sovereignty of Law* (n 10) ch 7.

[68] See Allan, *Sovereignty of Law* (n 10) *passim*, but especially ch 7.

[69] ibid ch 7, especially 242–44.

[70] Allan, 'Interpretation' (n 15) 74.

[71] See eg PP Craig, 'Legislative Intent and Legislative Supremacy: A Reply to Professor Allan' (2004) 24 *OJLS* 585.

[72] See eg TRS Allan, 'Common Law Reason and the Limits of Judicial Deference' in D Dyzenhaus (ed), *The Unity of Public Law* (Oxford, Hart Publishing, 2004) 289 and TRS Allan 'Human Rights and Judicial Review:

readily accepts that the considerations people associate with deference – democratic legitimacy and institutional competence – are already built into ordinary interpretative legal reasoning.[73] One might again say: plus ça change. Indeed, as with the grounds of review, we might make a positive case for doctrine without detracting from the principled substance of the debate. As Kyritsis argues, there may be moral and epistemic reasons to determine, in advance of particular decisions, the proper way to assign decisions to different branches of government.[74] As he sees it, doctrines of deference may strengthen the necessary assurance within a political community of 'more or less stable and systematic' principles of separation of powers.[75]

Allan's readiness to challenge orthodox understandings is symptomatic, I think, of his exclusive style of protestant argument. It is not obvious that his defence of collaborative interpretation does much to temper that style of argument. To close this section, I shall allow Allan himself to provide the best argument for treating even the most desiccated canons of constitutional orthodoxy as morally engaged views. As he puts it, there is no

> neutral, detached, descriptive ground on which a lawyer may stand in drawing conclusions about the requirements of English (or Scottish or European) law, in general, or the content of the British constitution, in particular … any statement or law is always a matter of interpretation, and … interpretation is (in the present context) necessarily normative: it draws on moral and political ideas and values to support one reading rather than another.[76]

This is the correct view. It is, as Allan suggests, *not possible* for a lawyer (or anyone else) to stand outside of their practice.[77] To adapt Dworkin's celebrated aphorism, morally engaged arguments are 'silent prologue to *any* decision at law'(emphasis added).[78] But Allan cannot have it both ways. If he subscribes to the view just put, then he cannot, consistently with that view, seek to disqualify views on the law and constitution here, there and everywhere as being external and detached.[79] I do not deny that it is often far from straightforward to make moral sense of theories whose advocates either vehemently resist such moral recasting, or who seek to recast in a questionable way.[80] But there is already plenty of impetus and inspiration for this endeavour. Kyritsis's emphases on political settlement, mutual responsiveness among branches of government, and

A Critique of Due Deference' (2006) 65 *CLJ* 671. For a wider argument against doctrine, see Allan, *Sovereignty of Law* (n 10) ch 7.

[73] ibid.

[74] See Kyritsis, *Where Our Protection Lies* (n 44) ch 7.

[75] Kyritsis gives the example of the principles laid down in *International Transport Roth GmbH v Secretary of State for the Home Department* [2003] QB 728. See Kyritsis, *Where Our Protection Lies* (n 44) 163.

[76] Allan, *Sovereignty of Law* (n 10) 9.

[77] cf the 'Archimedean' position rejected by Ronald Dworkin: Dworkin, *Justice in Robes* (n 41) ch 6.

[78] Dworkin, *Law's Empire* (n 3) 90.

[79] I think Allan and Dworkin differ on this point. A willingness to 'recast' positivist theories is central to Dworkin's work. See eg Dworkin, *Law's Empire* (n 3) ch 4 (recasting positivism as 'conventionalism'); R Dworkin, *Justice in Robes* (n 42) ch 7 'Thirty Years On' (arguing for 'interpretive positivism'); and 198–212 and 227–331 (recasting Joseph Raz's 'hard' positivism). I explore these possibilities in S Lakin, 'Defending and Contesting the Sovereignty of Law: The Public Lawyer as Interpretivist' (2015) 78 *MLR* 549.

[80] For an attempt in the latter category, see J Goldsworthy, *The Sovereignty of Parliament, History and Philosophy* (Oxford, Clarendon Press, 1999) 254. I criticise this attempt in S Lakin 'Why Common Law Constitutionalism is Correct (If It Is)' in Kyritsis and Lakin (eds), *Methodology* (n 13) 149.

the need for stable separation of powers doctrines, are redolent of many positivist-style claims within orthodox constitutional theory. Others have offered similarly rich moral stories about Diceyan orthodoxy to rival the views of Allan.[81] To my mind, this is conciliatory protestantism *par excellence*.

3. The Inclusive British Constitution

At the start of this chapter, I posed a conundrum: How may an interpreter argue from their own convictions about their community's moral commitments, while simultaneously arguing with, or on behalf of, the many other interpreters with whom they may deeply disagree? I have argued at length above about *how* we might reconcile these two perspectives. An interpreter, I have said, must adopt an inclusive and conciliatory attitude towards other interpreters or interpretations. We shall need to say more about this below. Before doing so, it is worth briefly pausing to consider *why* we should seek to reconcile these two faces of protestant argument. Is an inclusive, conciliatory attitude merely a matter of good manners, or does it capture something of moral importance about the rule of law? We may take our lead from Ronald Dworkin who describes an 'expressive' value of integrity:

> [T]he expressive value of integrity is confirmed when people in good faith try to treat one another in a way appropriate to common membership in a community … and to see each other as making this attempt even when they disagree about exactly what integrity requires in particular circumstances.[82]

This is to say that an attitude of good faith – or, as I have put it, inclusion and conciliation – towards each other's interpretations is itself *partly constitutive of political community*.[83] We treat people as equals precisely when we respect their arguments about legitimacy: when we treat no one's convictions about the moral commitments of their community as being any less genuine than anyone else's. The exclusive protestantism I have attributed to Allan I think fails in this regard. It views protestant argument as 'each person for himself' – a cudgel with which to beat a path for his vision of the constitution over all others. It is this style of protestantism, I suggest, that explains the troubling tendency in contemporary legal and political argument to 'cheer or boo' a decision, rather than view (opposing) winning or losing arguments as good faith interpretations of a common practice.

In the remaining space in this chapter, I shall attempt to sketch the sense of inclusiveness, conciliation and collaboration that, as I see it, is necessary for legal and constitutional practice to flourish. Or to put this in more solemn terms: the conditions

[81] See, for instance, M Gordon, *Parliamentary Sovereignty in the UK Constitution: Process, Politics and Democracy* (Oxford, Hart Publishing, 2015).

[82] Dworkin, *Law's Empire* (n 3) 190. cf GJ Postema's value of 'fidelity', closely allied to integrity: 'Duties of fidelity are owed to *people*, not to theories, principles, rules or events. Fidelity is a matter of keeping faith with our common past as the appropriate way of keeping faith with each other as comembers of the community to which we are committed': Postema, 'Justice in Workclothes' (n 6) 308.

[83] '[T]he general acceptance of [political integrity], even among people who otherwise disagree about political morality, [is] constitutive of political community': Dworkin, *Law's Empire* (n 3) 211.

under which we may co-exist in an interpretative community of principle. I emphasise the word 'sketch'. My limited ambition for this part of the chapter is to explore some tentative directions in which the arguments above might proceed.

I begin with the premise, defended at length above, that people within the same community (including judges in the higher courts) may interpret their community's history and practice in radically different but no less 'resolutely interpretative' ways. It follows from this assumption, I suggest, that judges and other interpreters must in some sense be *receptive* to the reasonable interpretations of others. They must actively *respect* others' moral views as rival but *concurrent* visions of law and the constitution.[84] As Allan puts it, they must see their collective views as a 'consensus of independent *conviction*'.[85] How do these responsibilities bear on the freedom of an interpreter to challenge entrenched paradigms or orthodox understandings? My (tentative) answer is that the interpreter should not challenge a decision or argument if it is *reasonable*, in the sense that it expresses or presupposes some plausible moral reading of their community's record. This is so *even if* they fundamentally disagree with it from the point of view of their own theory.[86]

This may all sound, at first blush, like a call for interpreters routinely to suppress their own convictions and defer to the arguments of others. That is not my position. The interpreter must maintain their responsibility to argue from their convictions for the correct understanding of their community's public, moral commitments; but they must do so in a way appropriate to being a member of a community whose members disagree deeply about the nature of those commitments. They must not compromise on the full rigour of their moral theory, but must compromise on *how they pursue* that theory. They will not, like the exclusive protestant, readily treat decisions, paradigms or understandings at odds with their theory as 'mistakes', obscuring the true natural Law underlying the practice. Their vehicle for pursuing their own moral vision is to convince judges and others of their aspirations for the practice, while accepting that rival moral theories will prevail along the way. They plant their convictions through arguments in and out of court, in the hope that they take seed in legislation, judicial decisions and dissenting judgments. Of course, the attitude I defend must have its limits. An interpreter does not owe their allegiance to a regime simply because there are some who defend it. They owe allegiance *in so far as* they judge there to be reasonable scope for moral argument about the community's past practice and history. They may think with Dworkin, then, that post-bellum US allowed for such disagreement; but will surely think that Nazi Germany did not.

[84] For a fascinating realisation of the inclusive style of interpretivism defended here and throughout this chapter, see MD Walters, 'Toward the Unity of Constitutional Value – Or, How to Capture a Pluralistic Hedgehog' (2017) 63 *McGill Law Journal* 419, especially 434–38. Walters argues that an interpretive theory of law must be pluralistic and 'circular' about value. As he puts it at 435: 'The unity of value to emerge through interpretation must accept all differences that are necessary to accept in order to make a coherent sense of a world full of diversity'. For Walters's very original notion of 'circular' interpretation, see MD Walters, 'The Unwritten Constitution as a Legal Concept' in D Dyzenhaus and M Thorburn (eds), *Philosophical Foundations of Constitutional Law* (Oxford, Oxford University Press, 2016) 33.

[85] Allan, 'Paradox' (n 15) 706.

[86] For an intriguing defence of this type of approach in the context of Northern Ireland, see A Schwartz, 'Patriotism or Integrity? Constitutional Community in Divided Societies' (2011) 3 *OJLS* 503, 522.

I now come to a stage in the argument that will no doubt leave many people behind (assuming that any were with me until now). If interpreters (including senior judges) adopt this type of receptive attitude to diverse, reasonable interpretations, then I think we must be prepared to expect and accept that *different theories will take root in the practice*. Our practice is likely to be something of a 'patchwork quilt' of competing moral theories, with orthodoxy, common law constitutionalism, and perhaps other theories vying for supremacy. Now many will see immediate difficulties with this view, some of which I shall attempt to anticipate and meet below; but I think this is the natural way for an inclusive protestant interpreter to understand their practice. Indeed, I think this is an intuitive, common understanding of contemporary constitutional practices. It is widely thought, for instance, that the British constitution reflects two or more competing visions.[87] The Human Rights Act gestures towards Allan's common law constitutionalist view of democracy, rights and adjudication in section 3, but towards a political constitutionalist, republican view in section 4.[88] Decisions of the higher courts plausibly oscillate between the robust judicial protection of fundamental rights and deference to Parliament.[89] Allan is determined to refute this bipolar understanding of the constitution. He says:

> It is important to rescue a 'natural law' understanding of the common law from Dworkin's errors; our view of common law reasoning will otherwise remain obscured by its legal positivist characterisation, giving pride of place to posited rules. Parallel to Dworkin's unstable 'third theory' of law, as it has been dubbed, lies the erratic behaviour characteristic of judges when required to interpret statutes consistently with common law or human rights principles. Veering from bold affirmations of the rule of law, on one hand, to obsequious invocations of absolute parliamentary sovereignty, on the other, their attempted reconciliations of justice and 'legislative intent' appear to reflect insecure foundations in constitutional theory. Just as we must resolve any fundamental conflict within legal and constitutional doctrine, so we must also reject any muddled combination of theoretical viewpoints in our analysis of the common law.[90]

The argument here is that orthodox constitutional doctrines (such as the so-called 'principle of legality')[91] presuppose the flawed, positivist-leaning legal theory of Ronald Dworkin. Just as Dworkin's 'third theory' of law allows that some features of a constitution may obtain as a matter of brute-fact, so British constitutional orthodoxy takes some features to be brute facts. If we replace Dworkin's theory with Allan's natural law account of the common law then, Allan implies, we can peel away the confused, orthodox parts of constitutional practice to reveal a coherent scheme of justice. We need not reject

[87] See eg D Feldman, 'None, One or Several? Perspectives on the UK's Constitution(s)' (2005) 64 *CLJ* 329. cf Allan, *Sovereignty of Law* (n 10) 1–4.

[88] As Allan puts it, the Human Rights Act 'actually enshrines the ambivalence that [contrasting accounts of the constitution] engender': *Sovereignty of Law* (n 10) 4.

[89] A particularly good example, often used by Allan, is the contrasting reasoning of the Court of Appeal and House of Lords in *R (Prolife Alliance) v British Broadcasting Corporation* [2002] WECA Civ 297, [2003] UKHL 23. Allan says of these decisions: 'The competing approaches reflect rival interpretations of British constitutionalism, which in turn embody rival conceptions of law …': Allan, *Sovereignty of Law* (n 10) 25.

[90] Allan, 'Interpretation' (n 15) 60 (footnotes omitted). See further, Allan, *Sovereignty of Law* (n 10) ch 5.

[91] As articulated, for instance, in *R v Secretary of State for the Home Department, ex p. Simms* [2000] 2 AC 115 at 131.

Dicey's celebrated account of the constitution in doing so, says Allan.[92] Properly understood, Dicey was himself a full-blooded common law constitutionalist.[93]

I hope I have said enough in this chapter to expose the problems with these arguments. Briefly, Dworkin's theory of law is not, as Allan claims, a confused hybrid between positivism and natural law; it is an interpretative theory about how the different branches of political morality interact at different times, and in different places and contexts. On one plausible view of how these principles interact within British constitutional practice, political fairness takes priority over justice. That type of view, I have suggested, is apt to supply the interpretative underpinnings for any number of claims within orthodox constitutional theory. This is to say that the two 'theoretical viewpoints' of orthodoxy and common law constitutionalism co-exist, not as a 'muddled combination', but as *rival*, concurrent, interpretations.[94]

Allan may object at this point that we cannot just leave

> the conflict [between these two interpretations] unresolved. Any decent theory must show how principles of legislative supremacy and legality are properly reconciled and brought into harmony. It would otherwise be a theory of two competing constitutions, leaving us without any guidance about how to choose between them.[95]

I disagree. I have offered an argument as to why we can and should embrace competing moral visions of the constitution rather than seek to resolve them into a single theory – even if such a thing were possible.[96] There is nothing in the nature of interpretivism to require a univocal view as to the scheme of principle underlying a practice.[97] It may be true that interpreters should *imagine* that the government speaks with one voice; but this is, as Postema says, no more than a heuristic device.[98] *How* a community speaks with one voice, I have argued, depends on widely practised attitudes of inclusion, conciliation and collaboration. It is this 'expressive' dimension of integrity that binds us together as community, rather than the scheme of principle which *in fact* underlies our practice.[99]

[92] AV Dicey, *Introduction to the Study of the Law of the Constitution*, 10th edn (London, Macmillan, 1964).

[93] For Allan's common law constitutionalist interpretation of Dicey, see Allan, *Sovereignty of Law* (n 10) passim, but especially chs 3 and 5. For similar treatment of Dicey, see MD Walters, *AV Dicey and the Common Law Constitutional Tradition: A Legal Turn of Mind* (Cambridge, Cambridge University Press, 2020) especially ch 10. cf Goldsworthy's chapter in this volume and, generally, Goldsworthy, *Sovereignty of Parliament* (n 80) and J Goldsworthy, *Parliamentary Sovereignty, Contemporary Debates* (Cambridge, Cambridge University Press, 2010).

[94] See further Lakin, 'Why Common Law Constitutionalism is Correct' (n 81).

[95] Allan, *Sovereignty of Law* (n 10) 23.

[96] 'We know that our own legal structure constantly violates integrity in this less dramatic way … We cannot bring all the various statutory and common law rules our judges enforce under a single coherent scheme of principle': Dworkin, *Law's Empire* (n 3) 184.

[97] It should be emphasised that Dworkin's 'right answers' thesis does not so require. See Dworkin, *Taking Rights Seriously* (n 5) 216. As Waldron says, moral objectivity 'underwrites' the arguments we make. Indeed, it makes disagreements between interpreters who espouse different moral theories intelligible. The protestant interpreter will hardly engage his fellow interpreters simply by dressing his theory as the true, objectively correct one. See J Waldron, 'The Rule of Law as a Theatre of Debate' in J Burley (ed), *Dworkin and His Critics* (Hoboken, Wiley-Blackwell, 2004) 326, J Waldron, *Law and Disagreement* (n 32) ch 8, R Dworkin, 'Objectivity and Truth: You'd Better Believe It' (1996) 25 *Philosophy and Public Affairs* 87, and Walters, 'Pluralistic Hedgehog' (n 84) 435–38.

[98] Postema, 'Justice in Workclothes' (n 6) 294.

[99] The expressive value of integrity 'is not exhausted … when citizens disagree about which scheme of justice is *in fact embedded* in the community's explicit decisions. For the expressive value is confirmed when people in

We are just about in a position to close the argument of this chapter. Before doing so, I briefly want to explore a possible parallel between what I have been saying, and the arguments that Dworkin makes in the last chapter of *Law's Empire*. In that chapter Dworkin distinguishes between 'inclusive' and 'pure' integrity. As he says:

> The law we have, the actual concrete law for us, is fixed by inclusive integrity. This is the law for the judge, the law he is obliged to declare and enforce. Present law, however, contains another law, which marks out its ambitions for itself; this purer law is defined by pure integrity. It consists in the principles of justice that offer the best justification for the present law seen from the perspective of no institution in particular and thus abstracting from all the constraints of fairness and process that inclusive integrity requires.[100]

Dworkin's distinction here supposes that we can separate, with at least some certainty, the theory of justice and fairness *actually instantiated* in the law, from the aspirational visions of justice that different philosophers may have for the law in abstraction from separation of powers considerations. He says of these visions of justice: 'We cannot defeat these other visions by measuring out and comparing the tracts of law that fit ours and theirs. None fits well enough to dominate present law overall; all fit well enough to claim a base within it'.[101]

Like Dworkin, I am taken with the image of there being different moral visions or 'dreams' pushing their way to the surface of legal and constitutional practice. But, in my view, such dreams or visions represent the *sum total* of legal argument for inclusive protestants. There is no separate 'actual concrete law' – at least at the level of our day to day arguments and disagreements – checking the many different ways in which interpreters may 'meld' together the different branches of political morality.[102] Here we see a further difference. The dreams of inclusive protestants are not just dreams of *justice*. They are dreams of how justice and separation of powers properly interact. In my opinion, this is how we must view the various interpretative theories considered in this chapter (and others besides). Allan's judge-centric vision jostles with Kyritsis's assurance vision, which jostles with Bellamy's political constitutionalist's vision,[103] and so on. No vision 'dominates' present law overall; each plausibly has a base within it. Each vision aspires to colonise the practice.

4. Conclusion

I shall not attempt to rehearse the different stages of argument in this chapter. I have argued for a particular understanding of protestant argument within an interpretative

good faith try to treat one another in a way appropriate to common membership in a community … and to see each other as making this attempt even when they disagree about exactly what integrity requires in particular circumstances' (emphasis added): Dworkin *Law's Empire* (n 3) 190.

[100] ibid 406–407.

[101] ibid 408.

[102] cf Allan, 'Paradox' (n 15) 709. This recalls the point made about 'fit' above.

[103] R Bellamy, *Political Constitutionalism: A Republican Defence of the Constitutionality of Democracy* (Cambridge, Cambridge University Press, 2007).

theory of law, one that demands an inclusive, conciliatory and collaborative attitude on the part of each interpreter. I have argued further that if this attitude successfully holds among interpreters, then we should expect and embrace an inclusive constitution, one in which different moral theories justify different parts of the practice. Indeed, I suggest that this is a plausible way to understand the British constitution.[104] I have advanced these arguments for inclusion and reconciliation by way of a refutation of an exclusive form of protestantism found in the work of Trevor Allan. This latter form of interpretivism, I have argued, is non-inclusive in that it fixates on one moral vision to the exclusion of all others. It is non-conciliatory in that it seeks to bar opposing views from the interpretative arena. In my view, only the inclusive form of protestantism can live up to the collaborative ideals to which both forms are wedded, and to which a political community of principle must aspire.

[104] I think my argument bears some relation to Dworkin's account of law and disagreement in the US constitution, but I shall not pursue that point here. See, for instance, R Dworkin, *Is Democracy Possible Here? Principles for a New Political Debate* (Princeton, Princeton University Press, 2006).

5

Unwritten Constitutional Principles and the Argument from Extreme Cases

HAN-RU ZHOU*

1. Introduction

While it is commonplace to divide the world between written and 'unwritten' constitutions, it would be more accurate to say that national constitutions are partly written, partly unwritten. The inevitable limitations of constitutional instruments, as detailed as some may be, stem from the fact that their framers could not envisage, and could not have conceivably envisaged, all the situations for which each constitutional provision may apply, nor how it should apply. When faced with a situation that the interpreter concludes is not completely governed by the provisions of the constitution, they can apply an (unwritten) interpretative *a contrario sensu* rule, ie that what is not prohibited is permitted, or what is not included is excluded, or some variant thereof. Alternatively, one may seek another interpretation by venturing further into the unwritten part of the constitution.

In jurisdictions where there is a constitutional instrument (or a set thereof) identified as forming the supreme law of the land, the unwritten part has drawn intense scrutiny. Unwritten constitutional principles (UCPs) have been defined as those norms that are 'not derived by normal processes of textual interpretation from the written Constitution'.[1] One author has spoken of legally binding principles 'that *no* reasonable reader could claim to extract or infer from … the Constitution's language by anything like standard "legal" arguments'.[2] Expressions such as 'normal processes of textual interpretation' and 'standard legal arguments' seem to refer to reasoning from constitutional provisions that is mainly based on logic, notably deduction, induction, and analogy.[3]

* I thank Geneviève Cartier and Mark Walters for their comments on an earlier draft. This research was supported by the Social Sciences and Humanities Research Council of Canada.

[1] PW Hogg and WK Wright, *Constitutional Law of Canada*, 5th edn, loose-leaf (Toronto, Carswell, 2007) 15–51. The authors appear to have borrowed the definition by TC Grey, 'Do We Have an Unwritten Constitution?' (1975) 27 *Stanford Law Review* 703, 703–704.

[2] LH Tribe, *The Invisible Constitution* (Oxford, Oxford University Press, 2008) 28–29.

[3] See HR Zhou, 'Legal Principles, Constitutional Principles and Judicial Review' (2019) 67 *American Journal of Comparative Law* 889, 908, 912–13, 929.

In common law countries, lengthy debates have covered every aspect of UCPs, from their legitimacy and desirability to their sources, origins, and interpretation, and have given rise to two main but somewhat paradoxical positions.

The first – in line with the standard account of judicial review of legislation according to which its exercise must be grounded in the provisions of the constitution[4] – is the prevalent view that courts cannot use and have never used so-called UCPs to invalidate a law. At most, defenders of the standard account accept such a use of rules and principles that are necessarily implied from the terms of the constitution (in light of its structure). The second is a consensus that, in the last resort, egregious laws should not be upheld or applied by the courts, even in the absence of conflict with a constitutional provision. While their contours might defy definition, such egregious laws – or what has been more commonly referred to as 'extreme cases' – are recognisable by the grave challenge they pose to fundamentals of our democratic system of government. Concern with extreme cases has long figured in the case law and literature, including throughout TRS Allan's work,[5] especially where it was determined that the terms of the constitution did not fully regulate those cases.

The argument from extreme cases has been countered or dismissed in several ways, notably by suggesting that they cannot be resolved judicially or that their occurrence is so rare in modern democracies that further discussion is purely academic. Consequently, many legal scholars have turned their efforts to the broader inquiry of where and how to trace the line between judicial deference to legislative authority and judicial intervention against an impugned law based on UCPs. In continuing the enterprise of redefining or fine-tuning the boundaries of legislative and judicial authority, one should heed Allan's warning that 'the constitutional limits to legislative power cannot be definitively stated. They remain to be refined and tested in future instances'.[6] In fact, challenges to legislation based on UCPs have, from time to time, been made before the courts of many common law jurisdictions and have generated a rich but at times contradictory body of cases, which, in turn, has generated a broad range of legal commentary.

This chapter seeks a possible broader consensus regarding the exercise of judicial review based on UCPs by taking a 'bottom-up' or practice-based approach in examining

[4] See eg WN Eskridge and JA Ferejohn, *A Republic of Statutes: The New American Constitution* (New Haven, Yale University Press, 2010) 34, 59–60 (implying from the standard account of American constitutionalism that 'Constitutional claims must be linked to the written Constitution'); J Goldsworthy, '*Kable*, *Kirk* and Judicial Statesmanship' (2014) 40 *Monash Law Review* 75, 104–107 (identifying as part of current Australian orthodox constitutional doctrine the proposition 'that state Parliaments possess plenary power subject only to limits entrenched in our written constitutions'); Hogg and Wright, *Constitutional Law* (n 1) 15-52 (Canadian lawyers normally assume 'that only the text of the Constitution … creates enforceable rights and obligations').

[5] See eg TRS Allan, 'Constitutional Rights and Judicial Review' (2018) 9 *Jurisprudence* 138, 141–42; TRS Allan, 'The Limits of Parliamentary Sovereignty' [1985] *PL* 614, 620–21; TRS Allan, *Law, Liberty, and Justice: The Legal Foundations of British Constitutionalism* (Oxford, Oxford University Press, 1993) 282; TRS Allan, *Constitutional Justice: A Liberal Theory of the Rule of Law* (Oxford, Oxford University Press, 2001) 216, 219; TRS Allan, 'Questions of Legality and Legitimacy: Form and Substance in British Constitutionalism' (2011) 9 *International Journal of Constitutional Law* 155, 162; TRS Allan, *The Sovereignty of Law: Freedom, Constitution, and Common Law* (Oxford, Oxford University Press, 2013) 34, 40–41, 173–74, 301.

[6] Allan, *Law, Liberty and Justice* (n 5) 270. See also Allan, *Sovereignty of Law* (n 5) 41: 'The distinction between an interpretation of statute that avoids the infliction of serious harm on individuals, out of all proportion to any advancement of the public good, on the one hand, and the non-application [or invalidation] of a wicked statute, on the other, is only a distinction of degree'.

and connecting a series of leading cases that are considered to exemplify the prevailing position under Westminster constitutions.[7] From this perspective, the argument from extreme cases can offer some renewed potential.

Section 2 presents two well-known types of extreme cases that involve *ad hominem* criminal laws and 'full' privative (or ouster) clauses. Despite extensive judicial and academic efforts to portray the resulting decisions as the product of a standard interpretation of the constitutional instrument, these decisions evidence the use, across the Commonwealth, of UCPs as a basis for the exercise of judicial review. Section 3 seeks to explain and justify the use of UCPs by identifying, mainly from Allan's work, three characteristics of extreme cases and then testing them on the constitutional evaluation of *ad hominem* laws and privative clauses. It should follow that, in legal systems with a Westminster constitution, there are cases, identifiable by three characteristics, that require the intervention of UCPs failing the application of relevant constitutional provisions. While there will always be deep disagreements regarding UCPs, it is hoped the fact of their unavoidability in conducting judicial review can be generally accepted and future debates can better focus on the search for a methodology or the conditions of their operation.

2. Judicial Review of *Ad hominem* Criminal Laws and Full Privative Clauses

A. Two Types of Extreme Cases

Liyanage v The Queen[8] has been considered 'the leading modern authority for the proposition that under a written constitution based on the separation of powers, the legislature may not determine by statute the outcome of particular judicial proceedings'.[9] The case was set against the backdrop of great political and social unrest in Ceylon (today Sri Lanka) and followed a failed coup d'état on 27 January 1962. Before the beginning of the trial of the alleged conspirators, the Ceylonese Parliament passed in March the Criminal Law (Special Provisions) Act, No 1 of 1962, a retroactive statute that was 'limited in its application to any offence against the state alleged to have been committed on or about January 27, 1962' (section 17). For cases coming within its purview, the 1962 Act

[7] In almost every British colony, a system of government whose essential features were based on the British system was eventually established. When the colonies later became independent, many of them formalised their new political and legal position through a constituent instrument, which sought to preserve their existing common law system and tradition. The content of these instruments typically borrowed from the relevant Imperial constitutional legislation of the second half of the nineteenth century or the first half of the twentieth century, and the Acts establishing the prewar Dominions. The result was a set of national constitutions considered to be based on the 'Westminster model'. See generally W Dale, 'The Making and Remaking of Commonwealth Constitutions' (1993) 42 *International and Comparative Law Quarterly* 67; SA de Smith, *The New Commonwealth and Its Constitutions* (London, Stevens, 1964) ch 3; A Harding, 'The "Westminster Model" Constitution Overseas: Transplantation, Adaptation and Development in Commonwealth States' (2004) 4 *Oxford University Commonwealth Law Journal* 143.

[8] *Liyanage v The Queen* [1967] 1 AC 259 (PC).

[9] *Ferguson v AG of Trinidad and Tobago* [2016] UKPC 2 at [21].

(along with an amendment passed later in the year) lifted the requirement of a warrant for arrest; set aside the right to habeas corpus by authorising detention for 60 days; amended the elements of the existing offence of conspiracy to target the failed coup; replaced the maximum sentence of 20 years of imprisonment with the death penalty or a minimum sentence of ten years and forfeiture of property; permitted to receive into evidence statements made to police officers, to co-defendants or while in police custody; and removed the right to a jury trial and the right to appeal.

Counsel for the accused argued that the two 1962 Acts 'constituted an unjustifiable assumption of judicial power by the legislature, or an interference with judicial power, which is outside the legislature's competence and is inconsistent with the severance of power between legislature, executive, and judiciary which the Constitution ordains'.[10] The Judicial Committee of the Privy Council essentially agreed with the accused's submission in concluding that the impugned bill of attainder[11] unduly interfered with the functions of the judiciary and therefore was inconsistent with Part VI of the Constitution of 1946 (titled 'The Judicature').

One would think that, in common law-based systems, to say nothing of mature democracies, the type of law struck down by the Privy Council in *Liyanage* belonged to a bygone era. Such belief made the classic 1996 case of *Kable v DPP (NSW)*[12] all the more extraordinary.

In *Kable*, the High Court of Australia was asked to rule on the validity of the Community Protection Act 1994 passed by the Parliament of New South Wales pending the appellant's imminent release from custody at the end of his sentence for manslaughter. The Act created a power for the State Supreme Court to order the detention of persons found to be 'more likely than not to commit a serious act of violence'. Its most unusual feature was in section 3, which specifically targeted Kable. Subsection 3(1) bluntly proclaimed that 'the object of this Act' was to 'provid[e] for the preventive detention … of Gregory Wayne Kable', while subsection 3(3) stated that '[t]his Act authorises the making of a detention order against Gregory Wayne Kable and does not authorise the making of a detention order against any other person'. Section 5 provided for a maximum period of detention of six months renewable on application by the Director of Public Prosecutions. A majority of the High Court found the Act to be inconsistent with the exercise of judicial power pursuant to Chapter III (ss 71–80) of the Australian Constitution (also titled 'The Judicature').

Privative clauses are well-known legislative provisions that seek to limit judicial review of executive or administrative action or decisions rendered by non-superior courts or tribunals. In jurisdictions with a written constitution like Canada and Australia, courts have not recognised legislative authority to enact 'full' privative clauses, ie that would completely shield an adjudicative body's decision from judicial review. In the landmark case of *Crevier v Quebec (AG)*, the Supreme Court of Canada for the first time held unconstitutional a privative clause that barred judicial review on questions of jurisdiction against any proceedings taken by a professional regulatory body or a tribunal.

[10] *Liyanage* (n 8) 285.
[11] ibid 289.
[12] *Kable v DPP (NSW)* (1996) 189 CLR 51.

The same clause also excluded recourse to the superintending and reforming power of the Superior Court. In a unanimous judgment, the Supreme Court declared that:

> where a provincial Legislature purports to insulate one of its statutory tribunals from any curial review of its adjudicative functions, the insulation encompassing jurisdiction, such provincial legislation must be struck down as unconstitutional by reason of having the effect of constituting the tribunal a s. 96 [of the Constitution Act 1867] court.[13]

The Australian position regarding the validity or effectiveness of privative clauses is similar to the holding in *Crevier* despite the somewhat different sets of constitutional provisions dealing with judicature. At issue in *Kirk v Industrial Relations Commission (NSW)*[14] was the interpretation of subsection 179(1) of the Industrial Relations Act 1996 of New South Wales, which provides that a decision of the Industrial Court 'is final and may not be appealed against, reviewed, quashed or called into question by any court or tribunal', and subsection 179(5) that prohibits 'proceedings brought in a court or tribunal for any relief or remedy, whether by order in the nature of prohibition, certiorari or mandamus, by injunction or declaration or otherwise'. Invoking section 73 of the Constitution of Australia, which defines its appellate jurisdiction, including over appeals from a state Supreme Court, the High Court held that state laws could not eviscerate a state Supreme Court's power to grant relief on account of jurisdictional error. It interpreted section 179 as not precluding the grant of certiorari for jurisdictional error and consequently quashed the lower court orders.

B. Compatibility with the Standard Account

On the surface, the four cases seem to fit the standard account of judicial review of legislation. Indeed, *Crevier* stands for the rule that full privative clauses are unconstitutional in Canada pursuant to section 96 of the Constitution of 1867. In *Kirk*, the High Court arrived at the same result through its interpretation of section 73 of the Australian Constitution read in conjunction with subsection 75(v) (which defines the original jurisdiction of the High Court). In *Kable* and *Liyanage*, the courts stated that their invalidation of the impugned law was based on the judicature provisions of the relevant constitutions.

Under the standard account, emphasis is often placed on the proposition that the court's interpretation of the constitution was the one dictated by the framers' intent and is consonant with the historical context. Particularly telling is the Privy Council's remark in *Liyanage* that:

> [The provisions of Part VI of the Constitution] manifest an *intention* to secure in the judiciary a freedom from political, legislative and executive control. They are wholly appropriate in a Constitution which *intends* that judicial power shall be vested only in the judicature .... The Constitution's silence as to the vesting of judicial power ... is not consistent with any *intention*

[13] *Crevier v Québec (AG)* [1981] 2 SCR 220, 234. Section 96 of the Constitution Act 1867 states as follows: 'The Governor General shall appoint the Judges of the Superior, District, and County Courts in each Province, except those of the Courts of Probate in Nova Scotia and New Brunswick.'

[14] *Kirk v Industrial Relations Commission (NSW)* (2010) 239 CLR 531.

> that henceforth it should pass to or be shared by, the executive or the legislature. … And thus judicial power may be eroded. Such an erosion is contrary to the *clear intention* of the Constitution.[15] (emphasis added)

The High Court in *Kirk* also contended that its interpretation of the meaning of state 'Supreme Courts' in section 73 was historically sound. According to the Court, their jurisdiction at federation included that of the English Court of Queen's Bench, which consists in the supervisory jurisdiction over decisions of non-superior courts.[16]

Courts also backed their interpretation and decision by appealing to logic, in that both were necessarily implied from the relevant constitutional provisions. In *Crevier*, the Court agreed with the proposition that 'the restrictions on the legislative power of the province to confer jurisdiction on boards must be derived by implication from the provisions of s. 96' of the Canadian Constitution.[17] It even opined that its reading of section 96 'is so evident that it has no need of demonstration'[18] and that 'it would make a mockery of it to treat it in non-functional formal terms as a mere appointing power'.[19]

C. 'Not Derived by Normal Processes of Textual Interpretation'

However, a closer examination of the judgments under examination reveals that they do not exactly fit the standard account of judicial review. At the outset, both courts in *Liyanage* and *Kable* were unable to point to a specific constitutional provision that had been infringed, thereby requiring them to engage in more complex reasoning.

Part VI of the Ceylonese Constitution conferred on Supreme Court judges the traditional guarantees of judicial independence, namely security of tenure and financial security, but did not expressly vest judicial power in the courts. Still, the Privy Council found that 'the importance of securing the independence of judges and of maintaining the dividing line between the judiciary and the executive was appreciated by those who framed the Constitution'.[20] To so conclude, the Privy Council reached back to the country's Charter of Justice 1833, which did include a provision that vested the administration of justice in the courts. It interpreted the Ceylonese Constitution as the continuation of the judicial system established in Ceylon by the 1833 Charter.[21] In this context, the Privy Council read the Constitution of 1946 as containing an implied general principle of separation of powers and judicial independence. However, it admitted 'the almost impossible task of tracing where the line is to be drawn between what

[15] *Liyanage* (n 8) 287–88, 291–92.

[16] *Kirk* (n 14) paras 97–98.

[17] *Crevier* (n 13) 235, citing *Farrell v Workmen's Compensation Board* [1962] SCR 48, 52. See also *Kable* (n 12) 111, 119 (McHugh J).

[18] *Crevier* (n 13) 235, citing *Alliance des professeurs catholiques de Montréal v Quebec Labour Relations Board* [1953] 2 SCR 140, 155.

[19] *Crevier* (n 13) 237. See also *Kable* (n 12) 118 (McHugh J) (opining that it 'would make a mockery of the principles contained in Ch III of the Constitution' if they allowed a State to freely alter the jurisdiction of its Supreme Court). For a recent example of judicial insistence that the 'substantive legal force [of UCPs] must arise by necessary implication from the Constitution's text', see *Toronto v Ontario* [2021] 2 SCR 845 at [48]–[84].

[20] *Bribery Commissioner v Ranasinghe* [1965] AC 172 (PC) 190.

[21] *Liyanage* (n 8) 286.

will and what will not constitute' an inadmissible interference in judicial power.[22] That task was unnecessary with regard to the 1962 statutes, as they amounted to a deliberate usurpation of judicial power. The Privy Council added that '[i]f such Acts as these were valid the judicial power could be wholly absorbed by the legislature and taken out of the hands of the judges'.[23]

By contrast, section 71 in Chapter III of the Australian Constitution does vest judicial power in federal courts and 'such other courts as [the Commonwealth Parliament] invests with federal jurisdiction'. At the outset, the High Court in *Kable* inferred from Chapter III the principles of the separation of powers and judicial independence to be applicable to all federal courts, although only some justices commented briefly on the nature of that inference. McHugh J stated that '[o]ne of the basic principles which underlie Chapter III and to which it gives effect is that the judges of the federal courts must be, and must be perceived to be, independent of the legislature and the executive government'.[24] For Toohey J, Chapter III 'reflects an aspect of the doctrine of separation of powers, serving to protect [judicial independence]'.[25] Only Brennan CJ went into some particulars, stating in his dissenting judgment that:

> Chapter III of the *Constitution* of the Commonwealth both limits the repositories of the judicial power of the Commonwealth and, in context, prescribes a separation of the function of the High Court and of other federal courts from the functions of the political branches of government. The separation of functions is derived from the structure of the Constitution and, in particular, from the distribution of legislative power to the Federal Parliament (s 1), of executive power to the Queen for exercise by the Governor-General (s 61) and of judicial power to the courts referred to in s 71.[26]

In concluding that the NSW Parliament did not have jurisdiction to pass the impugned law, the majority justices needed to further infer that the federal constitutional requirements of the separation of powers extend to state courts when they exercise federal jurisdiction. There again, little explanation was given regarding how the justices inferred the extension to state courts of the (also inferred) principle of the separation of powers. Only two justices addressed the matter. While he recognised that 'the Commonwealth doctrine of separation of powers cannot apply to the State', McHugh J still found that 'it necessarily follows that those [State] courts must also be, and be perceived to be, independent of the legislature and executive government in the exercise of federal jurisdiction'.[27] For Gummow J, it is 'the structure of the *Australian Constitution*, especially Chapter III',[28] that does not permit the division of the Australian judiciary into two classes: one that is imposed the exercise of non-judicial functions that are repugnant to the judicial process and one that is not imposed such exercise.

[22] ibid 289–90.
[23] ibid 291.
[24] *Kable* (n 12) 117.
[25] ibid 99.
[26] ibid 67.
[27] ibid 117. See also 119 ('it is a necessary implication of the Constitution's plan of an Australian judicial system with State courts invested with federal jurisdiction that no government can act in a way that might undermine public confidence in the impartial administration of the judicial functions of State courts').
[28] ibid 128.

Chapter III as a whole has also been invoked in the determination of the constitutionality of full privative clauses enacted at the state level. Subsection 75(v) confers on the High Court original jurisdiction in all matters 'in which a writ of Mandamus or prohibition or an injunction is sought against an officer of the Commonwealth'. In a 2003 case, the Court interpreted subsection 75(v) as 'introduc[ing] into the Constitution of the Commonwealth an entrenched minimum provision of judicial review'.[29] However, the Constitution does not expressly contain an equivalent provision applicable to state Supreme Courts. Nevertheless, the High Court in *Kirk* interpreted Chapter III to include an equivalent requirement applicable to state laws, that was inferred from the mention of state 'Supreme Courts' in section 73 of the Constitution. That mention, the Court explained, refers to the supervisory jurisdiction of the English Court of Queen's Bench over 'the exercise of state executive and judicial power by persons and bodies other than the Supreme Court'.[30]

Under the Canadian Constitution, the Supreme Court's reasoning concerning the unconstitutionality of full privative clauses has unfolded in two related ways. Under one line of reasoning, a superior court has an inherent power to perform its supervisory and controlling power over inferior tribunals; this (unwritten) constitutional power necessarily implies the power to review whether a statutory court or tribunal has exceeded its jurisdiction; pursuant to section 96 (in Part VII of the 1867 Constitution, titled 'Judicature'), the appointment of superior court judges is made by the Governor General; since the members of statutory courts and tribunals are not appointed by the Governor General, they are not superior courts; therefore, their decisions cannot be shielded from judicial review of a purported excess of jurisdiction. In *Crevier*, following this line of reasoning, the Supreme Court held that the tribunal whose decision was challenged 'cannot constitutionally be immunised from review of decisions on questions of jurisdiction'.[31]

A second and related line of reasoning engages the principle of the rule of law and one of its core elements, namely, protection from arbitrary government action. The purpose of a privative clause is to limit or bar judicial review. If it successfully ousts judicial review of the decisions of tribunals or the government, then nothing, save legislative intervention, can prevent them from making unreviewable arbitrary decisions. Chapter III of the Australian Constitution and Part VII of Canada's Constitution Act 1867 have established in their respective countries the English model of High Courts with their inherent power of supervision over tribunals and administrative bodies. However, the judicature provisions *per se* do not say which level of judicial review is constitutionally protected and, correlatively, which types of privative clauses pass constitutional muster. While one could argue that Chapter III and Part VII expressly or impliedly constitutionalise *some* level of judicial review, it is the rule of law which traces the line between constitutionally permissible and impermissible privative clauses: those that preclude judicial oversight of arbitrary decisions impermissibly offend the

[29] *Plaintiff S157/2002 v Commonwealth* (2003) 211 CLR 476 at [98].
[30] *Kirk* (n 14) para 98.
[31] *Crevier* (n 13) 236.

rule of law and therefore are contrary to the judicature provisions of the Australian and Canadian constitutions.

The cases just discussed could be read as illustrations of the old distinction between what courts do and what they say they do. In each case, the judges asserted that their decisions declaring laws invalid or, in *Kirk*, 'constructing' the impugned clause, were mandated by the terms of the constitution. However, upon closer analysis, the decisions were based on principles that 'do not follow from the Constitution's language by any standard legal argument':[32] UCPs. With respect to full privative clauses, even the United Kingdom and New Zealand Supreme Courts have thus far declined to accept that their Parliaments could completely shield the government or a tribunal from judicial review, despite the principle of Parliamentary sovereignty.[33]

One would think that bills of attainder and full privative clauses[34] are among the most egregious laws that could be found in a democracy, and therefore could only be considered as the rarest of occurrences, or extreme cases. Extending the comparative analysis would show other lines of cases of judicial review where the courts used a similar type of reasoning, in particular, vis-à-vis statutes that authorised discretionary or indefinite detention imposed by executive decision[35] or attempted to bar challenges of the constitutionality of laws or other state action.[36] Section 3 turns to what characterises these extreme cases that have consistently warranted judicial intervention.

3. Characteristics of Extreme Cases

Discussions of principle-based judicial review of legislation inevitably entail consideration of what are qualified as core, basic, essential, central or fundamental tenets or the bedrock of our constitutional system, in particular, the rule of law, democracy, the separation of powers, and individual rights and freedoms. While their role cannot be overstated, and without underestimating the importance of reasoning from first principles, there is a risk, given their universality and generality, of deriving too much from constitutional fundamentals to bolster all sorts of arguments about the extent of judicial review.

An alternative approach would be to identify, from case studies and in light of Allan's theory of constitutional law and adjudication, characteristics common to extreme cases that call for the application of countervailing UCPs. Aside from the consensus on the

[32] Tribe, *Invisible Constitution* (n 2) 29.

[33] See eg P Craig, *Administrative Law*, 9th edn (Wellington, Sweet & Maxwell, 2021) 895–96; PA Joseph, *Joseph on Constitutional and Administrative Law*, 5th edn (Toronto, Thomson Reuters, 2021) 648, 932, 962–63.

[34] Compare Goldsworthy, '*Kable*, *Kirk* and Judicial Statesmanship' (n 4) 114 (opining that the privative clause in *Kirk* was not exceptional and extreme but at the same time acknowledging that '[t]he history of judicial resistance to strong privative clauses certainly suggests that judges regard them as exceptional and extreme').

[35] See eg *Hinds v The Queen* [1977] AC 195 (PC); *Chu Kheng Lim v Minister for Immigration* (1992) 176 CLR 1; *Browne v The Queen* [2000] 1 AC 45 (PC); *DPP of Jamaica v Mollison* [2003] 2 AC 411 (PC); *Griffith v The Queen* [2005] 2 AC 235 (PC) at [24].

[36] See eg *Amax Potash Ltd v Saskatchewan* [1977] 2 SCR 576, 591–92, citing *Antill Ranger and Co Proprietary Ltd v Commissioner for Motor Transport* (1955) 93 CLR 83, affd [1956] AC 527 (PC).

ultimate outcomes of extreme cases, the value of focusing on these cases is to avoid getting entangled in the complexity of those characteristics, given that they figure prominently in each case under examination. One may suggest that the extreme cases examined present three characteristics relevant to principle-based judicial review.

A. Rights, Separation of Powers, Proportionality

A first characteristic is the violation of certain basic individual human rights that are placed 'beyond serious legislative encroachment',[37] even if their exercise may injure the public interest, and whether or not they are guaranteed in a bill of rights. For Allan, these basic rights would be 'the enjoyment of freedoms of conscience and expression, personal liberty and bodily integrity, rights of access to the courts and to confidential legal advice, and other well-established rights that have their foundation in settled common law doctrine and practice'.[38] They have typically been enshrined in international rights instruments and national constitutions.[39] Allan qualified the right not to be subjected to cruel or unusual or arbitrary punishment, which can be traced back to the Bill of Rights 1689, as '"the right of rights" in a true democracy'.[40] His opinion is supported by the prevailing Canadian position that this right, guaranteed at section 12 of the Canadian Charter of Rights and Freedoms 1982, has never been, and is unlikely to be, justifiably limited 'in a free and democratic society'.[41] It also accords with the absolute and non-derogable nature of the right not to be subjected to torture or cruel, inhuman or degrading treatment or punishment under international law.[42]

A second characteristic of extreme cases is their subversion of the separation of powers that cannot be viewed as serving the public good. Allan's conception of the separation of powers draws on some of the basic elements of Locke's theory of government. As the sole body entrusted by consent of the people to make laws for the public good, the legislative branch 'cannot assume to itself a power to rule by extemporary arbitrary decrees' or 'transfer the power of making laws to any other hands'.[43] For Allan, the gravest violation of the separation of powers (and of the rule of law) is the bill of attainder when Parliament acts as prosecutor, judge and jury, which would 'lie beyond the boundaries of any notion of legislative supremacy acceptable today', whatever the

[37] TRS Allan, 'Parliamentary Sovereignty: Law, Politics, and Revolution' (1997) 113 *LQR* 443, 449. See also Allan, *Sovereignty of Law* (n 5) 297 and Allan, 'Form and Substance in British Constitutionalism' (n 5) 158.

[38] Allan, 'Form and Substance in British Constitutionalism' (n 5) 158.

[39] DS Law and M Versteeg, 'The Declining Influence of the United States Constitution' (2012) 87 *New York University Law Review* 762, 773–79.

[40] TRS Allan, 'Democracy, Legality, and Proportionality' in G Huscroft, BW Miller and G Webber (eds), *Proportionality and the Rule of Law: Rights, Justification, Reasoning* (Cambridge, Cambridge University Press, 2014) 215.

[41] Hogg and Wright, *Constitutional Law* (n 1) 38–52.

[42] Convention against Torture and Other Cruel, Inhuman or Degrading Treatment or Punishment (adopted 10 December 1984, entered into force 26 June 1987) 1465 UNTS 85; UN Committee against Torture 'General Comment No 2: Implementation of Article 2 by States Parties' (24 January 2008) UN Doc CAT/C/GC/2.

[43] J Locke, *Two Treatises of Government: And a Letter Concerning Toleration*, Ian Shapiro (ed) (New Haven, Yale University Press, 2003) 156, 160–61, 163. See also Allan, *Sovereignty of Law* (n 5) 77, 298.

historical precedents.[44] Another basic precept of the separation of powers (and the rule of law) is the right of access to the courts, the removal of which (for instance, through a privative clause) would lead to a constitutional breakdown and the destruction of the legal order.[45]

Third, the extreme case fails what can be regarded as the least stringent proportionality test between the public and individual interests, which is 'intrinsic to the interpretative process'[46] (under a written or unwritten constitution). A law will fail the test if its purpose is the suppression of rights;[47] if it amounts to irrationality in the sense that 'the means are so far removed from any defensible connection with the purported ends as to call the legitimacy or bona fides of such ends into question [or] curtail[s] basic rights without any plausible justification';[48] or if the public benefit derived from the law is wholly disproportionate to the individual harm that it causes.[49]

A law that displays those three characteristics not only flouts the fundamental principles of our democratic constitutional systems but, allowing it to stand (on the basis of the silence or purported silence of the constitutional instrument) and to be used or enforced would imperil the 'character or stability of the legal order'[50] and set the course for a constitutional crisis. In the final analysis, judges are pragmatists. As Marshall CJ famously stated in *McCulloch v Maryland*, '[t]he Constitution was intended to endure for ages to come, and, consequently, to be adapted to the various crises of human affairs'.[51] When necessary, law and theory will reconcile with reality.

B. Applications

Re-examining the *ad hominem* criminal laws and full privative clauses from the perspective of the three characteristics of extreme cases should give a clearer sense of the extreme nature of the cases. The impugned laws in *Liyanage* and *Kable* subjected the defendants to arbitrary punishment and were violations of the 'right of rights' (and, in *Liyanage*, of at least half a dozen other basic rights). In *Kable*, the NSW statute also allowed the government to apply for detention orders against Kable that could amount to indefinite detention. The bill of attainder and *ad hominem* criminal statute are said to be the most flagrant violations of the separation of powers. The Privy Council in *Liyanage* quoted approvingly from the 1799 case of *Calder v Bull* where the US Supreme Court declared that '[t]hese acts were legislative judgments; and an exercise of judicial power'.[52] In the view of the Privy Council, the 1962 Ceylonese Acts constituted a usurpation of judicial

[44] Allan, *Sovereignty of Law* (n 5) 34, 93–94; Allan, *Law, Liberty and Justice* (n 5) 73.
[45] Allan, *Constitutional Justice* (n 5) 213.
[46] Allan, *Sovereignty of Law* (n 5) 184.
[47] Allan, 'Democracy, Legality, and Proportionality' (n 40) 231.
[48] Allan, *Sovereignty of Law* (n 5) 185.
[49] ibid 173–74, 185.
[50] ibid 301. See also Allan, *Constitutional Justice* (n 5) 213; Allan, 'The Limits of Parliamentary Sovereignty' (n 5) 620–21.
[51] *McCulloch v Maryland* 17 US 316 (1819) 415.
[52] *Liyanage* (n 8) 291, citing *Calder v Bull* 3 Dallas 386 (1799).

power and were not 'designed as any improvement of the general law'.[53] In *Kable*, the NSW statute required the judiciary to exercise non-judicial powers, turning it into 'an instrument of executive government policy'.[54] Two High Court justices denounced it as 'a mockery of the judicial process', 'extraordinary' and 'repugnant to the judicial process in a fundamental degree'.[55]

The Ceylonese and NSW statutes also failed each step of the minimal proportionality test. Their purpose was to interfere with the judicial process and further deprive the detainees of their freedom (in addition to the confiscation of their property in *Liyanage*). As regards the Ceylonese Acts, the Privy Council stated that they sought to compel the judges to impose the prescribed harsher sentences to each offender, 'even though his part in the conspiracy might have been trivial'.[56] In *Kable*, the NSW statute required the court to make a 'guess … whether the defendant will commit a … serious act of violence',[57] based on evidence that, as in *Liyanage*, would have been inadmissible in normal legal proceedings. To the extent that the impugned law in *Liyanage* and *Kable* amounted to '[a]rbitrary punishment, inconsistent with the general principles of law', it 'is inherently irrational; it imposes burdens on the individual that cannot be justified as necessary for the public good'.[58]

The full privative clauses also possessed the three characteristics of extreme cases. At their core, they denied the right of access to courts, and, consequently, the benefit of other individual rights that state action may have infringed. For instance, in *Kirk*, the High Court held that the charges against the appellants did not disclose any act or omission on their part nor identify any measure that they should have taken, thus violating their common law right to make full answer and defence.[59] It also found that, by calling the accused to give evidence, the prosecution violated his legislative right against compellability.[60] The High Court quashed the convictions and sentences entered by the Industrial Court judge despite the full privative clause.

The legislative removal (as opposed to a permissible restriction) of judicial review negates the superior courts' long-recognised inherent authority to supervise and control the legality of decisions made by inferior courts, tribunals, administrative bodies and public officials, in addition to the courts' generally assumed authority in common law jurisdictions as the 'ultimate interpreters' of the constitution.[61] In *Kirk*, the High Court recognised that the supervisory role of state Supreme Courts, 'was, and is, a defining characteristic of those courts'.[62] In *Crevier*, the Supreme Court of Canada opined that there was 'nothing that is more the hallmark of a superior court' than the vesting of

[53] *Liyanage* (n 8) 289.
[54] *Kable* (n 12) 123, 125 (McHugh J), 133 (Gummow J).
[55] ibid 109 (Gaudron J), 133–35 (Gummow J).
[56] *Liyanage* (n 8) 291.
[57] *Kable* (n 12) 107 (Gaudron J).
[58] Allan, 'Democracy, Legality, and Proportionality' (n 40) 215–16.
[59] See *Kirk* (n 14) paras 26–28, 74.
[60] See ibid paras 50–54, 76.
[61] *Crevier* (n 13) 237–38. See also *Baker v Carr* 369 US 186 (1962) 201; *Re Griffin; Ex p Professional Radio & Electronics Institute (Aust)* (1988) 167 CLR 37, 40 (Brennan J); *Plaintiff S157/2002* (n 29) para 104; *Canadian Western Bank v Alberta* [2007] 2 SCR 3 at [24]; *AG of Trinidad and Tobago v Dumas* [2017] 1 WLR 1978 (PC) at [15], citing *State of Rajasthan v Union of India* 1977 AIR 1361 at [143].
[62] *Kirk* (n 14) paras 55, 98–99.

power to determine the limits of a tribunal's jurisdiction.[63] In its view, the legislative limitation on tribunals' power to determine their own jurisdiction 'stands on the same footing' as the limitation on the power of tribunals to make unreviewable determinations of constitutionality.[64]

The full privative clauses also failed the minimal proportionality test. As it was already noted, not only their legislative purpose was the denial of access to courts, but such clauses further denied the exercise of other rights and permitted arbitrary decisions to stand. In *Kirk*, the High Court noted that: '[t]o deprive a state Supreme Court of its supervisory jurisdiction enforcing the limits on the exercise of state executive and judicial power by persons and bodies other than that court would be to create islands of power immune from supervision and restraint'.[65] All value in a privative clause vanishes when it renders a public body or official legally unaccountable for its decisions.

Conversely, the analysis from extreme cases sheds additional light on, and perhaps makes some sense of, the Privy Council's decision to uphold the mandatory death penalty in several Caribbean countries even though it appears to be (or is) at least as egregious as a bill of attainder or a full privative clause.

In *Chandler v Trinidad and Tobago*,[66] the Privy Council examined whether the mandatory death penalty for murder imposed by a 1925 colonial statute violated the Constitution of Trinidad and Tobago of 1976. It was not contested that the penalty was contrary to subsections 4(a) and 5(2)(b) of the Constitution, which guarantee the right to life and the right not to be subjected to cruel and unusual treatment or punishment. In addition, the Privy Council suggested that it was disproportionate and unjust. However, the Constitution included a savings clause that the Privy Council interpreted as 'disapplying'[67] sections 4–5 to all existing laws at the date of the adoption of the Constitution. It also rejected the appellant's alternative argument that the mandatory death penalty breached the separation of powers. For the Privy Council, a legislature that prescribes a fixed penalty to be imposed on all persons found guilty of a defined offence, is an 'inherently legislative power' and thus consistent with the principle of the separation of powers in the Trinidad and Tobago Constitution 'and in many other Constitutions on the Westminster model'.[68]

Proponents of the standard account of judicial review will point to judicial statements from *Chandler (No 2)* that the separation of powers is not an 'overriding', 'freestanding', 'independent' principle that can invalidate legislation, but one that 'operates through the terms of a Constitution'.[69] However, surely the savings clause could not give Parliament unlimited licence to violate any and all of the two dozen rights found in sections 4–5 that make up the heart of the nation's constitutional bill of rights. At the outset, a broad interpretation of the clause would run contrary to the Privy Council's recognition in *Chandler (No 2)* that '[i]t is a tenet of the jurisprudence of both the Board and the

[63] *Crevier* (n 13) 237.
[64] ibid 236.
[65] *Kirk* (n 14) para 99.
[66] *Chandler v Trinidad and Tobago* [2023] AC 285 (PC) (*Chandler No 2*).
[67] ibid paras 32, 94.
[68] ibid paras 32, 79, 81, 91.
[69] ibid paras 75, 78, 81.

CCJ [Caribbean Court of Justice] that savings clauses are to be given a strict or narrow interpretation'.[70] Later in its judgment, the Privy Council also reiterated the longstanding principle from *Liyanage* as follows: 'What has been recognised as constitutionally unacceptable is that a legislature should prescribe the penalty that is to be imposed on any particular individual'.[71] In the end, *Chandler (No 2)* does not perfectly fit the above notion of extreme cases (and perhaps shows its limits) to the extent that, contrary to the *ad hominem* criminal laws and full privative clauses, no contravention of the separation of powers had been demonstrated in respect of the mandatory death penalty for murder. Had it been enacted in contravention of the separation of powers, one can believe that the mandatory death penalty for murder would not have been upheld.

4. Conclusion

This chapter focused on what is regarded as the most contentious use of UCPs in common law-based countries, namely as grounds for the exercise of judicial review of legislation. It sought to identify the characteristics that called for the use of these principles, as inferred from landmark and extreme cases where principle-based review was unavoidable and necessary in the absence of applicable constitutional provisions.

As Charles Black once stated, '[e]very legal method starts with extreme cases'.[72] Reference to extreme cases has been a regular feature in the work of TRS Allan. When the logical inferences from the terms of the constitution can no longer rationally explain or justify the fact of judicial intervention in such cases, it is time to confront more squarely the flaws of the standard account of judicial review and realign the doctrinal and theoretical debate concerning UCPs.

Absent a bill of rights or an applicable right stated therein, courts under Westminster constitutions have invoked UCPs in conducting judicial review of legislation. *Ad hominem* criminal laws and full privative clauses present three characteristics: a denial of basic individual rights, a subversion of the separation of powers without evidence that it serves the public good, and failure to satisfy a minimal proportionality test. Despite the different jurisdictions and periods, the similarities in the judicial reasoning and conclusions suggest that those UCPs, as 'fundamental common law principles',[73] form part of a 'supra-jurisdictional', 'common stock of constitutional common law'.[74]

The three characteristics of extreme cases may not be exhaustive, given that they were elaborated and examined mainly with respect to *ad hominem* criminal laws and full privative clauses. Definitions of extreme cases can also develop. For centuries, courts have played their part in adapting, when necessary, the written and unwritten

[70] ibid para 69.
[71] ibid para 79.
[72] CL Black, *Structure and Relationship in Constitutional Law* (Baton Rouge, Louisiana State University Press, 1969) 12.
[73] Allan, *Sovereignty of Law* (n 5) 40, 299.
[74] JW Harris, 'The Privy Council and the Common Law' (1990) 106 LQR 574, 574, 588–90. See also J Waldron, *'Partly Laws Common to All Mankind': Foreign Law in American Courts* (New Haven, Yale University Press, 2012) 2–3 (defining *ius gentium* as 'a body of legal principles constituted by those positive laws common to the various national legal systems').

constitution to the relevant changes in society.[75] Some extreme cases were not considered as such in the past and some today may cease to be in the future while new ones emerge. Extreme cases undoubtedly remain infrequent but some of them do not appear to be exceptional outliers and, to such an extent, their name may be a misnomer.

Principle-based judicial review of legislation need not be, and is not, confined to extreme cases. The constitutionalisation of the mechanism of judicial review is *lex non scripta*, as are most, if almost all, of the rules and principles governing its operation. It has been said that the statement that unwritten law cannot be used as a standalone basis to invalidate legislation is itself a proposition of unwritten constitutional law. One way or another, UCPs are inevitable. Facing more squarely their reality, as TRS Allan has in his works, would allow franker critical engagement with the crucial issue of what their role in judicial review is and should be.

[75] See eg *McCulloch v. Maryland* (n 51) 415; *Stockdale v Hansard* (1839) 9 A&E 1; 112 ER 1112, 1155 ('The Constitution of this country being framed on abstract principles: there cannot be a doubt that it adapted itself to the exigencies of the several occasions that arose, and gradually grew into that form which the ends of good government require') and *Edwards v Canada (AG)* [1930] AC 124 (CP) 136 (introducing the famous 'living tree' metaphor).

PART II

Law, Morality, and Justice

6

The Rule of Law and Respect for Persons

THOMAS ADAMS*

1. Introduction

A common thought about the rule of law is that its observance ensures a baseline of respect for the individual – in standing against, for example, punishment in accordance with secret laws or conviction by kangaroo courts – and that it is therefore of moral value. This way of understanding the notion treats it as a good-making feature of social arrangements because of its connection with the autonomy of the legal subject. When the law addresses its requirements to you in a way that is coherent and intelligible and enforces them in the same spirit it treats you, on this view, with dignity and in this way does something right. Perhaps it also does a number of things wrong. The demagogue may operate under the rule of law as much as the democrat and rule of law compliant norms are capable of being deeply unjust; clear, prospective, coherent and yet exploitative or discriminatory. Adherence to the rule of law would not correct for these ills but it would ensure that whatever else the law did, it would show some degree of respect for those that it governed.

It is this conception of the rule of law that Trevor Allan attributes to Joseph Raz and he thinks it is unstable.[1] For once we notice the rule of law's special connection with autonomy, Allan argues, we will also notice its relationship with other values, such as liberty and equality:

> [C]onstitutional theory cannot rest content with a narrow, formal conception of the rule of law … The formal conception directs our attention to matters of individual right and

* Thanks to Trevor Allan, Geneviève Cartier, Ruby Daily, Hasan Dindjer, Felipe Jimenez, Kacper Majewski, Javier Gallego Saade, Nigel Simmonds, Mark Walters, Fred Wilmot-Smith, participants at the Sherbrooke and Queen's University joint conference in honour of Trevor Allan, the Queen's University Colloquium in Legal and Political Philosophy, the Oxford Philosophy Society and the Permanent Workshop of the Lisbon Legal Theory Group.

[1] TRS Allan, *Law, Liberty, and Justice: The Legal Foundations of British Constitutionalism* (Oxford, Clarendon Press, 1993) 39. Did Raz in fact embrace such a view? I think the answer here is no. While Raz does hold that 'observance of the rule of law is necessary if the law is to respect human dignity' he is nonetheless clear that compliance with its precepts does not establish that there exists 'some moral value in every legal system'. Why? Because the rule of law is a 'negative value', designed to prevent wrong, not to do right. See J Raz, *The Authority of Law: Essays on Law and Morality*, 2nd edn (Oxford, Oxford University Press, 2009) 221, 224. For a different reading of Raz's argument see K Rundle, *Forms Liberate: Reclaiming the Jurisprudence of Lon L Fuller* (Oxford, Hart Publishing, 2012) 148–54.

> human dignity. [But we] are obliged to confront wider questions of liberty [and] equality … in order to make concrete our commitment to the rule of law in the circumstances of particular cases.[2]

To mobilise his argument, Allan offers as an example a regime for the indefinite detention without trial of non-nationals suspected of terrorist offences.[3] This, he suggests, would offend against the rule of law for three reasons. Through potentially unjustified detention it would threaten the liberty of the individual.[4] In singling out non-nationals for internment it would offend against equality before the law.[5] Finally, through the failure to allow the individual to challenge their detention it would infringe on the autonomy of the legal subject.[6] No doubt each of these is an important objection to legislation of this form, but are they rule of law objections?

The rule of law unquestionably stands as a bulwark against certain interferences with liberty – the warrantless arrest, for example – but it so doing is coincidental to the value of freedom. From the perspective of the rule of law, the problem in the example is the absence of a warrant not the fact of arrest. Similarly, practices such as solitary confinement and mandatory whole life sentences stand as serious affronts to liberty but only become concerns for the rule of law if imposed arbitrarily or absent appropriate checks. For the defender of legality the issue with the carceral state lies in its administration, not in its existence.

One response to this type of argument is to suggest that it focuses on too narrow a conception of liberty. For while the rule of law does not guarantee the fundamental freedoms of those subject to it, it nonetheless preserves their liberty in the sense that it ensures that power over them is exercised only through a stable network of rules and principles. So Nigel Simmonds argues:

> When a citizen lives under the rule of law, it is conceivable that the duties imposed upon him or her will be very extensive and onerous … Yet, if the rule of law is a reality, the duties will have limits and the limits will not be dependent upon the will of any other person.[7]

So, while it is true that under the rule of law an individual might, say, be placed in prison or else ordered to surrender their possessions, these acts would be a consequence of the application of legal standards as opposed to the whim of some person or another. 'In claiming that the rule of law is intrinsically linked to liberty', Simmonds suggests, we are concerned not with 'the range of options available to us without interference' – something he admits that the law may seriously curtail – but with 'the degree to which that range of options is itself dependent upon the will of another.'[8]

[2] Allan, *Law, Liberty, and Justice* (n 1) 39.

[3] TRS Allan, *The Sovereignty of Law: Freedom, Constitution, and Common Law* (Oxord, Oxford University Press, 2013) 114. Allan's discussion is framed around the infamous Anti-Terrorism, Crime and Security Act 2001. This legislation was declared contrary to the European Convention on Human Rights in the celebrated case of *A (FC) and others (FC) v Secretary of State for the Home Department* [2004] UKHL 56 (*A (FC) and others*).

[4] Allan, *Sovereignty of Law* (n 3) 114–15.

[5] ibid 123–24.

[6] ibid 115–16.

[7] NE Simmonds, *Law as a Moral Idea* (Oxford, Oxford University Press, 2007) 101.

[8] ibid 101.

There are a number of difficulties with this. For one, law just is the systematised, institutionalised expression of will – the will of Parliament, judge or founder, for example – and so the question becomes one about our relative exposure to the controlling influence of others, not about whether we are so exposed.[9] True, law may involve limits on the capacity of these authorities to curtail liberties, for example through bills of rights or other constitutional instruments. But any such protections form a contingent part of the practices of particular legal systems and are not implied by an account of the rule of law. At best we can say that the rule of law's tendency towards publicity and constancy will put on notice those who are likely to fall foul of the law's prohibitions. But knowing the demands that we must choose to live under on pain of force is not a form of freedom. Instead, it marks a choice between different ways of being unfree.

Consider next the argument from equality. Allan holds that the rule of law speaks in favour of this value by standing against arbitrary distinctions between individuals:

> Measures that draw distinctions between persons, or groups of persons, that cannot be justified on grounds that all could recognize – grounds consistent with equal citizenship – are no different from bills of attainder, singling out individuals for special punishment or inferior treatment. Renouncing the idea of legal equality, in the fundamental sense of equal citizenship, they flout the ideal of the rule of law.[10]

Just as a bill of attainder would deny the equal standing of the person it targets so, Allan suggests, an unjustified distinction between nationals and non-nationals in terror legislation would threaten the legal equality of the latter group.[11] A bill of attainder runs contrary to the rule of law, however, not because it singles out a particular individual for divergent treatment but because it amounts to a denial of due process, and a transferring of the responsibility to determine breach of the law from the judge to the politician.[12] Similarly, a regime for the detention of foreign nationals offends against the requirements of legality not because of the distinction it draws between nationals and non-nationals – things would hardly be better from the perspective of the rule of law if such a regime applied equally to all – but because it involves an unregulated power to incarcerate individuals.[13] The rule of law is threatened in these situations because of the ways in which those subject to the relevant measures are treated and not because of the fact that they, as opposed to others, are so treated.

Surely, however, the rule of law, with its insistence on uniform application of the law, speaks in favour of some form of equality, if not equal standing or citizenship then at

[9] A fact that Simmonds himself recognises as qualifying his original claim. The law, he concedes, might depend on the 'will of a sovereign law-maker'. Nonetheless he suggests 'one needs to remember here that laws must be prospective, and must not be subject to constant change'. As such, he suggests, 'the law may conflict with the present will of the sovereign lawmaker'. And certainly this is true. The rule of law *may* operate to limit the present power of one over another. But where the legislative will is constant, promulgated and prospective the rule of law stands as no objection to subjection of the individual to the will of the lawmaker. See ibid.

[10] Allan, *Sovereignty of Law* (n 3) 124.

[11] ibid 116.

[12] Something Allan himself is of course aware of. See ibid 93–94.

[13] None of this is to deny that post 9/11 systems of detention and criminalisation have created classes of person to varying degrees outside of the law's protection, and that this is a serious injustice to those in the outgroup. It is to note, however, that rule of law objections to such regimes lie elsewhere and are not well encapsulated by notions of equal citizenship.

least a more formal notion of equality before the law. There is a sense in which it inevitably must. By urging congruence between the letter of the law and the actions of legal officials, the rule of law enjoins that like cases be treated alike, where likeness is determined by the standards of the law in force. But does this formal equality engender any measure of substantive value? No doubt when the law itself is just, formal equality functions as a justice maximiser, extending the benefits of the law to all of those to whom it rightfully applies. But formal equality may also act as an injustice maximiser, extending the burdens of the law to all unfortunate enough to fall under its reach. Where the law's aspirations towards equal treatment manifest in the rigorous application of draconian criminal laws it is no justification to those subject to such requirements that they are at least all in it together.[14]

What of the argument from autonomy? Certainly, as Allan notes, the rule of law requires that individuals have access to the courts and in this sense detention without trial is an anathema to it.[15] But it is important to understand the reason why such a regime offends against the requirements of legality. Detention without trial is not a problem for the rule of law because it interferes with the autonomy of the legal subject. Indeed, detention consequent on trial is also likely to have such an effect. Rather, the absence of recourse to courts runs contrary to the core idea of the rule of law: that of government subject to law. Indeed, it is this notion that provides the unifying thread running through the various examples discussed above: secret laws, warrantless arrests and extrajudicial detention are all means through which governmental power might be exercised without legal constraint. It also explains the rule of law's intrinsic, albeit derivative, connection with the autonomy of the legal subject. We can take these points in turn.

It is sometimes argued that the rule of law means that all must live their lives in accordance with the law, that the rule of law means the law's rule. This involves several mistakes. For one, it ignores the special connection the principle has with the affairs of government. For the haulage company to breach their contract or for the individual to defame their neighbour is no threat to the rule of law. Legal institutions, however, stand capable of directly undermining the principle, for example through the enactment of retrospective criminal sanctions or the practice of extrajudicial detention. The rule of law functions in this way as a constraint on government, not the governed. Second, the rule of law means more than that the government must act within the bounds of the law. For although this idea – sometimes described as the bare principle of legality – captures some obvious ways in which the rule of law might be undermined – for example, through the illicit diversion of public funds into private accounts or through state sanctioned but unlawful killings – it fails to explain the breadth of the principle. After all, the retrospective criminal statute is still a statute, and the legal regime for detention without trial is still a legal regime. The rule of law means not merely that government must

[14] See, for further criticism of those who might be tempted to identify justice according to the law with justice simpliciter, L Green, *The Germ of Justice – Essays in General Jurisprudence* (Oxford, Oxford University Press, 2023) 153–70.

[15] Notice that it was on this ground and this ground only that the Judicial Committee of the House of Lords considered the regime under the Anti-Terrorism, Crime and Security Act 2001 to be contrary to the rule of law. See *A (FC) and others* (n 3) paras 42, 74.

act according to the law, but that its actions must be appropriately constrained by law. New criminal offences should be promulgated and announced in advance. The power to detain must be answerable to public standards and subject to independent oversight. In turn the courts must always be available to enforce the law at the suit of the individual. These are possibilities that the law is capable of securing, but also possibilities that it can take away. The rule of law is in this way both an ideal for law and something that the law is uniquely positioned to place in jeopardy. Its contrast case lies not in the lawless society, but in the society where the law and its protections are flouted, escaped from, ignored or otherwise undermined by its institutions of government.

Given its central concern with the affairs of government, how then is the rule of law connected with the autonomy of the legal subject? By specifying a mode of government – subject to and through general rules – the rule of law implies a means of interacting with the governed, as rational agents capable of responding to the law's demands.[16] To require that the law be clear, prospective, and constant is both to constrain the institutions of government and to render the norms they produce capable of being obeyed, enforced, or otherwise engaged with by the governed. True, not every legal norm specifies a two-way relation between ruler and ruled – consider, for example, laws specifying the conditions of political office – and so we should not reduce the rule of law's government-constraining function to its citizen-guiding function. Nonetheless, all legal systems extend their reach into the lives of their subjects and when they do so in a rule-of-law compliant manner they engage them in a way which recognises their agency. This recognition is, as we have noted, consistent with the gross denial of liberty and with the failure to respect the moral equality of those to whom the law applies. But it does involve the law treating its subjects as subjects.[17]

The rule of law, then, bears an intrinsic connection with the autonomy of the individual. The question I want to explore in this chapter is what follows from this fact. For it might seem as though once we've established a necessary connection between the rule of law and individual autonomy that we have thereby shown the rule of law to be of positive moral value. We have reason to care about the conditions of human

[16] Consider in this regard Hayek's influential statement of the principle: 'Stripped of technicalities [the rule of law] means that government … is bound by rules fixed and announced beforehand – rules that make it possible to foresee with fair certainty how the authority will use its coercive powers in given circumstances and to plan one's individual affairs on the basis of this knowledge.' Hayek is famous for having made too much of the latter part of this equation, believing that the rule of law stood in opposition to state discretion and the planned economy. Why did he think this? Like Dicey before him, Hayek contrasted rule-based and discretionary decision-making, believing that only the former was consistent with the rule of law. But the contrast is a false one because discretion conferred through law and subject to legal control is itself a rule-based form of decision-making. The rule of law finds its antithesis not in discretion but in uncontrolled power. See FA Hayek, *The Road to Serfdom* (London, Routledge & Kegan Paul, 1944) 57.

[17] Some treat arguments of this form as establishing a necessary connection not between the rule of law and autonomy but the rule of law and human dignity. There are of course important differences between these concepts. A person can have a dignified death, for example, but not an autonomous one. And it is possible to offend against the dignity of another without compromising their autonomy, for example by insulting their culture. So far as the present dialectic is concerned, however, I take this to be a distinction without a difference. To the extent that the rule of law affords individuals dignity it does so by treating them as autonomous, and hence capable of understanding and responding to its demands. See, for a similar argument, Raz, *Authority of Law* (n 1) 221: 'observance of the rule of law is necessary if the law is to respect human dignity. Respecting human dignity entails treating humans as persons capable of planning and plotting their future. Thus, respecting people's dignity includes respecting their autonomy.'

agency and so we have reason to cultivate systems of clear, prospective, and enforceable law. This would not be to suggest that the rule of law counts as the ultimate value realisable through law, or that it should operate as a side constraint on all that we aim to accomplish through legal means. It is consistent with holding that there is always some autonomy-based value associated with the rule of law that there be weightier reasons favouring its sacrifice in particular cases, for example where the requirements of legality come into conflict with the demands of justice. What it would be to suggest, however, is that we always have some reason to treat the legal system that upholds the principle as a moral achievement because it so doing involves respect for the agency of those who live under the law. This is, I think, the most powerful and pervasive argument for the moral value of the rule of law. Prominent in the work of Lon Fuller,[18] it underlies much of Allan's constitutional theory, as well as contemporary natural law[19] and liberal theorising about the rule of law.[20] In what follows I want to make three points about this thesis: one clarificatory, one critical, and one about the consequence of its failure.

2. Means not Ends

The rule of law is a principle that orders law's means not its ends.[21] It instructs the law's agents as to how to regulate social life – to impose new offences prospectively not retrospectively, to make coherent as opposed to contradictory demands, and to be faithful to the law when adjudicating disputes – but not what to regulate. This is why respect for the rule of law is no guarantee of justice. We can as well have a clear, coherent, and promulgated system of racial discrimination as we can have a clear, coherent, and promulgated system of fair distribution.[22] Notice that this contrast – between means and ends – is different from that between form and content. Many have been attracted by the idea

[18] LL Fuller, *The Morality of Law*, rev edn (New Haven, Yale University Press, 1969) 162. For an insightful elaboration of Fuller's core idea see Rundle, *Forms Liberate* (n 1) 97–100. See also C Murphy, 'Lon Fuller and the Moral Value of the Rule of Law' (2005) 24 *Law and Philosophy* 239.

[19] See, eg J Finnis, *Natural Law and Natural Rights*, 2nd edn (Oxford, Oxford University Press 2011) 272–73.

[20] See J Waldron, 'How Law Protects Dignity' (2012) 71 *CLJ* 200.

[21] See J Gardner, *Law as a Leap of Faith: Essays on Law in General* (Oxford, Oxford University Press, 2012) 205–11.

[22] True some have been tempted by a speculative anthropology according to which the rule of law is more conducive to good government than bad, that adherence to legality will naturally incline lawmakers in the direction of better and more just results and away from more odious ends. This was certainly Fuller's view. He believed, for example, that apartheid South Africa was bedevilled by rule of law issues in part because of the wicked ends of its government. The South African government's attempts to create a racialised society in absence of 'any uniform or scientific basis of race classification' led to a plethora of definitions and understandings of racial concepts in different aspects of the law and hence, Fuller suggested, to 'gross departure from the standards of the inner morality of law'. That the rule of law problems associated with apartheid law follow more obviously from the open ended and contested nature of racial definitions as opposed to their iniquity is a fact that appears to have passed Fuller by. So too that similar such issues would likely bedevil any positive attempt to make up for this history through programmes of racially targeted affirmative action. Certainly we should agree with Fuller that the moral weight of rule of law problems is often more pronounced in the context of unjust regimes. This is different, however, from suggesting that their injustice is itself the cause of such problems. Fuller, *The Morality of Law* (n 18) 160. For criticism see HLA Hart, 'Review of The Morality of Law' (1965) 78 *Harvard Law Review* 1281, 1288 and Gardner, *Law as a Leap of Faith* (n 21) 219–20.

that the rule of law is a formal ideal for law, one that regulates the law's form but not its content. As John Gardner reminded us, however, a retrospective law is only a retrospective law because of its content and a vague law only vague because comprised of vague requirements.[23] By contrast retrospectivity cannot be the end of any statute, but it can certainly be a means through which some goal or social policy is achieved.

Perhaps this is too quick. For surely the rule of law's aversion to impossible demands and contradictory requirements involves a prohibition on certain ends, namely those that individuals are incapable of adhering to or which cannot be jointly satisfied?[24] And, equally, does the rule of law's insistence on impartial enforcement of norms not require that legal systems actively take up certain ends, namely those conducive to the independence of the judiciary and access to justice?[25] To require that lawmakers refrain from imposing impossible demands is not in any meaningful way to restrict the range of end-states that the legal system might be oriented towards, however, for an impossible state of affairs cannot be the end of any rational system of government. So too the prohibition on contradictory demands rules out neither the requirement that p nor the requirement that not p. What it does rule out is the imposition of both requirements on the same individuals in the same context at the same time. What of the rule of law's insistence on judicial independence and impartiality? Surely these should be classified as important ends for any legal system? No doubt such requirements are capable of being designated as such for, as Gardner argued, 'all means are capable of serving as subsidiary ends, as intermediate destinations on the way to [some final] destination.'[26] What they cannot be classified as, however, is ends in and of themselves. Enforceability is only a coherent ideal if we have something to enforce, and judicial independence only meaningful in the context of a system of legal standards oriented to further ends. That the means specified by the rule of law can be characterised, in this way, as subsidiary or intermediate ends in no way disturbs our understanding of it as a modal kind,[27] or of such requirements as constraints on the means of government.

That the rule of law is a modal constraint implies that any value associated with it lies in realising the means it commends as opposed to the ends achieved through such means. As subject I can know everything about whether a particular norm complies with the requirements of the rule of law and yet know nothing about whether I should conform to it. True, the rule of law places a defeasible duty on the judge to apply the law and in this way it asks them to treat the law's ends as their ends.[28] But to speak in favour

[23] See Gardner, *Law as a Leap of Faith* (n 21) 198–201.

[24] See, for an argument of this kind, MP Foran, 'The Rule of Good Law: Form, Substance and Fundamental Rights' (2019) 78 *CLJ* 570, 585–89.

[25] For an excellent analysis of the implications of the rule of law for access to legal resources see F Wilmot-Smith, *Equal Justice: Fair Legal Systems in an Unfair World* (Cambridge, Harvard University Press, 2019) esp 78–86.

[26] Gardner, *Law as a Leap of Faith* (n 21) 205.

[27] The term is Leslie Green's. See Green, *Germ of Justice* (n 14) 58.

[28] Why defeasible? Because, as we have noted, the rule of law can be subverted through legal means and so a judge faced with legal provisions that undermine the ideal would be presented with a trade-off between different aspects of the rule of law. Consider in this regard a situation in which judicial review of administrative bodies is ousted by statute. In such circumstances there would exist an inevitable tension between judicial respect for the requirements of the law as contained in the relevant ouster and the need for the administrative body not to become a power unto itself.

of decision-making in accordance with law – a generic – is not yet to speak in favour of the law – a particular. To the extent that the argument from autonomy does normative work, then, it speaks in favour of a means of regulating society as opposed to any particular act of regulation.

To some this will seem like an unnecessary concession, a retreat from an account of the rule of law that would ground the citizen's obligation of fidelity to law.[29] In fact, however, it strengthens any such account because it avoids the absurd implication that we have some reason to submit to the law merely because of its generality, prospectivity, etc. To point to facts of this kind in answer to the question of why the law ought to be obeyed would seem to involve, at best, a misunderstanding of that which was being asked and at worst a perverse fetishising of form over substance. If the rule of law is of moral value this means that it ought to be respected, not the law.

It might be suggested that this argument moves too quickly and in two different ways. First, it is quite possible for factors other than the content of the law to bear upon our reasons for allegiance. It is commonly thought, for example, that the democratic pedigree of the law gives us some reason to comply with it. So too, it might be suggested, with the system's adherence to legality. Second, although the demands of the rule of law fall in the first place on governments as opposed to legal subjects, it is often the case that we have reason to support others in their moral endeavours; to aid, assist, or encourage them to do the right thing. For the citizen to bolster the rule of law compliant state through a commitment to obey the law, it could be suggested, would be for them to do just this.[30]

It is true that we often have reason to support, or at the least not undermine, morally valuable institutions. The question is what this entails. In the case of democracy, for example, it seems highly implausible to suggest that support for democratic institutions speaks in favour of even *pro tanto* support for every law passed by such bodies. By crossing the red signal when alone at night we do not bite our thumb at representative government. Short of slavish adherence to the law, however, there are a range of more plausible possibilities: supporting the value and outcome of elections and not undermining the overall effectiveness of democratic institutions. None of this comes close to justifying a general attitude of obedience to law. The point applies *mutatis mutandis* to the rule of law. On the assumption of its moral value we would have reason not to destabilise institutions committed to the principle. Short of this, however, the rule of law can coexist with substantial indifference to and disregard of the law. For although the law requires us to keep our contracts and pay our fines the rule of law requires neither.[31]

[29] See LL Fuller, 'Positivism and Fidelity to Law: A Reply to Professor Hart' (1958) 71 *Harvard Law Review* 630, esp 632: 'Law, as something deserving loyalty, must represent a human achievement; it cannot be a simple fiat of power or a repetitive pattern discernible in the behavior of state officials …'. See similarly Allan, *Sovereignty of Law* (n 3) 128: 'The rule of law is ultimately an ideal of legitimate governance that explains the citizen's moral obligation of obedience'.

[30] For an argument of this form see F Jiménez, *Legality and Commitment* (unpublished manuscript).

[31] Is it likely that the rule of law would survive long in a society in which subjects had little respect for the law? Perhaps not. But this hardly shows that the rule of law requires individual compliance with the law. Rome fell without its empire, but no one should conclude from this that the existence of Rome necessitated the Roman Empire. I thank Mark Walters for pushing me on this point.

Fuller believed that respect for the rule of law on the part of the government and the citizen's obedience to the law constituted a bond of reciprocity, an informal pact in accordance with which rule-maker and rule-taker were mutually accountable: 'Government says to the citizen in effect "These are the rules we expect you to follow. If you follow them you have our assurance that they are the rules that will be applied to your conduct"'.[32] 'When this bond of reciprocity is completely ruptured by government', he suggested – for example, through the enactment of secret directives,[33] or by legislating for impossible standards of conduct[34] – there would be 'nothing … left on which to ground the citizen's duty to obey the rules.'[35] But while it is certainly true that obedience is out of the question in the case of hidden commandments or instructions to spin hay into gold, the reason for this is not that some bond of trust has been broken but because it is impossible to comply with such requirements. Moreover, in holding that the citizen's obligation to obey would be undermined by the government's failure to abide by the rule of law, Fuller assumed that which he needed to prove: that compliance with the rule of law on the part of government in the first place generates such an obligation on the part of the governed.

3. Necessary not Sufficient for Respect

To value the rule of law is not to value the law. But should we recognise the rule of law as itself instantiating some positive moral value? As with Allan, Fuller believed that there were a number of reasons for so doing. First and foremost among these was 'the view of man implicit in the internal morality of law':

> To embark on the enterprise of subjecting human conduct to the governance of rules involves of necessity a commitment to the view that man is … a responsible agent, capable of understanding and following rules, and answerable for his defaults … Every departure from the principles of the law's inner morality is an affront to man's dignity as responsible agent. To judge his actions by unpublished or retrospective laws, or to order him to do an act that is impossible, is to convey to him your indifference to his powers of self-determination.[36]

Is this enough to show, as Fuller thought it did, that the rule of law functions as 'a morality'? Certainly Fuller is right to suggest that rule-of-law compliant law is law that treats the individual as autonomous, as a thinking agent capable of understanding and responding to its dictates. Rather than goad and prod it instructs and demands response, holding itself accountable to the standards contained in its instructions. In this way the rule-of-law compliant legal system is a system that engages the autonomy of those it governs. From this it might be thought short order to the conclusion that the rule of law involves respect for the agency of the legal subject, the showing of respect being if not 'a morality' then at the very least a morally valuable attribute.[37]

[32] Fuller, *Morality of Law* (n 18) 39–40.
[33] ibid 34–35.
[34] ibid 36–37.
[35] ibid 39–40.
[36] ibid 162.
[37] See, for an argument of this form, Waldron, 'How Law Protects Dignity' (n 20).

In fact, however, there is a gulf between these ideas. For while treating someone as an agent is a necessary condition of respecting their autonomy – you cannot respect someone's agency if you do not recognise their agency – it is very far from sufficient. The gun-wielding outlaw who demands 'your money or your life' is someone who engages the autonomous capacities of their victim. But they haven't by the very same token shown respect for their target. Respect for the agency of the individual means giving due weight to their preferences and views. This is precisely what the robber does not do. Indeed, it is part of the logic of coercive practices such as this that they involve a recognition of agency that at the same time undermines it. By threatening their victim, the coercer presents them with reason to do as they say, a move that presupposes the agentive capacities of the coercee. But by this act the coercer also manipulates the agency of their victim, upsetting or undermining their preferences through threat of force. This is why coercion is so morally problematic.

Now it is certainly true that law is more than 'the gunman writ large'[38] – how much more being the subject of enduring debate[39] – but there is nothing in this that transforms the aspirations of the rule of law from those of engagement to respect. Prospective law certainly involves the agency of the individual in a way that retrospective law does not, but it may well do so in a manner totally inconsistent with the autonomous wishes of that person. When the law criminalises the expression of one's sexuality, it is scant comfort to be told that at least this will not be backdated. So too the law may be clear, coherent, and well publicised – all means that would make it better able to engage the agency of those who live under it – and yet in firm opposition to the projects that make life meaningful. Respecting the agency of others requires not just that we interact with them in an appropriate manner – explaining rather than cajoling, directing rather than pushing – but that we give appropriate credence to the decisions they make about how to live their lives. If the law is to do this for us it must sometimes support us in our projects, for example by ensuring that we have the resources to carry them through or by preventing others from interfering with our decisions. At other times the law does best by leaving us to go our own way, restricting its jurisdiction for the sake of our own. Legality, as a means rather than end-state principle, ensures none of this.

Perhaps the closest the rule of law comes to ensuring respect for the autonomy of the individual involves its insistence on access to independent adjudicative institutions, and on norms of procedural fairness in the context of dispute. Does the right of defence in a criminal trial or ability to hold government to account through judicial review not show that the rule of law speaks to the value of autonomy? Jeremy Waldron thinks so. 'The operation of a court', he suggests:

> involves a way of proceeding which offers to those who are immediately concerned an opportunity to make submissions and present evidence … In the course of all of this, both sides are treated respectfully, and above all listened to by a tribunal which is bound in some manner to attend to the evidence presented and respond to the submissions that are made … These are abstract characteristics. But they are not arbitrary abstractions. They capture a deep and

[38] HLA Hart, *The Concept of Law*, 3rd edn (Oxford, Oxford University Press, 2012) 7.

[39] For some recent additions see FF Schauer, *The Force of Law* (Cambridge, Harvard University Press, 2015) and KE Himma, *Coercion and the Nature of Law* (Oxford, Oxford University Press, 2020).

> important sense associated foundationally with the idea of a legal system, that law is a mode of governing people that acknowledges that they have a view or perspective of their own to present on the application of the norm to their conduct and situation … As such it embodies a crucial dignitarian idea – respecting the dignity of those to whom the norms are applied as beings capable of explaining themselves.[40]

It is not every courtroom that treats those who come before it respectfully, however. And it is unlikely to be of autonomy enhancing value for those whose action is in clear violation of law that they reject to be offered the opportunity to explain why the inevitable – foreclosure, jail, death – should not befall them. For such individuals the trial may indeed be the first part of the punishment. This is not to say that standards of procedural fairness and judicial impartiality can be set aside without doing serious wrong to those subject to the law. As I will try to explain momentarily, to deny that the rule of law instantiates a positive moral value is not the same as holding that departures from it are morally unproblematic or *ceteris paribus* justifiable. Nor is it to deny that for many their day in court – their chance to be heard, and to hold accountable or be held to account – really is part of what it means for their autonomy to be respected. What it is to deny, however, is that respect for the individual is necessarily instantiated by adjudicative institutions that live up to the demands of the rule of law.

4. Failure?

The failure of arguments for the positive moral value of the rule of law might tempt us to deny the independent force of the ideal. Perhaps, as Hart argued, the rule of law only takes on worth when conjoined with valuable ends, inheriting its authority from that of the law where the law is oriented towards the good.[41] On such a view when we have both justice and the rule of law we have two good things, but when we have injustice and the rule of law we don't yet have one. No doubt when legality combines with just law this will often have a multiplier effect, with the legal system benefitting from the efficacy gains and goodwill engendered by its respect for the rule of law. However, it also seems that we would want to hold an exploitative, lawless government doubly accountable, first for their exploitation and second for their exercise of power unconstrained by law. On Hart's view, the second criticism loses its force in light of the first.

It is true that in the face of serious injustice the protections associated with the rule of law might turn out to be of little worth to those subject to such measures. And it is also possible for the rule of law to operate as a tool for oppressor groups, ensuring that their position of dominance in society is ruthlessly and effectively maintained. In such a case, if we cannot force change in the law we might, on balance, favour degradation of the rule of law. Nonetheless, to say that the protections associated with the rule of law may in certain contexts turn out to be of little worth is not the same as saying they are of no worth. That a law criminalising the sexuality of a minority group applies only prospectively does not prevent that law from ruining the lives of those to whom it

[40] Waldron, 'How Law Protects Dignity' (n 20) 209–210.
[41] See Hart, 'Review of The Morality of Law' (n 22) 1285–86.

applies, but it does prevent such individuals from being held responsible for behaviours that were at the time lawful. And that the individual is put on notice of the fact that their home is to be seized is morally different from it just being taken. This is so despite the fact that they will end up destitute either way.

If respect for the rule of law does not itself constitute a moral value then what explains these facts? To answer this question, we should return to Fuller. Recall that he held the rule of law to involve 'a commitment to the view that man is … a responsible agent, capable of understanding and following rules …'.[42] And in this he was essentially right. A rule-of-law compliant legal system is one that maximises the possibilities for agential interaction with the law. The problem for Fuller, as we have seen, is that engagement falls far short of respect for individual autonomy, the most plausible candidate value associated with the rule of law. Be this as it may, treating someone as an agent is certainly a necessary part of respecting them and the failure to do so a plausible condition for disrespect. Fuller believed it to be sufficient, holding 'every departure from the principles of the law's inner morality [to be an] affront to man's dignity as responsible agent.'[43] Notice that if a claim in this vicinity is right we would have an argument, not for the positive moral value of the rule of law, but for why undermining it is wrong. While compliance with the precepts of legality would not ensure respect for those living under law, departure would nonetheless signal disrespect.

Should we accept Fuller's claim? Leslie Green suggests not. It is, he argues, too extreme to consider '*every* single departure from the principles of legality [to be] an insult to the dignity of people as responsible beings':

> It is as unreasonable as holding that any failure to say 'thank you' to the bartender is an insult to their humanity. Disrespect, insults, etc. are all subject to threshold conditions, and minor slights, especially if unintended, do not undermine our dignity as responsible beings.[44]

But does disrespect have threshold conditions? When I briefly trail off during my friend's rundown of their recent holiday it seems right to say I have disrespected them, albeit in a relatively trivial manner. Perhaps what I did does not rise to the level of affront to their dignity *qua* responsible agent, but it is something that ideally I would have avoided. Equally we can imagine minor infractions of the rule of law, for example the failure to promulgate a variation to an existing parking ordinance, that would arouse in us little more than annoyance with the institutions of government. Does a legal system that engages in such practices deny our very agency as responsible beings? No, but it does show us some level of disrespect.

One reason why we might be tempted by Green's line on these issues is if we have in mind a fetishistic understanding of the rule of law according to which every infelicity in our legal code or imprecision in its language counts as a violation of the requirements of legality. If the rule of law is so easily breached, then it might seem as though, on this argument, government disrespects us not just occasionally but continuously. But the rule of law no more requires that we eliminate uncertainty as a property of legal orders than norms of punctuality require that we turn up to our various engagements on time

[42] Fuller, *Morality of Law* (n 18) 162.
[43] ibid 162. See also Raz, *Authority of Law* (n 1) 223–24.
[44] Green, *Germ of Justice* (n 14) 72.

to the second. Were the rule of law to require, for example, the total precision of legal norms or the elimination of administrative discretion it would not only be unhelpful but impossible.[45] Fortunately the idea of government subject to law does not depend on any such absolutist notions. For the exercise of discretion to occur under the law it must be constrained by rules, but it need not be eliminated by them. And a vague standard may still be a binding standard even if it does not completely remove the element of human choice. The rule of law requires that government is controlled by and operate through law. Such an idea is both general and subject to borderline incidents. All that need be shown is that in the clear case of violation government commits a wrong.

Now, of course, the wrong involved in breach of the rule of law is only *pro tanto* and so it is possible for some social arrangement to be both in violation of the principle and yet on balance justified. Consider in this regard a retrospective fix to the tax code designed to close an exploited loophole. In order to be warranted in departing from the rule of law, however, government must provide special justification. It is an important fact about law that it stands in constant need of justification. As a coercive imposition there should be no law that cannot be justified in appropriate terms. But in making law that departs from the requirements of the rule of law government must offer a distinct form of justification, one which speaks to its particular need to exercise authority in a way that is inconsistent with the autonomy of its subjects. If it cannot do this then it cannot justifiably infringe on the requirements of the rule of law.

A final concern about the argument is that it might seem to falsely align the failure to engage some individual with disrespect for them. But we know that these two can come apart. Perhaps it is arguable whether we owe the bartender a 'thanks' when making our exit at the end of the night. However, we certainly do not owe the stranger with wandering eyes sat at the opposite end of the bar anything. And when we walk away without acknowledging their advances we have done nothing to disrespect them. Isn't it possible for law too to fail to engage us as agents without yet disrespecting our agency? Certainly the law might not regulate a given aspect of social life and in its absence no rule of law issue can arise. However, once we have legal norms and directives on the table we have only two possibilities. Either the law regulates our lives in a manner that recognises our autonomous capacities or it does so in a manner that does not. That is, the law either engages our lives while engaging our agency or engages our lives without engaging our agency. If it does the latter, it disrespects us.

5. Conclusion

Allan has long argued that we understand the value of law by first understanding the value of the rule of law. Indeed, he comes close at points to suggesting that there is nothing more to our law than that which lives up to the idea of legality.[46] For those of us of a more sceptical disposition, this will seem like double folly. For one, we will want

[45] See, on which, T Endicott, *Vagueness In Law* (Oxford, Oxford University Press, 2000) 186–90.

[46] See Allan, *Sovereignty of Law* (n 3) 110–11 and TRS Allan, 'Why the Law is What it Ought to Be' (2020) 11 *Jurisprudence* 574.

to suggest that law can well exist without legality, and to propose that in many legal systems it is the law itself that poses the greatest threat to the rule of law. Second, the belief that the rule of law instantiates some positive good will seem like a step too far in the direction of legalism, too much of a commitment to the idea that forms in the end will liberate us. Nonetheless I have tried to make a case, consistent with these two sceptical propositions, for why the rule of law matters: not as determinative of law's ends, but as regulative of its means, not as respectful of autonomy, but as necessary for the law to avoid disrespecting our agency. The argument implies an account of the rule of law very different from Allan's, both in shape and substance. But I hope, even in disagreement, that it reflects the enduring importance of his work for mine.

7

Outsiders and Trevor Allan's Rule of Law

EVAN FOX-DECENT*

> [Parliamentary sovereignty] expresses a commitment to honour the reasonable decisions of elected representatives, in accordance with the proper demands of democratic equality. In a society marked by a wide divergence of moral and political viewpoints, the category of the 'reasonable' may have to be very broad; but we need the qualification, nonetheless, because no one could accept an obligation to obey any decision at all, however seriously it contradicted his most basic ideas of justice or fairness. He must be able to sustain his loyalty to a reasonably just political order, so that Parliament speaks or decides for him as well as other citizens even when he disagrees with its particular decisions; he is otherwise an outsider, lacking allegiance to a constitution that is not, in any real sense, his own.[1]

1. Introduction

I first read Trevor Allan's scholarship some 30 years ago, and recall being as struck then as I am now by its depth, originality and rigour. But even more than the impression left by those qualities, I was struck by his project's ambition, and still am. That ambition, of course, is to explain comprehensively the nature of common law constitutionalism from an internal point of view, taking into account and elaborating common law constitutionalism's core principles, doctrines and practices. Drawing on Albert Venn Dicey, Lon Fuller, Ronald Dworkin, Friedrich Hayek and others, Allan plumbs constitutional cases and doctrines to illuminate salient connections between law, liberty and justice. With one foot in history and the common law, and another in morality and philosophical inquiry, Allan's interpretive method sublimely mirrors the common law tradition itself. Within his framework, public law cases provide starting points for inquiry, while

* I'm especially grateful to Oliver Chan, Marie-Laure Dufour and Joanne Murray for outstanding research assistance. I owe a similar debt to participants in McGill University's Research Group on Constitutional Studies' Work-in-Progress workshop series, a session of which was dedicated to discussing a prior draft. I thank the Social Science and Humanities Research Council for financial support that helped make this chapter possible through its support of the Canada Research Chair in Cosmopolitan Law and Justice.

[1] TRS Allan, *The Sovereignty of Law: Freedom, Constitution, and Common Law* (Oxford, Oxford University Press, 2013) 32. My discussion throughout will rely mainly on *The Sovereignty of Law*, Allan's most recent monograph.

constitutional organising principles – parliamentary sovereignty, the separation of powers, and the rule of law – govern respectively the practices of legislative law-making, executive decision-making, and judicial review of administrative action. On Allan's view, these constitutional principles reflect moral precepts such as liberty as independence (freedom as non-domination) and equal citizenship, and these moral precepts in turn ground the legitimacy of legal order under common law constitutionalism.

With an ecumenical and generous approach to sources, Allan develops HLA Hart's idea of an internal point of view and distinguishes it from what he describes as an external viewpoint.[2] Likewise, he borrows at times from Joseph Raz's treatment of reasons and authority, insisting that obedience to law must not be blind,[3] but departs from Raz by insisting that the reasons for obedience must reflect allegiance to the constitutional principles that make it possible for the regime to live up to the claim to legitimacy it necessarily makes as a legal regime.[4] We shall see that Allan's understanding of legal obligation places at the forefront the citizen's critical capacity for interpreting and assessing their government's efforts to meet the demands of legality. Allan takes on board the Rawlsian idea that free and equal citizens of a reasonably just liberal democracy have a duty to obey the law and support its institutions. But he adds to it a crucial representational element, as evident in the epigraph to this chapter.

Allan insists that Parliament's law-making authority must be limited by some conception of the reasonable. If Parliament's authority is not so limited – if Parliament could legally enact very unjust laws – then Parliament's authority to speak and decide for its citizens (even when they disagree with Parliament) would be subverted. A truly unfettered and absolute Parliament would regard the citizen as an 'outsider,' as someone 'lacking allegiance to a constitution that is not, in any real sense, his own.' In other words, an absolute Parliament untethered to the rule of law and constitutional principle would not be a legal Parliament capable of passing statutes that place its subjects under legal obligation, since an absolute Parliament would treat the subject as an 'outsider' for whom its legislation could not purport to speak. In short, a Parliament with unqualified and absolute power could not be said to represent its subjects or otherwise legislate in their names.

Allan suggests, then, that genuine representation as a legal institution means, among other things, taking seriously constitutional principles and doctrines so that citizens can justifiably believe that their representatives are in fact acting for publicly avowable ends in which they are counted as free and equal. Put slightly differently, Allan's thought is that we deploy constitutional norms as markers of bona fide representation to assess whether purported authorities are acting as genuine authorities, and whether their purported official acts can properly count as valid legal acts. In a healthy legal order, citizens are invited to engage in interpretation and reflection on constitutional norms and decisions, confident that their participation in a legal culture of justification will be taken seriously. This is an enormously helpful contribution to how we can profitably think about the authority of legal institutions and public law more generally.

[2] HLA Hart, *The Concept of Law*, 3rd edn (Oxford, Oxford University Press, 2012) 7 (critiquing Austin and affirming that law is not 'a gunman situation writ large').

[3] J Raz, *The Morality of Freedom* (Oxford, Oxford University Press, 1986) 42 and J Raz, *Ethics in the Public Domain* (Oxford, Oxford University Press, 1994) 213.

[4] TRS Allan, 'Citizenship and Obligation: Civil Disobedience and Civil Dissent' (1996) 55 *CLJ* 89, 94.

Allan does not, however, extend this framework to embrace all the persons amenable to a national legal order's jurisdiction. He distinguishes citizens from outsiders who in the epigraph seem to lack any sense of belonging to the constitutional order. An unfortunate implication of this distinction is that foreign nationals or non-citizens who do not belong to the constitutional order – at least not in the way citizens belong – are left unrepresented by the legal institutions to which they are nonetheless subject. By making a hard citizen/outsider distinction, Allan risks depriving himself of the constitutional resources necessary to explain how commonwealth legal institutions can govern outsiders justly and lawfully. If legislatures are incapable of speaking for and representing outsiders amenable to their jurisdiction, it is unclear how they are to relate to outsiders as anything other than the absolute Schmittian sovereigns Allan is determined to banish from legal order.

I will suggest ultimately that Allan can extend his representational framework to outsiders. First, however, in Section 2, I provide a brief exposition of Allan's conception of equal citizenship and the role it plays in his theory. Outsiders receive relatively little attention by Allan *qua* constitutional theorist (the theorist who reflects insightfully on the normative grounds of legal obligation and the nature of constitutional authority), though Allan *qua* constitutional lawyer plainly does not think they should be left without legal protection (Allan-the-lawyer addresses the doctrines and principles of constitutional law). Still, the status and role of outsiders within Allan's theory must be inferred indirectly, by contrasting their position and attributes to those of citizens who benefit directly from the principle of equal citizenship. In Section 3, I elaborate on some of the challenges outsiders pose for Allan. In Section 4, I suggest a way to bring them under the common law constitutionalist's aegis. The way forward is to develop common law constitutionalism so that it embraces cosmopolitan constitutionalism, the substantive elements of which, happily enough, are already in Allan's theory.[5]

2. Equal Citizenship

For Allan, equal citizenship is the liberal ideal that 'everyone is of equal intrinsic worth, regardless of racial or ethnic origin or colour or class or talent or religion'.[6] Allan

[5] In her chapter for this volume, 'Persons, Not Citizens', Joanna Langille also targets Allan's use of citizenship as a building block of legality. She argues that the idea of the person rather than the citizen offers better resources for an interpretive account of legality, pointing out that persons rather than citizens are the bilateral right and duty bearers of private law. And, as I try to do, she offers a reconstruction of Allan's account that does not draw on citizenship, and uses Allan's understanding of autonomy and dignity to do so. Langille ultimately concludes, however, that the reconstruction effort fails because Allan's account cannot explain why the law of a particular state (rather than some other state) applies to a particular dispute; some other state might meet the demands of autonomy and dignity better. My reconstruction of Allan is porous to the roles autonomy and dignity may play in helping us to understand and interpret positive law, but subsumes such principles within a framework that affirms an authority relation between law-giver and legal subject. The authority relation is one of representation, and demands of law-givers that their pronouncements or other actions be intelligible as actions taken in the name of or on behalf of the individuals subject to them. On this reconstruction, due regard for autonomy and dignity makes legality possible, whereas representation of particular legal subjects by particular law-givers makes it actual in particular states.

[6] Allan, *Sovereignty of Law* (n 1) 33.

announces the significance of this ideal to his conception of constitutionalism at the outset of *The Sovereignty of Law*. He criticises '[a] purely formal conception of the rule of law, affirming a merely formal equality before the law'[7] for implicitly regarding parliamentary sovereignty as parliamentary absolutism, and for adopting the posture of the political constitutionalist who sees politics as the sole antidote to very unjust laws. For the legal constitutionalist who sees law itself as 'a shield against arbitrary power,' Allan claims, a 'deeper' and substantive conception of equality is required, one he develops under the aegis of equal citizenship.[8] Within his robust conception of the rule of law supported by this account of equality, the 'primary function' of the judge is to sustain a regime of liberal principle that includes 'a range of familiar liberal rights and freedoms intended to guarantee each person's autonomy or independence'.[9] And as we shall see, this means that the judicial role involves much more than simply enforcing, as might a textualist or formalist, 'whatever rules have been duly enacted by the legislature, without fear or favour'.[10] On Allan's understanding, legislative supremacy is 'subject to certain assumptions about the equal dignity of every citizen, which demands respect for basic common law rights, definitive of the British tradition of liberal democracy and the rule of law'.[11]

In working out the contours of equal citizenship, Allan brings a republican understanding of liberty to bear on his interpretation and use of Dicey. Dicey's antipathy to arbitrary power aligns congenially with the republican conception of freedom. For republicans, liberty as independence (or freedom as non-domination) consists in the ability to act as one wishes without the threat of arbitrary power or interference hanging overhead, consistent with a like freedom for all. The rule of law, Allan says, not only makes equal freedom under law possible, but in fact 'upholds the freedom and dignity of those independent citizens who comprise the political community'.[12] In short, Allan's rule of law, in a well-ordered liberal democracy, charges judges and others with responsibility for securing liberal rights and freedoms, and these rights and freedoms in turn are the public law building blocks of a regime of equal citizenship.

Importantly, Allan expressly grounds the rule of law's requirement of equal freedom on citizenship: '[f]reedom or liberty inheres … in each individual's status as citizen: the rule of law in a just state secures an equal liberty, consonant with a basic equality of citizenship'.[13] In practice this means that legal rules should 'be ones that all citizens can affirm without loss of self-respect,' and that distinctions between persons must be justified on the basis of 'defensible public purposes – purposes consistent with a vision of equal, independent citizens who cooperate to secure the enjoyment of their civil and political freedoms'.[14] Citizens must be able to see themselves in the public purposes and rules enacted by Parliament, implemented by the executive, and interpreted and applied by the judiciary.

[7] ibid 2.
[8] ibid 2–3.
[9] ibid 2.
[10] ibid.
[11] ibid 323.
[12] ibid 91.
[13] ibid 93.
[14] ibid 93.

At the level of doctrine, Allan's treatment of proportionality reflects how an overarching duty of justification may be thought to flow from his principle of equal citizenship. In most cases, implementation of policy that conforms demonstrably to a proportionality standard will provide a 'defensible moral balance' between individual and collective interests.[15] But in an extreme case, Allan says, if 'a measure discriminates between groups of citizens on grounds that are quite irrelevant to its supposed rationale – or to any legitimate rationale, consistent with constitutional equality – it is hard to treat it as *law*, imposing genuine obligations'.[16] Such a measure resembles a bill of attainder that singles out an individual or group for punishment without trial, a measure that violates the separation of powers because the judicial role is eliminated. And, arguably, such a measure would also violate the idea that the legislature is in any meaningful way acting as a representative of the targeted persons. They are targeted for abuse by a legislature that acts with impunity, for a purpose its victims cannot reasonably be expected to share, and contrary to the separation of powers.

Allan adds that the requirement of proportionality is also 'a demand of *rationality*, implicit in the idea of equal citizenship internal to our basic concept of law'.[17] A rational measure, Allan continues, is 'one that respects equality; and the maintenance of a fair balance between individual and collective interests is a dimension of rationality or reasonableness, sensitive to the constitutional context in point'.[18] Proportionality, then, is a common law constitutional doctrine that reflects the rule of law's imposition on officials and judges of 'a requirement of *justification*, connecting restrictions on liberty to a public or common good, open to fearless debate and challenge'.[19]

The duty or requirement of justification under Allan's account of constitutionalism is itself an indispensable organising principle. As just indicated, it is this duty that licenses public decision-makers to pursue policies that may either benefit or prejudice some groups and not others. Offering reasons in line with proportionality gives officials the opportunity to show that they are treating all citizens with equal concern and respect, even when they are treating some citizens differently than others. Allan thus brings together Dworkin's idea of equality as equal concern and respect and Fuller's view that legal order relies on a certain form of reciprocity between the governors and the governed. For Fuller, Allan notes, '[l]aw is the product of cooperation and collaboration – by legislators, officials, judges, and citizens – in search of a public good that can elicit the necessary support'.[20]

We are now able to appreciate the central role of the citizen in Allan's account of constitutionalism. Allan's interpretivism is thoroughgoing, countenancing no polity in which citizens are so 'deplorably sheeplike' that 'the sheep might end in the slaughterhouse'.[21] Parliamentarians, administrative officials and judges must enact and interpret law in good faith and with some view of the public good in mind. Citizens should

[15] ibid 184.
[16] ibid 185.
[17] ibid.
[18] ibid.
[19] ibid 91.
[20] ibid 47.
[21] Compare Hart, *Concept of Law* (n 1) 117 (asserting that the internal point of view applies to officials alone, so that even in a genuine legal regime law's subjects may be led like sheep to slaughter).

generally reciprocate such efforts by acknowledging the value of a legal order that regards them with equal concern and respect.[22] But the citizen's reciprocal obedience is not intended to be a creature of habit or arise from fear of sanction, but is instead to emerge from critical reflection on the constitutional merits of a given law or measure. When a statute plausibly imperils a basic right, the citizen occupies an interpretive role akin to a judge or official, and is vested with a demanding responsibility: 'every citizen is a guardian of the constitution he affirms, entitled – indeed bound – to consider whether his cooperation with dubious state demands is, in all circumstances, really justified'.[23] And, Allan claims, 'our sensitivity to the resistance of the principled dissentient or conscientious objector' stems from 'our recognition of the citizen's ultimate responsibility to determine the validity of the state's claim to his obedience'.[24]

Allan gives as an example *Minersville School District v Gobitis*,[25] where the Supreme Court of the United States upheld a state law requiring school children to salute the American flag. Jehovah's Witnesses refused to accept the Court's decision, claiming they were protected by freedoms of belief and conscience enshrined in the US Constitution. Allan follows Dworkin and defends their disobedience on the grounds that, in the circumstances, they were entitled to come to their own determination of the matter. They were so entitled because,

> no one could concede an *unqualified* power to courts to change the law without abandoning his allegiance to the constitution. His allegiance depends on the preservation and protection of certain fundamental rights and values; their infringement ruptures the essential harmony between his moral obligation of civic loyalty, on the one hand, and respect for justice and the public good, on the other.[26]

Still, to be clear, Allan does maintain that 'it is critical to the maintenance of the rule of law, and hence individual liberty, that people honour their legal obligations, even when they doubt the wisdom or the justice of the laws (as inevitably they often will)'.[27] Citizens owe each other 'moral duties of cooperation,' and the law 'imposes a general obligation of obedience that reflects the citizen's duty to cooperate in maintaining a viable and flourishing legal order, capable of securing liberty for all on a fair and equal basis'.[28] Legal obligation is for Allan as species of moral obligation, and this means that the limits of a citizen's legal obligations 'are ultimately a matter of his own responsibility and judgement'.[29] If a public authority threatens grave injustice, 'we cannot escape the obligation to decide … whether we should maintain our cooperation or, on the contrary, engage in civil disobedience'.[30]

Allan is right to observe that the conscientious citizen cannot escape deciding whether to become an objector if confronted with the enforcement of a law she views

[22] Allan, *Sovereignty of Law* (n 1) 39.
[23] ibid 161.
[24] Allan, 'Citizenship and Obligation' (n 4) 119.
[25] *Minersville School District v Gobitis* 310 US 586 (1940) (rev'd by *West Virginia Board of Education v Barnette* 319 US 624 (1943)).
[26] Allan, *Sovereignty of Law* (n 1) 161.
[27] ibid 39.
[28] ibid.
[29] ibid.
[30] ibid 40.

as very unjust. It does not follow, however, that the individual is entitled to act as final arbiter of the justice or legitimacy of a measure she considers abhorrent. If a liberal democracy were to collapse into a state of nature in which there were no effective legal institutions and rampant insecurity, individuals would have a straightforward claim to rely on their own sense of justice and self-help: by hypothesis, there would be no alternative. But ordinarily, within liberal democracies, rights-infringing statutes or decisions are not extinction-level events for the rule of law and its institutions. Assuming that reasonably liberal and just institutions remain in place, the possibility of reasonable disagreement between citizens over the merits of a contentious law suggests we may need a further argument to explain why objectors might be entitled to deny an impugned law's authority and claim to their obedience.

Toward the end of *The Sovereignty of Law*, Allan sets out such an argument as he defends Dworkin's idea of constitutional democracy against Jeremy Waldron's critique of judicial review.[31] Dworkin argues that majoritarianism within a political community can provide legitimate self-government only if every member of the community is a full 'moral member,' by which he means the community gives every member a '*part* in any collective decision, a *stake* in it, and *independence* from it'.[32] Moral membership means, among other things, being treated as a member by others, while the requirement of independence 'sustains the self-respect of those who are encouraged to regard themselves as partners in a joint venture'.[33] This allows for the possibility of '[a] genuine political community,' since this kind of community 'must be composed of independent moral agents'[34] who are then provided 'circumstances that encourage them to arrive at beliefs on these matters through their own reflective and finally individual conviction'.[35]

It follows from this understanding of political community and moral membership in it that 'government can have only qualified authority,' and that 'respect for individual rights is a background condition of the legitimacy of representative majoritarian decision-making'.[36] Allan concludes that '[i]t is only when people are treated fairly by their political institutions, as citizens entitled to equal concern and respect, that they have reason to accept the legitimacy of majority decisions on matters in dispute'.[37]

Before considering some of the challenges outsiders may be thought to pose to this understanding of constitutionalism, it is important to note that Allan qualifies his focus on citizens in important ways. He claims that '[s]ince we assume lawfully resident non-citizens are entitled to the same protections as citizens demand for themselves – especially respect for their human rights, fundamental to human dignity – discrimination between the two groups needs justification consonant with its scale or severity'.[38]

[31] ibid 328–30 citing R Dworkin, *Freedom's Law: The Moral Reading of the American Constitution* (Oxford, Oxford University Press, 1996) 15–35.

[32] Dworkin, *Freedom's Law* (n 31) 24 cited by Allan, *Sovereignty of Law* (n 1) 329.

[33] Allan, *The Sovereignty of Law* (n 1) 330.

[34] ibid.

[35] Dworkin, *Freedom's Law* (n 31) 26 cited by Allan, *Sovereignty of Law* (n 1) 330.

[36] Allan, *Sovereignty of Law* (n 1) 330.

[37] ibid.

[38] ibid 93 fn 13. Allan refers to *A v Secretary of State for the Home Department* [2004] UKHL 56 (*Belmarsh 9*). Strictly speaking, Allan's qualification of 'lawfully resident' leaves out irregular non-citizens whose residence is not lawful, but we will see in the text immediately below that Allan plainly believes the human rights of all non-citizens merit respect by the state.

His discussion of the *Belmarsh 9* case applauds the House of Lords criticism of the indefinite detention regime. The court found that indefinite detention of nine foreign nationals was not 'strictly required' and therefore offside the relevant doctrine on emergency derogation grounded in the European Convention on Human Rights. The House of Lords found that British nationals as well as foreign nationals threatened terrorism, and that if indefinite detention without formal charge was not necessary in the former case – British nationals were not subject to the relevant national security law – then it was unclear why such an extreme measure was necessary with respect to foreign nationals. Allan criticises the House of Lords, however, for not ordering the detainees' release and for not striking down or at least ignoring the impugned provisions of the statute. The court itself had concluded that there is no rational basis for a power to detain outsiders while allowing equally dangerous British nationals to remain at large.[39] The treatment of citizens thus sets a standard from which departures in the case of outsiders requires significant justification.

Allan further opens the door to outsiders by connecting liberty as independence to human dignity, by treating liberty 'as a requirement of respect for human dignity'.[40] Following Dworkin's understanding, Allan takes human dignity to mean that every human life has intrinsic value, and therefore 'the state must honour everyone's human rights, including those of non-citizens'.[41] Even with these qualifications in place, however, Allan's reiterated lionising of the citizen and membership in a political community suggests the position he takes in the epigraph to this chapter regarding the outsider was not a slip. The position sketched in the epigraph comes perilously close to situating the outsider and national authorities in a political but not legal order vis-à-vis one another; political because the outsider is subject to the state's raw political power, but not legal because the outsider is treated as someone to whom the constitution does not apply, or applies in a lesser or even sham form.[42]

3. Outsiders

Allan affirms that respect for human dignity means that states must respect the human rights of outsiders as well as citizens. But he then faces the following dilemma. Either respect for equal dignity and human rights – including the dignity and human rights of outsiders – is sufficient to explain and justify common law constitutionalism and its principles of qualified parliamentary sovereignty and a robust rule of law, or it is not. If equal dignity is sufficient, then Allan's foundational principle of equal citizenship is superfluous. Further, Allan would need to modify his account of legal obligation and

[39] ibid 116.
[40] ibid 91 fn 8.
[41] ibid, paraphrasing R Dworkin, *Is Democracy Possible Here? Principles for a New Political Debate* (Princeton, Princeton University Press, 2006) 9–21.
[42] See D Dyzenhaus, *The Constitution of Law: Legality in a Time of Emergency* (Cambridge, Cambridge University Press, 2006) 196–220 (discussing 'legal black holes' created by legislation in which terror suspects are held without genuine due process, but with some procedure to give the detention regime a veneer of legality).

its role within his theory. His present account is tied to the idea that citizens owe each other 'moral duties of cooperation' that are reciprocal and needful of a bounded political community. If respect for human dignity and human rights can justify qualified legislative supremacy and the rule of law – understood broadly as Allan understands them to include the law's claim to legitimacy and a duty to obey – then, again, the emphasis on equal citizenship and membership in a political community is under-motivated. Allan's defence of Dworkin's conception of constitutional democracy would also be superfluous, because the associational requirements and features of 'moral membership' in 'a genuine political community' would not be necessary to any extent further than could be defended on the basis of equal human dignity.

The other horn of the dilemma has its own unpleasantness. If respect for equal human dignity is not sufficient to explain and justify a generous understanding of qualified legislative supremacy and the rule of law, Allan can attempt to fill in the gaps using equal citizenship, his citizen-dependent account of legal obligation, and Dworkin's conception of constitutional democracy. The difficulty on this side of the dilemma is that equal citizenship, a conception of legal obligation that depends on citizenship, and Dworkin's 'moral membership' theory of constitutional democracy all, by definition, exclude outsiders.

The immediate effect of the exclusion, as the epigraph makes clear, is that common law constitutionalism is barred from claiming the kind of legitimacy vis-à-vis outsiders that it claims over citizens. Citizens but not outsiders can have and benefit from legal obligations grounded on 'moral duties of cooperation' with other citizens. For citizens whose allegiance must be earned by public authorities, but not outsiders, a justification can be marshalled to qualify Parliamentary sovereignty. For citizens but not outsiders, legal order encourages them to see themselves as 'partners in a joint venture'.[43] And yet, outsiders within the territorial jurisdiction of a state are every bit as subject to its laws and jurisdictional claims as citizens; indeed, more so, since they ordinarily remain subject to deportation unless and until such time as they naturalise and become citizens.

Consider then the relationship between national authorities and outsiders under Allan's theory. We take on board the exclusion of outsiders within Allan's theory and their lack of capacity, as foreign nationals, to participate in electoral politics or hold office. But we also assume with Allan that non-citizens' human rights be respected, and that differential treatment of outsiders requires special justification. The resulting relationship seems to be one in which national authorities have a series of human rights obligations to outsiders, but a form of public authority over them, if any, that is not matched by a correlative legal obligation or an expectation of reciprocity. Recall from the epigraph that legal obligation is the centrepiece of Allan's argument in favour of a qualified as opposed to absolute conception of parliamentary sovereignty. For Allan, a citizen cannot have a legal obligation to do anything whatsoever an absolute legislature declares law, such as a purported law to 'kill all blue-eyed babies'.[44] The conscientious citizen 'should subject putative laws, enacted in pursuance (or purported pursuance) of

[43] Allan, *Sovereignty of Law* (n 1) 330.

[44] ibid 120 citing AV Dicey, *Introduction to the Study of the Law of the Constitution*, 10th edn (London, Macmillan, 1964) 81 (quoting L Stephen, *Science of Ethics* (London, Smith, Elder & Co, 1882) 143).

recognised authority, to an overriding judgment of justice before granting their claim to obedience'.[45] And as the epigraph suggests, an absolute power to legislate would disqualify the legislature from being entitled to speak on behalf of citizens. On Allan's view, citizens have no rational or moral ground to recognise the authority of a legislature that claims an unqualified legal power to treat them howsoever it wishes, including harshly.

Put another way, if a legislature has lawmaking authority, in the ordinary case its statutes produce legal obligations or some other normative change in the positions of the relevant citizens; those citizens gain or lose legal powers, claim rights, liberties, immunities, etc. Allan thus subscribes to the correlativity thesis of authority according to which a citizen has a duty to obey the law if, and only if, her state has legal authority over her. On this view, if a legislature has law-making authority, properly understood, then its citizens must be liable to have their normative positions changed by an ordinary exercise of that authority (eg they might acquire rights, duties, powers, etc).[46] Conversely, if citizens are liable to have their normative positions changed, under the correlativity thesis it follows that they are subject to a legal authority with standing to bring about that change. The outsider from the epigraph who appears to stand outside the constitutional legal order, however, complicates this account.

Because for Allan's outsider the constitution that empowers the legislature to make law 'is not, in any real sense, his own', the constitution is incapable of attracting the outsider's allegiance and attributing to him legal obligations. From this incapacity it follows that the legislature does not have legal authority, properly understood, over the outsider. On this interpretation, the outsider is arguably ruled by force rather than law. That the state must respect the outsider's human rights shows that the state has various obligations to the outsider, but those obligations do not show without more that the state has general legal authority over the outsider. For example, human rights obligations alone do not entail an authority to tax a foreign national, subject her to surveillance or detention, impose on her permit regimes that limit her ability to study and work, or simply deport her for policy reasons unrelated to her conduct. The purported authority for such regimes comes from the national constitution's authorisation of its legislative power. However, if that constitution cannot be said to represent or speak for the outsider, and can be called on and amended at any time without her participation, then the foreign national suffers a compromise of her liberty as independence – she suffers domination – living as she does under a sword of Damocles.

Allan faces the following tension. On the one hand, an outsider cannot have legal obligation of the kind Allan envisions as necessary to maintain legal order, since the outsider is not a citizen and is presumed to lack allegiance to the national constitution. On the other hand, constitutions in fact purport to regulate by law the relationship between public authorities and outsiders. It follows that national legal orders necessarily claim authority over the outsider, even though the outsider may have just arrived and never participated in the political life of the receiving state. Furthermore, *pace* Allan,

[45] Allan, 'Citizenship and Obligation' (n 4) 102.

[46] See, eg J Finnis, *Natural Law and Natural Rights* (Oxford, Oxford University Press, 1980) 231–34; Raz, *The Morality of Freedom* (n 3) 23–28; AJ Simmons, *Justification and Legitimacy* (New York, Cambridge University Press, 2001) 106–07, 130–31.

with the law's claim of authority comes a claim of obedience; the outsider is expected to obey the law and is liable for transgressions. These rudimentary features of public law are difficult to explain with Allan's theory due to the sharp distinction he draws between citizens and non-citizens. Nonetheless, we can return once again to the epigraph and develop from it an ideal of public representation, extending the concept to outsiders so as to bring them into the constitutional fold.

4. Representing Outsiders

The key idea in the epigraph is not that the qualification of parliamentary sovereignty is necessary to prevent citizens from being regarded as neglected outsiders, but that Parliament's legislative authority itself depends on qualification so citizens can understand that Parliament's law-making is conducted on behalf of all of them. In other words, we can read the epigraph to say that qualification of expansive legislative authority attentive to constitutional principle is necessary for exercises of that authority to constitute legitimate acts of law-making conducted on behalf of all citizens. Principled qualification allows a purported law-making power to count as a genuine law-making authority by making it possible for the authority to credibly claim to act as a public law-making representative of all citizens. We can expand this idea in two ways to bring in outsiders.

First, we can insist that principled qualification of legislative supremacy is necessary for exercises of legislative authority to constitute legitimate acts of law-making conducted on behalf of all legal subjects, citizens and non-citizens alike. Evan Criddle and I have defended an idea along these lines. We have argued that for state action to count as legitimate – whether legislative, administrative or judicial – it must be intelligible as action undertaken in the name of or on behalf of the affected group or individual, whether citizen or non-citizen.[47] This criterion of legitimacy is also a standard of adequacy for testing the legality of a given act of public authority, and stands to be much improved by Allan's discussion of the need to qualify legislative supremacy with constitutional principle. The underlying idea at its most abstract is that genuine public representation is the institutional realisation of moral standing to announce and enforce law over citizens and non-citizens amenable to the jurisdiction of a given state. While the constitutive norms of public representation may vary across time and from place to place, the basic idea is that there is a robust morality of role that empowers lawgivers to govern in a manner consistent with publicly avowable values and principles, and therefore on behalf of the persons subject to their power. In liberal democracies, these principles and values include respect for equal human dignity and human rights, democratic self-determination, procedural and substantive doctrines found in judicial review of administrative action, and (where applicable) review of legislation for conformity with an entrenched Charter or Bill of Rights. The idea that states are obligated to abide

[47] E Criddle and E Fox-Decent, *Fiduciaries of Humanity: How International Law Constitutes Authority* (New York, Oxford University Press, 2016) 3, 99–100, 131, 217, 240, 268, 288.

by these norms by both their constitutions and the nature of public representation helps explain how law can turn might into right in the service of the legal subject. The pairing of constitutional principle with public representation explains how public law can be law for citizen and outsider alike; it can be so because the relevant law is intelligible as law made on behalf of and in the name of both. The structure of representation makes it possible for the lawgiver to have the appropriate standing to announce and enforce law; constitutional principle grounds the exercise of public power within a legal order that serves the legal subject and their publicly avowable values.

The second expansion of Allan's idea of representation concerns how we are to imagine authorities of a national legal order to be capable of representing outsiders and having legal authority over them. This is where common law constitutionalism must take a cosmopolitan turn and look outside its home jurisdiction if it wishes to embody a form of constitutionalism credibly capable of governing outsiders with authority. For a state to claim that its constitution alone authorises it to deal with outsiders howsoever it wishes would immediately raise the question David Dyzenhaus rightly says must be at the centre of legal philosophy; that is, the question posed by the legal subject: 'But, how can that be law for me?'[48] Allan's concern to qualify legislative supremacy with respect to citizens is responsive to this very question.

Regarding outsiders, one way forward is to reimagine states from a global perspective. From this perspective, Criddle and I have argued that we can think of states as co-stewards under international law charged with governing jointly the common interests and patrimony of humanity, including the earth's surface.[49] While international law clearly affirms that a state's primary responsibilities are to its citizens, international law also holds receiving states to a range of obligations concerning outsiders fleeing persecution and others who have established family lives and long-term ties to a host state. In the case of asylum-seekers, we claim that the duty not to deport such persons to a place of danger (the duty of *non-refoulement*) should be regarded as a peremptory and non-derogable norm of *jus cogens*. Without this duty securely in place and shared by all states, refugees would suffer incurable domination, since their mere physical presence anywhere in the world could be treated as a trespass.

The joint responsibility for the international refugee regime falls to states that international law has authorised to govern the world. At the same time, international law authorises states to govern all outsiders within their borders, subject to respecting their human rights and, at least in the case of refugees, a principle of non-differentiation very similar to the principle relied on in *Belmarsh 9*.[50] Most states offer outsiders various paths to citizenship. Before they are eligible to become citizens of their host state, however, they each may be understood as a cosmopolitan 'citizen of the world',[51] since

[48] See, eg D Dyzenhaus, *The Long Arc of Legality* (Cambridge, Cambridge University Press, 2022) 2–3.

[49] Convention Relating to the Status of Refugees (Geneva, 28 July 1951); Protocol Relating to the Status of Refugees (New York, 31 January 1967); Convention on the Rights of the Child (New York, 20 November 1989).

[50] *Belmarsh 9* (n 38).

[51] I Kant, *The Metaphysics of Morals*, translated by M Gregor (New York, Cambridge University Press, 1991 [1797]) 98–99 (6:281) (characterising the newborn as a 'citizen of the world' who on that basis alone cannot be neglected by her parents).

on this understanding the authority of national states over them is ultimately delegated by international law. Accordingly, receiving states that comply with the rule of law and their human rights obligations vis-à-vis an outsider may be thought to rule in a manner that 'speaks for him as well as all other' outsiders within the state's jurisdiction.

Although non-citizens cannot vote or sit in Parliament, Parliament can act and speak for them because Parliament enjoys international authorisation to do so. Or more precisely, international law authorises states to develop national constitutions that claim authority over outsiders. Those constitutions, in turn, authorise their respective legislatures and other legal institutions to govern outsiders. So, in the case of common law constitutionalism, the principle of equality we saw used in *Belmarsh 9* can be understood not as an act of mercy by the House of Lords, but rather as the court's respect for a constitutional principle that is also a core constitutive aspect of the authority the UK constitution claims over foreign nationals. And this may let us recover, to some extent, the principle of equal citizenship, so long as citizenship is understood to include citizens of the world.

In the conference discussion of a prior draft of this chapter, Allan suggested that perhaps outsiders could be considered quasi-citizens, and in that way brought into his theory. This is most plausible when we think of long-term resident foreign nationals who live and work among citizens, pay taxes, own homes, run businesses, send their children to public schools, develop ties of kinship and friendship, and so on. As we have seen, Allan thinks that constitutional legal order depends on the conscientious citizen who is entitled to question whether the law she is asked to obey is law that lives up to the demands of constitutional principle. When Dyzenhaus asks the subject's question, 'But, how can that be law for me?', he in a way makes explicit for legal philosophy an important idea implicit within Allan's constitutional theory: for the official to properly adopt law's internal point of view, she must make law for which a satisfactory reply can be given to the subject's question. It is only by satisfying this requirement that the official can produce law that carries with it a duty to obey. In a sense, the official must take up the perspective of the subject to make and interpret law from the internal point of view, and thereby transform might into right.[52]

There is no impediment in principle to applying this framework to denizen outsiders. For Dyzenhaus, the fundamental person from the point of view of constitutional theory and legal philosophy is not the citizen, but the legal subject.[53] Every person amenable to the law of a given legal regime, whether citizen or non-citizen, is a legal subject of that regime. By understanding law's authority as dependent on its relation to the subject, and by specifying that relation in terms of a justification that takes constitutional principle and representation seriously, we can commodiously bring outsider's within the sovereignty of Allan's legal theory.

[52] I am grateful to Joanne Murray for suggesting this point. The idea, as I understand it, is not that every law and regulation must be explicitly justified to every legal subject, but that all laws should be amenable to a justification that explains the standing and authority of the lawgiver vis-à-vis the legal subject, from the perspective of the subject.

[53] Dyzenhaus, *Long Arc of Legality* (n 48) 30–31, 414–17.

5. Conclusion

I have tried to show that Allan offers a compelling account of common law constitutionalism that brings constitutional principles into close contact with core liberal principles, such as human dignity and liberty. Holding it all together at the doctrinal level is the idea that departures from equality and constitutional principle must satisfy a demanding requirement of justification that points to a significant public good. At the level of theory, one of Allan's most illuminating insights is the idea that we must be able to understand lawgivers as speaking for or otherwise representing their subjects for them to count properly as lawgivers, and they can be so understood only if their powers are conditioned by principle. While Allan elaborates his project through an ideal of equal citizenship that may appear to exclude outsiders, there is no reason in principle for such an exclusion to occur. A cosmopolitan antidote is available to bring outsiders in, as legal subjects and citizens of the world, and as such, as legal subjects worthy of equal citizenship.

8

The Rule of Law without Law

HILLARY NYE*

1. Introduction

TRS Allan argues that the past matters. Our institutional history is important for figuring out what moral obligations we have. One reason this might be true is predictability and fairness; ensuring people know what is expected of them might affect the moral obligations we have. But Allan seems to hold that there are deeper reasons why the very fact that our community has decided something in some way will give us a reason for action. He says that '[t]he backward-looking aspect of adjudication is intrinsic not merely to considerations of fairness as between the litigants, who will have acted in the light of previous institutional decisions, but also to the ideal of justice itself'.[1] But why should we think that the past gives us any reason for action?

Allan claims both that the law is moral, and that it is linked to our actual practices. This is a difficult needle to thread. He says: 'In common law theory there is no gap between legal and political obligation – no scope for conflict between the law's demands and those of political morality'.[2] For Allan, the rule of law is an integral part of the concept of law. They are intertwined, and law is a moral entity that gives us real obligations. But there is a serious impasse in legal philosophy about the nature of law. If we cannot settle that question, then connecting the rule of law to the nature of law will provide little to no information about what is to be done. The better path, in my view, is to adopt eliminativism about law.[3] Much of what Allan says is true and important, and his focus on the moral questions is right. But we need not follow him in insisting that such moral questions are 'legal' ones. Attempting to attach that label to them is a source of confusion.

* I wish to thank the participants at the workshop 'The Promise of Legality: Critical Reflections on the Work of TRS Allan', 16–17 September 2022, co-hosted by the University of Sherbrooke and Queen's University. I also wish to thank Sina Akbari, Matt Lewans, and Grace Nye for discussion. Some parts of this chapter draw on an earlier draft paper that was presented at the Edinburgh Legal Theory Research Group Seminar Series at The University of Edinburgh, and I thank the participants at that workshop as well.

[1] TRS Allan, 'Law as a Branch of Morality: The Unity of Practice and Principle' (2020) 65 *American Journal of Jurisprudence* 1, 10.

[2] ibid 12.

[3] I explain this concept in more depth below – see Section 2. But briefly, it is the idea that we should drop questions about the nature of law and refocus our attention on questions about, for example, what differently-situated agents should do.

We should ask instead: What does it mean for a judge to make a decision that complies with the rule of law? And, in particular, what does the rule of law mean if we adopt eliminativism and do not talk in terms of 'law' at all? I will argue here that we can develop an account of the rule of law, and that Allan's work is a rich source for such an account. We can accept much of what Allan says about the rule of law without taking a position about the concept or nature of law. Indeed, tying the rule of law too closely to law is problematic. Doing so results in a theory of the rule of law that cannot serve the purposes we need it to.

2. Eliminativism

In a recent article,[4] Allan has engaged with the growing movement known as 'eliminativism'. I have defended eliminativism,[5] as has Scott Hershovitz,[6] and Lewis Kornhauser.[7] I won't present the whole argument for adopting eliminativism here, for reasons of space. I will simply say that a core motivation for the movement is the worry that the impasse about the nature of law is unresolvable.[8] Intuitions drive the various views, and the same facts about the world can be redescribed under either view, such that there is no way to settle who is 'right' about the nature of law.[9]

Though there is ambiguity about precisely what eliminativism commits us to, on Hershovitz's view it means there is no distinct domain of legal normativity.[10] As Allan puts it, describing Hershovitz's position, '[l]egal obligations are simply moral obligations, which may sometimes clash with other moral obligations'.[11] Eliminativism implies that we can drop all talk of law and proceed by talking about relevant practical questions. Eliminativists do, however, agree that we can point to matters of social fact – what those in power have done and said – and then draw conclusions about what should be done. They simply deny that we need the intermediate step of saying 'what the law is'.[12]

[4] Allan, 'Law as a Branch of Morality' (n 1) 10.

[5] H Nye, 'Does Law "Exist"? Eliminativism in Legal Philosophy' (2022) 15 *Washington University Jurisprudence Review* 29.

[6] See S Hershovitz, 'The End of Jurisprudence' (2015) 124 *Yale Law Journal* 1160.

[7] LA Kornhauser, 'Doing Without the Concept of Law' [2015] NYU School of Law, Public Law Research Paper No. 15-33 at papers.ssrn.com/abstract=2640605.

[8] See L Murphy, *What Makes Law: An Introduction to the Philosophy of Law* (Cambridge, Cambridge University Press, 2014). Though he does not defend eliminativism, he sees the debate as having reached an impasse. Murphy argues that the two camps in legal philosophy 'represent two fundamentally opposed visions of the kind of thing law is, and that nothing so much as an argument is likely to move either side closer to the other': ibid 3.

[9] See Nye, 'Does Law "Exist"?' (n 5) 48–50. A related objection is why we should be eliminativists about law but not about morality, when moral questions are similarly subject to disagreement. I thank David Dyzenhaus for pressing me on this point. I cannot fully answer it here. But in brief, I think there is an answer in the fact that the moral questions are not inert: something important turns on them, and we cannot give them up, the way that we can simply drop legal questions without losing anything important. I discuss this briefly in ibid 58 fn 107, and I attempt to expand on it in draft work.

[10] Hershovitz, 'The End of Jurisprudence' (n 6) 1193.

[11] Allan, 'Law as a Branch of Morality' (n 1) 3.

[12] Kornhauser, 'Doing Without the Concept of Law' (n 7) 15. One objection is that, if you can talk about statutes, precedents and all the materials we typically call legal, you have essentially recreated law, and so eliminativism is doing no work. I thank Jeffrey Goldsworthy for raising this point. I think, however, that

Allan, however, resists eliminativism. He maintains that it is important to be able to say what the law is: '[w]e cannot eliminate law as a special site of normative contestation'.[13] Instead, we should understand law in a way that aligns with the natural law tradition: '[a]n allegedly wicked law … is either no law at all or must be interpreted (whatever its authors' intentions) in accordance with general principles of law and justice'.[14] Allan argues that a truly interpretative view does not permit us to conclude that the law is deeply unjust: 'a wicked law is, on an interpretative view, a contradiction in terms'.[15] Allan also critiques Raz for 'separating the idea of law from the ideal of the rule of law'.[16] Allan argues that 'the rule of law is an ideal that helps to define what we mean by law itself',[17] and further that we can learn about the rule of law through reflecting on the concept of law.[18] In other words, for Allan, it is crucial to keep law in our theory, and to link it to the rule of law.

I will argue in what follows that we can eliminate law, and that we can do so in a way that preserves many of Allan's core intuitions and insights about the role of institutional history and practices. Further, we can avoid the problematic impasse that results if we insist on debating what truly counts as law, properly so-called. (As I mentioned above, the argument for why we *should* eliminate law is reserved for other work. Here I just want to show that we *can* talk profitably about the rule of law without settling the nature of law debate.)

3. Why Starting with Law is Unhelpful

In a very general sense, the rule of law is often understood as the idea of government *according to law*, as opposed to the arbitrary government of people. This idea comes from AV Dicey. He argues that the rule of law demands that no punishment occur except in accordance with law, established before courts. This is contrasted with discretionary decision-making.[19] Joseph Raz, too, argues that the rule of law means 'that people should be ruled by the law and obey it'.[20]

Many theorists, even if they go beyond this idea of 'compliance with law', do include it as a foundational element of their account. Allan's theory contains this idea. He says that the rule of law means 'as far as possible that *law* rules, rather than prominent

eliminativism does help us avoid the dispute about whether *all that stuff* really counts as law, or whether there is a further moral constraint on what counts. We may use the word 'law' if we wish, but we should be clear we are using it stipulatively. Otherwise we will find that we are still stuck in a disagreement about the boundaries of law.

[13] Allan, 'Law as a Branch of Morality' (n 1) 5.

[14] ibid 4.

[15] ibid 4–5.

[16] TRS Allan, *The Sovereignty of Law: Freedom, Constitution, and Common Law* (Oxford, Oxford University Press, 2013) 111.

[17] ibid.

[18] ibid 112.

[19] See AV Dicey, *Introduction to the Study of the Law of the Constitution*, 8th edn (London, Macmillan, 1915) 149.

[20] J Raz, *The Authority of Law: Essays on Law and Morality* (Oxford, Oxford University Press, 2009) 213.

men or women'.[21] However, as I will show below, his view includes more substantive elements as well.

Thus, we might think that on any view of the rule of law, we need to understand what law is first. Even if we adopt a thicker view of the rule of law, it will nevertheless include the idea of being ruled by law as central. This suggests that any theory of the rule of law must necessarily include an account of law. We are talking about the rule of *law* – so a focus on law seems natural. One way to figure out what the rule of law is would be to break down the composite phrase and ask first what 'law' is and then what it might mean for that thing, properly understood, to rule.[22]

However, I want to argue here that we can and should theorise about the rule of law without settling the question of what the concept or nature of law is.[23] Any vision of the rule of law that is tied to a concept of law will provide insufficient guidance about what ought to be done, due to persistent disagreement about the meaning of 'law'. We should take law out of the picture because the term 'law' is the subject of substantial dispute. Positivists argue that it is a matter of social fact, and non-positivists argue that it has a necessary moral element.

Building our account of the rule of law on a foundation that includes a particular view of law will likely lead to one of two problems. First, there is the concern that taking a positivist or nonpositivist view about the nature of law alienates half of one's potential audience. If we can frame our views about the rule of law in a more neutral way, we need not speak only to positivists or nonpositivists. Let's take Allan's view as an example here. On Allan's view, true law is necessarily intertwined with morality, and provides real reasons for action: '[w]e should insist that legal obligations are genuine moral obligations, underpinned by principles affirmed by legal practice as a whole'.[24] When Allan describes law in this way, a large contingent of legal philosophers will immediately refuse to get on board with the project at the ground floor. Positivists will disagree that '[l]aw is plainly different from brute power'.[25] They will define law as a matter of social fact.[26] If we can talk about the rule of law without starting from a commitment to a controversial view of law, we may reach a larger audience.

The second problem is that if we aren't explicit about what we mean by law, we may end up gaining a kind of illusory agreement: people will think they agree about the rule of law, but are in fact talking past each other because they mean different things by law.

[21] TRS Allan, 'The Rule of Law' in D Dyzenhaus and M Thorburn (eds), *Philosophical Foundations of Constitutional Law* (Oxford, Oxford University Press, 2016) 215. See also Allan, *Sovereignty of Law* (n 16) 90.

[22] Raz can be interpreted as taking this approach. He says that the rule of law exists only 'to minimize the danger created by the law itself', suggesting that we need to understand what law is before understanding the rule of law: Raz, *Authority of Law* (n 20) 224. But Jeremy Waldron objects to this. He argues that the rule of law can be understood as the value that is associated with controlling *governmental power*. It need not be understood as the value that controls *law*. See J Waldron, 'The Concept and the Rule of Law' (2008) 43 *Georgia Law Review* 11.

[23] Some theorists talk about 'concept' and some about 'nature'. For Raz, the two are connected. See my discussion of this in H Nye, 'A Critique of the Concept–Nature Nexus in Joseph Raz's Methodology' (2017) 37 *OJLS* 48.

[24] Allan, 'Law as a Branch of Morality' (n 1) 8.

[25] ibid 6.

[26] Many positivists take it to be a virtue of their view that it highlights a connection between law and power. Liam Murphy makes this point: 'It is an important aim of positivists to bring to the surface (what they regard as) the fact that judges have the authority to change the law'. See Murphy, *What Makes Law* (n 8) 93.

'Yes', we might all say, 'of course judges must apply the law'. Agreement on that point is easily won.[27] But that is a hollow victory: it does not mean anything without an account of law to back it up, and then our disagreement immediately resurfaces.[28] The idea that we should 'apply the law' tells us nothing at all, given our disagreements about what 'law' is. We can't know if we should endorse it until we have a fleshed-out account of law, which is a tall order. So, since we seem not to be able to settle the question of what law is, we have good reason to sidestep it if possible.[29]

If we adopt eliminativism, the next question is what an eliminativist might be able to say about the rule of law. I will argue that, far from impoverishing our discussions, the eliminativist impulse to do without reference to law actually helps us to be clearer about the normative ideal we mean to appeal to when we talk about the rule of law. We can't fall back on the idea of 'applying the law' or 'being controlled by law' in giving our account of the rule of law, and this actually sharpens our discussion of how we should govern ourselves.

In stripping the 'apply the law' version of the rule of law of its usefulness, eliminativism orients us towards more profitable questions.[30] In the judicial realm, we have to ask what we mean when we demand that judges apply the law. What behaviour is it that is endorsed or objected to? We might think that the underlying idea is that judges should be constrained – that their decisions be made only in accordance with rules we have specified in advance. But not everything can be settled in advance. So we have to ask what the judge should do in cases of uncertainty. What kinds of normative principles should guide their decision? Further, we may not always think the morally right thing to do is to follow the rule that has been established. So constraint can only be part of the story.

One might object at this point that the debate about the nature of law isn't relevant here. Perhaps we don't agree about the nature of law, but we do agree about what we

[27] Indeed, the idea that judges ought to apply the law has strong and widespread appeal in legal philosophy. Allan says that 'the court must in each case apply the law': TRS Allan, 'The Moral Unity of Public Law' (2017) 67 *University of Toronto Law Journal* 1, 29. See also R Dworkin, *Justice in Robes* (Cambridge, Belknap Press, 2008) 2: 'judges … are thought to have a responsibility to decide only as required or licensed by true propositions of law'; Raz, *Authority of Law* (n 20) 96: 'Courts have a duty to apply the laws of the system when they are applicable'; J Waldron, 'Separation of Powers in Thought and Practice' (2013) 54 *Boston College Law Review* 433, 462: 'The role of a court is to settle disputes according to law'; L Murphy, 'Better to See Law This Way' (2008) 83 *New York University Law Review* 1088, 1106: 'it seems that almost all judges believe that their duty is to figure out what the law is and apply it'.

[28] To return to the previously quoted phrase from Allan, let's now read the full sentence: 'The balance of moral considerations is intrinsic to the relevant questions of law; and the court must in each case apply the law'. Allan, 'Moral Unity of Public Law' (n 27) 29. It will be easy to get agreement on the second half – that we should apply the law – and much harder to get agreement on the first half – that moral considerations are part of the law.

[29] One need not endorse eliminativism to draw something from the present argument. We might think the debate may one day be solved. But we can still see that there is (so far) no consensus about the nature of law. And in the face of serious disagreement about the nature of law, any account of the rule of law that relies on 'law' as a central element will have to first settle the question of what law is, which centuries of debate have not resolved. Thus, even if the reader does not share my pessimism about the ultimate fate of the debate, they still have good reason to agree that proceeding in this way is valuable. In what follows, however, I will talk in terms of adopting eliminativism.

[30] In general, it tells us to focus on the substance of certain ways of cabining and controlling governmental power. I am here concerned with the question of what judges should do, but there is a broader set of questions that could be asked.

mean by law when we're talking about the rule of law; in that context, we've always meant to refer to positive law.[31] However, some rule of law theorists would disagree. Ronald Dworkin, for instance, thinks that the rule of law means rule by law that meets a particular moral standard.[32] And, of particular relevance for this chapter, Allan does not agree that the rule of law means rule by positive law.

But putting aside what particular people have meant by the rule of law, we might still think that we can make progress by stipulating that the rule of law means the demand that power be exercised in accordance with *positive law*, and thus avoid the debate about what law is. We can, of course, stipulate a meaning for the sake of argument. But it is not clear that 'rule by positive law' has much moral force as an ideal, given that positive law can be unjust. So, if we decide to stipulate that 'law' means 'positive law', we may withdraw our assent to the principle that judges should always and only apply the law. At any rate, if the 'rule by positive law' account is morally defensible, work must be done to demonstrate this, and to explain its limits and its interaction with other values. Thus, saying that we should talk about positive law is only the start, not the end, of the discussion. The normative question of what judges *ought to do* is the question we should really care about. And whether they should endorse a moral ideal that requires them to comply with positive law is an open moral question.

The view that the rule of law demands that we 'apply the law' is unhelpful because it opens up a centuries-old debate about what 'law' is. And the view that it demands that we 'apply positive law' is not an obviously appealing moral ideal, at least without much more justification. In light of this, the next section aims to build a moral account of the rule of law, without reference to the troubled concept of law.

4. The Rule of Law without Law?

We are now left in a tricky position. The rule of law is, after all, the rule of *law*. What could that mean without an account of law in the background? I want to see what we can draw from Allan's work to answer this question. Allan argues that:

> Properly understood, the rule of law is not a shield against the abuse of *law*, as it is sometimes portrayed. It is the moral ideal of governance according to *law in its primary sense* – the sense in which it enforces a scheme of rights and duties that provides for each individual a domain of liberty, secure from the threat of domination either by public officials or powerful private interests.[33]

The rule of law, for Allan, protects us against arbitrary power.[34] But this also has implications for the substance of law: 'the scheme of rights, duties and powers established by

[31] I thank Luís Duarte d'Almeida for raising this point.

[32] See R Dworkin, *A Matter of Principle* (Cambridge, Harvard University Press, 1985) ch 1 'Political Judges and the Rule of Law'.

[33] Allan, 'The Rule of Law' (n 21) 218. The same idea about freedom is articulated elsewhere. See Allan, *Sovereignty of Law* (n 16) 89. See also Allan, 'The Rule of Law' (n 21) 208, for discussion of the ideal of governing in a way that maximises the freedom of all.

[34] Allan, *Sovereignty of Law* (n 16) 93.

legal rules must itself be non-arbitrary, in the sense that it is justified in terms of a *public or common good* – one that we can fairly suppose favours a similar freedom for all'.[35] The idea of substantive commitments as part of the rule of law is a frequent point for Allan: 'The rule of law embraces both procedure and substance'.[36]

One important theme in Allan's writing is coherence. In his article 'The Moral Unity of Public Law', he argues that we should see our public law as a unified sphere in which we are attentive to concerns of legitimacy, rights, the rule of law, and human dignity. None of these concerns can be elevated above the others or isolated. He says: '[w]e may understand the rule of law as the basic requirement that each person should be fairly treated according to the law as a whole – the law interpreted as a coherent set of standards, amounting to an intelligible and attractive scheme of justice'.[37]

This quotation invokes a rich vision of the law as something morally defensible. Again, not all readers will agree with this as a statement of *what the law is, properly understood*. Positivists may resist this, and they often do so not just as a matter of correct description, but as a rhetorical move to highlight power and the fact that it is often used in abusive ways. While Allan would not, I think, deny this, he would characterise such uses of power as not law, strictly speaking. As I argued above, though, debate over this point quickly ends in an impasse. We are better off avoiding it.

We should, then, draw what we can from Allan's account of the rule of law, while excising the part that describes law as a matter of justice. We can present his view as follows, with just a minor edit: '[w]e may understand the rule of law as the basic requirement that each person should be fairly treated according to … a coherent set of standards, amounting to an intelligible and attractive scheme of justice'.[38] This side-steps the question of whether that coherent set of standards properly amounts to law, but still provides rich resources for our vision of the rule of law. For Allan, the rule of law is a moral ideal. It is an 'ideal of governance'[39] according to 'a scheme of rights and duties that provides for each individual a domain of liberty'.[40] We can appeal to the same values that Allan does – substantive equality of citizenship,[41] dignity,[42] etc – without saying that this is equivalent to 'equal protection of the law'.[43]

One statement from Allan is, in my view, particularly illuminating: '[a]ny doctrinal statement of the common law, even when contained in the judgment of a superior court, is only as sound as the reasons that underpin and justify it'.[44] A judge, then, must ask what reasons justify their taking an action. Some of those reasons may have to do with predictability and expectations. But reasons having to do with justice must also be weighed and balanced here.

[35] ibid.
[36] Allan, 'The Moral Unity of Public Law' (n 27) 2.
[37] ibid 4.
[38] ibid.
[39] Allan, 'The Rule of Law' (n 21) 218.
[40] ibid. Here again I am quoting from Allan but removing references to law.
[41] Allan, *Sovereignty of Law* (n 16) 90.
[42] ibid 96.
[43] ibid 90.
[44] ibid 121.

In other words, for Allan, it is always the judge's obligation to reason morally. Moral reasoning doesn't just come in at the margins; it is always relevant. 'Legal judgment is moral judgment in which doctrinal legal argument serves to focus the moral dialogue, making every question of law, in the final analysis, a matter of interpretation of the larger scheme of justice in which it arises'.[45] Or, as he puts it later, '[i]f the earlier reasons are persuasive, they are *morally* persuasive – consonant with justice … Legal reasoning embodies our ideal of moral reasoning as that ideal applies when we try to reason in the name of the whole society'.[46]

An eliminativist can agree with the substance here, while sidestepping the definitional dispute about whether what Allan is describing is really 'legal reasoning'. What Allan says is right, as a description of 'what ought to be done'. Judges ought to reason morally, and they ought to do so in a way that does not ignore the social facts and institutional history that we live with. But ultimately, they must give those facts and that history exactly the weight that morality requires they give them. They must make a moral judgment about what ought to be done. That moral judgment is sensitive to statutes, precedents, etc., but only insofar as they are morally justifiable.[47] The relevant attitude is not an unquestioning deference to those materials, but a deep questioning about exactly what those materials morally require of us.[48]

What *do* those materials require of us? What does the rule of law tell judges that is different from simply saying 'do what is right'?[49] The task of weighing the many values Allan talks about is a heavy one. It demands that judges exercise *judgment*. The rule of law cannot be a mechanistic set of guidelines that can be applied without thoughtfulness. The values Allan draws our attention to are big: liberty, dignity, justice, rights. We can't devise a system of weighing that puts one above the other. Some liberties will be absolutely central to us, and others will be trivial. And so not much can be said in the abstract without attention to a concrete situation. But there are some things we can say. Deciding well in the name of others is not just a matter of following rules. It is about showing respect to people.

What the rule of law is really about is how to decide in the name of others in a way that is *sensitive* to the fact that we are engaged in a collective endeavour that has a history, but not *bound* to that history. It is about how we treat people fairly while

[45] Allan, 'The Moral Unity of Public Law' (n 27) 6.

[46] ibid 16.

[47] I discuss this idea in more depth in H Nye, '"It's Not Right, But It's Okay": Role Morality and Judicial Decision-Making' (unpublished manuscript, on file with author, 2023).

[48] This view shares much with M Greenberg, 'The Moral Impact Theory of Law' (2014) 123 *Yale Law Journal* 1288, but it is ultimately different in resisting the move to label the moral upshots of those materials 'the law'.

[49] I am focused here on the perspective of the judge, but I want to briefly mention the citizen's perspective. Allan says that if there is injustice in our rules or practices, 'we must defend an interpretation of practice that alleviates the threat': TRS Allan, 'Why the Law Is What It Ought to Be' (2020) 11 *Jurisprudence* 574, 594. It makes good sense for the judge to take such a perspective: they are wielding power over others and thus should do the best they can to exercise that power in a way that is legitimate. But Allan often speaks as though the citizen, too, should take such a perspective: Allan, *Sovereignty of Law* (n 16) 91. He says: '[t]he rule of law is ultimately an ideal of legitimate governance that explains the citizen's moral obligation of obedience': ibid 128. But why think a citizen has such an obligation? If we take an 'external, non-interpretive stance', Allan says, 'we would … [succumb] to wholesale scepticism': Allan, 'Why the Law Is What It Ought to Be' 594. I fail to see why taking that kind of external or sceptical attitude is something to regret or avoid, especially as a citizen.

participating in a system that is imperfect. It requires taking seriously the demands of justice while being conscious that we disagree about what justice requires.

What this means is that the rule of law will not always demand compliance with what is set down in statute or what has been done in the past. It often will, because there is fairness in honouring expectations. But there are times when past practice is too unjust to be followed. What we really want is for the government's pronouncements to be applied when it is just to do so, and resisted when it is not.

Allan acknowledges that judges may sometimes disregard the enacted rules. For Allan, the rule of law tolerates departures from established rules, as long as such departures are justified, and the state's aims are legitimate.[50] When such invalidation happens, there may be a loss to certainty, but 'the risks of being misled by taking enacted rules at face value are offset by the greater assurance that acknowledged principles of justice will be reliably upheld'.[51]

There is, Allan says, often a tension between certainty and predictability on the one hand, and justice on the other.[52] The relationship between certainty and justice is complex: '[w]hile an authority's failure to adhere to its own rules or statements of intention may cause injustice, it is equally a source of injustice for rules or policies to be applied inflexibly, with insufficient attention to the circumstances of the particular case'.[53] In other words, sticking to the rules can be as problematic as changing them, depending on the context and the rule in question. We tend to place great importance on certainty and predictability. But 'there is always scope for adaptation of the rules when justice requires it'.[54] In striking this balance, we look to context: for example, we may be stricter about sticking to established expectations in the criminal context.[55]

But even in that context, the rules are not absolute. Allan uses the example of *R v R*,[56] the case which removed the bar to prosecution of husbands for rape of their wives. He argues that this is justifiable and in line with the rule of law because it was a development that could and should have been reasonably foreseen by people.[57] I think the underlying justification drawn from Allan – his attention to dignity and freedom – actually pushes us further than this. Even if the change came out of the blue, and was not preceded by any hints that the rule would be overturned, we might nevertheless say that the change is permissible because the value of protecting people from rape – protecting their liberty and dignity interests – outweighs the predictability interests of those who expect immunity for rape.[58]

This brings us back to the point made above, about the relevance of the past. Allan says a judge's 'opinions about legal rights and duties will be heavily dependent (if she is a good judge) on her grasp of the implications of a shared tradition'.[59] Can it be right that

[50] Allan, 'The Rule of Law' (n 21) 207.
[51] ibid.
[52] Allan, *Sovereignty of Law* (n 16) 99.
[53] ibid 109.
[54] ibid.
[55] ibid 99.
[56] *R v R* [1992] 1 AC 599.
[57] Allan, *Sovereignty of Law* (n 16) 122.
[58] I argue elsewhere that judicial decisions must always be all-things-considered decisions. See Nye, '"It's Not Right, But It's Okay"' (n 47).
[59] Allan, *Sovereignty of Law* (n 16) 125.

a good judge's opinion about what ought to be done will depend on facts about what happened in the past, which may be anywhere from arbitrary to morally abhorrent?

The fact that something has been done in the past does not give it any special moral force. The act being contemplated can only have the moral valence that it has. Is it the right thing to do? The mere fact that it has been done before means nothing. The fact that it has been done before may lead to *other* facts worth considering – that people have formed the expectation that it would be done again. This, certainly, is part of the rule of law. But ultimately the act in question cannot have more weight *simply* because it was done in the past. Reliance matters, but only as far as it matters: is it valuable to protect the reliance interests of the rapist? I think it is legitimate to say: 'not at all'. The past and our practices matter, but, as Allan says, a judgment is only as sound as the reasons that justify it. Ultimately a judge must do what is right. It will not be often that what is right is convicting someone of a crime contrary to their expectations. But it may sometimes be the case.

Of course, a judge cannot wholly ignore the past. Nor can an ordinary person making moral decisions in their own life. We look at all the circumstances, and decide what ought to be done. But our shared tradition may be morally indefensible, and a judge should be alive to that possibility. Our past cannot give a decision any greater moral weight than it earns.

To be fair, perhaps this is precisely what Allan means. There are times, he says, where 'the conscientious interpreter, whether private citizen or public official, should repudiate the whole system as irredeemably unjust, deserving resistance rather than loyalty'.[60] But I think before we get to repudiation, judges should always do the morally right thing, and that will be influenced, but not determined, by the past. Perhaps this is what Allan means when he says that judgments are only as sound as the reasons that underpin them.[61] I agree with this, though I think it is difficult to square that way of putting the point with Allan's emphasis on our past, our practices, and our 'law' as genuine sources of moral force. For that reason, I prefer to view things as I have articulated them here: to make claims about what the rule of law requires that do not commit us to a view of law, and do not necessarily tie us to doing what was done before.

5. Objections

A. The Rule of Law is Distinct from Justice

Raz objects to substantive accounts of the rule of law. He says: '[i]f the rule of law is the rule of the good law then to explain its nature is to propound a complete social philosophy. But if so the term lacks any useful function. We have no need to be converted to the rule of law just in order to discover that to believe in it is to believe that good should triumph'.[62]

[60] ibid 127.
[61] ibid 121.
[62] Raz, *Authority of Law* (n 20) 211.

Allan sees and responds to the objection: 'Admittedly, the defence of a substantive conception of the rule of law invites the objection that the separate ideals of legality and justice are being conflated and confused. We generally suppose that there is a difference between acting justly and acting within the law: an unjust enactment or decision may nonetheless be lawfully made'.[63] His response is that there is some inevitability to the substantive dimension of the rule of law. The rule of law is underpinned by the ideal of liberty, which limits what governments can do.[64] The commitment to treating people fairly under the rules expands to the idea of treating them fairly in terms of the substance of the law.[65]

I think there is something to this idea: the rule of law has a kind of substantive 'creep', once we pay attention to the values that underpin it. But is Raz right that we are using words in obfuscating ways if we lump all of justice into the rule of law? In line with my eliminativist tendencies, I don't think the view I've put forward here captures the 'true nature' of the rule of law, and I think we could equally use different terms to describe 'good governance'. If someone wanted to debate about the metaphysical essence of the rule of law, I would decline to engage in that dispute just like the dispute about the nature of law. The fundamental question is simply the question of what we ought to do, all things considered, in any given situation.

But I do frame the discussion here in terms of the rule of law, and I think it can be reasonable to continue talking in those terms. The term 'rule of law' has rhetorical force, and we may not want to let go of talking about it. The question of the 'true nature' of the rule of law might well be a verbal dispute. But a point from David Chalmers is important here. He says:

> In cases where words have fixed connotations and associations, too, verbal issues often have serious practical import. *This applies especially when those connotations are normative.* What counts as 'torture' or as 'terrorism' might be, at one level, a verbal issue that a philosopher can resolve by distinguishing senses. But in a rhetorical or political context, words have power that transcends these distinctions. If the community counts an act as falling into the extension of 'torture' or 'terrorism', this may make a grave difference to our attitudes toward that act. As such, there may be a serious practical question about what we *ought* to count as falling into the extension of these terms.[66] (first emphasis added)

The point is not that we should conclude that a spurious-seeming question is actually a viable one because it has this sort of upshot. That is, we should not think the metaphysical 'what *is* torture' – or 'what is the rule of law' – question becomes truth-apt simply because it matters rhetorically how we use the term. Instead, if we see that term as operating as a normative one, we exit the metaphysical realm and rephrase the question as a normative one about how we *ought to* conceive of torture.

The thought is that we have identified a term with more normative weight than descriptive weight. The 'badness' of torture, the 'not-to-be-done-ness' of it is somehow

[63] Allan, 'The Rule of Law' (n 21) 203 (citations omitted).
[64] ibid.
[65] ibid. He makes a similar point elsewhere. See Allan, 'Why the Law Is What It Ought to Be' (n 49) 578.
[66] DJ Chalmers, 'Verbal Disputes' (2011) 120 *Philosophical Review* 515.

primary to the description of acts that might fall under the category.[67] This feature is what makes us shift from the 'what is x?' question to the 'how should we normatively understand x?' question.

Is the rule of law like this? We disagree about what it means, but we do seem to agree that it is morally valuable. The idea that judges should adhere to the rule of law is a widely shared commitment. Given that the idea of the rule of law has so much purchase in our society as a value that is worth preserving and upholding, it may be better to keep the term and argue for our preferred moral understanding of it. If we were to accept that the rule of law just means applying all rules put forward by government, even if they are bad, then we would likely resist the idea that the rule of law should be a guiding principle for judges. Instead, we may wish to keep it as a judicial guidepost and flesh it out, as Allan does, such that it is morally worthy of judges' adherence. This runs the risk of conflating the rule of law with justice, but it keeps our discussion on normative territory where the important questions can be discussed.

B. Eliminativism Misses Something Important

Allan resists eliminativism. He would, I think, insist that we should keep speaking about 'law', and that we should keep defining law as he does, as something that serves the public good and respects the dignity of legal subjects. Part of this is his commitment to the idea that the law comes along with obligation: 'If we adopt a non-moral concept of law, identifying law with the factual content of officially authorised rules or rulings, it is very hard to account for political obligation'.[68] But those who are drawn to a positivist view will simply say that that is right: there is no general obligation to obey the law, and it is not something we need to account for.

Allan's way of describing things is, I think, less simple and intuitive than the eliminativist's. He says that the 'duty to obey the law is a duty to act as the law requires *when correctly discerned* – interpreted in the light of the moral principles that justify her conditional, critical, allegiance' (emphasis added).[69] But is that not just a duty to do the right thing, all things considered? Why call that a duty to obey the *law*? On the eliminativist's view, we sidestep making claims about what the law is, and simply talk about the moral and political obligations of various agents.

Allan is committed to the idea that the rule of law is an inherent part of law.[70] I do not have an argument to convince him that these two things are *not* intertwined; that would involve entering the nature of law debate and engaging in a dispute that I think is unresolvable. I can simply offer an alternative way to view things, which seems simpler and clearer to me. We can talk about the rule of law as a value, just as he does, without insisting that it is connected to the correct understanding of law.

[67] See Waldron, 'The Concept and the Rule of Law' (n 22) 36–38, discussing the use of the concept of law as a term of commendation. See also Dworkin, *Justice in Robes* (n 27) 148: 'Almost everyone agrees that the values in question are of at least some importance, and perhaps very great importance, but that agreement leaves open crucial substantive issues about what more precisely these values are or mean'.

[68] Allan, 'Why the Law Is What It Ought to Be' (n 49) 584.

[69] ibid 586.

[70] Allan, *Sovereignty of Law* (n 16) 88.

Nevertheless, it might still seem that we are missing something if we go the eliminativist route. If we think of the judge's decision as an all-things-considered one, doesn't that miss the nuanced way in which a judge reasons? Allan is concerned to preserve law as a special domain of normative reasoning. It is a subset of the normative domain in which specific considerations apply.[71] We should, in other words, pay attention to the distinctiveness of the legal domain, and the worry is that eliminativists are likely to miss this, in seeing legal obligations as no different from our ordinary moral obligations.

Connor Crummey reads Dworkin in a way that highlights this. He says:

> When read as a one-system theory, Law as Integrity offers an account of the moral value of legal practice that motivates the view that the subset of our moral obligations whose enforcement in court is justifiable is *morally distinct* from the rest of our moral obligations. This moral distinction is what motivates the thesis that it is this subset that we should think of as *legal* obligations.[72]

Crummey helpfully draws attention to the fact that there are different subsets of moral rights and obligations, and that it can be valuable to pay attention to certain subsets in certain contexts. But he too recognises that the labelling of a right as legal or non-legal is ultimately of little or no importance.[73] Ultimately, one can be an eliminativist and still be attuned to the nuanced terrain of the moral domain, and the many subsets within it.

We are asking what someone should do when they exercise power over others, which is different from what they should do when they are making a decision for themselves. We can develop an account of the rule of law that sharpens the focus for judges, as I aimed to do in the previous section. Ultimately, it is an all-things-considered decision, but the rule of law brings certain considerations to the fore.

C. Judicial Power

A further objection is that this approach puts too much power into the hands of judges. The worry is that if we define the rule of law as we did above – as the 'requirement that each person should be fairly treated according to … a coherent set of standards, amounting to an intelligible and attractive scheme of justice'[74] – then we allow judges to determine what constitutes an attractive scheme of justice, and that this is undemocratic and may lead to bad outcomes. We don't want, in other words, to be beholden to others' judgment, and a view of this sort might elevate judges' private beliefs above the norms we have decided on together.[75] Reasons of space constrain me from answering this worry in depth, but it is a serious one: there is no shortage, even in recent history, of examples of judges making morally problematic decisions. I discuss this in more

[71] I thank Peter Cane, Hasan Dindjer, and George Letsas for raising versions of this objection. There are domains within morality – we have obligations qua parent, for example. But on my view, parents too must make all-things-considered decisions. What the idea of a domain does is make salient certain special considerations, but it cannot exempt one from considering the broader demands of morality.

[72] C Crummey, 'One-System Integrity and the Legal Domain of Morality' (2022) 28 *Legal Theory* 269, 288.

[73] ibid 295.

[74] Allan, 'The Moral Unity of Public Law' (n 27) 4. Again, this is Allan's phrasing without the law talk.

[75] I thank Joanna Langille for putting the point in this way. Jeffrey Goldsworthy also raised this objection.

depth in a draft article.[76] What I will say is that the view I put forward here, drawing on Allan, invites this problem no more than Raz's view does. Raz says we should keep the rule of law narrow and not incorporate justice and other values within it. Nevertheless, Raz accepts that judges are permitted to appeal to justice. They simply do so under the separate umbrella of justice and not under the banner of the rule of law. So any view that permits judges to take account of questions of justice has to face this worry; it is not unique to the view presented here. Judges engage in moral deliberations as it stands. Nothing in my view gives them more power than they have on other views, and a virtue of my view is that it makes explicit the role of morality.

6. Conclusion

Allan argues that the fact that our community has decided something in some way gives us real reasons for action. Law, properly understood, is the rules of our community when they respect the rule of law and promote our liberty and dignity. I have argued that this way of seeing things requires us to settle a question that has so far eluded us: the question of the nature of law. Instead, we should adopt eliminativism about law. We can be eliminativists, I have argued, and still take much from Allan's view about the rule of law. We should understand the rule of law as the guiding principle that tells us that we must treat people fairly according to the demands of justice. Judges, then, should do what is morally right – their judgment must be driven by the soundness of the reasons that justify it. This much we can take from Allan, while avoiding the fraught claim that, when we abide by these principles, we are also 'following the law'. We should understand the rule of law as a moral and political principle that guides judges, and we can do so while endorsing eliminativism.

[76] Nye, '"It's Not Right, But It's Okay"' (n 47).

9

Against the Juridicalisation of Political Philosophy: Equality, Morality, and the Rule of Law

CHRISTINE SYPNOWICH

1. Introduction

Debates about the meaning of the rule of law are often couched in terms of liberty – the freedom that is protected by the authority of the state in times of unrest or instability, or the freedom that is safeguarded when the state's authority is restrained by procedural checks. However, there is an obvious sense in which equality is also at the heart of the rule of law ideal. At its most basic, the rule of law means that all are equally subject to the law, and all are equal in their entreaties before it.

Trevor Allan's scholarly contribution is distinguished by a subtle appreciation for how the rule of law is not a mere formal principle, but reflects important political values, of freedom, but also equality. When judges adjudicate cases, he says, they must see their role requiring interpretation of legislation in light of respect for common law and constitutional rights which safeguard citizens' equal entitlements to dignity and independence. Parliamentary supremacy, on this view, is unqualified only within the sphere of legitimate governmental authority, which requires abiding by fundamental legal principles.[1]

Allan is concerned that his theory of law be agnostic on questions of policy and politics. Yet is it? On the one hand, his rich moral understanding of the rule of law might be compatible with, perhaps even facilitate, progressive political approaches to law which seek equality, not just in law's application, but also its content. On the other hand, Allan's ideal of legality has contrary elements too. His Hayekian-inspired emphasis on warding off state intervention that risks infringing individual liberty may imply some unease with redistributive policies, and in particular a dissonance with an ambitious egalitarianism which understands the political community's role as seeking to make human flourishing more equal.

[1] TRS Allan, *The Sovereignty of Law: Freedom, Constitution, and Common Law* (Oxford, Oxford University Press, 2013) 324.

In this chapter I argue that an appreciation for the value of the rule of law need not mean the 'juridicalisation' of political philosophy, which thwarts a progressive ideal where the community provides the material resources, but also the cultural context, needed for each member to flourish equally. One can affirm the protections of legality and yet resist the unfortunate influence of a proceduralist ethic on egalitarianism which has prevented engagement with questions of human wellbeing. Indeed, I will suggest that such a project is ultimately in keeping with Allan's nuanced appreciation for the moral complexity of the ideas of both legality and equality.

2. Equality before the Law

The phrase 'the rule of law' has a multitude of meanings. In popular discourse, it is often associated with the coercive power of the state and its absolute authority over citizens. Liberal democratic governments will sometimes invoke the rule of law to communicate a concern for order and stability – for example to justify the deployment of exceptional police powers of arrest and detention in times of public unrest. Thus, a Canadian news headline invokes the power of the state to override dissent: 'rule of law applies, pipeline will proceed despite opposition'.[2] There is obviously a widely shared interest in stability and security. Yet the rule of law may pull in different directions. A focus on the state's authority can, on the one hand, serve the interests of the powerful and the freedom to pursue profit; it can assure the unimpeded flow of commodities, and exclude members of the public from private property when the state uses its coercive powers in such cases. On the other hand, appeal to the rule of law may well be made by precisely those protestors whose actions are being restricted in the name of law's authority. The rule of law is principally understood to mean a set of procedural guidelines that dictates properly formed rules, such that it is law, and not arbitrary decree or the whims of the sovereign, that governs us. State power, then, must be regulated and controlled on behalf of the people to whom the state is accountable.[3] Thus, we also see this headline: 'Shackling judges: Europe confronts Poland over its trampling on the rule of law'.[4]

The rule of law thus refers to *ruling*, and the state's coercive authority, but also the idea of *law*, whereby restrictions are imposed on the state's use of force and power. The two conceptions of the rule of law – that law *rule* or that *law* rule – may seem in tension. However, it is precisely the proclivity of leaders in times of crisis to 'crack down' with the might of the state that renders the rule of law so vital. A state that claims to be democratic and legitimate ultimately finds its authority to rely on fidelity to the rule of law. That is, we as citizens grant the state legitimacy and submit to law because of law's procedural character; the state rules us, yes, but it does so by means of rules.

The rule of law ideal which challenges the authority of the state does so in the name of the equality of citizens. No one is above the law, even those who make or enforce it.

[2] 'Rule of law applies, pipeline will proceed despite opposition' *APTN News* (13 January 2020) aptnnews.ca/2020/01/13/horgan-says-rule-of-law-applies-lng-pipeline-will-proceed-despite-opposition/.

[3] J Waldron, 'The Rule of Law and the Importance of Procedure' (2011) *Nomos* 3.

[4] 'Shackling judges: Europe confronts Poland over its trampling on the rule of law' *The Economist* (23 January 2020) www.economist.com/europe/2020/01/23/europe-confronts-poland-over-its-trampling-on-the-rule-of-law.

Even the more authoritarian variant of the rule of law relies on the idea that citizens are equal in their shared obligation to respect law's authority. In the words of the celebrated constitutional theorist AV Dicey, 'every man, whatever his rank or condition, is subject to the ordinary law of the realm and amenable to the jurisdiction of the ordinary tribunals'.[5] The law rules us all: citizens, government, police, and judges; rulers as well as the ruled, all must submit to the rule of law.

If law is to command obedience, we must know its dictates. Key to the rule of law is that law be so designed that we can obey it. We cannot obey the law if it is secret, or if it tells us that what we did yesterday is illegal today. Procedural strictures ensure people can understand the law's requirements, adjust their plans and act accordingly. An unpredictable, arbitrary political order, whatever its purposes, undermines our capacity to choose how to live. Thus, perhaps paradoxically, freedom to act involves knowing what actions are not permitted, since in order to be able conduct oneself without fear of violating the community's rules, one must understand those rules as they are encapsulated in law.

The rule of law's meaning is captured by a range of overlapping ideas: due process, procedural justice, legal formality, procedural rationality or justice as regularity. These all involve the idea that law should be general, that law take the form of rules directed to more than a particular situation or individual. As Lon Fuller notes, the rule of law requires that law be relatively certain, clearly expressed, open, prospective, and adequately publicised. If law fails to meet these criteria, it is self-defeating.[6] Fuller thus ventures a natural law view of the validity of law based on its fidelity to a morality of legality. Joseph Raz, however, contends that the rule of law's virtue is like the virtue of a sharp knife; it enables the law to fulfil its function, whatever that function may be. The rule of law, he says, is not needed to believe that 'good should triumph', a riposte to more substantive moral conceptions of the rule of law.[7]

Allan counters that the rule of law is a foundational moral principle of constitutionalism, going beyond procedural fairness and impartial administration of the law. In requiring that the state govern by rules rather than arbitrary decrees, the rule of law provides a measure of consistency, predictability and rationality in the state's actions. Indeed, as Mark Walters argues, properly understood, Dicey too conceived of the rule of law as imposing moral aspirations on the sovereignty of law.[8] The egalitarian essence of the rule of law consists in securing equality before the law by preventing unregulated discretion, and this is not without moral significance. Indeed, according to Allan, the rule of law expresses 'ideas of human dignity and respect for persons'. Common law constitutions, particularly the British one, have a particular shape owing to the 'continuing effort, over many generations' to achieve a reconciliation between parliamentary sovereignty and the rule of law. Thus judges, when reasoning about constitutional matters, do so in the context of both principles and practice, to interpret legislation in

[5] AV Dicey, *Introduction to the Study of the Law of the Constitution*, 10th edn (London, Macmillan, 1964) 193.

[6] LL Fuller, *The Morality of Law* (New Haven, Yale University Press,1969) 33–94.

[7] J Raz, *The Authority of Law* (Oxford, Clarendon Press, 1979) 211.

[8] MD Walters, *AV Dicey and the Common Law Constitutional Tradition: A Legal Turn of Mind* (Cambridge, Cambridge University Press, 2020).

such a way that individuals' equality and liberty before the law are affirmed. There is no clear distinction, Allan contends, between political ideals and legal principles, since interpretation seeks to bring public law closer to the realisation of the connected ideals of freedom, equality, and legality.[9]

3. Hayek, Allan, and the Left

How substantive is the egalitarianism of the rule of law? The idea of the equality of citizens before the law might be thought to be 'merely formal', consistent with significant inequality in the law's policies or purposes. Allan, however, insists that consistent application of the law equally to all inevitably constitutes a 'route to a larger, more substantive equality of legal principle'. He purports that the idea that 'like cases should be decided alike' is a 'pertinent principle of equality' and that rule of law principles make it possible for a legal order to come 'closer to an ideal of substantive justice'. Indeed, the commitment to equality before the law means 'there must be no discrimination between persons or groups inconsistent with a coherent and plausible account of the public interest'.[10]

Such views are important in their insistence that arbitrary distinctions, prejudice and discrimination, have no place in the application of law. Yet Allan's ideal of the rule of law is a theory of constitutional interpretation, not a philosophy of social justice, perhaps inevitably thin gruel for political egalitarianism. The idea that procedural guarantees yield substantive equality might seem like wishful thinking; equality before the law does not entail, after all, more thorough-going ideas of equality pertaining to, eg, the distribution of wealth, the rights of workers, or the elimination of disadvantage for historically marginalised groups.

Indeed, classical Marxism has tended to view the rule of law as, not just indifferent to substantive equality, but a handmaiden to the inequality that pervades a class-divided society such as capitalism. The Left notes the law's connection to class inequality in two ways. First, it is argued that the legal form is designed to express and protect the interests of property owners and thus is useless as a resource for challenging the parameters of private property in the first place. The 'bourgeois egoism' view was advanced by the influential Bolshevik legal theorist, Evgeny Pashukanis, who developed the 'Commodity Theory of Law' to articulate the idea of how commodity exchange was the essence of legality.[11] A second view understands the inequalities of social class as integral to the rule of law insofar as law enforces the shared interests of the dominant class. The procedural guarantees of the rule of law are an ideological mask behind which lies the naked

[9] TRS Allan, 'Freedom, Equality, Legality' in JR Silkenat, JE Hickey and PD Barenboim (eds), *The Legal Doctrines of the Rule of Law and the Legal State (Rechtsstaat)*, Ius gentium. Comparative perspectives on law and justice (Berlin, Springer, 2014) 155, 155–57.

[10] ibid 156–58. See also Allan, *Sovereignty of Law* (n 1) 100.

[11] E Pashukanis, *Selected Writings on Marxism and Law*, P Beirne and R Sharlet ed, PB Magg trans (London, Academic Press, 1980) 76–77; see also C Sypnowich, *The Concept of Socialist Law* (Oxford, Clarendon Press, 1990) ch 1; C Sypnowich, 'The Left and Wrongs: Marxism, Law and Torts' in M Lobban and J Moses (eds), *The Impact of Ideas on Legal Development, Comparative Studies in the Development of the Law on Torts in Europe* (Cambridge, Cambridge University Press, 2012) 150–66.

power of the bourgeois class under capitalism.[12] At their most polemical, Marx and Engels proclaimed law to be 'the will of your [the bourgeois] class made into a law for all'.[13] In sum, legality provides the bourgeoisie with a means of securing its class interests, first by setting out individual rights to property and exchange, and second, by conferring the power of class rule.

Paradoxically, the Marxist idea that law serves capitalist economic relations was endorsed by some thinkers on the Right. In his argument against state intervention in the capitalist economy, Hayek contended that the rule of law, in its protection of individual liberty against unaccountable state power, is wedded to the policies of a market economy. Hayek's view rested on the conviction that individual liberty is secure so long as, not just the assaults of private individuals, but also the intrusions of government are constrained; the idea that concentrations of economic power can also undermine people's freedom is not considered.[14]

Allan's focus on the substantive morality of the rule of law as a bulwark against state power owes much to Hayek, in fact. Allan shares Hayek's preoccupation with a private sphere insulated from illegitimate coercion, where the state enjoys a monopoly of force, but individuals enjoy a realm of freedom so long as they and their fellow citizens are equally subject only to the law.[15] Thus he sounds a Hayekian note of concern regarding the pitfalls of the interventionist state and associated ideas of official discretion in the following passage:

> It would be foolish … to ignore or deny the real threat to liberty that such discretionary powers present; they leave the citizen at the mercy of the judgement of public officials, who may have little incentive to allow even reasonable objections to thwart their pursuit of their own policy agendas. There is a danger of oppression or unfairness, even when officials are well intentioned and act in good faith in (what they deem) the public interest.
>
> The principle of the rule of law requires that a grant of official discretion should be no greater than strictly necessary for the tasks in view: the scope of a power must be confined by its proper purposes, as those purposes are ascertained by interpretation of the empowering statute.[16]

Similarly:

> When the modern welfare-regulatory state confers extensive discretionary powers on public agencies, enabling them to perform wide-ranging and perhaps loosely-defined public functions, the clear-cut distinction between law and administration, or law and public policy, dissolves. The simple and idealised version of the separation of powers is inapplicable … The traditional conception of the rule of law is undermined.[17]

[12] H Collins, *Marxism and Law* (Oxford, Oxford University Press, 1984) 141.

[13] K Marx and F Engels, 'Manifesto of the Communist Party' in R Tucker (ed), *The Marx-Engels Reader* (New York, Norton, 1978) 487; Sypnowich, *Concept of Socialist Law* (n 11) 17.

[14] FA Hayek, *The Road to Serfdom* (London, Routledge and Kegan Paul, 1971) 57–59.

[15] Allan, *Sovereignty of Law* (n 1) 97.

[16] Allan, 'Freedom, Equality, Liberty' (n 9) 160. Interestingly, Allan voiced these Hayekian worries early in his career. See also Allan, 'Legislative Supremacy and the Rule of Law: Democracy and Constitutionalism' (1985) 44 *CLJ* 113–14.

[17] TRS Allan, 'Doctrine and Theory in Administrative Law: The Elusive Quest for Jurisdiction' [2003] *PL* 429.

Thus Allan, when admitting of the possibility of 'interpretations that enable rules to be applied to novel and unforeseen instances' notes the importance of context; for example, a 'strictness of approach' may be required 'appropriate to the needs of business confidence'.[18]

So long as the rule of law is understood in this way, as a source of restraint on political and legal power, it can imply that these public forms of power are the only forms that exist, or at least the only ones that matter. Moreover, in assuring subjects of the law that law is applied with generality and certainty, the rule of law also seems to imply that formal justice is the only relevant kind of justice; that equality before the law is identical to equality per se. Allan's reference to the needs of business confidence makes explicit the idea that legal proceduralism aids the capitalist enterprise. One critic has therefore argued that Allan cannot help but offer a doctrine of legality that is 'dogmatically liberal in the Hayekian mold'. According to Thomas Poole, Allan's ideal of the common law owes too much to Hayek's rule of law ideal that demands law organically evolve with no overt human design, akin to Adam Smith's hidden hand in the unfettered market, a position that seems to provide little scope for the administration of policies that might further social justice.[19]

Nonetheless, Allan's debt to Hayek can be overstated. Though eschewing Raz's thin, positivistic account, he sought to be 'more ecumenical' than Hayek, steering clear of his heavy, rightwing political prescriptions, acknowledging that Hayek leaves 'no scope for legitimate political debate and action' and commending a more 'suitably modest definition' of the rule of law.[20] Allan acknowledges the criticisms made of Hayek and Dicey in failing to realise 'the benefits of flexibility that the conferment of discretionary powers on officials may bring'.[21] Indeed there are collectivist themes in Allan's position, eg, his idea that the legality of the state's actions 'depends on its being shown to serve a defensible view of the common good' which he explained meant 'the good a community whose members are accorded equal respect and dignity, according to some rational account of their collective well-being'.[22]

Moreover, Allan stresses the centrality of the ideal of equality in the principles of the rule of law in a range of cases that have preoccupied progressive lawyers. The state tends to act arbitrarily against disadvantaged persons who are the target of discrimination and prejudice, eg in the denial of due process to those accused under the Prevention of Terrorism Act in the UK; or to immigrants or refugees seeking entry into Canada.[23] As Allan eloquently puts the point in the terrorism cases, 'urgent questions about fundamental equality and discrimination are raised, in particular, by the restriction of the liberty of persons who, though suspected of planning serious crime, have not been convicted of any offence'. Allan's natural law approach rings through in his claim that the denial of the opportunity to know the charges one faces means a person is 'made only tenuously subject to the law'; to uphold such a practice means 'abandoning the first principles of legality'.[24]

[18] Allan, *Sovereignty of Law* (n 1) 99.
[19] T Poole, 'Dogmatic Liberalism? TRS Allan and the Common Law Constitution' (2002) 65 *MLR* 467–69.
[20] TRS Allan, *Constitutional Justice: A Liberal Theory of the Rule of Law* (Oxford, Oxford University Press, 2001) 15.
[21] Allan, 'Freedom, Equality, Liberty' (n 9) 160.
[22] Allan, *Constitutional Justice* (n 20) 2.
[23] TRS Allan, 'The Moral Unity of Public Law' (2017) 67 *University of Toronto Law Journal* 13–14.
[24] ibid 12–13.

Such cases remind us that the rule of law cannot serve as ideology unless it does indeed perform a moral function with significant, emancipatory consequences.[25] Ideology is a complex phenomenon. Marx uses the metaphor of a *camera obscura*, where the image projected by the camera is upside down but is otherwise an accurate reflection of the object being photographed.[26] This suggests that ideological phenomena such as the ideal of equality before the law can dissemble or divert attention from inequality only if it has genuine efficacy. Legality can function to mask injustice only if it provides some measure of justice. Engels noted that it would 'offend' the conception of right for law to be mere domination. Intrinsic to the ideological function of the rule of law is its capacity to impose inhibitions on unequal economic power, even if far-reaching inequality persists.[27] As the socialist EP Thompson put it, 'if the law is evidently partial and unjust, it will mask nothing, legitimise nothing, contribute nothing to any class's hegemony.' The procedural virtues of the rule of law render it, as he said with some controversy, 'an unqualified human good' and a 'cultural achievement of universal significance'.[28] On this view, compatible with any legal order, be it radical egalitarian or laissez faire, the rule of law exercises a constraint on any hierarchies that might be afoot, even if it is only a procedural constraint.

In requiring that the law apply with equal weight to all, the rule of law prevents law from being used by the strong to oppress the weak and safeguards, not just liberty, but equality of liberty. This equal protection of liberty may be formal and negative – leaving untouched, for example, the systemic racism experienced by refugees and immigrants whose legal interests are nonetheless safeguarded in proper processes. But there are dangerous consequences in discarding formal protections, whatever their limitations. Formal equality is not a sufficient condition, but it is a necessary one, for substantive justice. The Left-wing jurist Franz Neumann thus contends that the rule of law 'transcends both the economic and political contexts in which it operates'.[29]

4. Moralising and Morality

Allan's view of the moral foundations of legality shares much with Ronald Dworkin's philosophy of law, according to which 'law and morality should be understood as parts of a unified normative domain'.[30] According to David Dyzenhaus, Dworkin understands

[25] See Sypnowich, *Concept of Socialist Law* (n 11) 8–16; C Sypnowich, 'Law and Ideology' in *Stanford Encyclopedia of Philosophy* (2019) plato.stanford.edu/entries/law-ideology/.

[26] K Marx and F Engels, 'The German Ideology' in Tucker (ed), *The Marx-Engels Reader* (n 13) 154.

[27] F Engels, 'Letter to C Schmidt' 27 October 1890, *Marx-Engels Selected Works III* (Moscow, Progress Publishers, 1973) 483–84, 492. See also A Gramsci, *Selections from the Prison Notebooks*, Q Hoare and GN Smitt ed and trans (New York, International Publishers, 1971) 246 and C Sumner, 'Rule of Law and Civil Rights in Contemporary Marxist Theory' (1981) 9 *Kapitalistate* 63.

[28] EP Thompson, *Whigs and Hunters: the Origins of the Black Act* (New York, Pantheon Books, 1975) 263–65.

[29] F Neumann, *The Democratic and Authoritarian State* (London, Free Press, 1964) 170 and F Neumann, 'The governance of the rule of law: an investigation into the relationship between the political theories, the legal system, and the social background in competitive society' (PhD thesis, London School of Economics, 1936).

[30] TRS Allan, 'Law as a Branch of Morality: The Unity of Practice and Principle' (2020) 65 *American Journal of Jurisprudence* 1.

law in terms of a 'constitutional morality', in which legislation must meet the test of the judge's understanding of the moral principles which underlie it. As the arbiter of principle, judges thus have special authority to decide cases insulated from the demands of the political majority.[31] Judicial review is famously likened by Dworkin to a chain novel, where judges interpret the law with reference to the constitutional narrative wrought thus far, but with ambitious moral aims to enable law to 'work itself pure'. Judges must go beyond positivist sources to ask themselves which interpretation 'provides a better justification of the decisions from the point of view of political morality'.[32] Dworkin's approach took issue with the positivist emphasis on law's source in 'facts' – the dictates of statutes, precedents, common law or constitutional materials. Indeed, he contended that his interpretive view provided a theory of law that could take on 'conservative positivists' in American courts who refused to find legal materials to protect minorities.

The test of 'political morality' in cases where the minority's freedom is at stake, for example, is a Millian principle that respects individuals' privacy. For Dworkin, neutrality is key in his understanding of moral individualism: law's 'ambitions for itself' rule out appeals to common understandings of 'what justice and fairness and a decent and valuable life require'.[33] Dworkin's concern that law eschew moralising dictates about how to live found a provocative repudiation in the ideas of the British jurist, Patrick Devlin. In *The Enforcement of Morals*, published in 1961, Devlin responded to the call for the liberalisation of laws on sexual matters with a passionate case for the idea of 'public morality' by which the community could legitimately criminalise 'immoral' private sexual activity such as homosexual sex or prostitution. 'I do not think one can talk sensibly of a public and private morality any more than one can of a public or private highway', Devlin argued. It is the duty of a legal system to enforce morals. What counts as moral or immoral, he contended, could be defined in light of 'the limits of tolerance' of society, indicated, he famously suggested, by the views of the typical 'man on the Clapham omnibus'.[34]

Dworkin's rebuttal to Devlin required some complex moves; after all, in his own legal philosophy he had also insisted that the law be interpreted by means of moral principles, though he repudiated conventional morality for the morality that judges are uniquely qualified to discern and elaborate in a society's legal record. On what basis should Dworkin's political morality win out against Devlin's public morality? 'What is shocking and wrong is not his idea that the community's morality counts, but Devlin's idea of what counts as the community's morality', says Dworkin. As to how to properly determine what should count as the community's morality, Dworkin offers only the mysterious counsel that legislators should 'test' the credentials of a moral consensus, and that if legislators find them wanting, they should seek 'to enforce a distinct, and fundamentally important, part' of the community's morality, 'a consensus more essential to society's existence in the form we know it' than the opinion recommended by Devlin. Interestingly, in his argument with Devlin, Dworkin avoids making a case for

[31] D Dyzenhaus, 'The Rule of Law as the Rule of Liberal Principle' in A Ripstein (ed), *Ronald Dworkin, Contemporary Philosophy in Focus* (Cambridge, Cambridge University Press, 2007) 66–67, 63.
[32] R Dworkin, *Law's Empire* (London, Fontana Press, 1986) 225–32, 400.
[33] R Dworkin, 'Law's Ambitions for Itself' (1985) 71 *Virginia Law Review* 173, 185–87.
[34] P Devlin, *The Enforcement of Morals* (Oxford, Oxford University Press, 1965) 15–16.

the obvious unifying moral claim in his own position about the centrality of individual autonomy, let alone a claim that the proscribed practices are in fact benign. Instead, he proceeds by discrediting Devlin's populist approach, contending that Devlin's public morality relies on prejudice, emotional responses such as disgust or repugnance, rationalisation based on dubious claims of fact, or the parroting of others' views.[35]

However, the idea that law should reflect the community's morality could be couched without such problematic argumentative strategies. And indeed, some liberals have defended, not Devlin's conservative views, but his position that law should engage with questions of personal morality. Gerald Dworkin contends that, contra Devlin's critics, there is 'no principled line' between harmful and immoral conduct; if liberals want to dispute criminalisation of homosexual acts, for example, they will have to argue, not that moral questions are outside the state's purview, but that there is nothing immoral about gay sex.[36]

Allan, though sharing Ronald Dworkin's view of law in many respects, endorses Devlin's project from the standpoint of an anti-positivist, robust understanding of the morality of legality. Allan concedes that Devlin's particular view, that conventional morality, and the feelings of disgust and intolerance that attended it, is a poor basis for an understanding of the morality of law. Nonetheless, he contends that the liberal view, inherited from Mill, that there should be a protected realm of private morals outside the domain of law looks both 'unwelcome and elusive'. Such views follow from the 'futile quest for ethical neutrality' attending, not just the ideas of Mill, but also 'Rawls's narrow conception of public reason'. Allan argues that law is an expression of community, where one identifies one's own wellbeing with that of others. A community should seek to forge an understanding of morality in all its laws, subject to checks and balances provided by the consciences of legislators, judges and jurors. The rule of law, then, is not the deliverance of a merely formal understanding of law that rules out any moral precepts, but rather a procedural framework where restrictions on liberty must be justified 'according to a coherent and consistently defended vision of the common good'.[37] These are fighting words on the liberal political landscape dominated by Dworkin and Rawls.

It is worth considering further the role of ethical neutrality in the ideas of left-wing liberals such as Rawls and Dworkin. Both draw on this idea of citizens' moral obligations to each other, as commended by Allan above, in their insistence that the community properly plays a role in remedying economic disadvantage. Rawls was concerned that citizens enjoy the genuine 'worth' or 'fair value' of equal political liberties,[38] and famously defended a 'difference principle' where inequalities would only be permitted if they benefitted the worse off. Moreover, Rawls also took the view that both liberal democratic socialism and a property-owning democracy were candidates

[35] R Dworkin, 'Lord Devlin and the Enforcement of Morals' (1966) 75 *Yale Law Journal* 986, 1001–02. Dworkin's later work, in contrast, develops a theory of law that involves a general theory of morality based on 'interpretivism' in which a society's morality is understood within a broader, critical account that seeks to identify objective moral truths. See Dworkin, *Law's Empire* (n 32) and R Dworkin, *Justice for Hedgehogs* (Cambridge, Harvard University Press, 2011). Nonetheless, Dworkin continued to resist the idea of a community morality, as I argue below.

[36] G Dworkin, 'Devlin was Right: Law and the Enforcement of Morality' (1990) 40 *William and Mary Law Review* 927, 928.

[37] Allan, *Constitutional Justice* (n 20) 296–300.

[38] J Rawls, *Lectures on the History of Political Philosophy*, S Freeman ed (Cambridge, Harvard University Press, 2007) 148–49.

for realising his principles of justice, articulating this as the effort to find an 'alternative to capitalism'.[39]

Nonetheless, Rawls's political liberalism does not reject Hayek's counsel altogether, retaining a preoccupation with keeping the state at bay, albeit without Hayek's libertarian rationale.[40] The spectre of Devlin-style repressive moral views animating democratic legal orders arguably accounts at least in part for the preoccupation with impartial proceduralism in political philosophy, a preoccupation which grew apace in the years that followed. Rawls advocates 'neutrality of aim', whereby 'the basic institutions and public policies of justice' should be understood as 'neutral with respect to comprehensive doctrines and their associated conceptions of the good'.[41] In order to respect individuals' capacity to choose how to live, the state (and indeed political philosophy itself) should be agnostic about what counts as a good life. Dubbed an 'epistemic withdrawal from the fray',[42] Rawls's position dictates that the scope of the political be constrained by formal procedures: that is, the decision process of the original position, the tenets of public reason, or political liberalism's explicit exclusion of considerations about the good life. Indeed, Rawls's proceduralist ethic became especially prominent in his later work, where the focus on constitutional questions rather than the remedy of economic disadvantage attracted much critical comment.[43]

5. Dworkin's Neutralist Egalitarianism

For all his insistence on the morality of law, Dworkin, like Rawls, took a neutralist view about the political community's role in human wellbeing. It is well known that Dworkin's corpus includes not just his philosophy of law, but an influential, neutralist theory of distributive justice: equality of resources. What is to be made equal, Dworkin argues, are the goods or resources possessed by individuals, apportioned along the lines of an auction, supplemented by an insurance scheme that models social welfare benefits. Dworkin commended the resources approach for respecting individuals' rights to choose how to live, going so far as to say that there is an egalitarian principle at the heart of the mechanism of the market, suitably understood, whereby each person, and their choices, count for as much as any other, and the state cannot betray any preferential consideration for some plans of life over others.[44] The 'beer-drinking, television-watching' citizen's plan of life should not count any less than the plans of life of the intellectual or the aesthete. 'A liberal theory of equality rules out … appeal to the inherent value of one theory of what is good in life'.[45]

[39] J Rawls, *Justice as Fairness: A Restatement*, EI Kelly ed (Cambridge, Belknap Press, 2001) 135–36.

[40] This discussion draws on Sypnowich, 'Law and Ideology' (n 25).

[41] Rawls, *Justice as Fairness* (n 39) 153 fn 27.

[42] J Raz, *Ethics in the Public Domain* (Oxford, Clarendon, 1994) 46.

[43] See B Barry, 'John Rawls and the Search for Stability' (1995) 105 *Ethics* 874; SM Okin, Book Review of *Political Liberalism* by John Rawls' (1993) 87 *American Political Science Review* 1010; B Williams, 'A fair State', *London Review of Books* (13 May 1993).

[44] R Dworkin, 'Liberalism' in S Hampshire (ed), *Public and Private Morality* (Cambridge, Cambridge University Press, 1978) 136.

[45] ibid.

Rawls's political liberal view stipulated that a theory of justice should be detached from any comprehensive ethical view about the good life. Dworkin, however, took his position to be 'comprehensive' rather than political, committed to a particular liberal ethical view, which stresses the importance of the individual choosing how to live, independent of any political influence.[46] The endorsement of one's ethical ideas are essential for one's life to be a success, and coercion to enable a better life, he argues, is self-defeating. The upshot, however, is Rawlsian: politics should refrain from engaging in questions about the good life.

True, Rawls put much store by 'the good' of a well-ordered political society[47] and admitted that views about valuable ways of living might play a role in legislative decisions about 'suitably circumscribed questions' such as the protection of wildlife habitat.[48] However, he retained a traditional view of perfectionism as in principle inegalitarian, involving the idea that 'some people have special claims because their greater gifts enable them to engage in the higher activities that realise perfectionist values'.[49] Dworkin too, was prepared to discuss the nature of living well, even if he contended the state should take no part in promoting it, advocating in his later writings what he called the 'challenge model,' where living well is akin to an inherently valuable skilful performance bound up with being self-determining, developing one's capacities and talents and finding self-mastery.[50] Like Rawls, when confronting sources of the good that are vulnerable or threatened, such as natural wilderness areas or historical artefacts, he also agreed the state should offer support, not because these are sources of valuable options, but for the sake of neutrality, so that these pursuits remain options for future individuals. Funding for the arts, though apparently at odds with liberal neutrality, is permitted to provide 'complex and diverse' cultural forms. Thus, society should, as 'trustees for the future complexity of our own culture,' protect the 'structure of our intellectual culture' rather than 'particular aesthetic events'.[51]

Nonetheless, in all his writing Dworkin retained a squeamishness about the political community promoting valuable ways of life, a squeamishness which he repeatedly expounded. 'Paternalism is misguided because it wrongly treats convictions as limitations or handicaps'. Genuine endorsement, we are cautioned, cannot be the product of being hypnotised, brainwashed, or frightened. The agent's endorsement is not 'the result of another person's thoughts being piped into his brain'. Individuals cannot use the law to 'forbid anyone to lead the life he wants, or punish him for doing so,' out of a belief that a person's ethical convictions are 'profoundly wrong'.[52] Dworkin encourages

[46] R Dworkin, *Sovereign Virtue: The Theory and Practice of Equality* (Cambridge, Harvard University Press, 2000) 5.

[47] Rawls, *Justice as Fairness* (n 39) 198–99.

[48] ibid 152 fn 26.

[49] ibid 152.

[50] Dworkin, *Sovereign Virtue* (n 46) 253–76.

[51] R Dworkin, *A Matter of Principle* (Cambridge, Harvard University Press, 1985) 195, 232. See also R Dworkin, *Life's Dominion: An Argument about Abortion, Euthanasia, and Individual Freedom* (New York, Alfred A Knopf, 199) 154. H Brighouse discusses the obstacle posed by 'the neutrality constraint' in H Brighouse, 'Neutrality, Publicity and State Funding of the Arts' (1995) 24 *Philosophy and Public Affairs* 35, 63. J Quong insists that demand should dictate the provision of cultural goods, which should be paid for 'at the point of consumption': J Quong, *Liberalism Without Perfection* (Oxford, Oxford University Press, 2010) 90–91.

[52] Dworkin, *Sovereign Virtue* (n 46) 274, 283, 269.

individuals who possess 'strong convictions' instead to 'campaign for the good as they see it.' In his final work, *Justice for Hedgehogs*, Dworkin again warns against 'imposing on everyone its collective judgement of what lives are good and how to live well'; to do so would 'annihilate personal responsibility' since it would 'aim to insure that people are equal in the designated welfare commodity'. An appropriate 'test of equality' should be 'as shorn of assumptions about welfare or well-being as possible', focussing on people's 'impersonal resources', that is 'wealth, measured as abstractly as possible'.[53]

Here it's worth returning to Allan, who found Dworkin's philosophy of law too much at the mercy of statutory practices. Dworkin puts faith in Herculean judges to reason in light of moral principle when adjudicating cases, but admits of, as Allan puts it, the possibility of 'gravely unjust' law, which judges are bound to uphold.[54] For Allan, in contrast, an interpretive theory must be 'moral through and through', so that 'grave breaches of justice should be accounted departures from legality – illegitimate acts or threats of coercion that violate legal and constitutional principle'. On Allan's view, 'common law reasoning means that nothing is placed beyond challenge – all aspects of legal and constitutional doctrine have only provisional authority'. The interpretation and application of law must draw on a community's legal practices, but to 'vindicate justice'. Founded on 'the fundamental assumption' of 'the equal dignity of all members of the community' a legal system will have 'in-built defenses against iniquity'.[55] There is 'no impartial basis for distinguishing principle from prejudice'; judge and legislator will need to make their 'own judgement of the moral and intellectual merits' of rival views in public debate.[56] For Allan, the construction, application and interpretation of law does not admit of 'neutral' constraints.

6. Human Flourishing and Legality

Dworkin should hardly be commended for the insight that it is wrong to brainwash or punish people if we disapprove of their pursuits. Such truisms are hard to avoid, perhaps, in a society where ideas of the good life include the right to bear arms, not being 'unAmerican', denying women bodily autonomy, bible-thumping and repressive notions of salvation. Certainly, Dworkin is understandably exercised by the possibility of bigoted moral views being enforced on others; the example he uses most often is an antipathy to homosexuality. American liberals like Dworkin are caught, perhaps, in what might be called a Hugh Hefner model of progressivism: a 1960s view that reduced the quest for a moral consensus to Victorian repression.

Yet equality requires mechanisms for enriching the public domain, not to coerce sexual minorities into living by the majority's code, but to foster a cultural environment that enables a range of worthwhile choices. Inequality is, after all, relevantly manifest in the kinds of lives people are acculturated to pursue. We shouldn't snub the

[53] Dworkin, *Justice for Hedgehogs* (n 35) 355–56.
[54] Allan, 'Law as a Branch of Morality' (n 30) 2.
[55] ibid 4–8.
[56] Allan, *Constitutional Justice* (n 20) 299.

beer-drinking, television-watching citizen, and certainly we shouldn't force such citizens to give up their pleasures. But we might think about how society can enable other kinds of pleasures that would allow a diversity of ways of living well.

The neutralist position seems to suggest that our ways of life are either immune to influence or putty in the hands of others, as though human agency means that one is only freely choosing if untouched by social influences. Of course, life goes better, as Will Kymlicka puts it, if one is 'leading it from the inside, according to my beliefs about value'.[57] One cannot 'make people's lives better against their own convictions'.[58] A life can only be lived from the 'inside,' but who one is 'on the inside' is affected by her situation on the outside, the influence of a social milieu. Thus, the debate about choice must take account of this modest 'social thesis'.[59] The idea of responsiveness to reasons, at the heart of the ideal of autonomy so central to Dworkin's view, means that grounds for choice lie beyond the self; the choosing self is not pure will, but a being who considers how to act by reflecting on external sources of information. The values of friends, parents and those with authority or influence, formative experiences in one's life, superficial factors such as the symbolic value of a pursuit, all contribute to choices about how to live.[60]

In making the case for equality of resources, Dworkin famously argued against catering to those whose welfare involved 'expensive tastes', portraying such tastes as the frivolous pursuits of the privileged few; his example of a penchant for plover's eggs is revealing.[61] But what of tastes for green spaces, a culture of civility, historic buildings, access to the arts? These goods may be costly, but they merit support, not so the elite might enjoy them, but so that they may be accessible to all. They are constituents of the public good, a rich and diverse cultural environment that enables a plurality of genuinely valuable choices. Dyzenhaus notes how Dworkin's legal philosophy focuses on courts, excluding administrative agencies from the domain of legal principle.[62] Dworkin's political philosophy reflects this myopia, since it is those agencies that play a crucial role in normatively rich dimensions of egalitarian social policy.

Dworkin's argument suggests the individual is a consumer in an idealised marketplace, making unfettered choices in full knowledge of their effects. There is no mention of the deleterious effect that real markets have on human pursuits, even measured on a simple scale of expressions of satisfaction,[63] where the loftiest goods are victims of

[57] W Kymlicka, *Contemporary Political Philosophy* (Oxford, Oxford University Press, 2002) 216.

[58] R Dworkin, 'Foundations of Liberal Equality' in GB Peterson (ed), *Tanner Lectures on Human Values XI* (Salt Lake City, University of Utah Press, 1990) 118.

[59] See C Taylor, 'Atomism' in A Kontos (ed), *Essays in Honour of C.B. Macpherson: Powers, Possessions and Freedoms* (Toronto, University of Toronto Press, 1979).

[60] In this we must, as David Bakhurst puts it, 'wean ourselves off the idea that the self is something purely inner and psychological': D Bakhurst, *The Formation of Reason* (Oxford, Wiley-Blackwell, 2001) 64. See also D Bakhurst and C Sypnowich (eds), *The Social Self* (London, Sage Publications, 1995).

[61] Dworkin, *Sovereign Virtue* (n 46) 49–52.

[62] Dyzenhaus, 'Rule of Law' (n 31) 71.

[63] This is borne out by some interesting recent work in economics: A Offer, *The Challenge of Affluence: Self-Control and Wellbeing in the United States and Britain Since 1950* (Oxford, Oxford University Press 2006); PA Victor, *Managing Without Growth: Slower by Design, Not Disaster* (Cheltenham, Edward Elgar, 2008); R Frank, *Luxury Fever: Money and Happiness in an Era of Excess* (Princeton, Princeton University Press, 1999). See also 'happiness studies' such as D Gilbert, *Stumbling on Happiness* (New York, Knopf, 2007); D Nettle, *Happiness: the Science Behind Your Smile* (Oxford, Oxford University Press, 2006); and R Layard, *Happiness: Lessons from a New Science* (London, Penguin, 2005).

market failure, economies of scale, the exploitation of resources, the commodification of culture. In market societies, advertising, product differentiation, brand promotions, packaging or 'imaging' mitigate against conscious, considered choices, what the anti-perfectionist liberal Jonathan Quong calls 'the paternalizee's capacity to effectively advance his or her own interests'.[64] In his theory of equality, Dworkin proposes a robust social insurance distributive system that corrects for the disadvantage that accrues from the capitalist economy; moreover, in his final writings he emphasised the importance of state regulation of the economy to address abuses of power and externalities.[65] Nonetheless, he commends the market as a mechanism for the expression of preferences, free of state interference.[66] The market is thought to support the neutralism of the liberal state because its exchanges are conducted according to the supposedly contentless measure of profitability, but this in fact makes for significant consequences for the kinds of values one can pursue. Moreover, market actors who influence choices are not typically held to public account or democratic control. Thus, it is particularly damning of neutralist positions that they continue to evoke the 'marketplace of ideas' in making their case. The political community is denied a role in supporting worthwhile choices, but there is no attention paid to the immense private and unaccountable forces shaping people's preferences. Devlin's position against pornography, for all his prudishness and sexism, contained a truth about how values may be corrupted.

Back in 1966, Judith Shklar wrote that legalism was an 'intrusive ideology' producing an 'uncompromising policy of judicialization', which takes the important proceduralist ideal about the independence of the judiciary and gives it unlimited warrant. The impact was to denude both social theory and governmental authority of important moral considerations.[67] Indeed, the increasing domination of 'neutralist' approaches to distributive justice in liberal political philosophy seems a symptom of the idea that state power be constrained by formal rules. The highly valuable rule of law ideal, designed to ensure democracies rule accountably, became a straight jacket for normative theorising about politics.

Allan's defence of Devlin's view that the community should engage with questions of how people live is a salutary, and perhaps surprising, source of sustenance to a more imaginative egalitarian view. I have argued elsewhere that a philosophy of 'egalitarian perfectionism', which focuses on human flourishing as the metric for equality, is compatible with a robust understanding of the rule of law. But this is only possible if the concern for impartiality in the law is not permitted to have imperialistic designs on all political questions, so that the community forfeits its responsibility to seek to foster equal human wellbeing.[68] The impressive contribution of egalitarian liberals like Dworkin to legal and political philosophy has performed a disservice in the insistence that the community should refrain from promoting the good.

[64] Quong, *Liberalism Without Perfection* (n 51) 83.

[65] Dworkin, *Justice for Hedgehogs* (n 35) 357.

[66] Dworkin, *Sovereign Virtue* (n 46) 65–119.

[67] J Shklar, 'In Defense of Legalism' (1966) 19 *Journal of Legal Education* 56.

[68] See C Sypnowich, *Equality Renewed: Justice, Flourishing and the Egalitarian Ideal* (London, Routledge, 2017) 85–87; see also C Sypnowich 'The Rule of Law and the Social Ethos' in M Sevel (ed), *Handbook on the Rule of Law* (London, Routledge, 2024).

Dworkin's philosophy displays the pitfalls of what I call the juridicalisation of political philosophy, where legalistic notions of neutrality prevent an engagement with questions of inequalities in human wellbeing. This should be distinguished from the critique of the 'judicialisation' of politics. The juridical refers to judicial proceedings and the administration of law, whereas the judicial means appropriate to a law court or judge. A subtle difference, perhaps, but by juridicalising political philosophy I mean reducing normative political questions to the terms of an impartial legal process, barring questions of substantive value. This does not mean such proceedings in the domain of law are unimportant, nor does it oppose empowering the judiciary to decide important moral questions.

Critics of the judicialisation of politics worry about the conduct of courts rather than the theory of politics, and their complaint is that matters of policy are being decided through the process of judicial review, where courts find legislation invalid in light of constitutional considerations. This can mean a matter of policy is found improper on procedural grounds, but the greater grievance is often that courts are engaging in weighty moral questions – eg, whether women have a constitutional right to abortion – questions, it is argued, better left to the people to decide through their elected representatives. The question of whether unelected judges are usurping the role of democratic legislatures has spawned a great deal of debate which I won't enter into here, but Allan's case for understanding how the rule of law enables accountability to ordinary citizens is a useful riposte to often simplistic claims regarding courts and democracy.

7. Conclusion

It is telling how both Right and Left have invoked the rule of law in the fallout of the US Supreme Court's striking down of *Roe v Wade*. A conservative opined that the decision, acting against 'administrative overreach', is a 'victory for the rule of law'.[69] A progressive, on the other hand, proposed the decision was the action of a 'post-legal' Supreme Court, asking, 'what happens if the Court rejects the rule of law?'[70] It will be apparent that the author of this chapter favours the latter interpretation. The rule of law should not be weaponised by the Right to prevent courts from protecting the rights of vulnerable persons, be they refugees, immigrants, or pregnant women.

Contra Hayek, I contend the rule of law would fare well in a radical egalitarian society, since equality before the law would be furthered by equal access to adequate legal representation, or a judiciary that is not the prerogative of a wealthy elite.[71] Yet vulnerable persons can also find themselves in need of legality when it comes to the potentially arbitrary processes of the progressive administrative state; in this, Hayek was not entirely misguided, as Allan recognises. The richness of Allan's legal theory lies

[69] J McClaughry 'A Victory for the Rule of Law' *Vermont Biz* (28 July 2022) vermontbiz.com/news/2022/july/28/mcclaughry-victory-rule-law.

[70] I Millhiser, 'The post-legal Supreme Court' *Vox* (9 July 2022) www.vox.com/23180634/supreme-court-rule-of-law-abortion-voting-rights-guns-epa.

[71] See Sypnowich, *Concept of Socialist Law* (n 11) 74–78.

in its nuanced grasp of these issues. First, he appreciates the importance of constraining the state's interference with individual liberty, particularly when it comes to fundamental freedoms such as guarantees of fair judicial process, rights to mobility, expression and conscience. Yet Allan also emphasised the law's role as an ethical domain which promotes the common good and enables all people to live well, with equal dignity. The pursuit of equal human flourishing through social policy, which was the ideal that underlay the origins of the welfare state, certainly needs legality to keep it in check. The rule of law is crucial for a society guided by the institutions and culture of a robust egalitarianism to ensure that proper processes structure the pursuit of equal human wellbeing. Yet appreciating the value of procedural justice should not mean forfeiting the ideal of a political community that provides the material resources, but also the cultural context, to ensure people are fully equal before the law.

10

The Essence of Rights and the Limits of Proportionality

JACOB WEINRIB*

> Where the constitution permits the restriction of a fundamental right by law, the law must leave the fundamental right in its essence untouched.[1]

1. The Bifurcated Model

Constitutional rights have two structural features, scope and strength. The scope of a right consists in the particular protections that fall within its reach. The *strength* of a right consists in its power to withstand opposing considerations. My aim in this chapter is to formulate an account of the strength of constitutional rights.

In debates about the strength of rights, constitutional theory and practice have become disconnected. As a matter of constitutional practice, in recent decades a *bifurcated model* of the strength of constitutional rights has assumed increasing prominence. The model divides the scope of a right into a core (or an essence) and a periphery.[2] The core possesses absolute strength and is therefore not susceptible to limitations. In contrast, the periphery is subject to limitations that satisfy the doctrine of proportionality.[3] In some jurisdictions, these commitments appear explicitly in

* I am grateful to Oliver Flis for exceptional research assistance and to Geneviève Cartier, Hasan Dindjer, George Letsas, Evan Fox-Decent, Joanna Langille, Mark Walters, Lorraine Weinrib, and Ernest J Weinrib for comments. This project was supported by a SSHRC IDG grant.

[1] W Jellinek, 'Grundrechte und Gesetzesvorbehalt' (1946) 1 *Deutsche Rechts-Zeitschrift* 4, 6.

[2] In a pathbreaking article on the essence of rights, Esin Örücü outlines the structure in terms of a core, circumjacence, and an outer edge, before adding that the core is 'that part of a right which is essential to its definition'. See E Örücü, 'The Core of Rights and Freedoms: The Limits of Limits' in T Campbell (ed), *Human Rights: From Rhetoric to Reality* (New York, Blackwell, 1986) 37, 38. I accept this structure, but to avoid cumbersome and archaic formulations, I will simply refer to the core (or essence) and the periphery that lies beyond it.

[3] According to a prominent formulation of the doctrine, when government seeks to justify the limitation of a constitutional right, it must demonstrate that the limitation pursues an appropriate objective, that it employs means that are rationally connected to this objective and minimally impairing of the right, and, finally, that the extent to which the objective is furthered justifies the extent of the right's restriction.

constitutional texts[4] and human rights instruments.[5] In others, these commitments emerge through interpretation.[6] This bifurcated model of the strength of rights is presented in Figure 1.

Figure 1 The Bifurcated Model

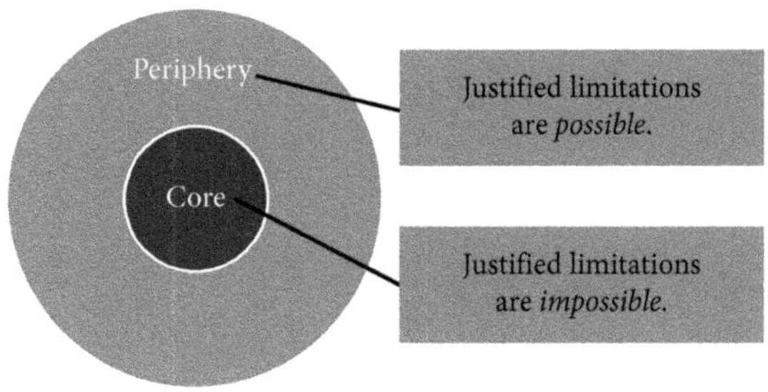

Each of the leading models of constitutional rights rejects the bifurcated model. What I will call the *absolutist* model conceives of rights as unlimited in strength but limited in scope.[7] When the scope of an absolute right is appropriately specified, it binds without exception. Accordingly, any restriction to any absolute right is necessarily unjustified. In this way, absolute rights maintain a categorical distinction between permissible and impermissible state actions and omissions. What I will call

[4] See eg the constitutions of the Czech Republic at art 4(4); Estonia at art 11; Germany at art 19(2) [Grundgesetz]; Hungary at art I(3); Namibia at art 22(a); Poland at art 31(3); Portugal at art 18(3); Romania at art 53(2); Spain at art 53(1); Switzerland at art 36; and Turkey at art 13.

[5] See, eg UN Commission on Human Rights, The Siracusa Principles on the Limitation and Derogation Provisions in the International Covenant on Civil and Political Rights, 28 September 1984, E/CN.4/1985/4 (art I(A)(2)); Charter of Fundamental Rights of the European Union, Oct 26, 2012, 2012 OJ (C 326), art 52(1).

[6] The European Convention on Human Rights does not contain a provision explicitly protecting the essence of the rights that it sets out, but such a restriction has emerged in its case law. For discussion, see M Brkan, 'The Concept of Essence of Fundamental Rights in the EU Legal Order: Peeling the Onion to its Core' (2018) 14 *European Constitutional Law Review* 332, 333–34; K Lenaerts, 'Limits on Limitations: The Essence of Fundamental Rights in the EU' (2019) 20 *German Law Journal* 779, 780; T Ojanen, 'Making the Essence of Fundamental Rights Real: The Court of Justice of the European Union Clarifies the Structure of Fundamental Rights under the Charter' (2016) 12 *European Constitutional Law Review* 318, 323. Following the enactment of the *Canadian Charter of Rights and Freedoms*, the Supreme Court of Canada expressed initial support for the bifurcated model. See *A.G. (Que.) v Quebec Protestant School Boards*, [1984] 2 SCR 66, 86: 'An Act of Parliament or of a legislature which, for example, purported to impose the beliefs of a State religion would be in direct conflict with s. 2(a) of the *Charter*, which guarantees freedom of conscience and religion, and would have to be ruled of no force or effect without the necessity of even considering whether such legislation could be legitimised by s. 1'. For discussion, see LE Weinrib, 'The Supreme Court and Section One of the Charter' (1988) 10 *Supreme Court Law Review* 469, 479–83. More recently, the Court has adopted the position that even where the essence of the right is breached, justification remains possible. See, eg *Charkaoui v Canada (Citizenship and Immigration)*, 2007 SCC 9, [2007] 1 SCR 350 at para 64, McLachlin CJ (describing the principle that a 'person whose liberty is in jeopardy must know the case to meet' as having 'not merely been limited' but 'effectively gutted') and *Sauvé v Canada (Chief Electoral Officer)*, 2002 SCC 68, [2002] 3 SCR 519 at para 46, McLachlin CJ (describing the deprivation of the right of prisoners to vote as 'unmodulated'). In each of these cases, the court held that justification failed, not that justification was precluded.

[7] The absolutist camp includes Hugo Black, Russell Brown, Suzanne Côté, John Finnis, Laurent B Frantz, Jürgen Habermas, George Letsas, Bradley W Miller, John Oberdiek, Neomi Rao, Stavros Tsakyrakis, Francisco J Urbina, Grégoire Webber, Paul Yowell, and the later works of Ronald Dworkin. The label *absolutism* captures this camp's conception of the strength of rights, while the alternative label *specificationism* captures this camp's narrow conception of scope.

the *relativist* model reverses this structure.[8] Relative rights are unlimited in scope but limited in strength. Persons have a relative right to engage in any conceivable form of conduct. Because this right inevitably conflicts with other rights and interests, this right is subject to justified limitations, as determined by the doctrine of proportionality. Each of these models offers a non-bifurcated account of the strength of rights: the entire scope of an absolute right is immune from incursion; the entire scope of a relative right might be balanced away.

These non-bifurcated models have received extensive exploration by legal, political, and constitutional theorists. In contrast, the bifurcated model has been the preserve of constitutional lawyers and judges elaborating legal doctrine, disconnected from an explicit overarching theoretical framework. Trevor Allan's innovative and illuminating engagements in the world of constitutional theory form an important exception to this trend.

In discussing the strength of rights, Allan distances himself from both the absolutist and relativist models. On the one hand, he rejects the absolutist tradition by claiming that the subjection of rights to proportional limits is integral to constitutional justice:

> Because justice consists in the correct regulation of affairs or resolution of disputes, according to the moral principles applicable, it invokes the notion of proportionality: there must be an appropriate weighting of relevant principles to reflect their proper balance in all the circumstances. Principles of justice are always dependent on context in the sense that what they permit or require must be determined by analysis of all the relevant facts … Restrictions of individual rights must be *proportionate* to the aims and benefits envisaged.[9]

On the other, Allan rejects the relativist model by maintaining that each right has an 'irreducible core' that may never be breached regardless of the benefits to be attained or the burdens to be avoided.[10] Referring to the right to procedural fairness, he explains that a limitation of a right's periphery might be justified or unjustified, but a limitation of a right's core is unjustifiable:

> [P]owerful considerations of public interest may properly qualify the procedural rights that would otherwise apply: reasons of national security, in particular, may justify restrictions on the disclosure of evidence or relevant sources. But such limitations or qualifications must not be so extensive as wholly to undermine procedural rights, making a trial or hearing unfair … Like other fundamental rights, procedural fairness has a conceptual core that cannot properly be ignored or overridden.[11]

[8] The relativist camp includes Robert Alexy, Aharon Barak, David Beatty, Moshe Cohen-Eliya, Jamal Greene, Matthias Klatt, Mattias Kumm, Moritz Meister, Kai Möller, Jud Mathews, Iddo Porat, Julian Rivers, Alec Stone Sweet, Lorenzo Zucca, and the early works of Ronald Dworkin. The label *relativism* captures this camp's conception of the strength of rights, while the alternative label *inflationism* captures this camp's broad conception of scope.

[9] TRS Allan, 'Democracy, Legality, and Proportionality' in G Huscroft, BW Miller and G Webber (eds), *Proportionality and the Rule of Law: Rights, Justification, Reasoning* (Cambridge, Cambridge University Press, 2014) 205, 205, 209. See also TRS Allan, *The Sovereignty of Law: Freedom, Constitution, and Common Law* (Oxford, Oxford University Press, 2013) 185.

[10] Allan, 'Democracy, Legality, and Proportionality' (n 9) 222.

[11] ibid 220, 222. For a parallel passage, see Allan, *Sovereignty of Law* (n 9) 132: '[L]egislation … may *regulate* the transmission of party election broadcasts or the time and place of public meetings, it cannot *abrogate* the freedom of political speech' (emphasis added).

For Allan, the limitations to which procedural fairness and other rights are subject must cease wherever the core of the right begins. As he puts the point: 'No matter how important the countervailing interests,' the essence of rights 'must be preserved'.[12]

Allan's pioneering account of the strength of rights joins what the leading theories sever: a commitment to the absolute strength of rights *and* to the idea of justified limitations, as determined through doctrine of proportionality. Within Allan's bifurcated account, these ideas can be combined because each takes a different object. The idea that rights possess absolute strength applies solely to the core of a right, while the idea that rights are subject to proportional limits applies solely to the periphery.

In a recent article, Koen Lenaerts, the President of the Court of Justice of the European Union (CJEU), makes the following methodological remark about the bifurcated model:

> [T]he case law of the CJEU reflects the fact that that court will first examine whether the measure in question respects the essence of the fundamental rights at stake and will only carry out a proportionality assessment if the answer to that first question is in the affirmative. The application of that method of analysis is not simply empty formalism, but rather seeks to emphasise the point that the essence of a fundamental right is absolute and not subject to balancing.[13]

In this passage, Lenaerts identifies two methodological pillars on which the bifurcated model rests. The first is that one can determine whether a measure has respected the essence of a right without engaging in balancing. The second is that when a measure breaches the essence of a right, proportionality justification is precluded. Each pillar has attracted extensive criticism.

The claim that the bifurcated model offers a method of identifying the essence of a right without engaging in balancing is attacked on both doctrinal and theoretical grounds.[14] As a doctrinal matter, critics of the bifurcated model observe that the case law surrounding the essence of rights is 'rife with ambiguities and inconsistencies'[15] and fails to disclose 'a consistent methodology'.[16] As a theoretical matter, critics claim that the bifurcated model is doomed from the outset: 'The problem with the "very essence" is that it is almost impossible to define usefully without reference to competing public interests' that might override the right in a particular setting.[17] But if the essence cannot be determined without considering the reasons that oppose constitutional protection in a given context, then the 'final untouchable areas of a right' will depend upon the

[12] Allan, *Sovereignty of Law* (n 9) 188.

[13] Lenaerts, 'Limits on Limitations' (n 6) 787–88, 793.

[14] A Barak, *Proportionality: Constitutional Rights and their Limitation* (Cambridge, Cambridge University Press, 2012) 498; Brkan, 'The Concept of Essence of Fundamental Rights' (n 6) 349; J Van Bernstorff, 'Proportionality Without Balancing' in L Lazarus, C McCrudden and N Bowles (eds), *Reasoning Rights: Comparative Judicial Engagement* (Oxford, Hart Publishing, 2016) 63, 83; O Scarcello, 'Preserving the "Essence" of Fundamental Rights under Article 52(1) of the Charter: A Sisyphean Task?' (2020) 16 *European Constitutional Law Review* 647, 654.

[15] S Van Drooghenbroeck and C Rizcallah, 'The ECHR and the Essence of Fundamental Rights: Searching for Sugar in Hot Milk?' (2019) 20 *German Law Journal* 904, 910.

[16] M Dawson, O Lynskey and E Muir, 'What is the Added Value of the Concept of the "Essence" of EU Fundamental Rights?' (2019) 20 *German Law Journal* 763, 771.

[17] J Rivers, 'Proportionality and Variable Intensity of Review' (2006) 65 *CLJ* 174, 186–87; R Alexy, *A Theory of Constitutional Rights* (Oxford, Oxford University Press, 2002) 195.

balance of reasons that support and oppose constitutional protection.[18] With this, critics conclude that the bifurcated model short-circuits by relying on balancing, the very method that the model repudiates.

The second methodological challenge concerns the status of the doctrine of proportionality within the bifurcated model. As we have seen, the bifurcated model claims that when the essence of a right is breached, justification is impossible and the doctrine of proportionality is inapplicable. Relativist critics of the bifurcated model regard these claims as baseless. Even when a right is restricted in its entirety, it remains possible that the breach will be justified because the reasons that oppose the right might outweigh the reasons that support it. Accordingly, critics claim that where a right is restricted, the restriction might be *justified* or *unjustified* depending on the interplay of the reasons apposite to that context. But there is no basis, critics conclude, for the bifurcated model's claim that the restriction of the essence of any right is *unjustifiable* as such.[19]

My overarching aim in this chapter is to continue Allan's project of elaborating the bifurcated model by confronting the methodical challenges that surround it. If one proceeds on the assumption that a general balancing of interests represents the exclusive method of justifying claims about rights, then these methodological challenges will seem irresolvable. However, this assumption need not be accepted. Our constitutional practices present doctrines concerning the scope and strength of rights that both form an alternative to a general balancing of interests and illuminate the inner workings of the bifurcated model. These doctrines explain how the methodological challenges surrounding the bifurcated model can be overcome.

I proceed as follows. Section 2 explores the diverging structures of the non-bifurcated models of rights and shows that each converges on the idea that balancing is the method of identifying the essence of rights. Section 3 shows how purposive interpretation offers resources for identifying the essence of rights without engaging in balancing. Section 4 explains why justification is impossible when the essence of a right is breached, by articulating the distinctive conception of proportionality on which the bifurcated model relies. Section 5 concludes that the key to elucidating the bifurcated model lies in identifying and elaborating the distinctive doctrines that animate it.

2. The Non-Bifurcated Models

Debates between the absolutist and relativist models of rights are often staged as though relativists support and absolutists oppose the idea that rights hang in the balance. This is not the case. Here, I contrast the structure of each model, locate their fundamental dispute, and explain why both models are ultimately committed to the idea that every judgment about what constitutional rights demand ultimately depends on balancing.

[18] M Klatt and M Meister, *The Constitutional Structure of Proportionality* (Oxford, Oxford University Press, 2012) 68.

[19] For versions of this objection, see, eg ibid 67–8; Alexy, *A Theory of Constitutional Rights* (n 17) 192–6; Rivers, 'Proportionality and Variable Intensity of Review' (n 17) 186–7.

The absolutist and relativist models mirror the other's structure. Absolute rights are indefeasible in strength but narrow in scope, while relative rights are boundless in scope but defeasible in strength. Table 1 contrasts the structure of these models.

Table 1 Models of Constitutional Rights

	Absolute Rights	**Relative Rights**
Scope	Limited	Unlimited
Strength	Unlimited	Limited

Each of these models draws our attention to different justificatory projects.

From the standpoint of the relativist model, what stands in need of justification are claims about the strength of rights rather than their scope. Since the eighteenth century, relativists have claimed that, as a matter of the scope of rights, persons have a 'right to everything indiscriminately'.[20] Contemporary proponents of rights relativism embrace the radical ramifications of this idea by claiming that wherever a constitution protects liberty or autonomy, persons possess a prima facie right to engage in any conceivable form of conduct, including theft and even murder.[21] This claim about the scope of rights has ramifications for their strength: 'rights do not have a special importance, and precisely because of the lack of special importance they do not have special normative force'.[22] Because relative rights encompass conduct that is virtuous, vacuous, and even vicious, such rights enjoy no necessary primacy over opposing claims.[23] From this standpoint, the justificatory task that rights present involves determining their strength, that is, their capacity to withstand whatever reasons oppose constitutional protection in a given context.

In contrast, the absolutist model insists that if we are to retain the simple idea that constitutional rights distinguish between permissible and prohibited conduct, then the relativist understanding of rights must be inverted. Constitutional rights must be regarded not as *prima facie* claims that are forfeited whenever the opposing reasons are sufficiently weighty, but as categorical claims. Once rights are conceived of as prevailing over any opposing consideration, the protections that rights afford must be confined to specific claims of overriding importance.[24] Absolute rights are 'specific high-priority requirements, and thus though their force is great, their scope is narrow'.[25]

What divides the leading models of constitutional rights is the question of what it is about rights that stands in need of moral justification. Absolutists insist that it is their

[20] D Edelstein, *On the Spirit of Rights* (Chicago, University of Chicago Press, 2018) 75 (quoting F Quesnay, an 18th century French physiocrat who developed the relativist conception of rights).

[21] Barak, *Proportionality* (n 14) 42; Alexy, *A Theory of Constitutional Rights* (n 17) 214–15; K Möller, 'Proportionality and Rights Inflation' in Huscroft, Miller and Webber, *Proportionality and the Rule of Law* (n 9) 165.

[22] Möller, 'Proportionality and Rights Inflation' (n 21) 165–66.

[23] M Kumm, 'Political Liberalism and the Structure of Rights: On the Place and Limits of Proportionality Requirement' in G Pavlakos (ed), *Law, Rights, and Discourse: The Legal Philosophy of Robert Alexy* (Oxford, Hart Publishing, 2007) 131, 139; Möller, 'Proportionality and Rights Inflation' (n 21) 156.

[24] R Dworkin, *Taking Rights Seriously* (Cambridge, Harvard University Press, 1977) 261: 'The more limited the range of a principle, the more plausibly it may be said to be absolute'.

[25] FJ Urbina, *A Critique of Balancing and Proportionality* (Cambridge, Cambridge University Press, 2017) 221.

scope, while relativists maintain that it is their strength. However, when it comes to the method of identifying what rights demand, each of these models endorses balancing.

Absolutists often attack their relativist counterparts for being unable to accommodate the idea that rights have a 'core content that cannot be compromised under any circumstances'.[26] Once constitutional rights are subject to balancing, '[a]nything which the Constitution says *cannot* be done *can* be done if … the interests thereby served outweighed those which were sacrificed'.[27] Because relative rights occupy a constitutional world devoid of categorical constraints, even the right not to be tortured or enslaved may, in principle, be set aside in contexts where the benefits obtained (or the burdens avoided) are sufficiently weighty. Thus, absolutists conclude that wherever the relative model prevails, 'everything, even those aspects of our life most closely associated with our status as free and equal, is, in principle, up for grabs'.[28]

Defenders of relative rights respond to this charge in two ways. The first seeks to accommodate the objection by stipulating that certain constitutional rights – for example, those that protect persons from torture and enslavement – are exempt from balancing.[29] I will set this response aside as it stands in tension with relativism's organising idea: 'Constitutional judgments are only correct if they correspond to the outcome of an appropriate balancing of principles'.[30] The second response follows this idea to its conclusion: 'There is no such thing as an absolute principle'.[31] From this standpoint, even the prohibition of torture 'is only an apparently categorical claim,' true in most circumstances but susceptible to being 'outweighed'.[32]

When proponents of rights relativism encounter constitutional provisions that proclaim that the core or the essential content of a constitutional right may not be restricted, they maintain that balancing is the method of identifying the essence of a right. Consider, for example, article 19(2) of Germany's Basic Law, which imposes a limit on the restrictions to which rights may be subject: 'In no case may the essence of a basic right be affected'.[33] Robert Alexy, the leading theorist of the relativist model, interprets this provision as follows:

> [T]he essential core is what is left over after the balancing test has been carried out. Limitations which correspond to the principle of proportionality do not infringe the essential core, even

[26] S Tsakyrakis, 'Proportionality: An Assault on Human Rights' (2009) 7 *International Journal of Constitutional Law* 468, 492. See also Urbina, *A Critique of Balancing and Proportionality* (n 25) 113.

[27] LB Frantz, 'The First Amendment in the Balance' (1962) 71 *Yale Law Journal* 1424, 1445. See also J Habermas, *Between Facts and Norms: Contributions to a Discourse Theory of Democracy* (Cambridge, MIT Press, 1996) 258–59; G Kateb, *Human Dignity* (Cambridge, Belknap Press, 2011) 30–31; N Rao, 'On the Use and Abuse of Dignity in Constitutional Law' (2008) 14 *Columbia Journal of European Law* 201, 232–38; Urbina, *A Critique of Balancing and Proportionality* (n 25) 113.

[28] Tsakyrakis, 'Proportionality: An Assault on Human Rights' (n 26) 489.

[29] M Kumm, 'Is the Structure of Human Rights Defensible? Three Puzzles and Their Solutions' in VC Jackson and M Tushnet (eds), *Proportionality: New Frontiers, New Challenges* (Cambridge, Cambridge University Press, 2018) 51, 59; K Möller, 'US Constitutional Law, Proportionality, and the Global Model' in ibid 130, 136.

[30] Alexy, *A Theory of Constitutional Rights* (n 17) 210.

[31] Klatt and Meister, *The Constitutional Structure of Proportionality* (n 18) 32.

[32] ibid 31.

[33] Grundgesetz art 19(2). For illuminating exploration of the history, scope, and significance of this provision, see I Leijten, *Core Socio-Economic Rights and the European Court of Human Rights* (Cambridge, Cambridge University Press, 2017).

> if they leave nothing left of the constitutional right in an individual case. This reduces the guarantee of an essential core to the principle of proportionality. Since this applies anyways, this would mean that article 19(2) Basic Law simply has declaratory effect.[34]

When confronted by a provision that prohibits restricting the essence of any right, relativists explain that the essence of the right is what (if anything) survives balancing in a given context. Since balancing determines the extent to which rights may be restricted, rights are susceptible to being balanced away in their entirety.[35] From this standpoint, a constitutional prohibition against restricting the essence of a right has no impact on the constitution's meaning.[36]

When absolutists repudiate relativism for placing categorical rights in the balance, relativists respond that absolutism does not know itself. Absolutists insist that a right is 'designated only after the *final* interaction of *all* of the reasons bearing upon the justifiability of a given action'.[37] Once this designation occurs, whatever falls within the scope of the right is essential to it, conclusive in strength, and exempt from balancing. Relativists object that the absolutist opposition to balancing is more apparent than real: wherever the reasons bearing upon the justifiability of a given action divide into supporting and opposing reasons, there is no alternative to assessing the weight of the competing reasons, and that is what balancing is. Even if absolute rights cannot be balanced away, the scope of each right is nevertheless 'the outcome of an underlying balancing approach'.[38] Far from offering an alternative to balancing, absolutism merely resists applying the label *rights* until after the task of balancing all of the reasons bearing upon the justifiability of a given act has concluded.

Ultimately, rights relativists and absolutists conceive of claims about the essence of rights as dependent on balancing. Relative rights are the *inputs* of balancing, and whatever aspect of a right is not balanced away in a given context constitutes its essence. Absolute rights are the *outputs* of balancing, and what is essential to the right is whatever the balance assigns to its scope.[39] Thus, each of these opposing models converges on the same conclusion: balancing is the method for identifying the essence of a right. If this conclusion is inescapable, then the bifurcated model finds itself in the hopeless position both of requiring the essence of a right to be identified and of repudiating the only method for identifying it.

[34] Alexy, *A Theory of Constitutional Rights* (n 17) 193. See also Klatt and Meister, *The Constitutional Structure of Proportionality* (n 18) 67–68.

[35] Alexy, *A Theory of Constitutional Rights* (n 17) 193, 196. For a parallel passage indicating that, in the German constitutional context, even the 'inviolable' ['unantastbar'] right to human dignity may be balanced away, see Klatt and Meister, *The Constitutional Structure of Proportionality* (n 18) 30.

[36] Alexy, *A Theory of Constitutional Rights* (n 17) 193, 196.

[37] J Oberdiek, 'Specifying Rights Out of Necessity' (2008) 28 *OJLS* 127, 135. For endorsements of this idea in the constitutional context, see JM Finnis, 'A Bill of Rights for Britain? The Moral of Contemporary Jurisprudence' (1985) 71 *Proceedings of the British Academy* 303, 329; G Webber, 'The Loss of Rights' in Huscroft, Miller and Webber (eds), *Proportionality and the Rule of Law Proportionality and the Rule of Law* (n 9) 123, 131.

[38] Rivers, 'Proportionality and Variable Intensity of Review' (n 17) 184.

[39] For a powerful exposition of the same contrast with respect to theories of moral rights, see A Zylberman, 'Moral Rights without Balancing' (2022) 179 *Philosophical Studies* 549, 554.

3. Identifying the Essence

However, as I will now argue, there is a familiar constitutional doctrine that enables the essence of a right to be identified without engaging in balancing. What then is that method?

Proponents of the bifurcated model usually shy away from this question. On those rare occasions where an answer is advanced, the magnetic pull of balancing proves overwhelming. In a recent article, Takis Tridimas and Giulia Gentile embrace the bifurcated model and reject rights relativism when they write: 'Respect for essence is … best understood as an autonomous condition that must be satisfied separately from the requirement of proportionality'.[40] However, when turning to the question of how the essence of a right is to be identified, the authors state: 'Although the concept of essence as a legal threshold must be understood as an autonomous limit, in effect, it is impossible to determine it without engaging in a balancing process which is best carried out through a proportionality analysis'.[41] With this, the authors' allegiance to the bifurcated model collapses into a hardboiled relativism.

When lawyers and judges claim that the essence of a right has been breached, they set aside the language of infringement or limitation and speak of the right being abolished,[42] destroyed,[43] extinguished,[44] emptied of its contents,[45] or having its very existence called into question.[46] What unites these formulations is the idea that the essence of a right is breached by public acts and omissions that treat the purpose of the right as a nullity and public power as plenary with respect to it. In what follows, I explain how purposive interpretation determines the essence of a constitutional right without engaging in balancing.

Purposive interpretation is a method of determining the scope of a constitutional right. This doctrine integrates a series of ideas.[47] First, a charter of rights is a system of standards (or what we might call *purposes*) that regulate the relationship between public authorities and the free persons subject to their governance. Second, purposive interpretation is interpretive insofar as its task is not to determine *which* provisions in a charter of rights are to be given effect, but to explain how *each* provision can be given effect. Accordingly, when imputing purposes to provisions, purposive interpretation eschews purposes that render particular provisions inert or duplicative of others and instead seeks to formulate an interlocking set of general and particular purposes that

[40] T Tridimas and G Gentile, 'The Essence of Rights: An Unreliable Boundary?' (2019) 20 *German Law Journal* 794, 804.

[41] ibid.

[42] ibid 348.

[43] *Othman (Abu Qatada) v. United Kingdom*, (2012) App. No. 8139/09, Eur Ct H R (2012), para 260.

[44] *Regner v the Czech Republic*, 19 September 2017, Application No. 35829/11, para 50.

[45] Lenaerts, 'Limits on Limitations' (n 6) 784.

[46] Jellinek, 'Grundrechte und Gesetzesvorbehalt' (n 1) 5; K Gutman, 'The Essence of the Fundamental Right to an Effective Remedy and to a Fair Trial in the Case-Law of the Court of Justice of the European Union: The Best is Yet to Come?' (2019) 20 *German Law Journal* 884, 889.

[47] For elaboration of the ideas sketched here, see J Weinrib, 'What is Purposive Interpretation?' (2024) 74 *University of Toronto Law Journal* 74.

make sense of a charter of rights in whole and part. Because different constellations of purposes may inform different charters of rights, both the scope of rights and the boundary delineating the core and the periphery of rights may vary from one jurisdiction to the next. Third, the purpose of each right must be fulfilled by public authorities in the context of a constantly changing world. Thus, the 'social reality' to which a provision applies 'becomes an integral part of interpretation'.[48] Fourth, a right is fulfilled when the acts and omissions of public authorities conform to what the relevant purpose demands in a given context. In contrast, a right is breached to the extent that public acts or omissions deviate from what that purpose demands. So conceived, purposive interpretation identifies the purposes that animate a charter of rights and requires the legal order to live up to them.

A right might be breached in two ways. The first *limits* some aspect of the right's purpose. The second *negates* that purpose and thereby compromises the right's essence. An illustration of the distinction between a limitation and a negation arises in *Schrems v Data Commissioner* with respect to the rights to private life and to access effective judicial protection.[49]

Schrems is the first case in which the CJEU declared a measure invalid because it compromised the essence of rights held under the Charter of Fundamental Rights of the European Union (the EU Charter). The case concerned the transfer of personal data of Facebook users in Europe to the United States where the company's servers are located. The European Union's General Data Protection Regulation authorises the transfer of data to third countries that ensure an adequate level of data protection.[50] In its Safe Harbour Decision, the European Union determined that the United States provided adequate protection, and authorised companies to store the personal data of Europeans in the United States.[51] In the aftermath of Edward Snowden's disclosures regarding the access that public authorities in the United States had to personal data transferred from Europe, an Austrian national challenged the Safe Harbour Decision.[52] In *Schrems*, the CJEU interpreted the General Data Protection Regulation as requiring third countries to provide 'a level of protection of fundamental rights essentially equivalent to that guaranteed in the EU legal order'.[53] On this basis, the CJEU declared the Safe Harbour Decision invalid because the Commission failed to ensure that the United States offered equivalent protection. More specifically, the decision breached the essence of two rights held under the EU Charter.

First, the decision breached the essence of the right to private life. *Schrems* was handed down a few months after *Digital Rights Ireland*, in which the CJEU held that the retention of metadata[54] constituted a 'particularly serious interference' with the

[48] D Grimm, 'The Basic Law at 60 – Identity and Change' (2010) 11 *German Law Journal* 33, 44.

[49] ECJ, Case C-362/14 *Schrems v Data Commissioner* ECLI:EU:C:2015:650, Judgment of 8 October 2015. For discussion, see, eg Lenaerts, 'Limits on Limitations' (n 6) 786 and M Brkan, 'The Essence of Fundamental Rights to Privacy and Data Protection: Finding the Way Though the Maze of the CJEU's Constitutional Reasoning' (2019) 20 *German Law Journal* 864.

[50] Regulation (EU) 2016/679 of the European Parliament and of the Council of 27 April 2016.

[51] Commission Decision of 26 July 2000.

[52] Brkan, 'Essence of Fundamental Rights' (n 49) 874.

[53] *Schrems* (n 49) para 96.

[54] 'Metadata' is data about data. Although metadata does not include the content of a given data, it might reveal its author, the date of its creation or modification, where it is located on a computer network, the process used to create the data, its size, format, and so on.

right to private life,[55] but did not breach that right's essence because 'the content of the electronic communications' remained private.[56] In *Schrems*, the Safe Harbour Decision enabled public authorities in the United States, such as the National Security Agency, to access *both* metadata *and* the content of all personal data transferred from the European Union to the United States.[57] As the CJEU noted, the Safe Harbour Decision 'does not contain any finding regarding the existence, in the United States, of rules adopted by the State intended to limit any interference with the fundamental rights of the persons whose data is transferred from the European Union to the United States'.[58] Because the subjection of the content of personal communications to unrestricted surveillance by public authorities treats the right to private life as a nullity – an empty claim imposing no constraint on the exercise of public authority – the decision breached the essence of the right.[59]

Second, the CJEU held that the essence of the right to effective judicial protection was breached because domestic legislation in the United States failed to provide individuals with an 'administrative or judicial means' of pursuing 'legal remedies in order to have access to personal data … or to obtain the rectification or erasure of such data'.[60] Accordingly, the right of individuals to seek a remedy to protect their rights was treated as non-existent because persons were left without any mode of legal recourse to constrain the use of their personal data.[61]

As these examples show, the essence is breached in contexts where the purpose of the right is not limited but denied. This idea extends in two directions. First, where the purpose of the right requires public authorities to exercise restraint, the essence of the right is breached where a public authority acknowledges no limit on its power to interfere with that purpose. The prospect of an unrestricted invasion of privacy in *Schrems* illustrates this possibility. Second, where the purpose of the right demands state action, the essence of the right is breached where the public authority fails to act to create the conditions of the right's protection. In *Schrems*, the absence of any mode of legal recourse negates the right to effective judicial protection. Similarly, the European Court

[55] ECJ, Joined Cases C-293 & C-594/12 *Digital Rights Ireland Ltd v Minister for Communications* ECLI:EU:C:2014:238, Judgment of 8 April 2014 at para 65.

[56] ibid para 39.

[57] *Schrems* (n 49) paras 92–94.

[58] ibid para 88.

[59] ibid para 94. Admittedly, the reasoning in *Schrems* is not as analytically clear as it might be. On what we might call the *relativist reading* of the case, the court employs considerations apposite to proportionality to determine that the essence of the right is breached. This view could be supported by the fact that para 94, which explicitly states that the essence of the right was breached, follows paras 92–93, which refer to elements of the proportionality analysis. In contrast, on what we might call the *bifurcated reading*, para 94 merely restates a conclusion established earlier in the judgment. While para 88 does not explicitly refer to the *essence* of the right, it maintains that Decision afforded no protection to the privacy rights of persons whose personal data is transferred from the European Union to the United States. In other words, the decision treats the right to privacy as a nullity that imposes no constraint on public authorities. In turn, para 91 elaborates what the right to privacy guarantees, while paras 92 and 93 formulate justificatory standards that must be satisfied if the periphery of the right is breached. On this reading, the conclusion in para 94 that the essence of the right to privacy has been breached does not rely on the considerations of proportionality discussed in paras 92 and 93, but instead simply restates the conclusion established in para 88. For further exposition of the bifurcated reading of *Schrems*, see Lenaerts, 'Limits on Limitations' (n 6) 782.

[60] *Schrems* (n 49) paras 90, 95.

[61] Brkan, 'The Concept of Essence of Fundamental Rights in the EU Legal Order' (n 6) 353.

of Human Rights has held that the essence of the right to vote is 'completely denied' in contexts where a state creates no mechanism for its exercise.[62]

Of course, the distinction between limits and denials will not always be easy to draw. The structure of constitutional adjudication addresses this ambiguity by placing the onus on the party seeking to establish the breach of a constitutional right. In cases where the claimant fails to establish that the breach compromises the essence of a right, justification remains possible. Whether it is actual depends upon considerations of proportionality.

Purposive interpretation is not a form of balancing. Balancing seeks to resolve conflicts between competing principles by considering the intensity of the interference to one principle, the importance of satisfying a competing principle, and, finally, whether the 'importance of satisfying the competing principle justifies the detriment to, or non-satisfaction of the first'.[63] Purposive interpretation is not a form of balancing because it does not apply to competing principles. As we have seen, purposive interpretation concerns the relationship between the purpose of a right and the context in which public authorities must give effect to it. Purpose and context are not principles that compete against one another. Rather, context must conform to purpose. From the standpoint of purposive interpretation, the opposite idea – that there is some context to which the purpose of rights must conform – is inadmissible because it would render rights powerless to protect persons from the various social realities to which they apply, including historical traditions, societal consensus, and policy preferences. Because determinations about whether (and the extent to which) context conforms to purpose does not involve competing principles, purposive interpretation is not a form of balancing.

One might object that the bifurcated model is incapable of accommodating non-derogable rights, such as the right not to be tortured or enslaved. Because these rights may not be restricted under any circumstances, they resist the distinction between a core that is immune from restriction and a periphery that may be restricted in accordance with the doctrine of proportionality. In the terminology of the birfurcated model, a non-derogable right has a core but no periphery. And so, it would seem, non-derogable rights cannot be reconciled with the bifurcated model. My response to this objection hinges on an earlier claim: purposive interpretation presumes that a charter of rights is an interlocking set of general and particular standards that regulate the acts and omissions of public authorities. From this standpoint, the rights not to be tortured or enslaved are not stand-alone rights, but instead form the core of a standard embodied by a more general right. For example, torture violates the core of the broader right to security of the person, while enslavement violates the core of the broader right to liberty. These rights are *derogable* insofar as their peripheries remain subject to justified limitations. However, the cores of these rights are *non-derogable* insofar as their breach cannot be justified. In this way, the bifurcated model subsumes the distinction between derogable and non-derogable rights.

[62] *Matthews v United Kingdom* (1999) 28 EHRR 361 at para 63.
[63] Alexy, *A Theory of Constitutional Rights* (n 17) 401.

The bifurcated model offers a distinctive answer to the question: What exceptionless rights do we have? Relativists answer that because the strength of every right is determined through balancing, there are no exceptionless rights. In contrast, absolutists answer that because what is susceptible to restriction is not a right, there are only 'a small number of rights,' such as 'the right not to be tortured, not to be subject to cruel and unusual punishment, and not to be held in slavery or servitude'.[64] All other supposed rights are subject to the vicissitudes of the political process. The bifurcated model departs from each of these approaches by maintaining that the core of *every* right imposes an unconditional obligation, including the right to privacy, the right to effective judicial protection, the right to vote, and – as Allan reminds us – the right to procedural fairness.[65]

4. Why the Essence is Absolute

The bifurcated model claims that when the essence of a right is breached, the breach is not *unjustified* but *unjustifiable*. I will now explain why the bifurcated model is entitled to the claim that derogation from the essence of the right is unjustifiable.

Relativist critics of the bifurcated model insist that '[t]he conviction that there must be rights which even in the most extreme circumstances are not outweighed … cannot be maintained as a matter of constitutional law'.[66] Relativists buttress this conclusion with a series of familiar ideas: *rights* are reasons that support constitutional protection; *limits* are reasons that oppose constitutional protection; and *balancing* is the appropriate method of determining the relative moral weight of these reasons in a given context.[67] If the strength that constitutional rights possess is determined by balancing, then it follows that every claim of right is subject to balancing, that rights may be balanced against any consideration that opposes them, and that rights are susceptible to being outweighed in part and whole.

To be sure, the relativist claim is that rights always hang in the balance, not that rights will always be balanced away. Within the relativist model, the more a right is restricted, the stronger the countervailing reason must be if that restriction is to be justified. Accordingly, as the severity of a restriction increases, the likelihood of its justification diminishes.[68] What relativists resist is the further claim that certain restrictions on rights are not merely unlikely to be justified but unjustifiable as such. From the relativist standpoint, this further claim cannot be maintained because it conflates improbability with impossibility. From the relativist standpoint, the bifurcated model rests on a simple error.

[64] G Webber, 'Proportionality and Absolute Rights' in Jackson and Tushnet (eds), *Proportionality: New Frontiers, New Challenges New Frontiers* (n 29) 75, 77. For a similarly compact list of absolute rights, see J Finnis, *Natural Law and Natural Rights* (Oxford, Oxford University Press, 1980) 225.

[65] Allan, *Sovereignty of Law* (n 9) 188.

[66] Alexy, *A Theory of Constitutional Rights* (n 17) 196.

[67] ibid 210.

[68] ibid 195. On this point, proponents of rights relativism and the bifurcated model stand in agreement. See, for example, Lenaerts, 'Limits on Limitations' (n 6) 793; Allan, 'Democracy, Legality, and Proportionality' (n 9) 222.

This objection takes the form of a conditional: *if* the bifurcated model relies on the relativist account of justification, *then* the bifurcated model would not get off the ground. However, if the bifurcated model had something of its own to say about why it is that justification is impossible when the essence of a right is breached, then it is the objection that would not get off the ground. After all, the objection does not show that the bifurcated model cannot succeed on its own terms. The objection simply observes that the bifurcated model is committed to a conclusion that does not follow from relativist premises.

In claiming that there is no justification for breaching the essence of a right, the bifurcated model relies on its own distinctive understanding of what justification means in the realm of constitutional rights.[69] This understanding proceeds from the organising idea that constitutional rights, by virtue of their status as supreme law, enjoy categorical priority over any legal norm that lacks the same pre-eminence. This idea has ramifications for both the scope and strength of constitutional rights. With respect to the *scope* of rights, the bifurcated model resists the relativist idea that the function of constitutional rights is to 'put every conceivable form of conduct under their special protection'.[70] Instead, a charter of rights articulates a set of purposes integral to the relations of free and equal persons, elevates these purposes to the rank of supreme law, and looks to these purposes to distinguish what the constitution protects from what 'is left to the rules and remedies of ordinary law'.[71] With respect to the *strength* of rights, the bifurcated model rejects the relativist idea that rights enjoy no priority over sub-constitutional considerations of policy, preference, expediency, and tradition.[72] Instead, the bifurcated model preserves the priority of rights by maintaining that a right may be limited only to provide 'equivalent protection to the rights and freedoms of others, or for the protection of other legal interests which are essential if man is to continue to enjoy his rights and freedoms'.[73] In this way, the bifurcated model resists the twin tendencies of rights relativism to reduce all rights into interests and to elevate all government interests to the rank of rights.[74]

The bifurcated model's commitment to the priority of rights generates a distinctive account of the final proportionality substage.[75] This substage presupposes a series of prior determinations: that one member of the system of rights has been breached, that

[69] Here I rely on a conception of the strength of rights that I explore more fully in J Weinrib, *Escaping the Impasse in Constitutional Rights Theory* (Cambridge, Cambridge University Press, forthcoming).

[70] BVerfGE 80, 137(1989) (*Reiten im Walde*) para 99, Grimm J, dissenting.

[71] ibid para 100.

[72] R Alexy, 'Proportionality and Rationality' in Jackson and Tushnet (eds), *Proportionality: New Frontiers, New Challenges* (n 29) 13, 19.

[73] R Marcic, 'Duties and Limitations Upon Rights' (1968) 9 *Journal of the International Commission of Jurists* 59, 67.

[74] JE Fleming, 'Securing Deliberative Democracy' (2004) 72 *Fordham Law Review* 1435, 1446. But see Rivers, 'Proportionality and Variable Intensity of Review' (n 17) 180.

[75] This understanding of proportionality's final substage appears under different labels, such as *reconciliation* or *practical concordance*. See, for example, Frank Iacobucci, '"Reconciling Rights": The Supreme Court of Canada's Approach to Competing Charter Rights' (2003) 20 *The Supreme Court Law Review* 137; T Marauhn and N Ruppel, 'Balancing Conflicting Rights: Konrad Hesse's Notion of '*Praktische Konkordanz*' and the German Federal Constitutional Court' in E Brems (ed), *Conflicts Between Fundamental Rights* (Antwerp, Intersentia, 2008) 273; H Bielefeldt, 'Limiting Permissible Limitations: How to Preserve the Substance of Religious Freedom' (2020) 15 *Religion and Human Rights* 3.

the breach furthers the fulfilment of the purpose of another member of that system (appropriate objective and rational connection), and that there is no means of fulfilling the purpose of each member of the system of rights undiminished (minimal impairment). At issue in the final proportionality substage is the question of how conflicts between members of the system of rights are to be resolved where the constitution presents each member as possessing 'equal validity and rank' and offers 'no specific limitations clauses' for resolving conflicts that might arise between them.[76]

These conflicts may not be resolved by appealing to the familiar idea that rights are trumps. This idea is decisive when a constitutional right is confronted by a sub-constitutional consideration, but the idea offers no resources for resolving conflicts in which opposing claims issue from the normative apex of law's hierarchy. Nor may these conflicts be resolved by 'postulating an abstract hierarchy' in which one member of the system of rights, say, freedom of expression, is always prioritised over another, say, the right to a fair trial.[77] As an interpretive matter, this approach is precluded wherever the constitutional text presents particular rights not as standing in relations of superior and inferior, but as making an equally valid claim to 'effective implementation'.[78]

Where conflicts arise between members of the system of rights, the task 'is not to determine which one prevails but to find a solution which leaves the greatest possible effect to both of them (*Pracktische Konkordanz*)'.[79] Accordingly, where each member of the system of rights issues an equally valid claim to fulfilment, conflicts may not be resolved by negating one member of the system in order to advance another. The sacrifice of any member of the system of rights is unjustifiable because it violates the idea that animates the final proportionality substage, namely, that each member of the system of rights makes an equally valid claim to implementation. Thus, when the essence of a right is breached, it is not the case that, given the severity of the interference, an adequate justification remains possible but is unlikely to materialise. Rather, justification is impossible because the nullification of a member of the system of rights can neither be justified by appealing to a sub-constitutional consideration nor to another member of the system of rights. In the former case, justification is precluded by the priority of each member of the system of rights over any sub-constitutional legal norm. In the latter, justification is precluded because if each member of the system of rights makes an equally valid claim to fulfilment, no member can justify another's nullification. Thus, where the essence of a right is breached, the final proportionality substage necessarily remains unsatisfied because there is no kind of consideration capable of justifying the breach.

In our collective constitutional terminology and imagination, the metaphor of balancing has become enmeshed with the final proportionality substage. From the standpoint of the bifurcated model, this metaphor is misleading because it denies the priority of the system of rights by subjecting each of its members to a general balancing of interests, in which rights may be restricted by any sub-constitutional consideration,

[76] Marauhn and Ruppel, 'Balancing Conflicting Rights' (n 75) 296.
[77] Bielefeldt, 'Limiting Permissible Limitations' (n 75) 13–14.
[78] Marauhn and Ruppel, 'Balancing Conflicting Rights' (n 75) 281.
[79] D Grimm, 'Human Rights and Judicial Review in Germany' in D Beatty (ed), *Human Rights and Judicial Review: A Comparative Perspective* (Dordrecht, Martinus Nijhoff Publishers, 1994) 267, 273.

whether political or economic, social or cultural.[80] Further, the metaphor suggests that rights may be balanced away in their entirety whenever the benefits to be achieved or the burdens to be avoided possess sufficient magnitude. The relativist model embraces both of these ideas. The bifurcated model rejects both, but for its own distinctive reasons. On the one hand, the priority of rights precludes restricting any right to advance any consideration that does not sound in a constitutional register. Each member of the system of rights possesses absolute strength against any sub-constitutional consideration. On the other, where the members of the system of rights possess an equal claim to fulfilment, no member may be nullified to advance another. Instead, members of the system of rights may be restricted at their periphery to ensure that no member is breached at its core.

5. Conclusion

Allan's immense contributions to the world of constitutional theory include his articulation of the bifurcated model of constitutional rights. This model leads a double life. As a matter of constitutional practice, judges and lawyers in jurisdictions around the world appeal to the model to conceptualise the strength of rights. As a matter of constitutional theory, however, the model has come in for a rough ride. Critics claim that the model is defective both because it offers no method of identifying the essence of a right and because it provides no basis for its claim that when the essence of a right is breached, justification is impossible. This chapter argues that the key to overcoming these methodological challenges lies in appreciating the distinctive doctrines on which the model relies. On the one hand, purposive interpretation identifies the essence of a right with its purpose. Any public act or omission that treats the purpose of a right as a nullity breaches its essence. On the other, there is a conception of proportionality that explains why justification is impossible when the essence of a right is breached. Where each member of the system of rights makes an equally valid claim to implementation, no member may justify the nullification of any other. Uniting each of these doctrines is the shared idea that a constitutional right enjoys priority over any legal norm that lacks the same pre-eminence. These doctrines and the shared idea that animates them are, as Allan might say, 'implicit in our existing constitutional arrangements'.[81]

[80] J Rawls, *Political Liberalism* (New York, Columbia University Press, 2005) 358.
[81] Allan, *Sovereignty of Law* (n 9) 91.

PART III

Common Law Constitutionalism and Parliamentary Sovereignty

11

Foundations, Theory and Doctrine

PAUL CRAIG*

1. Introduction

Trevor Allan has written with commitment and vigour on a range of public law topics over the years, and he has been at the forefront of common law constitutionalism. He has challenged accepted modes of thinking on a range of topics, and his work is thought-provoking. This is just as it should be within the academic world. His work should, by the same token, be subject to the same critical scrutiny that he routinely brings to bear on others. This is more especially so, given the breadth of the claims that he makes.

In this spirit of academic engagement, this chapter will consider three dimensions of Trevor Allan's work. The analysis begins with consideration of legal theory, more particularly the claim made in recent work that there is coherence between what the law is and what it ought to be. This is followed by examination of his attack on the utility of Administrative law doctrine. The final section of the chapter addresses Trevor Allan's critique of deference in Administrative law.

2. Legal Theory: Legal Reasoning, Legal Obligation and Moral Obligation

Trevor Allan's work on constitutional law is underpinned by a Dworkinian vision of legal theory. He has also written more directly on legal theory, in which he has challenged certain aspects of Dworkin's theory, with the conclusions informing his view about the relationship between legal and moral obligation. The work is stimulating and challenging. The focus of the ensuing inquiry is on Allan's recent work, in which he argues that there is congruence between the law as it is and the law as it ought to be.[1]

* I am grateful for comments from Mark Walters and Alison Young.

[1] TRS Allan, 'Why the Law is What it Ought to Be' (2020) 11 *Jurisprudence* 574, 574.

A. Thesis

Trevor Allan's central claim is that 'our legal obligations are precisely the moral obligations we owe as citizens, faithful to that community'.[2] The nature of this claim is explicated at the outset.

> It is widely supposed by lawyers and legal theorists alike that the law, as it is understood and applied in practice, falls short of what it ought to be. It falls short in the sense of being morally deficient, failing to match the standards of justice or political morality by which it must be measured. If, however, we often disagree about what those standards require, at least in particular cases or contexts, the law may provide a legitimate basis for governance, capable of eliciting our support in spite of its many imperfections. When the necessary conditions are met, the law is in an important sense what it ought to be. The law's content may diverge from what each of us may in our private capacities consider that justice, ideally conceived, would ordain. But we should nonetheless accept the law's demands in our public capacities as members of the political community, allowing it to determine disputes between people whose moral and political disagreements extend far beyond the specific issues immediately in point. While we must not abandon our moral ideals, as external critics, we may nevertheless be morally required to obey the law as it is correctly interpreted – consistently with the principles that underpin its legitimacy. If, moreover, those principles determine the lawful exercise of official state power, defining basic rights of persons against improper coercive interference, the law is what it ought to be.[3]

Equality is central to this vision. It is the normative condition precedent that underscores the argument. This is readily apparent from Allan's analysis. Thus, we are told that 'as the public scheme or charter of justice, the law must respect the equal dignity of all those within its coercive embrace'.[4] The idea of legal integrity is posited on the assumption that participants in the legal system are orientated by 'principles that affirm the equal dignity of persons'.[5] When the 'equal dignity of persons is a basic presumption of legal reasoning, the law is what, for the political community concerned, it ought to be', such that the rule of law obtains in contradistinction to the rule of persons.[6]

The law's application to particular cases may on occasion, be unsatisfactory, but the law itself is morally what it ought to be because it is 'the public scheme of justice constructed and maintained by a legal and political culture that honours the moral independence and equal dignity of persons'.[7] This claim in turn is premised on the assumption that 'everyone has a voice in the debates over justice that political arrangements facilitate', and 'no one may be subjected to legal requirements that could not be justified by recourse to principles that provide the principal currency of that debate'.[8] This demands the equal protection of the law, which constitutes an implicit limitation on anyone's duty of obedience.[9]

[2] ibid 574, 595.
[3] ibid 574.
[4] ibid 575.
[5] ibid.
[6] ibid 577, 595.
[7] ibid 576.
[8] ibid.
[9] ibid 577, 579.

Trevor Allan accepts that there will perforce be disagreement as to the best way to proceed on a particular issue, and acknowledges that there must, nonetheless, be cooperation to maintain legitimate governance in spite of moral disagreement. However, law 'informed and disciplined by its internal, conceptual moral ideal of equality'[10] furnishes the way forward, at least in circumstances where disagreement is not so divisive as to defeat collaborative effort.

Allan denies there is any space for conflict between integrity and justice, or what the law is and what it ought to be.[11] He regards 'Dworkin's anxiety to preserve a clear distinction between what the law is and what it ought to be, though consistent with orthodoxy', to be 'at war with his larger vision'.[12] Thus, a 'full-blooded interpretative approach to integrity erases the distinction between questions about the law's content, on the one hand, and questions about obedience, on the other'.[13] There is then, for Allan, 'no point at which we must abandon the law in favour of justice or qualify the law by extraneous moral considerations', since 'legal reasoning is a moral exercise through and through'.[14] It follows that 'if a statute cannot be interpreted consistently with fundamental principles, it has no power to affect the court's conclusions in the particular case'.[15]

Allan concludes that the primary focus must be on issues of interpretation rather than validity, and that 'interpretation is never a matter of what any lawmaker envisaged or intended, as regards the disposition of any particular case, but rather what the law itself requires when correctly understood'.[16] It is then unsurprising that Allan adheres to the declaratory theory of the common law, stating that this is 'a myth or "fairy tale" only for those who view the law as constituted by specific rules and rulings, ignoring the moral basis of those rules and rulings in general principle'.[17]

There is a qualification to the preceding argument. Allan acknowledges that legislative intervention may on occasion be necessary because the courts are unable to resolve the case as justice requires, since they are 'impeded by an exaggerated deference to erroneous precedents, which betray past prejudices or questionable assumption', and that the 'law may fall short of what, ideally, it ought to be'.[18] This qualification does not, for Allan, derail the principal argument:

> While the law's administration may, on this view, be morally deficient, it awaits internal challenge and correction. If the law's application to particular cases is sometimes inaccurate or unreliable or otherwise unsatisfactory, the law itself is morally what it ought to be. It is, at root, the public scheme of justice constructed and maintained by a legal and political culture that honours the moral independence and equal dignity of persons. Everyone has a voice in the debates over justice that political arrangements facilitate.[19]

[10] ibid 594.
[11] ibid 575.
[12] ibid.
[13] ibid.
[14] ibid 593.
[15] ibid.
[16] ibid 596.
[17] ibid 576.
[18] ibid.
[19] ibid.

B. Temporal Perspective

There is much that is of interest in Trevor Allan's argument, which he develops in greater detail than can be recounted here. There are, nonetheless, difficulties with central aspects of the thesis, which will be explored in this section and those which follow.

The initial difficulty concerns equality/equal dignity/equal concern and respect, which constitute, as seen above, the normative cornerstone to the argument. The difficulty is empirical and temporal. The moral foundation of the law is said to be predicated on such equality. However, in the United Kingdom prior to 1832, only 5–10 per cent of the male population could vote, and women were not accorded the vote before 1928. The problem is indeed more far-reaching, since the prevalence of equality legislation from the 1960s onwards attests to the difficulties of ensuring equal treatment based on gender, race, sexuality, age and the like. Allan's assumption that 'everyone has a voice in the debates over justice that political arrangements facilitate', and 'no one may be subjected to legal requirements that could not be justified by recourse to principles that provide the principal currency of that debate',[20] clearly has no purchase in circumstances where 50–80 per cent of the population were excluded from the franchise. They were not part of the debate and had no voice. The common law viewed historically did not, moreover, contain a free-standing principle of equality, whereby the equal dignity of persons was secured. There are two possible responses to this argument, but both are problematic in their own right.

It might be contended that we should consider equality/equal dignity/equal concern and respect in inter-temporal terms, such that we judge such matters in accord with understandings of equality prevalent at the time. Thus, insofar as slavery, lack of the franchise, a married woman's property passing to her spouse, and a multitude of other such matters, were accepted by earlier societies, then we accept this and make our assessment of equality in those societies accordingly. This temporal relativity comes at a price. The price is that if you buy into this argument, you must also accept its possible application in the modern day. Thus, it might then be argued that differential treatment of, for example, trans-gender persons does not offend conceptions of equal dignity, if and insofar as a society does not accept such parity of treatment.

It might alternatively be contended that such equality exists now and that this suffices for the purposes of Allan's argument. This response is doubly problematic. The obvious counter argument is that it begs the question as to whether such equality does exist now. This raises a plethora of interesting issues, which are part empirical, concerning the extent to which there really is such equal respect; and partly normative, concerning the level of abstraction or specificity with which one views the very idea of equal dignity, since it will be more easily satisfied, albeit less meaningful, the more abstract the level at which it is cast.

There is, however, a less obvious, but equally important problem with this argument, which is that it does not fit with the declaratory theory of adjudication that Trevor Allan espouses. That theory has by its very nature a temporal and historical dimension. It is indeed difficult to discern what a declaratory theory would mean if it

[20] ibid.

did not have such a component. I believe that constitutional principles do and should inform adjudication, but I do not subscribe to the declaratory theory.[21] I also believe that we should be honest in understanding the principles developed and applied by the courts, and not reason on the basis of some vision that bears scant relation to reality. The salient point for present purposes is that if you subscribe to the declaratory theory then you cannot view equality/equal concern and respect/equal dignity through a temporal lens limited to the last 20 years. You are driven to confront the past, which includes, inter alia, the common law's acceptance of the inequalities that persisted, combined with the common law's creation of offences, such as seditious libel, which were used to buttress the established and unequal hierarchy in society. The idea that invocation of the declaratory theory can be the platform for some pristine tale of common law courts upholding constitutional principles that cemented foundational ideals of equal concern and respect is to be blind to reality.

The argument is not saved by Allan's qualification set out above.[22] Allan cannot maintain as his principal thesis that the law is what it ought to be and then say at the same time that the law may not always work itself perfect in the manner for which he argues such that legislative intervention is required. It begs the obvious rejoinder that the qualification to the principal thesis undermines the thesis itself. You cannot use the qualification to the thesis as an 'excuse' every time that the principal thesis does not get you where you want to go, without denuding that thesis of all content. The qualification is further undermined by the erroneous distinction between the 'law's administration' and the 'law itself'.[23] For Allan, when adjudication goes awry, this is simply a defect in the law's administration, which does not touch the law itself, which remains morally pure. This is so even though legislative intervention is required to redress the imperfection in 'administration', and even though the purity of the law itself is premised once again on the untenable assumption that everyone has a voice in the debates that inform the content of the law.

C. Interpretive Perspective

The second tension in Trevor Allan's argument is substantive. It concerns the limits of what can be achieved by and through interpretation. It is central to Allan's claim that pretty much everything that needs to be done can be done in this manner, without recourse to troublesome issues of validity, and without the need for a judge to feel the tensions described by Dworkin when faced with a morally questionable statute.

It is not entirely clear whether Trevor Allan thinks that there are any limits as to what can be achieved through interpretation, because his precise language varies in the article. There are, however, numerous points in the analysis where the interpretive potential in service of the background precept of equal dignity is cast very broadly. Thus, he rejects

[21] See eg Lord Reid, 'The Judge as Lawmaker' (1972–73) *Journal of the Society of Public Law Teachers* 22; PS Atiyah, 'Judges and Policy' (1980) *Israel Law Review* 346. For defence of the theory, see A Beever, 'The Declaratory Theory of the Law' (2013) 33 *OJLS* 421.

[22] See text to nn 18–19.

[23] See text to n 19.

any hard and fast distinction between what the law is and what it ought to be.[24] We are told that a 'full-blooded interpretative approach to integrity erases the distinction between questions about the law's content, on the one hand, and questions about obedience, on the other';[25] that there is 'no point at which we must abandon the law in favour of justice or qualify the law by extraneous moral considerations', since 'legal reasoning is a moral exercise through and through';[26] that 'if a statute cannot be interpreted consistently with fundamental principles, it has no power to affect the court's conclusions in the particular case'; and that if 'the rules cannot be interpreted in a manner that serves the public good, consistently with fundamental equality, they are invalid: they are an abuse of legal forms, incapable of generating obligations of obedience'.[27] There are two related difficulties with this view.

In empirical terms, it does not cohere with judicial practice, certainly not in the UK. The UK courts will, to be sure, read down legislation that infringes rights/ important interests, or where it has some serious deleterious consequence, but they do not believe that the law can always be read to be what it ought to be through creative interpretation pursuant to constitutional principle. There is no evidence presented by Allan to suggest that they do and there is multiple evidence to the contrary. Thus, even when the courts are acting pursuant to the broadened interpretive powers under the Human Rights Act, section 3, there are numerous cases where they have issued a declaration of incompatibility, because they do not feel that the language of the legislation can be read consistently with HRA rights.[28] To take another example, related albeit distinct, the courts have been cautious in their application of the principle of legality, and have declined to apply the principle on a large number of occasions, either because the asserted right did not qualify in this regard, or because it was clear that Parliament had indeed cast its mind to the issue and meant to limit the right in the manner suggested by the legislation.[29]

In normative terms, Allan's argument runs into difficulties of constitutional principle in the UK. It is the flip side to the empirical argument. The point could undoubtedly occupy an article in itself, space which I do not have, so I will cut to the chase directly. The UK has a principle of parliamentary sovereignty. You may like it, or you may not, but the legal reality is that courts eschewed the power to strike down primary legislation 400 hundred years ago.[30] The principle of parliamentary sovereignty must be

[24] ibid 575.
[25] ibid.
[26] ibid 593.
[27] ibid 582.
[28] Trevor Allan seeks to argue, ibid 592 fn 79, that declarations of incompatibility should be regarded 'as remedies of last resort, applicable where judicial interpretation alone is unable to secure perfect alignment between domestic and international law'. To be sure they can be so regarded, but it does not alter the fact that the courts do not believe that they can always achieve the desired result through interpretation, even in rights-based cases where more expansive rules of interpretation apply, and they do not view the statute as something that can be cast aside if it does not cohere with judicial understanding of fundamental principles. Nor does it alter the fact that the courts do not believe that they could do anything more through the common law, independent of the HRA, as evidenced by the judicial limits to the principle of legality.
[29] P Craig, 'Judicial Review, Methodology and Reform' [2022] *PL* 19.
[30] J Goldsworthy, *The Sovereignty of Parliament, History and Philosophy* (Oxford, Oxford University Press, 2001); P Craig, *English Administrative Law from 1550: Continuity and Change* (Oxford, Oxford University Press, 2024) ch 11.

read in tandem with the rule of law. Trevor Allan would contend that this provides the normative window through which sovereignty can be tamed by recourse to a substantive conception of the rule of law, enabling courts to deploy their interpretive tools so as always to ensure fit between background moral principles of equal concern and respect and the statutory text, hence his disavowal of any distinction between the law as it is and the law as it ought to be. He also contends that courts have the power to declare statutory rules invalid. The normative reality is that this is but one reading of a substantive conception of the rule of law. It is not shared by Dworkin. It is not shared by the UK courts.[31] They do not think that anything and everything can be achieved through interpretation, where this would undermine parliamentary sovereignty by reading language in such a way as to exceed its textual boundaries, even taking account of accepted principles of interpretation. Viewed from this perspective, parliamentary sovereignty constitutes a background element of fit, which provides normative limits to the courts' interpretive capacity. This remains so notwithstanding judicial dicta to the effect that the courts might re-think their position if Parliament did the unthinkable, such as the purported abolition of judicial review.

D. Substantive Perspective

Trevor Allan's argument also warrants reflection from a substantive perspective, which connotes in this respect the meaning ascribed to ideas of equal dignity/equal concern and respect. This is important, since it is determinative of what we 'get' by subscribing to the ideal that the law as it is coheres with the law as it ought to be. There are three possibilities in this respect.

The first might be labelled thin, and bears the following connotation. Trevor Allan's thesis is predicated on twin assumptions, the need for equal dignity/equal concern and respect, and the fact that moral disagreement is prevalent in society, such that people might legitimately disagree as to the desired outcome on a particular issue. It would then follow that, provided the relevant choice is applied equally, the law thus declared would cohere with the law as it ought to be, since no individual could expect his or her own preferred choice always to be embodied in the legal rule. There is much in Allan's analysis that is suggestive of this outcome. If this is the substantive outcome it is pretty thin for reasons that are readily apparent. We, the academic community, routinely criticise decisions where the nub of the analysis is that the law is not what it ought to be, even where there is no equality issue as such. The pages of law reviews, past and present, are shot through with argumentation to the effect that, for example, the courts or legislature opted for an interpretation of free speech or freedom of assembly that was unduly narrow, irrespective of whether the chosen definition pertains equally to all. Now it may be that the academic community has been wrong in these instances, such that provided the equality dimension is safely secured, the outcome thereafter is simply

[31] See, eg *BRB v Pickin* [1974] AC 765; *R v Secretary of State for the Home Department, ex p Simms and O'Brien* [2000] 2 AC 115; A Le Sueur, M Sunkin and J Murkens, *Public Law, Text, Cases and Materials*, 5th edn (Oxford, Oxford University Press, 2023) ch 3.

reflective of the choice attendant on moral disagreement. This is, however, unlikely. To the contrary, most would contend that the equality dimension is a necessary but not sufficient dimension when determining what the law ought to be, and that other moral considerations circumscribe the room for reasoned disagreement.

The second possibility is to thicken the baseline conditions that serve as the foundation for the argument that the law as it is coheres with the law as it ought to be. Equality/equal dignity would, on this view, constitute a necessary, but not sufficient condition, to be complemented by more general ideas of liberty. This may be what Trevor Allan intended, as suggested by his analysis of wicked laws, such as those of the Nazi regime, and more generally by some of his earlier writing.[32] The circumstances of societal moral disagreement still prevail, but they are now addressed within a richer intellectual framework that includes liberty as well as equal dignity. This is certainly possible, but the thickness brings greater attendant contestation as to the meaning and application of these base line conditions, with the consequence that there is room for more controversy as to whether the judicial/legislative outcome comes within the sphere of acceptable reasonable disagreement. This in turn means that there can be no ready assumption that the law as it is coheres with the law as it ought to be. This is reflected in academic scholarship where there are often divergent views as to whether the existing law captures the law that ought to prevail in a particular area.

The third possibility raises somewhat different issues, and concerns the substantive reach of Trevor Allan's thesis. The general focus of the analysis, whether in its thin or thick format, is the individual claim against the state, where the claimant raises a rights-based argument of the kind commonly found in the HRA or analogous document. There is, however, a very great deal of judicial and legislative activity that does not fit this mould, even though individuals may be directly affected by the outcome, as exemplified by areas such as social welfare, immigration and asylum, planning, the environment, employment law and the like. These issues matter a very great deal in the lives of those affected by the relevant rules. The numbers are often numerically large, extending in the realm of, for example, climate change to the entire population. The laws might be considered unjust in certain respects, irrespective of whether they would generate a traditional rights-based claim. There are then two ways of addressing such matters. It might be argued that they should be brought within the remit of Trevor Allan's argument, in which case the challenge would be to decide how to apply such reasoning to these areas. It might alternatively be argued that the subject matter precludes consideration of such cases in rights-based terms, or anything akin thereto, but the consequences for Allan's general thesis would be profound. The reach of the principle that the law as it is matches the law that it ought to be, would be significantly circumscribed. The fact that there might be serious mismatch between the two would be excluded from the analysis in these areas, which would be intellectually 'packaged off' into a different room, notwithstanding the fact that the mismatch might have serious consequences for those affected.

[32] See, eg, TRS Allan, *Constitutional Justice: A Liberal Theory of the Rule of Law* (Oxford, Oxford University Press, 2001) 2 ('the basic liberties of thought, speech, conscience, and association are, in their main applications, necessary constituents of the rule of law').

3. Administrative Law: Doctrine, Theory and Value

A. Thesis

The focus now shifts to prominent aspects of Trevor Allan's work in Administrative law, with discussion of his views on doctrine in this section, and deference in the section hereafter. Paul Daly[33] has also addressed this dimension of Allan's scholarship. I agree with much of Daly's analysis, but the points that I make, though related, are distinct. Trevor Allan is sceptical as to the value of Administrative law doctrine, and subjects it to a litany of criticism.[34]

General conceptions of legality, rationality and procedural propriety are said to do little work, since so much depends on the particular context to which they are applied.[35] There is the related claim that Administrative law conceived as a body of doctrine to be interpreted by public lawyers does not have any 'genuine content that could be usefully distinguished either from constitutional law or political theory on the one hand, or the pertinent statutory context, on the other'.[36] For Allan, the legitimacy of judicial review must be defended by appeal to both political theory and settled constitutional tradition, but legal doctrine has 'only very limited capacity to translate fundamental values into concrete judgments in particular cases'.[37] Legal doctrine therefore offers 'no refuge from substantive moral or political judgment; conceptual analysis merely articulates a conclusion reached independently'.[38]

Administrative law should, therefore, 'break free of its exaggerated dependence on conceptual reasoning and its largely formal interpretation of the rule of law; and debates over the foundations of judicial review must move from conceptual abstraction to legal and political substance'.[39] There is, for Allan, no clear distinction between legal judgment and the merits of the salient governmental policy determination when a court undertakes balancing of interests.[40] There is, so he contends, little rhyme or reason to the law concerning jurisdictional error, and the relevant jurisdictional limits could not be identified without recourse to constitutional or political values.[41] There is no clear divide between jurisdictional limits and other public law constraints.[42] The law relating to invalidity is also subject to criticism, such that exceptions to retrospective invalidity are said to rob the doctrinal concept of consistency and integrity.[43]

[33] P Daly, 'A Defence of Administrative Law Doctrine' ch 19 in this volume.
[34] TRS Allan, 'Doctrine and Theory in Administrative Law: The Elusive Quest for Jurisdiction' [2003] *PL* 429.
[35] ibid 431, 434, 438, 439.
[36] ibid 431, 435.
[37] ibid 435.
[38] ibid 436.
[39] ibid 434.
[40] ibid 435.
[41] ibid 439.
[42] ibid 441.
[43] ibid 445–50.

B. Doctrinal *Status Quo*

Trevor Allan expresses his argument forcefully. It should be taken seriously. It should also be subject to careful scrutiny. It is important to begin with reflection on the doctrinal status quo. It would be impossible within the exigencies of space to deal in detail with Allan's arguments concerning existing doctrine. Suffice it to say the following.

We are presented with a picture in which courts are damned if they do, and damned equally if they do not. Thus, they are condemned either because they are said to reason doctrinally in a purely formal manner, or they are condemned because they are cognizant of the complexities entailed, the need to be mindful of context, with the consequence that there are exceptions and qualifications to particular doctrine, but this too is said to reveal the limits of doctrinal reasoning. The impression repeatedly conveyed to the reader is that courts have been missing the real issues from time immemorial, reaching decisions pursuant to doctrinal concepts in a formal manner, without being cognizant of the salient underlying values. This is matched by an analogous view concerning academic discourse, whereby the academic community is said to conceive of doctrine as if it were self-executing, without being mindful of the contestable values thereby entailed.

This picture of the doctrinal status quo is misconceived, with respect to both courts and academia. Let us begin with courts. It is helpful to take a step back to clear the ground. Every legal doctrine, whether in public or private law, is based on certain values. There are no exceptions to this. The values that do and should underpin particular legal doctrines may well be contestable. We shall return to this point in due course. The salient point for present purposes is that when the courts created the doctrines of judicial review 400 years ago, they did so because they believed that they were normatively warranted. They did not do so for some formal reason, whatsoever that might connote. The foundational precepts of review for law, fact, discretion, natural justice, remedies and the like, were created because they embodied values that were felt to be important. They were developed in the centuries thereafter, as the courts refined the doctrine, and adapted it to altered circumstance.[44] Allan's characterisation of legal doctrine, as comprising the bare invocation of, for example, natural justice, without more bares scant relation to legal reality. To the contrary, courts added sub-parts to each legal doctrine as the jurisprudence evolved over the years, as exemplified by the rules relating to matters such as notice, the nature of hearings, reason-giving, appeals and the like that form part of the doctrinal fabric that is natural justice.[45]

The courts were, moreover, fully mindful of the functional complexities of the subject. This is not a modern insight; it has been there from the outset of Administrative law. They did not, for example, believe that natural justice applied in the same way in all instances, and commonly held that the type of hearing would depend on the subject matter, viewed against the statutory backdrop. This was also so in relation to standing, where the courts acknowledged that who could bring a direct challenge for judicial

[44] Craig, *English Administrative Law from 1550* (n 30) chs 8–21.
[45] P Craig, *Administrative Law*, 9th edn (London, Sweet and Maxwell, 2021) chs 12–13.

review would depend, in part, on context and the legislative framework. The same point can be made in the modern context, where the courts have been clear that different normative considerations are relevant in different types of legitimate expectation case. They were, in addition, acutely aware of the difficulties that could arise in relation to invalidity, if, for example, a poor relief rate was declared retrospectively null.

There could be judicial disagreement on these and other issues, and the case law could be messy. This is, however, to say no more than that judges could take different views as to the values underpinning a particular legal doctrine, which is endemic in any realm of law, public or private. There could also be general judicial agreement on the particular doctrinal issue, which might nonetheless be contested by academic scholarship.

This then is the fitting point to consider briefly the academic dimension. There is, as is well known, a very considerable academic literature on judicial review doctrine. There are a plethora of views on just about all aspects of the law and the academic debates can be fierce. There is, however, no one, to my knowledge who believes that, for example, the meaning of jurisdictional error is self-defining, or that the application of natural justice is self-executing, or that the demands of reasonableness review can be expressed in one size fits all terms. There is, to the contrary, a veritable library of literature concerning what should be the intensity of review for error of law. This is no different from the very extensive scholarship in private law, as to the meaning of corrective justice and its implications for tortious liability. The idea that academics are labouring under some narrow and formalistic conception of Administrative law doctrine bears no relation to reality.

It is, moreover, noteworthy, when reflecting on Trevor Allan's critique, to recognise that the UK doctrinal tableau is replicated, albeit with some differences, across all common law systems.[46] It is also noteworthy that the general doctrinal categories used in common law systems will be found in many civil law regimes, subject, once again, to some differences in substance and nomenclature.[47]

C. Alternative Doctrinal Vision

We move then to consider Trevor Allan's alternative doctrinal vision. This is intellectually intriguing, since his preferred replacement for the doctrinal status quo, which he marked gamma, is not immediately clear. There can by definition only be an alternative doctrinal vision, but it is then instructive to consider three possibilities as to what form this might assume.

The first possibility is that we wipe the doctrinal slate clean and create doctrine afresh from the preferred constitutional values. Let us call this 'world 2.0', which is the same as ours in all respects, save for the fact that the doctrinal hard drive has been cleansed in readiness for the new world order. There are doubtless endless fascinating narratives that

[46] See eg H Wilberg and M Elliott (eds), *The Scope and Intensity of Substantive Review: Traversing Taggart's Rainbow* (Oxford, Hart Publishing, 2015).

[47] See eg P Cane et al (eds), *The Oxford Handbook of Comparative Administrative Law* (Oxford, Oxford University Press, 2020).

one could run in this respect, but word limits necessitate that I cut to the chase. There is no legal system that subscribes to 'world 2.0'. The exercise is doomed to failure because the preferred constitutional values, whatsoever they might be, are too abstract to create the doctrinal architecture required by Administrative law. Constitutional ideals of, for example, equal concern and respect, or liberty, do not, in and of themselves, dictate the existence of all doctrinal heads of review, nor do they provide definitive guidance as to the content of any such particular ground. Thus, they furnish scant guidance as to the intensity of review for law, fact or discretion. To put the same point from the converse perspective, the constitutional ideals could only furnish the requisite detail if they replicated the same discussion of values that underpins existing doctrine.[48]

The second possibility is that we wipe the doctrinal slate clean, abjure any doctrinal replacement and determine cases based solely on foundational constitutional values. Let us call this 'world 2.01', which once again is the same in all respects as our world, save for the change proposed here. Doctrine is regarded as a thing of the past, and the courts are duly instructed to decide individual cases based solely on fact, context and constitutional values. There is no legal system that subscribes to 'world 2.01'. It is doomed to failure for a plethora of reasons.[49] There are rule of law concerns as to like being treated alike. There are attendant difficulties of legal certainty. There is the fact that the foundational constitutional values provide no certain guide to many of the issues that arise in Administrative law, such as when a contract made by a public body should be regarded as fettering other powers, the bounds of discretionary power, or the criteria for damages liability. There is the additional problem that the very latitude for differences based on context would be undefined.

The third possibility is that we supplement the existing doctrinal slate, through more rigorous recourse to fundamental values. We call this 'world 2.02'. It is less radical than the previous possibilities. There is much to be said for resort to constitutional value as part of judicial review, and the meaning accorded to such values can be affected by background views on political theory.[50] We should, however, pause for a moment and reflect on the degree of difference between this and the doctrinal status quo. We have already seen that courts have, from the very inception of Administrative law, created doctrine that embodies values regarded as normatively important. They underpin every pillar that constitutes the overall doctrinal architecture. The values that inform different doctrine perforce varied, for the good reason that the doctrinal function was different. It is, however, manifestly clear that the values included protection of liberty and property, as exemplified in the doctrinal case law on rights as a constraint on administrative action. It is equally clear that separation of powers concerns were not treated in some formalistic manner, to the contrary they were centre-stage in the elaboration of limits to judicial review of discretionary determinations, whether for reasonableness

[48] Which seems to be acknowledged in TRS Allan, *The Sovereignty of Law: Freedom, Constitution, and Common Law* (Oxford University Press, 2013) ch 6.

[49] In later work, such as *Sovereignty of Law*, Allan works with doctrine, and does not therefore seem to favour world 2.01.

[50] P Craig, *Public Law and Democracy in the United Kingdom and the United States of America* (Oxford, Oxford University Press, 1993).

or proportionality. It may be that 'more rigorous recourse' to such values would cause a significant re-think of a particular doctrine. This is possible in principle, but unlikely in practice, given that courts already expressly advert to, for example, the importance of the interest affected when applying reasonableness review, and are cognizant of the fact that not all rights are equally important for the purposes of the Human Rights Act 1998. It should in any event be recognised that the doctrinal implications of increased resort to such values will be contestable, more especially so where they are couched in abstract terms. There is, moreover, nothing in 'world 2.02', as compared to the doctrinal status quo, that would help a court to decide how to modify application of particular doctrine in accord with context.

It is fitting to conclude this section with a final word concerning Trevor Allan's doctrinal critique and common law constitutionalism. He would no doubt regard the two as compatible and complementary. He would see the increased recourse to fundamental values as strengthening doctrine and enhancing common law constitutionalism. This is, however, predicated on the assumption that the alternative vision is 'world 2.02', although the extent to which this makes a difference to the doctrinal status quo is doubtful for the reasons set out above. If, however, we go for either of the other possibilities the tension is very real. They both entail, albeit in different ways, a very significant diminution in the role played by doctrine. The common law evolves by and through the development of doctrine in all legal areas, public and private alike. It is through the creation, development and change of causes of action that common law values are expressed. To espouse a concept with the nomenclature of common law constitutionalism, which is predicated on the radical curtailment of the doctrine that gives life to the common law, is problematic to say the least.

4. Administrative Law: Deference, Standards of Review and Application

The final section of this chapter is concerned with deference, a topic on which Trevor Allan has written on a number of occasions.[51] There is, as will be seen, a paradox concerning his critique of Administrative law doctrine, and that directed at deference. We shall return to this in due course after we have addressed the argument concerning deference. There is a large academic literature on the topic, which is reflective of an extensive jurisprudence.[52] This is not the place for any general exegesis on this topic. The focus is on Trevor Allan's view, which he has expressed and defended with vigour. There are two principal strands to the argument, which should be disaggregated for the sake of analytical clarity. They are related, but distinct.

[51] TRS Allan, 'Common Law Reason and the Limits of Judicial Deference', in D Dyzenhaus (ed), *The Unity of Public Law* (Oxford, Hart Publishing, 2004); 'Human Rights and Judicial Review: A Critique of "Due Deference"' [2006] *CLJ* 671; 'Judicial Deference and Judicial Review: Legal Doctrine and Legal Theory' (2011) 127 *LQR* 96.

[52] The literature is cited in Craig, *Administrative Law* (n 45) ch 20 fn 265.

A. Standards of Review and Application

Trevor Allan does not object to the idea that the courts should show some restraint when reviewing the exercise of discretionary power in a rights-based or non-rights-based context, but nonetheless contends that there is no need for any special doctrine of deference, since the factors that the courts consider when showing judicial restraint are properly addressed through application of the normal processes of judicial review. It is this that gives rise to Allan's well-known conclusion, to the effect that any doctrine of deference is either empty in merely repeating what is currently done within standard judicial review doctrine, or it is pernicious if it accords latitude over and beyond this, since this is unwarranted and leads to the vice of double counting, whereby weight is given to considerations such as administrative expertise twice over.[53]

The argument is predicated on the assumption that the normal process of judicial review is exhausted by the articulation of distinctive standards of review, each of which embodies conclusions as to the appropriate degree of leeway accorded to the primary decision-maker. Thus, for example, classic *Wednesbury* reasonableness review is premised on the assumption that an administrative decision that does not impact on rights should only be overturned if the claimant can show some manifest unreasonableness by the public body. For Allan, any talk of deference over and beyond this is either otiose, through repetition of what is already entailed by adherence to the *Wednesbury* test, or pernicious in according the public body some extra element of deference over and beyond what is already entailed by that standard of review.

This is an important argument, and we should clear the ground at the outset. It can readily be accepted that deference/respect/weight must be located within the standard fabric of judicial review. They are not and cannot be free-standing concepts. Deference/respect/weight are not in and of themselves tests for review at all, and this is so whatever their content. They are considerations that inform the way in which a test for review, such as reasonableness or proportionality, should be applied. It would, therefore, be meaningless to conclude that considerable weight should be accorded to the primary decision-maker without posing the inquiry in the context of a test for review, since no answer could logically be forthcoming. Deference and respect modulate application of, for example, proportionality. They are not in themselves tests for review. While Trevor Allan is assuredly correct in this respect, no one argues to the contrary.[54]

The substance of Allan's argument is, nonetheless, misconceived, since it misses the distinction between choice as to the standard of review and choice as to the manner of its application. A version of this distinction was articulated by Mark Elliott, when he distinguished between intrinsic deference and adjudicative deference.[55] The former concerns the relative degree of deference that should be afforded to the

[53] Allan, 'A Critique of "Due Deference"' (n 51) 675–76.

[54] See eg P Daly, *A Theory of Deference in Administrative Law: Basis, Application and Scope* (Cambridge, Cambridge University Press, 2012); M Lewans, *Administrative Law and Judicial Deference* (Oxford, Hart Publishing, 2016).

[55] M Elliott, 'From Bifurcation to Calibration: Twin-Track Deference and the Culture of Justification', in Wilberg and Elliott (eds), *Scope and Intensity of Substantive Review* (n 46) ch 4.

primary decision-maker for a particular type of case by reason of the subject matter involved; it will be affected by 'the normative significance of the value impacted by the impugned decision';[56] and will be relatively abstract in nature.[57] The latter is expressive of reasons for affording more fine-tuned calibration of the chosen standard.

This point can be exemplified by the standard of review and its application in rights-based cases in the UK.[58] The UK uses a proportionality test for review under the Human Rights Act 1998. The paradigm case is a prima facie breach of a Convention right, to which the government proffers a defence. The Strasbourg Court requires proof that the government action constitutes a proportionate response to the limitation of the right on one of the specified grounds. The proportionality standard of review will commonly require strict scrutiny by the reviewing court, and this embodies the normative assumption that rights should be carefully safeguarded.

There is, however, variance in the application of this standard. There are two related rationales for doing so. Not all rights are regarded as equally important: thus, for example, a right to property is not as important as a right to life. Not all invasions of the same right are equally important: thus, for example, invocation of the right to free speech to protect the sale of pornography will not be treated as significant as curtailment of the right during elections.[59]

The salient point for present purposes is that adjudicative deference fine tunes the basic standard of proportionality review as it applies to rights-based cases, and in doing so affects the intensity of judicial review.[60] This is illustrative of a theme that stretches across the entire terrain of review. The wider the prima facie remit of the standard of review, the greater the need for modulation in its application, because the heterogeneity of cases that fall within the standard preclude a one size fits all answer.

This begs the obvious question as to why the standard of review should not be fine-tuned, thereby alleviating the need for variance in application. This does occur in some instances, as exemplified by refinement in the standards of EU proportionality review. However, the HRA exemplifies the difficulty of fine-tuning the standard itself. It would require demarcation of what rights should be regarded as more important, *and* which invasions of significant rights should be treated as more pressing, followed by specification of the distinctive standard of review for each such category. The difficulties of this exercise are self-evident.

Adjudicative deference as conceptualised above is the norm when the courts use deference/respect/weight. It is not otiose, since it does not merely repeat what is already contained in the standard of review itself. It is not pernicious, since the fine-tuning of application of the standard of review is normatively warranted, embodying conclusions as to the more particular considerations that are relevant when applying a relatively abstract standard of review to a more concrete situation.

[56] ibid 76.

[57] ibid 81.

[58] Analogous techniques are evident in the EU: P Craig, *EU Administrative Law*, 3rd edn (Oxford, Oxford University Press, 2018) chs 16, 19.

[59] Compare *Belfast City Council v Miss Behavin' Ltd* [2007] 1 WLR 1420, and *R (ProLife Alliance) v BBC* [2004] 1 AC 185.

[60] P Craig, 'Varying Intensity of Judicial Review: A Conceptual Analysis' [2022] *PL* 442.

B. Internal and External Perspectives

There is a second strand to Trevor Allan's discourse on deference, which is the distinction between the internal and the external perspective. He rejects the idea that the courts should be swayed by factors that might be regarded as 'external' to the intrinsic quality of the decision under review. The judge should only defer to the extent that the reasons proffered are persuasive, and any deference should be regarded as 'internal' to the ordinary principles of review applied by the courts, with due regard for the particularities and circumstances of the case.

It is important once again to clear the ground. Allan is undoubtedly correct that deference should not be regarded as some trump, such that the mere mention of 'democratic credential' leads the court to refrain from judicial review, or accept without more the view taken by the legislature or executive. There is, however, no academic who maintains such a position, nor is it the view taken by the courts, who have made clear that deference has to be earned through reasoned argument.

The crucial issue is the factors regarded as relevant in deciding on the latitude afforded to the primary decision-maker. There is room for debate about this issue, both in terms of the substantive factors considered to be legitimate in deciding on deference, and the nomenclature accorded to them. Thus, while it is generally agreed, including by Allan, that expertise should be a relevant factor in this regard, there is more debate as to whether constitutional considerations should be relevant. There is much to be gained by making such factors explicit, both in terms of transparency per se and because it thereby facilitates dialogue as to their legitimacy.

The salient point for present purposes is the meaning and utility of the distinction between the 'internal' and the 'external' when making this determination. The difficulty in this regard is exemplified by the fact that while Allan is content for factors such as expertise to be considered, this is predicated on the assumption that they are warranted on the facts and conceptualised as internal to the 'intrinsic quality' of the decision when applying the ordinary precepts of judicial review, rather than as 'external factors'. The difficulty is that the distinction between matters that are 'internal' to the determination of the legal right and those that are 'external' is an imperfect guide in relation to epistemic, institutional or constitutional rationales for restraint. It presupposes a neat two-step inquiry in which the meaning of the right is elaborated, the internal inquiry, and there is then a further determination as to whether that might be modified through taking cognizance of epistemic, institutional or constitutional considerations, the external inquiry. This neat two-step sequence is belied by the reality of much adjudication in rights-based cases.

Thus, in cases such as *Animal Defenders* the House of Lords did not make an abstract determination of whether freedom of speech was violated by the legislative constraint, and then consider any possible legislative excuse.[61] To the contrary, the legislative rationale for placing this constraint was crucial to the judicial inquiry as to whether the right had been violated and whether there were justifications for the

[61] *R (Animal Defenders International) v Secretary of State for Culture, Media and Sport* [2008] 1 AC 1312.

limitation. The same is true for the mode of judicial inquiry in most cases where epistemic or institutional considerations are taken into account in deciding whether a limitation of a right was proportionate or not, such factors being part of the initial legal determination on this issue, not something undertaken as an external inquiry after an internal assessment has been made.[62] The fact that it is the democratically elected legislature that made the initial choice is not determinative of its legality, but nor is it something external to the intrinsic quality of the decision. To accord respect to the legislative determination does not mean submission,[63] nor does it entail judicial abdication of responsibility. It is reflective of the contested nature of rights determinations, and a judicial willingness to consider seriously the interpretation given to a right by the democratic branch of government.

C. Doctrine, Deference and Paradox

We can now address the paradox, adverted to earlier, that underpins Allan's arguments concerning Administrative law doctrine and that concerning deference. A cornerstone of the argument against judicial review doctrine is, as we have seen, that the doctrinal heads are vacuous and devoid of meaningful substance. The arguments to the contrary have been set out above.

The paradox is then as follows. Judicial considerations of deference/respect/weight are designed to give greater guidance as to the application of standards of review in the manner adumbrated above. In conceptual terms, deference/respect/weight are predicated on the assumption that there are limits as to how far one can fine tune the standards of review themselves, and that there should therefore be tools that help to determine the application of any such standard in a particular case. Insofar as Trevor Allan feels that doctrine is defective because it is vacuous, overly formal and the like, he should then welcome tools designed to imbue the application of such standards of review with greater content, more especially given that the factors considered in this respect embody important constitutional values.

The same point can be put from the converse perspective. Let us imagine that the language of deference/respect/weight had never been legally invented. Let us imagine also that courts mindful of Allan's critique of doctrine seek to furnish more guidance on the constitutional values that underpin doctrine. They articulate and develop such values. The values are very likely to include, inter alia, considerations relating to matters such as expertise, institutional function, and constitutional legitimacy, and their role would, in substance, be no different from that performed by such factors under the nomenclature of deference/respect/weight.

[62] See from among many examples, *Samaroo v Secretary of State for the Home Department* [2001] UKHRR 1150; *R (Bloggs 61) v Secretary of State for the Home Department* [2003] 1 WLR 2724; *R (Begum) v Denbigh High School Governors* [2007] 1 AC 100.

[63] D Dyzenhaus, 'The Politics of Deference: Judicial Review and Democracy', in M Taggart (ed), *The Province of Administrative Law* (Oxford, Hart Publishing, 1997) 279.

5. Conclusion

Trevor Allan has over the years written on big issues within public law broadly conceived. He has made important contributions to the academic literature and that is assuredly so notwithstanding the fact that I disagree with some of the arguments. They merit close scrutiny and careful evaluation, in accord with the basic intellectual principle that the more far-reaching the argument, the more secure must be its foundations.

12

Common Law and the Common Good

MICHAEL FORAN

> It is necessarily implicit that ... a legislature, even if sovereign ... must act for the public good.[1]

> The law must be regarded as a public asset, intended to serve the public good: it cannot be merely an instrument for promoting the interests of a ruling elite.[2]

> Political obligation is a matter of what we owe to other members of the community, who collaborate with us in pursuit of the public good and in defence of the rule of law.[3]

One might be forgiven for presuming that the author of these quotes was none other than Adrian Vermeule, the Harvard professor who has emerged as a leading natural law critic of originalism and a proponent of what he terms 'Common Good Constitutionalism'.[4] They are, in fact, the words of Trevor Allan, grounded within common *law* constitutionalism. In one sense, this should come as no surprise. Common law constitutionalism draws quite explicitly upon an anti-positivist perspective which embraces a morally engaged approach to legal reasoning, rejecting any neat divide between legal and political principle.[5] Yet, in another sense, the similarities between these statements and the emerging theory of common good constitutionalism invite reflection, particularly in light of some of the alarmed criticism that Vermeule has faced, even from those who would ordinarily be quite sympathetic to Allan.[6]

[1] TRS Allan, *The Sovereignty of Law: Freedom, Constitution, and Common Law* (Oxford, Oxford University Press 2013) 293.

[2] TRS Allan, 'Why the Law Is What It Ought to Be' (2020) 11 *Jurisprudence* 574, 575.

[3] ibid 577.

[4] A Vermeule, *Common Good Constitutionalism* (Medford, Polity Press, 2022).

[5] See TRS Allan, 'Principle, Practice, and Precedent: Vindicating Justice, According to Law' (2018) 77 *CLJ* 269; J Laws, 'The Constitution, Morals and Rights' [1996] *PL* 622; J Laws, 'Law and Democracy' [1995] *PL* 72.

[6] See D Dyzenhaus, 'The Snake Charmers' (*Verfassungsblog*, 7 March 2022) verfassungsblog.de/os5-snake-charmers/. One explanation for this is the belief that an opposition to liberalism is necessarily an endorsement of autocracy, tyranny, or totalitarianism, a point Vermeule ardently rejects, the premise of *Common Good Constitutionalism* being that there is an older tradition of constitutionalism which predates liberalism and which does not collapse into totalitarianism. As Welikala notes, 'it should be clear that the necessarily unitary conceptualisation of the "common good" in the classical tradition is no licence whatsoever for authoritarianism, theocracy, or purely majoritarian forms of political monism ...': A Welikala '"Administrative Law Imagination" and "Legality without Liberalism" in New Emergencies: Some Reflections from Comparative

The connection between the common good and the common law tradition, including common law constitutionalism, remains somewhat underexplored. Drawing on the work of TRS Allan, I hope to bridge some of this divide in emphasis by exploring the role of the common law within the classical natural law tradition. However, I also wish to suggest that neutrality on questions of the good life, a hallmark of Dworkin's political liberalism, is not sustainable in light of the commitment, embraced by both him and Allan, that law must serve the public good. If law is to be a public asset – a common good – it cannot refuse to take a stand on the flourishing of legal subjects. Allan's political liberalism, to the extent that it embraces this neutrality principle, is therefore open to challenge for failing to provide adequate content to the concept of the public good which does so much work within his work. To constitute a defensible scheme of justice, law must be defended as a plausible attempt at the common good, intended to improve the lives of its subjects by facilitating their flourishing among a community of moral equals. With this in mind, common good constitutionalism presents a challenge and a rallying cry to anti-positivists, encouraging them to follow through on their commitment to the idea that the rule of law demands good government in the best interests of the governed. To do this, we must think seriously about what those interests require, paying sufficient attention to the specific context and institutional history of our law. Good government cannot be neutral on the good life any more than it can be neutral on the nature and scope of fundamental rights.

A substantive conception of the good life, appropriately respectful of the diverse ways such a life might be lived, is necessary if law is to truly pursue the common good. Requirements of fundamental legal equality, manifesting a commitment to the equal dignity of persons, grounds the rule of law as a defensible scheme of public justice.[7] But this commitment also demands that law be ordered towards a politics which views the flourishing of each and every member of our community as an essential feature of its own success. Put simply, the normative commitments latent within the ideal of legality are not and cannot be neutral as to the ends of just government. There is an internal moral standard within the rule of law which manifests principled constraints on what officials can do in pursuit of the common good. This much is a hallmark of Allan's extensive and richly nuanced jurisprudence and should serve as a benchmark against which we are to determine whether the common good is genuinely common; whether it is

Constitutional Law' (2023) 27 *Edinburgh Law Review* 364, 369. Another cause of alarm may be the fact that Vermeule has endorsed the descriptive accuracy of the work of Carl Schmitt. Vermeule has also described Schmitt as having fallen into an 'apostasy to Nazism' and has never endorsed Schmitt's positive moral vision beyond his critique of liberalism and his descriptive predictions of the collapse of modernist technocracy: A Vermeule, 'The Ark of Tradition' (*kirkcentre*, 19 Nov 2017), kirkcenter.org/reviews/the-ark-of-tradition. Further still, some may look to the fact that Vermeule is Catholic and has written about Catholic political theory in the past as evidence that *Common Good Constitutionalism* is a prelude to theocracy. Again, this is explicitly rejected by Vermeule, who argues that his theory does not depend upon any theological account of ultimate ends but does draw upon the natural law tradition which has its roots in ancient Greece and in no way presupposes or necessitates a commitment to Catholic legal theory: A Vermeule, 'The Common Good as a Universal Framework' (*Balkinization*, 27 July 2022) balkin.blogspot.com/2022/07/the-common-good-as-universal-framework.html; Vermeule, *Common Good Constitutionalism* (n 4) 29. One may be left thinking that some of this alarm has come from a lack of academic charity. But scholarship is far better served by responding to the best version of an opponent's argument.

[7] See M Foran, 'Equal Dignity and the Common Good' (2023) 46 *Harvard Journal of Law & Public Policy* 1009.

appropriately respectful of the fundamental rights of persons. But there must also be plausible limits on what constitutes the common good which are not only grounded in constraints but in what the law can enable and facilitate. This aspect of legality – what law must be directed towards if it is to meet its internal standards of just governance – warrants as detailed elaboration as Allan has provided for the common law method of rights protection.

1. The Classical Legal Tradition

It is hard to extract common good constitutionalism from its American context. This is partially due to the focus Vermeule places on using this theory as a foil for originalism, a phenomenon almost unique to the United States of America, that has thankfully not had much influence within the British common law system.[8] Indeed, a recurring criticism of this project has been the somewhat parochial nature of much of the surrounding debate and discussion. Yet this parochialism is driven as much by the response that has been engendered as by anything that Vermeule himself has consciously encouraged. Indeed, the stated aim of his book is to shift US constitutional theory out of its parochialism by recovering a lost international tradition within which it once operated.[9] That tradition, referred to as the Classical Legal Tradition, is one which is grounded explicitly within a natural law framework, rejecting legal positivism on both theoretical and historical grounds as inconsistent with our practice from the ancient world through to the modern common law. In this, he draws upon the largely forgotten natural law bedrock of western jurisprudence which, in subtly different guises, has influenced much of our historic and existing constitutional practice.[10]

In the classical legal tradition, law is understood in a distinctly anti-positivist manner, one that rejects any account which conflates it with brute political will. Instead, to use Aquinas' famous description, law is an ordinance of reason for the common good and promulgated by a legitimate political authority who demonstrates appropriate care for the community.[11] This should not be taken to mean that the classical legal tradition, or the natural law tradition which informs it, collapses into Thomism.[12] Aquinas'

[8] Vermeule began this project by calling on constitutional scholars and practitioners to move beyond originalism: A Vermeule, 'Beyond Originalism' *The Atlantic* (31 March 2020), www.theatlantic.com/ideas/archive/2020/03/common-good-constitutionalism/609037/. See also Vermeule, *Common Good Constitutionalism* (n 4) ch 3; A Vermeule, 'Pickwickian Originalism' (*Ius & Iustitium*, 22 March 2022), iusetiustitium.com/pickwickian-originalism/; C Casey and A Vermeule, 'If Every Judge Is an Originalist, Originalism Is Meaningless' *The Washington Post* (25 March 2022) www.washingtonpost.com/outlook/2022/03/25/if-every-judge-is-an-originalist-originalism-is-meaningless/.

[9] Vermeule, *Common Good Constitutionalism* (n 4) 1–3.

[10] See RH Helmholz, *Natural Law in Court: A History of Legal Theory in Practice* (Cambridge, Harvard University Press 2015).

[11] T Aquinas, *Summa Theologica*, pt I-II, q 90 art 4. See also Vermeule, *Common Good Constitutionalism* (n 4) 3–4.

[12] Indeed, Vermeule expressly rejects this contention, arguing that the conception of the common good embraced by the classical legal tradition is a *legal* one, not a philosophical or theological one: A Vermeule, 'The Common Good as a *Legal* Concept' (*Ius & Iustitium*, 16 Nov 2022), iusetiustitium.com/the-common-good-as-a-legal-concept/.

account of law is a useful summary of a tradition which stretches back to ancient Greece and Rome, associated with the thought of Aristotle,[13] Cicero,[14] Augustine,[15] and more recently the likes of Heinrich Rommen,[16] Yves Simons,[17] and John Finnis.[18] The classical tradition is concerned with, in very broad terms, 'the requirements of practical reasonableness in relation to the good of human beings who, because they live in community with one another, are confronted with problems of justice and rights, of authority, law, and obligation'.[19] A major focus of the jurisprudential aspect of the tradition has been inquiry into the 'nature, purpose, and obligation of human law'.[20] At that level of abstraction, a broadly defined conception of the common good as a political or moral concept can be advanced. This is not what Vermeule is thinking of when describing the common good as a distinctly legal concept, worked out within our existing and historic legal practice, understood not as a mere positivistic social practice but as a living tradition informed by moral reason.[21]

A rejection of positivism entails a conception of legal order which expands beyond mere rules and rulings to include moral and political principles which help to inform their content, placing limits on plausible conceptions of such rules and rulings by reference to reason and justice. To Aquinas, right is the object of justice, a rational ordering of social behaviour, directing us in our relations with fellow members of our community.[22] This ordering – right – is either natural, 'existing in some sense apart from, and normative for, human artifice and institutions', or it is positive, 'the product of consensus in the community or of institution by the *princeps*'.[23] This being said, positive right, on this understanding, is not the mere product of will, it is an attempt by a community or a political authority to interpret and provide greater specification to the requirements of justice within their given context.[24]

Within the classical tradition, the relationship between law and right, be it natural or positive, is complex. Here, the distinction between *lex* and *ius* is illustrative. The classical tradition distinguishes, as many languages do, between these two senses of 'law'.[25] On this view, *lex* is positive law and *ius* is the body of law generally, 'including and subsuming *lex* but transcending it, and containing general principles of jurisprudence

[13] G Duke, *Aristotle and Law: On the Politics of Nomos* (Cambridge, Cambridge University Press, 2019).

[14] Cicero, *The Republic and the Laws* (London, Penguin Classics, 2008).

[15] MM Kundmueller and JJ Castle, 'When a Law Is No Law at All: Martin Luther King, Jr.'s Use of Augustine and Aquinas in the Battle Against Segregation' in BZ Kabala, A Menchaca-Bagnulo and N Pinkoski (eds), *Augustine in a Time of Crisis: Politics and Religion Contested* (London, Palgrave MacMillan 2021).

[16] HA Rommen, *The Natural Law: A Study in Legal and Social History and Philosophy*, TR Hanley trans (Indianapolis, Liberty Fund 1998).

[17] YR Simons, *A General Theory of Authority* (South Bend, Notre Dame University Press, 1980) and MD Torre (ed), *The Philosopher's Calling: An Yves Simon Reader* (South Bend, Notre Dame University Press, 2021).

[18] J Finnis, *Natural Law and Natural Rights* (Oxford, Oxford University Press 1980).

[19] J Pojanowski and K Walsh, 'Enduring Originalism' (2016) 105 *The Georgetown Law Journal* 97, 120.

[20] Finnis, *Natural Law* (n 18) 351.

[21] Vermeule, 'Common Good as a *Legal* Concept' (n 12).

[22] Aquinas, *Summa Theologica* (n 11) pt II-II, q 57 art 1.

[23] G Postema, *Bentham and the Common Law Tradition* (Oxford, Oxford University Press, 1986) 40. See also Aquinas (n 11) pt II-II, q 57 art 2.

[24] As such Aquinas is explicit that human will can, by common agreement, make something just only if it is not, in itself, contrary to natural justice: Aquinas (n 11) pr II-II, q 57 art 2.

[25] In French, *loi* and *droit*; in Spanish, *ley* and *derecho*, etc.

and legal justice'.[26] Posited law is, to Vermeule, a body of precepts or ordinances defined with respect to principles of justice – right – but also the product of attempts by political authority and legal officials to apply these general principles to particular contexts. *Lex* and *ius* are thus co-constitutive: posited law is an application or interpretation of principles of right which are themselves given clearer meaning in the process of interpretation and application.[27] As such, *ius* is not simply a body of principles external to our law which acts upon it, even if justice and the common good are the proper ends of law. Rather, *ius* is law in its entirety; a public scheme of justice directed towards the common good. A full understanding of *ius* includes its implementation or application within a given political context: *lex*. Neither can be understood in abstraction from the other. As such, '*lex* is a source of *ius* but does not exhaust its content'.[28]

On this view, law, in its fullest sense, cannot be separated from the ends that it is to be put to.[29] It is not a mere means to pursue whatever ends a political authority wishes. Rather, to rule through law is to adopt a distinctive attitude towards legal subjects, one which views their collective flourishing as a central feature of the systems success as law. The common good is thus the proper end of any juridical order, manifesting within legal officials a requirement to act as custodians for the interests of the governed.[30] Within common good constitutionalism this manifests as an overarching constitutional duty, and entailed authority, upon legal officials to pursue a public good.[31] Public authority 'is bounded and limited by the very condition that gives it legitimacy: that the ruling authority always act through reasoned ordinances conducing to the common good, to public rather than private interest'.[32]

This may seem like a banal statement. Few constitutional theorists would argue that public authorities can or should act to further their own private interest. What differentiates the classical legal tradition from more liberal forms of constitutionalism is the rejection of an account of the public good which purports to be neutral on questions of the good life or the proper ends of just government. On the classical view, the public interest is not simply a constraint on state power, it is also an end to which it should be oriented, defined by the natural law triptych of peace, justice, and abundance.[33] Central to this is a robust understanding of the communal nature of political and legal obligation. As TH Green notes, '[A]n interest in the common good is the ground of political society, in the sense that without it no body of people would recognise any authority as having a claim on their common obedience'.[34] This does not mean that the individual must be absorbed into the political community or subjected to it. Indeed, Vermeule expressly rejects this claim, describing it as the opposite error to that made by

[26] Vermeule, *Common Good Constitutionalism* (n 4) 4.

[27] Aquinas, *Summa Theologica* (n 11) I-II, q 95 art 2. See also Finnis, *Natural Law* (n 18) 284–85.

[28] Vermeule, *Common Good Constitutionalism* (n 4) 4.

[29] See Finnis, *Natural Law* (n 18) ch 1.

[30] Raz associates this with the rule of law as distinct from the concept of law, but neatly captures the idea nevertheless: J Raz, 'The Law's Own Virtue' (2019) 39 *OJLS* 1.

[31] Subject, as any constitutional order must be, to considerations of comity and respect for institutional role morality: Vermeule, *Common Good Constitutionalism* (n 4) 43–47.

[32] ibid 7.

[33] ibid 30–38. See also M Foran 'Legality Without Liberalism: The Rule of Law and the Environmental Emergency' (2023) 27 *Edinburgh Law Review* 345.

[34] TH Green, *Lectures on the Principles of Political Obligation* (London, Longman, Green and Co, 1950) 109.

the libertarian who views political morality as wholly contained within the interests of atomistic individuals severed from communal goods.[35]

How then does the common law fit into this picture? Vermeule draws quite explicitly upon Roman and civilian jurisprudence in describing the classical legal tradition.[36] For someone operating within a common law system, this might seem strange. Yet to Vermeule, the common law is 'a local variant' of the classical Roman and European tradition, the *ius commune*.[37] His claim is that common law shares 'the classical legal cosmology in which civil positive law gives specification to, and is interpreted in light of, general background principles of natural law and the law of nations, understood as enduring commitments of the legal order'.[38] But does this characterisation match how common law theorists would themselves view the common law?

2. Situating the Common Law

Classical common law theory drew upon medieval understanding that law is not made exclusively by a political authority such as a King or a Parliament, but is rather 'the expression of a deeper reality which is merely discovered and publicly declared by them'.[39] To classical common law theorists, this deeper reality was not primarily a set of abstract principles of justice but rather the concrete working out of such principles through the customs and practices of the community.

The presumption is that the traditions and customs of the land maintain their usage through time precisely because they are just and reasonable, accepted by political community as worthy of their allegiance.[40] Unjust or unreasonable practices will be abandoned such that the common law 'works itself pure'.[41] But this reveals a tension within common law theory between rival interpretations of its foundational commitments: on the one hand, a positivism focused on social facts, history, and practice, and, on the other, an anti-positivism more attuned to reason, tradition, and justice. If understood in a positivist guise, common law theory ostensibly conflicts with natural law theory because the source of these underlying principles is not a wholly external set of rational principles but instead historically evidenced national custom. Yet, if framed entirely by reference to reason and justification, common law theory collapses into external morality or private politics, unconnected to the practice that it seeks to justify.

[35] Vermeule, *Common Good Constitutionalism* (n 4) 29.

[36] ibid 6–8, 18, 54–56, 84–89, 136–37, 177.

[37] ibid 5. Indeed, the very name 'Common Law' derives from the *ius commune*; F Pollock and F Maitland, *The History of English Law before the Time of Edward I*, 2nd edn (Liberty Fund, 2010 [1895]) 176. See also: TJ McSweeney, *Priests of the Law: Roman Law and the Making of the Common Law's First Professionals* (Oxford, Oxford University Press 2019).

[38] Vermeule, *Common Good Constitutionalism* (n 4) 55.

[39] Postema, *Bentham and the Common Law Tradition* (n 23) 4; See also FA Hayek, *The Constitution of Liberty* (London, Routledge & Kegan Paul, 1960) 163.

[40] Allan, 'Why the Law Is What It Ought to Be' (n 2) 575; See also R Dworkin, *Law's Empire* (Cambridge, Harvard University Press, 1986) 90–94.

[41] *Omychund v Barker* (1744), 1 Atk 22, 33; 26 ER 15, 23. See also *James v Price* (1773), Lofft 219, 220; 98 ER 619, 621; *Jones v Randall* (1774), 1 Cowp 37; 98 ER 954, 955.

It is here where Allan does some of his best work: resolving this tension by challenging its frame, premised upon a sharp distinction between legal practice and moral reason. To Allan, legal practice is a moral – not merely social – practice: 'legal argument is simply moral argument within the context of a specific tradition … legal practice giving detailed content to what would otherwise be an appeal to very abstract and indeterminate moral standards'.[42] Each of these aspects of legality is essential. Morally inert description of social practice fails to distinguish between specific rules or rulings and the moral basis of those rules or rulings within general principle.[43] But moral reason abstracted from legal practice fails to give adequate expression of the law of a given community: '[l]egality qualifies justice, as it might otherwise be understood, by rooting it in practice – the practice of the particular community in which justice is sought as a collaborative endeavor, grounded in a shared tradition'.[44] As such, '[t]he law is always in a process of transition, acquiring greater determinacy and precision as it is applied to novel circumstances'.[45]

We can make sense of this only if we understand that for the classical Common Law theorist, custom is not simply a collection of practices, social facts which can be determined without recourse to moral deliberation.[46] To constitute a custom capable of grounding legal doctrine, social practices must be underpinned by moral reasons which entail political obligations that bind members of the social community. These customs form an important source of Common Law which are taken to be authoritative expressions of the principles which inform our customary practices. As Postema notes, 'Common Law is seen to be the *expression* or manifestation of commonly shared values and conceptions of reasonableness and the common good'.[47] Under the Common Law, custom is a valid source of law, not because it is the *mere* practice of the community, but because it is the *moral* practice of the community, informed by considerations of justice.

Once the common law is understood in this manner, the contention that it is a local variant of a wider classical legal framework grounded within natural law jurisprudence becomes easier to comprehend. This is because, the ostensible conflict between custom and orders promulgated by a *princeps* falls away once one accounts for the role that Aquinas attributed to custom within his own framework:

> A law, properly speaking regards first and foremost the order to the common good. Now to order anything to the common good, belongs either to the whole people, or to someone who is the viceregent of the whole people. And therefore the making of a law belongs wither to the whole people or to a public personage who has care of the whole people.[48]

[42] Allan, 'Why the Law Is What It Ought to Be' (n 2) 579.

[43] ibid 576.

[44] TRS Allan, 'Law as a Branch of Morality: The Unity of Practice and Principle' (2020) 65 *American Journal of Jurisprudence* 1, 6.

[45] Allan, 'Why the Law Is What It Ought to Be' (n 2) 578.

[46] See F Jiménez, 'Legal Principles, Law, and Tradition' (2022) 33 *Yale Journal of Law and the Humanities* 59. Jiménez does recognise moral judgement as a part of custom but sees it was a historical social fact about the views held by members of a community rather than something that demands the engagement of our own moral judgement for its full understanding.

[47] Postema, *Bentham and the Common Law Tradition* (n 23) 7.

[48] Aquinas, *Summa Theologica* (n 11) I-II, q 90, art 3.

As such, custom – the moral practices that evolve and maintain themselves within community – can properly be accounted for within a natural law framework as a people's collective but diffuse practice of determination, applying general moral principles to concrete social context. Custom then becomes a source of common law because it is rooted in the moral practice of the community. Legitimate political authorities in the form of common law judges, or even Parliament, are then tasked with interpreting those principles, where there is dispute, by reference to moral reasons capable of commanding the support of the community. Thus we see classical common law theorists presenting the legislative acts of Parliament as 'declarative and remedial of ancient Common Law, perhaps enlarging or restricting this ancient custom, but not essentially altering or adding to it'.[49] Allan, representing the best of this tradition, similarly argues that statute must be seen as a contribution to and interpretation of the principles which underpin previous practices, correcting errors in the law that it amends by reference to the law's own principles.[50] Legislative rules are thus 'subsumed into the larger body of the law', their content interpreted by reference to background, unwritten principles of justice.[51]

This interpretation must extend beyond a detached description of practice or what has come before. The interaction between reason and precedent is a hallmark of common law adjudication which also reveals an important feature of the classical legal tradition: the rejection of an account of law which collapses into either positivistic convention or pure moral judgement.[52] No natural lawyer working within the classical tradition described by Vermeule would disagree with Allan when he stresses that '[w]e cannot properly classify the common law as either critical (universal) or positive morality. It is a complex admixture of both'.[53]

David Dyzenhaus is thus mistaken when he claims that Vermeule has abandoned the dimension of fit within his theory.[54] Just as Allan does, Vermeule sees law as reliant upon a complex admixture of critical and positive morality. It is for this reason that he stresses that '[c]ommon good constitutionalism shares the [Dworkinian] view that the positive provisions of the *ius civile* … can only be interpreted in light of principles of political morality that are themselves part of the law'. With this in mind, he stresses that '[t]he point is not to reclaim the insights of the classical tradition out of nostalgia', but because it is 'the best of our tradition, with the emphasis on both "best" (justification) and "tradition" (fit)'.[55] Thus, '[d]eveloping constitutionalism celebrates continuity with the enduring principles of the past; it recognizes change in applications only insofar as necessary in order for those principles to unfold in accordance

[49] Postema, *Bentham and the Common Law Tradition* (n 23) 17. See also Sir William Blackstone, Commentaries on the Laws of England, W Prest ed (Oxford, Oxford University Press, 2016 [1783]) 73–74, 127–28; Sir Matthew Hale, *The History of the Common Law of England*, CM Gray ed (Chicago, University of Chicago Press, 1973 [1739]) 17.

[50] Allan, 'Why the Law Is What It Ought to Be' (n 2) 576; Allan, 'Law as a Branch of Morality: The Unity of Practice and Principle' (n 54) 14.

[51] Allan, 'Law as a Branch of Morality' (n 44) 14–15.

[52] ibid 15.

[53] Allan, *Sovereignty of Law* (n 1) 64.

[54] D Dyzenhaus, 'More Protestant than Luther or Dworkin? TRS Allan on Law and Morals', ch 2 in this volume.

[55] Vermeule, *Common Good Constitutionalism* (n 4) 5–6.

with their true natures and to retain those natures in new environments'.[56] This is contrasted with corruptions, where 'the relevant principle is *itself* taken to change', representing 'a break with the past that mutilates or fundamentally transforms the core and essence of the doctrine'.[57] Far from abandoning requirements of fit, Vermeule posits a theory of constitutionalism with the express purpose 'to preserve the rational principles of the constitutional order as the circumstances of the political, social, and economic environment change'.[58]

This being the case, the frequent references that Vermeule makes to natural law theory in his book are perfectly germane, given the deep and intimate connection between common law and natural law as a matter of both history and theory. The Natural Law was heavily influential to the development of the common law and the doctrine of common law rights, at least as they were traditionally understood.[59] Far from being something to contrast the common law with, natural law was integral to its development, both as a source of common law and as a model for the systematic interconnectedness of legal concepts.[60] It was widely accepted at the seminal points of common law exegesis and by the seminal institutional writers, from Coke to Hale to Blackstone, that 'Natural Law was a body of self-evidently valid ideas antecedent to the Common Law and in some way superior to it'.[61] Coke and his contemporaries, in their description of common law, constantly referenced the law of nature as a source of common law doctrine.[62] General understanding that the natural law was integral to the common law was so widespread as to be banal.[63]

The fusion of critical and positive morality within classical common law is illustrated by the role that natural law principles played within common law doctrine, being invoked in hard cases to help further or correct the common law and tacitly accepted in ordinary legal practice. As such, natural law informed settled doctrine and could also be relied upon as a source of common law where no positive law could be found. Its general principles could be drawn upon to answer concrete questions.[64] They were not themselves independently justiciable when freed from common law principle or rule, however. Even in some of the more blatant examples of natural law directly informing common law principle such as the neighbour principle grounding the law of negligence, one needed to concretise such arguments into more discrete doctrine.

Yet this is precisely how natural law theory envisages the process of application, concretising general principles of *ius* into posited rules and doctrines of *lex*, understood

[56] ibid 118.

[57] ibid 122–23.

[58] ibid 122. See also A Vermeule, 'The Theory and Practice of Common Good Constitutionalism' (*Ius & Iustitium*, 8 August 2022) iusetiustitium.com/the-theory-and-practice-of-common-good-constitutionalism/.

[59] See the many examples provided in DJ Ibbetson, 'Natural Law and Common Law' (2001) 5 *Edinburgh Law Review* 4. See also Helmholz, *Natural Law in Court* (n 10).

[60] Ibbetson, 'Natural Law and Common Law' (n 59) 6–7.

[61] ibid 8.

[62] AD Boyer, '"Understanding, Authority, and Will": Sir Edward Coke and the Elizabethan Origins of Judicial Review' (1997) 43 *Boston College Law Review* 43.

[63] See Helmholz, *Natural Law in Court* (n 10) 96–100; Ibbetson, 'Natural Law and Common Law' (n 59) 7–9.

[64] See eg *Manby v Scot* (1661–1662), 1 Keb 69, 363; 83 ER 826, 996: 'There being no presidents we must resort to the law of Nature'.

not merely as an act of will, but as an interpretation of *ius*. The classical legal method is virtually identical to the common law method, at least with regard to the interplay between critical and posited morality. Most of the positivistic criticism of natural law theory is premised upon the false contention that the natural law is a creature of pure speculative morality and that natural law theorists wish to impose this morality onto our existing, morally inert practice. But this is a mistake, compounded by the co-opting of the phrase 'natural law' to describe the speculative theories of enlightenment liberals and their progeny. Indeed, many prominent common law writers drew heavily upon these speculative theories in their description of natural rights, to be contrasted with the embedded nature of common law rights. This can be described as a 'Hobbesian turn' within common law theory, whereby natural rights began to be conceived as a-social, a-political, external entitlements which are then filtered through the practice of the common law.[65] The pre-Hobbesian natural law tradition is distinct from the natural rights tradition which grew up around the common law as an external set of rights which may or may not be reflected in common law. Those rights were then presented as given up or set aside 'for the sake of justice and the general good'.[66] Thus, while there is general agreement among classical common law theorists that natural law is a source of common law, there was disagreement over the nature of natural rights as creatures of pure speculative morality and their relationship with the embedded nature of common law rights. On one view, natural rights are an expression of natural law and are set aside or given up when common law doctrine developed ways to balance these absolute entitlements against the needs of the community. On another, this balancing is the working out of the requirements of natural law within context.

This speculative turn is in sharp contrast with the practice-centred methodology of the classical legal tradition, including perhaps especially the common law tradition, from Bracton to Allan. Thus Wu laments

> that practically all of the seventeenth, eighteenth and nineteenth century philosophers of Natural Law departed from this great tradition. They proceeded *more geometrico*; they wove whole systems of so-called Natural Law just as a spider would weave a net out of its own belly. To mention a few, Hobbes, Spinoza, Locke, Pufendorf, … Kant, Hegel, and even Bentham with his felicific calculus, all belong to the speculative group.[67]

If anything represents an abandonment of the requirement of fit, it is this speculative philosophy. Natural law has historically been intimately connected to the common law and it remains so today, even if the term 'natural law' has fallen out of favour. There remains a steady continuity between this history and the underlying principles of justice which inform, to use but one example, our conceptions of reasonableness and the principles of natural justice within modern administrative law. As Justice Farwell noted in *Bradford v Ferrand*, 'the conception of *aequum et bonum* and the rights flowing therefrom which are included in the *ius naturale* underly a great part of English

[65] See M Foran 'A Great Forgetting: Natural Law, Common Law, and the Human Rights Act' in R Johnson and Y Yi Zhu (eds), *Sceptical Perspectives on the Changing Constitution of the United Kingdom* (Oxford, Hart Publishing, 2023) 77–105, 88–93.
[66] *Entick v Carrington* [1765] EWHC J98; 95 ER 807.
[67] JCH Wu, 'The Natural Law and Our Common Law' (1954) 23 *Fordham Law Review* 13, 22.

Common Law; although it is not usual to find "the law of nature" or "natural law" referred to in so many words in English cases'.[68] This is entirely to be expected, given that development of doctrine involves recourse to the moral principles embodied within our practice rather than abstract notions of natural reason. Indeed, this forms the foundation of Coke's notion of artificial reason; the application of natural reason to a shared tradition.[69] Thus, Wu notes that '[n]atural law must be supplemented by human law, for art perfects nature; and this too is a precept of the natural law'.[70] As our system has matured, the principles of the common law have built upon and concretised the principles of natural reason and justice such that recourse can be made to them in the resolution of disputes in most cases.

Within the classical legal tradition there is a similar scepticism of speculative theorising. To Vermeule, the precise content of the common good is worked out as a developing and evolving legal concept through time, informed by background principles of justice but attuned to the context and history of a given community. It is a distinctly *legal* concept, not an abstract moral or political (or theological) one. Principles of natural reason are not external to our practice but a central aspect of it, our practice being the working out of a public scheme of justice. It only makes sense to describe reliance on these principles as an abandonment of fit if our law collapses into the mere practices of the community – a positivism – rather than the moral practices of the community which are guided by considerations of justice according to law. Decisions of common law courts are *lex* – but the content of the common law, its general principles, are the principles of justice – this is how common law theory can rest both on a seemingly positivistic commitment to customary practice and a natural law foundation of reason: the practice is a moral one, custom is the community's attempt at determination, providing concrete application of principles of justice to their specific context; applying the general law and making it more concrete, eventually being shaped and interpreted by legal and political authorities into doctrine and statute. It is only when viewed as such that we can account for why certain customs or practices are abandoned over time. Time is a great test for custom precisely because it is expected that unreasonable custom will be jettisoned such that the common law can work itself pure. When Lord Mansfield held that the Common Law 'works itself pure by rules drawn from the fountain of justice',[71] he meant the law of nature.[72]

Dyzenhaus suggests that Vermeule is drawing his conception of the natural law from outside of the law – what he sees as timeless principles, abstracted from our practice. But this characterisation is in danger of collapsing into positivism, by presuming that our law consists only in the decisions of courts or the proclamations of legislatures. Unwritten principles of justice are internal to the concept of law itself. They are constantly being

[68] *Bradford v Ferrand* 2 Ch. D. 655, 662 (1902).

[69] *Prohibitions Del Roy*, 12 Co. Rep. 63 (KB 1612). On legal practice as a collaborative endeavour, grounded in a shared tradition, see Allan, 'Law as a Branch of Morality' (n 44) 5; G Postema, 'Integrity: Justice in Workclothes' (1997) 82 *Iowa Law Review* 821, 851.

[70] Wu, 'The Natural Law and Our Common Law' (n 67) 27.

[71] *Omychund v Barker* (1744), 1 Atk 22, 33; 26 ER 15, 23. See also *James v Price* (1773), Lofft 219, 220; 98 ER 619, 621; *Jones V Randall* (1774), 1 Cowp 37; 98 ER 954, 955.

[72] See NS Poser, *Lord Mansfield: Justice in the Age of Reason* (Montreal, McGill-Queen's University Press 2013) 214–16.

refined and applied to changing contexts, even if certain commitments – such as to the equal dignity of subjects – remain constant. These commitments, because they are fixed at such a general level, must be interpreted and applied to our developing context, remaining true to the values which justify our practice in so doing. They are not external to law. The natural law is an important part of our practice. It fits.

3. Legal Reasoning and the Common Good

Allan has rightly argued that 'constitutional theory cannot rest content with a narrow, formal conception of the rule of law, neutral between different accounts of justice and fairness … Both judge and legal theorist must address substantive questions of political philosophy in seeking justification of legal decisions'.[73] Yet, this stands in tension with aspects of Ronald Dworkin's political liberalism which have informed the distinction that Allan relies on between principle and policy within his work.[74] The sharp contrast drawn between the rights of legal subjects and the pursuit of their collective flourishing in the form of 'policy' misconstrues the basis of each. If the rule of law sets limits upon plausible conceptions of the public good, as Allan rightly contends, then it cannot remain neutral on questions of the good life. Legal principle must be grounded within an understanding of law as 'a set of collaborative arrangements for the pursuit of justice and the public good'[75] wherein the public – common – good is the ground of justice. Neutrality on the good is not compatible with this.

Dworkin characterises liberal constitutionalism by the neutrality principle: the requirement 'that governments must be neutral on what might be called questions of the good life … that political decisions must be, so far as is possible, independent of any particular conception of the good life or of what gives value to life … liberalism takes [this] as its constitutive political morality'.[76] Dworkin argued that this neutrality is what distinguishes liberalism from rival left-wing and right-wing doctrines which all embrace non-neutral conceptions of the good life and attempt to mobilise state power to establish a flourishing society.[77] Yet this is difficult to reconcile with his account of policy, informed by arguments pertaining to how a given decision will work to promote the general welfare or the public interest.[78] How can it be the case that government must remain neutral on the good life while policy decisions about the public interest remain the unique purview of government? This only makes sense if the public interest is not related to members of the public leading good lives. Indeed, this is exactly how Dworkin

[73] TRS Allan, *Law, Liberty, and Justice: The Legal Foundations of British Constitutionalism* (Oxford, Clarendon Press, 1993) 39. See also M Foran, 'The Rule of Good Law: Form, Substance and Fundamental Rights' (2019) 78 *CLJ* 570.

[74] Allan, *Law, Liberty, and Justice* (n 73) 54–55.

[75] Allan, 'Law as a Branch of Morality' (n 44) 7–8.

[76] R Dworkin, 'Liberalism' in S Hampshire (ed), *Public and Private Morality* (Cambridge, Cambridge University Press, 1978) 127.

[77] ibid 128.

[78] R Dworkin, *A Matter of Principle* (Oxford, Clarendon Press, 1986) ch 4; Dworkin, *Law's Empire* (n 40) 221 ff. See also Allan, *Law, Liberty, and Justice* (n 73) 54.

construes the public interest; either a utilitarian calculus or an aggregate of majoritarian preferences.[79]

If framed in this way, it is easy to see why one might argue for the primacy of the right over the good: the public or common good is conflated with an aggregative idea of the 'greater' good,[80] to be contrasted with rights under justice which can then act as 'trumps' against the collective will.[81] But this conception of both rights and the common good is mistaken. Properly understood, rights and the common good do not conflict.[82] This can only be fully understood once one breaks from the mistaken belief that the common good is some utilitarian aggregative concept.[83] Thus, while Laws contends that '[p]oliticians, governments, are by necessity utilitarians',[84] this should be replaced with an understanding that legislatures and governments are engaged in reasoned deliberation in pursuit of the common good, which can include deliberation over rights, obligations, and goals.[85] As Vermeule notes, 'Classical law treats enacted texts as products of the reasoned deliberation of public authorities who give specific content to the law where background legal principles need specificity or leave relevant issues to discretionary choice'.[86]

This understanding of the legislative and administrative process is far more closely aligned with Allan's more recent work, akin to the classical common law tradition, than with the Dworkinian view of policy. Properly understood, political authority in the form of legislative or administrative action is reasoned action, furthering the principles which underpin our existing practice, and not a mere act of aggregative will.[87] But if we accept that 'policy' cannot be sharply distinguished from principle, then neutrality on the good life or on the common good of the community is unsustainable. The commitment to a morally engaged legal practice is not compatible with attempts to remain neutral on the good life. Moral neutrality is impossible on matters of legal principle and the actions of legislatures and executives when they pursue the common good are far more a matter of legal principle than they are of aggregative will.

This does not mean that judges should necessarily create 'policy' or pursue some private version of the public good, however. The role of the common law judge is not to 'decide' within a realm of discretion how best to order society to the common good

[79] See R Dworkin, 'Social Sciences and Constitutional Rights – the Consequences of Uncertainty' (1977) 6 *Journal of Law and Education* 1, 10; Dworkin, *A Matter of Principle* (n 78) 366; R Dworkin, *Taking Rights Seriously* (Cambridge, Harvard University Press, 1977) 22, 90.

[80] See JS Mill, 'Utilitarianism' in JM Robson (ed), *The Collected Works of John Stuart Mill, Vol X, Essays on Ethics, Religion and Society* (Toronto, University of Toronto Press 1969); P Singer, *Practical Ethics*, 2nd edn (Cambridge, Cambridge University Press, 1993); R Hare, *Moral Thinking: Its Levels, Method, and Point* (Oxford, Clarendon Press 1981). cf D Brink, 'The Separateness of Persons, Distributive Norms, and Moral Theory' in RG Frey and C Morris (eds), *Value, Welfare, and Morality* (Cambridge, Cambridge University Press, 1993).

[81] See Dworkin, *Taking Rights Seriously* (n 79).

[82] See M Foran, 'Rights, Common Good, and The Separation of Powers' (2023) 86 *MLR* 599–628.

[83] See P Yowell, 'A Critical Examination of Dworkin's Theory of Rights' (2007) 52 *American Journal of Jurisprudence* 93.

[84] J Laws, *The Constitutional Balance* (Oxford, Hart Publishing, 2021) 41.

[85] See G Webber and P Yowell, 'Securing Human Rights through Legislation' in G Webber and others (eds), *Legislated Rights: Securing Human Rights through Legislation* (Cambridge, Cambridge University Press, 2018).

[86] Vermeule, *Common Good Constitutionalism* (n 4) 3.

[87] Allan, 'Why the Law Is What It Ought to Be' (n 2) 576; Allan, 'Law as a Branch of Morality' (n 44) 14.

but rather to interpret the decisions or actions of other actors, either political authorities such as legislatures or the community as a whole in their customs, presuming that such decisions are reasonably directed towards the common good. There is a space for political authority to engage in reasoned action to pursue the common good within a realm of discretion which may even involve a degree of arbitrary choice among a range of defensible options.[88] But this should not be sharply removed from the reasoned elaboration of legal principle that Allan associates with the determination of legal rights and duties.[89] In all areas of legal reasoning, including legislative or administrative reasoning, will and reason must operate in harmony, reflecting the vital admixture of critical and positive morality such that no action of a legal authority can be described as a mere act of will. This is so, even if courts must respect the legitimate acts of legitimate political authority to make choices in pursuit of the common good: that respect must be given, but it cannot amount to an abandonment of a court's duty to uphold the rule of law and the related commitment that government proceed in the interests of the governed.

The forced depopulation of Diego Garcia, the largest of the Chagos Islands, serves as a powerful illustration. The Commissioner, established as a legislature for the colony under the British Indian Ocean Territories Order 1965, made an Immigration Ordinance in 1971, providing that no one could enter or remain in the territory without a permit which would not be granted as by this time the British government had already removed the population of the island to make way for the construction of a military base by the United States of America. In 2000, the High Court quashed this provision, holding that this exclusion was not within the Commissioner's power to make law for the 'peace, order and good government' of the territory.[90]

Initially the government accepted the ruling, lifting the restrictions, but subsequently reimposed them by Order in Council. The Court of Appeal upheld the conclusion of the High Court that these restrictions were invalid, but eventually a majority of the House of Lords disagreed. The Court agreed that the legality of the Order in Council was subject to judicial review, rejecting the argument that this exercise of the royal prerogative was immune from judicial oversight: the ordinary principles of legality, reasonableness and natural justice applied.[91] Nevertheless, the majority concluded that the Order was not irrational. The decision of the majority reflected a refusal to accept that the legislative powers of the Crown were limited by the requirement that laws must be ordered towards the 'peace, order and good government' of the territory. Rather than placing restrictions on government power, informed by the rule of law, this clause was construed exclusively as an empowering provision, 'the traditional formula by which legislative powers are conferred upon the legislature of a colony or a former colony upon the attainment of independence'.[92]

Allan is right to question these conclusions, stressing that even though it is claimed that 'a power to make laws for the peace, order, and good government of a territory

[88] A Vermeule, 'Rationally Arbitrary Decisions in Administrative Law' (2015) 44 *The Journal of Legal Studies* S475.

[89] Allan, *Law, Liberty, and Justice* (n 73) 55.

[90] *R (Bancoult) v Secretary of State for Foreign and Commonwealth Affairs* [2001] QB 1067.

[91] ibid para 57 per Laws LJ.

[92] ibid para 47.

connotes "the widest lawmaking power appropriate to a Sovereign",[93] it is necessary to ask whether there are inherent limits to "sovereign" legislative power'.[94] As such Sedley LJ was correct to distinguish in *Bancoult (No 2)*, between what the British government claimed to be in the well-being of the colony and what, as a matter of law, fell within the constitutional limits of a legal order directed towards furthering the interests of its citizens. It is not appropriate for the court 'to substitute their own view of what is best for a colony'. But it is nevertheless 'their constitutional function to decide whether what has been enacted, or what it is proposed to enact, is rationally and legally capable of providing for a colony's well-being'.[95]

Allan is thus entirely correct to stress that '[i]t is one thing to deny a broad judicial power to question the wisdom of legislative determination of the public interest, made in good faith, especially when the legislature is properly representative of the people; it is quite another to suppose that a legislature (democratic or otherwise) might act for purposes entirely inimical to the well-being of all or some of its subjects'.[96] But it is simply not possible to conceive of this constraint if one remains neutral as to what constitutes the well-being of legal subjects. The protection of fundamental rights is a centrally important aspect of this.[97] But this does not capture those considerations of peace, order and good governance which are not confined to individual rights claims and which are instead grounded in considerations of the collective wellbeing and flourishing of the polity. The *Bancoult* cases can be described exclusively by reference to an individual constitutional right of abode, but this would be an impoverished account that would not give due regard to the requirements of peace, order, and good government. It is only when examined by reference to the effect this policy had on the community as a whole that it can be said that the Orders fell foul of standards which, while generally requiring comity, demand that the authority of political bodies rests on their legitimate and reasonable pursuit of the common good.

Common good constitutionalism offers a framework for thinking about cases such as this which place emphasis on the common good as the ultimate guiding ideal for legal and political institutions. It grounds a theory of constitutionalism, and thus the interpretation and legitimacy of constitutional principles and structures, in a manner which is conducive to the flourishing of all members of a given community. This will demand reasoned and principled interpretation of our legal practice in a manner which rejects any attempt to remain neutral between rival accounts of justice and fairness, as Allan has himself stressed. But is also rejects neutrality on what constitutes flourishing, well-being, or a good life. One cannot make full sense of requirements of good governance if one refuses to think critically about the good. Common law constitutionalism has been a shining light for analysis of the connection between the rule of law and fundamental rights protection. But it has neglected analysis of the enabling function of constitutional principle which demands reasoned interpretation of the proper ends of government:

[93] *Ibralebbe v R* [1964] AC 900, 923.

[94] Allan, *Sovereignty of Law* (n 1) 291–92.

[95] *Bancoult (No 2)* [2007] EWCA Civ 498 at para 51.

[96] Allan, *The Sovereignty of Law* (n 1) 293.

[97] ibid 294; TRS Allan, 'Constitutional Rights and Common Law' (1991) 11 *OJLS* 453; Foran, 'The Rule of Good Law' (n 73).

what the flourishing of a community requires, always attentive to our shared practice, customs, and traditions. This has occurred, in my view, because of the false distinction that Dworkin drew between principle and policy and the insistence that government must remain neutral on questions relating to human well-being or flourishing. Properly understood, legislative and governmental action cannot be utilitarian or aggregative, sacrificing the minority for the sake of the majority. Instead, legal officials, including courts, must proceed from the presumption that political authority is exercised reasonably as acts of law: not brute will, not unmoored reason, but the careful fusion of each. When viewed in that manner, law *qua* law is properly ordered towards the best interests of the governed, duly respectful of their fundamental rights but not aloof to the quality of their lives.

Legality demands that presumptions are made about the reasonableness of public authority, rejecting any attempt to conflate law with the mere will of a sovereign. This cannot be confined to rights analysis on the basis that rights are the product of principled reason and that legislation or executive policy is not. Once we accept that policy is also the product of reasoned deliberation about how best to achieve peace, order, and good governance (necessary aspects of the common good),[98] then reason is demanded from judges: presumptions are and have been made on the basis that acts purported to be in the public interest are simply not in any such interest. This is so, not necessarily because they have breached fundamental rights, but because they are not directed towards any plausible vision of the common good. Our legal practice has all of the resources needed to facilitate reasoned interpretation of the requirements of peace, order and good government. Our administrative law principles of legality, reasonableness, and natural justice can just as easily enable the pursuit of the public good as they restrict abuses of power. That is the foundation of our law, grounded in the customs and traditions of the community, founded upon principles of justice and fairness. A commitment to the common law is a commitment to the common good.

[98] Vermeule, *Common Good Constitutionalism* (n 4) ch 1.

13

Persons, not Citizens

JOANNA LANGILLE

In a vast body of work, Trevor Allan has developed his well-known theory of common law constitutionalism.[1] Throughout this work, one of Allan's central projects has been to offer a comprehensive account of the conditions under which legal authority can be justified and thus accord with the rule of law. This account is intended to apply generally, to all domains of law,[2] and is rooted in an interpretive account of positive law.[3]

Underlying Allan's account is an assumption about how to conceptualise the legal relationship between ruler and ruled which requires a justification. Allan assumes that it is the state that exercises legal authority, and that the subjects of that authority are the citizens of that state. This assumption is problematic, however, because the state-citizen relation is not the relevant jural relation in all domains of law, nor is the legal subject always the citizen. Indeed, as the case of private law most dramatically makes clear, this is not necessarily how the law itself mediates relationships of authority. In the context of private law, being a legal subject – being a person to whom the law's coercive force can apply – does not necessarily turn on citizenship. Instead, the subjects of private law are universal persons, not the citizens of a particular polity.[4] This does not mean that all states have authority over all private law disputes. On the contrary, private law requires there be particular facts that generate an authority relationship between the law's subjects and the applicable law. But it is rarely the status of the law's subjects *as citizens* that generates this legitimate authority relationship. In this way, citizenship plays no role in legitimating state authority. (And not only is this the case in private law, but it is the case in many domains of public law as well.)

[1] Allan's corpus is immense and rich. His primary monographs are TRS Allan, *Law, Liberty, and Justice: The Legal Foundations of British Constitutionalism* (Oxford, Oxford University Press, 1994); TRS Allan, *Constitutional Justice: A Liberal Theory of the Rule of Law* (Oxford, Oxford University Press, 2001); TRS Allan, *The Sovereignty of Law: Freedom, Constitution, and Common Law* (Oxford, Oxford University Press, 2013).

[2] Allan, *Law, Liberty, and Justice* (n 1) 5. See also TRS Allan, 'The Rule of Law as the Rule of Private Law' in LM Austin and D Klimchuk (eds), *Private Law and the Rule of Law* (Oxford, Oxford University Press, 2014); TRS Allan, 'The Rule of Law' in D Dyzenhaus and M Thorburn (eds), *Philosophical Foundations of Constitutional Law* (Oxford, Oxford University Press, 2016).

[3] This approach is evident throughout Allan's work. See eg Allan, *Sovereignty of Law* (n 1).

[4] I develop this point further in relation to tort law in J Langille, 'The Subjects of Tort Law' (draft on file with author). This chapter borrows in places from that article.

Since it justifies legal authority on grounds that apply only to citizens, there are aspects of Allan's account that are deficient and cannot achieve his objective of developing a comprehensive and unified account of legal authority. We can try to reconstruct the core of his account to justify legal authority to the universal legal subject – the person. Once we remove the idea of citizenship, however, the reconstructed version of Allan's account ultimately flounders, because it offers no way to explain why the law holds that only certain states are authoritative in certain disputes, depending on the facts at issue. Ultimately Allan lacks an account of how jural relations can be particularised in a legitimate and normatively justifiable way.

In Section 1, I describe what Allan takes to be the salient instance of legal subjecthood in need of justification in the face of law's coercive authority: the citizen. In Section 2, I take up the example of private law to show how the subjects of legal authority are often persons, not citizens. In Section 3, I reconstruct Allan's account of justification to apply to the universal legal subject, jettisoning the aspects of his theory that justify law only to citizens. I conclude that, in so doing, we encounter a different problem: his account now lacks the resources to particularise legal authority.

1. The Citizenship Paradigm

For Trevor Allan, a central question is how to justify law's use of coercive force and how to distinguish between legitimate and illegitimate uses of state power.[5] The need to justify law's coercive force arises in the following way. Normally we do not think it is acceptable for some people to use force to compel others to behave in a certain way; typically we understand the use of force to be merely arbitrary power or violence, because we assume that people have a right to be free from coercive interference on the basis of their autonomy and dignity.[6] But the law is different. We think it is sometimes appropriate and indeed legitimate for public legal authorities to wield coercive power.

The core question for the rule of law theorist, then, is what distinguishes the law from arbitrary power?[7] Allan's body of work seeks to answer this question, articulating an account of the rule of law that can justify legal authority vis-à-vis the law's subjects. And Allan's ambition is comprehensive. He does not see his project as limited to the classic domains of public law, such as constitutional and administrative law, but wishes to develop an account of the rule of law that applies to private law as well.[8] In addition, Allan does not want to develop an account of legitimate authority and the rule of law in the abstract. Instead, his claim is broadly interpretive and rooted in legal doctrine. Indeed, he claims that the law itself has articulated the conditions necessary to ensure that the application of legal authority is legitimate, and that the development of the

[5] Allan repeatedly mentions the need to justify the law's use of coercive force. See eg Allan, *Sovereignty of Law* (n 1) ch 3; Allan, 'Rule of Private Law' (n 2).

[6] Allan, *Constitutional Justice* (n 1) ch 3; Allan, *Sovereignty of Law* (n 1); Allan, 'Rule of Law' (n 2).

[7] Allan, *Constitutional Justice* (n 1); Allan, *Sovereignty of Law* (n 1).

[8] Allan characterises his account as 'a radically different perspective on the rule of law that moves private law to centre-stage,' and continually emphasises the importance of the ordinary civil law to a system governed by principles of legality: Allan, 'Rule of Private Law' (n 2) 67.

common law over centuries has established an account of the limits of authority and the nature of the rule of law on which judges can rely.[9]

Allan also assumes that the authority question is not one to be asked in the ether. Whether an authority is legitimate is a relational question – the issue is whether one entity has the right to use coercive force to tell another entity what to do. And whether authority is legitimate will depend on how things stand between the putative authority and the subject of the law. This leads us to an important question: Who are the subjects of legal authority to whom a justification for the state's coercive force is due?

At the heart of Allan's account is an assumption about who is the legal subject entitled to justification. In his work, Allan regularly describes the legal subject entitled to a justification as the citizen of a state whose law is to apply. The entitlement to autonomy and dignity is possessed, he says, by the citizen: 'The *citizen* of a constitutional democracy is to be honoured as an equal, autonomous, moral agent'[10] (emphasis added). The law must 'uphold … the freedom and dignity of those independent *citizens* who comprise the political community'[11] (emphasis added). As such, the law 'must be justified *to the citizen* – shown to be worthy of his assent'[12] (emphasis added). This commitment to justifying law to citizens, and to protecting their dignity and autonomy, informs Allan's definition of the rule of law. The rule of law is the 'fundamental principle that people are entitled to be treated with the respect that their equal dignity *as citizens* demands'[13] (emphasis added). Or, '[t]he rule of law is ultimately an ideal of legitimate governance that explains the *citizen's* moral obligation of obedience. It seeks to reconcile governmental authority with individual autonomy, revealing the conditions under which compliance with positive state law is consistent with the freedom and self-respect of the morally responsible *citizen*'[14] (emphasis added). Ultimately, '[t]he equal dignity *of citizens*, with its implications for fair treatment and respect for individual autonomy, is the basic premise of liberal constitutionalism, and accordingly the ultimate meaning of the rule of law'[15] (emphasis added).

This use of the term 'citizen' to characterise the legal subject who is entitled to respect for her dignity and autonomy, and to whom a justification for legal authority is owed, is pervasive throughout Allan's work. Allan also regularly characterises the relationship in need of justification as that between a citizen and her state.[16] He does not typically (although there are some offhand exceptions in his writings[17]) couch the legal subject as a generic 'person', but rather explicitly limits his analysis to the citizens of a particular

[9] For this gloss on Allan, see S Lakin, 'Defending and Contesting the Sovereignty of Law: The Public Lawyer as Interpretivist' (2015) 78 *MLR* 549.

[10] Allan, *Constitutional Justice* (n 1) 6.

[11] Allan, *Sovereignty of Law* (n 1) 91.

[12] Allan, *Constitutional Justice* (n 1) 8.

[13] ibid 39.

[14] Allan, *Sovereignty of Law* (n 1) 128.

[15] Allan, *Constitutional Justice* (n 1) 2.

[16] ibid at 38 ('it is the first principle of constitutionalism, that, in its interactions with the citizen, the state must satisfy the requirement of the rule of law'), 84 ('constitutional relationship between state and citizen'). It is the 'nature of the relation between citizen and state' that constitutional and rule of law theorists must explain; they must address the potential 'case of conflict between citizen and state': ibid 87; TRS Allan, 'Legislative Supremacy and the Rule of Law: Democracy and Constitutionalism' (1985) 44 *CLJ* 111, 143.

[17] See eg TRS Allan, 'Why the Law is What it Ought to Be' (2020) 11 *Jurisprudence* 574 ('equality of persons'); Allan, *Sovereignty of Law* (n 1) (occasionally saying 'person' instead of 'citizen').

state and their legal relationship to that state's laws. So the image Allan presents of the legal relationship in need of normative justification is that between a state and its citizens, within the confines of a single domestic legal order.

One may contend, however, that Allan's use of the term 'citizen' in these contexts is normatively inert, not revealing any important aspect of his view; perhaps the term 'citizen' is just a meaningless linguistic choice.[18] While an author may use the word 'he' when invoking the generic third person singular, we would not necessarily assume that the author's intent is to limit his comments to men and concomitantly to exclude women. Perhaps Allan's choice to use the word 'citizen' to describe the legal subject is not driven by any substantive view about the persons to whom a justification for legal authority is owed.

There are two reasons to think Allan intentionally identifies citizens as the legal subjects to whom authority must be justified. First, Allan argues at various points that the problem of justifying legal authority to the citizens of a democracy is particularly challenging given the aspiration to self-rule in a democracy.[19] Power in a democracy is derived ultimately from citizens,[20] Allan contends, and thus any coercive force used against them must be understood as having been something to which they have (at least in some sense) consented.[21] For this reason, Allan appears to assume there is an additional burden when the law applies to citizens (as opposed to non-citizens), who are owed a special justification when law applies to them.[22] Likewise, democracies do not merely seek compliance with their laws. Rather, they claim a special duty of moral obedience and cooperation in the law's common projects from the law's subjects.[23] And these claims, Allan argues, are made only of citizens, not mere persons: 'The law is addressed not merely to an individual, who must choose between compliance and punishment for disobedience. It is addressed to the *citizen*, seeking his co-operation in the legitimate pursuit of the common good'.[24] If the law of a democracy is to seek this kind of moral obedience from its citizens, we must offer them a particular type of justification.

Second, some of the reasons that Allan gives to justify legal authority apply readily to citizens but are difficult to generalise to other types of legal subjects (without significantly more analysis).[25] Or, to put the point another way, some of the conditions under which legal authority can be justified on Allan's account are capable of being realised when legal subjects are citizens but can only be realised with difficulty by other types of legal subjects.

[18] As Linda Bosniak has discussed, sometimes 'citizen' is used in constitutional scholarship as a stand-in for person. L Bosniak, 'Persons and Citizens in Constitutional Thought' (2010) 8 *International Journal of Constitutional Law* 9.

[19] See eg Allan, 'Legislative Supremacy' (n 16).

[20] See eg ibid.

[21] Allan, *Constitutional Justice* (n 1); TRS Allan, 'Citizenship and Obligation: Civil Disobedience and Civil Dissent' (1996) 55 *CLJ* 89.

[22] Allan, *Constitutional Justice* (n 1) 75.

[23] See eg Allan, 'Why the Law is What it Ought to Be' (n 17); Allan, *Constitutional Justice* (n 1).

[24] TRS Allan, 'Constitutional Justice and the Concept of Law' in G Huscroft (ed), *Expounding the Constitution: Essays in Constitutional Theory* (Cambridge, Cambridge University Press, 2009) 219, 222.

[25] However, in my view, while Allan regularly makes these arguments, they are in some ways peripheral to the core of Allan's republican account of legal authority and the common law constitution. I offer a reconstruction of this account below, which does not make reference to these arguments.

Allan regularly argues that legal authority can be distinguished from arbitrary force, and thus justified, when the ends for which the law acts can be understood as furthering a conception of the *common good* for a particular community that the law's subject, the citizen who is a long-standing member of that community, can endorse.[26] When the law's purpose is connected to a reasonable conception of the common good for the community, citizens can be legitimately subjected to the law's authority. 'Governance according to law,' Allan writes, 'ultimately is distinguished from arbitrary rule by its commitment to justification: The law imposes its demands on the citizen in the interests of the common good – a good that he can affirm in virtue of his allegiance to the political community'.[27] According to this logic, justification framed in terms of the common good need only convince the citizen; if you are not a member of the political community – not someone with an allegiance to the political community – this rationale is not directed at you. Thus presumably this justification for legal authority has no bearing on non-citizens.

Likewise and relatedly, Allan borrows from Rawls to justify legal authority through the notion of *imagined consent*. Law can legitimately govern the citizens of a democracy, who are meant to be self-governing, when the substance of the law is something to which they can be taken to have consented – typically when the law protects fundamental rights or furthers a purpose connected to a community-based common good. On this basis, 'the rule of law constitutes an ideal of consent, wherein the law seeks the citizen's acceptance of its demands as morally justified: he is invited to acknowledge that obedience is the appropriate response in the light of his obligation to further the legitimate needs of the common good'.[28] But again, Allan does not worry explicitly about the imagined consent of non-citizens, who presumably do not necessarily endorse the common goals of a community of which they are not a part.

Finally, Allan also suggests that legal authority can be justified under democratic conditions in which citizens have an opportunity to *participate* in the law's formation.[29] If citizens have an equal opportunity to shape the law's content through participatory democratic procedures, this helps to justify the ultimate application of that law's authority to them, consistent with their equal dignity as citizens and the ideal of self-government. But this rationale is also not helpful when justifying legal authority to non-citizens who typically do not have the full panoply of democratic participation rights, such as voting in elections, that are available to citizens.

Ultimately, it is not surprising that Allan assumes that the legal relationship in need of justification is that between a state and its citizens, within the confines of a single domestic legal order, as this is the way in which most other legal and political theorists have traditionally framed the issue of how to justify legal authority. This assumption is perhaps best exemplified in contemporary political thought with Rawls,[30]

[26] This theme is evident throughout Allan's work. See eg TRS Allan, 'Constitutional Justice and the Concept of Law' (n 24); 'Constitutional Rights and the Rule of Law,' in M Klatt (ed), *Institutionalized Reason* (Oxford, Oxford University Press, 2012) 132; Allan, *Sovereignty of Law* (n 1).

[27] Allan, 'Constitutional Justice and the Concept of Law' (n 24) 223.

[28] Allan, *Constitutional Justice* (n 1) 6.

[29] See ibid 26ff.

[30] J Rawls, *A Theory of Justice*, revd edn (Cambridge, Belknap Press, 1999) 7. For a succinct rejection of this premise, see L Bosniak, 'Status Non-Citizens' in A Shachar et al (eds), *The Oxford Handbook of Citizenship*

who makes this assumption explicit, but other scholars have implicitly made the same assumption.[31] Likewise, public law scholars often assume that the normative relationship of significance to constitutional law is the state-citizen relationship. As Linda Bosniak has detailed, there is a strand of constitutional law thinking that identifies citizens as rights-bearers, rather than persons, and thus considers citizens to be the relevant legal subjects of constitutional authority.[32] So Allan is in good company when assuming that the problem of legal authority is typically cashed out as justifying a state's power vis-à-vis its citizens.

2. How Private Law Constructs Relationships of Authority

In this Section, I will argue that Allan's assumption about the relational structure of legal authority is problematic, particularly for a scholar who wishes to offer a comprehensive and interpretive approach. This is because the state-citizen relation is not the relevant jural relation in all domains of law; nor is the legal subject always the citizen. As such, an attempt to offer an account of legal authority that roots legal authority in the relationship between a state and its citizens is necessarily incomplete, because citizenship is not always germane to how law constructs relationships of authority. Here I will use private law as an example of where authority relationships between state and subject are constituted without reference to citizenship, and thus where we cannot justify legal authority on the grounds that the subject is a citizen.[33] But it is worth noting that it is not just private law in which citizenship does not ground legal authority; many domains of public law, such as criminal law, function this way too. However, due to the distinctive structure of private law relationships, private law is a particularly striking example of where citizenship does not ground law's authority.

A. The Triangular Structure of Private Law Relationships

Private law establishes the legal rights and duties that individuals have vis-à-vis other private persons.[34] As such, private law disputes are bilateral – they are between (at least) two private persons, understood as equals, on a horizontal plane. They define our

(Oxford, Oxford University Press, 2017) 314. Indeed, one might contend that the standard way of theorising about law and authority has been, for centuries, to focus on the relationship between rulers and the members of a political community.

[31] For example, Ronald Dworkin – a scholar whose work has profoundly influenced Allan's thinking – also tends to make this assumption, theorising about law's authority for the most part within particular political communities. See eg R Dworkin, *Law's Empire* (Cambridge, Belknap Press, 1986).

[32] Bosniak, 'Persons and Citizens' (n 18).

[33] A claim I develop more fully in Langille, 'The Subjects of Tort Law' (n 4), from which this Section will draw.

[34] In the paradigmatic context. This is not to deny that private persons cannot make private law claims against public authorities – this is of course legally possible, and in such context public authorities are essentially conceived of as private actors standing in the same horizontal relationship to other private persons. Such claims raise important conceptual difficulties from the point of view of private law, however, as scholars have recently pointed out. See M Oza, 'The Personality of Public Authorities' (2024) 43 *Law and Philosophy* 415.

mutual, interpersonal obligations to respect, *inter alia*, the bodily integrity and property of other private persons.

These bilateral private law relationships between persons are not confined to the boundaries of a particular state. This can be, for example, because the two 'poles' of the bilateral relationship are individuals from different places. Private persons who are citizens of one state regularly interact with private persons who are citizens of another state, in ways that can either respect, change, or violate the private rights of those other persons. A citizen of Canada may travel to the United States and may tortiously interfere with the bodily integrity or property of a US citizen. A Canadian may interfere with the reputation of an American by posting defamatory material online. A Canadian may enter into a contract with an American, or marry an American, or divorce an American, or have a child with an American. In this way, private legal relationships do not map onto traditional political boundaries. Our private rights are regularly respected and violated by those who are not our fellow citizens, and thus can be transnational in nature.

Likewise, private disputes can be transnational – ie factually connected to multiple political jurisdictions – even if both parties to a private law dispute are from the same political jurisdiction. Two Canadians can drive together to the US, where the driver can tortiously injure the passenger. Two Canadians can form a contract, which they can agree to have governed by New York law under a choice of law clause. Two Canadians can marry in the US.

However, even though private law relationships can cross traditional political boundaries with ease, the law of a particular state is still essential to constituting those relationships. The law does not understand us as having, say, tort law duties in the abstract. They are not purely moral, untethered to the positive law of any state. Likewise, the law does not assume that all states are authoritative in all instances. Instead, each private law matter is to be determined by the law of a *particular* state. The question, then, in transnational private law disputes, is which state's law *in particular* defines the rights and obligations of the parties. This is, of course, the classic and central 'choice of law' question of the field of law that directly addresses transnational private law disputes: private international law.

In this way, private law relationships can be imagined as triangular: they are bilateral disputes between two private persons, as mediated by the positive law of a particular state. There are, of course, instances in which all three points on the triangle are confined to the purely domestic arena of a particular state. But it is equally possible that one of the points of the triangle – one or both of the two parties, or the applicable law – is from outside the confines of one state, and thus the dispute is transnational in nature.

B. Legal Authority in Private Law

Given the triangular structure of private law, how does a particular dispute about private law rights come under the authority of a particular state's private law? That is, when and why does a particular state's private law apply to a particular dispute? And, on that basis, who are the legal subjects of a particular state's private law? This question is answered doctrinally by choice of law, which defines when a state's law applies to a particular dispute and thus identifies who are the legal subjects of a particular state's positive law, and what law is authoritative, in a particular instance.

A foundational assumption of choice of law doctrine is that a court hearing a dispute will not assume that the law of the state in which the court sits must apply to the dispute. Just because a court has jurisdiction over a dispute does not determine what law applies. Unlike in public law contexts, courts hearing private law matters regularly apply *foreign* private law – the law of some other state – to decide a dispute.[35] So a particular state's private law can be applied and can authoritatively decide private law matters in disputes that take place far beyond its borders.

If a court must decide, then, which state's private law applies to a particular transnational dispute before them (and thus what law can authoritatively govern), how does a court go about this? The answer is complex, and varies both between jurisdictions and among domains of private law, but one dominant paradigm is territorial: Courts frequently apply the law of the place where the rights of the parties were changed. For example, in tort law, courts will apply the law of the place of the wrong.[36] So in the case of two Canadians who drive to New York and are involved in a car accident, a Canadian court would hold that New York state tort law would apply to authoritatively define the rights and duties of the parties to one another.[37]

Absent in much of common law choice of law analysis, however, is any consideration of the citizenship of the parties to the dispute.[38] As Karen Knop has argued, the public law idea of citizenship is not relevant to which state's private law is authoritative.[39] Thus becoming a subject of a particular state's law does not generally turn on one's status as a citizen.

In this way, the legal subjects of private law are persons, not citizens. Any human in the world could become the legal subject of any state's private law, depending on the facts at issue. The public law of citizenship does not typically mediate one's legal subjecthood in private international law, and thus law is potentially applicable to and authoritative vis-à-vis all persons in the world, regardless of their status as members of a particular political community. Private law subjecthood is conceptually universal, not citizenship-based; it does not map on to the boundaries of membership, inclusion, and allegiance established by public law.

This does not mean, though, that all states are authoritative in all private law disputes. Instead, one state has the most authoritative claim to govern a particular private law dispute, and this state is identified by examining the facts underlying the dispute and

[35] There is some dispute in the literature as to whether a state ever 'actually' applies foreign law, or whether it simply applies its own law as informed by the norms of foreign law. This debate is interesting, but it is not germane to the contention that legal subjecthood in private law is never constituted by citizenship.

[36] In Canada, the classic proposition in support of this claim is *Tolofson v Jensen*, [1994] 3 SCR 1022.

[37] *Wong v Li* [2002] OJ No 885.

[38] As I demonstrate more conclusively in Langille, 'The Subjects of Tort Law' (n 4). One might argue, as I explore in ibid Section 3, that citizenship or political membership can still get us part of the way to an account of legitimate authority in private law. We can use citizenship-based accounts to justify law to citizens, and then add a different account for non-citizens. But as I argue, the law does not offer different grounds of authority to citizens and non-citizens. Instead, the account of law's authority is transactional – it relates to the nature of the wrong itself. Thus the public membership of the particular parties plays no role, at least in choice of law contexts.

[39] K Knop, 'Citizenship, Public and Private' (2008) 71 *Law and Contemporary Problems* 309.

their connection to a particular state. These facts justify the normative authority of a particular state over the particular subjects of the dispute with respect to that dispute. But one's personal status *as a citizen* does not generally determine who are the subjects of a particular state's law.

3. A Return to Allan's Account

If legal subjecthood in private law is not necessarily mediated by citizenship, then theories of legal authority that aim to explain law's authority in all domains must offer an account that does not condition law's legitimacy on law's application to a state's citizens. That is, legal authority cannot be rendered legitimate exclusively on the grounds that the law that is to apply to a particular person is the law of the state of which the person is a citizen, because that is not how legal authority operates. On this basis, Allan's arguments for legitimate authority that are organized around citizens as the law's subjects cannot give us a comprehensive account.

However, on closer examination, the core of Allan's account can be reconstructed to justify legal authority to persons. Or to put it another way, there are important components of Allan's account of the rule of law that do not discriminate on the basis of citizenship, and that therefore do not limit legitimate exercises of legal authority to citizens. We can refine his account in a way that better achieves his broader objective, which is to explain the conditions in which legal authority can be exercised legitimately across all domains of law – including private law – and therefore in relation to all of the law's subjects. But this reconstruction comes with a price. Once we remove the idea of citizenship from Allan's account, we lack a way to determine which particular state is authoritative in a particular instance. Thus Allan's account is ultimately incomplete.

A. Justifying Legal Authority to the Universal Subject

Recall that Allan begins his inquiry into what constitutes legitimate authority and the rule of law with a puzzle: how can the law have the power to tell people what to do, consistent with their dignity and autonomy? Allan starts from the initial 'basic premise'[40] that it is the dignity and autonomy of *citizens* that matters. But we can modify this premise to include a concern for the dignity and autonomy of *all persons*. And indeed, there are aspects of Allan's view which suggest that he would endorse this modification. Allan suggests at certain points that the rights of non-citizens must be respected.[41] And he argues that any legal distinctions between nationals and non-nationals are suspect.[42] While he does not explicitly stress the need to justify legal authority to non-citizens,

[40] Allan, *Constitutional Justice* (n 1) 2.

[41] Allan, *Sovereignty of Law* (n 1) 91, 93 fn 13 ('the state must honour everyone's human rights, including non-citizens,' and 'we assume that lawfully resident non-citizens are entitled to the same protections as citizens demand for themselves – especially respect for their human rights, fundamental to human dignity').

[42] ibid 114–15.

Allan does not adopt the inverse proposition: that non-citizens are mere objects in the eyes of the law, against whom any use of coercive force can be legitimate, without justification. For these reasons, we can offer a friendly amendment to Allan's theory: we should assume that for legal authority to be justified, it must reckon with the dignity and autonomy of *all persons* against whom legal authority is exercised.[43]

With this premise altered, we can now return to our elaboration of Allan's view. The rule of law theorist, Allan argues, must identify the conditions in which coercive force can be distinguished from mere arbitrary power, and thus authority can be rendered legitimate.[44] What are the features of law that are necessary to ensure that any use of force against the law's subjects is legitimate and authoritative and is not merely arbitrary power inflicted by some people against others?[45] When the problem of legal authority is posed in this way, an essential characteristic of the rule of law becomes clear – at a minimum, the law must provide a bulwark against arbitrary exercises of power.[46] It must 'protect … each [person] from the arbitrary will of others'[47] and 'shield against domination by powerful private interests or public officials'.[48] We can understand the rule of law, then, as a means by which persons can be protected from arbitrary coercive force. It is thus the task of the rule of law theorist to distinguish between arbitrary and non-arbitrary coercive interference in the lives of persons.

Drawing from the republican tradition in political theory, Allan argues that what non-arbitrariness requires is for the law to protect and constitute the freedom (or liberty) as independence of the law's subjects.[49] In this view, the rule of law must ensure that individuals are free from the domination of others, which includes both actual interference with one's choices and the threat of arbitrary interference.[50] Preventing individuals from being subject to arbitrary interference (and thus preserving their independence) has two dimensions: a liberty dimension and an equality dimension.[51] On the liberty dimension, Allan argues that the concept of law requires individuals to be treated as responsible moral agents and with respect for their human dignity.[52] To meet this requirement, the state must secure for each person a sphere of autonomy and independence so that each is not subject to the choices of others as a matter of right – so each person is her own master. Among other requirements,[53] certain constitutional or human rights are essential to this project. They include fundamental rights of freedom of expression, freedom of conscience, and freedom of association. They also include the right to bodily integrity, on the basis that no one else should decide what is done to your body, and thus slavery and torture must be prohibited.

[43] What follows here is drawn in part from J Langille, 'Frontiers of Legality: Understanding the Public Policy Exception in Choice of Law' (2023) 73 *University of Toronto Law Journal* 216.

[44] See eg Allan, *Sovereignty of Law* (n 1) ch 3; Allan, 'Rule of Private Law' (n 2).

[45] Allan, *Constitutional Justice* (n 1); Allan, *Sovereignty of Law* (n 1).

[46] Allan, *Constitutional Justice* (n 1); Allan, *Sovereignty of Law* (n 1); Allan, 'Rule of Private Law' (n 2).

[47] Allan, *Law, Liberty, and Justice* (n 1) 22.

[48] Allan, 'Rule of Law' (n 2) 203.

[49] ibid; Allan, 'Rule of Private Law' (n 2); Allan, *Sovereignty of Law* (n 1) ch 3.

[50] Allan, *Sovereignty of Law* (n 1) 96; Allan, 'Rule of Private Law' (n 2) 72, 74, 85; Allan, 'Rule of Law' (n 2) 205.

[51] As I have argued elsewhere. See, eg Langille, 'Frontiers of Legality' (n 43).

[52] Allan, 'Rule of Private Law' (n 2) 68.

[53] Such as procedural fairness.

On the equality dimension, Allan's argument is that any distinction in the way that people are treated by the law (or granted rights) must be non-arbitrary, lest it deny the *equal* freedom of persons. Freedom as independence must be granted to all of the law's subjects, securing 'as far as possible an equal freedom for all'.[54] And Allan thinks that there are some types of distinctions in the rights and freedoms accorded to persons that are *prima facie* arbitrary and thus violate the rule of law.[55] He states that legal discrimination on the basis of sex, race, or sexual orientation is almost certainly arbitrary.[56] So distinctions made on the basis of immutable (or constructively immutable) characteristics are the type of arbitrary and unequal treatment that constitutes a violation of the rule of law. Constitutional/human rights protections against discrimination are therefore also central to the rule of law.

However, it is not only human or constitutional rights which realise the freedom as independence of persons. Legally enshrined human rights guarantees typically shield individuals from arbitrary interference by the *state*. But it is not only the state that can subject individuals to domination or arbitrary force: private persons are also capable of such interference. For example, chattel slavery, in which one person asserts a right to 'own' another as a matter of the private law of property, is a private relationship that exemplifies the type of domination and arbitrary power that freedom as independence is meant to prohibit.[57] It violates both the liberty and the equality dimensions of freedom of independence, by subjecting one person to the domination of another, and by failing to protect the freedom of persons *equally*. Likewise, a violation of the bodily integrity of one person by another, such as a battery, is another instance of the domination of one private person over another, in which the aggressor subjects the victim to arbitrary force, violating the victim's liberty and equality. As such, Allan's account of legitimate authority is comprehensive; it articulates necessary substantive implications for the content of both public and private law.

In identifying these implications for both public and private law, Allan's account of legitimate authority differs sharply from formal or 'thin' accounts of the rule of law,[58] which claim that rules posited by legal authorities can have any normative content and still constitute law.[59] By contrast, Allan's account of the rule of law is thickly substantive and normative. The rule of law should be understood as a 'moral ideal of legality' – a normative theory of justice that ensures that the exercise of coercive political authority is justified, legitimate, and respectful of the autonomy and dignity of persons.[60] The law is not just whatever officials happen to say it is, nor what is merely posited; rather, it is a means by which the equal freedom of persons can be both protected and constituted.[61]

[54] Allan, 'Rule of Law' (n 2) 204.

[55] See eg Allan's discussion of discrimination against gay men by the British armed forces in Allan, 'Rule of Private Law' (n 2) 85.

[56] See ibid.

[57] Allan, 'Rule of Private Law' (n 2).

[58] The classic articulation of such a view is J Raz, *The Authority of Law: Essays on Law and Morality* (Oxford, Clarendon Press, 1979). See also PP Craig, 'Formal and Substantive Conceptions of the Rule of Law: An Analytical Framework' (1997) 21 *PL* 467.

[59] Raz, ibid 214.

[60] Allan, 'Rule of Private Law' (n 2) 67.

[61] Allan, 'Rule of Law' (n 2).

As such, the law's content and reasoning must respect certain substantive moral values: it must protect certain substantive commitments to the liberty and equality of persons, in both public and private contexts.

But how should these substantive rule of law values, or principles of legality, be realised in the positive law? Allan's answer to that question is complex, and relates to his distinctive view of judges, constitutionalism, and the common law.

For Allan, judges are central to instantiating rule of law values in the law, and thus ensuring that legal authority is legitimate. Their primary role is interpretive: to construe positive law in a way that best gives effect to rule of law values/principle of legality. In this mode, the rule of law operates as an ideal that informs and infuses the interpretation of positive law. And because it is an ideal, the rule of law can be instantiated in different ways in different legal systems, at both the legislative and judicial level. He writes, 'The ideal of legality is compatible with a great diversity of opinion about the social, economic, and cultural conditions that best uphold human dignity'.[62] The rule of law, he argues, 'does not prescribe the detailed content of the laws … there are many different arrangements compatible with liberty and equality'.[63] A judge's job is to take seriously rule of law values and try to interpret the law in light of them, in a way that makes the law make moral sense and that also accords with the way in which rule of law values have been understood in his or her community.

But Allan also insists that in extreme circumstances, courts must have the power to strike down laws that violate fundamental principles of the rule of law, to properly guard against arbitrary power and secure freedom as independence, and thus ensure that the law exercises only legitimate authority.[64] And courts must have this power even if they are not granted it through formal judicial review, and even if these principles of legality are not enshrined in a written constitution. This is because the principles of legality are constitutive of law's legitimacy even if they have not been enacted through legislation.[65] If a government wishes to rule through law, these non-derogable, constitutional principles of legality must be complied with. Indeed, it is these principles that make the exercise of legal authority legitimate.[66]

So for Allan, the rule of law operates both as an ideal, guiding interpretation and capable of plural instantiation, and a floor, guaranteeing certain principles of legality. This sounds somewhat mysterious – how can the rule of law be both a goal and a minimal guarantee? But, Allan tells us, this is not really mysterious at all, because courts do this all the time. Indeed, this is just the regular practice of common law courts, which typically seek to interpret the law in a coherent way that brings it into accordance with the requirements of justice. The practice of common law courts has also developed in positive law principles of legality which can operate as a floor, and which have been incorporated into the adjudicatory process through the practice of common law courts

[62] Allan makes this point repeatedly throughout his work. See eg Allan, 'Rule of Law' (n 2); Allan, *Constitutional Justice* (n 1).

[63] Allan, *Sovereignty of Law* (n 1) 123.

[64] ibid 117; TRS Allan, 'In Defence of the Common Law Constitution: Unwritten Rights as Fundamental Law' (2009) 22 *Canadian Journal of Law and Jurisprudence* 187.

[65] Allan, 'Rule of Law' (n 2).

[66] 'Adherence to the rule of law converts what would otherwise be an assertion of governmental will or power into an exercise of legitimate authority': Allan, *Sovereignty of Law* (n 1) 119.

over centuries. This process of adjudicatory accretion has developed a series of unwritten principles that together form the 'common law constitution'. And judges maintain discretion to exercise interpretive judgment to ensure that the positive law complies with the fundamental values of legality that inhere in the common law constitution.

We can summarise Allan's account as follows. In order for legal authority to be legitimate, it must operate as a bulwark against arbitrary power, from public and private sources alike. This means that the substance of public and private law must both protect and constitute the liberty and equality of persons. The rule of law is thus a thick, substantive idea, which has important implications for the law's content, across all legal domains. It is not a complete account of justice – it is a morally pluralist idea, which allows different instantiations of these ideals – but it operates as both an interpretive ideal and a floor for the content of law.

In reconstructing Allan's account here, I have not used the term 'citizen' to describe the law's subjects, despite the fact that Allan himself does so in much of his work. But we can see that it was not necessary for me to do so. Nothing in the above discussion turns on citizenship. His account of the rule of law does not reference membership in a political community, and can be reconstructed without employing the more citizenship-focused arguments rooted in imagined consent, the common good, or participation. While Allan starts from the initial 'basic premise' that it is the dignity and autonomy of *citizens* that matters, we can find the resources in his account to recognise that it is the dignity and autonomy of *persons* that is relevant to law's authority.

B. The Missing Factual Particulars

But Allan's theory, as reconstructed above, is ultimately unable to provide a comprehensive account of when legal authority is legitimate. While it identifies some of the conditions necessary for law to apply legitimately to persons, it lacks an account of how *particular* authority relationships are normatively justified. As discussed above, the law does not assume that every state is authoritative in relation to every dispute. Instead, authority relationships are particularised. The law requires there to be sufficient facts connecting the state and the law's subjects to normatively justify the exercise of authority of a particular state's law in relation to a particular dispute/particular legal subjects.

While Allan recognises that authority is relational, as discussed above, he identifies the wrong relationship as justifying its scope. And once we remove the idea of citizenship, Allan's account says nothing about why a *particular* state would have the authority to decide a *particular* dispute. His reconstructed account of authority is entirely general: if the law is substantively correct in certain ways, it has the right to rule. But this seems to mean that any state's law is potentially authoritative in the context of any dispute. This is not doctrinally correct, of course, because the law itself insists that one state's law is more authoritative than another in every instance. And it is also normatively unattractive. We do not think that *any* state's law has the normative authority to decide *any* dispute. The inability to determine which state is authoritative over a particular dispute is also problematic since Allan's account – and the law itself – accept a degree of pluralism as to what private laws a state can adopt. That is, states are permitted by law to have different substantive approaches to legal issues enshrined in their positive law. But if *any* state's laws could apply to *any* dispute, we would all be without certainty as to how we are legally permitted to treat one another, because we would not know which of these plural norms govern our behaviour.

Allan's account, shorn of citizenship, does not have the resources to grapple with these issues. Consequently, we need a more robust theory of the grounds on which authoritative legal relationships are particularised, beyond just identifying the law's necessary substantive content. Future work will have to fill in this aspect of his account, to determine how we can account for authority relationships in instances in which citizenship does not provide the necessary nexus between state and subject.[67]

4. Conclusion

In Allan's extensive body of work, he embraces an ambitious project: to provide a comprehensive account of what makes legal authority legitimate. However, by focusing only on authority relationships between a state and its citizens, he fails to offer a comprehensive account of the nature of legal authority in practice, as the example of private law makes clear. In private law, citizenship does not mediate the exercise of legal authority. Instead, all persons can potentially be the subjects of a particular state's law, depending on the factual connections between the dispute and the law.

Yet despite describing the relationship in need of justification as the state-citizen relationship, Allan's account offers resources to reach the potentially universal legal subject. His substantive account of the rule of law and legitimate authority is not predicated on membership of the law's subjects in a particular political community, and offers an important and distinctive account of how and when legal authority may be legitimate. Reconstructed in this way, however, Allan's account flounders, because when the idea of citizenship as the connective tissue between state and subject is removed, his account cannot explain how particular facts generate a more legitimate claim for authority for one state's law over another.

Despite this lacuna, however, scholars of both private and public law have much to learn from Allan's work. First, as this analysis reveals, Allan is right to insist that inquiries into the nature of legitimate authority and the rule of law are relational questions that cannot be asked in the abstract.

Second, this analysis has also helped us to draw out two aspects of authority relationships, at least in the context of private law. Private law understands the legal subject as the universal, undifferentiated person. It then narrows in on which state is authoritative in a particular dispute by examining particular facts that normatively justify a state exercising authority, such as the territory on which the alleged wrong took place. For this reason, we need an account of when legal authority is legitimate that applies to the potentially universal legal subject, but that also identifies a particular relationship of authority. Although it has not been my focus in this chapter, this lesson applies equally in the context of public law, where legal authority is also not necessarily conditioned

[67] I attempt to offer the beginnings of such an account in the context of tort law in Langille, 'The Subjects of Tort Law' (n 4).

on citizenship. Think, for example, of contemporary criminal law, where jurisdiction is typically territorial, and acts are criminalised within a state's borders no matter who commits them.[68] A theory of authority that sought to justify criminal law would lack explanatory power if it constrained itself to citizens as subjects, or if it did not address why territory is so significant.[69]

Third, when we move beyond the assumption that the law's subjects are citizens and instead appreciate that legal authority must often be justified to the universal, undifferentiated person, Allan may offer an important substantive theory of when legal authority can be legitimate. As described in Section 3 above, Allan's account is not in principle limited to citizens, and offers an important theory of how law must protect and constitute a particular conception of the person – as equally free – in order to be authoritative. As such, a substantive account of law's content may be a necessary aspect of justifying law's authority.

Finally, my analysis here should push us to do more of our constitutional, political, and legal theorising outside of the confines of a single state. The assumption that we can effectively conduct our justificatory analysis within the purely domestic context is misleading. For this reason, theorising about authority must remove assumptions like the one that law is only applied to citizens within the confines of a particular state. Theory must explore how law can be justified to persons, not citizens.

[68] See, eg L Farmer, 'Territorial Jurisdiction and Criminalization' (2013) 63 *University of Toronto Law Journal* 225.

[69] For a discussion of the difficulties of developing a citizenship-based account in the context of territorially focused criminal law, see RA Duff, *The Realm of Criminal Law* (Oxford, Oxford University Press, 2018). Relatedly, while constitutional law is often conceptualised as mediating the relationship between state and citizen, this does not actually capture the practice of constitutional law, wherein (most) constitutional rights are typically guaranteed to all persons. See Bosniak, 'Persons and Citizens in Constitutional Thought' (n 18).

14

What's Good about Parliamentary Sovereignty?

GEORGE LETSAS*

1. The Interpretive Turn in Public Law

Parliament is not sovereign; law is. This aphorism captures much of the interpretive turn in UK public law that we owe to the work of Trevor Allan. It is a turn away from two closely related ideas, one methodological and one substantive, which only three decades ago were treated as dogmas by most UK lawyers. The first is the idea that giving an account of the UK Constitution is a morally neutral endeavour, a matter of reporting a set of facts or doctrines about constitutional practice in the UK. The second is the idea that Parliament in the UK is sovereign in an absolutist fashion, having the power to make or unmake any law without constraints imposed by the judiciary, or other bodies. That these ideas are no longer accepted as dogmas is a mark of the intellectual health of the discipline. What has come to be known, following the influence of the work of Ronald Dworkin,[1] as legal interpretivism[2] puts forward a radically different idea: Parliament gets to rule only in so far as it is justified by moral principles that are embedded in the common law, and that it is the courts' constitutional duty to uphold.

The interpretivist turn in UK public law theory is not accidental. It reflects deeper changes in domestic and international politics as well as theoretical developments within general jurisprudence and constitutional theory. Legal theory in Britain had to grapple inevitably with the process of European integration, globalisation, the proliferation of international law norms and the incorporation of the European

* I am extremely grateful to the organisers and all the participants to the conference 'The Promise of Legality: Critical Reflections on the work of TRS Allan', for the opportunity to engage with Professor Allan's work and for all the comments and suggestions. Special thanks to the editors, Geneviève Cartier and Mark Walters, for their very helpful comments on an earlier draft. Above all, I am deeply grateful to Professor Allan for detailed discussion and comments. The debt of intellectual gratitude owed to his work, and to his integrity as an academic scholar, far exceeds what is paid in this chapter.

[1] See R Dworkin, *Law's Empire* (Cambridge, Belknap Press, 1986); R Dworkin, *Justice for Hedgehogs* (Cambridge, Harvard University Press, 2013).

[2] See N Stavropoulos, 'Legal Interpretivism', entry in the *Stanford Encyclopedia of Philosophy* available at: plato.stanford.edu/entries/law-interpretivist/.

Convention on Human Rights (ECHR) into domestic law by the Labour government in 1998.[3] These developments did not quite fit the traditional theoretical model of parliamentary sovereignty, which had to be stretched at breaking point in order to accommodate them. The judicial application of Section 3 of the Human Rights Act in particular made it clear that courts are giving effect to the will of Parliament only in the very thin sense that they respect Parliament's abstract commitment to the values underlying human rights. And it raised the further question of whether it is completely up to Parliament to undertake the legal commitment to respect fundamental rights, or whether it is in the nature of its role to be constitutionally bound by those rights, whether or not it has expressed so in a legislative enactment like the HRA 1998.

However, political developments alone would not have been sufficient to challenge the traditional understanding of parliamentary sovereignty without the difference that particular scholars have made. Ronald Dworkin's work, starting with his *Model of Rules I* in 1967, shook the foundations of the theoretical tradition of legal positivism, which had predominantly been an English product. Furthermore, Trevor Allan's work has in the last three decades offered a vision of the British constitution that in significant respects was ahead of its time; it articulates elements of constitutional practice that few UK public lawyers had appreciated, or are yet willing to endorse. And it does so in a bottom-up way, inviting reasoned engagement by anyone who claims to take constitutional practice seriously. Public lawyers in the UK can no longer assert the above two dogmas without addressing Allan's powerful theoretical objections and his alternative conception. His work has inspired not only a growing number of interpretivists within UK Public Law, but also sophisticated critics who aim to defend a positivist account of the British Constitution that aims to answer these objections.

As someone who is on Allan's side in the jurisprudential and constitutional battles, I shall not here attempt to revisit his arguments against a positivist conception of the UK Constitution. Instead, I want to ask what is left of the doctrine of parliamentary sovereignty once it is stripped of its positivistic understanding. This is a friendly critique, in that its aim is to expose the positivistic underpinnings of the very concept of parliamentary sovereignty as the main *explanandum* of constitutional theory. Interpretivism, as a methodology, works in a very distinctive way. It invites us to place law within political morality, to see it in the light of what demands are legitimate to enforce collectively against people. Consider a simple case such as that of a protester holding a sign 'Not my King' getting arrested by the police under the Public Order Act 1986 during King Charles's coronation. The interpretivist lawyer must start with the question of what – if any – moral principles could possibly justify censoring a protester's republican views, looking at common law as a whole, and then gradually work their way to the question of what Parliament decided by enacting the Public Order Act. We ask what is legitimate for government to enforce in order to find out what the law is, not the other way around. We do not assume that the Public Order Act allows the censoring of anti-monarchical protests and then ask whether that is legitimate.

How this general interpretivist thesis is meant to play out in the context of the British Constitution, and the doctrine of parliamentary sovereignty, is not obvious,

[3] Human Rights Act 1998 (HRA 1998).

however. In this piece, I want to sketch two possible ways, a weak one and a strong one, that an interpretivist reading of the doctrine might go. The weak reading salvages the doctrine, albeit truncated. It holds that Parliament's supremacy is neither absolute, nor axiomatic, but nevertheless an objectively valuable feature of the British constitution. The weak interpretivist model insists that, properly understood, parliamentary sovereignty is a distinct and central aspect of the political morality that underpins the Constitution, even if it is qualified by principles to do with human rights and other rule of law standards. The strong reading, by contrast, holds that the doctrine of parliamentary sovereignty is a historic relic that serves merely as a shorthand for a variety of principles of political morality that may justify paying attention to legislative practice. The strong reading seeks to *debunk* the doctrine of parliamentary sovereignty, in the apt phrase used by Stuart Lakin;[4] it tells us to do away with the doctrine altogether and to talk instead of the underlying moral principles (such as democracy, equality, stability, good governance, transparency) that may be binding on the judge at each given time. Put differently, the strong reading seeks to disaggregate the doctrine of parliamentary sovereignty into more finely-grained principles of political morality, of which democracy is just one.

I want to begin with the disclaimer that it is not clear to me which of the two readings Trevor Allan favours; if pressed to attribute one to him, I think that the weak reading is more in line with his writings. But my understanding from personal conversations with him is quite different and I believe that the stronger model is closer to his heart. During the proceedings for this volume, he expressed his frustration that the stronger model – even though superior – would have no chance of engaging other public lawyers, wedded as they are to the doctrine of parliamentary sovereignty. Be that as it may, my main aim here is not biographical, or exegetical. Rather, I want to highlight these two interpretivist accounts of the doctrine of parliamentary sovereignty and ask what reasons we might have for favouring one over the other. My plea will be that we have very good reasons, both moral and pragmatic, to opt for the stronger, debunking, model. More specifically, I will seek to unpack the stronger model in terms of the need to disaggregate the many reasons that courts have to pay attention to Parliament as a constitutional actor.

2. Is the Doctrine of Parliamentary Sovereignty a Shorthand for the Value of Democracy?

It was once thought that the power of kings was absolute, having the divine right to rule on earth. This religious idea, dominant for centuries, is still very much alive in the UK at a symbolic and cultural level, despite the long process of democratisation and secularisation of British politics. It is also there at a constitutional level, evident in the absence of a strict separation between church and state, in the role of the monarch as a constitutional actor (eg, in giving ascent to Bills passed by Parliament, or exercising

[4] See S Lakin, 'Debunking the Idea of Parliamentary Sovereignty: The Controlling Factor of Legality in the British Constitution' (2008) 28 *OJLS* 709.

powers under the royal prerogative), in the hereditary nature of (many) members of the House of Lords and much else. It is also there, of course, in the doctrine of parliamentary sovereignty. Formally, sovereignty does not lie with Parliament, but with the King in Parliament. At a symbolic level, Parliament did not so much take power away from the monarch, but rather joined His Majesty as holders of the divine right to rule. The pedigree of parliamentary sovereignty as a legal doctrine is deeply rooted in pre-modern conceptions of legitimacy and justice, in religious ideas of social rank and status. It is against these conceptions that ideas of equality and liberty emerged during the Enlightenment and gradually took root politically and legally within western liberal democracies, especially with the emergence of the human rights movement. And it is within the moral outlook of the Enlightenment that we should situate legal interpretivism as a philosophical school of thought.[5]

How should then a modern-day interpretivist, committed to objective principles of political morality, approach a doctrine with a tainted past and a compromised presence? In his work, Trevor Allan is primarily pre-occupied with establishing a negative thesis about this doctrine: parliamentary sovereignty is not absolute, nor is it in conflict with the rule of law. The rule of law shapes the scope and limits of Parliament's power and grants it whatever normative weight it has. It contains sovereignty within the remit of things that it is legitimate for Parliament to decide, under common law principles. He writes:

> Treated as a general principle of legislative supremacy, the doctrine of parliamentary sovereignty is perfectly consistent with the rule of law because it does not threaten the integrity of basic constitutional values.[6]
>
> [S]overeignty or supremacy is a political idea and legal construct: it asserts a duty of obedience or allegiance whose validity is always a matter of moral judgement, albeit one made within the context of an established constitutional tradition.[7]

But what about the positive side of the doctrine? What does the doctrine have going for it morally speaking in the first place? Here, Allan stresses time and again the democratic basis of the justification for the doctrine. He writes:

> A doctrine or principle of legislative supremacy, fit for a theory of British constitutionalism, must be defensible as an interpretation of legal practice, informed by considerations of legitimacy. The doctrine must be much more closely related to popular sovereignty, or conceptions of democracy, than the merely contingent connection that Dicey was apparently willing to concede.[8]

And elsewhere: 'Parliament's supremacy reflects its role as the collective voice of the people, given expression through their elected representatives'.[9]

[5] Ronald Dworkin, for example, has been clear that his legal philosophy is part of his liberal moral and political philosophy, which is committed to the idea of ethical individualism. See R Dworkin, *Sovereign Virtue: The Theory and Practice of Equality* (Cambridge, Harvard University Press, 2000) 5.

[6] TRS Allan, *The Sovereignty of Law: Freedom, Constitution, and Common Law* (Oxford, Oxford University Press, 2013) 174.

[7] ibid 36.

[8] ibid 172.

[9] ibid 132.

This is, no doubt, the type of analysis in which the interpretivist is meant to engage. Democracy is an objective value of political morality, itself an expression of the more abstract value of human equality. The normative connection to equality is inherent to the value of democracy, not contingent. We all have an equal right to participate in collective governance and a corresponding duty to respect procedures that give a reasonable institutional expression to this right, including arguably the UK's first-past-the-post system. I say 'arguably' because alternative models of co-relating votes and seats, such as mixed models of proportional representation for example, offer a more egalitarian conception of representative democracy. Be that as it may, political morality constrains in any case what we may collectively decide through our elected representatives. I have no right to control, through my representatives, what my fellow citizens may read, think, worship, or express; no right to stop others from expressing ideas that may 'shock, disturb or offend'.[10] If I were so minded, I would be denying the very premise of representative democracy. We are all equals and enjoy strong moral rights to personal autonomy. The moral value of democracy is therefore not a justification for Parliament's authority to decide anything it wants, but a substantive constraint on what it may decide, as well as on what it has *already* decided.[11] Allan's analysis is characteristically lucid on this point:

> Parliament's supremacy reflects its role as the collective voice of the people, given expression through their elected representatives. It is only when Parliament determines how state power shall be deployed to secure the general conditions of freedom that the law is truly binding, representing the general will. In giving concrete form to that ideal of freedom, of course, Parliament cannot violate the moral rights it is supposed to be affirming .... Democracy is not a principle that operates in a vacuum: its power derives from our related commitments to equality and justice; and these values govern the *interpretation* of statutes.[12]

Should interpretivists then be content with the invocation of representative democracy as the normative foundation of parliamentary sovereignty? There are difficulties here and Allan is very much attuned to them. The first difficulty is to do with the very label of the doctrine, which suggests that the legislature is 'sovereign', albeit only within a circumscribed domain. Parliament enacts statutes but the contribution these enactments make to the content of the law is necessarily tentative and can hardly be described as the exercise of a sovereign power. This is because legislation in force at any given time has been passed by successive Parliaments and, seen holistically, contains language that inevitably has normative tensions and ambiguities. What Parliament said in a statute enacted in 1967 may be in tension with what Parliament said in a statute enacted in 1977, both of which contain ambiguous and abstract terms that have been interpreted and applied in hundreds of cases by courts. For instance, in 1967,

[10] This apt phrase comes from the *Handyside* judgment of the European Court of Human Rights: *Handyside v the United Kingdom* App no 5493/72 (1976) para 49.

[11] Nicos Stavropoulos is right to distinguish interpretivism from what he calls the 'moral filter view', ie the idea that we just look at legislative enactments, descriptively identified, and then disregard those that are on their face morally wicked, like the familiar example of law mandating the murdering of blue-eyed babies. Interpretivism is not Radbruch's formula by a different name. See Stavropoulos, 'Legal Interpretivism' (n 2).

[12] Allan, *Sovereignty of Law* (n 6) 132, 139.

the UK passed the Sexual Offences Act, which decriminalised same-sex acts. And in 1977, it passed the Rent Act, which provided that the spouse of a deceased person can succeed them in a statutory tenancy. Did Parliament also decide that same-sex couples have the right to protected tenancy in case one of them dies?[13]

The Court here must exercise a moral judgment and rely on normative assumptions about how to *assign* meaning to democratically-passed enactments, across time. In other words, the text of a statutory enactment is just the beginning, not the end, of an inquiry as to what rights are enforceable in court. And the inquiry – the one undertaken by courts, though anyone can apply themselves to it – must be a moral one, simply because the issue at stake is one of political morality: which party should prevail in court when it is never clear what Parliament 'decided', thus availing themselves of the possibility of coercive enforcement?

It makes no sense here to reply: courts should just enforce what the democratically enacted legislature decided. This reply would be question-begging because we are precisely asking what it is that Parliament decided in the first place. This point is entirely missed by republican theorists who hail the value of democracy as a constraint on courts, arguing against strong forms of judicial review.[14] They assume, wrongly, that once democratic institutions are properly set-up and well-functioning, then the role of courts will be limited to giving effect to the will of the elected branch of government. They presuppose, in other words, a very positivistic understanding of legal interpretation which is at great odds with the common law. As any good lawyer knows, there is no such thing as the 'will' of the legislature, clearly expressed in a statute and waiting to be pronounced unmediated by the judge, without any evaluative judgment. People reasonably disagree about what that 'will' is because they disagree about what it is legitimate to enforce in court. The so-called 'will' of the legislator – even a democratically elected one – is a fiction, something that the court constructs, and arrives at, after offering finely crafted arguments about the normative significance of this or that aspect of the constitutional history. For example, the question of whether the word 'spouse' in the Rent Act 1997 means 'partner' is a question about whether it is legitimate for the law to exclude same-sex partners from a benefit granted to married couples, given that Parliament has already abandoned the despicable practice of criminalising same-sex acts. This legal question is not some low-level technicality in the mechanics of statutory interpretation. It is not an exercise in linguistics or sociology. Nor is it a question that can be returned to Parliament by the court, asking it whether *it* now thinks that it is legitimate to exclude same-sex couples, given the legal history that we have. Even if Parliament were to hear individual petitions (which it does not), it would be in no better position than the court to construct a valid answer to this moral question. This is why the term 'sovereignty' is so misleading: it suggests that the decisions of one branch of government (preferably Parliament's) settle the moral question of what should be enforced through courts. But the only thing that can settle a moral question is morality itself.

[13] See *Ghaidan v Godin-Mendoza* [2004] 2 AC 557.

[14] See R Bellamy, *Political Constitutionalism: A Republican Defence of the Constitutionality of Democracy* (Cambridge, Cambridge University Press, 2007).

Still, might there be a sense in which the task of the court is to discover, case-by-case, how far the sovereignty of the democratically-elected Parliament extends, morally speaking? Surely, one might argue, a democratically-elected legislature has the 'sovereign' power to decide whether to grant protected tenancy in the first place, and if so, whether to extend it to the partners of a deceased tenant. Even when the court may legitimately extend this legal benefit to cover same-sex couples, they are still in principle upholding the sovereignty of a democratic body.

I am far from convinced that the legitimacy of an elected parliament to enact and pursue housing policies, subject to legal constraints, is best described as a 'sovereign power'. This is because there is no area of public policy that, in principle, will be free from the constraints imposed by legality and the rule of law, which is the role of courts to discover. For example, suppose that Parliament does not enact a policy of protected tenancy. A person may still have a legal right to protected tenancy, say when they will otherwise be left destitute under inhuman and degrading conditions of the kind that the common law already finds unacceptable. In advance of knowing the specifics of a case, real or hypothetical, we cannot offer a list of domains or areas of public policy where a democratically-elected body will be 'sovereign', precisely because its 'will' must in any case be the product of assessing multiple moral principles at play.

We might at best say that the value of democracy creates a strong presumption. It requires taking legislative enactments seriously and placing prima facie weight on them. But the actual relevance and weight of these enactments can only be established after they have passed the moral test of the rule of law. As it has been pointed out so often, the constitutional relevance of a statutory provision abolishing judicial review or election is only presumptive, not real. It is of course true that the outcome of an interpretivist process most often results in statutory language receiving both relevance and weight by the court. And we can call such outcomes instances where the sovereignty of a democratic parliament has prevailed. But the problem remains that the concept of 'sovereignty' has done no normative work in that process. It is simply a conclusory label for a moral judgment about the interplay between democracy and other values, and the way that judgment feeds into the judicial determination of a person's rights.

3. Disaggregating Parliamentary Sovereignty

I propose that we should genuinely question whether Parliament's power, normatively understood, is worthy of the noun 'sovereignty', whether – that is – the legal doctrine is one of parliamentary 'sovereignty' or something else altogether. I do not mean to sound provocative by this statement. Lawyers know that doctrines are rough labels that are continuously unpacked with care and precision by each generation of lawyers in the context of ever evolving case-law.

I think that Allan shares the above scepticism, considering parliamentary sovereignty an 'infelicitous' British label because 'it attributes to one institution an authority that should strictly attach to the constitution from which Parliament derives its very extensive powers'.[15] It is constitutional law that is sovereign, not Parliament. The explanation he gives for why the term is infelicitous is that the noun 'sovereignty' should be understood in a justificatory sense, as a reference to the normative basis of whatever powers Parliament has. And, thus understood, he finds that the reference fails because it is circular: Parliament's constitutional powers are not axiomatic, a self-evident empirical or social fact, but derivative normatively from moral values. Parliamentary sovereignty, we might say, is the *explanandum* not the *explanans*. We must ask why, and when, Parliament should be sovereign, not accept its powers *because* it is sovereign.

But it is at this point that I am slightly puzzled by how Allan's account proceeds. He does not move on to propose that we should substitute the label 'parliamentary sovereignty' with 'parliamentary democracy', given that he treats democracy as the main constitutional foundation for the unquestionable, yet prima facie, contribution that parliamentary enactments make to our laws. One would expect Allan to say at this stage that 'parliamentary sovereignty' is an infelicitous British name for parliamentary *democracy* or, more accurately, for representative democracy. Instead, Allan expresses his preference for the term 'parliamentary *supremacy*'. But isn't the term 'supremacy' even more infelicitous than sovereignty? It is far from a justification as to why parliamentary enactments make a moral difference, when they do. The concept of democracy, by contrast, has direct evaluative connotations, particularly if understood as an institutional manifestation of the value of human equality.

The term 'supremacy' moreover seems totally out of place within an interpretivist framework. Within that framework, there is no institution over which Parliament reigns supreme, and certainly not courts. The courts' role is to ensure that coercive force is authorised against an individual only when it is legitimate to do so under operative moral principles embedded in the common law. Their task is individualised to a specific case and litigant party; it is backward-looking, assessing the normative effect of past institutional actions. By contrast, the task of legislatures is non-individualised and forward-looking; they aim to effect social change so as to bring a country closer to a vision of distributive justice that, in a democratic polity, has been chosen by the electorate. My own view is that we should not see any competition between Parliament and the courts. It is not that their roles can be harmonised practically, with each branch showing proper respect for the power of the other. Rather, it is that the job of the courts is fundamentally different in kind to that of legislatures. Courts interpret the political history of a country, with a view to identifying which individual rights are enforceable in a given case. Legislatures simply add data-points to that history, without controlling normatively how they fit with the rest of the record. If that is true, then their respective roles are not comparable such that we can ask who is better at it, who is more legitimate, or who should prevail when their views diverge.[16] Courts' role as guardians of enforceable claim is therefore not an institutional choice that some jurisdictions

[15] Allan, *Sovereignty of Law* (n 6) 133.

[16] At times Allan does seem to find them comparable. See eg Allan, *Sovereignty of Law* (n 6) 177: '[T]here are good democratic reasons for accepting legislative supremacy and its concomitant system of general rules: within the broad constraints imposed by respect for human dignity and fundamental rights, Parliament's solution to a question of justice or public policy can usually claim a legitimacy that an unelected court's determination cannot.'

might make, or a consequentialist calculation as to which branch is likely to produce better outcomes. It is a role justified in political morality under a specific conception of the value of the rule of law. The fact that many public lawyers still talk about 'judicial supremacy' or 'juristocracy' is I think a sign of the lingering failure to understand the substance of interpretivism. The interpretivist is not someone who wants courts rather that legislatures to be supreme. It is someone who believes that the question 'who decides?' or 'who should have the last word?' is the wrong one to ask. The moral question courts, but not legislatures, face is this: how should one figure out what rights are enforceable, given that the outcome of the judicial process will result in state coercion against the losing party? If the question posed by the rule of law is a moral one, then *no-one* decides. Courts can get it wrong, just like anyone else can.

It also makes little sense to say that Parliament is at least supreme vis-à-vis other law-enacting bodies, like the European Union or the United Nations. The familiar idea that international law is binding on domestic courts only in so far as common law permits, is a type of absolute dualism that makes no sense within an interpretivist framework. One could try to point to Brexit to defend this dualism, but examples where domestic courts cannot turn a blind eye to international law abound, from the Northern Ireland Protocol to the current government's attempt to detain asylum seekers arbitrarily under the Illegal Migration Bill 2023. The practice of international and supranational institutions is clearly relevant to what individual rights are enforceable by domestic courts. What these examples show is not merely that democracy circumscribes the limits of parliamentary power (as it does for instance in the tired example of blocking a statute mandating the murder of blue-eyed babies), such that, once it is circumscribed, it rules supreme; rather, they show that parliamentary legislation is simply one amongst many areas of political practice that legality makes relevant to the question of what can be judicially enforced.

One might here object: all this is terminological. It does not matter if we keep using the term 'parliamentary sovereignty' and 'parliamentary supremacy' so long as we make clear, as Trevor Allan does, that its constitutional significance is derivative from the value of representative democracy. Besides, it is a common feature of legal practice that doctrines evolve and often end up serving as a shorthand for principles that bear little conceptual resemblance to the original label. There are, moreover, clear upsides to keep using the label 'parliamentary sovereignty', despite its infelicity. Constitutional interpretivists should try to engage their opponents, those who treat the doctrine of parliamentary sovereignty as the ultimate foundation of the British Constitution. Telling them that there is no such thing as parliamentary sovereignty is hardly a good start for a constructive dialogue. They are more likely to listen if one tells them that the doctrine, though central, cannot stand as an empirical or conceptual truth, but must instead be defended on normative grounds. This is the gist of what we might call the *weak* interpretivist approach to the doctrine of parliamentary sovereignty: keep its pride of place within the constitutional imagery, but hasten to add that it's democracy that calls all the shots.

This is a pragmatic argument rather than an argument from first principles. It invites public lawyers who endorse interpretivism not to debunk the doctrine of parliamentary sovereignty, on the basis that retaining it will make the prospect of an interpretivist understanding of the UK constitution more likely. Put differently, positivists and non-positivists alike can be seen as equally committed to the same doctrine, and that is no small thing. As the saying goes, we have to have something in common in order to be able to disagree.

I worry, however, that the benefits of retaining the centrality of the doctrine of parliamentary sovereignty as the *locus* of constitutional theory within the UK are not as significant as the costs. And this is because law thrives when citizens can reliably identify the normative rationale of its doctrines.[17] In my view, the proposition that Parliament is sovereign (or supreme) does not adequately project the values of democracy, equality and liberty which make whatever Parliament does relevant to our lives as equal citizens. In fact, I worry that it projects a message in the opposite direction. Parliamentary practice in the UK, unlike that of many newly-founded democracies, still contains a number of inegalitarian elements. The upper house is still unelected and the monarch's role – though mainly ceremonial – is part and parcel of an inegalitarian medieval outlook based on rank and status. These elements exert indirect influence in the attitudes and actions of officials, whose pernicious effects are not always visible. The speed and eagerness with which police officers clamped down on republican protests to King Charles' succession to the throne is a helpful reminder of this.

These concerns aside, the bigger worry I have is that there is only so much that the principle of representative democracy can justify from what falls within the doctrine of parliamentary sovereignty, as it is conventionally understood in the UK. Representative democracy does not *require* bicameralism, let alone bicameralism with an unelected upper house. Nor is the value of democracy indifferent to whether ceremonial constitutional roles should be assigned on a hereditary basis. It is all nice and good to say that parliamentary supremacy is ultimately grounded on democratic legitimacy. But for a sizeable part of UK parliamentary practice, this normative justification would be over-inclusive. There is nothing democratic about hereditary peers. Nor can the value of democracy condone the crucial role that the Crown may play, under certain circumstances, in deciding whom to appoint or retain as prime minister.[18]

Here, one might object that an interpretivist approach to the British Constitution cannot do away with the not-so-noble aspects of its history. In Dworkin's familiar vocabulary, an interpretation of legal practice must both fit the history and have independent moral appeal. Interpretivism, the objection goes, cannot do away with the central role that the House of Lords has within the British Constitution; nor can it turn a constitutional monarchy into a republic. Such suggestions would fall at the first stage of the interpretive methodology, the requirement that a legal interpretation must 'fit' with existing practice.

In answering this objection, we must recall that it is only if we have substantive reasons of political morality that we should assign weight to less-than-ideal aspects of constitutional practice. And since democracy does not speak in favour of any self-standing notion of parliamentary sovereignty (in fact it speaks against much of what falls within it), it is not clear to me where else we might look for normative support. Ideas of the so-called 'common good constitutionalism', based on national or religious

[17] See SV Shiffrin, *Democratic Law* (Oxford, Oxford University Press, 2021).
[18] I am grateful to Mark Walters for this point.

identity, are antithetical with so many common law principles, as they have developed in recent decades, so as to make them ineligible as a conception of the constitution. These ideas have resurfaced recently in academic circles,[19] but they are far from novel; rather, they belong to the counter-Enlightenment tradition against which liberalism sought to define itself. Liberal democracies cannot take these ideas seriously without abandoning their commitment to rights-based constitutionalism.

Other options exist of course. Liberal political morality has ample space for the values of tradition, patriotism, community, stability, accountability and effective governance. One can attempt to justify treating the doctrine of parliamentary sovereignty as a central feature of the British Constitution by invoking this plurality of values. These values might not justify everything one finds in UK parliamentary practice, but they will justify much more than what democracy alone can. For instance, it might be – though I am sceptical – that the value of tradition could justify hereditary privileges or ceremonial roles. Or that the value of accountability can justify an unelected second chamber. I now worry, however, that we are down the path of packaging so much normative theorising under one single doctrine for no reason at all. Why not go straight to these other values? Why not say that the UK Constitution, like those of other countries, has several core principles including representative democracy, accountability, checks and balances, stability and tradition. Why do we need the detour of a tired legal doctrine, whose arteries have become so clogged?

The gist of what we might call the *strong* interpretivist reading is that there is no such thing as a one-to-one correlation between normative principles and the doctrine of parliamentary supremacy. Seeking to find a normative justification for the doctrine is bound to cause confusion and obscure the normative basis for paying attention to (or ignoring) facts about parliamentary practice. The risk of confusion is a genuine concern to the citizen, who has to be able to understand the justification for giving the legislature the significance that it has in a democracy. And this speaks in favour of the strong interpretivist reading, which invites us to disaggregate the various aspects of the UK Constitution and to point separately, one by one, to the various normative principles that lend support to them. There is no such thing as parliamentary sovereignty or supremacy, we might say: it's too crude a notion to serve as the *explanandum* of a value-laden approach to the British constitution.

I have no illusion of course that the strong interpretivist reading will find support amongst constitutional theorists, let alone the British public, any time soon. I have seen people roll their eyes at the suggestion that the doctrine of parliamentary sovereignty is a myth, too archaic an idea to do any explanatory work. A weak interpretivist approach to the doctrine of parliamentary sovereignty, of the kind that I think Allan's work puts forward, is already thought radical by many UK public lawyers. But I do believe that strong interpretivism might be the most honest and consistent approach for those who reject a positivistic understanding of the British Constitution. Disaggregating parliamentary sovereignty into different normative principles (with democracy being one amongst others) has both intrinsic and instrumental benefits. It invites citizens and judges to be more engaged with the constitution and to demand a

[19] For a recent defence of common good constitutionalism, see Michael Foran in this volume, ch 12.

more detailed justification by courts when they hear cases. Citizens should, for example, be able to understand why the Supreme Court decided against the government in *Miller 1*[20] and *Miller 2*,[21] both of which were of immense political and legal significance. They are no wiser if they are simply told: the court found against the government on the basis of the doctrine of parliamentary sovereignty. They are likely to become suspicious that courts are usurping their power. Dropping this label and pointing to more basic principles that citizens can grasp is a much better justificatory process, since it does not seek to shoehorn everything that Parliament may legitimately do into a single normative foundation. It helps citizens to understand that each of these principles (rights, equality, fair warning, representative democracy, protected expectations) place different constraints on politics and on what can be enforced in courts. Perhaps more importantly, it helps citizens to understand that the question facing the courts is never of a binary nature, say either to uphold parliamentary sovereignty, or to curtail it and uphold individual rights instead. Courts must interpret many normative principles, see one in the light of the other as that famous metaphor goes. Suppose that Parliament were to enact a statute whose clear language makes anti-monarchical protests during succession of the Crown a criminal offence and that courts upheld, as they ought to, the individual right to hold up the sign 'Not my King'. It is one thing to say that the value of democracy is not undermined by courts upholding the right to individual protest, and that it is in fact undemocratic to censor political views. But it is a different proposition altogether to say that parliamentary *sovereignty* is not undermined by upholding that right. Citizens who are told that parliamentary sovereignty is the pillar of the UK constitution will struggle to see that such an offence would be unconstitutional, *qua* undemocratic.

I should like to end by saying that there should hardly be any disagreement on Allan's part about the outcomes that a constitutional interpretivist should reach on this or that case. What I am not sure about is whether he would agree with me that whether we should continue to treat parliamentary supremacy as a constitutional doctrine is *itself* a normative question, one that goes beyond pragmatic concerns about how the academic debate in UK public law is likely to go in the coming decades. I wanted to emphasise, instead, that whether we should retain the label of this doctrine is itself a normative question, one that admits of a principled answer. We have good moral reasons, both as citizens and as scholars, to make constitutional arguments without any reference to the doctrine parliamentary sovereignty, invoking instead first principles of political morality. If constitutional discourse in the UK ever develops in this direction, it is the groundbreaking vision of constitutionalism which Trevor Allan has offered us that will have made it possible.

[20] *Miller v Secretary of State for Exiting the European Union* [2017] UKSC 5, [2018] AC 61.
[21] *R (Miller) v Prime Minister* [2019] UKSC 4, [2019] 3 WLR 589.

15

Constitutional Balance and the Common Law Constitution

ALISON L YOUNG

Trevor Allan and I adopt different accounts of the United Kingdom constitution. Allan is the main advocate of common law constitutionalism in the UK. My theory is one of constitutional balance, resting on a series of inter-institutional interactions between the legislature, the executive, and the courts. This may appear to be a simple, if arguably vague, distinction. However, the more we investigate these differences, the more we realise that they are more than superficial, resting on distinct approaches to constitutional theory.

We often distinguish between accounts of legal and political constitutionalism. Common law constitutionalism is an example of legal constitutionalism. The common law provides the main and most important means of holding the executive to account. Political constitutionalism, however, is regarded as the polar opposite. Democracy is more important than the rule of law. Political checks and balances, therefore, should play a larger and a more important role when holding the executive to account. Balanced constitutionalism, as its name implies, argues that constitutions require a balance of political and legal controls over the executive.

There are problems with this taxonomy. First, it suggests that balanced constitutionalism occupies a middle ground between legal and political constitutionalism. Yet, when we look closer at both legal and political constitutionalism, it is hard to find a stable middle ground between the two. Accounts of legal constitutionalism do not argue that there should be no political controls over the executive, and likewise political constitutionalism does not argue that the executive should not be subject to legal controls. Moreover, accounts of balanced constitutionalism tend to use the same arguments as those used by advocates of legal and political constitutionalism in order to justify a particular legal or political control over the executive. Surely, therefore, any distinction between common law and balanced constitutionalism is, at best, a matter of degree and, at worst, non-existent.

The purpose of this chapter is to argue that there is a sustainable distinction between common law constitutionalism developed by Allan and the idea of balanced constitutionalism that I advance. It will do so by, first, setting out ways in which our accounts appear similar, but are different from one another. Second, it will set out how both our theories differ from other accounts of constitutionalism. It will argue that these differences and similarities depend upon an adoption of divergent assumptions about the nature of the rule of law, democracy, and the separation of powers. I will argue that this analysis calls into question the way in which we distinguish between constitutional theories. There is a need for more sophistication in our accounts both to ensure accuracy and to prevent talking at cross-purposes. I will argue that this is best achieved through adopting a model-theoretic account to constitutional theory.

1. Differently Similar

There are two elements of our theories that appear to be the same, but where there are nevertheless subtle differences. The first relates to how we analyse the UK constitution. Both Allan and I are advocates of bi-polar sovereignty. We both argue that sovereignty is shared between Parliament and the courts. The second similarity is broader, applying more generally to common law legal systems. Both Allan and I adopt a dynamic as opposed to a static analysis of law. What I mean by this is that we both examine how law evolves and changes over time, rather than providing an account of general, stable, legal principles. We both look at institutional interactions. However, the interactions that we examine are different. In addition, we adopt different understandings of inter-institutional interactions. My theory explains that interactions can determine the content of legal outcomes. It also argues that interactions can be used to refine the separation of powers between institutions of the constitution. Allan's theory examines broader interactions, using these to determine the content of the rule of law which, in turn, determines legal outcomes.

A. Bi-polar Sovereignty

Although bi-polar sovereignty is referred to by both Allan and me, neither of us invented the term. Its origins can be traced to Sir Stephen Sedley, who, in 1995, argued that the most accurate description of the UK constitution was one of 'bi-polar sovereignty of the Crown in Parliament and the Crown in its courts, to each of which the Crown's ministers are answerable – politically to Parliament, legally to the courts'.[1]

Given this account of bi-polar sovereignty, it would appear odd to describe Allan as subscribing to this theory. Allan's account of common law constitutionalism is centred on the rule of law. If Parliament is sovereign, it is because the laws enacted by Parliament are ones that uphold principles of justice that are part of the rule of law. Here, the rule of law is understood as being determined through a process of practical reasoning. Legislatures should enact laws that use this process of practical reasoning, harnessing general principles of due process and equal citizenship which underpin Allan's conceptions of procedural and substantive equality. Without this, the law enacted by Parliament

[1] S Sedley 'Human Rights: a Twenty-First Century Agenda' [1995] *PL* 386, 389.

does not have the required qualities such that it should be obeyed by those governed by the law. It is not legislation in its true sense.[2]

This would appear to imply that, applying Sedley's account, Allan's theory would be best understood as one which prioritised the rule of law over parliamentary sovereignty, rather than providing an account of bi-polar sovereignty.[3] However, it is important to recognise that Allan does not argue that, as a current matter of UK law, courts would be able to strike down legislation which breached the rule of law. Nor does Allan argue that there is a *general* principle – regardless of whether this is currently recognised in UK law – that courts should *always* strike down legislation which contravenes the rule of law. Allan's argument is more subtle. Whilst it is possible that courts could strike down legislation which contravenes the rule of law, this depends on the circumstances of the case before the court.

Moreover, Allan argues that conflicts between parliamentary sovereignty and the rule of law should arise rarely, given his approach to statutory interpretation. Courts should interpret legislation in a manner that upholds the rule of law. They are not required to solely focus on determining the will of the legislature. Judges should make normative conclusions when interpreting legislation, drawing on the general presumed intention of Parliament to act according to the requirements of the rule of law.[4] This is how sovereignty is shared between Parliament and the courts. Parliament enacts legislation. However, we only understand fully what this legislation means, and how it applies to a particular set of circumstances, when the legislation has been interpreted by the courts. It is in this sense that sovereignty is bi-polar. For Allan 'the interpretative power of the superior courts is as fundamental as Parliament's legislative supremacy: shared sovereignty is intrinsic to constitutional government'.[5]

In a similar manner to Allan, I also argue that sovereignty is shared between Parliament and the courts because the meaning of legislation, and its application to specific circumstances, depends on both the wording of legislation and how it is interpreted by the courts. However, my theory adds a further dimension to bi-polar sovereignty, one which focuses not on how we interpret legislation, but on how Parliament and the courts share sovereignty when determining foundational constitutional rules, concepts, and principles – for example, how a legal system recognises law, the definition of Parliament, and the nature of parliamentary sovereignty itself. To explain this further dimension requires a slight detour discussing the nature of rules and of parliamentary sovereignty.

[2] See TRS Allan, *Law, Liberty, and Justice: The Legal Foundations of British Constitutionalism* (Oxford, Oxford University Press, 1994) ch 1; TRS Allan, *Constitutional Justice: A Liberal Theory of the Rule of Law* (Oxford, Oxford University Press, 2003) chs 1, 9; and TRS Allan, *The Sovereignty of Law: Freedom, Constitution, and Common Law* (Oxford, Oxford University Press, 2013) chs 3, 8.

[3] Christopher Knight argues that it is possible for bi-polar accounts of parliamentary sovereignty to include the power of courts to strike down legislation. See CJS Knight, 'Striking Down Legislation under Bi-polar Sovereignty' [2011] *PL* 90, 106–107.

[4] For the most recent account of this argument, see TRS Allan, *Sovereignty of Law* (n 2), especially chs 1, 5. See also TRS Allan, 'Legislative Supremacy and Legislative Intention: Interpretation, Meaning and Authority' (2004) *CLJ* 685 and TRS Allan, 'Parliament's Will and the Justice of the Common Law: The Human Rights Act in Constitutional Perspective' (2006) *Current Legal Problems* 27.

[5] TRS Allan, 'Parliament's Will' (n 4) 35.

First, we need to revisit Hart's distinction between primary and secondary rules.[6] Primary rules regulate behaviour, be that through granting a permission, regulating how individuals enter into legal relationships, or criminalising behaviour. Secondary rules are rules about rules. Hart's most famous example of a secondary rule is the rule of recognition. This rule explains how we identify law – its content being said in the UK to consist of the rule that whatever the King-in-Parliament enacts is law. Other examples of secondary rules include rules that regulate conflicts between rules – for example the principle that later legislation overrides earlier legislation with the same content. My theory of bi-polar sovereignty argues that legislatures and courts share sovereignty when it comes to determining the content of secondary as well as primary rules. These secondary rules are formed in the UK constitution when both Parliament and courts agree on their content.

This can be explained further when we examine differences between accounts of parliamentary sovereignty. One such distinction is that between continuing and self-embracing theories of parliamentary sovereignty. The most common way of explaining this distinction is through asking whether it is legally possible for Parliament to bind its successors. Theories of continuing parliamentary legislative supremacy conclude that this is not possible. Self-embracing theories of parliamentary sovereignty conclude that Parliament can bind its successors as to the manner and form in which legislation is enacted. This only partially encapsulates the difference between continuing and self-embracing theories of Parliament.[7] It does not account for theories of parliamentary sovereignty that enable Parliament to redefine itself.

A better means of drawing this distinction focuses on whether Parliament has sovereignty over secondary as well as primary rules.[8] Parliament can bind its successors when it has sovereignty over secondary rules. This can be achieved either through modifying the manner and form in which legislation is enacted, or through modifying how we define Parliament. Theories of continuing parliamentary legislative supremacy conclude that Parliament does not have sovereignty over secondary rules. This prevents Parliament from binding its successors through unilaterally modifying either the definition of Parliament, or the manner and form in which legislation is enacted.[9]

My account of bi-polar sovereignty fits with a theory of continuing parliamentary legislative supremacy. Parliamentary sovereignty does not extend to secondary rules, particularly those concerning the definition of Parliament and how legislation is enacted. Sovereignty over these rules is shared between Parliament and the courts. Both must accept the content of these rules. Courts incorporate these rules into the common law. However, this does not mean that these rules are developed by the courts in the same way that they develop the common law. Courts recognise these rules, rather like they recognise constitutional conventions or political facts. This recognition influences and grounds principles of the common law. Parliament recognises these rules through

[6] HLA Hart, *The Concept of Law* (Oxford, Oxford University Press, 1961) 79.

[7] AL Young, *Parliamentary Sovereignty and the Human Rights Act 1998* (Oxford, Hart Publishing, 2009).

[8] See JL Mackie, 'Evil and Omnipotence' (1955) 64 *Mind New Series* 200 and JW Harris, 'When and Why does the Grundnorm Change?' (1971) 29 *CLJ* 103.

[9] See G Winterton, 'The British Grundnorm: Parliamentary Sovereignty Re-examined' (1976) 82 *LQR* 591, 604–605.

enacting legislation in a manner that complies with the secondary rules that define Parliament and legislation, including how it is validly enacted. Whilst Parliament can initiate a change to these rules through modifying legislation – for example, through enacting a manner and form provision designed to bind its successors – such a change will only occur if this is accepted by courts recognising and accepting that the underlying rules have changed, not through a simple process of statutory interpretation.[10]

Allan, however, would not make this distinction. If courts were to accept that parliamentary sovereignty enabled Parliament to bind its successors, this would be because this was now recognised by the common law. If Parliament were to enact legislation purporting to bind its successors as to the manner and form in which legislation is enacted, this would succeed if this was the best interpretation of that legislation, read in line with the rule of law incorporating fundamental principles of justice and equality.

This distinction in our accounts of bi-polar sovereignty explains why our theories adopt different accounts of the justification of judicial review in English administrative law. We both reject a modified ultra vires account of judicial review, which argues that courts have the power to review decisions of the administration because, in doing so, courts are enforcing Parliament's implied intentions. This implied intention can arise either through the interpretation of legislation,[11] or because Parliament has specifically delegated to the courts the ability to develop principles of judicial review.[12] The modified ultra vires theory was developed to preserve parliamentary sovereignty. This theory argues that, if courts could develop their own principles of judicial review through developing the common law, it may mean that courts could strike down as unlawful an act of the administration that Parliament would consider to be lawful. This possibility would undermine the sovereignty of Parliament. However, if courts only strike down as unlawful those provisions that were outside the powers granted to the administration as set out in the express or implied will of Parliament, then parliamentary sovereignty is preserved.

As Allan rightly points out, this theory only makes sense if we understand references to parliamentary sovereignty as referring to the sovereignty of Parliament as a legally omnipotent institution, as opposed to an interpretation that recognises legislation as the highest source of law. Allan's theory of bi-polar sovereignty rejects this account of the sovereignty of Parliament. Allan advocates a strong common law justification of judicial review. This includes the possibility that courts could strike down legislation were it to breach the rule of law. As discussed above, however, in Allan's view the exercise of this judicial power is best understood as a possibility and not a requirement.

I also reject a modified ultra vires theory of judicial review. This is because modified theories of ultra vires rest on a conception of parliamentary sovereignty that requires Parliament to be sovereign over secondary rules. Without this assumption, there would be no justification for the argument that the development of common law principles

[10] For a more detailed discussion of this theory, see AL Young, 'Parliamentary Sovereignty Redefined' in R Rawlings, P Leyland and AL Young (eds), *Sovereignty and the Law: Domestic, European and International Law Perspectives* (Oxford, Oxford University Press, 2013) and AL Young, *Democratic Dialogue and the Constitution* (Oxford, Oxford University Press, 2017) ch 6.

[11] C Forsyth, 'Of Fig Leaves and Fairy Tales: The Ultra Vires Doctrine, the Sovereignty of Parliament and Judicial Review' (1996) 55 *CLJ* 122.

[12] M Elliott, *Constitutional Foundations of Judicial Review* (Oxford, Hart Publishing, 2001).

of judicial review may undermine the sovereignty of Parliament. Instead, I argue that the justification of judicial review derives from fundamental constitutional principles relating to the separation of powers. These principles are determined by interactions between Parliament and the courts, in a similar manner to the determination of the sovereignty of Parliament or the rule of law. My theory, therefore, supports a weak as opposed to a strong common law justification of judicial review. Courts should develop the common law to develop principles of judicial review. However, they should not contradict the express will of Parliament when doing so.[13]

B. Dialogue and Inter-institutional Interactions

It would seem odd to describe Allan's theory as one that advocates dialogue between institutions. We normally see dialogue theories as relating to the protection of human rights, particularly to those advocating a commonwealth model of human rights protections. These theories explain how the legislature may respond to human rights decisions of the judiciary with the result that courts do not always have the final say over the content of rights.[14] Allan, however, does not advocate this model. He is critical of the Human Rights Act 1998 and the associated dialogue theory about defining rights because he believes the common law provides a better protection of rights.[15]

Dialogue can refer more broadly, however, to any accounts of law which rely on interactions between institutional actors. Unlike other substantive accounts of the rule of law, Allan's account does not provide a definitive list of substantive principles. Instead, he says courts determine these principles in the UK through the dynamic process of common law reasoning which is akin to practical reasoning.[16] General principles of due process and equal citizenship determine the content of the rule of law. But these principles are insufficiently precise to determine the detailed content of laws. Rather, in his view, law's content crystallises on a case-by-case basis. Each case before the court has a novel set of facts. Courts draw on the principles of due process and equal citizenship, as refined in previous legal cases, using this past learning to determine the specific content of the rule of law as it applies to the current set of facts before the court.[17]

Allan's theory is thus dynamic, but does it include inter-institutional interactions? The clearest example of these interactions can be seen in Allan's account of how courts should interpret legislation. As discussed above, Parliament also plays a role in determining specific applications of the rule of law.[18] However, legislation provides general rules that are over and under inclusive. Courts should take account of

[13] See AL Young, 'The Relationship between Parliament, the Executive and the Judiciary' in J Jowell and C O'Cinneide (eds), *The Changing Constitution* (Oxford, Oxford University Press, 2019) and AL Young, 'Law and Politics: Standing on Shifting Sand' in K Gromec-Bloc (ed), *Public Law in a Troubled Era: a Tribute to Patrick Birkinshaw* (Alphen aan den Rijn, Wolters Kluwer, 2023).

[14] S Gardbaum, *The New Commonwealth Model of Constitutionalism: Theory and Practice* (Cambridge, Cambridge University Press, 2013).

[15] TRS Allan, 'Constitutional Rights and Common Law' (1991) 11 *OJLS* 453.

[16] Allan, *Constitutional Justice* (n 2) ch 1 and 290–292; Allan, *Sovereignty of Law* (n 2) ch 3.

[17] See, *Sovereignty of Law* (n 2) 91–92 and 121 in particular.

[18] ibid ch 3.

Parliament's assessment of how the rule of law applies generally, but they should interpret these general provisions to ensure that the rule of law applies correctly in specific circumstances.[19] The legislature and the judiciary thus work together to determine the requirements of the rule of law. This is a form of dialogue occurring through inter-institutional interactions.[20] However, it is one where courts have the final say over the content of the rule of law in the specific case before the court.

Interactions also occur when courts determine the content of the common law. For Allan, the content of the rule of law is refined as courts look at past decisions, not because they serve as precedents, but because they provide previous examples of how these general principles of the rule of law apply to specific situations. This is an interactive process, determining how the rule of law applies in a particular society, derived from legislation, previous case law, and other examples of how that society substantiates the general principles of the rule of law. Allan argues that this dialogue does not just concern interactions between institutions. It can also involve the public. As courts decide cases, and government and Parliament respond to these cases, the public can also play a role in discussing principles, helping to refine the content of the rule of law.[21]

My theory is also dynamic, relying on dialogue and inter-institutional interactions. Where our theories differ concerns the purposes of these interactions. I argue that inter-institutional interactions may serve two purposes. First, these interactions may enable institutions to work together to determine the content of the law – for example to determine the content of a particular human right. I refer to this as constitutional collaboration. This is similar to the account of interactions found in Allan's theory – although we would give different roles to the institutions of the constitution, as discussed further below.

Second, these interactions may be used by institutions to protect their role in the constitution. This role-protecting may be through constructive interactions, where institutions work together, or exercise self-restraint to facilitate mutual trust. It may also occur through institutions defending their constitutional role more proactively. I refer to these as constitutional counterbalancing.[22] These interactions do not merely apply to the determination of rights. They are relevant to the determination of the content of secondary as well as primary rules. They are a means through which the UK constitution determines the content of the rule of law, and also of parliamentary sovereignty and the separation of powers between the legislature, the executive, and the courts. It is this additional form of inter-institutional interaction that distinguishes Allan's account of dialogue from my own.

2. Similarly Different

The previous section set out situations in which Allan and I may appear to make the same argument, but where there are nevertheless differences between these apparent

[19] ibid 177–79.

[20] For a more detailed account of how this may take place, see Allan's discussion of *R (Pretty) v Director of Public Prosecutions* [2001] UKHL 61, [2002] 1 AC 800 in Allan, *Sovereignty of Law* (n 2) 179–84.

[21] ibid 184.

[22] Young, *Democratic Dialogue and the Constitution* (n 10) ch 3.

points of commonality. This section develops these differences further, setting out elements that distinguish our theories from those of other theorists. The first difference follows on closely from the previous section, explaining our distinct approaches to judicial reasoning, both when interpreting legislation and when developing the common law. The second is more abstract, it explains how we adopt different methodologies of constitutional theory.

A. Legal Reasoning

Allan's account of legal reasoning is well-known. Allan draws a distinction between the internal and the external perspective. Lawyers and legal theorists can only adopt the internal viewpoint. All accounts of law from this viewpoint are an interpretative process. As discussed above, this occurs through a process of practical reasoning. General principles are interpreted and applied to the facts of the case before the court. This applies to both reasoning in the common law and statutory interpretation. We do not know how the common law regulates a particular situation until common law precedents have been evaluated in light of the rule of law and applied to the particular situation before the court. Any conclusion as to what the law is before this evaluative process has occurred is, for Allan, an external account of academic opinion about the law.[23]

This process of interpretation is necessarily normative. It requires an evaluation of first principles. For Allan these are the principle of equal citizenship and due process central to the rule of law. Allan states that 'We cannot, then, distinguish (as is often supposed) between an account of the present law, as it simply is for the time being, and our opinions about what, ideally, it ought to be, if the statutes and precedents were better understood'.[24] This is not to argue that lawyers and academics provide their own account of law according to their own personal system of values. Rather, it is to recognise that a determination of the law requires an evaluation of precedent and general rules against the rule of law. The rule of law itself requires an evaluation of how the broad principles of formal and substantive equality, understood in line with the principle of equal citizenship, apply to the scenario before the court. This determination is less concerned with how any decision fits with previous precedents than it is with ensuring integrity in the law.[25]

My theory of legal reasoning differs from that of Allan precisely because it does take account of what Allan would classify as external as well as internal factors. These external factors focus on the different institutional and constitutional features of the legislature, the executive and the courts. Specifically, this requires an analysis of the relative strengths and weaknesses of these institutions in terms of their ability to reason about law and public policy. In addition, it assesses whether there are

[23] Allan, *Sovereignty of Law* (n 2) 6.

[24] ibid 7.

[25] See TRS Allan, 'Text, Context, and Constitution: The Common Law as Public Reason' in DE Edlin (ed), *Common Law Theory* (Cambridge, Cambridge University Press, 2007) 185 and TRS Allan, 'Principle, Practice, and Precedent: Vindicating Justice, According to Law' (2018) 77 *CLJ* 269.

prima facie arguments for concluding that either the legislature or the courts have greater constitutional legitimacy.[26] These factors play a predominant role in statutory interpretation. They also influence how courts develop the common law as well as interpret legislation. However, I would also argue that there are additional factors in play, focusing on the relative importance in a particular case of legal certainty and justice. The greater the importance of legal certainty, the stronger the case for courts to rely on precedent. The greater the importance of justice, the more courts should focus on reasoning from first principles.[27]

The differences between our two theories are best explained through an example. I will use the *Evans* case, as we have a clear account of how Allan would reason about this case.[28] It can also illustrate our distinct accounts of dialogue. *Evans* concerned a freedom of information request from a *Guardian* journalist, seeking disclosure of correspondence between Prince Charles and various ministers – known as the 'black spider' memos. The request was originally refused. Evans appealed unsuccessfully to the Information Commissioner. His appeal to the Upper Tribunal was, however, partially successful, enabling some of the memos to be disclosed. However, section 53(2) of the Freedom of Information Act 2000 empowered an appropriate person – in this instance the Attorney General – to issue a certificate to prevent disclosure of this information, if, on 'reasonable grounds', the Attorney General had formed the opinion that disclosure was not required. The Attorney General exercised this power, overriding the decision of the Upper Tribunal. This triggered further legal action challenging the decision of the Attorney General to issue the certificate. This challenge was unsuccessful in the divisional court but succeeded in both the Court of Appeal and the Supreme Court.

Lord Neuberger concluded that a power to issue a certificate on 'reasonable grounds' did not enable the Attorney General to issue a certificate merely because he had a different opinion as to whether public policy was better served by overriding the decision to disclose some of the memos. Lord Mance, giving the other majority judgment in the case, also agreed with this analysis. Lord Neuberger went further, concluding that the Attorney General would only have 'reasonable grounds' to form an opinion which would justify the issuing of a certificate where there was a material change of circumstances, or where there were demonstrable flaws in fact or law.[29] Both Allan and I argue that the majority judgment of Lord Neuberger is not an example of judicial activism. However, we do so for different reasons.

Allan argues that the decision of Lord Neuberger is correct through an analysis of background constitutional principles, including the rule of law, applying the principle of legality. This principle applies to statutory interpretation, incorporating an interpretative presumption that Parliament would not wish to legislate contrary to fundamental

[26] Young, *Democratic Dialogue and the Constitution* (n 10).

[27] AL Young, 'Public Law Cases and the Common Law: A Unique Relationship?' in E Fisher, J King and AL Young (eds), *The Foundations and Future of Public Law* (Oxford, Oxford University Press, 2020) and AL Young, 'Stuck at a Crossroads? Substantive Legitimate Expectations in Public Law' (2021) 80 *CLJ* s179.

[28] *R (Evans) v Attorney General* [2015] UKSC 21, [2015] 1 AC 1787.

[29] TRS Allan, 'Law, Democracy, and Constitutionalism: Reflections on *Evans v Attorney General*' (2016) 75 *CLJ* 38.

common law rights. This provides the means through which courts ensure that legislation is interpreted in a manner compatible with the rule of law, applied to the specific facts of *Evans*. In this case, the rule of law, and the specific principle of *res judicata* justify Lord Neuberger's narrow interpretation of 'reasonable grounds'.

Allan recognises that there are disadvantages to this interpretation – not least that this may come as a surprise to the legislature given that this interpretation may not fit the literal meaning of 'reasonable grounds'.[30] He argues that this does not undermine parliamentary sovereignty. Parliament's legislation should be interpreted by the courts in a manner that is compatible with the rule of law, as refined through interactions between general principles of the rule of law and previous case law, applied to the facts before the court. Otherwise, the legislation is not capable of requiring citizens to obey its provisions.[31]

My defence of Lord Neuberger's judgment is different. It relies upon an interpretation of 'reasonable grounds' that takes account of institutional and constitutional features of the legislature and the courts, incorporating constitutional counterbalancing as well as constitutional collaboration. I agree with Allan that the legislation undermined the principle of *res judicata* by empowering a Minister to overturn a decision of the Upper Tribunal. An interpretation of this statutory provision, therefore, directly engages the principle of the separation of powers. The provision can be interpreted as an intrusion into the proper constitutional role of the judiciary.

These roles are determined through an analysis of their institutional features as well as their constitutional legitimacy. The determination of 'reasonable grounds' is a legal issue. As such, it should, prima facie, be determined by the courts. It is possible that courts may make a mistake and that this mistake has consequences that can be determined by the Attorney General. It may be, for example, that as a member of the Government, the Attorney General is aware of information that is unavailable to the court, or that new circumstances have come to light and the disclosure of information would no longer be in the public interest.

Lord Neuberger's judgment interprets 'reasonable grounds' in a manner that provides a means for the Attorney General to correct errors that may have been made by the Upper Tribunal that would undermine the legal authority of their decision – where the decision was demonstrably wrong in fact or law, or where the material change in circumstances was such as to undermine the reasons for the decision of the Upper Tribunal. This interpretation of 'reasonable grounds' reinforces mutual respect between the legislature and the courts, as well as enabling a possible correction of errors that the Attorney General may be able to correct. It therefore facilitates constitutional collaboration, as well as being an example of constitutional counterbalancing.

Evans, however, does not explain our different approaches to common law reasoning, which stem from the different role each of us gives to precedent. Allan does not see past legal cases as providing a reason in and of themselves for reaching a particular conclusion in a current case. Previous cases provide examples of how courts have applied general principles of the rule of law to specific facts in the past. In this sense,

[30] ibid 44.
[31] ibid 47–48.

they may aid the courts in determining the specific meaning of the rule of law in the UK constitution, as well as providing examples that may help the judge determine the outcome of a particular conclusion.[32] However, they have no specific weight beyond this. A statement of 'the law' according to precedent is an external account of the law. It is not an internal assessment of what the law requires in the case before the court.

My theory provides for a stronger role for precedent. However, it does not argue that precedent should always take priority. Rather, it examines the relative importance of legal certainty, achieved through the application of precedent, and ensuring that the court reaches the right answer through an application of principles of justice. How this works in practice depends on the legal issue before the court.

For example, I have argued in previous work that, in public law cases that have constitutional significance, there may be good reasons for courts to focus on using background constitutional principles, applied to the specific facts before the court, in order to reach their conclusion.[33] This reasoning process is similar to that used by Allan. This is particularly the case when courts are determining whether there has been a shift in the content of fundamental background constitutional principles of the rule of law, parliamentary sovereignty, and the separation of powers. In these situations, reasoning from first principles, drawing on previous examples where possible, helps to provide legitimacy to the determination of fundamental constitutional principles. Institutional features of the judiciary mean that they are more likely to reach conclusions as to the content of these principles that uphold good normative principles of constitutional government as they evolve over time. In agreement with Allan, I argue that this determination of normative principles is more legitimate given the independence of the judiciary. However, differently from Allan, I argue that these fundamental constitutional principles also need to be accepted by Parliament. This provides a form of democratic legitimacy.[34]

The purpose of a provision of public law may also influence whether courts should prioritise legal certainty over determining the normatively correct outcome – whether courts should rely predominantly on precedent or reason from first principles. For example, in cases involving substantive legitimate expectations, legal certainty is more important when it comes to determining whether the administration should be able to renege on a specific promise made to an individual about the substantive outcome of their application or decision relating to that individual. Legal certainty helps to ensure that individuals can rely on promises, promoting personal autonomy, as well as building trust in the administration. It also helps provide clarity to public bodies as to when the promise they make will have legal consequences. However, other situations arise in which the criteria of substantive legitimate expectations are not met, but where there is nevertheless injustice for an individual who relied on a promise as to a substantive outcome. Here, the courts can rely on background legal principles to determine whether the common law should intervene to protect the individual in these circumstances. I've argued that this may explain why the courts developed the principle in *Mandalia*,

[32] Young, 'Stuck at a Crossroads?' (n 27).
[33] Young, 'Public Law Cases' (n 27).
[34] AL Young, '*Miller* and the Future of Constitutional Litigation' in M Elliott, J Williams and AL Young (eds), *The UK Constitution after Miller: Brexit and Beyond* (Oxford, Hart Publishing, 2018).

for example, that a public body should be required to apply a policy to an individual, unless there are good reasons not to, even when no specific promise has been made and the individual is unaware of the policy.[35] This upholds fairness and facilitates good administration.[36]

B. Methodology

Allan adopts an interpretative methodology. I adopt a model-theoretic approach to constitutional theory. These distinctions can be partially explained through references to Barber's threefold taxonomy of methodologies in constitutional theory: the historically minded; the critical constitutional approach; and the interpretative approach.[37] An interpretative approach aims to provide an account of constitutional principles, explaining their meaning. This is contrasted with a historically minded approach, which provides an account of the historical origins of a constitution, or an historical account of key constitutional principles. A critical constitutional approach differs from an interpretative approach as it is designed to provide a normative framework from which to evaluate constitutions.

Whilst Allan adopts an interpretative approach, it is different from that set out, and adopted, by Barber. Barber's theory provides common understandings of constitutional principles – for example, the rule of law or the separation of powers.[38] These common understandings underpin other approaches to constitutional theory. For example, Barber would argue that a common understanding of the rule of law is necessary before a theorist could then provide a historical account of the origins of the rule of law in the UK constitution, or a critical constitutional account of the rule of law that can then be used to assess the extent to which the UK upholds principles of the rule of law in the UK constitution.

Allan would argue that Barber adopts an external approach. However, legal scholars can only adopt an internal perspective. Allan's approach to constitutional theory is interpretive as, in common with Dworkin, he regards law as an interpretive concept. It can only be understood in terms of an interpretative process to determine the content of the rule of law and how this applies to the case before the court. Allan argues that there is 'no simple fact-of-the-matter about any questions of public law … a statement of law is always the conclusion of an interpretative argument over how best to read the relevant legal materials'.[39]

Perhaps a better way of reading Allan is to argue that he would regard constitutional theory as external to public law. His theory does not provide a methodological account of constitutional theory as, to do so, would be to provide an account that is external to law. This explains why Allan's account is not best classified as a critical constitutionalism approach. His theory is normative, in the sense that he sees the provisions of the rule

[35] *Mandalia v Secretary of State for the Home Department* [2015] UKSC 59, [2015] 1 WLR 1456.
[36] Young, 'Stuck at a Crossroads?' (n 27).
[37] NW Barber, *The Constitutional State* (Oxford, Oxford University Press, 2010) ch 1.
[38] NW Barber, 'The Significance of the Common Understanding in Legal Theory' (2015) 35 *OJLS* 799.
[39] Allan, *Sovereignty of Law* (n 2) 7–8.

of law as valuable and necessary. However, this normative claim is abstract. Allan does not provide a specific set of normative principles against which to judge the law. Rather, Allan's theory explains how judges, and legal commentators, should reason in public law. It is a methodology of law, not of legal theory. If Allan's theory is critical of the law, it is critical of approaches that adopt an external point of view, failing to apply the rule of law, or of cases that do not reach the right conclusion in terms of the application of the rule of law.

In this sense, Allan's theory falls outside of Barber's taxonomy of approaches to constitutional theory. My approach to constitutional theory also falls outside of Barber's taxonomy. However, Allan would also dismiss my theory as external as opposed to internal to the law. I adopt a model-theoretic approach to constitutional theory.[40] This approach relies on developing theoretical models of the constitution. These models are neither a purely heuristic device, aiming to explain or describe the constitution, nor an ideal type, aiming to providing a normative account of an ideal of constitutionalism. Rather, these models are best understood as constructed-type models.

Constructed-type models are both descriptive and normative. In common with heuristic models, constructed-type models aim to provide a realistic account of a constitution. However, a constructed-type model need not provide a fully accurate model of the constitution. It does, however, need to provide a model based on realistic factual assumptions. In common with ideal-types, constructed-type models aim to provide a model that has normative values. However, ideal-type models propose a model that may be possible to achieve, but there is no requirement that it is probable that the normative values proposed by an ideal-type will be achieved in any particular constitution. Constructed-type models propose normative values that are probable.

Model-theoretic approaches also provide for different ways in which models can be evaluated. First, models can be evaluated in terms of how well they fit with a particular constitution. Here, the evaluation is not concerned with whether there is a perfect match between a particular model of the constitution and reality, but whether the assumptions on which a model is based are feasible, such that the model can be applied to that constitution.

Second, models can be evaluated in terms of their own internal consistency. Constructed-type models advocate values. The achievement of these values should be facilitated if institutions of the constitution act in the manner proposed by a particular model of the constitution. However, it is possible that a model has made a logical error, setting out a consequence that would not be achieved by the behaviour it advocates. The model would not, therefore, be internally consistent.

Third, models can be assessed in terms of the normative values they advocate. Constructed-type models need to set out the values advocated by a particular model, explaining why these values are normatively justified. Different models of the constitution may advocate different values, with different theorists advocating different models in terms of the relative value of the normative principles on which the model rests.

[40] AL Young, 'Constitutional Methodology and Brexit: Adopting a Model-Theoretic Approach' in D Kyritsis and S Larkin (eds), *The Methodology of Constitutional Theory* (Oxford, Hart Publishing, 2022).

3. A 'Small' Difference?

The previous sections set out the ways in which my theory and that of Trevor Allan both appear to be similar, and yet are distinct, and ways in which both theories differ from each other and yet do so in a manner that makes our theories similarly different from other accounts of constitutional theory. Allan would, arguably, provide two possible explanations for these differences. First, he might argue that these differences arise because we have different conceptions of law. Second, he may argue that these differences arise because I think rights are contestable and Allan does not. Whilst both provide a partial explanation, I will argue that the real distinction is that I propose that many of the concepts used in constitutional theory are essentially contestable, whereas Allan would argue that they may be vague, or open textured, and perhaps even contestable, but they are definitely not essentially contestable.

A. Conceptions of Law

In his analysis of *Evans*, Allan states that the reason the majority and the minority reach different conclusions is because they have diverse conceptions of law which, in turn, influence the balance between the rule of law and the sovereignty of Parliament. As Allan and I reach different conclusions as to the relative importance of these concepts, this would appear to be a good place to start to find an explanation for why we have adopted different general theories of the constitution, and specifically different accounts of the UK constitution.

Allan sees law as an interpretive concept. There is no clear distinction between law and morality as normative principles and values of the rule of law are part of his conception of law. My theory does not stem from an adoption of a particular conception of law. However, it would be fair to classify my theory as being compatible with soft positivism. I argue that there is a distinction between law and morality. My theory of the UK constitution distinguishes between legal, political and moral sources of the constitution, and the determination of constitutional law rests on an acceptance of a rule of recognition underpinning the UK legal system. My conception of law, therefore, is source-based. However, I argue it is possible for principles to be validly recognised as forming part of UK constitutional law.

This distinction may appear to provide an explanation for the differences between our theories. In particular, it explains Allan's focus on internal and external approaches to law. This also explains the more subtle and more obvious differences between our theories. In relation to our common acceptance of bi-polar sovereignty, Allan focuses on how Parliament and the courts share sovereignty when it comes to determining the content of legislation. Whilst accepting this account, my theory gives a greater role to the determination of the intention of Parliament than Allan's theory, based on the relative constitutional legitimacy of Parliament and the courts. Allan would argue that this would be to take account of external factors and arises because we adopt different conceptions of law. More fundamentally, I argue that Parliament and the courts share sovereignty when it comes to determining the content of the rule of law, parliamentary sovereignty, and the separation of powers. My theory looks at these elements as it is influenced by the need to establish a rule of recognition. This would not be necessary were I to adopt Allan's conception of law.

Similar arguments can be used to explain our distinct understandings of dialogue and of legal reasoning, as well as our different methodologies. As regards dialogue, Allan accepts constitutional collaboration as this is a means through which institutions can reason to determine the content of the rule of law. He would not accept constitutional counterbalancing as this would take account of factors external to determining the content of the rule of law. Similarly, precedent plays less of a role in Allan's account of legal reasoning, as this may detract from the determination of the content of the rule of law and how this applies to the situation before the court. There is no need for any form of methodology of constitutional theory other than through the process of practical reasoning. A model-theoretic approach is external to this process.

Whilst this may explain the differences between our theories, I would argue that it does not provide a full explanation. In particular, it does not explain why Allan and I adopt different conceptions of law and why I would argue that arguments that Allan considers to be external to his conception of law are fundamentally important not only to my conception of law and my account of the UK constitution, but also to conceptions of constitutional theory more generally.

B. Essential Contestability

In an email exchange discussing deference, Allan suggested that there was one small difference between his theory and mine. I think that rights are contestable. Allan argues that they are not. This difference explains why we take different approaches to deference, ie, the idea that interpreters of law (like judges) should extend at least some deference to the views on rights expressed by other decision-makers (like legislators or administrators). Allan argues that there is no need for a distinct account of deference when determining the content of rights. Any general theory of deference is unnecessary and could give rise to double counting. Courts should focus on determining the content of the right in the case before the court. Every case before the court is unique and the application of the criteria of deference are fact-dependent, making a general theory of deference untenable.

Moreover, Allan argues that the factors that may influence the content of deference have already been considered through reasoning about rights. The rule of law recognises that there are some situations in which the content of a legal right embraces a range of correct interpretations. The legislature or the executive can choose from among these interpretations without breaching the rule of law. My theory of deference uses the constitutional and institutional features of the legislature, the executive, and the courts to assess whether, and to what extent, courts should defer for constitutional, institutional, and epistemic reasons. In other words, it takes account of what Allan would consider to be external features.[41] Because I believe rights are contestable, I rely on external

[41] AL Young, 'In Defence of Due Deference' (2009) 72 *MLR* 554; AL Young, 'Deference, Dialogue and the Search for Legitimacy' [2010] *OJLS* 815.

features to help determine the extent to which courts should defer to the executive or the legislature. These features focus on when one institution is better able to correct the other, or when one institution has greater legitimacy to determine the content of a right. However, whilst this distinction provides a good starting point for explaining why Allan and I adopt different constitutional theories, it needs to be refined further. In order to do this, we need to explore the idea of essentially contestable concepts.

WB Gallie first coined the phrase 'essentially contested concept' in the mid 1950s.[42] According to Gallie, there are seven criteria of an essentially contested concept. First, the concept needs to be appraisive. Achieving the concept must have value or worth. Gallie saw this as an intrinsic value. However, I would agree with the modification of Waldron that the appraisive element of an essentially contested concept may also derive from its ability to provide a solution to a problem. Consequently, essentially contested concepts may also be achievement concepts.[43] I would argue that the rule of law, democracy and the separation of powers are all essentially contestable achievement concepts.

Second, essentially contested concepts are internally complex. Third, the worth of these concepts derives from their features. Fourth, the value of essentially contested concepts changes according to changes in circumstances. Fifth, those who use essentially contested concepts accept that the concept is contested and appreciate that differences between distinct conceptions of these concepts stem from the diverse criteria of essentially contested concepts. Sixth, essentially contestable concepts can be traced to some original exemplar, or, alternatively, it is possible to distinguish between historical and current conceptions of an essentially contested concept.[44] Seventh, essentially contested concepts rely on discussion to ensure that these original or historical exemplars are sustained. There is no need for a universal answer to provide a definitive determination of an essentially contested concept. The value of essentially contested concepts lies in their ability to facilitate genuine discussion, thereby enriching debate.[45]

One of the examples of an essentially contested concept provided by Gallie is the concept of democracy.[46] Waldron argues that the rule of law is also an essentially contested concept.[47] I agree. I would also add the separation of powers as a further example of an essentially contested concept. The assumption that these principles are essentially contestable concepts underpins my model of the UK constitution based on constitutional balance. As essentially contested concepts, it is not only reasonable to

[42] WB Gallie, 'IX – Essentially Contested Concepts', (1955–56) 56 *Proceedings of the Aristotelian Society, New Series* 167.

[43] J Waldron, 'Is the rule of law an essentially contested concept (in Florida)?' (2002) 21 *Law and Philosophy* 137.

[44] See ibid and J Gray, 'On Liberty, Liberalism and Essential Contestability' (1978) 8 *British Journal of Political Science* 385.

[45] Waldron, 'Is the rule of law an essentially contested concept (in Florida)?' (n 43); Gray, 'On Liberty' (n 44) and K Ehrenberg, 'Law is not (best considered) an essentially contestable concept' (2011) 7 *Journal of Law in Context* 209.

[46] Gallie, 'IX – Essentially Contested Concepts' (n 42).

[47] Waldron, 'Is the rule of law an essentially contested concept (in Florida)?' (n 43) and J Waldron, 'The Rule of Law as an essentially contested concept' in J Meierhenrich and M Loughlin (eds), *The Cambridge Companion to the Rule of Law* (Cambridge, Cambridge University Press, 2021) 121. This is also suggested by Fallon in R Fallon, '"The Rule of Law" as a Concept in Constitutional Discourse' (1997) 97 *Columbia Law Review* 1.

disagree about meanings of democracy, the rule of law, and the separation of powers, but also continued debate about the content of these concepts is valuable, helping to refine the specific conceptions that become part of the ever-evolving principles of the UK constitution. This is not to argue that we cannot distinguish between good and bad conceptions of democracy, the rule of law, and the separation of powers. Rather, my theory accepts both that there is a variety of conceptions of these concepts and that there is no warrant to believe that any one conception is the best conception.[48]

Allan's theory rests on an assumption that there is one correct, though evolving, conception of the rule of law in the UK constitution. His approach is similar to that of Dworkin, particularly his 'right answer thesis' which states that there is a right answer as to the correct conception of a particular concept in specific circumstances.[49] For Allan, the right answer is determined through the process of practical reasoning applied by the courts when deciding cases. Allan accepts that there can be different conceptions of the rule of law. It may even be reasonable to disagree as to the best conception of the rule of law from a range of correct conceptions. In this sense, a conception of the rule of law may be contestable. However, these conceptions are refined through the process of practical reasoning, with courts reaching what will become the right answer as to the specific conception of the rule of law in the UK constitution.

Conceptions of rights may also have open texture. This explains why Allan's account of deference accepts that the determination of a right may give rise to a range of possible answers – for example there may be a range of ways in which the right to freedom of expression and the right of privacy may be balanced. However, this vagueness or open texture is within a set of means of balancing these rights that recognises the right answer as to the conception of both the right to freedom of expression and of privacy in the UK constitution, as determined by the courts' reasoning through applying the rule of law.

It is in this sense that Allan, as ever, was right that the difference between our theories is related to contestability. However, this contestability is not limited to the determination of rights. I argue that democracy, the rule of law, and the separation of powers are also contestable. In addition, I argue that these concepts are not just contestable but are best understood as essentially contestable. Their content is refined through deliberation. This deliberation is valuable and should be sustained.

This explains why I adopt a theory which relies on dialogue through inter-institutional interactions. It also explains why I want both Parliament and the courts to play a role in determining these concepts in the UK constitution. This inter-institutional dialogue should include the determination of parliamentary sovereignty as, otherwise, either Parliament or the courts could have the final say on how the UK constitution determines a key principle of the UK constitution which in turn rests on understandings of democracy, the rule of law, and the separation of powers. If this were the case, then it would be possible for one institution to authoritatively and unilaterally determine the meaning of these conceptions, inhibiting the way in which deliberation as to their meanings adds value and helps to continually refine their meanings in changing circumstances.

[48] C Swanton, 'On the "Essential Contestedness" of Political Concepts' (1985) 95 *Ethics* 811.

[49] R Dworkin, *Taking Rights Seriously* (Cambridge, Harvard University Press, 1978) ch 4 and R Dworkin, *Law's Empire* (London, Fontana Press, 1986) ch 7.

4. Conclusion

This chapter aimed to distinguish between Allan's account of common law constitutionalism and my account of balanced constitutionalism. It argued that, whilst both Allan and I adopt a dynamic approach and accept that the UK constitution is best understood as exemplifying a form of bi-polar sovereignty, we have divergent accounts of legal reasoning and of constitutional theory. Whilst these divergences stem, in part, from the fact that we adopt different conceptions of law, this provides only a partial explanation. The deeper explanation rests on whether you accept that a series of principles are essentially contestable. I would argue that democracy, the rule of law, and the separation of powers are all essentially contestable concepts. Allan would argue that the rule of law is not essentially contestable and, given his adoption of an interpretative conception of law, he would argue that democracy and the separation of powers are to be read in light of the principles of the rule of law. Whilst it is possible that the question as to the specific application of the rule of law to the case before the court may be vague, or open-textured, and so it may be reasonable to disagree about what specific conception of the rule of law should be applied from within a range of possible legally correct conceptions, the rule of law is not essentially contestable.

My hope is that this chapter prompts a re-thinking of how we classify different accounts of constitutionalism more generally, and accounts of the UK constitution more specifically. I would argue that not only can the rule of law, democracy, and the separation of powers be understood as essentially contestable concepts, but that this is also true of different constitutional theories. As such, there is value in debating different accounts of constitutionalism and of the UK constitution. However, if this debate is to refine our understanding, it must be done in a manner that helps to provide a full explanation of the distinctions between different accounts of constitutionalism. To rely on a distinction between legal and political constitutionalism is too vague and may cause confusion as opposed to furthering understanding. Adopting a model-theoretic account of constitutionalism, including its trifold account of comparing, contrasting, and evaluating models, provides a better means of facilitating debate and furthering understanding.

When I presented this chapter, Trevor Allan provided another reason for the difference between our theories which I think is really an extension of his first possible justification – that we disagree about the nature of law. Allan is a legal theorist. He classified my work as being more akin to that of a political theorist. Others suggested that I was a pragmatist. In truth, Allan and I are asking different questions. My account of the UK constitution is not an account of law, or of judicial reasoning designed to discover law once properly defined. My account seeks to determine and defend a justifiable account of what institutions of the constitution do and what they should do, given their institutional features and constitutional roles. Whilst these features may be external to an account of law, they are intrinsic to an account of a legitimate constitution.

This is not to say that one approach is more, or less, valid than the other. But it does make it clear that, if constitutional theory is to move on, we also need to think carefully about the questions we are asking. Trevor Allan has provided the definitive account of the UK constitution based on his theory of law. Other accounts may well rest on other theories of law. Adopting a model-theoretic account may help to weigh up the relative advantages and disadvantages of these theories – something Allan would definitely regard as external to law. However, maybe constitutional theory is not just about constitutional law. Maybe it is also legitimate to draw on political theory, particularly when we are seeking to define legitimate models of constitutionalism.

PART IV

Administrative Law and the Administrative State

16

Reasons to Give Reasons

HASAN DINDJER*

1. Giving Reasons to Give Reasons

People subject to adverse decisions almost invariably want to know why things did not go their way. They seek an explanation of the decision-maker's reasons. Of course, that people want something does not by itself give them any moral claim to it. But moral reasons for government agencies to provide reasons for their decisions are not hard to come by. Knowing the reasons for a decision equips an affected party with the information they need to evaluate their prospects for an administrative appeal or judicial review and to formulate a complaint. If the case is litigated, a contemporaneous statement of reasons will help the court adjudicate the claim, since the reasons for a decision may disclose a legal error. The reasons may also assist the court by demonstrating the extent of the agency's relative expertise, or lack of it, and so inform how far the court should defer to the agency's judgement.[1] And a requirement or practice of official reason-giving will tend to improve decisions *ab initio* by focusing the decision-maker's mind.[2] If a rationale has to be articulable, it is more likely to be relevant and cogent and less likely to be based on prejudice or hunch – especially if it might later be scrutinised by a court.

A difficulty with this familiar instrumental case for reason-giving is that the practice has costs as well as benefits. It is, first, literally costly. Agreeing reasons, recording them, and communicating them requires time, personnel, and money. Second, reason-giving can sometimes be incompatible with a need for confidentiality or secrecy. Moreover, reason-giving requirements may have perverse consequences if they encourage pretexts, instead of genuine explanations, to be given. And they may tie administrators to articulated principles and policies that they would do better to treat as flexible.[3]

* For discussion, my thanks to Thomas Adams, Trevor Allan, Geneviève Cartier, Paul Daly, James Edwards, Linda Eggert, Kate Greasley, Joanna Langille, Tess Little, George Letsas, Adam Perry, Sandy Steel, Jonathan Turner, Mark Walters, Jacob Weinrib, and to attendees at the conference 'The Promise of Legality: Critical Reflections on the work of TRS Allan'.

[1] A Perry and F Ahmed, 'Expertise, Deference, and Giving Reasons' (2012) 2 *PL* 221.

[2] See *R v Higher Education Funding Council, ex p Institute of Dental Surgery* [1994] 1 WLR 242, 256 (Sedley J).

[3] See F Schauer, 'Giving Reasons' (1995) 47 *Stanford Law Review* 633.

One response to this mix of instrumental values and disvalues is to accept that, in administration and administrative law, there should be no *universal* insistence on reason-giving.[4] Another response is to stress the importance of non-instrumental values served by reason-giving, such as respect and dignity.

The richest and most penetrating account of this kind is TRS Allan's.[5] Allan argues that a duty of respect compels the giving of reasons. Giving reasons, says Allan, 'enables people to understand their treatment'.[6] It is 'an integral part of treating a disappointed applicant with the respect which his dignity as a citizen demands',[7] particularly by 'acknowledg[ing] his special (even unique) position and his independence of mind'[8] – 'his status as a rational agent'.[9] Crucially, for Allan, this is not only important for its own sake but also 'as a prelude to [the citizen's] acceptance' of the decision.[10] A theme of Allan's work on reason-giving and procedural justice generally is that fairness norms, when embodied in a process of decision-making, can ground the legitimacy of the *outcome*, so that, within reasonable limits, the citizen has an obligation to abide by it.[11] Reason-giving achieves this by constituting an aspect of the justification of state action to which, Allan believes, assent is normally the appropriate response.[12] In making a claim on citizens and ultimately being prepared to act coercively against them, the state must, Allan holds, do so in a way that is somehow acceptable to them, even if they are the disappointed party.

Allan's account is full of insight but, I will suggest, we should reject significant aspects of it. I propose an alternative account of the value of reason-giving, one that I hope does justice to the impulses animating Allan's view, but which is ultimately quite different from it. I begin by considering arguments from respect and from the idea of justification. Despite their considerable intuitive appeal, I suggest neither idea can do much to justify reason-giving in public administration. My conclusions are not entirely sceptical, however, and I identify some important truths these ideas contain.

My alternative account takes as its starting point not the goodness realised when reasons are provided but the badness that obtains when they are absent. It is sometimes said that being denied reasons is 'Kafkaesque',[13] and I seek to explore and vindicate that idea. The denial of reasons can create a kind of unintelligibility, one that is particularly objectionable because it can interrupt the formation of one's identity and understanding of the story of one's life. The second limb of my account more explicitly concerns the political relationship between government and the governed. I argue that the failure to give reasons can make the exercise of power arbitrary.

[4] See eg M Elliott, 'Has the Common Law Duty to Give Reasons Come of Age Yet?' [2011] *PL* 56.

[5] See especially TRS Allan, 'Procedural Fairness and the Duty of Respect' (1998) 18 *OJLS* 20; see also TRS Allan, 'Requiring Reasons for Reasons of Fairness and Reasonableness' (1994) 53 *CLJ* 207 and TRS Allan, *Constitutional Justice: A Liberal Theory of the Rule of Law* (Oxford, Oxford University Press, 2003) ch 3. Allan is sometimes concerned in these works with reasons given at the close of a formal hearing, but many of the same points of principle apply broadly.

[6] Allan, 'Duty of Respect' (n 5) 499.

[7] ibid.

[8] ibid 500.

[9] TRS Allan, *Law, Liberty, and Justice: The Legal Foundations of British Constitutionalism* (Oxford, Oxford University Press, 1994) 29, quoting JR Lucas, *The Principles of Politics* (Oxford, Clarendon Press, 1966) 132.

[10] Allan, 'Duty of Respect' (n 5) 499.

[11] See eg ibid 508–09; Allan, *Constitutional Justice* (n 5) 80.

[12] See especially Allan, *Constitutional Justice* (n 5).

[13] See eg Elliott, 'Common Law Duty to Give Reasons' (n 4) 62–63.

I confine myself to the question of providing reasons when a decision is made, rather than in the course of litigation. And as far as possible I consider reason-giving alone, rather than as simply one aspect of participation in general.[14] Since reason-giving need not be preceded or followed by an affected person's involvement, such as through hearings or consultation, and since courts face reasons challenges that do not also implicate other modes of participation, I will focus on reason-giving as a relatively discrete phenomenon.

Like Allan, I will be concerned with non-instrumental moral reasons to give reasons. 'Non-instrumental' can mean different things depending on what it is contrasted with. In the *axiological* sense, something is instrumentally valuable just if it is a means to another end of final value, and non-instrumentally valuable just if it is otherwise valuable.[15] In another, *procedural* sense, something is instrumentally valuable just if it tends to improve the 'accuracy or soundness of the substantive decision or verdict'[16] and non-instrumentally valuable just if it is otherwise valuable. There is overlap, but the two senses differ. The argument that reason-giving promotes trust in government is exclusively non-instrumental in the procedural sense, since public trust in government does not bear on the accuracy or soundness of the instant decision, but might be exclusively instrumental in the axiological sense, since public trust might be valuable only as an instrument to some other end, such as political stability or legitimacy. My focus will be on reasons that are non-instrumental at least in the procedural sense and, save in exceptional circumstances, also in the axiological sense.[17]

I put these claims in terms of reasons rather than duties, but I take it that such reasons will generally be morally weighty and will often also constitute at least pro tanto duties. Such reasons or pro tanto duties are not indefeasible, so my argument leaves room for circumstances in which, all things considered, it may be permissible or even morally required to withhold reasons, such as where providing them would be extraordinarily costly or compromise an ongoing investigation. This should not be controversial: even proponents of a general legal duty to give reasons do not think it should be exceptionless.[18] Nevertheless, we cannot judge when the moral case in favour of reason-giving should yield to such countervailing considerations until we understand the nature and strength of that case.

2. Respect

Let us begin with Allan's idea that respecting persons requires giving reasons. The relevant notion of respect cannot be what Stephen Darwall calls 'appraisal respect', the respect we give to someone on account of some achievement or virtue; rather it is

[14] I will later highlight one way in which the value of reason-giving can depend on a decision-maker's willingness to listen to the affected person's response to those reasons: see Section 5.

[15] For discussion of some complications, see CM Korsgaard, 'Two Distinctions in Goodness' (1983) 92 *Philosophical Review* 169.

[16] Allan, 'Duty of Respect' (n 5) 498.

[17] See Section 4.

[18] See eg Elliott, 'Common Law Duty to Give Reasons' (n 4).

'recognition respect'.[19] This involves 'giving appropriate consideration or recognition to some feature of its object in deliberating about what to do'.[20] If persons are entitled to recognition respect, they are 'entitled to have other persons take seriously and weigh appropriately the fact that they are persons' in those deliberations.[21] That persons – all persons – are entitled to such respect is a central idea in contemporary ethical thought, and it is not empty. But it is very nearly empty. For everything depends on how one fills in the variables: what about a person merits respect, and what is the appropriate response to it? As Darwall says, 'what it requires as appropriate is not a matter of general agreement, for this is just the question of what our moral obligations or duties to other persons consist in'.[22] If one thinks respecting others is a matter of recognising their capacity to experience pleasure and pain, and that the appropriate response is to aim to maximise their pleasure and minimise their pain, then one will be a utilitarian. That is not a theory that offers much hope for non-instrumental, respect-based reasons to give reasons. To make progress, then, we should consider what other features of persons might be thought to ground reason-giving as the appropriate response.

A. Rationality

Rationality is the most natural starting point. Someone's capacity to understand and act on reasons seems most obviously relevant to the proposal that we should furnish them with reasons. It is an idea Allan himself explicitly appeals to.[23] And it fits best the language of *respect* of *persons* (rather than 'things')[24] – of beings possessed of *dignity* – within which respect-based arguments are typically couched.[25] This interlocking set of concepts is owed most clearly to Kant, and on Kant's view human rationality is the foundation of personhood and moral agency, and is therefore the basis of respect.[26]

But is giving someone reasons necessary to recognise their rationality? Does withholding reasons treat someone as non-rational? The answer is that it does not. Indeed, intentionally withholding reasons might appeal to a decision-maker precisely *because* they recognise the rationality of the would-be addressee. A decision-maker who fears scrutiny may cynically prefer not to give reasons, or to give reasons so terse as to be uninformative, because they know that any reasons they give might be used to challenge the decision. Mounting a challenge, of course, would be an exercise of rationality *par excellence*: it would involve comprehending reasons, deliberating about them, deciding that they are insufficient, and formulating and articulating objections to them. Far

[19] SL Darwall, 'Two Kinds of Respect' (1977) 88 *Ethics* 36.
[20] ibid 38.
[21] ibid.
[22] ibid.
[23] See eg Allan, 'Duty of Respect' (n 5) 504; Allan, *Law, Liberty, and Justice* (n 9) 29.
[24] L Tribe, *American Constitutional Law*, 2nd edn (New York, Foundation Press 1988) 666.
[25] I will not deal separately with the idea of dignity, since on the most plausible view dignity is a status one has as a person possessed of rationality, and perhaps other features, and who is therefore owed respect. See J Waldron, 'How Law Protects Dignity' (2012) 71 *CLJ* 200, 202. I will simply directly discuss the features of persons that may plausibly be thought to explain the status of dignity and the respect accordingly due.
[26] I Kant, *Groundwork of the Metaphysics of Morals* (London, Routledge, 2005 [1785]).

from failing to recognise rationality, withholding reasons from someone in this strategic way presupposes their rationality.

Now, it might be said that in such a case, although the decision-maker *recognises* that the affected person is rational, still they do not *respect* their rationality. For here the withholding of reasons uses the person's rationality, as it were, against them, even when they seem to have a good claim to the reasons. This response is not entirely satisfactory, insofar as the person's moral claim to the reasons is exactly what the respect-based argument seeks to explain. In any case, withholding reasons in a way that treats withholdees as rational is common in many contexts where it seems at least capable of being justified. It is the premise of state information control in contexts such as secret intelligence, where government agencies insist that even seemingly insignificant snippets of information can be used by the state's adversaries to piece together a 'mosaic' of information.[27] This not only presupposes but explicitly emphasises the rationality of those denied reasons. The same dynamic occurs across government – in policing, financial regulation, competition and tax enforcement, and in many other areas. Claims to state secrecy may often be overblown, but they are perfectly capable of being justified.

A decision-maker also treats a person as a rational agent, even when it does not provide them reasons, simply by issuing a decision at all. For an administrative decision is generally the exercise of a normative power that has the effect of changing rights, obligations, powers and so forth. To communicate that someone's licence is granted, or that someone is subject to an investigation, or that they must leave the country within 90 days – all of this presupposes a rational addressee, capable of understanding changes in normative arrangements and conforming their behaviour to the new norm accordingly.

One might still object that justifiably treating people as rational is not the same as respecting their rationality. Yet it is not clear exactly where that difference might lie. It has commonly been thought that the law itself, even without the provision of reasons for compliance, *already* treats people with the respect they deserve as rational beings – it does not simply evince a morally neutral, factual recognition of their rationality but actually respects it. Jeremy Waldron, for example, says that the legal system, in supposing that people will 'self-apply' legal norms before the question of official coercion arises, protects dignity. Legal norms 'work by using, rather than short-circuiting, the agency of ordinary human individuals'.[28] They 'count on people's capacities for practical understanding, for self-control, for self-monitoring and modulation of their own behaviour in relation to norms that they can grasp and understand'.[29] Administrative decisions equally 'count on' these rational capacities when they are not accompanied by reasons, and especially when reasons are withheld for fear that they may be misused.

Could it be that respecting rationality requires more than counting on it? Perhaps rationality must also be valued. Yet it may well be valued by a decision-maker who does

[27] DE Pozen, 'The Mosaic Theory, National Security, and the Freedom of Information Act' [2005] *Yale Law Journal* 52.

[28] Waldron, 'How Law Protects Dignity' (n 25) 206.

[29] ibid.

not give reasons. An agency may, for example, value a party's co-operation in other matters and accordingly value their rationality, and yet deem it necessary to keep some information, including reasons, confidential on some occasions. Or it may simply deem the articulating of reasons in a particular case to be too complicated or costly and prefer on balance not to give them; that is quite consistent with valuing the affected person's rationality.

It might now be suggested that an *attitude* of valuing a person's rationality is not enough – what is needed is *action* that shows one values it. What might that be? It would beg the question to assume that providing reasons is among the actions one must perform in order to show that one values a person's rationality. Perhaps rationality-valuing actions are those that somehow nourish a person's rationality by providing them with opportunities to exercise it, and providing reasons does this. But that is a non-starter. We do not respect someone's rationality by providing them with bad but fiendishly complicated reasons which, although totally insufficient to justify our decision, give the person ample opportunity to put their rational faculties to work.

This point exposes a further difficulty with the idea of respecting rationality as the foundation for reason-giving, namely that the addressee's rationality is implicated just as much whether they are disappointed or pleased by the outcome. Either way the giving of reasons is held to engage their rational capacities, which implies that the respect-based argument is as strong in both cases. Yet it is almost always true that receiving reasons is more important to the disappointed party. The argument from rationality does not explain why.

B. Views and Perspectives

Consider, then, the related idea, also present in Allan's work, that people ought to be respected as bearers of their own views and perspectives. I will trace a version of this argument due to Bernard Williams and John Rawls, before discussing Allan's account, which draws also on the ideas of autonomy and providing assurance.

Williams argued that respect requires regarding others in a particular, human way, and not from a merely 'aesthetic or technical' point of view.[30] Respect involves an attempt to understand someone as a whole person, with their own views and purposes; it means trying to 'see the world from [their] point of view'.[31] Williams casts respect as *empathy* for others as agents.

Rawls combined Williams's view of respect with a largely Kantian view of personhood and concluded that respect involves being prepared to give people reasons whenever their interests are 'materially affected'.[32] When we seek to understand a person's interests from their standpoint, Rawls thought, we seek 'to present him with considerations that enable him to accept the constraints on his conduct'.[33]

[30] B Williams, *Problems of the Self: Philosophical Papers 1956–1972* (Cambridge, Cambridge University Press 1973) 236.
[31] ibid.
[32] J Rawls, *A Theory of Justice* (Cambridge, Belknap Press, 1971) 337.
[33] ibid 338.

But how exactly is the inference from understanding others' perspectives to owing them reasons supposed to run? When we inhabit another's perspective, we may of course see that they would *like* reasons to be given. But that you desire something does not, by itself, imply that I owe it to you. A desire may be irrational, self-regarding, or simply a morally inert psychological instinct. The question is whether the desire for reasons sounds in morality. Rawls needs something more than the idea that the other seeks reasons; he must also rely on the idea that they do so by virtue of their 'moral personality' – that is, their possession of a conception of the good and, in particular, a 'sense of justice'.[34]

Rawls does not make the connection between moral personality and the claim to receive reasons very explicit, but the idea seems to be this. Someone in a possession of a sense of justice is disposed to 'apply and to act upon the principles of justice', at least minimally.[35] Such a person accordingly 'wishes … to regulate [their] actions on the basis of principles to which all could agree.'[36] That being so, they are entitled to receive 'relevant facts which explain the restrictions [on their actions] in this way'.[37]

This is all rather gnomic. If Rawls means only that the addressee wishes to see whether the other's reasons accord with justice, this does not take us much further than before: why does the desire to learn of the reasons matter? Nothing much follows from the addressee's own disposition to act justly. Perhaps Rawls means that learning of others' reasons will assist the addressee in recognising and acting on principles of justice. The putative epistemic mechanism is unclear, however. Others' reasons will be variously saintly, permissible, unwise, disgraceful, and so on; they will not necessarily provide the most promising basis for moral learning. It could be that if others' reasons are scrutable, this provides richer data, useful for honing one's moral sensibility – perhaps via the process of reflective equilibrium.[38] Still, it is difficult to believe that the value of respect realised in reason-giving lies in the more vivid examples it provides for moral education.

Other aspects of Rawls's remarks suggest his concern is with the ability of the addressee to *accept* the action for which reasons are offered.[39] Of course, since many actions are not adequately justified and have no claim to being accepted, the point cannot hold generally. In any case, it remains unclear why this should engage a person's moral personality. Does someone, *qua* moral agent, have some interest in accepting all those actions that are acceptable? Is their sense of justice diminished if there are acceptable actions yet to be accepted by them?

I return to the question of acceptance below, but there is a general difficulty in attempting to justify reason-giving via respect-as-empathy. The problem is not that the Williams-Rawls account of respect is false. The problem is that it instructs us to appreciate the other's perspective – and much as the idea of respect calls for specification of what about a person ought to be respected and how, the idea of empathy

[34] ibid 337.
[35] ibid 505.
[36] ibid 338.
[37] ibid.
[38] ibid 46–48.
[39] ibid 338.

needs an account of what in someone else's perspective calls for reasons to be given and why. Yet once we give such an account, it will explain the importance of reason-giving directly. To add that we can appreciate its urgency if we inhabit the other's perspective – if we respect them – adds nothing to the fundamental moral explanation. 'Put yourself in their shoes' may still be an excellent heuristic, a rule of thumb that helps real-world decision-makers see the need to give reasons where they ought to.[40] But it does not explain why they ought to in the first place.

C. Autonomy, Particular Interests, and Assurance

Allan writes that the duty of respect 'flows from the citizen's autonomy',[41] and that explaining the application of general rules to a person 'acknowlegd[es] his autonomy and individuality'.[42] How might this be so? Allan emphasises that reasons should respond to someone's '*particular* arguments' and recognise the addressee's 'special (even unique) position and his independence of mind'.[43] The thought seems to be this. Persons matter individually, for who they are, not just as bearers of fungible units of value. What makes them who they are, as individuals, is the particular perspectives they have adopted and interests they have, which are a result of their exercise of autonomy. That they are their own person, with their own interests and perspectives (Rawls might say 'conception of the good') *matters*: it ought to make a call on the deliberations of the decision-maker.

The question is why reason-giving should follow. After all, a decision-maker can recognise the distinctive perspectives of different parties by taking seriously their interests in the course of decision-making. A conscientious decision-maker will consider how different parties might be affected by a measure and weigh such reasons diligently along with other public interest considerations. A person's particular interests can thus be given as much weight in determining the decision as they merit.

Allan argues that this is not enough. Respect requires that the affected person be able to '*see* that his case has been given the careful consideration which it may deserve'[44] (emphasis added). He endorses JR Lucas's claim that reasons should 'make it manifest to anyone disappointed at the outcome that we were solicitous of his interests'.[45] One might wonder whether this really shows that giving reasons is valuable in itself, or only that it provides *evidence* of something valuable in itself. A bank statement that records a charitable donation makes manifest but does not constitute something of intrinsic value. But the giving of reasons is not merely the provision of evidence; it functions, as Allan says, as a kind of 'reassurance' that a person's interests were carefully considered.[46]

[40] Hence Geneviève Cartier's prescription for decision-makers to this effect is still attractive: G Cartier, 'Administrative Discretion as Dialogue: A Response to John Willis (or: From Theology to Secularization)' (2005) 55 *University of Toronto Law Journal* 629, 644.
[41] Allan, 'Duty of Respect' (n 5) 502.
[42] Allan, *Law, Liberty, and Justice* (n 9) 29.
[43] Allan, 'Duty of Respect' (n 5) 500.
[44] ibid.
[45] JR Lucas, *On Justice* (Oxford, Clarendon Press, 1980) 97, quoted in Allan, 'Duty of Respect' (n 5) 500.
[46] Allan, 'Duty of Respect' (n 5) 501.

Now, if reassurance, or just assurance, is construed only as a psychological state, then giving reasons may be only quite contingently connected to it: reason-giving might or might not produce the feeling of being reassured, depending on the psychology and disposition of the affected person. But assurance is better understood as an objective property of someone's epistemic position. By providing good reasons that show a person's interests were solicitously considered, the decision-maker can give the person sufficient reason to believe that they were treated as an autonomous person with their own important interests. If it is non-instrumentally valuable that one be treated in that way, then, it is natural to hypothesise, it is also non-instrumentally valuable to be assured that this is so. In fact, this inference requires an intermediate step – that one has a separate interest in understanding one's normative position – which the foregoing argument does not itself provide. To justify that premise, we will eventually need to appeal to the importance of intelligibility.

Be that as it may, in highlighting the value of reassurance, Allan identifies an important and deep truth about reason-giving. But, as he emphasises, the value of reassurance is conditional: '[n]o reassurance is given by the statement of invalid or inadequate reasons'.[47] If the reasons do no real justice to the person's interests, then they will not make manifest appropriate or conscientious regard for the person's situation. Such reasons will instead provide only *disaffirmation*. They will show how little store is put in their interests. If there is reason to provide affirmation, there must be reason against providing disaffirmation.

Hence Allan's reassurance argument is not a sound one for giving reasons as such. It is only an argument for giving reasons if they are good. There is nothing wrong with that conclusion, and Allan does not claim more for the argument than it shows. But it is important to see how it is not exactly suited to the general question whether decision-makers should give reasons. It is that general question that seems more salient, not only practically but theoretically. The decision-maker themselves is not necessarily a good judge of whether their own reasons are reassuring or disaffirming; the callous bureaucrat does not self-identify as callous. And, importantly, a person seeking reasons believes themselves entitled to them whatever their content, and perhaps especially if the reasons would reveal a form of wrongdoing that the person may suspect tainted the decision. Yet the reassurance argument cannot explain this; if anything, it has the surprising implication that, where reasons would disclose wrongdoing, the more respectful thing would be to withhold them.

3. Justification

A. Two Senses of Justification

Let us now consider a second strand in Allan's thought, and arguments for reason-giving more widely, that appeal to the idea of justification. It is common to claim that state power calls for justification, and it may seem a short step to conclude that administrative decisions, being exercises of state power, call for reasons to be offered.

[47] ibid.

Yet this argument is too quick. It trades off an ambiguity in the idea of justification, an idea that has at least two senses. The more fundamental is the *sufficient-reason* sense of justification: a positive normative status that an action (or attitude or emotion) can have in virtue of being supported by sufficient normative reasons, ie those that are stronger, or at least not weaker, than countervailing reasons. If an action is justified in this sense, it is worthy of being chosen. We also use 'justification' to refer to the act of explaining one's motivating reasons (the reasons one takes to be sufficient and for which one acts). A justification in this second, *explanation* sense is an act of communication, or the content that one communicates.

The two senses of justification are not always clearly distinguished by writers who favour a 'culture of justification'. When, for example, Etienne Mureinik introduced the idea, he wrote that:

> [The new Constitution] must lead to a culture of justification – a culture in which every exercise of power is expected to be justified; in which the leadership given by government rests on the cogency of the case offered in defence of its decisions, not the fear inspired by the force at its command. The new order must be a community built on persuasion, not coercion.[48]

The *cogency* of the case must be a matter of its being justified in the sufficient-reason sense.[49] Yet Mureinik also speaks of the case having to be *offered*, and of *persuasion*: these are communicative acts, which involve the explanation sense of justification. This is not to say Mureinik illegitimately elides the distinction between the two senses. He might insist that justification in both senses is required. Nevertheless, that is a substantive thesis in need of defence. One cannot start with the inescapable fact that (state) action generally must be justified, in the sense of being supported by sufficient reasons, and conclude without further ado that it must also be *explained*. Most justified actions are never explained to anyone, and need not be.

A tendency to conflate the senses of justification seriously afflicts some defences of giving reasons. It is the central difficulty in Rainer Forst's theory of the 'right to justification', which moves from the claim that humans demand justification in one sense to the conclusion that they must be furnished with justifications in another.[50] Forst offers a kind of transcendental argument: he says the question whether there is a right to justification is self-defeating because to ask moral questions is already to presuppose the necessity of justification.[51] But that could only be true of justification in the sufficient-reason sense, not in the explanation sense. Similarly, in a recent defence of the culture of justification, Kai Möller assumes the central plank of Forst's view vis-à-vis the state: persons 'have a right to be subjected to the authority of the state only if such authority

[48] E Mureinik, 'A Bridge to Where – Introducing the Interim Bill of Rights' (1994) 10 *South African Journal on Human Rights* 31, 32.

[49] Elsewhere Mureinik also seems to have the sufficient-reason sense in mind, as where he says that apartheid statutes' defining feature was their 'want of justification', and that '[r]acial discrimination is a term of censure, used to condemn racial differentiation that is not justified': ibid.

[50] R Forst, *The Right to Justification: Elements of a Constructivist Theory of Justice* (New York, Columbia University Press, 2012).

[51] See especially ibid 31–60.

is justifiable to them.'[52] 'This idea', says Moller, 'must be correct (and is widely shared)'.[53] Again, however, this premise can be taken for granted only if justification means support by sufficient reasons. The suggestion that this in turn requires justification in the sense of the institutionalised giving of explanations is precisely what needs to be explained.

B. Authority and Persuasion

Where might we look for what is needed – an argument for the offering of explanations to affected persons? An abiding theme in Mureinik's discussion is the contrast between authority and persuasion. On this view, authoritarian government is authoritarian precisely because it governs via authority – via the logic of 'because we said so'. Perhaps attempting to *persuade* the governed negates this objectionable reliance on authority. Perhaps, as Frederick Schauer suggests, '[t]he act of giving a reason is the antithesis of authority'.[54]

That thesis, however, does not hold generally. Some paradigmatic authorities, such as military commanders and parents, are indeed fond of 'because I said so' rhetoric. Yet others, such as sentencing judges and political leaders, are not; they are in the habit of explaining themselves. Authorities frequently give reasons to ensure they maintain the basis of support that allows them to subsist as authorities: no political regime lasts for long without large-scale reason-giving, whether in good faith or otherwise. It is true that authorities seldom *need* to give reasons to impose obligations, but it does not follow that giving reasons negates independently established authority. Moreover, giving certain reasons presupposes and therefore loudly announces the fact of authority. When the sentencing judge explains the aggravating and mitigating factors that moved them to set a particular sentence, they give the kind of explanation that can only intelligibly be given by someone with authority to take such reasons into account. Some reasons are only reasons *for* authorities. So reason-giving need not undercut authority or suggest its absence. It can coexist, and usually does, with the state's imposition of obligations via authority and its readiness to enforce them via coercion.

All this assumes, with Mureinik, that by 'authority' we mean de facto authority, not necessarily morally legitimate authority. But perhaps the importance of persuasion is not that it negates authority but rather that it stands to transform a merely de facto authority into a legitimate one, whose directives are moral obligations. This is apparently what Allan has in mind in saying that 'where justice is not seen to be done' and 'the requirement to justify [people's] treatment has been implicitly rejected or abandoned' then '[t]he exercise of authority … has become the exercise of power'.[55]

Where exactly does the value of persuasion, or attempted persuasion, lie? We have already considered the argument that the activity of offering reasons itself respects a person. A different approach locates the value not in the means but in the end

[52] K Möller, 'Justifying the Culture of Justification' (2019) 17 *International Journal of Constitutional Law* 1078, 1088.

[53] ibid.

[54] Schauer, 'Giving Reasons' (n 3) 636–67.

[55] Allan, 'Duty of Respect' (n 5) 506.

sought: perhaps it is good to try to persuade people because it is good that they be persuaded. Allan writes that reasons should 'enable a person to … more readily accept the outcome'.[56]

The problem is that the state cannot have a moral reason to seek assent in general. For the value of assent depends on what is assented to. Suppose that it is better, morally speaking, if affected persons assent to decisions that are lawful and justified. Still, not all government decisions meet those conditions. Some involve legal error, some are badly misconceived, some are seriously wrongful. One should assent to what warrants assent but withhold assent from what does not. The attempt to obtain unwarranted assent is itself unwarranted – something which, when undertaken at population level, we typically recognise on the spectrum from spin to propaganda. Where successful, such attempts propagate false beliefs and displace appropriate dissent.

Although Allan sometimes writes of affected persons accepting 'the result'[57] or 'the justice of the decision',[58] he elsewhere puts things more modestly: someone might be persuaded to accept the outcome 'as a legitimate decision'[59] or 'as a reasonable accommodation between private and public interests'.[60] Nonetheless, acceptance of legitimacy is not something that should be sought where the decision is not, in fact, legitimate. The difficulty persists unless one maintains that administrative decisions are indeed widely legitimate.

This is apparently Allan's approach. He holds that 'if [a person's] arguments are treated with the respect which is due to a fellow-citizen's opinions … his legal obligations can be accounted genuine, amounting (within reasonable limits) to moral duties of compliance'.[61] That is a strong claim. Notice that the issue here is not whether the administrative state is *in general* legitimate, or whether its existence is democratically acceptable. One need not be a global sceptic of that kind to recognise that many individual government decisions do not, by virtue of having been made, give every affected person a moral obligation to go along with what is decided. Affected persons almost invariably have prudential reasons to do so, and often other contingent, moral reasons; but the relevant question is whether the decision is such as to generate corresponding moral obligations of obedience. What, we might ask, might create such an obligation for a person deported and separated from their family by a draconian immigration policy, or for a person denied a subsistence level of social welfare because they have not been able to demonstrate a sufficiently zealous approach to job-seeking, or for a person made homeless because their local authority prefers to sell off public housing and fund tax cuts for the wealthy? How could the provision of reasons help?

It is not clear what Allan's account is committed to with respect to such cases – partly as it is not clear when a decision falls within 'reasonable limits' – although Allan is explicit that fair procedures can provide grounds for obedience even where

[56] ibid 500.
[57] ibid.
[58] ibid.
[59] ibid 501.
[60] ibid.
[61] ibid 510.

the decision is 'otherwise unjust'[62] and that 'it would *normally* be wrong to repudiate' a decision if 'reasonable standards of fair procedure have been applied'[63] (emphasis added). If Allan's view does not apply to cases such as this, it excludes from its scope a sizeable proportion of decisions in the administrative state as it actually operates in much of the world.

Why does Allan hold that reason-giving can generate obligations of obedience? Two connected explanations stand out. The first is that reason-giving can be part of a process in which 'questions of justice can be raised and answered, and where every rule is ultimately open to challenge and, accordingly, modification'.[64] The second, which reprises an idea already discussed, is that reasons may show the decision-maker's solicitous concern for the affected person's specific interests.[65]

It is difficult to see how these possibilities, when they obtain, could ground an obligation to accept a decision. The first idea, of norms being open to challenge, might be interpreted in different ways. It might mean that affected persons are capable of stopping the application of a norm to their case by contesting it. However, people practically never have such a power, except in very specialised contexts where agencies proceed by consent.[66] On this interpretation, the condition would practically never be satisfied (even if it would be better if it were).[67] If, however, the idea is simply that people can raise objections which must then be carefully considered, albeit ultimately rejected at the authority's say-so, it is unclear why obligations of obedience should result. Allan's analogy to democratic decision-making[68] is inapt because, whereas democratic procedures distribute decisional authority equally among relevant parties or their representatives, those affected by administrative decisions lack any decisional authority.

What of the idea that reasons evince respect for a person's interests and their autonomy, and thereby give them an obligation to obey? The problem is the final step. That someone respects you does not put you under an obligation to do as they say, still less to do as they say because they say it. That is especially clear when what they require is unjust (or, as Allan would say, otherwise unjust). It is quite possible for a decision-maker to think seriously and in good faith about a person's moral claims and yet to treat them unjustly – to simply make a moral mistake. Solicitous concern or efforts at right action cannot, by themselves, induce obligations of obedience. It is true, to reiterate, that Allan thinks a fair procedure generates duties of compliance only 'within reasonable limits'. Yet the difficulty is general: in *no* case can respect explain why those respected should obey the authority.

[62] ibid.

[63] Allan, *Constitutional Justice* (n 5) 80.

[64] Allan, 'Duty of Respect' (n 5) 510.

[65] ibid 501, 510–11.

[66] Of course, they can contest it by going to court, and a court does have the power to stop the decision. But Allan's respect-based obligation argument applies to courts too: see Allan, *Constitutional Justice* (n 5) 84–88. So contestation cannot always mean, for Allan, appealing to an independent arbiter with final authority.

[67] Allan is right to insist that a degree of flexibility should almost always be retained in the application of rules, yet the reasons for having any rules, as opposed to universal ad hoc decision-making, require that such flexibility is itself finite.

[68] Allan, *Constitutional Justice* (n 5) 79–80.

C. Legitimacy Redux

We have considered the argument that public authorities should give reasons so as to procure acceptance, which acceptance is generally warranted, and which is in part justified by reason-giving itself. We should, I argued, reject each step in that argument. However, Allan also in places hints at a different, though superficially similar argument.

'[T]here is value', Allan writes, 'in a person being able to judge for himself whether or not an exercise of authority over him is justified'.[69] The key words are 'whether or not'. Rather than supposing that there is a widespread fact of legitimacy which it is the job of reasons to convince people of, this argument is neutral on why and when persons may have obligations to obey administrative decisions. The point of giving reasons, on this account, is to supply people with the information they need to make up their minds for themselves.

This idea is both deep and narrow. It is deep because it identifies what is at least an important contributor to the legitimacy of government. Allan elsewhere says that '[b]y inhibiting a person's consideration of moral reasons for disobedience, the state undermines his obligation to obey its demands'.[70] At the very least, it is hard to see how a government could have the moral *standing* to make claims on people's obedience if it denies them the ability to judge whether such claims are legitimate. For that would be to demand a sacrifice of autonomy on the basis only of blind faith, and normally only an agent lacking in self-respect could make such a sacrifice.

The idea is narrow because reasons for administrative individual decisions can be uninformative with respect to whether the state's demands are legitimate or obligation-imposing. That is because the reasons for particular decisions often constitute only small fragments of a larger picture of political organisation. The person who is to be deported may learn simply that they were deemed not to have spent enough continuous years in the country to establish family ties under an existing administrative policy. The person denied benefits may learn that they were not deemed to have applied for enough jobs. Such explanations are not irrelevant to the question whether there is an obligation to accept the decisions in question, but often that will depend on policies and political decisions that lie further upstream. Learning how those policies apply in one's own case may be less informative than the knowledge of the policy's existence, or of its systemic effects, neither of which is gained from a statement of reasons.

4. Intelligibility

Let me propose a different approach. To see why reasons matter we can consider what it is like not to have them. This is brought out vividly in the English case of *Doody*.[71] The applicants had each received the mandatory life sentence for murder following separate convictions. Under the regime then applicable, the Home Secretary, after consulting the

[69] Allan, 'Duty of Respect' (n 5) 500.
[70] Allan, *Constitutional Justice* (n 5) 109.
[71] *R v Secretary of State for the Home Department, ex p Doody* [1993] UKHL 8, [1994] 1 AC 531.

trial judge and the Lord Chief Justice, determined the earliest date at which a prisoner's case would be reviewed with the possibility of release on licence. The periods assigned to the four applicants were respectively '15 years; not more than 20 years; 12 years; and 11 years'.[72] No reasons were given. This was, held the House of Lords, unacceptable. As Lord Mustill said of the prisoner's situation:

> He never sees the Home Secretary; he has no dialogue with him: he cannot fathom how his mind is working. There is no true tariff, or at least no tariff exposed to public view which might give the prisoner an idea of what to expect. The announcement of his first review date arrives out of thin air, wholly without explanation. The distant oracle has spoken, and that is that.[73]

What troubles us most here is that the prisoner's own situation is unintelligible to him. He knows his fate – knows *that* he is imprisoned for at least some number of years – but he does not know why it is his fate. He will not be able to fathom why, after serving some number of years, he could not have been released already, or why he is being detained for longer than others convicted of a similar crime.

A striking feature of situations in which people are denied reasons is that they tend to continually speculate, even where no information is forthcoming, about why they were treated as they were. They cannot stop posing questions in an effort to understand their situation. This is, not incidentally, precisely Joseph K.'s predicament in *The Trial*.[74] As K. is arrested without explanation, he puzzles: 'Who could these men be? What were they talking about? What authority could they represent?' [...] [W]ho dared seize him in his own dwelling?'[75] And when K. meets his ultimate fate, he notices an obscure human figure in a nearby house with arms outstretched. K. asks:

> Who was it? A friend? A good man? Someone who sympathized? Someone who wanted to help? Was it one person only? Or were they all there? Was help at hand? Were there some arguments in his favour that had been overlooked? Of course there must be.[76]

What is Kafkaesque in Kafka's portrayal is the inescapable, human need for intelligibility and the cruel and disorientating way it is denied. According to Fred Rush, it is not that reasons are absent in the world of *The Trial* but rather that it is 'teeming with reasons'.[77] 'The deeper one reasons and the more resolutely one pursues a systematic understanding of the world', says Rush, 'the more one finds oneself suspended over an abyss of further reasons'.[78] In fact, K.'s world is populated by endless *possible* or *apparent* reasons. What makes the situation radically unintelligible is that the agent is unable to tell which of the possible reasons are actual, unable to select from among all the more or less plausible explanations of official conduct the one that conforms to reality.

[72] ibid 551E.
[73] ibid 565C–D.
[74] F Kafka, *The Trial*, W Muir and E Muir trans (New York, Vintage, 2001 [1925]) 10.
[75] ibid 210.
[76] ibid.
[77] F Rush, 'Before the Law' in E Hammer (ed), *Kafka's The Trial: Philosophical Perspectives* (Oxford, Oxford University Press, 2018) 81.
[78] ibid.

This kind of unintelligibility has a special significance because of its connection to one's identity, to the story one is able to construct of one's life – what might be called one's *narrative identity*. One cannot, as an agent, help but seek to understand the course of one's life and the connections between it and the other people and communities to which one is related; to understand what kind of mark one has made on the world and what kind of mark the world has made on one; to understand, in short, what kind of life one has lived. The withholding of reasons interrupts the formation of that kind of story. For the relevant kind of understanding cannot be a bare cataloguing of outcomes – of ends achieved and fortunes and misfortunes that occurred – but must extend to the reasons underlying them. The projects one pursues, and the impediments others put in their way, are constituted by actions, and actions are only intelligible as the actions they are in virtue of the reasons that lie behind them.

It matters especially that one can understand one's *normative identity*, the kind of moral person one is, and, significantly, the moral status of the actions one is subject to. For the applicants in *Doody*, the question would eventually arise whether they were serving a just punishment or were instead unjustly, and perhaps unlawfully, detained. It matters to the course of a life whether a person was the victim of a wrong, and such knowledge matters to a person, therefore, in understanding the nature of their life. To deny a person reasons can be to deny them knowledge of the normative status of their lives, to produce a kind of normative ignorance.

These forms of unintelligibility, in the world-agent direction, might in turn produce unintelligibility in the agent-world direction. A person who has had an encounter with the state must be able to account for themselves to others in light of that encounter. Questions such as 'why did you leave the country?', 'why are you still in prison?', 'why did your business fail?', or 'how did you become homeless?' cannot, for those concerned, be avoided. To seek to explain oneself, to give an account of oneself, is something one cannot but do as an agent,[79] and it is in part through such telling that one can construct one's own narrative identity. Doing so is not just a matter of accounting for one's own actions but also the actions of others that have impinged on one's life. That is especially so where actions of the state threaten to undermine projects one was pursuing, so that one can only properly explain the success or failure of one's endeavours by reference to the reasons why the state has forestalled them.

The need for intelligibility is not, then, a bare psychological quirk but is rather fundamentally constitutive of agency.[80] Government officials, given the impact of their decisions and their moral duty to act for the benefit of the governed, will have reasons to ensure that they do not produce unintelligibility by their actions. These reasons will be weighty across a range of circumstances and will likely often amount to at least pro tanto duties. These reasons in turn count in favour of *giving* reasons: in view of the organisational complexity and generally non-transparent processes of public authorities, their actions will normally be otherwise inscrutable.

[79] For a related discussion in a different context, concentrating on an agent's own acts, see J Gardner, 'Relations of Responsibility' in R Cruft, MH Kramer and MR Reiff (eds), *Crime, Punishment, and Responsibility: The Jurisprudence of Antony Duff* (Oxford, Oxford University Press 2011) 88.

[80] Might one say, therefore, that I am giving an account of 'respect' for agency after all? Only in the sense that any moral wrong disrespects someone, and any moral consideration can be reframed as respect for some morally salient feature of persons.

Normally because exceptional cases are possible. An affected person might conceivably come to learn of the reasons from a leaked document, or by peering over the shoulder of an administrator and reading their confidential file. Putting such aberrant cases aside, is there any more systematic way an affected person might come to know of reasons which are not communicated? They might seek to *infer* the reasons from the background against which a decision is taken.[81] Of course, highly general inferences do not much assuage the concern with intelligibility: someone's inference that the Home Secretary thought their presence in the country was not 'conducive to the public good' is uninformative.[82] The question is whether it is plausible to make inferences that are both epistemically reliable and specific in content. This seems doubtful. Perhaps the most promising context is where a decision is made in light of a published administrative policy or statutory rule. Here the applicant might infer that the decision-maker's reasons are supplied by the rule or policy's perceived applicability or inapplicability. However, policies are not self-executing, and a given result under a policy is usually compatible with different interpretations of the policy, different factual findings, different weights being placed on the same or different factors, and so forth. Moreover, existing rules and policies are not always fairly or rationally applied, or applied at all.[83] Since there are almost always many routes from a given policy to a given decision, the existence of a policy will rarely eliminate the unintelligibility of a decision rendered without reasons, though it may mitigate it somewhat.[84]

Nevertheless, we should recognise the possibility of exceptional cases in which a person's situation is somehow intelligible even without communicated reasons. Equally, we can recognise exceptional situations in which unintelligibility persists despite communicated reasons: if, for instance, someone has strong grounds to doubt a public authority's honesty, they may lack sufficient reasons to believe the authority's account. In these cases, communicating reasons is not necessary or not sufficient for intelligibility. The temptation is therefore to say that reason-giving is only instrumentally valuable after all – a mere means to intelligibility.

This characterisation misses two points of importance. First, the intelligibility argument shows that reason-giving is non-instrumentally valuable in what I called the procedural sense. This is the sense of non-instrumentality that is centrally relevant for administrative behaviour and institutional design, since it counts powerfully in favour of reason-giving independently of any effects this may have for the accuracy or soundness of administrative decisions.

[81] Thanks to Adam Perry for discussion.

[82] See eg Immigration Rules, pt 9, para 320(6); British Nationality Act 1981, para 40(2).

[83] See eg *R (Lumba) v Secretary of State for the Home Department* [2011] UKSC 12, [2012] 1 AC 245, in which the government had applied the stricter criteria in a secret policy instead of those in the published policy.

[84] 'Rarely' but perhaps not 'never'. Suppose a decision-maker has previously communicated a policy such that there is only one salient criterion for reaching the instant decision, and that a negative decision is communicated without further reasons. Then the affected person might infer as follows: (1) decision, D, if and only if circumstance C (published policy); (2) not-D (communicated decision); (3) therefore not-C (inferred reason). As explained in the text, real-world cases will rarely be so clean. But if they are, this may well be because the decision-maker has itself made it unambiguous that C is a necessary and sufficient condition for D. If so, then by communicating the decision without more the decision-maker might itself pragmatically implicate (3). This would then be a case of the decision-maker communicating reasons after all, albeit not explicitly.

Second, in the normal cases that predominate overwhelmingly in practice, the connection between reason-giving and intelligibility is neither instrumental nor contingent but instead constitutive. To see this, we must appreciate that intelligibility is not a subjective psychological state. It is not the feeling or belief that one understands. Such feelings may be deeply mistaken. Conversely, one's situation may be perfectly intelligible because all the relevant information is at hand and yet one may not feel that one understands. Intelligibility is instead an objective epistemic state, the state in which one's evidence is such that one is able to understand one's position. In the present context, it is the state in which explanations are available, such that a person has sufficient reason to believe a decision was taken for such-and-such reasons. Unintelligibility is the state in which a person lacks such sufficient reasons. In the normal case, communicated reasons are constitutive of intelligibility because they directly make it the case that the affected person has sufficient grounds for believing that the decision was taken for certain reasons, viz. those communicated. Likewise, in the normal case, withholding reasons directly makes it the case that the person lacks such grounds for belief; to withhold reasons then just is to produce or guarantee unintelligibility. In all but the most deviant cases, reason-giving in government administration is valuable not as an instrument of intelligibility but as its essential constitutive element.

The idea of intelligibility, and its connection with agency, explains the basic thought that it is normally wrong to leave someone searching for answers which one could easily provide.[85] It shows why the reasons provided must be sufficiently detailed to allow a person to understand their treatment. It makes sense of the fact that the reasons given must be those that in fact motivated the decision-maker, since these are the reasons that explain the moral character of their decision, and hence its impact on an affected person's self-understanding. A false or misleading statement of the reasons will not produce understanding, but at best the false belief that one understands. The intelligibility argument shows, too, why reason-giving matters more to the disappointed party. Blocking a person from executing their projects means there is at least a blip in the story of a life, something in need of particular explanation, whereas simply being permitted to do what one wanted to do does not.

5. Arbitrary Power

Still, the intelligibility argument does not quite explain everything. In particular, it does not explain why the giving of reasons should be a form of directed address to the affected party: it is still objectionable if one learns of the reasons relevant to one's case from a leaked document, or only once they are reluctantly revealed in the course of litigation, even though either might satisfy the need for intelligibility. I will suggest presently that to explain such features, we must recognise, in addition, that withholding reasons can amount to the exercise of arbitrary power.

[85] It therefore makes perfect sense of issues discussed by Edmund Pincoffs which, despite his assertion to the contrary, have no connection to the Kantian 'mere-means' principle: EL Pincoffs, 'Due Process, Fraternity, and a Kantian Injunction' (1977) 18 *Nomos* 172.

By this I do not mean power exercised without sufficient or any justificatory basis. I mean power that does not stand in appropriate relations of accountability, power of the kind that, according to republican theorists, is apt to constitute domination. I claimed earlier that reason-giving is not necessarily the antithesis of authority. Nevertheless, it is true that failing to give reasons objectionably structures the link between government and the governed. It does so, I suggest, in making political power arbitrary.[86]

Both the giving and the withholding of reasons presuppose and in turn partly instantiate certain kinds of relationship. To give reasons is to make oneself vulnerable. For reasons, once laid bare, invite responses which might show one's decision to have been indefensible. The reason-giver is vulnerable, in the first place, to the addressee's reactive attitudes, such as anger or resentment, as well as to their ethical deliberations. The reason-giver is moreover liable to the addressee's making claims and demands. The nature and likely impact of such demands depend on background social and institutional conditions. Where a person affected by a government decision has a legal right to seek a judicial review or appeal, their demands may not only sound in morality or rationality but also trigger mechanisms of institutional scrutiny. If such scrutiny is largely effective – if it generally identifies and enforces a normatively significant range of duties on government – then a claimant's ability to engage it is a powerful tool.[87] A government decision-maker that withholds reasons renders itself substantially invulnerable to this range of responses on the part of affected persons.

In doing so, the decision-maker willingly inhabits a state of what Chrisopher McCammon usefully terms 'deliberative isolation'.[88] As McCammon suggests, such isolation is a hallmark of arbitrary power. Where A is deliberatively isolated then, if A thinks some reason is a good one for B, A 'need not reflect' about whether others think so: 'A need only consult A's sense of practical reason'.[89] Deliberative isolation is a matter of degree. A – an administrative agency, let us suppose – might be more or less isolated from what others think. A secret, non-justiciable decision involves almost total deliberative isolation. A justiciable decision communicated without reasons involves much less. But there is still a problematic degree. The decision is substantially isolated from the affected person's – B's – sense of practical reason.

Since B does not know the reasons for the agency's decision, B has nothing to reflect on beyond the bare outcome. The agency cannot be moved by B's view of the reasons because, by withholding them, the agency has prevented B from forming a view to begin with. In the ideal case, by contrast, the agency provides B with the reasons in a spirit of sensitivity and willingness to listen to B's appraisal of them. By considering

[86] Or more arbitrary than it would have been, on the plausible assumption that arbitrariness is a scalar property.

[87] As this suggests, the anti-arbitrariness argument depends partially, though by no means wholly, on the fact that the courts are a largely effective forum for scrutiny. In that way, it depends partly on an instrumental premise. But it is not therefore an instrumental argument: non-instrumental values are frequently conditional on instrumental values. See eg E Anderson, 'Democracy: Instrumental vs. Non-Instrumental Value' in T Christiano and J Christman (eds), *Contemporary Debates in Political Philosophy* (Hoboken, Wiley, 2009). The idea is that it can be wrong to make oneself invulnerable to an effective mechanism of scrutiny, yet not simply because of the avoided value of the scrutiny, but also because of the objectionable relationship thereby instantiated.

[88] C McCammon, 'Domination: A Rethinking' (2015) 125 *Ethics* 1028, 1046.

[89] ibid.

B's response, the agency might come to understand the impact of their decision, and be willing to revisit it or aspects of it if a mistake is pointed out, and if necessary to provide further explanations or reconsider the way similar decisions are made in future. And the agency would signal their willingness to undertake an appeal or submit to a judicial review of the decision if B seeks one. Rather than being deliberatively isolated from B, such an agency would be deliberatively engaged. But where the agency withholds reasons, it pre-empts such deliberative openness at the first step. The point here is not only the practical one that B may therefore find it hard to vindicate their legal rights concerning the underlying decision. After all, it is possible that B nevertheless makes it to court, whereupon the agency is finally compelled to explain themselves. Even here, however, the deliberative isolation with respect to B may persist if the agency regards itself accountable only, in the end, to the court, and not directly to B. The agency does not answer *to* the affected person, but instead answers to the court *about* the affected person. From the perspective of anti-arbitrariness, this will not do. It is not enough that the affected person comes somehow or other to learn of the authority's reasons; the authority must directly address the reasons to them so as to avoid deliberative isolation.

McCammon's own discussion of deliberative isolation centres not on the period after a decision is made but on the period leading up to it.[90] Does this disclose an important difference? One might worry that while *ex ante* deliberative isolation matters insofar as it renders a decision *uncontrolled* by the affected party, giving or withholding reasons for a decision that is already made cannot bear on control or arbitrary power.[91]

The concern is understandable but misplaced. First, *ex post* deliberative isolation can indeed bear on *ex ante* control. If a decision-maker knows in making a decision at t_1 they will at t_2 (be required to) give reasons for it, this knowledge already at t_1 operates as a constraint. The prospect of accountability later acts as a constraint now.[92] More fundamentally, *ex post* deliberative isolation can render a decision objectionably arbitrary independently of whether it makes it less controlled. *Ex post* and *ex ante* deliberative isolation implicate much the same moral concerns. The reason-withholder does not deign to explain themselves to others; they act solely on their own whim, on their own say-so. The protestations or potential protestations of those affected make no call on their practical deliberations. All of this is already arbitrary and already objectionable in the exercise of political power.[93] Even if we grant the republican thesis that arbitrary power is wrongful because of its impact on control and in turn freedom, it does not

[90] ibid.

[91] Thanks to Adam Perry for discussion here.

[92] This is precisely the mechanism that is commonly relied on in republican accounts of contestability. See eg P Pettit, *Republicanism: A Theory of Freedom and Government* (Oxford, Oxford University Press, 1999) 185. The point is not the (procedurally) instrumental one that such a constraint will reduce the incidence of poor decision-making but rather that it ensures that decision-making at t_1 does not have the morally objectionable quality of being unconstrained.

[93] The force of these points will depend to some extent on the degree of *ex ante* deliberative isolation. In a situation of thorough *ex ante* deliberative isolation, *ex post* deliberative isolation will tend to aggravate the problem. If *ex ante* the decision-making process has been deliberatively inclusive, then the overall degree of arbitrariness may be relatively modest even if reasons are withheld. Still, withholding reasons will imply a greater degree of arbitrariness than would providing them.

follow that it is wrongful for that reason alone. I am suggesting that the exercise of deliberatively isolated political power *per se* instantiates a defective relationship between government and the governed, quite apart from considerations of freedom and control.

I have emphasised *political* power since it would be excessive to claim there is a general moral requirement to avoid deliberative isolation or to explain ourselves for everything that we do. Many personal choices – for example about where to live, whom to associate with, which interests to pursue, or what to buy or consume – do not necessarily trigger reasons to account to others.[94] That holds even where such choices manifest power, such as social or economic power, and materially affect others. Not all power runs the risk of instantiating an objectionable relationship of arbitrariness. Much more, in the end, would need to be said to characterise relationships which do and do not trigger the anti-arbitrariness requirement. But for present purposes we may assume that the exercise of political power furnishes at least jointly sufficient conditions for the requirement, inasmuch as (i) coercion is always a standing possibility, (ii) the state purports to exercise such power authoritatively and (iii) the state has decisive duties to act for the good of those under its authority. Political power triggers the anti-arbitrariness requirement if anything does.

6. Pluralism

There are, I have argued, important non-instrumental reasons to give reasons. We could insist on the language of 'respect' to describe them without much linguistic awkwardness, but this notion does little explanatory work. Reasons to give reasons are not grounded, in any informative sense, in respect for others' rationality or autonomy. Attempts to ground reason-giving in a theory of political justification also face serious difficulties. But I have argued we should endorse two important claims of Allan's. First, although it does not provide a general basis for giving reasons whatever their content, public authorities should, where they can, provide assurance to affected persons that their particular interests were taken seriously. Second, I have defended the idea, sometimes suggested by Allan, that giving reasons allows the addressee to assess the legitimacy of government. I have also tried to identify two independent and, I believe, quite fundamental grounds for reason-giving. Government authorities have powerful reasons to provide reasons so as not to produce unintelligibility by their actions, and to eliminate or mitigate the risk that they exercise arbitrary power. The resulting outlook is overall, I hope, more pluralist than sceptical. Quite apart from the instrumental case for reason-giving, there is more than one reason to give reasons.

[94] Not always, of course. There may be strong reasons to give reasons in some cases falling within these categories, such as where one breaks off an existing relationship.

17

Administrative Law and the Internal Perspective

MATTHEW LEWANS

1. Introduction

TRS Allan has inspired public law theorists to reconsider common law doctrine and practice in a more rigorous, philosophical light. Among other things, his research highlights how judges can supervise administrative decisions through the mechanism of judicial review and thereby vindicate constitutional values of liberty and equality. These philosophical insights, grounded in the tradition of common law constitutionalism, are instructive for lawyers, judges, and scholars throughout the common law world.

One recurrent theme in Allan's scholarship is that common law doctrine and constitutional practices should be examined from an 'internal perspective'. At first glance, the methodological prescription that motivates Allan's broader theoretical arguments might seem odd, because it bears a striking resemblance to a jurisprudential term coined by the leading legal positivist of the twentieth century, HLA Hart.[1] Hart famously argued that John Austin's positivist theory of law was deficient, because it construed law's normativity exclusively from the external point of view of a detached observer as opposed to the internal point of view of critically-engaged participants (ie, legal subjects, officials, judges, etc) who consider and accept the laws of a particular legal system.[2]

Austin argued in the *Province of Jurisprudence Determined* that the concept of a command was 'the *key* to the sciences of jurisprudence and morals', whose meaning 'should be analysed with precision'.[3] A command, according to Austin, consists of an expression of a desire coupled with 'the power and the purpose of the party commanding to inflict an evil or pain in case the desire be disregarded',[4] which implies that a subject is obliged to comply with a legal rule that is enforced by a sanction for noncompliance. By claiming that a legal rule is a species of command, Austin explained law's normativity

[1] HLA Hart, *The Concept of Law*, 2nd edn (Oxford, Clarendon Press, 1994).

[2] J Austin, *The Province of Jurisprudence Determined*, W Rumble ed (Cambridge, Cambridge University Press, 1995 [1832]) Lecture VI.

[3] ibid 21.

[4] ibid.

by deriving it from the sovereign's power to enforce its commands as opposed to the substantive merits of a legal rule.[5] Using this definition, he claimed that the parameters of an independent political society[6] could be deduced by observing whether a sufficient proportion[7] of the general population rendered habitual obedience to a determinate institution possessing supreme legislative and executive powers.[8] Austin's main point is that any command anywhere – regardless of its substantive content – might nevertheless be valid legal rule provided that it is backed by the requisite sanction. Among other things this definition of law supports the separation thesis, which holds that there is no necessary connection between law and morality.[9]

By contrast, Hart argued that when one adopts the internal perspective of an engaged participant, it seems that law's normativity is grounded by a critical reflective attitude manifested in 'criticism (including self-criticism), demands for conformity, and in acknowledgements that such criticism and demands are justified'.[10] Thus, Hart shifted the focus of analytical jurisprudence away from external manifestations of habitual obedience and toward the internal perspectives of participants to probe their reasons for accepting legal standards and using them to guide their behaviour. Nevertheless, Hart claimed that understanding law in this way vindicates the separation thesis, because engaged participants could still accept substantively unjust laws that could be validated by the rule of recognition.[11]

Like Hart, Allan argues that common law doctrine and practice cannot be adequately understood from the external perspective of a detached observer. But he clearly rejects the separation thesis. For Allan, a participant's internal perspective on law extends beyond existing legal rules or common law doctrine validated by a rule of recognition, which can be inferred from observable patterns of judicial behaviour recorded in the law reports. While socially accepted legal rules, principles, doctrine, and related constitutional practices provide relevant pre-interpretive materials, they merely set the stage for a substantive normative debate between engaged participants about what justice requires in the context of a particular legal dispute.[12] As Allan puts it:

> [T]here is no law or legal practice (I shall argue) separate from, or independent of, the larger debates in constitutional theory and jurisprudence over basic doctrines and their moral and political justification. We cannot identify the content of law with a merely descriptive account of judicial practice, viewed as a matter of empirical fact: it is a product of normative judgement, in which we attempt to make good moral sense of an array of such familiar legal 'sources' as Acts of Parliament, judicial precedent and influential dicta. An account of English law on any specific subject is always a *theory* of how best to read the relevant legal materials, guided by notions of justice and coherence: we assume that the law, correctly interpreted,

[5] ibid 22.
[6] ibid 180.
[7] ibid 176–77.
[8] ibid 196–99.
[9] Austin, *The Province of Jurisprudence Determined* (n 2) 157.
[10] Hart, *The Concept of Law* (n 1) 57.
[11] HLA Hart, 'Positivism and the Separation of Law and Morals' (1958) 71 *Harvard Law Review* 593.
[12] In this respect, Allan's theory shares much in common with Ronald Dworkin's protestant and interpretive theory of law. See TRS Allan, *The Sovereignty of Law: Freedom, Constitution, and Common Law* (Oxford, Oxford University Press, 2013) 126–27, 162–67; R Dworkin, *Law's Empire* (Cambridge, Belknap Press, 1986) 65–68.

> should as far as possible serve the interests of justice, rather than injustice, and be broadly coherent rather than confused and contradictory. And this is true even when we disagree about what justice requires, or about what would make the law more coherent overall.[13]

Thus, while Allan shares Hart's methodological premise that legal theorists should examine law from the internal perspective of engaged participants, he argues that it leads inexorably to a morally-charged, normative debate about what justice requires in the context of a particular case. Furthermore, this debate can only be resolved by weighing the matters of principle that are at stake and cannot be short-circuited by appealing to conventional understandings about the law's content. According to Allan, Hart's positivistic understanding of the internal point of view is reductive and misleading, because it implies that law does not exist beyond the parameters of legal rules validated by a rule of recognition. The better view is that the moral resources of the law retain their normative traction or gravitational force even when legal subjects, legal officials, and judges disagree about what the law requires in a particular case, all things considered.[14]

When one considers common law doctrine and judicial review in the manner Allan recommends, it raises a series of intriguing questions regarding the interpretation of law in a constitutional democracy, in which free and equal individuals are actively engaged in the institutionally complex and argumentative project of self-government through law.[15] If, as Allan argues, the internal perspective reveals that interpretive disagreements regarding the content of law are more pervasive than Hart's theory suggests, how should judges exercise their power to review decisions rendered previously by administrative officials?[16] This basic question concerns the role of administrative law in an institutionally complex constitutional democracy, which is implicit in doctrinal tensions regarding whether and to what extent it is appropriate for judges to interfere with administrative decisions on procedural or substantive grounds when those decisions involve the exercise of statutorily delegated authority to resolve interpretive disagreements about the content of the law in the context of a particular case.

Amongst public law theorists, Allan offers the most sophisticated objection to arguments in favour of judicial deference to administrative interpretations of law. In *The Sovereignty of Law* he rejects theoretical arguments in favour of judicial deference, because 'the relevant considerations of constitutional legitimacy and institutional expertise are already implicit constraints on judicial review – reflected in ordinary legal reasoning or met by an application of legal principle sensitive to the circumstances of the particular case'.[17] Accordingly, Allan rejects Murray Hunt's plea for the development of a common law doctrine of deference in the United Kingdom, saying 'that the demand for special rules to curtail judicial "discretion"... reflects an outsider's external

[13] Allan, *The Sovereignty of Law* (n 12) 5.

[14] ibid 161–67; R Dworkin, *Taking Rights Seriously* (Cambridge, Harvard University Press, 1977) 111; Dworkin, *Law's Empire* (n 12) 183.

[15] H Richardson, *Democratic Autonomy: Public Reasoning about the Ends of Policy* (Oxford, Oxford University Press, 2002).

[16] J Waldron, 'Authority for Officials' in L Meyer, S Paulson and T Pogge (eds), *Rights, Culture, and the Law: Themes from the Legal and Practical Philosophy of Joseph Raz* (Oxford, Oxford University Press, 2003) 45.

[17] Allan, *The Sovereignty of Law* (n 12) 241.

viewpoint: it adopts an arm's length *detachment* that has no place within a fully internal, interpretative posture, appropriate to adjudication'.[18]

In this chapter, I want to examine different perspectives regarding constitutionalism and the legitimacy of administrative law, which shed additional light on the debate about judicial deference. Following Allan's lead, I will argue that examining law from an internal perspective raises important questions about legality and legitimacy that can be adequately addressed only by offering an explicitly normative argument. However, arguments about the legality of administrative decisions have significant democratic and institutional aspects that impact how engaged participants (legal subjects, administrative officials, and judges) interpret the law and approach questions about constitutional justice. These democratic and institutional aspects underpin administrative law from an internal perspective – a critically-reflective attitude that construes judicial review as a means of ensuring that administrative institutions are in good working order as opposed to reserving judges an exclusive right to determine what the law requires, all things considered.[19] Understanding administrative law from an internal perspective in this way suggests that there is an important, qualitative, and morally justified distinction between judges assessing an administrative decision to ensure that it is *reasonable* as opposed to judges assessing an administrative decision to determine whether it is *correct*. This qualitative distinction makes a practical difference in how judges assess the legality of administrative decisions and suggests that a common law doctrine of deference has important work to do in framing debates about the content of the law in the context of a particular interpretive dispute within a constitutional democracy.

2. Constitutionalism and Administrative Law

In the United States of America and Canada, there is a substantial body of common law doctrine[20] and public law scholarship,[21] which claims that administrative law is

[18] ibid. Murray Hunt develops his view of deference in M Hunt, 'Sovereignty's Blight: Why Contemporary Public Law Needs the Concept of "Due Deference"' in N Bamforth and P Leyland (eds), *Public Law in a Multi-Layered Constitution* (Oxford, Hart Publishing, 2003) 337.

[19] For a striking, but illuminating, example of this distinction, compare the opinions of Roberts CJ (for the majority) and Kagan J (dissenting) in *Loper Bright Enterprises v Raimondo* 603 US ____ (2024).

[20] See eg *Gray v Powell* 314 US 402 (1941); *National Labor Relations Board v Hearst* 211 US 111 (1944); *Skidmore v Swift & Co* 323 US 134 (1944); *Udall v Tallman* 380 US 1 (1965); *Canadian Union of Public Employees, Local 963 v New Brunswick Liquor Corporation* [1979] 2 SCR 227; *Chevron USA Inc v Natural Resources Defense Council Inc* 467 US 837 (1984); *National Corn Growers Association v Canada (Import Tribunal)* [1990] 2 SCR 1324; *Doré v Barreau du Québec* [2012] 1 SCR 395.

[21] See eg F Frankfurter, 'The Task of Administrative Law' (1926–1927) 75 *University of Pennsylvania Law Review* 614; F Frankfurter, *The Public and Its Government* (New Haven, Yale University Press, 1930); DM Gordon, 'Administrative Tribunals and the Courts' (1933) 49 *LQR* 94; J Willis, 'Three Approaches to Administrative Law: The Judicial, the Conceptual, and the Functional' (1935) 1 *University of Toronto Law Journal* 53; J Willis, 'Statute Interpretation in a Nutshell' (1938) 16 *Canadian Bar Review* 1; B Laskin, 'Certiorari to Labour Boards: The Apparent Futility of Privative Clauses' (1952) 30 *Canadian Bar Review* 986; J Willis, 'The McRuer Report: Lawyers' Values and Civil Servants' Values' (1968) 18 *University of Toronto Law Journal* 351; HW Arthurs, 'Rethinking Administrative Law: A Slightly Dicey Business' (1979) 17 *Osgoode Hall Law Journal* 1; M Bayles, 'The Justification of Administrative Authority' in JR Pennock and J Chapman (eds), *Authority Revisited* (1987) 29 *Nomos* 287 (New York, New York University Press, 1987); A Scalia, 'Judicial Deference to Administrative Interpretations of Law' (1989) 38 *Duke Law Journal* 511; M Allars, 'On Deference

a complementary source of law within a democratic constitutional order alongside legislation and the common law. Writing in 1927 amidst the constitutional commotion of the *Lochner* era[22] – a historical period when the United States Supreme Court held repeatedly that the due process clauses in the Fifth and Fourteenth Amendments to the Constitution of the United States entitled it to strike down state and federal legislation empowering administrative officials to regulate private economic relationships,[23] and constitutionally guaranteed *de novo* judicial review of administrative decisions[24] – Felix Frankfurter argued that it was high time for common lawyers to take administrative law seriously.[25] At the time, he observed that '[t]he widening area of what in effect is law-making authority, exercised by officials whose actions are not subject to ordinary court review, constitutes perhaps the most striking contemporary tendency of the Anglo-American legal order'.[26] He elaborated on this point by saying:

> Hardly a measure passes Congress the effective execution of which is not conditioned upon rules and regulations emanating from the enforcing authorities. These administrative complements are euphemistically called 'filling in the details' of a policy set forth in statutes. But the 'details' are of the essence; they give meaning and content to vague contours. The control of banking, insurance, public utilities, finance, industry, the professions, health and morals, in sum, the manifold response of government to the forces and needs of modern society, is building up a body of laws not written by legislatures, and of adjudications not made by courts and not subject to their revision. These powers are vested in a vast congeries of agencies. We are in the midst of a process, largely unconscious and certainly unscientific, of adjusting the exercise of these powers to the traditional system of Anglo-American law and courts. A systematic scrutiny of these issues and a conscious effort towards their wise solution are the concerns of administrative law.[27]

In effect, Frankfurter was exhorting public law theorists to examine administrative law from an internal perspective by highlighting the complementary value of administrative law in a constitutional democracy. By interpreting enabling legislation in a purposive and expert manner, administrative officials synthesise facts, legal principles, and public policy objectives to resolve significant social and economic problems.

to Tribunals, With Deference to Dworkin' (1995) 20 *Queen's Law Journal* 1; D Dyzenhaus, 'The Politics of Deference: Judicial Review and Democracy' in M Taggart (ed), *The Province of Administrative Law* (Oxford, Hart Publishing, 1997) 279; J Mashaw, *Creating the Administrative Constitution: The Lost One Hundred Years of American Administrative Law* (New Haven, Yale University Press, 2012).

[22] In *Lochner v New York* 198 US 45 (1905), the United States Supreme Court struck down legislation prescribing maximum work hours for bakers, which had been passed by the New York State Legislature, on the ground that it infringed the constitutional right to liberty of contract guaranteed by the Fourteenth Amendment. *Allgeyer v Louisiana* 165 US 578 (1897) is generally regarded as the starting point for *Lochner* period and *West Coast Hotel Co v Parrish* 300 US 279 (1937) is generally regarded as its ending point.

[23] See eg *Adkins v Children's Hospital* 261 US 626 (1923) (federal legislation establishing an administrative board to set minimum wages for women and children in the District of Columbia struck down on the ground it infringed the constitutional rights to property and due process guaranteed by the Fifth Amendment).

[24] See eg *Smyth v Ames* 169 US 466 (1898) (ratemaking decisions rendered by the Interstate Commerce Commission reviewable by federal courts on a *de novo* basis to determine whether they are confiscatory within the meaning of the Fourteenth Amendment).

[25] Frankfurter, 'The Task of Administrative Law' (n 21).

[26] ibid 614.

[27] ibid 614–15.

But despite de facto prevalence of administrative law in both the United States and the United Kingdom, Frankfurter noted that 'administrative law is hardly yet given *de jure* recognition by the English-speaking bar'[28] – an oversight he attributed to constitutional theorists like AV Dicey who denied the existence of administrative law under the English constitution.[29] Throughout his *Law of the Constitution*, Dicey used the concept of administrative law as an analytical foil to define the essential institutional and substantive attributes of the rule of law in England.[30] He argued that *droit administratif* 'rests on ideas foreign to the fundamental assumptions of our English common law, and especially to what we have termed the rule of law', because legal disputes between individuals and the state are (1) removed from ordinary courts, (2) adjudicated by administrative officials, and (3) determined in accordance with 'principles different from the considerations which fix the legal rights and duties of one citizen towards another'.[31] The essential characteristics that Dicey ascribed to administrative law were the very antithesis of his conception of the constitutional principle of the rule of law, which entailed (1) that no one 'can be made to suffer in body or goods except for a distinct breach of law established in the ordinary legal manner before the ordinary courts of the land',[32] (2) that 'every man, whatever be his rank or condition, is subject to the ordinary law of the realm and amenable to the jurisdiction of the ordinary tribunals',[33] and (3) that 'the general principles of the constitution … are with us the result of judicial decisions determining the rights of private persons in particular cases brought before the courts'.[34] The upshot, for Dicey, is that administrative law is an essential threat to the rule of law, which by definition requires common law judges to have a constitutional monopoly to adjudicate interpretive disputes regarding the meaning of legislation.

However, Dicey's perspective of constitutional law had a libertarian ideological underpinning, which might explain his rejection of administrative law.[35] In 1898, at the outset of the *Lochner* era in American constitutional law, Dicey accepted an invitation to deliver a series of lectures at Harvard Law School, which were later published as a monograph on *Law and Public Opinion in England During the Nineteenth Century*.[36] In addressing current issues in English constitutional law that would have resonated with his American audience at the time, Dicey condemned various legislative reforms that established the statutory foundation for the modern welfare state in the United Kingdom: legislation establishing old age pensions, unemployment insurance, trade

[28] ibid 615.

[29] AV Dicey, *Lectures Introductory to the Study of the Law of the Constitution*, JWF Allison ed (Oxford, Oxford University Press, 2013 [1885]).

[30] ibid ch 12.

[31] ibid 337–38.

[32] ibid 188.

[33] ibid 193.

[34] ibid 195.

[35] I Jennings, *The Law and the Constitution* (London, University of London Press, 1933) 252–63; JB Brebner, 'Laissez Faire and State Intervention in Nineteenth-Century Britain' (1948) 8 *The Journal of Economic History* 59; PWJ Bartrip, 'State Intervention in Mid-Nineteenth Century Britain: Fact or Fiction?' (1983) 23 *Journal of British Studies* 63; RL Crouch, 'Laissez-Faire in Nineteenth Century Britain: Myth or Reality' (1967) 35 *The Manchester School* 199.

[36] AV Dicey, *Lectures on the Relation Between Law and Public Opinion in England During the Nineteenth Century*, 2nd edn (London, Macmillan, 1914).

union legislation, property taxes, maximum hours of work, and minimum wages.[37] Like the United States Supreme Court, Dicey regarded these legislative programs as an extraordinary threat to liberty and the economic status quo, because they assumed an active role for the state in regulating the economy and redistributing wealth within society. Thus, in the preface to the second edition of *Law and Public Opinion*, which was published in 1914, Dicey observed that 'Englishmen will readily acknowledge that there are many cases in which the interference of the State really increases the personal liberty of the citizen' but qualified this point by saying that '[d]espotism may continue to be tyranny, even though it may have become both popular and benevolent'.[38]

Nevertheless, Dicey hoped that 'counter-currents' and 'cross-currents' of public opinion, including 'judge made law', would 'carry the individualistic virtues and laws of the nineteenth century into the twentieth century, and there blend them with the socialistic virtues of a coming age'.[39] Because English judges 'have always refused, in principle at least, to interpret an Act of Parliament otherwise than by reference to the words of the enactment',[40] judicial interpretation of legislation was characterised by 'a certain narrowness' that would preserve 'the authority of the judges and the fixity of the law'.[41] So long as Parliament retained a monopoly to legislate and judges retained a monopoly on interpreting legislation narrowly by focusing on the semantic content of statutory limits on administrative jurisdiction, there was no realistic prospect for the emergence of administrative law in England. Even though judges sitting in the House of Lords could not strike down enabling legislation like their counterparts on the United States Supreme Court, they could nevertheless parse legislative provisions narrowly to keep administrative officials on a short leash.

Against this backdrop, Frankfurter called on 'students trained in the common law and familiar with its history'[42] to develop 'instruments and processes at once adequate for social needs and the protection of individual freedom'.[43] For Frankfurter, the constitutional principles of liberty and equality imposed both positive constitutional duties and negative constitutional constraints on the state. This meant that public law theorists should reconsider constitutional doctrines and practices from a perspective that recognised the value of administrative law in building a more just and equitable society than the one which had prevailed during the *Lochner* era – a historical period characterised by unregulated economic activity, political corruption, and the unprecedented concentration of private wealth fuelled by the exploitation of individuals under the constitutional pretense of preserving liberty of contract.[44] But it also required public lawyers to develop an array of democratic guardrails to ensure responsible governance, public accountability, and prevent the enforcement of arbitrary administrative decisions: 'a highly professionalised civil service', 'an adequate technique of administrative

[37] ibid ch VIII.
[38] ibid lxxxi.
[39] ibid xcii.
[40] Dicey, *Law of the Constitution* (n 29) 407.
[41] ibid 408.
[42] Frankfurter, 'The Task of Administrative Law' (n 21) 621.
[43] ibid 617.
[44] R Pound, 'Liberty of Contract' (1909) 18 *Yale Law Journal* 454; M Horwitz, *The Transformation of American Law 1870–1960: The Crisis of Legal Orthodoxy* (Oxford, Oxford University Press, 1992).

application of legal standards', 'a flexible, appropriate and economical procedure' to ensure procedural regularity, 'easy access to public scrutiny', and 'a constant play of criticism by an informed and spirited bar'.[45]

Frankfurter's argument regarding the complementary relationship between legislation, the common law, and administrative law draws inspiration from James Thayer's highly influential article on American constitutionalism.[46] In 1893, Thayer argued that there had been a fundamental shift from an 'external' to an 'internal' perspective of American constitutional law after the War of Independence. Prior to the war, the purpose of judicial review of legislation was to maintain Crown sovereignty, which meant that judges were to assess whether legislation was ultra vires pursuant to the semantic meaning of terms included in colonial charters issued and enforced by the British Crown.[47] After the war, the purpose of judicial review was to facilitate a democratic project of constitutional self-government amongst free and equal citizens.[48] As Thayer put it, the state and federal constitutions 'were not so many orders from without, backed by an organized outside government … they were precepts from the people themselves who were to be governed, addressed to each of their own number, and especially to those who were charged with the duty of conducting the government'.[49]

Unlike Dicey, Thayer argued that common law judges did not have an exclusive monopoly over the interpretation of legislation or constitutional principles. Under the post-revolutionary constitutional settlement, the legislature had primary responsibility to interpret constitutional principles and enact legislation in accordance with those principles. This primary interpretive responsibility, Thayer argued, meant that 'the actual determinations of the body to whom it is intrusted are entitled to a corresponding respect; and this not on mere grounds of courtesy or conventional respect, but on very solid and significant grounds of policy and law'.[50] Judicial review was 'one of many safeguards'[51] available to uphold constitutional principles, which implied that the judiciary played an important, albeit secondary, constitutional role. When reviewing the constitutionality of legislation, judges were bound by 'a rule of administration', which

> recognises that, having regard to the great, complex, ever-unfolding exigencies of government, much which will seem unconstitutional to one man, or body of men, may reasonably not seem so to another; that the constitution often admits of different interpretations; that there is often a range of choice and judgment that in such cases the constitution does not impose upon the legislature any one specific opinion, but leaves open this range of choice and that whatever choice is rational is constitutional.[52]

The upshot of this idea is that the role of a reviewing court is to assess whether legislation and executive decisions reflected a 'reasonable' interpretation of constitutional

[45] Frankfurter, 'The Task of Administrative Law' (n 21) 618.

[46] J Thayer, 'The Origin and Scope of the American Doctrine of Constitutional Law' (1893–1894) 7 *Harvard Law Review* 129. For an examination of the relationship between Thayer's perspective of constitutional law and Frankfurter's perspective of administrative law, see M Lewans, *Administrative Law and Judicial Deference* (Oxford, Hart Publishing, 2018) ch 4.

[47] ibid 130.

[48] ibid 131.

[49] ibid 131.

[50] ibid 136.

[51] ibid 138.

[52] ibid 140.

principles.[53] As Thayer puts the point, '*the ultimate question is not what is the true meaning of the constitution, but whether the legislation is sustainable or not*'.[54] In other words, the role of a court is to assess whether a decision rendered by another governmental institution is *reasonable* as opposed to determining whether it is *correct*.

Thayer's internal perspective of American constitutional law and Frankfurter's recognition of administrative law mark important intellectual developments that still resonate with contemporary administrative law doctrine. In 1937, the United States Supreme Court radically changed its approach to assessing the constitutionality of President Franklin Roosevelt's New Deal package of legislative reforms,[55] which foreshadowed the demise of the short-lived non-delegation doctrine that prohibited the statutory delegation of administrative rule-making authority.[56] Instead of asking simply whether legislation or an administrative decision was ultra vires, infringed a negative conception of liberty, or violated a formal conception of the separation of powers between the legislative and executive branches of government, the practice of judicial review developed a greater sense of contextual sensitivity that acknowledged the potential legitimacy of administrative law. On this view, the primary focus of judicial review is not to determine the correct meaning of the law, but to assess whether an administrative decision is justified reasonably in light of statutory objectives and the context of a specific case.

This conception of judicial review has since become a fixture in both American and Canadian administrative law, and animates the reasoning in cases like *Chevron*[57] and *CUPE*,[58] which hold that judges should defer to administrative decisions that are not demonstrably unreasonable[59] because it is constitutionally legitimate for administrative officials to interpret the meaning of the law in light of the relevant social context. However, as the recent decision of the United States Supreme Court in *Loper Bright Enterprises v Raimondo* shows, the very notion that it is constitutionally appropriate for judges to defer to administrative interpretations of law remains controversial, because it conflicts with an assumption that attracted Dicey and other like-minded jurists: that the rule of law essentially requires judges to determine the meaning of the law.[60]

3. Common Law Constitutionalism and Judicial Review

Throughout the twentieth century, common law doctrine and public law scholarship in the United Kingdom followed a slightly different path. In 1929 (two years after Frankfurter's article was published), Lord Hewart of Bury, the Chief Justice of England

[53] ibid 144.
[54] ibid 150.
[55] *West Coast Hotel Co v Parrish* (n 22) upheld the constitutionality of State legislation authorising an administrative agency to set minimum wage standards for women, overruling *Adkins v Children's Hospital* (n 23).
[56] *Panama Refining Co v Ryan* 293 US 388 (1935); *Schechter Poultry Corp v United States* 295 US 495 (1935).
[57] *Chevron USA Inc v Natural Resources Defense Council Inc* (n 20).
[58] *Canadian Union of Public Employees Local 963 v New Brunswick Liquor Corporation* (n 20).
[59] *Chevron* (n 20) 844–845.
[60] *Loper Bright Enterprises* (n19).

and Wales, published *The New Despotism* – a polemic denouncing the prevalence of 'administrative lawlessness' in the United Kingdom, whereby Parliament enacted legislation establishing 'a large and increasing field of departmental authority and activity beyond the reach of ordinary law'.[61] Hewart argued that '[b]etween the "Rule of Law" and what is called "administrative law" (happily there is no English name for it) there is the sharpest possible contrast'.[62] Under the rule of law, interpretive disputes are determined exclusively by ordinary common law courts employing the common law method of adjudication, which guaranteed an individual's rights to a public hearing, cross-examine witnesses, a decision based on the evidence, and reasons.[63] By contrast, he said '[t]here are no rules or principles which can be said to be rules or principles of this astonishing variety of administrative "law", nor is there any regular course of procedure for its application'.[64] Citing Dicey, Hewart argued that the concept of administrative law was the antithesis of the rule of law. By passing enabling legislation and delegating discretionary power to administrative officials to fill in the gaps without direct political or judicial oversight, Parliament was unleashing a new despotism upon the world that rendered 'the will, or caprice, of the Executive unfettered and supreme'[65] and jeopardised 'those hardly won liberties which it has taken centuries to establish'.[66]

In retrospect, Hewart's argument seems hypocritical for two related reasons. First, in his previous career as a Member of Parliament (1913–1916), Solicitor-General (1916–1919), and Attorney General (1919–1922), Hewart supported exactly the type of enabling legislation he denounced in *The New Despotism*.[67] Most notably, in 1914 he was a recently-elected member of the Asquith government[68] that passed the Defence of the Realm Act, which gave the British government sweeping emergency powers including the power to pass regulations authorising the Secretary of State to detain any persons deemed to be a national security threat.[69] This might explain Hewart's relatively sanguine treatment[70] of the Defence of the Realm Act and the House of Lords' decision in *Rex v Halliday*[71] compared to the parade of horrible legislation regarding property taxes,[72] poor relief,[73] local government,[74] public utilities,[75] municipal planning,[76] labour boards,[77] unemployment insurance,[78] and personal income taxes.[79]

[61] Lord Hewart, *The New Despotism* (London, Ernst & Benn Ltd, 1929) 11.
[62] ibid 37.
[63] ibid ch 2.
[64] ibid 44.
[65] ibid 17.
[66] ibid 52.
[67] R Jackson, *The Chief: The Biography of Gordon Hewart Lord Chief Justice of England 1922–40* (London, George Harrap, 1959) 214.
[68] ibid ch 4.
[69] Defence of the Realm Act (Consolidation) Act 1914, 5 Geo V, c 8.
[70] Hewart, *The New Despotism* (n 61) 92, 167–168.
[71] *Rex v Halliday, ex parte Zadig* [1917] AC 260.
[72] Hewart, *The New Despotism* (n 61) 53, 61.
[73] ibid 66.
[74] ibid 57.
[75] ibid 67–68.
[76] ibid 64, 68.
[77] ibid 60.
[78] ibid 60–61, 68.
[79] ibid 92, 167–68.

Second, while serving as Lord Chief Justice, Hewart wrote a decision that limited the scope of judicial review, effectively immunising large swathes of administrative decisions from judicial review. In 1928 (the year immediately preceding the publication of *The New Despotism*), Lord Hewart held in *R v Legislative Committee of the Church Assembly* that administrative officials must possess a 'superadded' duty to act judicially in order to be subject to judicial review.[80] When this idea is coupled with doctrine of jurisdictional error, whereby non-jurisdictional issues are not justiciable,[81] the practical effect of Hewart's decision rendered a broad array of administrative decisions that did not concern questions of law inscrutable.[82] Like Dicey, Hewart believed that administrative law was, by definition, constitutionally illegitimate because administrative decisions occurred in a legal black hole.[83] The concept of administrative law simply could not be reconciled with the procedural and substantive attributes of the common law tradition.

Following the release of the Report of the Committee on Minister's Powers,[84] an inquiry provoked by Hewart's book, the extravagant claim that administrative law did not exist in England was no longer sustainable. The Committee concluded that, while statutory delegations of legislative and judicial powers to administrative officials was both 'legitimate' and 'inevitable',[85] this arrangement had 'definite advantages, provided that the statutory powers are exercised and statutory functions performed in the right way'.[86] To that end, the Committee recommended a broad range of constitutional safeguards: greater clarity in legislative drafting (especially when articulating statutory limits on discretionary powers),[87] exceptional use of statutory provisions granting legislative powers or restricting judicial review,[88] publication of administrative rules,[89] public consultation when administrative officials exercise rulemaking authority,[90] regular Parliamentary oversight of administrative rulemaking,[91] and a duty to provide reasons whenever administrative officials exercise judicial or quasi-judicial powers.[92] In commenting on the Committee's Report, William Robson echoed Frankfurter's plea for public lawyers to accept the constitutional legitimacy of administrative law, stating 'there can be little doubt that the great departments of state administering or supervising public health, public education, pension schemes, unemployment and health

[80] *R v Legislative Committee of the Church Assembly* [1928] 1 KB 411, 145.

[81] See, eg *Rex v Nat Bell Liquors Ltd* [1922] 2 AC 128 (JCPC).

[82] SA de Smith, 'The Limits of Judicial Review: Statutory Discretions and the Doctrine of Ultra Vires' (1948) 11 *MLR* 306.

[83] D Dyzenhaus, *The Constitution of Law: Legality in a Time of Emergency* (Cambridge, Cambridge University Press, 2006) 123. While Dicey later qualified his views regarding administrative law, Hewart's polemical argument was more categorical. See AV Dicey, 'The Development of Administrative Law in England' 31 *LQR* 148. For a detailed elaboration of Dicey's shifting perspective of administrative law, see MD Walters, *AV Dicey and the Common Law Constitutional Tradition: A Legal Turn of Mind* (Cambridge, Cambridge University Press, 2020) c 11.

[84] Committee on Ministers' Powers, *Report*, Cmd 4060, April 1932.

[85] ibid 58.

[86] ibid 5.

[87] ibid 64.

[88] ibid 65, 114.

[89] ibid 66.

[90] ibid.

[91] ibid 67.

[92] ibid 116.

insurance … are not only essential to the well-being of the great mass of the people, but also the most significant expressions of democracy in our time'.[93]

Nevertheless, the most influential English administrative lawyer of the twentieth century, HWR Wade, was far less optimistic. Like Hewart, Wade argued that the scope of judicial review tracked an analytical distinction between 'law' and 'policy'.[94] Questions of law concern an individual's pre-existing legal rights and obligations, whereas questions of policy are typically discretionary issues determined by 'the expediency of the moment'.[95] According to Wade, '[p]olicy cannot … be applied to the subject until duly transformed into law by proper constitutional procedure'.[96] While policy could be converted into law through the legislative process, 'once a rule has become *law* it must so continue (unless repealed by due process) irrespective of its rightness, wrongness, convenience or inconvenience'.[97]

Wade's distinction between law and policy entails important institutional implications regarding the adjudication of interpretive disputes. Wade emphasised that judges were entitled to control administrative officials exercising 'quasi-judicial' powers, by ensuring that administrative officials exercising those powers complied with the principles of natural justice so that 'the minister must allow any interested party to state his objections and that any such objections must be disposed of with at least an outward appearance of detachment and objectivity'.[98] However, because the substance of administrative decisions concerned matters of 'policy', judges could not pronounce upon the merits of an administrative decision any more than they could review the substance of Parliamentary legislation. As Wade puts it, '[a]rbitrary exercise of an administrative power the courts cannot control, for policy is in the last resort arbitrary'.[99] Accordingly, when the Judicial Committee of the Privy Council invoked Hewart's distinction in holding that a decision to cancel a textile licence did not involve the exercise of 'judicial' or 'quasi-judicial' power because it concerned a statutory privilege (as opposed to a legal right),[100] Wade lamented that the emergence of English administrative law occurred in the twilight of natural justice.[101]

What happened instead was a dramatic change of tack in English public law doctrine that was every bit as dramatic and profound as the constitutional revolution that occurred at the end of the *Lochner* era in American jurisprudence. Instead of parsing legislation and abstract concepts to delineate the scope of judicial, the House of Lords reasserted the supremacy of the common law and the authority of ordinary courts to determine questions of law. In *Ridge v Baldwin* Lord Reid famously rejected Hewart's distinction between administrative and quasi-judicial functions and the reasoning in

[93] W Robson, 'The Report of the Committee on Ministers' Powers' (1932) 3 *The Political Quarterly* 346, 349.
[94] HWR Wade, 'Quasi-Judicial and Its Background' (1949) 10 *CLJ* 216, 223.
[95] ibid.
[96] ibid 225.
[97] ibid.
[98] ibid 228.
[99] ibid 229.
[100] *Nakkuda Ali v Jayaratne* [1950] AC 66.
[101] Wade, 'Quasi-Judicial and Its Background' (n 94); HWR Wade, 'The Twilight of Natural Justice' (1951) 67 *LQR* 103. See also SA de Smith, 'The Right to a Hearing in English Administrative Law' (1954–1955) 68 *Harvard Law Review* 569; SA de Smith, *Judicial Review of Administrative Action* (London, Stevens & Sons Ltd, 1959) 14–122.

Nakkuda Ali, holding that the Watch Committee's decision to summarily dismiss Chief Constable Ridge was void because it had failed to notify Ridge of the allegations against him and an opportunity to respond.[102] While Lord Reid opined that '[w]e do not have a developed system of administrative law', he concluded that there was no reason for believing that 'our old methods are any less applicable today'.[103] In *Padfield v Ministry of Agriculture* Lord Reid rejected the distinction between administrative decisions involving legal rights and public policy, by directing the Minister of Agriculture to investigate milk producers' complaint against a Milk Marketing Board's determination of permissible profit margins. In doing so, he noted that 'Parliament must have conferred the [Minister's] discretion with the intention that it should be used to promote the policy and objects of the Act; the policy and the objects of the Act must be determined by construing the Act as a whole and construction is always a matter of law for the Court'.[104] Finally, in *Anisminic v Foreign Compensation Commission* Lord Reid articulated an expansive definition of jurisdictional error, holding that judges are entitled to quash an administrative decision whenever an administrative decision 'misconstrues' legislation.[105] While Lord Reid acknowledged that if an administrative tribunal 'decides a question remitted to it for decision without committing any … errors it is as much entitled to decide that question wrongly as it is to decide it rightly', it is difficult to see what logical space remains for administrative law under this model of judicial review.[106] As Wade himself noted, '[i]t comes perilously close to saying that there is jurisdiction if the decision is right but none if it is wrong'.[107]

4. Administrative Law and the Internal Perspective

This brief overview illustrates how contrasting perspectives regarding the nature of administrative law can be extrapolated from judicial practice, common law doctrine, and public law scholarship throughout the common law world. The perspective associated with Thayer's internal perspective of American constitutional law, Frankfurter's conception of administrative law, and judicial decisions like *Chevron* is anchored by a democratic and institutionally pluralist account of constitutionalism in which administrative law is a complementary source of law alongside legislation and the common law. From this vantage point, the legitimacy of the legal order is maintained through an array of safeguards (including, but not limited to, judicial review), which ensure that legislation, common law doctrine, and administrative law are publicly justifiable in light of constitutional values and principles. Furthermore, it acknowledges that it would be constitutionally inappropriate for judges to assume that they are exclusively entitled to determine the correct answer to interpretive disputes about law's content, because legislation and administrative law are 'entitled to a corresponding respect … on very

[102] *Ridge v Baldwin* [1964] AC 40, 74–75.
[103] ibid 72–73.
[104] *Padfield v Minister of Agriculture, Fisheries and Food* [1968] AC 997, 1030.
[105] *Anisminic Ltd v Foreign Compensation Commission* [1969] 2 AC 147, 170.
[106] ibid.
[107] HWR Wade, 'Constitutional and Administrative Aspects of the Anisminic Case' [1969] *LQR* 198, 211.

solid and significant grounds of policy and law'.[108] The constitutional responsibility of the judiciary is to maintain the conditions for fair and reasonable discourse between free and equal citizens about what the law and constitutional principles require in the context of a particular case. Therefore, if a particular administrative decision is rendered fairly and reasonably in light of relevant legal principles that decision provides good reasons for legal subjects, judges, and other legal officials to comply even if they might otherwise disagree with its substance.[109]

By contrast, the perspective associated with Dicey's understanding of English constitutional law, Wade's conception of administrative law, and judicial decisions like *Loper Bright Enterprises* and *Anisminic* perceives administrative law as an essential threat to the separation of powers and the rule of law, because it enables administrative officials to create binding legal rules or adjudicate interpretive disputes through the exercise of legally unconstrained discretionary power. In order to guard against this threat, they argue that an independent judiciary has exclusive interpretive authority to determine the answers to questions of law. Thus, they welcome judicial dicta that eviscerate privative clauses[110] and explode abstract formal distinctions (eg, between 'administrative' and 'quasi-judicial' functions or the distinction between 'jurisdictional' and 'non-jurisdictional' errors) that might otherwise constrain judicial review. However, they also overlook or discount the possibility that more principled arguments in favour of judicial deference might be based on the democratic delegation of authority to administrative officials, institutional expertise, or ensuring that citizens have efficient and affordable access to justice.[111] The very idea of judicial deference to administrative law is anathema, because it would entail a profound abdication of judicial responsibility under the constitution to determine what the law requires in the context of a particular case.[112]

The important point is that, despite the stark differences between these two constitutional perspectives, they cannot be mapped onto an analytical distinction between external and internal perspectives regarding law's normativity. Both perspectives are rooted in the idea that the normativity of law hinges, at least partially, on whether it is rendered fairly and can be justified substantively to individuals and other legal officials. Neither perspective resorts to Austin's more ham-fisted suggestion that the normativity of law, including administrative law, can be cinched by the state's power of enforcement.

Instead, it seems that this perspectival schism derives from a deeper tension between the micro-normativity of individuated legal norms (*gesetz*) and the macro-normativity of a legal order (*rechtsstaadt*) that afflicts both positivist and anti-positivist theories regarding the nature of law. For positivists, the validity of individuated legal norms depends on social facts like Austin's habit of obedience or Hart's rule of recognition. But once the focus of the inquiry shifts to larger questions regarding the normativity of the legal order writ large, the jurisprudential analysis becomes confused in ways that

[108] Thayer, 'The Origin and Scope of American Doctrine of Constitutional Law' (n 46) 136.
[109] Waldron, 'Authority for Officials' (n 16).
[110] Dyzenhaus, *The Constitution of Law* (n 83) 107–08.
[111] See, eg Frankfurter, *The Public and Its Government* (n 21); Willis, 'Three Approaches to Administrative Law' (n 21); Willis, 'Statute Interpretation in a Nutshell' (n 21); Bayles, 'The Justification of Administrative Authority' (n 21); Richardson, *Democratic Autonomy* (n 15); Waldron, 'Authority for Officials' (n 16); Allars, 'On Deference to Tribunals, With Deference to Dworkin' (n 21); Dyzenhaus, 'The Politics of Deference' (n 21).
[112] DJ Galligan, 'Judicial Review and the Textbook Writers' (1982) 2 *OJLS* 257, 265.

undermine the separation thesis. For example, when Hart shifts from examining the existence conditions for individuated legal rules in chapter V of the *Concept of Law* to broader questions concerning the relationship between political morality and the institutional attributes of a legal system in chapter IX, he highlights a series of 'characteristic judicial virtues' (like impartiality, fairness, and reasonableness) that are associated with the practice of legal interpretation in a stable legal order.[113] Hart concedes that, while 'it cannot be *demonstrated* that a decision is uniquely correct', an interpretation of law might nevertheless 'be made acceptable as the reasoned product of informed impartial choice'.[114] Hart's notion of reasonable acceptability suggests that, even though an engaged participant might disagree with the first-order substantive merits of a particular decision, he might still have good second-order reasons to accept it if the responsible decision-maker renders it fairly and reasonably in light of relevant legal standards.[115]

While Hart argued that this concession does not jeopardise the separation thesis, it obviously complicates the relationship between the separation thesis, rule acceptance, and the internal perspective. Lon L Fuller seized on this point when he examined the normative relationship between the practice of legal interpretation and the inner morality of legal order, which resonates with the institutionally pluralist understanding of constitutionalism from an internal perspective of constitutional law espoused by Thayer. Instead of resorting to the idea that judges have exclusive authority to interpret the law, Fuller elucidates how general principles of legality bolster 'fidelity to law', a critically-engaged perspective whereby legal subjects can respect the law 'even at the moment when it seems to us to miss its mark'.[116] This idea of fidelity to law shows how the normative character of a legal order can sustain a duty to comply even when the substance of a legal decision deviates from the principle of utility or otherwise conflicts with an engaged participant's first-order assessment of what ought to be done, all things considered. For Fuller, one does not answer this question simply on the basis of an assessment regarding the substantive merits of an individuated proposition of law, but by critically examining second-order reasons regarding the legitimacy of the broader legal order (ie, whether the legal order sustains a framework of laws that are sufficiently general, public, prospective, intelligible, consistent, practicable, stable, and administered congruently).[117] Thus, Fuller's ideas about fidelity to law leaves logical space for both individuals and judges to recognise the legitimacy of legislation and administrative law, by focusing attention on whether those laws can be justified in light of a reasonably acceptable scheme of legal obligations.

A similar tension crops up in Ronald Dworkin's interpretive theory of law, which begins with the puzzle posed by theoretical disagreement regarding the grounds or truth conditions for individuated propositions of law.[118] In order to resolve the puzzle, he advances the right answer thesis, according to which there are uniquely correct

[113] Hart, *The Concept of Law* (n 1) 205.
[114] ibid 205.
[115] J Raz, *Practical Reason and Norms*, 3rd edn (Oxford, Oxford University Press, 1999) 58–59.
[116] LL Fuller, 'Positivism and Fidelity to Law: A Reply to Professor Hart' (1958) 71 *Harvard Law Review* 630, 632.
[117] LL Fuller, *The Morality of Law* (New Haven, Yale University Press, 1969).
[118] Dworkin, *Law's Empire* (n 12).

answers to hard cases. That thesis advanced through a theory of adjudication modeled on the deliberations of a mythical judge (Hercules), who determines the correct answers to particular questions of law and thereby preserves the moral integrity of the constitutional order.[119] At first glance, this package of ideas seems to align with Dicey's and Wade's perspectives about judicial review.

However, elsewhere Dworkin argues that law's empire is 'an interpretive, self-reflective attitude addressed to politics in the broadest sense'.[120] He characterises this self-reflective attitude as 'protestant', because 'it makes each citizen responsible for imagining what his society's public commitments to principle are, and what these commitments require in new circumstances'.[121] Interestingly, while he advocates a moral reading of constitutional principles, he is equivocal about whether the judges should have the last word on debates regarding the interpretation of legislation and constitutional principles.[122] Most importantly, he acknowledges that constitutional justice entails a relatively complex and nuanced institutional arrangement, in which administrative officials share responsibility for vindicating constitutional principles of equality and liberty.[123]

Allan's objection to judicial deference weaves together many of the same jurisprudential threads in a manner that both replicates and obscures this underlying tension. Following Hart's lead, Allan draws a clear distinction between the external and internal points of view. He argues that one cannot fully understand the normativity of constitutional law from the external perspective of an observer who is content to merely describe law and legal practice in a manner that is 'detached from the relevant debates over meaning and interpretation'.[124] Furthermore, he argues that particular laws must be interpreted so as to maintain 'a coherent scheme of regulation for the attainment of justice'.[125] Other passages in *The Sovereignty of Law*, in which Allan cites *Anisminic* as an exemplar of judicial review[126] and approves AV Dicey's theory of statutory interpretation,[127] lend further support for the idea that judges have an exclusive right to determine the answers to questions of law.

The result is that, at times, it seems that Allan is arguing that the point of judicial review is for judges to determine the meaning of an individuated question of law in the context of a particular interpretive dispute and, in doing so, settle interpretive debates about its moral or political justification.[128] Writing in this vein, Allan rejects

[119] Dworkin, *Taking Rights Seriously* (n 14); R Dworkin, 'Law's Ambitions for Itself' (1985) 71 *Virginia Law Review* 173.

[120] Dworkin, *Law's Empire* (n 12) 413.

[121] ibid. See also D Dyzenhaus, 'More Protestant than Luther or Dworkin? TRS Allan on Law and Morals' ch 2 in this volume; G Postema, '"Protestant" Interpretation and Social Practices' (1987) 6 *Law and Philosophy* 283.

[122] R Dworkin, *Freedom's Law: The Moral Reading of the American Constitution* (Cambridge, Harvard University Press, 1996) 7.

[123] R Dworkin, *Sovereign Virtue: The Theory and Practice of Equality* (Cambridge, Harvard University Press, 2000).

[124] Allan, *The Sovereignty of Law* (n 12) 44.

[125] ibid 45.

[126] ibid 35–36.

[127] ibid 206–207.

[128] ibid 5.

the suggestion that judges might defer to administrative interpretations of law, saying that the legitimate scope of administrative authority 'depends on an appraisal of all the circumstances' to be conducted by an independent judiciary laser-focused on an 'analysis of the reasons for and against upholding the constitutional challenge presented'.[129] Accordingly, the legality of an administrative decision depends on whether a judge concludes that it is justified in light of all the circumstances, which renders doctrinal distinctions (eg, appeal/review, process/substance, administrative law/constitutional law, standards of review/standards of legality, *Wednesbury* reasonableness/proportionality, etc) distracting, unhelpful or misleading.[130] The responsibility of the judiciary, it seems, is to determine the correct constitutional balance between public policy and individual rights, and to assess the legality of an administrative decision according to that judicially-determined litmus test.

However, at other times, Allan appears to be more congenial to the suggestion that judges also have good reasons for deferring to administrative interpretations of law that are fair and reasonably justified. Writing in this vein, he concedes that '[c]ourts must … accept the legality of government action that lies within the jurisdiction of the public authority concerned', which implies 'a discretion to choose whichever one best accords in its own judgement with the public interest'.[131] Thus, 'a court may be dependent, to some degree, on the authority's own expertise or experience when it determines the range of permissible state action'.[132] Furthermore, he agrees that the legitimate scope of judicial review cannot be mapped onto anything like Wade's distinction between principle and policy, because 'judges and legislators alike must often address both kinds of standard'.[133] Nevertheless, he rejects arguments in favour of a common law doctrine of judicial deference, because 'the relevant considerations of constitutional legitimacy and institutional expertise are already implicit constraints on judicial review – reflected in ordinary legal reasoning or met by an application of legal principle sensitive to the circumstances of the particular case'.[134]

5. Conclusion

Regardless of one's jurisprudential leanings, there seems to be broad support for Allan's claim that in order to understand the normative foundations of law, one should consider the subject from the internal perspective of critically-engaged participants. Compliance with the law, on this view, is secured through legal reasoning rather than the sheer coercive power of the state. Furthermore, once one begins to consider the familiar sources of law that are the stock and trade of public lawyers – legislation, common law precedent, and administrative law – from an internal perspective, one will inevitably be drawn into substantive debates regarding moral or political justification of relevant legal principles in the context of a particular case.

[129] ibid 273.
[130] ibid 24–250.
[131] ibid 268.
[132] ibid.
[133] ibid 281.
[134] ibid 241.

However, the internal perspective also seems to involve another, equally important institutional dimension regarding the distribution of responsibility for resolving interpretive disputes. While it might be tempting to assume that common law courts have exclusive authority to determine the content of the law, we should probe the moral and political justification for that assumption from the internal perspective of critically-engaged participants as well. Among other things, participants deserve a reasonable account that explains the role of an independent judiciary in a constitutional democracy that includes legislatures and administrative decision-makers. Over the last century, administrative law scholars have provided principled responses to interesting and profound questions about the legitimacy of administrative law, which are of immense practical importance today. The answers we give to those questions directly impact how a constitutional democracy can effectively regulate market power and distribute public goods and services (like education and healthcare) that are essential to individual freedom and well-being. When considering these arguments, public law theorists should absolutely weigh and consider them from an internal perspective. But an internal perspective of administrative law might have important implications for the practice of judicial review.

18

The Public Service, Democracy and the Rule of Law

JANET McLEAN*

1. Introduction

In *The Sovereignty of Law*, Trevor Allan examines the constitutional foundations of judicial review of administrative action. He seeks to identify a nuanced path between those who argue that the rule of law is rooted exclusively in the common law, and those who seek to found the constitutional bedrock in legislative intent (treated as a place-holder for democracy). His argument is that the rule of law and democracy 'operate in harness, each affirming and reinforcing the other'.[1] He goes on to argue that 'the adherence of public authorities to certain elementary standards of legality is itself a democratic precept, operating within the constraints of the rule of law'.[2] In this chapter, I argue that a focus on the public service in Westminster systems may help us to elaborate some of the ways in which the rule of law and democracy work, or should work, in harness.

It is increasingly common in an age of extreme partisan politics to think of democracy and the rule of law in oppositional terms. If the part of public servants within this tension is considered at all, public servants tend to be viewed as having interests identical to their Ministers, to share their Ministers' democratic credentials, and to depend on democratic authorisation for all that they do. The rule of law tends to be viewed as constraining and modifying their actions in precisely the same way as it does political actors. Were public servants to act or counsel against the wishes of or independently of Ministers, according to this oppositional view, they would risk accusations of anti-democratic behaviour.

Such a view treats Ministers and public servants as an undifferentiated whole. It exaggerates the degree to which the functions of the public service are democratically authorised by legislation and by Ministerial direction (and often treats these as equivalents). It fails to distinguish between legislating and governing. It leaves unexamined

* Thanks to the Marsden Fund for supporting this project and to Nathan Pinder for research assistance.

[1] TRS Allan, *The Sovereignty of Law: Freedom, Constitution, and Common Law* (Oxford, Oxford University Press, 2013) 209.

[2] ibid 227.

and unacknowledged difficult questions about the different ways in which the legislature, Ministers and public servants are 'representative'[3] and also about whether and how it is possible to adapt government under direct democracy to government under representative democracy. This chapter asks what if instead of viewing public servants as a direct instrument of a Minister's will, we were to view the public service in Westminster systems as mediating between Parliament and Ministers on the one hand and citizens on the other? Once we disaggregate officials from Ministers it may be easier to discern democracy and the rule of law working together in harness.

Viewing the public service as separate from the politically elected executive helps us to consider executive power and its exercise as normatively distinct from legislative power, and as engaging different modes of deliberation. Rather than exclusively viewing the rule of law as constraining and modifying the actions of the executive as an undifferentiated whole, we should also regard the rule of law as constituting the relationship *between* Ministers and public servants. Obligations on public servants to obey the law, offer free and frank dispassionate advice, and to bring knowledge and evidence to policy-making, are a part of what transforms collective will into authority. And that is the case whether the sovereign will is manifested in a monarchy, aristocracy or democracy. A democratically elected legislature cannot eliminate nor cure all problems. It may indeed make some problems worse. Imagine how oppressive it would be if all administrative decisions were made according to majoritarian principles. That would turn everything into a kind of bill of attainder. General laws help maintain impersonal rule, but different legal techniques are required to maintain consistency of treatment and impartial impersonal rule and deliberation where individual administrative decision making is concerned.

Upon reflection we may also consider that the relationship between Ministers and public servants when governing rather than legislating in Westminster constitutions remains significantly monarchical in style and rationale. The rule of law may be viewed in that sphere as operating to support public servants when acting under the direction of and deliberating with elected politicians, as helping them to maintain a degree of protection from ministerial overreach, as supporting the maintenance of impersonal rule and professionalism among public servants themselves (constituting the official), and as enabling government in the public interest beyond the immediate electoral cycle. Law then has and should have a role in regulating the proper connection between sovereign right and its exercise – something the doctrine of ministerial responsibility cannot do on its own.

2. The Orthodox View: No Separate Constitutional Identity Apart from Ministers

New Zealand, British and Canadian constitutional lawyers do not routinely differentiate between the public service and Ministers when we talk about the central ministries and

[3] The classic work on this topic is still H Pitkin, *The Concept of Representation* (California, University of California Press, 1967).

departments of the executive.[4] We tend to treat the public service as synonymous with the political executive. In this way, Ministers lend their democratic credentials to public servants. The public service's interests are treated as the same as those of their Ministers whoever those ministers may be for the time being. Public servants owe Ministers the utmost loyalty. Indeed, the orthodox contemporary view has been that the public service as such has no constitutional personality or responsibility separate from the duly constituted government of the day.

There are several apparently authoritative statements to this effect. In the United Kingdom, the 1997 Armstrong statement on ministerial accountability noted that 'ministers have a duty to parliament to account, and be held to account, for the policies, decisions and actions of their departments and executive agencies'.[5] Armstrong went further to state that '[c]ivil servants are servants of the Crown. For all practical purposes the Crown in this context means and is represented by the Government of the Day. *The civil service as such has no constitutional personality or responsibility separate from the duly constituted government of the day*'[6] (emphasis added).

The Canadian Treasury Board seemed to adopt Armstrong's conclusion about the public service's absence of a distinct constitutional identity in its 2005 'Review of the Responsibilities and Accountabilities of Ministers and Civil Servants':

> The role of the Public Service is to advance loyally and efficiently the agenda of the government of the day without compromising the non-partisan status that is needed to provide continuity and service to successive governments with different political priorities and of different political stripes. In order to do this, public servants must provide candid, professional advice that is free of both partisan considerations and fear of political criticism, which in turn requires that they remain outside of the political realm. But, while public servants provide advice, the democratically elected Ministers have the final say, and public servants must obey the lawful directions of their Minister. In short, all government departments, and all public servants who work for them, must be responsible to a Minister who in turn is responsible to Parliament. Were this not so, the result would be government by the unelected. In keeping with these principles, *public servants have no identity independent of their Minister*.[7] (emphasis added)

The standard formal democratic account of the executive in Westminster jurisdictions, then, goes something like this: Ministers, by definition, enjoy the confidence of the House of elected Representatives. Ministers have a duty to parliament to account, and to be held to account, for the policies, decisions and actions of their departments and executive agencies. While Civil servants are at common law servants of the Crown, for all practical purposes the Crown in this context means and is represented by the Government of the day. Public servants do the legislature's bidding and failing that the Minister's bidding. Public servants have no minds of their own under this view. They are dependent on the animating minds of either the legislature or Ministers. Even on its

[4] Independent agencies, tribunals, commissions, and particular officials such as the police and law officers and statutorily empowered officials are more likely to have their constitutional independence recognised to varying degrees. My focus is on public servants directly answerable to Ministers.

[5] Sir Robert Armstrong, Note by the Head of the Home Civil Service, *The Duties and Responsibilities of Civil Servants in Relation to Ministers* (London, Cabinet Office, 1985, amended 1996) (Armstrong Memorandum).

[6] ibid.

[7] Treasury Board of Canada, 'Review of the Responsibilities and Accountabilities of Ministers and Senior Officials' *Treasury Board of Canada Website* (25 November 2009) tbs-sct.canada.ca.

face this formulation is perplexing – how can the public service provide independent professional advice when it has no separate identity?

Without acknowledging the dilemma, the *Carltona* doctrine apparently squares the circle by imputing the actions, and sometimes more problematically what is in the mind of the public servant, to the Minister.[8] The Minister remains responsible to Parliament for choosing a sufficiently senior and competent official to perform the task as well as for the decision itself. Lord Donaldson in *Oladehinde* suggested that 'the civil servant acts not as a delegate, but as the alter ego, of the secretary of state'.[9] This remarkable elision of the political figure of the Minister with the permanent impartial non-partisan official tends to discourage lawyers from looking inside the black box that contains the executive. The combined force of these doctrines suggests that the statutory authority conferred on Ministers is presumptively distributed throughout the bureaucracy, but political accountability for such actions is concentrated in the person of the Minister, as if that power had never been so distributed. Doubts have recently been raised about the presumptive status of the doctrine in the UK Supreme Court case of *R v Adams*.[10] And legislative delegation provisions may, of course, sometimes displace the *Carltona* doctrine.[11] The point remains that the *Carltona* doctrine contributes to the elision between the political and public service parts of the executive.

The orthodox approach thus imagines a kind of democratic chain of command – starting with the people, the legislature, then the executive as an undifferentiated whole. Treating the political executive and the public service administration as a single entity in this way has a certain logic. It lends democratic legitimacy to the public service, reinforces the political responsibility of Ministers, and is a pragmatic response to the complexities of modern government. But doing so also has the effect of underplaying the constitutional nature of the relationship *between* public servants and Ministers. There is also a great deal that these orthodox explanations of the executive's place in the democratic chain of command fail to capture or explain. For example:

1. Cabinet is not just another committee of Parliament. It is quite distinct in its origins, operation, status, powers and means of selection. And while it is true that in some Westminster constitutions Ministers have to be elected members of the lower House, this is not necessarily the case in the United Kingdom and Canada where Cabinet ministers can be drawn from the unelected Upper House.
2. Only a small percentage of legislation changes as government changes – most legislation stays in force regardless of the party in power. Government is worth winning because primary legislation does not always or usually incorporate government policy but as often allocates and defines powers among various officials – to facilitate, empower and proceduralise rather than to mandate particular policies or

[8] *Carltona v Commissioners of Works* [1943] 2 All ER 560. See the problems associated with this view explored by Sedley LJ in *R v National Association of Health Stores v Health Department* [2005] EWHC Civ 154 (2005).

[9] *R v Secretary of State, ex parte Oladehinde* [1991] 1 AC 254.

[10] *R v Adams* [2020] UKSC 19. The case considered whether to be valid an interim custody order under the detention of Terrorists Northern Ireland Order 1975 had to be considered personally by the Secretary of State.

[11] See eg Public Service Act 2020 (NZ) and Interpretation Act 1985 (Canada). For the latter see HL Molot, 'The Carltona Doctrine and Recent Amendments to the Interpretation Act' (1994) 26 *Ottawa Law Review* 257, 259.

decisions.[12] Legislation frequently contains provisions that leave open to different governments the exercise of wide discretion and the application of a range of policies.

3. There are an increasing number of government agencies for which Ministers have little direct responsibility. Even when there is a responsible Minister, public servant chief executives are increasingly delegated large powers and made publicly answerable for their exercise. Indeed, in the United Kingdom, permanent secretaries (in Australia and New Zealand called chief executives, and in Canada deputy Ministers) are now responsible and answerable in Parliament for their budgets. (The electorate's expectations of ministerial responsibility tend, however, to be resilient despite attempts to create independent agencies).
4. Only a small percentage of government policy originates within the contemporary party in government or is directly mandated by the electorate. Most executive activity is not directed from the top down but either originates in the bureaucracy, or continues despite changes in government.
5. Only a small percentage of the budget allocation changes when the government changes.[13]
6. Ministers routinely delegate their powers *to act* to the administration – which raises questions of what theory of representation should apply to their delegates so acting. Even more difficult to explain, is how the public service is able to provide independent, professional, free and frank *advice* to Ministers and to be protected when they do so if they enjoy no separate identity from the government of the day.
7. All the different forms of public service legislation in NZ, Australia, Canada and UK acknowledge that the public service owes duties directly to the public and not just through Ministers – though no one seems to be completely sure of what these duties are or how they should be made manifest.
8. Finally, how can it be that public servants do not have separate constitutional identity from that of the government of the day when it is public servants who have constitutional responsibility for keeping government working during caretaking periods between an election being held and a new government being formed, and serve key roles in the enforcement of other constitutional conventions. In what is their *most* democratic and constitutional role, public servants must *counsel* and at times *act* independently of Ministers holding legal but not constitutional powers.

In short, the fiction that the permanent public service has no separate identity from Ministers provides the public service with a degree of democratic camouflage. It exaggerates its credentials in terms of democratic *authorisation* and it does not allow any explicit place for its proper independence and professionalism in upholding the state's long-term values and interests. What if we were instead to imagine public servants as serving a mediating role between ministers and the public?

[12] EL Rubin, 'Law and Legislation in the Administrative State' (1989) 89 *Columbia Law Review* 369.

[13] J Heath, *The Machinery of Government: Administration and the Liberal State* (New York, Oxford University Press, 2020) 61; G Steele, *What I Learned About Politics* (Halifax, Nimbus, 2014) 120–21.

3. How Democratic is the Public Service?

If the idea that the public service is authorised and commanded through a chain of democratic command is an exaggeration of the way in which things work in practice, in which other respects can it be said that the public service qua public service manifests democratic qualities?

One important respect in which the public service in Westminster systems has often been described as democratic is that, while it is permanent in the sense that it does not change when the government changes, it is required 'to serve equally well governments of different political persuasions'.[14] The challenges involved in maintaining its capacity to advise a future government of different ideological hues should not be underestimated – especially given the immediate and ever-present demands of efficiency. A public service used to solving problems by leaving them to the market is unlikely to have well-developed strategies and capacities for government intervention, and a public service used to acting may not be good at supervising contractors. There will be difficult practical difficulties in maintaining government *capacity* to advise different sets of policies and in ensuring that political neutrality or more accurately 'serial partisanship' does not tip into partisanship simpliciter.[15]

The nineteenth century reforms to the UK public service instituting the appointment and later promotion of (male) public servants on merit were sometimes described as 'democratic' though the term was not necessarily used as a compliment at the time.[16] The Northcote and Trevelyan report and associated reforms,[17] adopted in other Westminster systems, were in part a response to the perceived aristocratic tory dominance of English officialdom, and to policies of patronage as well as religious exclusion.[18] By the twentieth century, public sector employment was often in the equality vanguard in attempting to attract a diverse and inclusive workforce representative of the polity more generally.

If the public service has over time become more internally representative of the polity, however, it is more difficult to identify whom it serves. We might have expected in a democracy that the public service should ultimately serve the public or perhaps even Parliament, and there are certain, mainly symbolic, acknowledgments that that is the case among Westminster jurisdictions.

Modern public service legislation in Australia, New Zealand, and Canada acknowledges in different ways that public servants ultimately serve the community, the people or the public. Section 3 (a) of the Australian Public Service Act 1999 mentions public

[14] Civil Service Code 2015: gov.uk/government/publications/civil-service-code/the-civil-service-code.

[15] Richard Mulgan suggests that it is more accurate to say that the public service demonstrates serial partisanship rather than impartiality: R Mulgan, 'How much responsiveness is too much or too little?' (2008) 67 *Australian Journal of Public Administration* 345–56. For the tensions that sometimes arise, see *Peters v Attorney-General* [2021] NZCA 355.

[16] Submission to Northcote-Trevelyan Report by Rev Charles Graves Professor of Maths Dublin University reproduced in Parliamentary Papers (1854) at 22.

[17] Northcote-Trevelyan Report on the Organisation of the Permanent Civil Service (London, Eyre and Spottiswoode, 1854) reproduced in Appendix 3, *Fulton Report 1968: The Civil Service 1: Report of the Committee* 1966–1968 (1968) 108–31.

[18] See evidence of Alfred Power Esq Chief Commissioner for Poor Laws Ireland to the Northcote-Trevelyan report (n 16) 87.

servants as serving Parliament and the Australian public along with Ministers. The preamble to the Canadian Act[19] refers to the public service as 'achieving results for Canadians' and recognises the accountability of public servants to the Public Service Commission and to Parliament (though surprisingly not explicitly to Ministers). In New Zealand there are legislative provisions which also require the public service to brief Ministers on the longer-term interests of the state beyond the short parliamentary term (independently of the views of the government of the day and through consultation with the public).[20]

Modern attempts to bolster the democratic workings of the public service have included techniques to connect the public service with the different publics they serve. These have included the adoption of freedom of information legislation and privacy codes, the creation of citizen's charters and service commitments, complaints procedures and the encouragement or requirement of public participation in policy development through statutory duties to consult. Human rights legislation serves to reinforce the equality of the individual, and special measures have been adopted (often legislatively) to encourage the participation of colonised indigenous peoples.[21] These initiatives tend to interrupt the hierarchical relationship between public servants and Ministers and create obligations directly between public servants and the public.

Despite these attempts to adapt the bureaucracy to modern representative democracy, in practice and by convention the public service owes its primary duties of loyalty and confidence to Ministers. Indeed, modern relationships between officials and rulers still bear a lot in common with those of monarchical times. The public service serves Ministers. The considerable resources of the public service are used almost exclusively to advise *Ministers*, not legislatures or the public more generally. Such advice happens mostly in private often under conditions of confidence and Ministers in large part maintain control over how much and which of that advice is revealed to Parliament and to the public – just as monarchs used to do. In Australia and the United Kingdom in particular, the most senior public servants are at risk of dismissal if they displease their Ministers.

Public servants are less anonymous than they once were and increasingly appear in the media, present evidence to Select Committees, and in the UK take responsibility for budgetary matters in Parliament. In all of these guises, however, public servants represent the Minister and their departments and are unable to defend themselves personally, or to defend any 'independent' role they may have. It is as the orthodox view predicts – public servants do not enjoy any distinct constitutional identity for these purposes.

From a public servant's perspective, their relationship with Ministers is in many ways like the relationship of officials and advisors to princesses or princes. Of course, in comparison to rule by hereditary princes, representative democracy takes some of the luck out of executive government. While the people need no longer only to rely

[19] Public Service Employment Act 2003 (Canada). The Act now codifies the extent to which public servants are able to pursue their own political views in Part 7.

[20] Public Service Act 2020 (NZ) Schedule 6 cls 8 and 9.

[21] See eg R Stacey, 'Honour in Sovereignty: Can Crown Consultations with Indigenous Peoples Erase Canada's Sovereignty Deficit?' (2018) 68 *University of Toronto Law Journal* 405.

on 'tears and prayers'[22] to protect them from the arbitrary qualities of the individual who happens to fill the office of ruler or to fear infant kings or childless monarchs, Ministers remain 'birds of passage' (as Bagehot called them).[23] Ministers switch in and out of roles and like princes vary greatly in their knowledge, education and capacity for good rule. And whereas the favourites of a monarch are few, the favourites who may be tempted to serve the private interests and kindred of an elected government are many.[24]

The mediating role of public servants is required for reasons which both long predate the advent of representative democracy as well as for reasons particular to democracy and the potential excesses associated with majority rule. It is the former reasons which relate to relationships between politicians and advisers which I am primarily concerned with here. Centuries of medieval and humanist thought considered the role of officials as being to lead princes to virtue, as the conveyors of knowledge to the omnipotent, as preserving stability as monarchs changed with the succession, as contributing capacity to legitimacy and as ensuring that the exercise of power was impersonal and hence not a form of arbitrary and capricious personal rule.[25] To be a judge in one's own cause was one of the earliest grounds on which to impugn a decision under the common law. Good counsel conveyed by officials was what distinguished the King from the tyrant. Counsel contributed to turning sovereign will (with its potential to be capricious, inconsistent, and arbitrary) into sovereign authority. In many respects public servants still serve these roles in representative democracies. Importantly, it is primarily the *law* that can and does assist them in doing so. Recourse to law helps to maintain trust between the ruler and official while at the same time defining limits in relation to what a loyal official may be called to do.

Democratic authorisation cannot and should not be treated as curing all the problems associated with governing. Among other things, principles of legality help to regulate the relationship between Ministers and officials and in doing so they encapsulate a collective view of morality rather than leaving matters to the individual conscience of a particular official, or, indeed, Minister.

Sometimes accounts of classical (direct) democracy are used to suggest that parliamentarians collectively bring their own rich knowledge and collective wisdom to bear on decision-making and thus there is no need for the mediating role formerly played by humanist counsel to Kings by a modern public service in a representative democracy. Such a view fails to distinguish between legislating and governing, between sovereign right and its exercise. In the next section, I explore further the ways in which sovereign right may be democratic but its exercise may be more monarchical in style, and how the law can help to align the public and private interests of Ministers and their officials.

[22] IWS Campbell, 'Calvinist Absolutism: Archbishop James Ussher and Royal Power' (2014) 53 *Journal of British Studies* 588, 590.

[23] W Bagehot, *The English Constitution* (Fontana Classics of History and Thought, 1973 [1867]) 200.

[24] Adapted from T Hobbes, *Leviathan* (Oxford, Clarendon Press, 1651) 195.

[25] See J McLean 'Good Counsel as a Constitutional Imperative' in E Carolan, JNE Varuhas and S Fulham-McQuillan, *The Making and Re-Making of Public Law* (Oxford, Hart Publishing, forthcoming).

4. A Distinction between Sovereignty and Government

Sovereign right in Westminster constitutions may have its foundations in democracy but the way sovereign power is exercised may, at times, scarcely resemble direct or representative democracy at all. This is an old and profound insight. There is a tradition going back to Jean Bodin, which maintains a distinction between sovereignty and government.[26] Bodin suggests that the sovereign can be a monarchy, a democracy or an aristocracy but the government need not share those same characteristics.[27] Indeed, he thinks that a separation between sovereignty and government helps to put in place a system of impersonal rule which is a way of avoiding tyranny. In a similar vein, Thomas Hobbes suggests that 'the advantages and disadvantages of a regime [meaning a monarchy, aristocracy or democracy] do not depend on him in whom the authority of the commonwealth resides but upon the Ministers of the sovereignty'.[28] By Ministers here, Hobbes means to refer to those who *exercise* the right or power rather than to those in whom the right or power resides.[29] Further, like Bodin, Hobbes emphasises the importance of maintaining this distinction. According to Hobbes the separation of right and its exercise is in the natural order of things. Just as God sets things in motion but leaves the actions of judging and deciding to others, right and its exercise ought to be distinguished.[30] Blackstone later reiterated this. Sovereigns ideally should not act.[31]

We can see how in practical as well as prudential terms a monarch is unlikely to be able to both make law and to execute it. Equally, as Rousseau suggests, it is difficult to see how without maintaining a distinction between sovereign right and sovereign exercise, ancient democracy could ever be given a modern representative institutional form. An ancient democracy where citizens were involved in deciding all of the policies could not even be implemented in a city the size of Geneva during Rousseau's time.[32]

Once we are prepared to accept that there is a distinction between sovereignty and government, the suggestion that the public service is not all that democratic does not necessarily convey a criticism. There is something almost inevitable about that. Maintaining a separation between sovereignty and government may also signal that government administration across different political systems may in many cases share a great deal more in common than we may have originally thought – as indeed Hobbes acknowledged.

[26] J Bodin, *Six Books of the Commonwealth*, MJ Tooley trans (Oxford, Basil Blackwell, 1967 [1606]) 74.

[27] J Bodin, *Six Bookes of a Commonweale*, R Knolles trans, K McRae ed (Cambridge, Harvard University Press, 1962 [1606]) 50.

[28] T Hobbes, *De Cive*, x 16 trans R Tuck, *The Sleeping Sovereign: The Invention of Modern Democracy* (Cambridge, Cambridge University Press, 2015) 92.

[29] ibid.

[30] ibid ch 13 (XIII.1) 96.

[31] Blackstone quoting Locke refers to the 'harm which the sovereign can do in his own person not being likely to happen often, nor to extend itself far, nor being able by his single strength to subvert the laws, nor oppress the body of his people': Sir William Blackstone, Book I *Commentaries on the Laws of England* (Dublin, Exshaw, 1765) 236.

[32] Rousseau Letter to Beaumont, Letters Written From the Mountain quoted by R Tuck, *The Sleeping Sovereign* (n 28) 2.

To illustrate the last point, consider the controversy about who public servants serve – Ministers, parliament or the public? At common law, public servants are regarded as servants of the Crown. This is still the position in the United Kingdom. The other Westminster jurisdictions by statute grant appointment powers to Public Service Commissions and heads of agencies – rather than Ministers directly. In the UK, Canada, Australia and NZ, the employee-like duties of loyalty and confidentiality of public servants to Ministers have their *origins* in constitutional conventions rather than deriving from the employer-employee relationship itself. The relationship between Ministers and civil servants then, is at its foundations constituted by constitutional norms.

These ambiguities about whom the public servant serves were explored in the Supreme Court of Canada case of *Fraser v Public Service Staff Relations Board*.[33] Dickson CJ would have allowed public servants a measure of legal protection when making certain kinds of public criticisms of governments (eg. about the legality of government's actions, or threats to the life, health or safety of the public) even in the absence of whistleblower legislation.[34] Lorne Sossin reads the Court as 'recognising that the civil servant's duty of loyalty to the Crown, and through the Crown to the public interest, must in some circumstances be a higher obligation than the duty of loyalty owed to the government of the day'.[35] Much of the case law actually finds against public servants who speak out[36] (that includes Mr Fraser whose concern was to warn against the evils of metrification). Nevertheless, the idea that public servants owe a higher duty to the public interest and the people (the contemporary political sovereign) 'will not die'.[37]

The notion that public servants are servants of the Crown representing the people owes as much to medieval and early modern theories of monarchy as it does to democracy. Judicial decisions can be found even in the eighteenth century which talk about the duties administrative officials owe to the public as servants of the Crown and emphasise that the concept of office recognises such obligations as a matter of law.[38]

The problem has long been acknowledged as an issue in political thought. Fully embracing the idea that public servants serve two masters (their political superior on the one hand, and the public interest on the other) is potentially a recipe for anarchy if it routinely leaves individual public servants to assess independently of Ministers where the public interest lies. How can we be sure that the public servant is not herself acting in self-interest or to usurp the ruler? The answer was at one time thought to lie in ensuring that both rulers and counsellors were wise and virtuous – by education, philosophy and religion. Hobbes was the first to offer a more modern solution.

The counsellor, Hobbes says, must advise the sovereign representative according to the sovereign's interests and not his own. The ends and interests of the counsellor should not be inconsistent with the ends and interests of 'him he counselleth'. Importantly for Hobbes the interests of the sovereign representative are always two-fold. The natural

[33] [1985] 2 SCR 455.

[34] There are now legislative provisions in Canadian Public Service Employment Act 2003, Part 7.

[35] L Sossin, 'Speaking Truth to Power? The Search for Bureaucratic Independence in Canada' (2005) 55 *University of Toronto Law Journal* 1,13.

[36] *Fraser v Public Service Staff Relations Board* [1985] 2 SCR 455; *Comcare v Banerji* [2019] HCA 23.

[37] RAW Rhodes and P Weller, *The Changing World of Top Officials* (Oxford, Oxford University Press, 2001) 118.

[38] See J McLean, 'Authority of the Administration' in E Fisher et al (eds), *The Foundations and Future of Public Law* (Oxford, Oxford University Press, 2020) 59–60.

person or persons who represent(s) the sovereign 'which person the Sovereign bears'[39] seeks to procure both the common interest as well as their own private good. The interests of the people whom the sovereign representative 'bears' go much further than mere self-preservation and include prosperity, riches, honour and reputation.[40] In other words, Hobbes ascribes good intentions to rulers. But, he suggests, if the public and private interests of the sovereign representative are in conflict, there is a real risk that the private interests of the sovereign representative are more likely to be served. The answer to this problem, according to Hobbes, is not to make the advisor choose the public over the private interest as a matter of individual conscience but rather to align the sovereign representative's private interests with the public interest as much as is possible.[41]

These then are problems that exist in all governments wherever the sovereign right resides. And it seems to me that many of the doctrines of judicial review, the general law, constitutional convention and the ethos of the permanent public service work to help align the public interest and the private interests of Ministers and public servants and to regulate the relationship between them. The rule of law enforces the idea of impersonal rule to protect the public from ministers or public servants exploiting power in their own self-interest, helps to guard against ministerial overreach in rewarding political allies or punishing opponents, contributes to conditions which maintain a certain degree of independence and professionalism in the public service (in fact finding, gathering evidence, producing reasoned advice, and interpreting legislation in accordance with fundamental understandings) and helps maintain stability. Public servants are better able properly to resist the demands of their Ministers to whom they owe loyalty and trust when they can rely on their *legal* obligations when doing so. AV Dicey's core rule of law insight still holds.[42] This enhances the ability of public servants to serve the public.

5. Execution and Interpretation and Advice by Officials

As we have already seen, maintaining a distinction between the making and execution of the laws has long been thought to create a system of impersonal rule. Blackstone advocated for the distinction on the basis that where the '*making* and *enforcing* the laws, is vested in one and the same man (or one and the same body of men) … there can be no public liberty'.[43] 'A total union of [legislative and executive functions] would be productive of tyranny', a 'total disjunction of them' would produce the same result given that 'the legislature would gradually assume to itself the rights of executive power'.[44] In terms

[39] Hobbes, *Leviathan* (n 24) 142.

[40] ibid 145.

[41] Hobbes uses these arguments to suggest that public and private interests are best aligned in a monarch. This is because a King's riches honour and glory are likely to arise from the richness strength and reputation of his people. In a democracy or aristocracy by contrast 'the publique prosperity does not confer so much by way of private fortune on one who is corrupt, or ambitious'. Perfidious advice, treacherous action or a civil war may better advance the private good of such natural persons: ibid 144.

[42] AV Dicey, *An Introduction to the Study of the Law of the Constitution*, 10th edn (London, MacMillan, 1959). See more recently MD Walters, *AV Dicey and the Common Law Constitutional Tradition – A Legal Turn of Mind* (Cambridge, Cambridge University Press, 2020).

[43] Blackstone (n 31)142.

[44] ibid 149–50.

reminiscent of Bodin, Blackstone describes certain officials (quite apart from judges) 'concerned in matters [affecting] the liberty of the people' as those whose '*business is to stand between the prerogative and the subject in the execution of the [ ] laws*'[45] (emphasis added). What are the practical implications of that for the mediating role of the public service in contemporary times?

Again Hobbes is helpful. When exercising the executive function, public service officials are representing the sovereign and Hobbes likens them to the joints of the body politic acting on its behalf. But he does not imagine a 'conveyor belt' or chain of sovereign command. When interpreting and applying their legislative powers, Hobbes explains that officials exercise a kind of memory (or we might say 'muscle memory') to so act consistently with longstanding legal principles on behalf of the body politic. Hobbes gives as a reason for this that to do otherwise would be to impute to the legislator an intention to act inconsistently with the law. Fundamentals of law help to align the public and private interests represented by the Minister as well as officials' own.

When advising rulers, by contrast, officials are not acting as sovereign representatives, but independently of them: 'For the advice is addressed to the sovereign only, whose person cannot in his own presence be represented to him, by another'.[46] Hobbes's solution to how the ruler remains in command and yet gives licence for free and frank counsel which licence cannot be withdrawn is innovative and helps to join together the counsellor and counselled while maintaining a distinction between them. The very act of asking for counsel, he says, gives licence to the counsellor to speak freely: 'He that asked it, cannot in equity accuse or punish it'.[47] He goes further to say '[a]nd generally he that demandeth counsel, is the *Author* of it and cannot punish it and what the sovereign cannot, no one else can'[48] (emphasis added). This use of the idea of authorship in contradistinction to representation (in a way that partially mirrors the discussion of authorship elsewhere in *Leviathan* to explain why subjects must obey the sovereign representative of whose actions they are authors) has the effect of maintaining sovereign right in the counselled but at the same time guaranteeing the conditions for free and frank advice even in cases in which the advice is contrary to majority opinion. Hobbes adds the important condition that counsel too needs to be lawful. This brings rationality into government because, Hobbes says, the reasons to act in accordance with counsel cannot be separated from the reasons offered in its support.[49]

6. Not Necessarily a Judge Looking Over One's Shoulder?

It follows then that the rule of law performs an important role in ensuring public servants obey the legislature through ultra vires doctrines while at the same time supporting

[45] ibid 335.
[46] Hobbes, *Leviathan* (n 24) 188.
[47] ibid 196.
[48] ibid.
[49] See J Paul, *Counsel and Command in Early Modern English Thought* (Cambridge, Cambridge University Press, 2020); M Walters, 'Judicial Review of Ministerial Advice to the Crown' (2016) 25 *Constitutional Forum* 33–42.

the public service's mediating role between the sovereign and the subject.[50] The rule of law, then, simultaneously protects the public against overreach by public servants *and* protects public servants from ministerial overreach.[51] It gives public servants the institutional resources to maintain a certain degree of independence. This is not always obvious. That is in part because an important means by which law does all of these things is by imputing good intentions to the ruler or legislator.[52]

The popular description of judicial review of administrative action performing the role of 'the judge looking over one's shoulder' fails to capture these nuances. The ethics and calling of public servants and the doctrines of judicial review are more aligned than we usually think. Consider the attributes listed in the UK civil service codes of conduct which are explicitly viewed as part of the civil servant's contract of employment.[53] These include: honesty, integrity, objectively 'basing your advice and decisions on rigorous analysis of the evidence', and impartiality defined as 'acting solely according to the merits of the case'. Many of these values are closely aligned to the doctrines of judicial review albeit stated in authentic public service language. Public servants acting consistently with such values are not merely obeying law imposed on them from outside by the courts by way of judicial review doctrine. These are norms made into law internalised by and sometimes even originating in the public service itself. They are norms which *constitute* the public service. Judicial review of administrative action (including human rights review) is capable of being considered a means by which to supervise, regulate and also to *support* the public service in maintaining a delicate balance between independence from and responsiveness to Ministers.

Judicial review, then, need not always be characterised as the external imposition on the public service of values and norms that it is commonly thought to be, nor necessarily as the sole source of those values. Focusing on the public service as a separate constitutional entity allows us to view judicial review not so much as an imposition on the public service or on democracy but as a support for public service impartiality and professionalism in the public interest.

Accountability in a public forum is a particular feature of direct democracy – as opposed to other systems of government. That being so, it is right for public lawyers in Westminster systems to highlight the importance of ministerial responsibility to parliament for the actions of their officials in the way that they do. Leaving aside the usual issues about whether ministerial responsibility to parliament is sufficiently adequate, consistent and detailed, it is hard to see how ministerial responsibility to parliament could support the relationship between public servants and ministers in the way that judicial review does.

There remains an outstanding question about what place constitutional conventions have within these rule of law norms. The most obvious example of an 'independence

[50] See further J McLean, 'Between Sovereign and Subject: The Constitutional Position of the Official' (2020) 70 *University of Toronto Law Journal* 167.

[51] ibid.

[52] D Dyzenhaus, 'Deliberative Constitutionalism Through the Lens of the Administrative State' in R Levy et al (eds), *Cambridge Handbook of Deliberative Constitutionalism* (Cambridge, Cambridge University Press, 2018) 44, 53.

[53] Made under Constitutional Reform and Governance Act 2010 (UK), s 5. There are separate codes for the devolved governments.

convention' which constrains a public servant's loyalty to the government of the day is the caretaking convention. In New Zealand the caretaking convention is understood to take effect after an election but before a new government is sworn in.[54] It operates to restrict the legally constituted outgoing government from initiating major new policies or taking major decisions. It is enforced by political actors and failing that by senior public servants rather than the courts. The ability of public servants to resist lawful instructions from a validly elected government during a caretaking government is assisted by the fact that the relationship between Ministers and civil servants is not strictly an employer-employee one. According to the common law of agency, an employee agent has little discretion but to follow the directions of his or her principal. Contextual agents though, which public servants arguably are, have a much greater ability to resist even lawful instructions.[55] This is an important practical respect in which the public service, like the Crown, has a permanence beyond that of the government of the day. This 'independence' convention, like that of the loyalty convention itself has a democratic rationale.

Created by the practices and norms of political and administrative officials,[56] these binding constitutional rules are specifically addressed to officials and are constitutive of sovereign institutions. On such constitutive principles public servants and Ministers respectively form their own critical internal points of view. Public servants do not simply reflect the views (or the commands) of Ministers in respect of such norms. What prospects are there for the public service to act independently of Ministers in accordance with their constitutional obligations when it really matters for democratic legitimacy, if they are unused to any degree of independence in the ordinary course of things? The political and legal aspects of the Constitution are intimately connected. In both political and legal spheres the public servant performs a mediating role.

7. Conclusion

We are not used to thinking of the public service as a constitutional entity separate from the government of the day: Ministers remain responsible for the actions of public servants in Parliament; public servants have no separate political accountability to the public. The orthodox view, however, does not fully acknowledge the constitutional aspects of the public service, its importance for the delivery of impersonal rule and its mediating role between rulers and the public when executing the law, or giving free and frank advice.

The rule of law and democracy operate in harness. But that does not necessarily mean that the rule of law always advances democracy per se. Many of the problems which the rule of law addresses arise in relation to government whether the form of

[54] New Zealand Cabinet Office *Cabinet Manual 2017* at para 1.30.

[55] F Reynolds and PG Watts, *Bowstead and Reynolds on Agency*, 22nd edn (online ed, Thomson Reuters, 2021) 2-031.

[56] On whether constitutional conventions are law, see J Waldron, 'Are Constitutional Norms Legal Norms?' (2006–2007) 75 *Fordham Law Review* 1697 and P Cane, 'Public Law in the Concept of Law' (2013) 33 *OJLS* 649.

government is democratic, aristocratic or monarchical. The rule of law has an essential role to play in regulating the relationships between those institutions in which sovereign right resides and those who exercise it.

A failure to distinguish between ministers and the public service as distinct constitutional entities results in an exaggeration of how much the public service is explicitly authorised by democratic means. Representative democracy cannot and does not by itself address every aspect of good rule. Once we acknowledge a distinction between sovereignty and government or sovereign right and its exercise, we can better discern how much contemporary government in Westminster systems owes to its monarchical origins, and the continued relevance of the need for officials to exercise a mediating role between rulers and the people in order to align the public and private interests of official actors.

Judicial review, in particular, plays an important role in aligning the public and private interests of individuals in power so that public servants do not have to choose for themselves which of those interests they must serve while at the same time maintaining loyalty to Ministers. It indirectly polices the degree to which the public service ought to be responsive to Ministers and acts as a buttress against undue political pressures that Ministers may be tempted to exert. In obeying both legislation and the common law, public servants have a legitimate means of maintaining their constitutional independence from Ministers on behalf of the public.

19

A Defence of Administrative Law Doctrine

PAUL DALY*

1. Introduction

In his poem 'Easter 1916', WB Yeats warns us: 'Too long a sacrifice / Can make a stone of the heart'. Yeats was writing of the culmination of revolutionary Irish nationalism in the bloody uprising of 1916. Dogged adherence to an ideal can cause true believers to lose sight of the human cost of their actions. When reading the scholarship of Professor TRS Allan, the ghost of Yeats often comes whispering to my mind.[1] Common law judges must, Professor Allan advises, engage in moral reasoning in each and every case that comes before them. Judges should not adhere to doctrinal rules that prevent case-by-case reasoning and close assessment of relevant moral considerations. Too long a sacrifice in adhering to doctrinal rules would make a stone of the heart by removing morality from common law adjudication.

But Yeats was ambivalent about Easter 1916, closing with a poignant observation: 'A terrible beauty is born'. We might also be ambivalent about an approach to common law adjudication that values morally optimal outcomes in individual cases over legal certainty. Reasoning from case-to-case without regard for doctrine is its own type of 'terrible beauty'.

As it happens, Professor Allan too is ambivalent about doctrine. Doctrine fits uneasily in his theory of law: on the one hand, for Professor Allan, 'law' is the *outcome* of a process of all-things-considered moral reasoning which takes account of all relevant factors; but on the other hand, Professor Allan's scholarship is firmly anchored in a common law tradition which limits the scope for moral reasoning by committing lawyers to protecting a 'set of norms'.[2] This uneasy fit is reflected in Professor Allan's scholarship: he has assailed administrative law doctrine as 'empty' and 'pernicious' but

* With thanks to Geneviève Cartier and Mark Walters for organising this wonderful collection. I have referred throughout to the excellent chapters of my fellow contributors.

[1] With apologies to Patrick Kavanagh: 'Epic' in P Kavanagh, *Collected Poems* (New York, Devin Adair, 1967).

[2] See P Cane, 'TRS Allan and Common Law Tradition' ch 1 in this volume, Section 1(B).

has nonetheless referred approvingly to 'doctrine' and 'general principles' as features of the common law.[3]

I will argue that there is a place for administrative law doctrine in Professor Allan's theory. Properly understood, administrative law doctrine is not empty, notwithstanding Professor Allan's powerful critiques. Nor is administrative law doctrine pernicious: on the contrary, setting out systemic conceptions of the principles, rules and standards of administrative law advances the rule of law. And, I argue, as long as administrative law doctrine rests on morally recognisable foundations it constrains judges *pro tanto* in their adjudication of individual cases. However, it remains open to the judge to revisit doctrine where their all-things-considered moral judgement demands making an exception to an existing principle, rule or standard or overruling a precedent. Professor Allan is right to channel Yeats's warnings: too long a sacrifice can make a stone of the heart, but one must beware the terrible beauties our philosophical commitments can create.

In Sections 2 and 3, I critically analyse his claim of emptiness, by reference to three propositions found in Professor Allan's work relating to the constitutional foundations of judicial review, the well-known 'heads' of judicial review in Commonwealth jurisdictions (legality, rationality and procedural propriety) and the general principles of judicial review.

In Section 4, I tackle the claim that administrative law doctrine is pernicious because it deflects judicial attention away from the moral, contextual judgement which must be exercised in judicial review cases. Rather, I argue, judicial and scholarly focus on doctrine in administrative law enhances the legitimacy of the judiciary: jurists who develop administrative law doctrine advance rule-of-law desiderata such as generality and clarity. Moreover, doctrine is not a straitjacket rendering the judge incapable of responding to injustice. Situating Professor Allan's scepticism of doctrine in relation to his sophisticated theory of law, I suggest that taking doctrine seriously is not at odds with the pursuit of justice.

On my account, 'doctrine' provides a 'systemic conception' of a particular area of law, setting out the relevant principles, rules and standards in a coherent fashion.[4] In the first instance, the focus of a researcher who is interested in doctrine will be on the 'basic question' of what the law is rather than what the law ought to be.[5] Developing a systemic conception involves 'the examination of primary materials in order to reach a conclusion about either a specific problem or a conclusion about a set of rules – a "doctrine" – of general application'.[6] Doctrine can be more or less ambitiously stated: the conclusion can take the form of the simple description of principles, the derivation of a series of principles, the organisation of principles into a coherent scheme, or the development of

[3] See below Section 4.

[4] L McDonald, 'Thinking about Doctrine in Administrative Law' in J Goudkamp, M Lunney and L McDonald (eds), *Taking Law Seriously: Essays in Honour of Peter Cane* (Oxford, Hart Publishing, 2021) 235, *passim*.

[5] J Varuhas, 'Mapping Doctrinal Methods' in P Daly and J Tomlinson (eds), *Researching Public Law in Common Law Systems* (Aldershot, Edward Elgar, 2023) 70, 70.

[6] M Dixon, 'A Doctrinal Approach to Property Law Scholarship: Who Cares and Why?' (2014) 3 *Property Law Review* 160, 162.

an interpretive framework based on the immanent rationality of the principles.[7] In all cases, the goal is to provide a systemic conception.

The target of the systemic conception may vary from the specific to the general. An author might attempt to provide an account of the law relating to 'reasons' as an aspect of the duty of fairness, or 'procedural fairness', or 'judicial review', or 'administrative law', or 'public law'. What I mean when I refer to 'doctrine' in the pages that follow is a systemic conception of the *general principles of judicial review of administrative action*. As I will explain in Sections 2 and 3, the general principles of judicial review of administrative action are an appropriate foil for Professor Allan, as he shows considerable scepticism towards systemic conceptions of administrative law.

There is one last terminological point to make. I use the phrase general principles of judicial review of administrative action interchangeably with the phrase general principles of administrative law. I do this only for ease of exposition: my focus is on judge-made principles, considered in abstraction of how public administration operates, which is sometimes called the 'legality' model of administrative law, in contrast to the 'governance' model targeted at what actually happens on the ground in administrative decision-making environments.[8] Focusing on judge-made principles can only ever give a partial view of the reality of public administration, writ large,[9] but it gives as full a view as possible of judicial review of administrative action, a valuable object of study in its own right.[10]

2. A Critique of Due Deference

Let us begin with 'Human Rights and Judicial Review: A Critique of Due Deference',[11] Professor Allan's extended critique of the burgeoning literature on 'deference' under the Human Rights Act 1998.

Contributors to the literature had suggested that the courts should develop a rigorous doctrinal approach to determining the limits of judicial review of allegedly rights-infringing governmental action.

Professor Allan is sceptical. In his view, the conclusions in any cases arising under the Human Rights Act 1998 'will (or should) be determined by the *substance* of the issues arising, rather than any set of principles operating independently'.[12] As such, any 'doctrine' of deference would invariably be empty or pernicious.[13]

Any 'doctrine' of deference would be empty because constitutional principles such as the separation of powers between the political branches and the judiciary

[7] Varuhas, 'Mapping Doctrinal Methods' (n 5).

[8] R Thomas, *Administrative Law in Action: Immigration Administration* (Oxford, Hart Publishing, 2022) 3–5.

[9] McDonald, 'Thinking about Doctrine in Administrative Law' (n 4).

[10] P Daly, *Understanding Administrative Law in the Common Law World* (Oxford, Oxford University Press, 2021) viii–ix.

[11] TRS Allan, 'Human Rights and Judicial Review: A Critique of Due Deference' (2006) 65 *CLJ* 671.

[12] ibid 674.

[13] ibid 675, 680.

'are already embodied in traditional doctrine' such as *Wednesbury* unreasonableness.[14] Moreover, traditional doctrines such as proportionality and *Wednesbury* unreasonableness involve, in any event, 'contextual analysis', as they are 'not truly distinct modes of review, but only labels for varying degrees of judicial scrutiny along a continuum', with 'more rigorous and sceptical … judicial scrutiny' applied in cases where the threat to and importance of protected rights are relatively greater.[15]

As for perniciousness, Professor Allan sees any 'doctrine' of deference as 'non-justiciability in pastel colours', as it would involve 'an abdication of judicial responsibility for the protection of rights' by virtue of 'reliance on the expertise or experience or public visibility of the decision-maker as opposed to the apparent quality of the decision itself'.[16] In all cases, the 'constitutional duty' of the courts is to 'decide each case, after hearing evidence and argument, in accordance with the reasons that it finds persuasive'.[17] What matters is an assessment of the 'intrinsic quality' of the decision under review.[18]

This is not to say that justifications for deference, such as expertise, which featured heavily in the literature, are irrelevant but simply that they are rolled into the assessment the court must undertake of the 'character and content of the legal questions arising in all the circumstances of the particular case'.[19] Therefore, an 'independent' analysis of deference factors is neither necessary nor appropriate.[20]

In the area of United Kingdom human rights law, Professor Allan's critique was immediately influential. Without citing to Professor Allan, the House of Lords considered it inapt to speak of 'deference' in relation to 'the ordinary judicial task of weighing up the competing considerations on each side and according appropriate weight to the judgment of a person with responsibility for a given subject matter and access to special sources of knowledge and advice'.[21]

I pushed back against Professor Allan's position about the emptiness and perniciousness of deference doctrines in my doctoral thesis. In order to counter the charge of emptiness, I accepted that I would have to demonstrate that 'a doctrine of curial deference is capable of precluding a court from reaching particular conclusions, on the assumption that the preclusion of particular conclusions demonstrates that a doctrine can have effect independently of the context of a particular case'.[22] I then argued by reference to American and Canadian jurisprudence that a doctrine of deference is not empty.[23]

[14] ibid 679.
[15] ibid 686.
[16] ibid 689.
[17] ibid 683.
[18] ibid 688.
[19] TRS Allan, 'Judicial Deference: Doctrine and Theory' (2011) 127 *LQR* 96, 105.
[20] ibid.
[21] *Huang v Secretary of State for the Home Department* [2007] 2 AC 167 para 16.
[22] P Daly, *A Theory of Deference in Administrative Law: Basis, Application and Scope* (Cambridge, Cambridge University Press, 2012) 27.
[23] ibid 30–31.

To address the charge of perniciousness, I posited that there is a declared constitutional principle[24] that courts must give effect to legislative intent.[25] The obligation to vindicate the legislature's intention gave rise to two inter-related justifications for a doctrine of deference. First, 'a delegation of power' to a body other than a court 'functions as a directive to courts to follow a restrained approach' to judicial review.[26] Second, courts should take into account practical justifications for deference, such as expertise, complexity, democratic legitimacy and participation: 'If reasons which explain the delegation of power can plausibly be inferred from a proper consideration of the relevant statutory provisions, then it can be argued that they influenced the legislative decision to delegate power to a body other than a court, and are thus factors that a reviewing court ought to consider'.[27] Put simply, a doctrine of deference based on legislative intent could not be pernicious.

In what follows, I go further and address not only deference but administrative law doctrine in general. For Professor Allan's scepticism about deference extended to the general principles of administrative law: these too could be empty and/or pernicious. In the next section, I will lay out Professor Allan's critique of administrative law doctrine, which focuses on its emptiness. Although I acknowledge that there is significant force to Professor Allan's critique, I nonetheless argue that doctrine in administrative law is not empty. In the subsequent section, I will take up the question of its potential perniciousness.

3. The Practical Utility of Administrative Law Doctrine

In his writings on deference, Professor Allan picks up on a theme he had first elaborated in 'Doctrine and theory in administrative law: an elusive quest for the limits of jurisdiction'.[28] As he later summarised his general position, doctrinal grounds of review 'express the *conclusions* of an analysis that depends, in each case, on a complex appraisal of interlocking matters of legal principle, factual assessment and policy choice: they articulate a distinction between review and appeal that varies in its nature and degree according to all the circumstances'.[29]

It seems to me that there are three propositions underpinning Professor Allan's scepticism about administrative law doctrine.

[24] A concept borrowed from Professor John Allison: 'a standard that is to be observed consistently as a requirement of justice or general political morality that has been authoritatively declared to establish, organise or rule governmental bodies': J Allison, *The English Historical Constitution* (Cambridge, Cambridge University Press, 2007) 76.

[25] Daly, *Theory of Deference* (n 22) 38–43.

[26] ibid 55.

[27] ibid 71.

[28] TRS Allan, 'Doctrine and Theory in Administrative Law: An Elusive Quest for the Limits of Jurisdiction' [2003] *PL* 429. See especially ch 6. I will refer to this article throughout this section. Although the issue is not addressed at length in Professor Allan's subsequent work, such as TRS Allan, *The Sovereignty of Law: Freedom, Constitution, and Common Law* (Oxford, Oxford University Press, 2013), I see little there to suggest that Professor Allan's views have changed markedly over the years.

[29] Allan, 'Judicial Deference' (n 19) 116.

First, that debates about the constitutional foundations of judicial review are largely irrelevant to the detail of administrative law and do not meaningfully constrain judges. Second, that the heads of judicial review – legality, rationality and procedural propriety – do not assist in the resolution of concrete cases. Third, that there are no general principles of administrative law, properly so-called, as the analysis in judicial review cases is invariably contextual.

I address these propositions, and develop my responses, in turn in the following sub-sections. My touchstone throughout – as it was in *A Theory of Deference* – will be whether doctrine precludes certain outcomes in judicial review cases. Although I accept Professor Allan's first proposition, I reject the second and third: judges must invariably make subjective judgement calls about whether lawfulness has been established in a given case, but the judgement call falls to be made within a doctrinal framework that imposes significant constraints.

A. The Constitutional Foundations of Judicial Review

Professor Allan's first proposition is that debates about the constitutional foundations of judicial review are a distraction which do not provide any concrete guidance about the disposition of individual cases, as they are 'powerless' to develop 'determinate criteria of legality'.[30] Debates about whether the 'ultra vires' doctrine or the 'common law approach' provide the constitutional foundations of judicial review are merely arguments about 'the substitution of one dubious dogma for another'.[31]

Here, I largely agree with Professor Allan. As I have argued elsewhere,[32] the debates generated more heat than light because participants were concerned with questions about the relationship between judicial and legislative power that have little bearing on concrete cases.[33] Ultimately, indeed, no one disagreed with Professor Craig's proposition that the judges may develop the common law when there is a 'reasoned justification' for doing so.[34] Further, the differing approaches advocated by participants in the debates were animated by different methodologies. Professor Forsyth's argument was normative; Professor Craig's was descriptive; and Professor Allan and Elliott's was interpretive. As methodologies can be evaluated only in their own terms – the proof of the pudding is always in the eating[35] – none of the participants could land a knock-out blow. A normative argument cannot be refuted by descriptive analysis; and interpretation cannot disprove description.

[30] Allan, 'Doctrine and Theory in Administrative Law' (n 28) 434.

[31] ibid 451.

[32] See further P Daly, 'Plural Public Law' (2020) 51 *Ottawa Law Review* 395, 412–14.

[33] For the most well-known contributions to the debate, see C Forsyth, 'Of Fig Leaves and Fairy Tales: The Ultra Vires Doctrine, the Sovereignty of Parliament and Judicial Review' (1996) 55 *CLJ* 122; P Craig, 'Ultra Vires and the Foundations of Judicial Review' (1998) 57 *CLJ* 63; M Elliott, *The Constitutional Foundations of Judicial Review* (Oxford, Hart Publishing, 2001); and TRS Allan, 'Constitutional Dialogue and the Justification of Judicial Review' (2003) 23 *OJLS* 563.

[34] Craig, 'Ultra Vires and the Foundations of Judicial Review' (n 33) 89.

[35] P Cane, *Controlling Administrative Power* (Cambridge, Cambridge University Press, 2016) 13–16.

Although the debates generated many useful insights into the permissible scope of judicial law-making and the deep philosophical commitments of the participants,[36] Professor Allan's scepticism about the practical utility of the debates was well founded.

B. Legality, Rationality, Procedural Propriety

The second proposition is that the heads of review – legality, rationality and procedural propriety – are too abstract to guide judges: 'Though a convenient summary of our conclusions in any particular case, the doctrine cannot provide any justifying ground for those conclusions',[37] as 'their application to the facts of any particular case – and hence their concrete meaning – is largely dependent on the specific context under review'.[38] They are not, in other words, capable of precluding particular outcomes in individual cases.

I propose to take the heads of review in the order in which the proposition has greatest force: rationality, legality and then procedural propriety. In respect of each head of review, however, I will suggest that Professor Allan's proposition can only be partially accepted.

i. Rationality

In *Wednesbury* unreasonableness, Professor Allan sees a 'flexible and contextual … standard of review' which permits 'varying levels of judicial scrutiny or substitution of judgment, according to context'.[39] Moreover, any difference between *Wednesbury* unreasonableness and proportionality 'depends on the degree to which the court is prepared to make its own assessment of the balance of interests in judging rationality', such that there is no difference between the two in concrete terms.[40]

There is no doubt that the various formulations of irrationality or unreasonableness which peppered the twentieth-century law reports are colourful but largely lacking in analytical content. They may be 'salutary reminders of the appropriate limits of judicial oversight'[41] but give little guidance in concrete cases:

- 'if a decision on a competent matter is so unreasonable that no reasonable authority could ever have come to it'.[42]
- 'whether the impugned decision plainly and unambiguously flies in the face of plain reason and common sense'.[43]

[36] See, eg D Dyzenhaus, 'Form and Substance in the Rule of Law: A Democratic Justification for Judicial Review?' in C Forsyth (ed), *Judicial Review and the Constitution* (Oxford, Hart Publishing, 2000); S Nason, 'Methodological Pluralism and Modern Administrative Law' in D Kyritsis and S Lakin (eds), *The Methodology of Constitutional Theory* (Oxford, Hart Publishing, 2022).

[37] Allan, 'Doctrine and Theory in Administrative Law' (n 28) 430.

[38] ibid 431.

[39] ibid 437.

[40] ibid 438.

[41] P Daly, 'The Language of Administrative Law' (2016) 94 *Canadian Bar Review* 519, 530.

[42] *Associated Provincial Picture Houses v Wednesbury Corporation* [1948] 1 KB 223, 230.

[43] *State (Keegan) v Stardust Victims' Compensation Tribunal* [1986] IR 642, 658.

- 'a decision which is so outrageous in its defiance of logic or of accepted moral standards that no sensible person who had applied his mind to the question to be decided could have arrived at'.[44]
- 'so flawed that no amount of curial deference can justify letting it stand'.[45]

Professor Allan is hardly the only scholar to have besmirched judicial articulations of rationality as a head or ground of review. The language of emptiness and perniciousness would be apt as applied to this list of formulations, which obscure more than they reveal and place 'insurmountable hurdles' between those subject to shoddy treatment and meaningful remedies: 'it is very difficult, if not impossible, to come up with real-world cases in which such extreme irrationality has been present'.[46] It is not enough to describe imagined instances of unreasonableness; it is necessary to provide criteria for determining why a particular act was unreasonable.[47]

Contemporary formulations which rely on the concept of 'intensity' or the metaphor of a 'range' of permissible, acceptable outcomes are little better in this regard than their twentieth-century forebears: they invite contextual analysis without necessarily constraining it. One must look to the pages of the law journals rather than the law reports for attempts to provide systematic accounts of the constraints inherent to rationality in its administrative law sense,[48] or for arguments in favour of displacing rationality with a more structured proportionality test.[49]

The Supreme Court of Canada's detailed articulation of a reasonableness standard in the *Vavilov* case is a notable exception. The majority judges set out two different types of unreasonableness: a want of reasoned explanation on the one hand; a failure to respect applicable legal and factual constraints on the other.[50] Some aspects of unreasonableness, Canada-style, might have to yield to an Allanite charge of emptiness: an administrative decision-maker's compliance with the governing statutory scheme and consideration of the important interests of the individual concerned are undoubtedly highly contextual.[51] Nonetheless, this detailed articulation of unreasonableness certainly guides and likely constrains reviewing courts. For example, an interpretation of a statute will be unreasonable if it is inconsistent with statutory text, context and purpose;[52] intervention will only be appropriate on factual matters where a decision-maker has 'fundamentally misapprehended' the evidence;[53] and an administrative decision-maker's departure from past practice will only be unreasonable where it lacks

[44] *Council of Civil Service Unions v Minister for Civil Service* [1985] AC 374, 410.
[45] *Law Society of New Brunswick v Ryan* [2003] 1 SCR 247 para 52.
[46] P Craig, 'Proportionality, Rationality and Review' [2010] *New Zealand Law Review* 265, 274.
[47] A Lester and J Jowell, 'Beyond *Wednesbury*: Substantive Principles of Administrative Law' [1987] *PL* 368, 371.
[48] See eg R Williams, 'Structuring Substantive Review' [2017] *PL* 99; H Dindjer, 'What Makes an Administrative Decision Unreasonable?' (2021) 84 *MLR* 265.
[49] See eg P Craig, 'Proportionality, Rationality and Review' (n 46).
[50] *Canada (Minister of Citizenship and Immigration) v Vavilov* 2019 SCC 65, [2019] 4 SCR 653 paras 105–38.
[51] ibid paras 108–10; 133–35.
[52] ibid para 120. cf the comments at paras 119, 122 and 123, which permit departures from the judicial standard of statutory interpretation.
[53] ibid para 126.

justification.[54] These tests for intervention constrain judges, precluding them from finding decisions to be reasonable or unreasonable unless the tests set out in *Vavilov* are satisfied.

Moreover, the majority decision in *Vavilov* does provide clear markers in relation to important issues: for one thing, the onus is on the applicant to demonstrate the unreasonableness of a decision;[55] for another, a reviewing court is forbidden from engaging in a de novo assessment of the underlying issue,[56] even on questions of statutory interpretation.[57]

Furthermore, the constraints set out in *Vavilov* have quickly become encrusted with jurisprudence. Judges in the Federal Court of Canada, for example, are constrained by virtue of horizontal stare decisis to apply their colleagues' understanding of the requirements of *Vavilov* as applied to the various subject-matter areas in which they hear judicial review applications, such as immigration, labour relations and environmental law. In concrete terms, the unreasonableness of a decision on immigration law (say) will turn as much if not more on Federal Court jurisprudence than on the majority reasons in *Vavilov*.

To the extent something similar can be said of other jurisdictions then the charge of emptiness must be qualified as far as rationality is concerned.

ii. Legality

As far as 'legality' is concerned, Professor Allan writes, '[t]he normative constraints that govern the exercise of an administrative discretion delimit an authority's jurisdiction as fully as the descriptive criteria that specify its functions; the relevant jurisdiction, properly understood, is simply that field of choice, if any, that remains when all applicable legal limits have been identified'.[58] Very simply, '[a]n error can be properly labelled or classified only in the light of the policies and purposes that inform the statute, construed as an intelligible whole, and the relevant consequences for the case in hand'.[59]

The force of this point has been demonstrated at considerable length, by reference to the caseload of the Administrative Court of England and Wales, by Dr Sarah Nason.[60] Her review of first-instance judicial review decisions highlights that judges rarely engage in detailed discussions of the doctrinal niceties which one finds in the textbooks or lectures on administrative law. Rather, first-instance decisions tend to turn on judicial judgement, informed by the judge's experience and the arguments of the parties, with the principles of statutory interpretation to the fore.

These findings about 'legality' are not especially surprising. In English administrative law, questions of law are invariably reviewed on a correctness standard, with no deference to administrative decision-makers. Questions of law, in turn, require the

[54] ibid para 131.
[55] ibid para 75.
[56] ibid para 83.
[57] ibid para 124.
[58] Allan, 'Doctrine and Theory in Administrative Law' (n 28) 441.
[59] ibid 442.
[60] S Nason, *Reconstructing Judicial Review* (Oxford, Hart Publishing, 2016).

application by the courts of the principles of statutory interpretation which, in their modern guise, involve an appreciation of text, purpose and context. Any exercise of divining statutory meaning undertaken by a contemporary court will involve careful consideration of a range of factors. Similarly, determining relevant considerations and proper purposes is a matter of statutory interpretation, to be addressed by reference to text, purpose and context so as 'to ascertain the statutory purpose or object which the draftsman had in mind'.[61]

However, it would go too far to state that doctrine is irrelevant in 'legality' cases. The general doctrine in English law states that questions of law are for the courts[62] and, accordingly, requires that the courts must give authoritative answers to legal questions. Even in Canada – a jurisdiction which embraces deference on questions of law, at least some of the time – a correctness standard calls for judicial application of the principles of statutory interpretation unencumbered by any requirement to defer to the analysis of an administrative decision-maker. Doctrine is unlikely to be debated in 'legality' cases, but absence of evidence is not evidence of absence: rather, the doctrine sets the framework in which matters of 'legality' fall to be assessed.

Moreover, in some cases involving relevant considerations, an administrative decision-maker will have discretion as to whether to take a particular consideration into account. Here, doctrine dictates how a court is to review the exercise of the discretion.[63] In addition, there are judicially developed doctrines about the consequences of an administrative decision-maker's reliance on an irrelevant consideration or improper purpose.[64]

In all events, these 'legality' doctrines act as constraints on what judges can do in judicial review cases, by ruling in or ruling out certain conclusions: judges cannot (where a correctness standard is appropriate) defer to an administrative decision-maker's reasonable view of the law; judges cannot add or subtract a relevant consideration unless the statute, properly interpreted, rules the relevant consideration in or out; and judges are not at liberty to determine the consequences of taking into account an irrelevant factor or relying on an improper purpose.

I acknowledge that the phrase 'properly interpreted' is doing a significant amount of work in the preceding paragraph. In many cases, the 'proper' interpretation of a statutory provision will involve the sort of wide-ranging consideration of context and constitutional principle that Professor Allan powerfully advocates. But the fact that context and constitutional principle should be (and generally are) taken into account as part of the statutory interpretation exercise does not mean that doctrine is irrelevant in 'legality' cases. Doctrine is, rather, inherent to the exercise.

[61] *R v Secretary of State for the Environment, Transport and the Regions, ex parte Spath Holme Ltd* [2001] 2 AC 349, 381, per Lord Bingham. See, eg *Tesco Stores v Secretary of State for the Environment* [1995] 1 WLR 759; *R (Palestine Solidarity Campaign Ltd) v Secretary of State for Housing, Communities and Local Government* [2020] UKSC 16, [2020] 1 WLR 1774.

[62] *R v Hull University Visitor, ex parte Page* [1993] AC 682.

[63] Lord Irvine of Lairg, 'Judges and Decision Makers: The Theory and Practice of Wednesbury Review' [1996] *PL* 59, 67–69. See, eg *R (Rogers) v Swindon NHS Primary Care Trust* [2006] EWCA Civ 392, [2006] 1 WLR 2649.

[64] Daly, *Understanding Administrative Law* (n 10) 141–43.

iii. Procedural Propriety

The contemporary, context-sensitive approach to procedural fairness has long since displaced the former rules of natural justice. These old hard-and-fast rules – *nemo iudex in sua causa* and *audi alteram partem* – were too inflexible for the burgeoning administrative state and were cast aside in the latter half of the twentieth century in favour of an avowedly contextual duty of 'fairness' calling for the application of a variety of criteria responsive to the circumstances of each individual case.

The move from natural justice to fairness has long been a source of angst for administrative lawyers. Professor Loughlin proclaimed a 'crisis' in administrative law theory in the late 1970s[65] and more recently Lord Justice Beatson has agonised about how a flexible approach to fairness might create a Tennysonian wilderness of single instances.[66]

Doctrine might, accordingly, seem to be conspicuous by its absence in this area. Indeed, high-level references to fairness and a multiplicity of factors will seldom guide the resolution of concrete cases. Yet it does not follow that doctrine does not matter. Consider the recent work of Dr Joanna Bell.[67] She describes the three features of administrative law which lend it an inherent complexity: administrative law cases involve the interpretation of discrete statutory provisions, not the articulation of sweeping general principles; in administrative law cases, judges juggle a plurality of principles, purposes or values and cannot rely on one unifying meta-concept; and the protagonists in administrative law cases find themselves in different relationships, sometimes tied together by general norms, sometimes by individualised decisions highly specific to the circumstances of the parties. This is the anatomy of administrative law and, she argues, we must appreciate it in order to understand the subject. She deconstructs the heads of judicial review in a manner which Professor Allan would doubtlessly appreciate.

But Dr Bell's is not simply an exercise in deconstruction. Recognising the complexity, diversity and variety of administrative law does not lead us to a wilderness of single instances. Rather, focusing on first-instance decisions on procedural fairness, legitimate expectation and standing, Dr Bell identifies a significant degree of coherence. Notably, procedural fairness is tied together by heavy reliance on procedural codes and the rights to receive notice and make representations: there is a 'series of patterns' in the jurisprudence.[68]

When addressing procedural fairness issues, judges are not and do not consider themselves to be at liberty to make 'all things considered' judgments about fairness based on the circumstances of individual cases: questions about compliance with the duty of fairness are 'not to be asked and answered simply by reference to context: more particular considerations attach to individual procedural fairness rights'.[69] No sensible litigant will go to court and argue that a procedure was 'unfair'. Rather, they will argue that a particular procedural right was not accorded, for example the right to notice. But

[65] M Loughlin, 'Procedural Fairness: A Study of the Crisis in Administrative Law Theory' (1978) 28 *University of Toronto Law Journal* 215.

[66] *R (L) v West London Mental Health NHS Trust* [2014] EWCA Civ 47 at para 72.

[67] J Bell, *The Anatomy of Administrative Law* (Oxford, Hart Publishing, 2020).

[68] ibid 127.

[69] Daly, *Understanding Administrative Law* (n 10) 81.

the right to notice (say) comes encrusted in particular contexts with past practice by the administrative decision-maker, policy guidance issued by the decision-maker or others and judicial decisions defining the scope of the right in question. Here, judges are not making decisions based only on context: they are constrained by soft law instruments, past administrative practice and binding judicial precedent. This is a doctrinal superstructure within which judgments about procedural fairness fall to be made.

One might make an analogy here to Professor Allan's discussion of constitutional conventions. He writes that 'interpretation involves *judgement*', with the decision-maker required to 'take sides between the competing theories or viewpoints'.[70] In respect of rationality, legality and procedural propriety, the judge 'takes the winning side' by providing a reasoned justification for his or her conclusions, grounded in the considerations revealed as relevant by doctrine. I suggest, accordingly, that the 'heads' of review are not empty but rather constrain judges, sometimes significantly.

C. General Principles of Judicial Review

Professor Allan's third proposition is that there are no general principles of judicial review. For him, the very proposition that general principles give administrative law a 'genuine sense' is 'actually a contradiction in terms'.[71] As a 'body of doctrine', administrative law lacks 'any genuine content',[72] because a 'contextual and disputable judgment' is necessary in all cases:[73] 'judicial definition of a statutory (or other) provision, however persuasive or authoritative as a matter of general understanding, can simply determine the result of future cases: new cases, involving unforeseen or novel circumstances, will arise to test (and so further elucidate) the true meaning or scope of the relevant provision'.[74] Therefore, to assess legality, rationality or procedural propriety requires the judge to determine whether it is appropriate to find a decision unlawful given all the circumstances.

It is necessary to begin by observing that the 'general principles' of administrative law are much more detailed than the 'heads' of legality, rationality and procedural propriety. Legality encompasses the principles relating to the delegation of authority and fettering, which contain hard-edged rules forbidding delegation and the elimination of discretion, as well as the doctrinal superstructure relating to jurisdictional error, error of law, and relevancy and propriety. Under rationality would come the principles of substantive review and, perhaps, legitimate expectation. Procedural propriety contains the principles of bias (including rules relating to automatic disqualification and legislative authorisation) and, as we have seen in Section 2(B)(iii), the particular criteria attached to particular procedural rights. Furthermore, these 'heads' do not comprise the totality of the general principles of administrative law: as noted below, the procedural requirements arising from the appeal/review distinction also need to

[70] Allan, *Sovereignty of Law* (n 28) 55.
[71] Allan, 'Doctrine and Theory in Administrative Law' (n 28) 435.
[72] ibid 431.
[73] ibid 441.
[74] ibid 444.

be considered; in addition, the (admittedly highly contextual) scope of review and the occasionally prescriptive principles about remedies need to be considered. There is no doubt that some of these areas are 'dominated by a contextual approach'.[75] But some of them are governed by detailed rules, imposing 'forensic limits' which significantly constrain the scope for judicial judgement.[76]

No one could sensibly deny that a judge hearing a judicial review application must exercise judgement in disposing of the application or that contextual factors will bear on this judgement. But it does not follow from the requirement to exercise judgement that the judgement is an 'all-the-circumstances' assessment of legality, rationality or procedural propriety in a given case. To pick up a thread from the previous section, procedural fairness cases involve the application of settled criteria relating to particular procedural rights. Respect for the right to notice requires disclosure of 'the essential facts and findings alleged' as well as the provision of 'a reasonable opportunity of presenting [a] response to that notice';[77] cross-examination is required where necessary to provide a 'fair opportunity' of commenting or contradicting adverse evidence;[78] and legal representation should be accorded where the proceedings are so important and complex that an individual would otherwise be unable to make his or her case effectively.[79] As I have remarked, '[s]ome judicial judgement will be required in determining the answers to the more specific questions relating to particular procedural rights, but judges are certainly not roving along a spectrum …', free to make a general contextual judgement about the fairness of the underlying process.[80] The judgement to be made is, in fact, constrained by doctrine. In other areas, such as rationality review or the scope of judicial review, judicial judgement is less constrained and context more important. But this does not mean that *all* cases *always* turn on context, such that there cannot be a 'genuine sense' to the general principles of administrative law.

There is more. Beyond legality, rationality and procedural propriety are a host of other important principles based on the appeal/review distinction.

Professor Allan observes that even '[t]he distinction between appeal and review is … necessarily one of degree: its existence is a function of the latitude accorded the public authority in respect of any particular decision'.[81] To the extent the appeal/review distinction tracks the merits/legality distinction, Professor Allan's observation is astute: courts can review decisions very intensively, with little deference, without necessarily providing an appeal; in Australia, where the merits/legality distinction is hardwired into the Constitution, the scope and intensity of judicial review have nonetheless varied over the years, with differing 'latitude' accorded even as the judges protest that they are not reviewing the 'merits' of administrative decisions.[82]

[75] Daly, *Understanding Administrative Law* (n 10) 254.

[76] *Four Aviation Security Service Employees v Minister of COVID-19 Response* [2021] NZHC 3012, [2022] 2 NZLR 26 para 85.

[77] *State (Gleeson) v Minister for Defence* [1976] IR 280, 296.

[78] *TA Miller Ltd v Minister for Housing and Local Government* [1968] 1 WLR 992, 995.

[79] *R v Secretary of State for the Home Office, ex parte Tarrant* [1985] QB 251.

[80] Daly, 'Language of Administrative Law' (n 41) 540.

[81] Allan, 'Doctrine and Theory in Administrative Law' (n 28) 441.

[82] See eg M Aronson, 'The Growth of Substantive Review: The Changes, their Causes and their Consequences' in J Bell, M Elliott, J Varuhas and P Murray (eds), *Public Law Adjudication in Common Law Systems: Process and Substance* (Oxford, Hart Publishing, 2016).

However, there is more to the appeal/review distinction than the unhelpful proposition that a 'review' should not become an 'appeal'. The appeal/review distinction is historically entrenched.[83] It is inherent to the process of judicial review. When a court is asked to assess the lawfulness of a decision, it does so based on its scrutiny of a paper record, assisted by the arguments of counsel.[84] The most important constraint on judicial decision-making in administrative law cases is that judges must base their decisions on limited material. With limited exceptions, there are no witnesses, no live evidence, no cross-examinations, no discovery. Even where – as rarely occurs – someone is cross-examined on the content of an affidavit, the permissible range of questions is limited, much more so than in a civil trial; and even allowing for the tendency to disclose larger amounts of material in judicial review cases, what is put before a judge is much less extensive than the material made available in an action between two private parties. Given that a judge cannot make decisions on material not properly before her, the appeal/review distinction operates as a significant constraint in administrative law cases, precluding a vast range of outcomes.

Related procedural restrictions further limit what a judge may do when reviewing administrative action. A judge has no role at all when an application for judicial review is made out of time (though admittedly might have discretion to entertain the application regardless).[85] Procedural exclusivity precludes judges from considering the lawfulness of administrative action where it is dressed up as a 'claim for judicial review with a thin pretence to a private wrong'.[86] Where an individual has not exhausted alternative avenues of appeal, reconsideration or review, judicial review remedies are not available. She who seeks judicial review must also have standing, which is generously accorded in contemporary times[87] but withheld in some scenarios, especially where a stranger to a process seeks to upset carefully balanced interests.[88]

The appeal/review distinction is, therefore, not a chimera. It exerts significant influence on what judges can do in judicial review cases. They do not have free rein to inquire in an abstract sense into the legality, rationality and procedural propriety of administrative action but rather must focus their attention on the lawfulness of that action as revealed by the record against the backdrop of the arguments of the parties. A priori, a vast array of conclusions is precluded in administrative law matters, by virtue of the procedural principles of judicial review of administrative action.

In my view, therefore, the 'genuine sense' of administrative law is the exercise of judicial judgement in individual cases, with due regard for context, within a doctrinal superstructure that constrains the scope of the judgement the judge may legitimately exercise.

[83] See especially SA de Smith, 'The Prerogative Writs' (1951) 11 *CLJ* 40, 48; SA de Smith, 'Wrongs and Remedies in Administrative Law' (1952) 15 *MLR* 189, 206.

[84] See eg *R v Titchmarsh* (1914) 22 DLR 272, 277–278; *R v Northumberland Compensation Appeal Tribunal, ex parte Shaw* [1952] 1 KB 338, 357.

[85] See eg *R v Stafford Justices* [1940] 2 KB 33.

[86] *Canada (Attorney General) v TeleZone Inc.*, 2010 SCC 62, [2010] 3 SCR 585 at para 78.

[87] See eg *R v Inland Revenue Commissioners, ex parte National Federation of Self-Employed and Small Businesses Ltd* [1982] AC 617.

[88] See eg *R (Chandler) v Secretary of State* [2009] EWCA Civ 1011; *Irving Shipbuilding Inc v Canada (Attorney General)* 2009 FCA 116, [2010] 2 FCR 488.

4. The Moral Character of Administrative Law Doctrine

I argued in Section 3 that administrative law doctrine is not empty, as it precludes judicial conclusions in concrete cases. In this section, I will argue that administrative law doctrine is not pernicious either. Setting out a systemic conception of doctrine is a useful activity whether undertaken by a scholar or a judge.[89] Taking doctrine seriously does not lead to an 'abdication of judicial responsibility', as Professor Allan feared.[90] There are two strands to my argument in this section, one about legal certainty, the other about legal legitimacy, and one fundamental point: administrative law doctrine does not stand in the way of contextual judgement but rather cabins it, helping to avoid muddled morality.

A. Legal Certainty

The role of doctrine is 'to provide a framework' for legal analysis.[91] Administrative law doctrine allows people to plan their affairs. Individuals better know, with the aid of legal assistance, when they have legitimate grounds on which to challenge administrative action. Those working in public administration are given tools to predict whether administrative action is likely to be seen as lawful or unlawful. Even legislatures can use the principles of judicial review of administrative action to adjudge how best (if at all) to legislate on substantive issues or the relationship between public administration and the courts. Judges, too, are able to draw on doctrine – assisted by the arguments of counsel – to perform their role accurately. Now, I do not want to overstate the extent to which legal doctrine can generate legal certainty: for as long as there has been law, there have been lawyers and judges precisely because no legal rule can be expressed with enough particularity to capture all of the instances to which it should apply. Nonetheless, as I explained in Section 3 by reference to administrative law, legal doctrine does provide a framework for analysis, ensuring at least *some* degree of certainty about how a dispute will be adjudicated.

Any systemic conception of the body of principles which bear on the lawfulness of administrative action should help to achieve the rule of law desiderata set out by Professor Fuller.[92] A systemic conception of administrative law will be general in nature, publicly accessible, non-contradictory, relatively stable and feature prospectively applicable rules and standards. To the extent that administrative law doctrine is not empty, a systemic conception of judicial review of administrative action will also be (tolerably) clear, capable of implementation and ensure congruence between the law in the books and the law in action. An approach emphasising case-by-case contextualism will have

[89] This is certainly more feasible for scholars than judges (see P Cane, 'Taking Disagreement Seriously: Courts, Legislatures and the Reform of Tort Law' (2005) 25 *OJLS* 393) but contemporary common law judges nonetheless spend significant time in their reasons on demonstrating how their analysis of a particular issue 'fits' with the decided cases.

[90] Allan, 'Human Rights and Judicial Review' (n 11) 689.

[91] Dixon, 'Doctrinal Approach' (n 6) 164.

[92] LL Fuller, *The Morality of Law*, rev edn (New Haven, Yale University Press, 1969).

greater difficulty satisfying the Fullerian desiderata:[93] 'Law thrives when citizens can reliably identify the normative rationale of its doctrines'.[94] Otherwise, a terrible beauty will indeed be born. There is therefore a role for 'les faiseurs de systèmes' in helping those who wish to assess the lawfulness of administrative action.[95]

B. Legal Legitimacy

I do not think that Professor Allan would quibble with the preceding subsection. In the scholarly work in which he sets out his theory of law (which sees moral and legal judgement as inextricably intertwined), he does not treat 'doctrinal development'[96] or 'general principles'[97] as evil. Indeed, analysis of leading cases with a view to establishing general propositions about adjudication is central to Professor Allan's scholarly method.

The difficulty with doctrine, from Professor Allan's viewpoint, is that it may impede moral judgement: 'legal certainty has value only when the rule of law is upheld, enforcing rules that serve an intelligible account of justice and the public good', such that 'wider considerations of justice' might require a rule to be modified to take account of the circumstances of an individual case.[98]

I would suggest, nonetheless, that the development and faithful application of administrative law doctrine enhances the legitimacy of judicial decisions (and, systematically, the legitimacy of the judiciary itself).

In the first place, doctrine helps to channel moral judgement. Understanding the doctrinal superstructure in which a particular case falls to be decided avoids muddled morality. Recent Australian experience with the 'materiality' doctrine is illuminating. In a series of decisions, the High Court of Australia has attempted to define what it means for an error of law or fact committed by an administrative decision-maker to be 'material' so as to justify a finding of unlawfulness and the granting of a remedy. These are murky doctrinal waters but in its most recent foray the justices were able to draw careful distinctions between different doctrinal senses of 'materiality' and make a clear-eyed judgment about where the 'onus' of proving materiality lies in any given case.[99] Where the onus lies can safely be described as a moral question, as it relates to the balance of power between the individual and the state; but without doctrinal clarity, there is a risk of muddled morality as judges attempt to determine on a variety of case-specific contextual factors where the onus ought to lie.

Furthermore, doctrine reduces the scope for judicial arbitrariness. Respect for doctrine will circumscribe the role of the judge: constrained by doctrine, the judge in an administrative law case is 'not a knight-errant, roaming at will in pursuit of his own

[93] D Knight, *Vigilance and Restraint in the Common Law of Judicial Review* (Cambridge, Cambridge University Press, 2018) chs 5 and 6.

[94] See G Letsas, 'What's Good About Parliamentary Sovereignty?' ch 14 in this volume, text to n 17.

[95] J Rivero, 'Apologie pour les « faiseurs de systèmes »' (1951) 23 *Dalloz* 99.

[96] Allan, *Sovereignty of Law* (n 28) 221.

[97] TRS Allan, 'Constitutional Rights, Moral Judgement, and the Rule of Law' in Goudkamp, Lunney and McDonald (eds), *Taking Law Seriously* (n 4) 95, 110.

[98] ibid 109–11.

[99] *MZAPC v Minister for Immigration and Border Protection* [2021] HCA 17.

ideal of beauty or of goodness'[100] and thus the risk of judicial arbitrariness is reduced.[101] Doctrine thereby enhances the legitimate authority of the judge, by helping her to fend off accusations that she seeks to advance personal interests based in public policy or ideology rather than justice and the common good. It helps to answer the critical question, 'But how can that be law for me?'[102]

Indeed, administrative law doctrine is valuable in its own right, as any systemic conception of administrative law will perforce set out a coherent basis for the organisation of the relevant principles, rules and standards; there is a commitment to showing administrative law in its best light. For example, I argue in a recent monograph that the general principles of judicial review of administrative action have a recognisably moral character drawn from the four values of individual self-realisation, good administration, electoral legitimacy and decisional autonomy which provide administrative law with an intelligible structure that 'facilitates the flourishing of individuals, of public administration and of the liberal democratic system'.[103] Again, the 'faiseurs de systèmes' have a role to play here in teasing out the recognisably moral principles 'embodied within our practice',[104] helping to ensure respect for the 'morally valuable' institution of judicial review.[105]

Ultimately, taking doctrine seriously would not prevent an Allanite judge from 'seeking coherence within the body of rules and principles that regulate the relationship between citizen and state',[106] as part of a 'continual process of adaptation and refinement'; rather, their task would be to interrogate 'the reasons that underpin and justify' a particular doctrine, in order to determine whether the doctrine should be revisited.[107] Just as stare decisis is not a straitjacket, administrative law doctrine does not eliminate judicial discretion to make changes where changes are justified: the balance of reasons relevant to the decision in a given case includes the utility of maintaining a doctrinal position and preserving legal certainty, as weighed against the consequences of an unjust result.

Just as there was nothing pernicious, in my view, about my doctrine of deference, there is nothing pernicious about the general principles of administrative law, properly understood. Far from being pernicious, administrative law doctrine can enhance judicial legitimacy even in cases where a judge seeks to revise doctrine. Any justification of a departure from doctrine based on an all-things-considered moral judgement will be stronger if the constraining force of doctrine is acknowledged and the overriding demands of justice clearly explained. The legitimacy of judicial development of doctrine and the resolution of individual cases can thereby be strongly defended. As such, respect for doctrine is not necessarily incompatible with Professor Allan's judicial ideal. Too long a sacrifice need not make a stone of the heart.

[100] B Cardozo, *The Nature of the Judicial Process* (New Haven, Yale University Press, 1921) 141.

[101] T Endicott, 'Arbitrariness' (2014) 27 *Canadian Journal of Law & Jurisprudence* 49.

[102] D Dyzenhaus, 'More Protestant than Luther or Dworkin? TRS Allan on Law and Morals' ch 2 in this volume, text to n 61. See also D Dyzenhaus, *The Long Arc of Legality. Hobbes, Kelsen, Hart* (Cambridge, Cambridge University Press, 2022).

[103] Daly, *Understanding Administrative Law* (n 10) 262.

[104] M Foran, 'Common Law and the Common Good' ch 12 in this volume, text to n 69.

[105] T Adams, 'The Rule of Law and Respect for Persons' ch 6 in this volume, text to n 30. See also J McLean, 'The Public Service, Democracy and the Rule of Law' ch 18 in this volume.

[106] Allan, 'Constitutional Rights, Moral Judgement, and the Rule of Law' (n 97) 121.

[107] Allan, *Sovereignty of Law* (n 28) 121. See also M Lewans, 'Administrative Law and the Internal Perspective' ch 17 in this volume.

20

Is TRS Allan Really that Popular? Sovereignty, Democracy and the Rule of Law

RICHARD STACEY

1. Introduction

How can a democratic political system ensure that its people are sovereign? In posing the question, I have tipped my hand to the view that popular sovereignty and democracy are not coextensive. My first objective in this chapter, then, is to make the case that a democratic system is not necessarily one in which its people are sovereign. Democracy and popular sovereignty are conceptually distinct. My second objective is of course to answer the question 'What makes a people sovereign?' My answer is the rule of law.

In this contribution to the celebration of TRS Allan's work, I argue that Allan's thinking on the rule of law helps to reveal a distinction between democracy and sovereignty.[1] More than that, it provides the foundation of an argument that the rule of law moves a democratic system towards popular sovereignty. For a people to be sovereign, or for a government to claim that it acts on the authority of a sovereign people, it is not enough that the political system be democratic or have democratic foundations. Beyond democracy, a political system must commit to and uphold the principles of the rule of law if its people are to be sovereign.

In making this argument, I deploy a particular rhetorical device. I work with a narrow conception of democracy, to illustrate more clearly what the rule of law adds to it. I introduce a conception of democracy understood in a strictly constituent sense, requiring only that people have an opportunity to participate in collective decisions about how they will be governed and by whom, and as Porky Pig might say at the end of a Looney Tunes cartoon, 'That's all, folks!'[2]

[1] In particular, I rely on Allan's opus from the early 2000s: *Constitutional Justice: A Liberal Theory of the Rule of Law* (Oxford, Oxford University Press, 2001). David Dyzenhaus has called this the most important commentary on the rule of law since Dicey.

[2] For this conception of democracy I draw both on John Locke's account of constitution-making in *The Second Treatise of Government*, P Laslett ed (Cambridge, Cambridge University Press, 1988 [1690]) esp ch X

Porky Pig democracy is a particular model of constituent power, then, to the extent that it demands a popular and majoritarian constitution-making exercise. Although some theorists understand constituent power to rest exclusively in the collective hands of the people,[3] there is no reason that constituent power – ie the power to make and impose a constitution on a people – cannot be exercised by a select few.[4] Using language that is familiar to theorists of democracy and constitutionalism, I think of these popular and majoritarian constitution-making processes as exercises of popular sovereignty *in the constituent sense.*

It does not follow, however, that the political order a people establishes through this exercise of popular sovereignty in the constituent sense will be democratic. It is just as democratic, in the constituent sense, to establish a liberal democracy as it is an authoritarian regime. In this chapter, I draw a distinction between popular sovereignty in this constituent sense and popular sovereignty in a society's day-to-day governance, or what I call popular sovereignty *under a constituted government*. A people is sovereign in the former sense as long as they have some capacity to make basic choices about the form of government to which they are subject, but that does not by itself guarantee that a people can be said to be sovereign while they are subject to that government's power.

Regardless of the form of everyday government a people constitutes – democratic or non-democratic – I argue here that they will be sovereign if that government respects and fulfils the substance of their original constituent decision: that is, if it upholds the rule of law.[5] When a people's collective decisions establish those rules and their government respects those rules, the people are the authors of the power to which they are subject. In a rule-of-law society, the people are sovereign not just in the constituent sense but under a constituted government as well, because the substance of their original decision continues to bind those whom they choose to wield political power over them.

If we care about popular sovereignty, then, our focus should be on the rule of law and not just on democracy. I argue that Allan's work highlights how this is the case. His conception of the rule of law requires governments to justify all exercises of power against widely held conceptions of the common good, and thus maintains the substance of a people's choice about how they want to be governed.[6]

(hereinafter Locke II, followed by paragraph references), and Joel Colón-Ríos's much more recent account of democratic constitutionalism in *Weak Constitutionalism: Democratic Legitimacy and the Question of Constituent Power* (London, Routledge, 2012).

[3] See eg A Kalyvas, 'Popular Sovereignty, Democracy, and the Constituent Power' (2005) 12 *Constellations* 223, LDA Corrias, 'Populism in a Constitutional Key: Constituent Power, Popular Sovereignty and Constitutional Identity' (2016) 12 *European Constitutional Law Review* 6, 10, and C Friedrich, *Constitutional Government and Democracy: Theory and Practice in Europe and America* (New York, Blaisdell, 1950) 132.

[4] Oran Doyle makes this argument, pointing out that even Carl Schmitt understood constituent power as both a capacity to make a constitution – exercisable by the people or some other entity – and as an entity that is necessarily the people: O Doyle, 'Populist Constitutionalism and Constituent Power' (2019) 20 *German Law Journal* 161, 166–69.

[5] Lon L Fuller described congruence between official conduct and previously declared rules to be the essence of the rule of law: LL Fuller, *The Morality of Law*, revd edn (New Haven, Yale University Press, 1969) 209–10.

[6] At the outset, I distinguish my own view – and Allan's – from the 'common good constitutionalism' that Adrian Vermeule has defended in the US (A Vermeule, *Common Good Constitutionalism: Recovering the Classical Legal Tradition* (Cambridge, Polity, 2022), that Michael Foran appears to defend in ch 12 in

The argument proceeds as follows. I begin in Section 2 with an account of Porky Pig democracy, locating its roots in classical theory and tracing it through to more contemporary work. I follow with Allan's conception of the rule of law in Section 3, emphasising how the rule of law is a foundation of legitimate government. I consider the connection between legitimacy and popular sovereignty in Section 4, using it to draw a clear distinction between democracy and popular sovereignty and emphasising that it is the rule of law, and not democracy, that paves the pathway to popular sovereignty.

2. Porky Pig Democracy

A. The Beginnings of Lawful Government

Consider, first, John Locke's ideas about the establishment of government. The limited, constituent form of democracy I call Porky Pig democracy rests largely on the back of the distinction Locke draws in *Two Treatises of Government* between a political system's foundations and its structures of everyday governance.

It is helpful in understanding this distinction to look at Locke's thoughts on the 'beginning of Political Societies' in Chapter VIII of *The Second Treatise*. There are, for Locke, two distinct steps in the establishment of a government. The first is the move that individuals make from the state of nature to a political community or a 'body politick'. The people make this move, Locke explains in a fashion similar to Hobbes, because it turns out to be nicer to live under a system of government than in the state of nature.[7]

Once a group of people has agreed in principle to constitute a political community, the second step is to design the institutions of government or as Locke says, 'to conclude the rest'.[8] It is crucial to decide on these details precisely because it is the authoritative prescriptions of a system of law and its enforcement that makes life under government

this volume, and with which a handful of young Canadian scholars also appear to have become enamoured (S Sérafin, K Sun and X Foccroulle Ménard, 'The Common Good and the Legal Interpretation' (2021) 30 *Constitutional Forum* 39). As far as I can tell, common good constitutionalism affords to the executive the power to pursue some free-standing conception of the common good with no regard to written instruments of law like the constitution or, crucially for my purposes, any obligation to justify or explain to subjects of their power how each exercise of power is congruent with public conceptions of the common good. Absolving the executive from obligations to justify exercises of power against democratically and publicly articulated conceptions of the good is distinctly anti-democratic in ways that make me deeply uncomfortable.

[7] Hobbes and Locke offer similar reasons for why people leave the state of nature where each is 'Lord of [their] own Person and Possessions,' and 'subject [themselves] to the Dominion and Controul of any other Power': Locke II (n 2)123. For Hobbes, people living without a 'common power to keep them all in awe' are in a state of war against one another. Where each person has no security against their enemies other than their own strength, and everyone is enemy to everyone else, there is no time for industry, agriculture, exploration, trade, science, art, literature, construction or community, and life is 'solitary, poor, nasty, brutish, and short': T Hobbes, *Leviathan*, R Tuck ed (Cambridge, Cambridge University Press, 1996 [1651]) XIII.62. Establishing a commonwealth, then, is motivated by individuals' 'foresight of their own preservation, and of a more contented life': Hobbes, *Leviathan*, XVII.85. For Locke, 'the great and *chief end*' of people uniting into commonwealths and putting themselves under the control of governments is the preservation of their property: 'The inconveniences, that they are therein exposed to, by the irregular and uncertain exercise of the Power every man has of punishing the transgressions of others, make them take Sanctuary under the establish'd Laws of Government, and therein seek the *preservation of their Property*': Locke II (n 2) 124, 127.

[8] Locke II (n 2) 95.

more attractive than life in the state of nature.[9] While Locke insists on unanimous consent for the agreement to form a political community, the institutional details of government – the rest – are to be decided by a majority. Only majoritarian constitutional design, on Locke's account, can 'give *beginning* to any *lawful Government*'.[10]

I take it that Locke uses the term 'lawful' here to mean what we might understand as legitimate: for Locke, a political system's legitimacy flows from the democracy of its origins.[11] While Locke does not deny that power can be wielded over a society in the absence of democratically established institutions, in Locke's eyes that would simply be power with no lawful foundation.[12]

Locke's commitment to majoritarianism does not go beyond the moment of origin, however. His concern is that the process of constitutional design is democratic, whether or not the resulting constitution is democratic. In Chapter X of the *Second Treatise*, for example, Locke admits that while the majority of a body politick could establish regularly elected legislative and executive institutions, it could also 'put the power of making Laws into the hands of a few select Men, and their Heirs or Successors' or 'into the hands of one Man'.[13] It is just as legitimate in Locke's view for the majority to establish a democracy as an authoritarian monarchy.[14]

Although Locke may not have insisted on democracy as a feature of everyday government, he took the democratic elements of his constitutional theory further in one important respect. Locke understood a people subject to government – whatever form that government took – to 'perpetually retain a Supream Power' of constitutional design. The government that a people constitutes to exercise power over them is 'only a Fiduciary Power to act for certain ends'. If the government betrays the people's trust by manifestly neglecting or opposing the ends for which the people authorised that government in the first place, power devolves to the people who are then free to reconstitute whatever structures of government they think best (presumably having learned something from their recent experience).[15]

Like George Lawson before him, Locke saw true sovereignty in the power to 'model the state'.[16] And like Sieyes who came after him, Locke distinguished the people's

[9] ibid 96. That which is one body, Locke says, must be capable of moving one way.

[10] ibid 99.

[11] Locke scholars agree on this point: John Dunn points out that democracy has become a vector for political legitimacy: J Dunn, *Setting the People Free: The Story of Democracy*, 2nd edn (Princeton, Princeton University Press, 2019) 27–28. Tom Poole in turn points out that democracy has become the 'central legitimating principle of most modern political communities': T Poole, 'Constitutional Exceptionalism and the Common Law' (2009) 7 *International Journal of Constitutional Law* 247, 254.

[12] In Chapter XVIII of the *Second Treatise*, 'Of Tyranny', Locke introduces a conception of unlawfulness. Tyranny, he says, 'is *the exercise of Power beyond Right*, which no Body can have a Right to do': Locke II (n 2) 199.

[13] ibid 132.

[14] Colón-Ríos accepts that an exercise of constituent power could, in theory, establish an autocratic regime. Regime may be undemocratic, even if it is democratically created. But he argues that to do so would be inconsistent with what he sees as the inherent conditions of democratic legitimacy: Colón-Ríos, *Weak Constitutionalism* (n 2) 58–59, 110. I think he slightly overstates his case in this regard: see further below under Section 3 of this chapter.

[15] Locke II (n 2) 149.

[16] G Lawson, *Political Sacra et Civilis*, C Condren ed (Cambridge, Cambridge University Press, 1992 [1660]) 47.

constituent power from the constituted powers the people establish through its exercise.[17] Although the people are subject to the constituted powers while they exist,[18] the constituted powers remain bound to act in pursuit of the ends for which the people constituted them in the first place. When the government breaches this fiduciary obligation, the people's constituent power re-emerges. The people remain sovereign in this constituent sense, regardless of the form of government they constitute.

B. Democratic Constitutionalism

A contemporary exponent of Porky Pig democracy is Joel Colón-Ríos. A constitution is democratic, he argues, if the people whose society it orders retain the capacity to fundamentally revise its terms and the revision process is inclusive and participatory. For Colón-Ríos, democratic constitutionalism rests on respect for the principles of openness to fundamental revision and maximum possible public participation in the process of revision.[19]

Colón-Ríos admits that while it would be preferable for a group of people to have had the opportunity to design their constitutional arrangements, that historical fact is not necessary for a polity's claim to democratic legitimacy. A moment of popular constitution-making might bolster a constitutional order's claim to democratic legitimacy, but it can never be enough to satisfy the demands of democratic legitimacy.[20] Indeed, many of the world's constitutions lack a democratic pedigree because the people they govern did not participate at all in formulating them. Think of the constitution the Allied powers imposed on Japan at the end of World War II or the 250-year old US Constitution.

Locke, for his part, also confronts the objection that most people are simply born into existing constitutional arrangements and do not have the opportunity to design them. His response is that a people's acquiescence to prevailing arrangements can be taken as a kind of fictional, reconstructive authorship of those arrangements and, moreover, because the people retain the supreme power to disestablish and reconstitute the system of government, a sign of their ongoing sovereign choice about what form of government to live under.[21]

There are important differences between Colón-Ríos's understanding of constituent democracy and Locke's, though. In the first place, Locke does not see the people's supreme power as exercisable at their instance, whenever they feel like a change. Rather,

[17] EJ Sieyes, 'What is the Third Estate?' in OW Lembcke and F Weber (eds), *Emmanuel Joseph Sieyes: The Essential Political Writings* (Leiden, Brill, 2014 [1789]). Locke draws attention to the distinction between constituent power and delegated, constituted powers in a footnote acknowledging his debt to Richard Hooker's 1632 work, *Of the Lawes of Ecclesiasticall Politie* (Locke II (n2) fn 134): 'The lawful Power of making Laws to Command whole Politick Societies of Men belonging to properly into the same intire Societies, that for any Prince or Potentate of what kind soever upon Earth, to exercise the same of himself, and not by express Commission immediately and personally received from God, or else by Authority derived at the first from their consent, upon whose persons they impose laws, it is no better than meer Tyranny.'

[18] Locke II (n2) 150.

[19] Colón-Ríos, *Weak Constitutionalism* (n 2) 6–7.

[20] ibid 108.

[21] Locke II (n 2) 100–22.

that power re-emerges only when the government betrays the people's trust and acts contrary to or neglects the public good.[22] For Colón-Ríos, there need not be a catastrophic constitutional crisis to trigger the people's power to fundamentally revise their constitutional arrangements. Implicit in popular sovereignty for Colón-Ríos is the people's ability to make fundamental constitutional changes whenever they want to.

Second, Locke does not foresee constitutional mechanisms for constitutional change. Rather, fundamental constitutional change takes place outside the ambit of the existing constitutional system. The popular sovereignty of these moments consists in the fact that the people themselves decide whether the government has neglected the public good, but the constitution itself need not provide the opportunity for that decision.

For Colón-Ríos, then, a constitutional order is democratically legitimate only if it provides an opening for popular revision. Even those constitutional regimes that were imposed or adopted centuries ago, or otherwise have no democratic pedigree, can rest a claim to democratic legitimacy on their 'susceptibility to re-constitution through mechanisms that facilitate the exercise of constituent power and that attempt to replicate a democratic constitution-making episode'.[23]

On Colón-Ríos's approach, a system that respects the two principles of openness and participation is democratically legitimate, and the people governed by such a system are sovereign in a constituent sense. But Colón-Ríos admits right at the outset of his work that he is not terribly interested in what he calls the 'first dimension' of democracy, or matters of daily governance. His focus is on democracy at the level of fundamental laws, the 'second dimension' of democracy,[24] or what I call Porky Pig democracy.

Just like Locke, then, Colón-Ríos is receptive to the idea that a people can choose to establish whatever forms of government they want, including non-democratic ones. Even regimes that are not democratic on the first dimension of everyday governance can be democratically legitimate on democracy's second dimension, if the people are able to initiate fundamental change and participate in making those changes. An authoritarian regime is just as democratically legitimate as a parliamentary democracy if it encodes the principles of openness and participation in its basic constitutional rules. Because a constitution need not commit to any particular substantive content or rules, Colón-Ríos calls his model 'weak constitutionalism', precisely because the constitution is easily changeable rather than permanent and inflexible.

My concern with weak constitutionalism is that while it may entrench popular sovereignty in this constituent sense, it does little to ensure that a people is sovereign during the tenure of the constituted powers. For Colón-Ríos as much as for Locke, it seems that the only way a people can act as sovereign masters of their own political destiny is to burn to the ground whatever constitution they end up with and rebuild from the ashes:

> A group of human beings engaged in the exercise of constituent power shows no respect for the established constitutional forms; such a group is simply putting into practice the (frequently violent) 'right of revolution', to use Carl Friedrich's formulation.[25]

[22] Colón-Ríos, *Weak Constitutionalism* (n 2) 80, 82. See Locke II (n 2) 149, 221–22, 240–43.
[23] ibid 9–10.
[24] ibid 6.
[25] Colón-Ríos, *Weak Constitutionalism* (n 2) 110, referring to Friedrich, *Constitutional Government* (n 3) 129.

And even so, Locke is careful to point out that the people are not going to take that extreme step unless subjected to ongoing and egregious breaches of the public trust.[26] Locke's constitutional theory does not lay a '*ferment* for frequent *Rebellion*'.[27]

If popular sovereignty exists only at these rare moments that we, the people, burn our existing institutions to the ground, and we are unlikely to go that far anyway, it is not clear that we can be said to be sovereign while we are subject to the authority of the constituted powers. My question is what makes a people sovereign under a constituted government rather than just at these exceptional moments of reconstitution.

3. Legitimacy and the Rule of Law

Locke's *Second Treatise of Government* is usually read as a theory of limited government and classical liberalism, but behind that ideological headline lie the foundations of a theory of the rule of law and legitimate government. For Locke, any government the people constitute is bound to uphold the trust the people put in it. The effect of a government's breach of trust, in turn, is a new exercise of sovereignty in the constituent sense: the people can constitute government anew. Locke is committed to this rule-of-law principle of congruence not for reasons of liberalism or even private property, but rather because it guarantees the people's sovereign choice to enter into a political community with a particular set of substantive commitments.

Similarly, Colón-Ríos sees a political system's democratic legitimacy not so much in the historical fact that it was established through an exercise of popular sovereignty in the constituent sense, but rather in the possibility that the people will be able to initiate and participate in making fundamental changes to the constitutional order.

Trevor Allan's project in *Constitutional Justice* aims to provide an account of the rule of law that vindicates its promise as a pathway to legitimate governmental authority. The conception of lawful authority that Allan describes requires a government to justify its conduct against the common good. The rule of law, Allan has famously said, is the 'rule of reason.' It amounts to

> a basic requirement of justification, or condition of legitimacy, whereby the legality of a person's treatment, at the hands of the state, depends on its being shown to serve a defensible view of the common good (broadly understood to mean for the good of a community whose members are accorded equal respect and dignity, according to some rational account of their collective well-being).[28]

Allan goes on to argue that the rule-of-law project of justification, and thus of legitimating the legal order, requires a set of conditions that we generally identify as liberal democracy: equality, freedom of expression and procedural fairness. For the government to justify its actions against the common good, people must be free to argue about the content of the common good and to raise questions about whether the government's

[26] Locke II (n 2) 223–30.
[27] ibid 224.
[28] Allan, *Constitutional Justice* (n 1) 2.

conduct is congruent with it. The rule of law, as the rule of reason, thus requires the liberal democratic conditions that make public reason possible.

On the back of Allan's work I make the case that liberal democracy is necessary for the rule of law to deliver on the Lockean promise of popular sovereignty, not just in the constituent sense but in the everyday sense, under a constituted government. However, I argue also that liberal democracy is not sufficient for popular sovereignty under constituted government.

I make this argument in two stages. In what follows I consider Allan's position on legitimacy, comparing it to Locke's requirements of lawfulness and Porky Pig conceptions of democracy. In Section 4 below, I trace Allan's rule-of-law argument for liberal democracy. I agree that a commitment to the rule of law implies a commitment to a set of rules and procedures we think of as liberal democratic, but I think that even a liberal democracy may want for popular sovereignty.

Both Allan as a theorist of the rule of law, and Locke and Colón-Ríos as Porky Pig democrats, are concerned with the conditions that make a government's use of force against its people legitimate. The Lockean commitment to democratic constitutional design and Allan's concern for the rule of law are connected by the concept of legitimacy. A significant part of Allan's contribution is that it shifts our thinking about legitimacy – and in turn popular sovereignty – from the constituent moment to the everyday experience of living under a constituted government.

For Locke, the lawfulness (or legitimacy) of a form of government depends on majoritarian constitutional design. It does not matter to the Lockean conception of legitimacy what form the government takes. A legitimate constitution is one that a majority of the people chooses or is at least able to revise, either when the government betrays its public trust or, on Colón-Ríos's approach, whenever the people feel like it.

Apart from these moments of constitutional design or revision, it is not clear how the people exercise sovereignty. The people's sovereignty emerges, in this constituent sense, only at discrete and rare (and burn-it-to-the-ground) moments of constitutional design or revision.

Embedded in Locke's account of popular sovereignty, however, is the people's right to judge whether the government has betrayed the public trust and whether a new constitutional framework is required.[29] It is therefore implicit in Locke's theory that legal rules allow people to arrive at this judgment. This is the kernel of Locke's prototypical conception of the rule of law: there must be some mechanism through which the people can hold the constituted government accountable to the public conception of the

[29] Locke is frustratingly obtuse on this point, saying at various points that there is 'no *Judge on Earth*' capable of deciding whether a constituted government has betrayed the public trust, and that the most a people can do when they believe that either the executive or the legislature has acted contrary to the public good is make an '*appeal to Heaven*': Locke II (n 2) 168. He does explain, though, that the 'appeal to heaven' is to be understood simply as casting the fate of the rebellion the people must mount against an illegitimate government to heaven (Locke II (n 2) 149, 219–20), and that it is nonetheless the people themselves who must decide whether to make that appeal to heaven (ie to foment rebellion) in the first place (Locke II (n 2)168). Finally, in the third-last paragraph of the *Second Treatise*, he asks, 'Who shall be Judge whether the Prince or Legislative act contrary to their Trust?' And he replies: 'To this I reply, *The People shall be Judge*; for who shall be *Judge* whether his Trustee or Deputy acts well, and according to the Trust reposed in him, but he who deputes him … ?': Locke II 240.

common good. A legitimate constitution is not just one that is designed or revisable by the people, but one where the government is ultimately accountable to the people.

Allan makes this implicit feature of Locke's theory of legitimate government explicit. Of course, to say that a government must act congruently with a set of constitutional principles is just to affirm the rule of law. But Allan does a great deal to explain how congruence works, mechanically, and what it means for a government to uphold the rule of law.

In short, a government must be able to explain how every one of its exercises of power is consistent with the common good. Any restraints a government imposes on its people in the form of laws, administrative decisions or executive action can only be said to be legitimate if the government can give people a compelling reason for why those restraints are necessary in the first place. A 'defensible scheme of justice', Allan goes on, is one where 'individual rights and countervailing public interests are brought into reasonable balance'.[30]

On this approach, there are two questions that the people must answer themselves. First, at a wholesale or macro level, what is the common good? Second, at the more case-specific, retail level, is each act of government power congruent with that conception of the common good?

The Porky Pig version of democracy is concerned only with the macro-level question – Colón-Ríos's 'second dimension' of democracy. A constitution is democratically legitimate on this approach if these conditions are met, regardless of what the government does every day, and whether or not specific acts of official power are congruent with basic values and principles.

Indeed, a great deal of constitutional theory, from Locke through Carl Schmitt and Bruce Ackermann to Colón-Ríos, posits a moment of fundamental constitutional design or revision, or at least the opportunity for one, distinct from processes of ordinary government, at which the people's sovereign constituent power exists. Colón-Ríos himself insists that the constituent power cannot be permanent. Quoting Ulrich Preuss, he understands it to be a 'transitory power that exists only in an evanescent moment of history'.[31]

Allan's emphasis on the rule of law, in contrast, demands that the government make constant reference to the common good. Unlike those who distinguish between extraordinary moments of design and ordinary government, or between different dimensions of democracy, Allan's theory does not set the moment of sovereignty aside into a distinct and isolated constituent moment.

Rather, settling on a substantive conception of the common good and assessing whether a specific act of official power is congruent with it can happen at the same moment. While for Porky Pig democrats the people's role is to determine a political community's basic structures, including substantive conceptions of the good (and that's all, folks), Allan's rule-of-law theory recognises that substantive conceptions of the good

[30] ibid 50.

[31] Colón-Ríos, *Weak Constitutionalism* (n 2) 113, quoting UK Preuss, 'The exercise of constituent power in Central and Eastern Europe', in M Loughlin and N Walker (eds), *The Paradox of Constitutionalism: Constituent Power and Constitutional Form* (Oxford, Oxford University Press, 2008) 211, 218.

must always be open to public debate, revision, refinement and development.[32] The people continuously determine both the public good and whether government conduct is congruent with it. The principle of congruence infuses popular sovereignty into both dimensions of democracy.

More than this, the very purpose of filling out a substantive conception of the public good is to provide a normative standard against which the acceptability of government conduct can be evaluated. A people's decision about their constitution's basic structures and principles is important as an exercise of their sovereignty, but it is surely meaningless if whatever government they establish is not bound to uphold them.

The constituent power, then, understood as a people's power to set the terms of their political association, is a form of sovereignty that is different to the sovereignty a people exercises in keeping a constituted government's conduct congruent with those terms.[33] If we understand popular sovereignty to mean that a people are subject to no political will but their own, whether constituting a political community or living under it, the people must have the means to hold the constituted powers accountable to their political will. It is therefore a mistake, in my view, to reduce popular sovereignty to the exercise of mere constituent power, precisely because the constituent power does not go beyond these exceptional moments of foundation.

The rule-of-law principle of congruence does this work for us. It ensures that a government acts only in accordance with previously established rules and principles. Where the people themselves set those rules and principles, in an exercise of popular sovereignty in the constituent sense, the rule of law extends popular sovereignty into constituted government. A rich and meaningful experience of popular sovereignty is not restricted to these distinct moments of constitutional design, but includes a people's capacity to constantly evaluate whether government conduct is congruent with the common good.

I should admit that the idea of a people constantly evaluating their government's congruence with the common good is something of a rhetorical fiction. I do not imagine that all of a political community's members are continuously thinking about the common good and collectively holding government accountable to it. All popular sovereignty under a constituted government ultimately requires is opportunities for the people to refine the conception of common good from time to time, and for some members of the community to question the government's compliance with it some of the time.

My intention in this chapter is not to catalogue the mechanisms by which people can make those periodic evaluations, and thereby exercise popular sovereignty under constituted government. It is enough at this point merely to nod towards some familiar rule-of-law features of modern constitutional democracy that allow the people to question the congruence of official conduct with fundamental principles.

The first is the doctrine of the separation of powers, through which each branch of government can itself scrutinise and evaluate the conduct of the other branches. The

[32] Allan, *Constitutional Justice* (n 1) 40.

[33] It is telling that Colón-Ríos goes to some trouble to distinguish his conception of 'democratic legitimacy', which he ties closely to constituent power, from legitimacy understood as justification: Colón-Ríos, *Weak Constitutionalism* (n 2) 104–06. And justification, as I argue on the back of Allan's work, is closely aligned with popular sovereignty in the constituted sense.

people are authors of the elected branches' conduct in this regard (notionally, at least), and are thus able, through their representatives, to consider the two questions on which a defensible scheme of justice depends.

People aggrieved by the government's conduct can also turn to the courts to inquire into the legitimacy of legislative or executive conduct. For the courts to perform this oversight role, though, they must be sufficiently independent from the other branches of government and institutionally powerful enough that court rulings are too consequential for the other branches to ignore.[34]

A second feature of modern constitutional democracies that foregrounds the people's evaluative role is the fourth branch of government: independent, arms-length institutions specifically mandated to police the constitutional acceptability of various forms of government conduct.[35] Institutions like human rights commissions, electoral commissions, auditors general and security services inspectorates are usually set up to respond directly to public complaints about individual exercises of state power. These institutions allow a people to question a government's conduct without having to rely on one of the established branches of government to represent their views.

Finally, consider how a referendum can be a mechanism of the rule of law. It is true, of course, that referendums have long been considered to be mechanisms of popular sovereignty. But the very fact that a referendum can also work to uphold the rule of law emphasises the connection I have tried to draw throughout this chapter between the rule of law and popular sovereignty.

While referendums are often used in the approval of entirely new constitutions – constitutional replacements – they are also used in constitutional amendment.[36] The rule of law requires that executive and administrative decisions be congruent with previously declared rules and justified against a substantive conception of the common good, but it also requires those previously declared laws and even constitutional principles to also be justified against a substantive conception of the common good.

A referendum can allow the people (or a majority of them, at least) to express their views about whether particular laws or constitutional rules are congruent with, or justifiable against, the substantive conception of the good that they hold. Assuming the government is bound by constitutional rules to accept the results of the referendum, the referendum is both a tool of the rule of law and of popular sovereignty because it allows the people to realign the direction or structure of government with their moral preferences.[37]

[34] Indeed, David Jenkins has argued that the nascent rule of law theory that Locke sets out is best manifested by the existence of an independent judiciary to whom the people can put questions about the government's compliance with fundamental values: D Jenkins, 'The Lockean Constitution: Separation of Powers and the Limits of Prerogative' (2011) 56 *McGill Law Journal* 543.

[35] See, generally, M Tushnet, 'Institutions Protecting Democracy: A Preliminary Inquiry' (2018) 12 *Law & Ethics of Human Rights* 181, and 'Institutions Protecting Constitutional Democracy: Some Conceptual and Methodological Preliminaries' (2020) 70 *University of Toronto Law Journal* 95.

[36] Z Elkins and A Hudson, 'The Strange Case of the Package Deal: Amendments and Replacements in Constitutional Reform' in R Albert and R Stacey (eds), *The Limits and Legitimacy of Referendums* (Oxford, Oxford University Press, 2022) 37.

[37] On the matter of a referendum's implications for a government, Richard Albert has helpfully pointed out that even referendums that are not formally binding on a government – such as the UK's Brexit referendum

In Ireland in the 2010s, for example, referendums twice resulted in the amendment of the Constitution, removing the prohibitions on abortion and same-sex marriage. In the US state of Kansas in 2022, referendum voters rejected a proposal to amend the state constitution to remove a right to abortion. In France in 1958, a majority of voters in a referendum preferred a semi-presidential system with a directly elected executive president over a parliamentary system with a ceremonial president.

There is no set formula or blueprint for how a political community can uphold the rule of law. At its core, the rule of law requires that the power that government exercises over a people be justified to those people. There are numerous mechanisms by which that might happen. All I have tried to illustrate in this brief account is that at least some of those rule-of-law mechanisms evince its connection to popular sovereignty.

4. Liberal Democracy and its Limits

I have so far argued that the rule of law, and not democracy as such, infuses a constitutional democracy with a full and rich form of popular sovereignty. The difficulty in making this claim is that liberal democracy turns out to be indispensable for the rule of law. Popular sovereignty and democracy are undeniably connected. The core of the argument is that even though liberal democracy is necessary for popular sovereignty understood in both the constituent and the everyday sense, it is not sufficient. To make this case I rely on the connections Allan's work draws between the rule of law and democracy.

While Joseph Raz conceives of the rule of law as a requirement that government exercise power in accordance with a set of formal, value-free principles,[38] Allan's conception of the rule of law presupposes a substantive conception of the common good against which all government conduct can be normatively evaluated. The rule of law just does not work without this normative element.

It does not matter to Allan what a particular community's substantive conception of the common good turns out to be. Locke happened to think that protection of private property was the common good, but a community of people might just as well think that the common good consists in reducing social inequality, or in living according to a set of religious principles, or in reducing the causes of climate change.

One of the implications of Allan's thick conception of the rule of law, then, is that it must preserve the space for a people to coalesce around whatever conception of the common good matters to them. Any legal order that is to uphold the rule of law must therefore create the conditions under which people can debate the substance of the common good and consider whether their government's conduct is congruent with it.

The human capacity for moral judgement is thus at the centre of Allan's conception of the rule of law. Individual moral autonomy and independence of mind is a critical

in 2016 – can be practically impossible for a government to ignore: R Albert, 'Discretionary referendums in constitutional amendment', in Albert and Stacey (eds), *The Limits and Legitimacy of Referendums* (n 36) 63, 65–69.

[38] J Raz, *The Authority of Law* (Oxford: Oxford University Press, 1979) ch 11, 'The Rule of Law and its Virtue'.

component of any assertion of legal authority or claim to legitimacy.[39] How does a legal system protect this capacity for moral judgment? By recognising that every legal subject is a morally autonomous agent and embedding that recognition in the law.

On a practical level this means, in the first place, a commitment to legal guarantees of equality. Every person must be treated with equal concern for their moral autonomy and independence of mind, and must be assured of the opportunities to participate in public life as an equally autonomous moral agent. A right to equality and prohibitions on unfair discrimination are thus necessary for the rule of law to do its work in legitimating a system of government.

Exercises of public power that undermine this basic equality in turn undermine the rule of law, by depriving some members of the political community of the opportunity to consider what the common good requires and whether official conduct is congruent with the common good. It is difficult to see how a constitutional system in which some of the people are unable or less able than others to evaluate official congruence with the common good cannot claim to be democratically legitimate.

Second, even if people are treated with equal concern for their moral autonomy, the legal system must allow for public discourse about the common good and whether government conduct is congruent with it. Beyond recognising that people are equally capable of thinking about what the common good is and what it requires government to do, the legal system must guarantee the formal mechanisms by which people are able to express their opinions, call attention to what they perceive to be government missteps, and freely criticise or support official conduct. This injunction is usually met through protections of rights to freedom of thought, conscience, access to information, and expression.

The commitments to equality, freedom of thought and free speech that follow from Allan's thick conception of the rule of law are at the core of what we think of as liberal democracy. Given that popular sovereignty understood in the everyday sense I present here requires a commitment to the rule of law, the necessary implication is that liberal democracy is necessary to a people's everyday sovereignty under a constituted government.

Joel Colón-Ríos comes to a similar conclusion about the necessity of liberal democracy, even though his focus is the Lockean constituent moment rather than Allan's requirement of everyday justification. The key element of Colón-Ríos's account of democratic legitimacy is the people's capacity to make fundamental changes to constitutional foundations whenever they like. This commitment has institutional implications, he goes on:

> The constitutional forms must provide the means for constituent power to reappear after the constitution is in place and, if needed, to put the entire institutional arrangement into question. To begin with, there must be some basic institutional guarantees in place: freedom of assembly, freedom of expression, the right to vote; in short, those rights of political participation necessary for the very existence of democracy.[40]

[39] Allan, *Constitutional Justice* (n 1) 89.
[40] Colón-Ríos, *Weak Constitutionalism* (n 2) 118.

It is not mere coincidence that Colón-Ríos's inquiry into what makes constituent power possible and Allan's rule-of-law theory end up at the same place. Although I have tried throughout this piece to distinguish popular sovereignty from constituent power, and indeed popular sovereignty from democracy, the concepts remain related. After all, constituent power on my view is just popular sovereignty limited to the exceptional moments of constitutional design and revision. It is not all that surprising that the conditions that allow a people to determine, on one hand, if government conduct is congruent with fundamental conceptions of the common good, or whether the constitution's fundamental structures and principles are still satisfactory on the other hand, turn out to be the same.

The more important point, though, is that while liberal democracy is necessary for popular sovereignty it is not sufficient. At best, we might be able to say that liberal democracy is sufficient for the attenuated form of popular sovereignty that Colón-Ríos and Locke are concerned with – that is, the constituent power to (re-)establish a political community and set the basic terms of a people's political association.

But if popular sovereignty is to live beyond the constituent moment and transcend a Porky Pig caricature of sovereignty, what matters is not a system's liberal democratic characteristics but its commitment to the rule of law. This is the point on which I rest the argument that democracy – even full-fledged, rights-protecting, modern liberal democracy – must be distinguished from popular sovereignty. It is not enough for a constitution to make the claim to the authority of popular sovereignty for it to entrench liberal democratic rights. More than this, those liberal democracy mechanisms must be directed at upholding the rule of law.

We need not look very far for examples of nominal democracies that fail to uphold the rule of law. All of the regimes variously described with the terms abusive constitutionalism, illiberal democracy, democratic dictatorship or competitive authoritarianism fit the bill.[41] It may be that in these systems the people are given meaningful opportunities, from time to time, to make decisions about the nature, design and direction of government. Elections for representative office are regularly held, and in some cases referendums on central questions of constitutional design or policy have been held. But it is rare that these systems create opportunities for the people to hold government accountable to prior commitments – even when the people themselves articulate those prior commitments.

Of course, you may object that these are not true democracies, and certainly not liberal democracies. Rights to free speech, to freedom of association, to hold political office and to access information are frequently breached in these regimes, if they are recognised at all. Where people are able to seek judicial protection of their rights or launch complaints against the government's conduct, they may confront a judiciary that

[41] See eg MA Graber, S Levinson and M Tushnet (eds), *Constitutional Democracy in Crisis* (New York, Oxford University Press, 2018); F Zakaria, *The Future of Freedom: Illiberal Democracy at Home and Abroad* (New York, WW Norton, 2003); D Landau, 'Abusive Constitutionalism' (2013) 47 *University of California Davis Law Review* 189; M Tushnet, 'Authoritarian Constitutionalism' (2015) 100 *Cornell Law Review* 391; B Vormann and MD Weinman (eds), *The Emergence of Illiberalism: Understanding a Global Phenomenon* (New York, Routledge, 2020); S Levitsky and LA Way, 'The New Competitive Authoritarianism' (2020) 31 *Journal of Democracy* 51.

has been co-opted by the government and thus neutralised as a mechanism of the rule of law.

It is perhaps obvious that these less than fully democratic systems are not rule-of-law systems. But my point is simply that it is possible for a constitutional system to combine elements of democracy – regular elections to political office, referendums – with a disrespect for the rule of law. A failure to uphold the rule of law prevents popular sovereignty under the constituted government, but it does not undermine entirely the system's democratic foundations.

This is especially true if we conceive of democracy in the Porky Pig sense. A constitutional system's failure to uphold the rule of law in matters of everyday governance does not detract from a people's constituent power, as long as the people get to decide when and how to revise the basic constitutional structure. Under these circumstances, the people's constituent power is unaffected by how the government behaves every day.

The question that remains, then, is whether an otherwise liberal democracy, which upholds and respects rights to equality, free speech, free association and political office, can continue to uphold democracy if it does not uphold the rule of law. My answer to that question is yes, and if that is correct, then a liberal democratic system by itself may still want for popular sovereignty in the everyday sense.

Consider, then, the three steps of this deductive argument. First, Porky Pig democracy of the form that Colón-Ríos and Locke argue for both require liberal democracy to work. The people will not be able to consider or come to a decision about whether to revise basic constitutional structures without legal forms protecting equality and free speech.

But, second, the constituent power that these liberal democratic freedoms allow a people to exercise is different from popular sovereignty in the everyday sense, under the constituted government. A constitution is democratically legitimate, and upholds popular sovereignty in that constituent sense, if it preserves the people's freedom to decide whether the constitution serves their interests or not, and whether or not they need to burn it to the ground and rebuild.

It must follow, finally, that liberal democratic freedoms do not by themselves guarantee popular sovereignty in that fuller, everyday sense, even if they do guarantee popular sovereignty in the constituent sense. Popular sovereignty under a constituted government demands a people's ability to hold government accountable to the substantive conception of the common good that they articulate without burning the constitution to the ground.

The objective of popular sovereignty under a constituted government, however, is maintenance rather than destruction. Liberal democratic rights are central to that, for sure, but it is the mechanisms of the rule of law that allow maintenance without having to resort to the wholesale replacement of the constitution.

The rule of law, in other words, is a distinct virtue that a liberal democracy may or may not possess. Whether a liberal democracy can be said to ensure a people's sovereignty is a question that depends on the extent to which it upholds a thick conception of the rule of law, like Trevor Allan's. It is not enough for a full and meaningful sense of popular sovereignty merely to establish a liberal democracy.

5. Conclusion

The position I advance in this chapter is that the rule of law, and the rule of law alone, generates popular sovereignty in a constitutional democracy. The argument I make in support of this position proceeds along two lines.

The first line of argument draws a conceptual distinction between democracy and popular sovereignty, arguing in turn that the people in a democracy – even a liberal democracy – cannot be said to be sovereign once they are subject to governmental authority if the constitutional system does not uphold the rule of law.

I anticipate that at this stage of the argument I might be accused of some semantic sleight of hand. The conception of popular sovereignty that I work with is different to the one many theorists of the constituent power, or even democracy more broadly rely on. It might appear, then, that I am helping myself to a loose and expansive definition of a concept that allows me to make the argument I want to.

The point is not so much that I may have defined popular sovereignty favourably, but rather that the prevailing conceptions of constituent power are themselves too narrow. Much of the theory about constituent power focuses exclusively on a people's constitutional origin story, without thinking about how the experience of a people under government is relevant to their sovereignty. Constituent democracy allows that a people can choose the basic conditions of their political association, and as long as they can do that, on this view, they are sovereign.

My view is that a people's power to constitute a political community – the constituent power – cannot be all that popular sovereignty requires. More than this, a constitutional system must hold a government to the decisions that a people make at this moment of origin, whatever those decisions turn out to be. Even if a people were to choose a non-democratic form of government at the constituent moment, their sovereign will would be undermined if the non-democratic government they constituted abandoned whatever forms of government or principles they did happen to choose.

A people's sovereignty, then, requires institutional mechanisms for the protection of the choices that the people made when they exercised their constituent power. It is on that basis that I come to the view that constituent power – and constituent democratic processes through which it is exercised – is distinct from the sovereignty a people can be said to exercise when constituted government continues to be bound by their will.

The second line of argument emerges from this distinction between popular sovereignty in the constituent sense and popular sovereignty under constituted government. The institutional mechanisms that protect a people's sovereign will under a constituted government are of course the principles of the rule of law, and I rely in particular on Trevor Allan's thick conception of the rule of law to illustrate how popular sovereignty and the rule of law are connected.

In Allan's view, the rule of law requires a government to justify each exercise of power against a substantive conception of the common good. Imagine that the people themselves define and redefine that conception of the common good through exercises of popular sovereignty in the constituent sense. Adherence to the rule-of-law principle that government justify its conduct against that conception of the common good upholds the people's sovereign will even after they have exercised constituent power.

It may be objected that the rhetorical device I use to make this argument – conceiving of democracy in a purely constituent or 'Porky Pig' sense – ignores the fact that liberal democracies do in fact give their subjects a significant say in their governance in an everyday sense, beyond the constituent moment. I agree, in turn, that the features of liberal democracy – equality, free speech, rights to vote and stand for public office – are necessary both for the democratic legitimacy that Colón-Ríos talks about and for the conception of the rule of law that Allan defends.

But liberal democracy, for both Colón-Ríos (and presumably Locke) and Allan, is merely instrumental. It allows a people to decide, for Colón-Ríos, if they should repudiate the constitution and replace it with a new one. It does not, by itself, guarantee the people any power to hold government to the decisions the people have already made.

For Allan, liberal democracy ensures that people are able to publicly debate and refine the conception of the common good and question whether their government's conduct is congruent with it. But simply having this debate is not what realises a people's sovereignty: rather, it is the institutional mechanisms that allow the people to hold government accountable to the outcome of that public debate.

Without the rule of law, then, even a democratically legitimate constitution that recognises and protects liberal democratic values and rights cannot claim that its people are sovereign beyond the constituent moment. What makes a people sovereign, under a liberal democracy as much as a hereditary monarchy or an autocracy, is the rule of law.

Reflections on Law and Legal Theory: A Response to Critics

TRS ALLAN

I am deeply grateful to all the contributors for their stimulating chapters and especially to the editors, Geneviève Cartier and Mark Walters, who also organised the conference that preceded this book. Confronted by such an array of interesting issues and challenges, I can only offer some general observations here to indicate the nature of my response.[1] I hope I shall be forgiven for neglecting matters that would certainly deserve more attention in a longer essay.

1. Legal and Political Theory

I have been seeking to articulate a conception of law that expresses an inherent commitment to the pursuit of justice and the public good. A sound theory of law is a necessary step towards a persuasive theory of legal practice, as it operates primarily within a certain jurisdiction but also, if possible, analogous jurisdictions pervaded by similar basic ideas and commitments. It must show the value of law as a distinctive form of governance, distinguishing legal practice from the assertion of a merely arbitrary superior force. If law is not, in Hart's expression, 'the gunman situation writ large', neither is it the consistent application of iniquitous rules that serve only the interests of a ruling élite.[2] Law is more than the systematic enforcement of publicly ascertainable rules. The rules must at least purport to serve the interests of justice and the public good; and, equally important, they must be interpreted and applied on that fundamental assumption.

A court cannot justify an adverse ruling to the affected party by citing the 'rule of recognition', which merely records the opinions or preferences of senior officials.[3] A legal judgment must appeal, instead, to a beneficial practice that the legal subject can reasonably be expected to acknowledge and endorse. It must seek to interpret the law in a manner that demonstrates its obligatory character. When correctly identified

[1] Unless otherwise indicated, references to the work of other contributors relate, primarily, to their chapters in this book.

[2] HLA Hart, *The Concept of Law*, 2nd edn (Oxford, Oxford University Press, 1994) 7.

[3] ibid chs 6, 7.

by recourse to an account of the legal order as a legitimate basis for governance, legal rules or rulings are morally binding. They express the requirements attached, in the relevant circumstances, to membership – whether permanent or temporary – of the organised political community. Legal theory is best understood as a dimension of moral and political theory. The most important questions about adjudication, legal interpretation and political obligation take us far from the sphere of descriptive analysis, obliging us to confront fundamental questions of value.

While Dworkin's theory of law-as-integrity correctly portrays legal judgment as moral judgment within the parameters of legal practice, it goes awry, in my view, in supposing that the constraints of 'fit' may sometimes preclude any morally acceptable interpretation. According to Dworkin, there may be valid legal requirements too wicked to be obeyed: political obligation is overridden by countervailing duties to resist injustice. The judge may confront an uncomfortable choice between strict obedience to law, misrepresentation of the law, or resignation from office.[4] As I have argued in detail elsewhere, these conclusions are not consistent with the idea of law as a coherent body of principle, affirming the fundamental equality of all persons subject to the state's jurisdiction – the very nerve of integrity.[5] A purported rule or ruling that cannot be interpreted consistently with general principle, even when necessary exceptions and qualifications are implied or imposed, is simply futile – a failure to alter the *corpus juris*, which cannot accommodate what from the perspective of justice is an aberration, lacking intelligible meaning. Either an official requirement is law, an integral part of the complex web of rules and principles, or it is not; and if it is genuine law it must carry with it the law's ordinary authority. Interpretation, then, is critical, fusing questions of content and obligatory force.[6]

We may invoke the idea of reflective equilibrium, treating legal reasoning as analogous to ethical reasoning as Rawls presents it.[7] We strive for moral coherence between our general principles and the judgments in specific instances – including judicial precedents – about which we have the requisite confidence. While our principles must find vindication in their implications for the decisions and doctrines that we think persuasive – the familiar paradigms of legal practice – those decisions and doctrines obtain their authority, in the last analysis, from the principles on which we draw in their support. Debate and deliberation proceed by reference to shared commitments, identified by reference to decisions, doctrines and assumptions that would be widely recognised as pertinent. While respect for settled doctrine or assumption rightly disciplines interpretative analysis, no paradigm is finally immune from review and reappraisal.[8] In the oscillation between general principles and specific instances, we affirm the connection between natural and artificial reason: the law consists in the rules and requirements that govern the circumstances immediately in view, interpreted consistently with legal doctrine at higher levels of abstraction.[9]

[4] R Dworkin, *Law's Empire* (London, Fontana, 1986) 219.

[5] TRS Allan, 'Law, Justice, and Integrity: The Paradox of Wicked Laws' (2009) 29 *OJLS* 705.

[6] TRS Allan, 'Interpretation, Injustice, and Integrity' (2016) 36 *OJLS* 58.

[7] J Rawls, 'Outline of a Decision Procedure for Ethics' (1951) 60 *Philosophical Review* 177; see also TRS Allan, 'Principle, Practice, and Precedent: Vindicating Justice, According to Law' [2018] *CLJ* 269.

[8] Compare Dworkin, *Law's Empire* (n 4) 72.

[9] Compare the account of early modern common law thought in MD Walters, 'Legal Humanism and Law-as-Integrity' [2008] *CLJ* 352. The analogy with reflective equilibrium is denied in J Waldron, 'Judges as

The link between natural and artificial reason, or between political morality and public law, is mirrored in the relationship between international human rights law, universally applicable, and domestic constitutional rights, tailored to more local experience and civic tradition. National law lends greater precision to the abstract standards of justice enshrined, for example, in the Universal Declaration of Human Rights. There can be no difference between citizens and others as regards the protection of basic human rights, which affirm the equal human dignity of all those subject to the power of the state. If we distinguish between the rights of citizens and those of non-citizens, the distinction should reflect the special obligations associated with membership of the political community; and such membership requires specific legal guarantees, such as those that ensure equality of access to democratic representation. We need not, however, tie the idea of equal citizenship exclusively to political representation (and Parliamentary authority) in the way that Evan Fox-Decent, in his interesting chapter, suggests. I envisage a more abstract idea of membership of the political community, extending to participation in social, economic, and cultural life and including all persons who enjoy the right of permanent, or even temporary, residence. The obligations of obedience to law are in all cases conditional on the justice of the treatment of those concerned. Discrimination between citizens and non-citizens, or between permanent and temporary residents, must be justified by reference to relevant features of the public good in the same manner as any other form of discrimination between persons. Even non-nationals whose presence in the community is considered a threat to public safety must not be arbitrarily detained – imprisoned in circumstances that would not justify the detention of a citizen who posed a similar threat.[10]

In challenging the distinction between citizens and others, in the context of a legitimate regime that honours the rule of Law, Joanna Langille reminds us of the importance of private law in securing the requisite independence of persons – their freedom from arbitrary interference of the kind that undermines their autonomy and dignity.[11] As I have previously acknowledged, the rule of Law is as much dependent on a defensible scheme of private law as it is on the enforcement of principles of public law. As the set of conditions under which equal freedom is secured, the rule of Law requires, above all, adherence to the principles that underpin and unify the ordinary civil and criminal law.[12] As Langille fairly observes, this complicates the picture because a legal relationship may involve nationals of different states and arise from events occurring outside the state asserting jurisdiction. It does not follow, however, that we must abandon our understanding of political obligation, which assumes an association with a specific political community. As Langille argues, we accept that a dispute must be determined in accordance with the law of a specific state, even if we must develop, ideally in concert

Moral Reasoners' (2009) 7 *International Journal of Constitutional Law* 2, but for my critique of Waldron's view, see TRS Allan, 'The Moral Unity of Public Law' (2017) 67 *University of Toronto Law Journal* 1, 14–9.

[10] See *A v Secretary of State for the Home Dept* [2004] UKHL 56, [2005] 2 AC 68; TRS Allan, *The Sovereignty of Law: Freedom, Constitution, and Common Law* (Oxford, Oxford University Press, 2013) 114–19. The distinction between citizen and 'outsider', to which Fox-Decent draws attention, was intended to distinguish between the committed legal subject, who honours the constitution as a legitimate source of obligation, and the interpretative sceptic, for whom purported obligations are only an assertion of illegitimate force.

[11] I have capitalised 'Law' to signify the status of the rule of Law as a basic precept of legitimate governance.

[12] TRS Allan, 'The Rule of Law as the Rule of Private Law' in LM Austin and D Klimchuk (eds), *Private Law and the Rule of Law* (Oxford, Oxford University Press, 2014) ch 3.

with other states, choice of law rules to enable us to decide which set of rules applies in which circumstances. If we acknowledge that different systems of private law may be equally legitimate, reflecting different national traditions, we must negotiate an appropriate regime of private international law. In this context, then, political theory certainly confronts some intriguing questions about the familiar distinction between citizens and persons.

The relationship between natural and artificial reason is helpfully explored by Michael Foran, who rightly insists that principles of natural reason, or natural law, are not external to legal practice but central to its task in developing a public scheme of justice. His analysis of the connection between *lex* and *ius* identifies the way in which the positive law gives determinate shape to the principles of natural law. I agree with him that we should not associate the distinction between legal principle and public policy with the imposition of constraints on a utilitarian conception of the common good. We should repudiate utilitarianism as inconsistent with the fundamental equality of persons, even if we accept that political decisions may sometimes legitimately reflect majority votes or preferences. We can nevertheless accept the distinction between principle and policy as an indication of the limits of public law, leaving scope for government officials and public agencies to serve the public interest as they perceive it, subject only to judicial review for excess or abuse of delegated power. The main form of that excess or abuse comprises breaches of legal and constitutional rights, protecting liberty and equality. While commitment to these rights is certainly not consistent with moral neutrality – they deny that certain sorts of state coercion are morally permissible – it does not follow that should we allow the state to promote and enforce a controversial view about the good (or common good). Our natural law commitments must not, for example, be contaminated by religious doctrine or tradition that non-adherents may reasonably reject. Liberals believe that a free society must accommodate a wide variety of different views about the best conditions for human flourishing. Government must not discriminate between persons on the grounds of their beliefs about the nature of a good life; it must protect people's freedom to live in accordance with their own convictions, at least insofar as everyone may enjoy a similar freedom. Public authorities may properly seek to promote a wide range of goods that serve the interests of all, especially by protecting the general environment and increasing opportunities for education or self-development. But such goods do not give rise to legal entitlements unless conferred by statute. Constitutional rights uphold the moral limits of state coercion; they do not dictate the procurement of certain preferred states of affairs.

Foran's discussion of the *Bancoult* case, relating to the exclusion of the inhabitants of the Chagos Islands from their homeland, rightly emphasises the constraints implicit in a power to make law for the 'peace, order and good government' of a territory.[13] In that context, however, the principal injury to the islanders' wellbeing or flourishing consisted in the flagrant denial of their fundamental rights. Insofar as the common good of the community includes protection of its members' constitutional rights, it was clearly undermined by the purported assertion of legislative power. It is in the guarantee of these basic rights against illegitimate coercion that we find the critical distinction between

[13] *R (Bancoult) v Secretary of State for Foreign and Commonwealth Affairs* [2008] UKHL 61, [2009] 1 AC 453. See also Allan, *Sovereignty of Law* (n 10) ch 8.

what the British government claimed to be for the well-being of the colony and what, as a matter of law, fell within the limits of a legal order intended to serve the interests of its citizens. As Laws LJ observed, the removal of a people from their land, in the absence of some natural catastrophe rendering the land uninhabitable, was inherently contrary to a duty of constitutional governance: the people were to be *governed*, not removed.[14]

In her wide-ranging and richly nuanced chapter, Christine Sypnowich makes a similar case against ethical neutrality, emphasising the law's role in making human flourishing more equal. The rule of Law certainly does not preclude the provision of the material and cultural resources necessary for all to thrive. A guarantee of formal equality need not frustrate the pursuit of a deeper substantive equality. A persuasive liberalism must recognise the legitimacy of state action in defence of a wide range of public goods, which enhance everyone's quality of life. We can straightforwardly acknowledge the importance of human life and public health, green spaces, historic buildings, access to the arts, a culture of civility, and many other elements of a valuable collective existence – an expansive common good – extending appropriate political and legal support. This is not, however, to endorse a *constitutional* common good, acknowledging rights to the enjoyment of specific material benefits independently of democratic choice and legislative action.

***

Paul Craig takes issue with my contention that the law, when correctly interpreted, is what it ought to be.[15] He observes that the law has in the past often offended the demands of basic equality. Moreover, we confront a choice, he suggests, between a thin version of equality, which would be undemanding, or a thicker version, which would be very controversial.

I do not claim, however, that the law is morally correct in some sense that would disallow or obviate disagreement. In my view, the legal process is in substance a moral dialogue, obliging us to reconsider every rule or ruling in the light of any reasonable challenge – a challenge drawing on principles we profess, as a society, to honour. The correct legal decision in any specific case coincides with what political morality commends, I argue, when we follow the directions given by a legitimate legal practice. The rules established by statute and precedent, as interpreted in the light of widely acknowledged general principles, may be taken to define the demands of justice and the public good. They do so, at least, when we grant the legitimacy of the legal order as a collaborative arrangement for the governance of free and equal persons. If we deny the wisdom or justice of a rule or ruling, we do so primarily as legal interpreters: our objections proceed from principles that we try to identify as common ground – elements of a shared practice or tradition. Basic equality requires adherence to a coherent body of legal principle, which embraces all the various dimensions of justice, including the controversial questions of liberty that Craig identifies.

Our moral disagreement is highly beneficial, invigorating legal practice and forcing it to evolve in the direction of justice by confronting us with faults and failings

[14] *R (Bancoult) v Secretary of State for Foreign and Commonwealth Affairs* [2001] QB 1067, para 57.
[15] TRS Allan, 'Why the Law is What it Ought to Be' (2020) 11 *Jurisprudence* 574.

that demand correction. It is characteristic of common-law practice that even well-established rules can be challenged in the very process of application, at least in the higher courts. There is constant appraisal of the current rules in the light of what we believe to be the appropriate moral standards, however far those standards may depart from the views of earlier judges and previous generations. The declaratory theory of the common law does not commit us to the perpetuation of injustice. It demands only that we strive to maintain a coherent body of legal doctrine, which will secure the contemporary unity of principle necessary to ensure that like cases are treated alike. It is a serious mistake to reject the declaratory theory, which is the bedrock of common law thought.[16]

My claim is that a court's judgment must be morally justified in the sense that it is consistent with the scheme of justice that the law, viewed as a whole, provides. Recourse to common law or statutory rules presupposes that such rules are morally justified, representing society's best effort to specify the pertinent demands of justice. Legislative supremacy and *stare decisis* are moral constraints: they discipline our interpretative efforts to further justice and the public good in a manner that treats everyone alike in the relevant respects. There is no gap between law and justice, as a matter of application, and hence no need for judges to countenance the unconscionable treatment of persons. An unjust rule – flouting basic principles – is only a purported rule, awaiting interpretative clarification (or, in the last resort, disapplication or annulment). The law always commands the inner resources to confront injustice of the kind that would challenge its commitment to fundamental equality. It articulates the details of the arrangements that bind us together as a political community, founded on equal respect for persons.[17]

2. The Rule of Law and Parliamentary Sovereignty

Paul Craig objects that my theory is inapplicable to the UK. The doctrine of Parliamentary sovereignty shows that it does not fit the facts. As I have argued elsewhere, however, the requirements of fit are finally responsive to the demands of the interpretation itself, which must identify those elements of practice that should command our primary allegiance. There are no fixed pre-interpretative facts, invulnerable to normative appraisal.[18] The critical issue, moreover, is not whether Parliament is 'sovereign', in some descriptive sense, but what such an attribution means in the context of legal reasoning and judgment. Statutes are properly read in the light of general principle: 'ordinary meaning', narrowly understood, gives way to more nuanced construction as far as necessary. That does not mean that statutes always impose the rules that a court might itself have chosen; judicial respect for legislative supremacy is a requirement of democratic

[16] Compare A Beever, 'The Declaratory Theory of Law' (2013) 33 *OJLS* 421, observing, at 443, that 'if the law cannot be true to the theory, then it cannot be true to itself'. See also J Finnis, *Philosophy of Law: Collected Essays*, vol IV (Oxford, Oxford University Press, 2011) ch 20, endorsing a version of the declaratory theory similar to that accepted by the House of Lords majority in *Kleinwort Benson Ltd v Lincoln City Council* [1999] 2 AC 349.

[17] The law also embodies our collaborative efforts to further the public good, embracing all the various matters that, as Craig observes, fall outside the sphere of individual right or justice, narrowly understood.

[18] Allan, 'Interpretation, Injustice, and Integrity' (n 6).

governance. But it does mean that there is always sufficient interpretative flexibility to counter potential infringements of the rule of Law. A statute that appears on its face to give executive officials a veto over unfavourable judicial decisions, for example, must be narrowly construed to apply only in very exceptional circumstances.[19] We cannot divorce the questions of meaning and application from the issue of justification: these matters are tightly interlocked in a rigorously interpretative approach to law.

When Parliamentary sovereignty is treated as a legal doctrine, representing the principle of legislative supremacy, it can be integrated into a larger vision of the unwritten constitution. Rather than the expression of an official consensus, as in Hartian accounts, 'sovereignty' becomes one element of a defensible conception of democracy, in which elected officials wield authority subject to limits that secure fundamental rights. The nature and limits of legislative supremacy are, in practice, negotiated according to context: a supposedly inflexible rule is displaced by interpretative nuance. The doctrine is explored and refined in every case in which the courts determine its interaction, in all the circumstances, with the equally important doctrines of the separation of powers and the rule of Law. In the absence of any power to strike down a potentially offensive statute, its meaning and application must be highly sensitive to the demands of constitutional principle. Questions of validity yield the dominance they enjoy in legal positivist theory in favour of interpretative judgment, focused on constitutional practice. An ouster clause, for example, may circumscribe judicial review of executive agencies only insofar as the integrity of the rule of Law permits in all the circumstances. The limits of 'sovereignty' are located by attributing a sense to the statute that enables it to operate as an integral part of the legal order, reconciling legitimate administrative autonomy and requisite judicial oversight.[20]

If we associate Dicey's view of Parliamentary sovereignty as a 'legal fact' with the absence of any judicial strike-down power, it is possible to develop his reconciliation between legislative supremacy and the rule of Law in the manner that Mark Walters suggests.[21] Even if a 'modern judge' would never entertain an argument that an Act was invalid because it was immoral, as Dicey asserted, she should still acknowledge that its application involves moral judgment, limiting its capacity to wreak injustice.[22] She should attempt to justify her decision, primarily to the litigants, by invoking relevant principles that exert their force throughout the law.[23]

Jeffrey Goldsworthy contends that even if courts must settle certain disputes about 'sovereignty' when they arise, they have no authority to question the doctrine's central

[19] *R (Evans) v Attorney General* [2015] UKSC 21, [2015] AC 1787; see TRS Allan, 'Law, Democracy, and Constitutionalism: Reflections on *Evans v Attorney General*' [2016] *CLJ* 38.

[20] See especially *Anisminic Ltd v Foreign Compensation Commission* [1969] 2 AC 147; *R (Privacy International) v Investigatory Powers Tribunal* [2019] UKSC 22, [2020] AC 491.

[21] MD Walters, *AV Dicey and the Common Law Constitutional Tradition: A Legal Turn of Mind* (Cambridge, Cambridge University Press, 2020) especially chs 8–10.

[22] AV Dicey, *Lectures Introductory to the Study of the Law of the Constitution*, JWF Allison ed (Oxford, Oxford University Press, 2013 [1885]) 39.

[23] Judicial decisions are determined by the 'ordinary' law, as Dicey characterised it. It is ordinary law in the sense that it is not derived from external sources, such as a rule of recognition, but rather from values immanent within law itself as a coherent scheme of governance, respectful of basic legal equality. Compare MD Walters, 'The Unwritten Constitution as a Legal Concept' in D Dyzenhaus and M Thorburn (eds), *Philosophical Foundations of Constitutional Law* (Oxford, Oxford University Press, 2016) ch 2.

core. But the distinction between core and penumbra is far too fragile to be of any practical value: it attempts to divide into separate categories what is in practice a simple continuum. Every dispute about the meaning and application of statute is inherently an argument about the nature and limits of legislative supremacy – the appropriate way to interpret an enactment in all the relevant circumstances. The decisions in *Anisminic* and *Privacy International* are fine examples.[24] They define the relationship between Parliament and the courts as it operates in the context of judicial review, where critical questions of legality and the separation of powers arise.

It is wrong to think that in the absence of explicit constitutional guarantees or safeguards statutes must be treated as orders or instructions that override all previous law. We should distinguish between the enacted text and the rules that can be justified by reference to it. If we suppose that a statute is intended to advance the interests of justice and the public good, it must be interpreted accordingly, consistently with the responsibilities that we attribute to the legislature. The statute must be integrated into the *corpus juris* by reference to its evident or declared purposes and the defects or deficiencies of the current law that need to be remedied. Just as a single clause obtains its true meaning from the surrounding context, appropriately explained, so a single statute acquires a determinate content when absorbed within the larger network of standards to which it contributes. Parliamentary 'sovereignty', or legislative supremacy, is in that way subservient to the rule of Law.

Although Dicey's account of statutory interpretation favoured the protection of liberty and the principles of international law, it did not, Goldsworthy observes, guarantee their integrity. Even fundamental rights could be abrogated by explicit legislation. When, however, we reject the model of legislation as sets of orders or instructions, detached from the reasons that might both justify and qualify them, we can attain a different understanding. When statutes are interpreted within their larger constitutional context, they cannot authorise what would amount to grave injustice in specific instances. The basic principles of due process and fundamental equality form the premises of our interpretative engagement with the pertinent texts. The deeper the intrusion into enjoyment of constitutional rights or liberties envisaged, the more compelling must be the purported justification. No language, then, could succeed in authorising iniquity: the killing of blue-eyed babies, in Stephen's famous example, would be unintelligible, having no bearing on any practical questions arising.[25] It is simply question-begging to dismiss this sort of interpretative sensitivity, or flexibility, as 'strained', as if it were legitimate to read a statute stripped from its legal and constitutional context. A truly strained interpretation would be one that attributed to legislation a meaning that undermined the rule of Law, displacing law by the arbitrary deployment of state coercion.

It is the failure to recognise the proper integration of legislative and judicial authority, in fulfilment of the rule of Law, that gives rise to the false opposition between Parliamentary and judicial supremacy. It is often presented as a matter of who should have the 'last word'. It is a false antithesis because while an enactment must be fairly

[24] See n 20.

[25] See Dicey, *The Law of the Constitution* (n 22) 47, citing L Stephen, *The Science of Ethics* (Cambridge, Cambridge University Press, 2011 [1882]).

interpreted, identifying the category of cases in which the statute alters the previous law, its application to the individual case must give due weight to general principle. If adjudication is dependent on reasons, which can be offered to the litigants by way of justification, obedience to statute must mean adherence to a defensible reading, consistent with justice as the legal order, viewed a whole, defines it. Sovereign authority is thereby diffused and divided.

The false antinomy between Parliamentary absolutism and judicial supremacy was paraded in Lord Sumption's opinion in *Privacy International*.[26] In the absence of a written constitution, he asserted, any qualification of legislative power would make judicial precedent a higher source of law than statute. But we may challenge the implicit assumption that law is finally the product of an exercise of will. The common law is, instead, the product of reasoned discourse, disciplined by rigorous requirements of moral and intellectual coherence. Notably, Sumption grants the 'conceptual' limits on Parliamentary sovereignty identified by Sir John Laws in *Cart*.[27] Parliament cannot dispense with the constitutional requirement of an authoritative judicial source of interpretation of laws. Sumption affirms that judicial review would be available, despite the ouster clause, if the tribunal exceeded its 'subject-matter competence' or contravened the principles of natural justice. The conceptual limits on legislative supremacy are by the same token *normative* limits: they reflect the constraints on all forms of authority imposed by a constitution that honours the rule of Law.[28]

3. Parliamentary Sovereignty as Legislative Supremacy

George Letsas acknowledges the pragmatic reasons for persisting with the term 'Parliamentary sovereignty', a doctrine widely embraced within the UK legal community, but argues, nonetheless, that we should reject it on grounds of principle. While a weak interpretative stance embraces the doctrine, albeit in a version consistent with the rule of Law and the separation of powers, a stronger account is better. If the moral relevance of legislation derives from the ideal of representative democracy, we should invoke that ideal directly along with other such values as accountability, checks and balances, stability, and tradition. We do not need the detour of a worn-out legal doctrine whose time has passed.

My own proposal was that we should treat references to Parliamentary sovereignty as invocations of the doctrine of *legislative supremacy*, which signifies merely that Parliament has final authority as lawmaker. While the courts must enforce existing law, Parliament may change it, breaking the continuity between past and present. And while

[26] [2019] UKSC 22, para 209.

[27] *R (Cart) v The Upper Tribunal (Public Law Project Intervening)* [2009] EWHC 3052 (Admin), [2010] 2 WLR 1012. Laws LJ identifies the requirement of an authoritative judicial interpreter as simultaneously a limit on, and an affirmation of, Parliamentary sovereignty, akin to the rule that prevents a Parliament from binding its successors: ibid para 38.

[28] When Sumption suggests that Parliament might escape the conceptual limitation by creating a tribunal of unlimited jurisdiction, beyond judicial control, he clearly contradicts himself. How could Parliament override the conceptual limits on its own legislative authority? See further TRS Allan, 'Constitutionalism at Common Law: The Rule of Law and Judicial Review' [2023] *CLJ* 236, 237–38, 248–50.

other official bodies make rules and regulations, whether under statutory power or the royal prerogative, their jurisdiction is subject to Parliamentary sanction or revocation. We use a grand, somewhat inappropriate term for a perfectly familiar doctrine, which enables the courts to correct the excess or abuse of power by government ministers and official agencies. Admittedly, it is often supposed that Parliamentary legislation routinely overrides the common law, whatever the context. But the recognition of common law rights shows this to be an oversimplification. There is in practice an accommodation, the common law giving way to statute insofar as that is a legitimate response to an enactment in all the circumstances.

When we understand the doctrine of 'Parliamentary sovereignty' in this way, it is harder to distinguish between the weak and strong approaches that Letsas identifies. That clarification may be enough to dissolve any apparent disagreement. I agree with him that there is no competition between Parliament and the courts: they have wholly different functions, the courts' role being justified in political morality under a certain conception of the ideal of the rule of Law. Legislative supremacy is perfectly compatible with the existence of limits on legislative power; and authority attaches to the statutory text, suitably interpreted, rather than to legislative officials or their intentions. Nor is a court precluded from invoking values beyond representative democracy, such as accountability. In the second *Miller* case, which recognised limits on the ministerial power of Prorogation, the UK Supreme Court invoked the value of accountability, insisting that ministers should remain answerable for their decisions in Parliament.[29] Legal force was given, in effect, to a prime constitutional convention, central to the proper functioning of British democracy.[30]

I am inclined to agree that there is more to this question than mere pragmatism. We must not appear to condone arrangements that substitute the will (or alleged will) of a temporary political majority for law. But we must also be wary of crossing the line between interpretation, duly sensitive to history and practice, and abstract moral reasoning, external to the practice. It is true that we must identify a basis in political morality for those features of our system of governance that retain our allegiance. But that is different from showing that democratic institutions, in general, give rise to obligations of obedience, or that recourse to a wider range of values can justify, without reference to our specific political tradition, the assertion of state force against recalcitrants.

A genuine interpreter, as Dworkin observes, must stand within the practice, alongside other practice-participants, whose arguments and considered opinions are normally entitled to respect. While we must each accept responsibility for our legal judgments, seeking a genuine moral coherence, we must not confuse the law, as we understand it, with the arrangements we might, if given the opportunity, have drafted on a clean slate. Dworkin's own work sometimes blurs or overrides that distinction. Hercules, as he is presented in *Law's Empire*, apparently reaches legal conclusions based on moral or political judgments that are largely disengaged from the practice itself – an echo of the Archimedean approach that Dworkin elsewhere condemns.[31]

[29] *R (Miller) v Prime Minister; Cherry v Advocate General for Scotland* [2019] UKSC 41, [2020] AC 373.

[30] See Allan, 'Constitutionalism at Common Law' (n 28) 253–54.

[31] Compare GJ Postema, 'Protestant Interpretation and Social Practices' (1987) 6 *Law and Philosophy* 283. For full discussion, see TRS Allan, 'The Law in Quest of Integrity: Interpretation, Invention and Internal

A denial of the doctrine of Parliamentary sovereignty, even in the form that I have tried to defend, might be thought equally insensitive to legal practice as we know it. While we may argue over the correct interpretation of statute, we generally agree that it does in normal circumstances make a difference. A statute's enactment is not merely an event that we may or may not think fit to weigh in the balance with a variety of other considerations. Legislative supremacy is binding on judges even when they may think that the common law would generally be better left alone, free from Parliamentary interference. It is true, as Letsas observes, that representative democracy does not require bicameralism, let alone bicameralism with an unelected upper house. But I do not think such considerations would be directly pertinent to legal reasoning or adjudication: neither a statute's authority nor its meaning depends on our appraisal of the comparative merits of British versus other models of representative democracy.

When the unelected upper house is finally subservient to the elected chamber and performs a mainly checking and revising role in the legislative process, there is a reasonable accommodation between political morality and national practice and tradition. If the history of Parliamentary sovereignty consists largely in the repudiation of autocratic monarchy in favour of a more egalitarian conception of legitimate governance, its invocation may continue to harness a worthy tradition in aid of moral judgment, forging at least a degree of mutual understanding within the moral debate that public law engenders. We can argue about the correct construction of a statute without having to establish, in a preliminary skirmish, whether to give it any weight at all in our deliberations. And we can honour the efforts of our representatives to further the public good, as they understand it, without supposing that they might choose to deny the constitutional rights that form the bedrock of any legitimate legal order.

4. The Rule of Law as the Rule of Reason

The more spartan one's conception of the rule of Law, the easier the reconciliation with legislative supremacy. On Joseph Raz's well-known account, the most egregious forms of injustice can be imposed consistently with clearly expressed and prospective general rules.[32] If, however, rule *by* law, in the sense of publicly ascertainable general rules, is part of the ideal of the rule of Law, it is certainly not the whole.[33] The underlying idea is that all forms of coercion, whether by government officials or others, should be justified by recourse to morally defensible criteria – criteria that presuppose the equal humanity and civic status of all those within the scope of the state's jurisdiction.[34] Arbitrary power

Critique' in T Bustamante and M Martin (eds), *New Essays on the Fish-Dworkin Debate* (Oxford, Hart Publishing, 2023) ch 7.

[32] J Raz, *The Authority of Law: Essays on Law and Morality* (Oxford, Oxford University Press, 1979) ch 11.

[33] The distinction is considered by Jeremy Waldron in his essay 'The Rule of Law and the Role of Courts' (2021) 10 *Global Constitutionalism* 91, 95–97. Waldron warns of the danger of the judiciary becoming a Hobbesian sovereign if it thinks of itself as a lawmaker, which he apparently associates with anything more than enforcing an enacted bill of rights, treated as a finite list of specific and unrelated entitlements.

[34] Compare J Waldron, 'How Law Protects Dignity' [2012] *CLJ* 200, 214, observing that the idea of law or of a legal system now 'embodies the assumption that everyone in a society ruled by law is treated as *sui juris*, as having full legal dignity'.

is excluded in the sense that everyone is equally accountable to everyone else, enjoying their freedom only within limits that secure a similar freedom for others. To the objection that the rule of Law, on that conception, cannot be distinguished from the idea of justice, about which we often disagree, we may answer that the rule of Law obtains when we adhere to a coherent scheme or charter of justice, adapted to the community's particular history and experience and responsive to internal critique – demands for the consistent treatment of persons, extending the application of acknowledged principles to all relevant cases. The rule of Law is ultimately the rule of reason, which denies any space for the exercise of will, untamed by respect for persons as equal beneficiaries of just governance and the public good.[35]

In his chapter for this collection, Thomas Adams follows Raz in treating Fuller's canons of formal and procedural legality as constitutive of the rule of Law.[36] If law is only the systematic enforcement of rules, the rule of Law must be viewed as a set of standards that govern their proper form and mode of application. When, however, law is understood as embracing the principles that justify those rules, where the rules are indeed morally justified, the rule of Law can be recognised as the ideal of adherence, by citizen and official alike, to publicly acknowledged standards of justice. The rule of Law is morally valuable, not merely because its violation involves disrespect for human agency and autonomy, but more broadly because it affirms the principles of justice that lend the law its moral coherence. I agree, of course, that formal equality before the law is logically compatible with grave injustice: my claim is that we prize formal equality as an essential element of substantive equality, or equal citizenship.[37] My account of the rule of Law is offered as the central core of a theory of liberal democracy and, more specifically, of UK and Commonwealth constitutionalism. The important role played by equality in the judgments in the *Belmarsh* case, mentioned above, supports my approach.[38] When, in response to Nigel Simmonds's account of the intrinsic connection between law and liberty, Adams asserts that law is finally only an expression of will, he makes a fundamental error.[39] That assertion undermines the law's implicit claim to legitimacy: law really is, then, only 'the gunman situation writ large'.[40] An instrumentalist account is, in my view, misguided. Law is not merely a means to the attainment of someone's chosen ends. Nor is the requirement of impartial and independent courts merely an intermediate end, as Adams insists. It is critical to the integrity of the scheme of justice that genuine law provides – a bulwark of the individual freedom and dignity that proper legal process protects.[41]

[35] Compare Postema's account of the rule of Law, which extends beyond the formal, procedural, and institutional standards of *legality* to include the relationships, responsibilities and commitments that define *fidelity*: GJ Postema, 'Fidelity in Law's Commonwealth' in LM Austin and D Klimchuk (eds), *Private Law and the Rule of Law* (Oxford, Oxford University Press, 2014) 17.

[36] LL Fuller, *The Morality of Law*, rev edn (New Haven, Yale University Press, 1969) ch 2.

[37] Fuller presumably agreed, which is why he thought that departures from the inner morality of law threatened the reciprocity between rulers and ruled on which the obligation of obedience depended. Respect for human agency is affirmed by a legitimate legal order on which genuine rights and duties are grounded.

[38] *A v Secretary of State for the Home Dept* [2004] UKHL 56; Allan, *Sovereignty of Law* (n 10) 114–19.

[39] N Simmonds, *Law as a Moral Idea* (Oxford, Oxford University Press, 2007).

[40] Hart, *The Concept of Law* (n 2) 7.

[41] See further Allan, *Sovereignty of Law* (n 10) ch 3.

The conceptual connections between law and liberty are illuminated by Han-Ru Zhou's illuminating chapter on unwritten constitutional principles. Drawing on insights derived from a study of several major Commonwealth cases concerning both *ad hominem* statutes and privative clauses, Zhou identifies important links between breaches of the separation of powers, violations of basic rights, and disproportionate state action – the pursuit of alleged public interests in a manner that could not plausibly justify the unconscionable treatment of specific individuals. When judicial appeal to the constitutional text is contestable and inconclusive, we must acknowledge the role of the general principles that transcend the text. These extreme or extraordinary cases provoke an appropriately robust judicial response to a threat of grave injustice. They exhibit the deficiencies of a narrow conception of the rule of Law, supposedly consistent with gross violations of fundamental equality.[42]

As Fuller's work shows, the scope for democratic decision-making, within the boundaries of legality, broadens as we move from form and procedure, at one end of the spectrum, to matters of substance, at the other. When principles of legality express the central precepts of natural law, applicable wherever legal order displaces the assertion of arbitrary power, they become implicit features of state law, affirming its legitimacy. An *ad hominem* statute or bill of attainder, intended to punish specific individuals, lacks even the form of a genuine law: the enactment of a general rule leaves matters of application to an independent judiciary. Fuller's canons of legality, or procedural morality, are safeguards against the unfairness that results from the enforcement of rules that lack sufficient clarity or publicity or consistency to provide intelligible guidance. Insofar as statutes threaten such unfairness they must be interpreted appropriately, confining their application within defensible boundaries: they must be read in the light of the demands of due process.

Common law presumptions, reflecting such basic safeguards as *nulla poena sine lege*, play a similar role, promoting the integration of statute law and common law principle. They are presumptions of 'legislative intent' only in the figurative sense that they enable the text to be read as a rational addition to the *corpus juris*. They surrender to explicit contrary enactment, accordingly, only insofar as a reconciliation between statutory purposes and the requirements of justice allows. There is no mere substitution of the legislative will for reasoned judgment, attuned to all the circumstances; there is no capitulation to anyone's orders or instructions, heedless of the consequences in particular instances. There is an analogy with the 'principle of legality' in English law, which governs the interpretation of statutory powers conferred on public officials. It permits only those limitations of basic freedoms that are strictly necessary to accommodate conflicting rights or legitimate countervailing public interests. If fundamental rights cannot be overridden by general or ambiguous words, it is not primarily because 'the full implications of their unqualified meaning may have passed unnoticed in the democratic process'.[43] More importantly, such implications can be ascertained only by study of the

[42] Such landmark cases as *Liyanage* and *Kable*, analysed by Zhou, show how variations on the bill of attainder lie at the core of a range of state action that violates fundamental equality – the implicit ground of unreasonableness or irrationality. See also TRS Allan, *Constitutional Justice: A Liberal Theory of the Rule of Law* (Oxford, Oxford University Press, 2001) chs 7, 8.

[43] *R v Secretary of State for the Home Dept, ex p Simms* [2000] 2 AC 115, 131 (Lord Hoffmann).

constitutional context in which specific questions of interpretation arise. While it would be unreasonable to expect Parliament to make explicit provision for every contingency, even when fundamental rights are likely to be engaged, it is also unnecessary. Basic rights and general principles are the taken-for-granted background to legislative action. It is an error to insist that all constraints on Parliament are 'ultimately political' rather than legal: the principle of legality is not simply a means of shifting blame from judges to politicians for injustices that would supposedly incur a 'political cost'.[44]

A consistently interpretative approach tries to make coherent sense of public law viewed as a whole, locating the respective roles of rights, duties, and powers within an overarching theory of legal practice. The critical test of any theory is its ability to justify each element of practice as a recognisable contribution to good governance, consonant with basic values of human freedom and dignity. As Jacob Weinrib's chapter ably shows, we cannot, for example, evaluate contrasting accounts of proportionality, as a standard of judicial review, in isolation from grander questions about the nature of constitutional rights and their mode of interaction with competing interests. A 'bifurcated' model of rights, in Weinrib's description, gives proportionality a role at the periphery of a basic right without denying the absolute strength of its essential core. An interpretative approach treats a charter of rights as an integrated system of standards that regulate the relationship between public agencies and those persons subject to their authority. We must construct an account that allows each right to be upheld according to its purpose: none may be wholly denied without violation of the charter itself. A right may be limited, in its essence, only to accommodate another right of equal status: it must be a proportionate restriction in that specific sense. I would add only that the charter of rights may be unwritten. Constitutional rights at common law exert a similar degree of resistance to the general interests or policy preferences that would otherwise infringe them. At their core, such rights possess absolute force, their denial or purported abrogation threatening the legitimacy of the legal order.

The right to a fair trial, when someone is alleged to have committed a criminal offence, is a necessary prelude to legitimate conviction and punishment. The right, more broadly, to natural justice or procedural fairness must be satisfied before decisions directly affecting individual rights or interests can be treated as binding.[45] In addition to ensuring that the law is correctly applied to the relevant circumstances, as these are ascertained by admissible evidence, a fair hearing allows for argument over the relevant legal criteria – the standards of judgment, which may well be a matter of dispute. Litigants or applicants may properly seek to present the law in a manner that reconciles their legitimate interests with the applicable rules or public policies.

[44] ibid. If the principle is treated as demanding explicit authority for a *disproportionate* interference with basic rights – one that cannot be strictly justified by reference to the relevant public interests – the standard rationale proves inapplicable. As Varuhas observes, it is neither realistic nor reasonable to expect legislation to provide for every possible circumstance in which powers conferred on a public agency may impinge on constitutional rights: JNE Varuhas, 'The Principle of Legality' [2020] *CLJ* 578, 605–06. See further Allan, 'Constitutionalism at Common Law' (n 28) 245–46.

[45] Where on its face a statute removes the ordinary requirement of procedural fairness it must be interpreted as qualifying such requirements only insofar as a fair trial is not rendered unattainable: see especially *R v A (no 2)* [2001] UKHL 25, [2002] 1 AC 45; *Secretary of State for the Home Dept v AF (no 3)* [2009] UKHL 28, [2010] 2 AC 269; *Canada (Citizenship and Immigration) v Harkat* 2014 SCC 37.

Procedural arrangements must accommodate the interpretative complexity of legal requirements, especially when there is scope for adaptation to meet unusual circumstances. A reasonable opportunity to participate in that way, where significant rights or interests are at stake, is a condition of respect for human dignity and, hence, of the rule of Law.[46]

In his very fine chapter, Hasan Dindjer reminds us of the centrality of reason-giving to the idea of natural justice. As he argues, a duty to give reasons to persons affected by an official decision is an important defence against arbitrary power. An administrative agency should regard itself as obliged to answer directly to those concerned, who may judge the cogency of the reasons given. And even when a decision is, in part, dictated by rules or policies adopted elsewhere – 'political decisions that lie further upstream', as Dindjer puts it – there is usually scope to consider what would be a fair application of the relevant criteria in all the circumstances. When the decision follows a hearing, the parties affected should be assured – if such assurance is warranted – that their arguments have been duly considered and weighed. As Dindjer observes, it is hard to see how a government could have the moral standing to make claims to people's obedience if it denies them the ability to judge whether its claims are legitimate.[47]

The closer a public function approximates a judicial one, narrowing the scope for exercise of official discretion, the more rigorous the demands of due process become. When decisions are made that have a direct bearing on the lives or liberties of identifiable individuals, the relevant criteria must be closely defined by law. A government minister, for example, entrusted with a power to determine what is, in effect, the sentence to be served by a convicted offender, must deliberate in the impartial manner of a professional judge, following judicial advice. No licence to wield arbitrary power is conferred by the statutory delegation of authority to an executive official.[48] And we should welcome the belated recognition that the power to pardon a convicted offender, in exercise of the Crown's prerogative of mercy, should be no exception to the ordinary principles of procedural fairness and judicial review. No one should be literally at the mercy of another: the rule of Law must not collapse into arbitrariness.[49]

5. Law as Practical Reason

It is important to distinguish clearly between true statements of law, on the one hand, and official (including judicial) opinion, on the other. Because legal judgment is ultimately moral judgment, even if closely focused on the demands of a legitimate social

[46] Compare Jeremy Waldron's argument that the law's susceptibility to rational analysis, as a unified system of governance subject to inquiry and debate, is an important public resource that promotes the ideal of human dignity: J Waldron, 'The Concept of Law and the Rule of Law' (2008) 43 *Georgia Law Review* 1, 35–36; Waldron, 'How Law Protects Dignity' (n 34) 208–12.

[47] As Dindjer argues, the failure to give reasons is intrinsically wrongful even if, in practice, we must rely on the availability of judicial review to secure the appropriate legal doctrinal foundations.

[48] See *R v Secretary of State for the Home Dept, ex p Venables* [1998] AC 407; *R v Secretary of State for the Home Dept, ex p Pierson* [1998] AC 539. See further Allan, *Constitutional Justice* (n 42) 142–48.

[49] *Lewis v Attorney General of Jamaica* [2000] 2 AC 50, repudiating the view expressed in *De Freitas v Benny* [1976] AC 239, 247, that mercy is intrinsically arbitrary, beginning 'where legal rights end' (Lord Diplock).

practice, there can be no escape from individual responsibility. The interpreter must be her own final judge, even if she should hesitate before rejecting the reasoning of other competent practice-participants. If the content of the practice – law or practical reasoning more widely – has a certain independence from anyone's views or opinions, even if those views or opinions are widely shared, each interpreter must strive to reach her own considered conclusions in specific instances. Acceptance of responsibility for judgment in the face of serious doubt and disagreement is critical to the role of the conscientious citizen, who grants the law's authority only insofar as it meets those fundamental requirements of justice that preserve its legitimacy.[50]

It is true, of course, that we should normally accept a court's decision as settling a specific legal dispute, subject only to any right of appeal. But it does not follow that we must endorse the court's reasoning or treat its decision as having unqualified authority for future cases. A precedent's bearing on another case is always a matter of judgment, attuned to all the circumstances. If, in our best judgment, the court's interpretation of the law is mistaken, we are entitled to say so, drawing attention to the pertinent rules or principles. The decision ought to be distinguished or overruled or otherwise repudiated in subsequent cases. Even if we should accord a limited, temporary authority to a doubtful decision, in the interests of local doctrinal coherence, we must not countenance any grave violation of basic principle.[51] Nor should we extend its influence any further than is required to ensure that like cases are decided alike – distinguishing other instances whenever we can draw reasonable distinctions that preserve overall coherence.[52] We can think of the legal process as a continuing debate over the appropriate criteria to determine disputes. Even when we are agreed about which statutes and precedents are relevant, scope for argument usually remains about their application to the facts. While legal doctrine gives general principles more concrete expression, fitted for the demands of practical instances, it cannot displace those principles even in particular cases. Every rule must give way, whether by adaptation or revocation, when its unqualified application would do real injustice. Such inherent doctrinal flexibility ensures that the law cannot move too far from the principles of justice that lend it moral coherence. Every invocation of a rule is an implicit affirmation of its *appropriateness* in all the circumstances: its application will not be an affront to fundamental equality.

I do not think David Dyzenhaus is correct, in his absorbing chapter, to distinguish so sharply between judges and ordinary citizens. A citizen's refusal to obey an illegitimate rule or ruling – one that he thinks violates constitutional principle – is plainly akin to a judge's repudiation of a measure on similar grounds. A person's obligation to obey the law is a duty to follow a defensible interpretation, consistent with basic principles of equality and due process. If there is a genuine moral dilemma, it need

[50] Compare Dworkin, *Law's Empire* (n 4) 190, defending an account of political obligation that requires 'fidelity to a scheme of principle each citizen has a responsibility to identify, ultimately for himself, as his community's scheme'.

[51] Dworkin defends a doctrine of 'local priority': ibid 250–54.

[52] I would not draw the line between principle and precedent as starkly as Alison Young suggests when she observes that I accord precedents no intrinsic weight in legal reasoning. I should prefer to say that precedent is influential insofar as it can be understood as giving specific doctrinal shape to a general scheme of legal principle, which satisfies basic moral requirements of due process and equal respect for persons. Principle and precedent are inextricably combined as abstract and specific dimensions of adherence to law.

not consist in a choice between obedience to law, on the one hand, and the dictates of conscience, on the other. A conscientious interpreter may nevertheless hesitate before rejecting an official or majority view of the law's demands because a serious division of opinion may weaken the bonds of community. A refusal to bow to the judgment of a court, which has heard full argument, is a particularly painful step towards what may turn out, sadly, to be an irreparable breach. The withdrawal of cooperation is a last resort when one's best arguments have been ignored or, insofar as one can fairly judge, unreasonably rejected.

It follows that civil disobedience does *not* normally involve resistance to an admittedly valid law on conscientious grounds. It is, in substance, a challenge on the ground of constitutional *legality*. It either denies the validity of a purported rule or ruling, as contrary to legal and constitutional principle, or contests the interpretation adopted by officials. The dissentient seeks to preserve her own integrity, arguing for an interpretation capable of maintaining her allegiance to (what she trusts remains) a legitimate legal order. No one can honourably acknowledge as binding – even prima facie – a rule or ruling that denies her status, or that of a fellow citizen, as an equal member of the political community, flouting fundamental rights. The moral force of her appeal lies in its steadfast adherence to a shared political tradition: it seeks to hold other citizens and state officials alike to the principles of justice that they profess to honour.[53]

Dyzenhaus asks whether I have gone too far in eliminating the productive tension between fit and justification, a tension which helps us to identify the moral authority that law derives from its nature as law. I agree with him that, in the hands of Greenberg and Hershovitz, the triumph of justification over fit comes at the expense of abandoning the puzzle of legal authority.[54] In my own theory, however, the Dworkinian paradigms remain to distinguish one legal order from another: the law is one among many possible instantiations of the rule of Law, the product of a common tradition as much as overlapping moral conviction.[55] There is law only insofar as moral argument can appeal to settled understandings and familiar practices, uniting interpreters in a joint deliberative endeavour. While considerations of fit are always subservient to those of justification, as I have argued above, they cannot be abandoned altogether. A threshold of fit operates to exclude bad faith interpretations that fail seriously to engage with practice and tradition; acknowledged paradigms serve to discipline interpretative debate even if each one is ultimately vulnerable to reappraisal and rejection. That threshold also delineates the boundaries of permissible cooperation. If a practice cannot reasonably be interpreted, in good faith, as one that embraces human dignity and equal liberty as core foundational values, it must be repudiated: it does not generate any genuine law.[56]

[53] See further Allan, *Sovereignty of Law* (n 10) ch 4. An analogy may be drawn with the role of conscientious civil servant, obliged to exercise a degree of independence, and hence interpretative responsibility, against ministerial instructions that threaten established constitutional standards: see Janet McLean's thoughtful chapter in this volume.

[54] M Greenberg, 'The Moral Impact Theory of Law' (2014) 123 *Yale Law Journal* 1288; S Hershovitz, 'The End of Jurisprudence' (2015) 124 *Yale Law Journal* 1160.

[55] See Allan, 'Principle, Practice, and Precedent' (n 7); TRS Allan, 'Law as a Branch of Morality: The Unity of Practice and Principle' (2020) 65 *American Journal of Jurisprudence* 1.

[56] Allan, 'Interpretation, Injustice, and Integrity' (n 6).

Although Dyzenhaus questions the general applicability of a theory of law focused on common law adjudication in a liberal democracy, he recognises, nonetheless, that legal and political theory must run in tandem. We are seeking to illuminate the nature of law when it carries moral authority, relevant to practical reasoning. Either legal positivism is misguided, unable to account for such authority, or it focuses on a different subject-matter, such as the means of control used by rulers in imposing their will on the ruled.[57] I do not mean to confine my legal theory to common law jurisdictions, which admittedly represent only one version of legal order, but rather to celebrate the role of reasoned judgments, which characteristically display the interpretative insight and flair required to preserve the critical link between law and justice. Common law constitutionalism is, in my view, a paradigm of legal liberalism. The law must guarantee the equal freedom and dignity of those over whom it purports to rule, according to a coherent understanding of the implications of those ideals in all the circumstances.

My theory of law, then, is also in substance a theory of the post-Westphalian state, as Dyzenhaus describes it. It is not contingent on whether the constitution is written or unwritten, or whether there is a formally enacted charter of rights and freedoms. Bills or charters of rights usually acknowledge principles of justice that already apply, as a matter of fundamental law, to any legitimate regime. While the relationship between the rule of Law and democracy is complex, much depending on how the latter ideal is understood, there is arguably a good deal of both conceptual and practical overlap. The principle of equality, or equal dignity, is foundational to both ideals, a principle that has extensive ramifications for both political arrangements and legal doctrine. Freedoms of thought, speech, and association, for example, are central features of both the rule of Law and democracy: each ideal presupposes an informed and conscientious citizen or subject, able and willing to subject official rules and rulings to appropriate scrutiny. Richard Stacey's interesting chapter for this collection develops a related connection between the rule of Law and popular sovereignty, arguing that only a fully developed, substantive account of the former can secure the conditions of the latter. As Stacey observes, a legal order in which some people are less able than others to evaluate official compliance with a vision of the public good cannot be democratically legitimate. The basic civil and political rights provide the foundations for both the rule of Law and democracy.

In his engagingly provocative contribution, Peter Cane suggests that the law, for my purposes, is only one among many considerations relevant to an overall assessment of what one ought to do. But that suggestion entails a distinction between the law and all-things-considered judgment, which is a distinction I would resist. The law's content, I argue, is a moral judgment that embraces all considerations relevant to the legitimacy of state action. And, when correctly ascertained, the law carries an obligation of obedience, which flows from the duty of civility or fidelity to the political community. In treating common law method as a form of practical reasoning apt to determine the conduct of any participant, whether judge or citizen, as Cane observes, I view statute

[57] Compare Dworkin's distinction between sociological and doctrinal concepts of law: R Dworkin, *Justice in Robes* (Cambridge, Harvard University Press, 2006) chs 1, 8.

and precedent as influential, if contestable, features of the deliberative process itself. They acquire their meaning from the interpretative exercise in which participants join to elucidate the character of their common practice. That meaning cannot be severed from the assumptions and commitments that animate the practice, which include the understanding that the law, when correctly ascertained, is morally binding.

As an adaptation of universal ideals of good governance to contemporary conditions, the law cannot intelligibly flout those ideals: it is an expression of political morality in the circumstances prevailing. In that sense, admittedly, the sovereignty of law is ultimately the sovereignty of reason. I am reluctant, however, to embrace Cane's distinction between practice-dependent and practice-independent conceptions of morality, or that between system-specific and other conceptions. I prefer the traditional common law approach, which sought to integrate natural law and legal tradition, artificial reason being finally a more detailed articulation of natural reason.[58] Even if we can, as I believe, intelligibly appeal to universal values, reflecting general ideas of human freedom and well-being, we must look to social practice to give them concrete expression. Legal judgment is only an aspect or dimension of that process, relevant to the justification of state action.

There is some 'slippage', in Cane's view, between my use of the term 'interpretation' to describe both a judicial method and a means of determining textual meaning. But the ambiguity arises only if such an authoritative meaning exists independently of the interpretative process itself; and that is an assumption I am inclined to reject. Even if there is an 'ordinary' linguistic meaning, dependent on the language read in the light of its immediate context, the legal meaning – what the text adds to the *corpus juris* – is something different, dependent on the principles that unify the law in general. A legal norm is no mere reflection of the text from which it, in part, derives: it is a product of the text's integration into the larger scheme of rules and principles. The treatment of Parliamentary sovereignty as a rule for resolving conflicts between statute and common law, as Cane describes it, is therefore an oversimplification. A statutory provision overrides, or modifies, a common law rule only to the extent that relevant general principles permit or require. These principles resolve the conflict by giving each rule, whatever its source, the effect that reasoned judgment prescribes in all the circumstances.

I readily acknowledge the possibility of a purely descriptive account of law, in the sense of an explanation of institutions and processes. Such an account may adopt what Cane calls a 'moderately' external perspective, which notices the insider's attitude to law without necessarily endorsing it. But I deny the possibility of a merely descriptive account of the law's content, which depends on moral judgment, sensitive to considerations of legitimacy. Being the product neither of judicial consensus nor official diktat, the law cannot be simply recorded without endorsement. When correctly identified, the law permits and requires what the best interpretation of legal practice indicates, even if that is often a matter of lively controversy. There is, then, no genuine question of 'descriptive accuracy': a true proposition of law rests on sound moral judgment, connecting observable practice and principled justification.

[58] Compare Walters, 'Legal Humanism and Law-as-Integrity' (n 9).

6. Law and the Rule of Law

I have some sympathy for Hillary Nye's contention that we should abandon intractable argument over the nature of law in favour of a focus on good governance in accordance with the rule of Law, understood as a political ideal. If the debate about law is irresolvable, it is surely because analytic legal theory cannot do much useful work without the context provided by moral and political theory. Debate over the nature of law is, at root, an argument in political theory – how best to grasp the idea of the rule of Law. Arguably, 'eliminativism' is only an acknowledgment of this inconvenient truth. We should frankly acknowledge that references to law, or the obligation of obedience to law, must be understood in the context of a theory of the rule of Law. A liberal-democratic constitutionalist concept of law carries substantive and procedural implications for legal practice that would be inapplicable elsewhere.

When Nye observes that, in considering what ought to be done, judges must take account of institutional history, she grants statutes and precedents no inherent moral importance. She adopts an externalist view, aligning the legal interpreter with the sceptical observer and critic. But the significance of the past is not confined to the promises or expectations that it has generated. It is arguably a presumptive guide to what justice means for the political community that legal practice has forged and nurtured. The law constitutes a distinct domain of morality, with its own unique rights and obligations, because it is the product of communal life, the fruit of a shared history marked by struggle against injustice in its numerous forms.[59]

The rule of Law, then, is the rule of *our* law, which gives a distinctive shape to abstract ideals that would otherwise prove indeterminate. The precedents, especially, help to define what our principles mean in practice, transforming sceptical critic into fully engaged interpreter. If a duty to obey the law is only a duty to do the right thing, all things considered – as Nye suggests – it is informed, nevertheless, by a shared tradition that steers and disciplines our deliberative efforts. When legal practice is sufficiently complex, natural reason supported by its artificial counterpart, judicial power is sharply constrained. Judges exercise only reason, which is subject to the standards of critical appraisal supplied by legal practice itself.[60]

Natural and artificial reason cannot be strictly separated: the latter is only a more precise specification of the former. I agree with Nye that we should hesitate to follow John Finnis in supposing that the 'intra-systemic' validity of an unjust measure could insulate it, even for limited purposes, against the ordinary critique supplied by practical reasoning, open to all relevant moral considerations.[61] It is not true, for example, that we may not usefully challenge the obligatory status of a rule affirmed as valid by the highest court.[62] There cannot, in particular, be an iniquitous rule or ruling that demands

[59] Compare GJ Postema, 'Integrity: Justice in Workclothes' (1997) 82 *Iowa Law Review* 821, arguing that justice is a public good attainable only through coordinated, collective action.

[60] See further Allan, 'Principle, Practice, and Precedent' (n 7). Compare FA Hayek, *Law, Legislation and Liberty* (London, Routledge & Kegan Paul, 1982) vol I, 115–19. Hayek observes that even when a judge is obliged to formulate a new rule, he remains 'a servant endeavouring to maintain and improve the functioning of an existing order': ibid 119.

[61] J Finnis, *Natural Law and Natural Rights* (Oxford, Oxford University Press, 1980) 314–20.

[62] ibid 357.

judicial obedience, on the one hand, but warrants civil disobedience, on the other.[63] When correctly interpreted, the law matches what political morality ordains because it operates in the same space: it fulfils and complements the general principles that regulate legitimate governance in the interests of the whole society.[64]

7. Justice, Fairness, and Integrity

Stuart Lakin objects that my interpretative mode of argument is insufficiently inclusive and conciliatory. My focus on justice, as law's essential aim, gives too little weight to such countervailing aspects of political morality as democratic choice and procedural fairness. My theory of law differs, admittedly, from the one Dworkin presents in *Law's Empire*. But I believe that my account is more faithful to the animating idea of integrity – the principle that all those subject to the state's jurisdiction must be treated with equal respect and concern.

Lakin resists my contention that the Fugitive Slave Acts were either invalid, from the perspective of integrity, or did not require what on a strictly literal reading they seemed to require. He favours Dworkin's suggestion that such wicked legislation might be valid, even if it should nevertheless by resisted, or disapplied, as morally abhorrent. But it is hard to see how the enforcement of slavery could have been legally required in any sense of law consistent with integrity. The point of integrity is to show how and why the law's enforcement is justified – why its subjects are morally obligated to obey – and the infliction of what is undeniably grave injustice is thereby logically precluded. A regime that flouts fundamental rights, implicit in the ideal of equal human dignity, is not legitimate. A legal interpreter who strives to preserve legitimacy must repudiate what purports to be law but, when judged by the standards of basic justice, is plainly not law. Admittedly, we often disagree about what justice requires. In fairness, we must try to accommodate reasonable disagreement, giving effect to statutes and precedents that complicate, even redirect, our efforts to interpret the law as a morally coherent set of standards overall. We must give a doubtful statute, for example, such force and effect as is consistent with our basic constitutional premise, bowing to considerations of democratic fairness as far as our commitment to basic justice allows. We cannot compromise, however, with grave injustice. We cannot acknowledge violations of fundamental equality without rejecting integrity – abandoning our efforts to integrate law and political morality.

Dworkin demonstrated a genuinely interpretative approach in his review of Robert Cover's book, *Justice Accused*. He argued that there were general principles of justice more central to the law than the 'particular and transitory policies of the slavery compromise' that the Northern states reluctantly enforced:

> The general structure of the American Constitution presupposed a conception of individual freedom antagonistic to slavery, a conception of procedural fairness that condemned the

[63] Compare H Nye, 'Finnis's Divided View of Law: Problems for Adjudicative Theory' (2020) 11 *Jurisprudence* 503.

[64] Compare J Finnis, 'Law and What I Truly Should Decide' (2003) 48 *American Journal of Jurisprudence* 107, 126.

> procedures established by the Fugitive Slave Acts, and a conception of federalism inconsistent with the idea that the State of Massachusetts had no power to supervise the capture of men and women within its territory.[65]

A resolutely interpretative approach dispenses for the most part with black-and-white judgments of validity. It grants all morally relevant considerations a role in the determination of statutory meaning and proper application. As the product of such inclusive moral judgment, the applicable law is inherently valid and binding: there is no intelligible question of valid law conflicting with moral or constitutional principle.

Lakin also complains that I seek to disqualify too many views about the law and the constitution in favour of my own 'justice-centric, judge-centric moral theory'. A theory of *public law*, however, must be grounded in a theory of the rule of Law, which on the most persuasive understanding requires that people's basic freedoms should be recognised and enforced in court. The judicial power to enforce constitutional rights cannot be merely contingent on the political arrangements currently in place, even if that view is commonly held. When state officials trample on constitutional rights in a manner that denies fundamental equality, the absence of legal remedy undermines legitimacy. The rule of Law, as integrity conceives it, is eviscerated.

The law cannot speak with one voice, moreover, if it is riven with internal contradiction. An oscillation between competing versions of the UK Human Rights Act offers a good example. Lakin argues that the courts oscillate between 'the robust judicial protection of fundamental rights and deference to Parliament', reflecting competing visions of the British constitution. But such oscillation is morally incoherent, flouting human rights in certain cases by removing the judicial protection that a more consistent interpretation would provide. However important the doctrines of Parliamentary sovereignty and the separation of powers may be, their correct interpretation must be sensitive to these fundamental points about the rule of Law. A political constitutionalist who denies the centrality of law to legitimate governance repudiates the ideal of integrity. Equal freedom and dignity are placed at the mercy of a temporary political majority, whose decisions need not satisfy the rigorous tests of good faith and non-discrimination that adherence to integrity entails. It is not enough that political decisions are usually just and fair. Legality is more demanding: each person's treatment must be defensible according to the standards of justice we jointly affirm.

8. Doctrine and Deference

Alison Young, in her wide-ranging discussion, contends that Parliament and courts must share authority over the content of Parliamentary sovereignty, the rule of Law, and the separation of powers. Her wish to incorporate within legal reasoning such matters of institutional and constitutional competence – the court giving way to official opinion that it might not share – explains why she endorses the general doctrine of deference that I reject. I cannot see, however, how these general principles of constitutional law

[65] R Dworkin, 'The Law of the Slave-Catchers', TLS (London, 5 December 1975) 1437, reviewing RM Cover, *Justice Accused: Antislavery and the Judicial Process* (New Haven 1975).

could properly be a matter of Parliamentary opinion or decision, or even how such an opinion or decision, supposedly shared by members of Parliament, could be ascertained. Legislative supremacy defines the nature and scope of Parliament's authority: it is a principle of law that the courts must identify consistently with their commitment to the rule of Law. The rule of Law requires adherence to legal principle, articulated by independent courts, appropriately detached from the pressures that accompany the pursuit of specific governmental ends. Perhaps we could infer from the enactment of an ouster clause, for example, that Parliamentary opinion, if only the opinion of a temporary majority, favoured some restriction of the scope of judicial review. We could not, however, infer any view about the implications of that clause for the statute's correct application to the facts of any specific instance. Those implications are a matter of judgment for the court in the light of the circumstances arising.[66] Deference to any supposed Parliamentary opinion would be as improper as it would be precarious, legal judgment giving way to political pressure or speculation.

I do not deny that any of our basic concepts, including fundamental rights, are highly contestable: public law is inherently controversial, dependent on a range of judgments about basic political values. It is nevertheless the duty of courts to decide disputes in accordance with their own best judgment of these matters, seeking the kind of reflective equilibrium between principle and precedent that I have described. To give judgment contrary to legal or constitutional rights, as the court understands them, is to abdicate responsibility for sustaining the rule of Law. And it makes no difference whether the abdication represents a surrender to the threat of political interference or deference to (what judges must consider) erroneous Parliamentary or executive opinion. It is one thing to make allowance for administrative expertise in determining the justifiability of an official rule or ruling. It is quite another to substitute an official view of the rights or principles at stake for what a court, in its considered judgment, believes is a better understanding, consistent with a morally coherent constitutional vision.[67] Nor may a court defer to another body on the basis that one conception of a contested concept is as good as another. On that approach there would be no legal rights at all, only conflicting claims: law would simply collapse into politics. An internal, interpretative theory of law, focused on a specific jurisdiction, imposes the discipline necessary to adjudicate fairly between competing claims.[68]

My objection to the so-called 'doctrine of deference' in administrative law concerns the risk that general questions of institutional competence or democratic accountability, applicable to the agency in question, will obscure the judicial focus on the specific

[66] Compare Lord Carnwath in *R (Privacy International) v Investigatory Powers Tribunal* [2019] UKSC 22, [2020] AC 491 at para 131, observing that 'it is ultimately for the courts, not the legislature, to determine the limits set by the rule of law to the power to exclude judicial review'.

[67] When a court permits an administrative agency to choose – recognising legitimate discretion – it does not surrender its judgment of the pertinent rights and duties. It determines that the decision impugned falls within the scope of that discretion, involving no breach of the complainant's rights.

[68] The essentially contested concepts that Young considers are plainly interpretative concepts, in Dworkin's sense. They obtain their meaning and significance from the practice in which they figure: see R Dworkin, *Justice for Hedgehogs* (Cambridge, Harvard University Press, 2011) ch 8. Legal concepts, accordingly, are integral to the theory of law on which an interpretative judgment of legal practice draws. Any interpretative judgment, of course, denies or opposes conflicting opinions or conclusions.

claim of injustice or illegality arising.[69] An expert or politically accountable body is, in principle, no more at liberty to act unfairly or unreasonably than an inexpert or unaccountable one. And this is true even if, in determining unfairness or unreasonableness, the court is careful to acknowledge its own comparative lack of expertise on some of the matters in contention. We should not confuse the acceptance of plausible arguments, which have not been plainly refuted, with reluctance to allow a challenge to administrative action on such extraneous grounds as comparative expertise or institutional competence. In the context of a human rights claim, a doctrine of deference threatens to weaken judicial protection by resurrecting the old fetters of non-justiciability – fetters that have fallen, one by one, in recent decades in the face of cogent legal objections to the abuse of executive, and especially prerogative, power.[70]

My argument, according to Paul Craig, misses a distinction between the standard of review and its manner of application: adjudicative deference 'fine-tunes' the standard of review. Such fine-tuning, however, is plainly dependent on the nature of the specific issues arising. It is a question of what the pertinent rights require in all the circumstances. There is a 'disproportionate' breach whenever an encroachment or restriction is unjustified: the measure impugned is either strictly unnecessary or, even worse, wholly inimical to the values under threat. If the proportionality test required a genuine balancing of interests – if rights could somehow be set off against utilitarian considerations that favoured their restriction – a doctrine of deference might, in the style of a justiciability test, dictate a somewhat arbitrary division of labour between court and public authority. But since rights cannot be balanced away in that manner, there is nothing beyond the analysis and application of rights for legal doctrine to regulate.[71]

I do not argue, as Craig supposes, that the courts should distinguish between internal and external factors in gauging the scope or intensity of judicial review. My contention is that these matters should be addressed – or rather displaced – by analysis of the rights or claims in issue, giving an authority's submissions such weight or credence as the context justifies. On certain questions, official expertise will enhance the prospect of meeting a claimant's objections; it will enable the agency to show, in appropriate detail, why those objections fail. Institutional or constitutional questions are directly relevant to the limits of the court's own jurisdiction. A determination of right must not eclipse legitimate discretion to formulate and implement public policy: a rights-violation occurs when the scope of that discretion has been exceeded. I cannot see that deference arises as a separate issue in need of doctrinal regimentation.[72]

The general grounds of review, moreover, offer little guidance in specific instances because they must be adapted, as appropriate, to a great variety of administrative contexts – many governed, in large part, by statutes that promote distinctive regulatory regimes. There was always some truth, at least, in the functionalist critique. What amounts to unfairness or unreasonableness, in their different forms, depends on all the

[69] TRS Allan, 'Human Rights and Judicial Review: A Critique of Due Deference' [2006] *CLJ* 671; TRS Allan, 'Judicial Deference and Judicial Review: Legal Doctrine and Legal Theory' (2011) 127 *LQR* 96.

[70] See Allan, *Constitutional Justice* (n 42) ch 6.

[71] Compare G Letsas, 'Rescuing Proportionality' in R Cruft, SM Liao and M Renzo (eds), *Philosophical Foundations of Human Rights* (Oxford, Oxford University Press, 2015) 316.

[72] For detailed analysis, see Allan, *Sovereignty of Law* (n 10) ch 7.

circumstances, which include the nature and purposes of the administrative jurisdiction in view. Even if, as Paul Daly contends, courts are not free, when deciding an issue of procedural fairness, to make an all-things-considered judgment on the facts, their moral judgment is fettered only in the sense that similar cases should be decided alike. But only by viewing the comparators in their wider constitutional context can we decide when a dissimilarity is significant. We need not be embarrassed to acknowledge that we can often do little more than observe that the requirements of natural justice depend on the nature of the public body, the kind of functions that it performs, and the statutory or non-statutory framework in which it operates.[73]

Daly's vigorous defence of legal doctrine rightly stresses its moral value as a necessary discipline in the context of judicial review. I readily acknowledge its role in sustaining the connection between legal and moral principle. The undoubted benefits of legal certainty and moral coherence, however, are not easily achieved. Doctrine must negotiate a path between constitutional principle, on the one hand, and the demands of a particular administrative regime, on the other. If doctrine is insufficiently sensitive to the varied pattern of administrative arrangements, it will give misleading direction in certain instances, the rules proving inapt in all the circumstances. English 'error of law' doctrine offers a telling example. It is not possible to distinguish between questions of law, on the one hand, and matters of fact and opinion, on the other, in a way that neatly tracks the different roles of court and public agency across a wide swathe of public functions. The standard view that so-called 'mistakes of law' are normally jurisdictional errors, subject to judicial correction, therefore belies the many instances in which certain questions of legal interpretation have for good reason been left in the hands of the public authority. The distinction between intra vires and ultra vires errors of law, then, simply reflects the division of authority considered appropriate in all the circumstances. The relevant doctrine serves merely to label a result reached on largely independent grounds.[74]

Matthew Lewans finds it hard to reconcile my insistence that a court must not abdicate its responsibility to determine the legality of an administrative decision with my acknowledgement that judges often have good reasons for accepting the reasonable determinations of law made by executive agencies. If, however, we cannot, in practice, draw any clear-cut distinction between general propositions of law and their application to specific instances of administrative action, we must grant that the proper distribution of interpretative authority will reflect a wide range of factors. The court does not defer to the relevant agency by withdrawal from the scene. It adopts the agency's reasoning and conclusions as its own just insofar as considerations of constitutional principle and specialist expertise permit or require. The various doctrinal distinctions that Lewans thinks I wrongly disparage are certainly helpful, at an abstract level, in articulating the nature and scope of judicial review. But their application to specific instances is

[73] Compare *Lloyd v McMahon* [1987] 1 AC 625, 702 (Lord Bridge). For a fine illustration of the application of general principle to a unique administrative context, see *R (Osborn) v Parole Board* [2013] UKSC 61, [2014] AC 1115.

[74] For further argument, see TRS Allan, 'Doctrine and Theory in Administrative Law: An Elusive Quest for the Limits of Jurisdiction' [2003] *PL* 429.

necessarily sensitive to context. They express, rather than direct, our judgments about how to identify the limits of administrative autonomy in all the circumstances.

My objective has been to show the limitations of doctrinal and conceptual approaches when detached from a broader interpretative inquiry. Scholarly discussion of the constitutional foundations of judicial review has been instructive. While the defenders of the ultra vires doctrine have been reluctant to concede, as they should, that an appeal to legislative 'intention' serves mainly to decorate judgments of legality made on other grounds, their opponents have been tempted to treat common law doctrine as largely self-contained, giving way only to explicit contrary statutory instruction. The debate has been impoverished by its divorce from the larger themes of democracy and legality, its animating purpose left obscure.[75] We can embrace ultra vires at a formal level, affirming the principle that statutory powers must be exercised within the limits of the jurisdiction conferred, while insisting at the same time that a finding of illegality or irrationality entails an application of common law principles to the specific administrative context. An ouster clause cannot confer immunity from judicial review in the case of ultra vires error because it is a principle of the rule of Law that executive bodies must act within the limits of their powers, limits that the court must define in the event of dispute. An ultra vires decision is in principle null and void, lacking any legal basis. In interpreting the statute to determine an agency's jurisdictional limits, however, we must have regard to common law principle, which identifies the pertinent grounds of review. When we move from conceptual to interpretative analysis, we can readily see that there is no more conflict between the ultra vires doctrine and common law principle than between legislative supremacy and the rule of Law. Administrative law doctrine, then, must be understood and applied as its wider constitutional framework indicates; and that framework in turn rests on a general theory of law or legality, applicable to every legal order that provides for the exercise of legitimate authority.

[75] See further TRS Allan, 'The Constitutional Foundations of Judicial Review: Conceptual Conundrum or Interpretative Inquiry?' [2002] *CLJ* 87; Allan, *Sovereignty of Law* (n 10) ch 6. While Adams acknowledges these points, he proposes an equally implausible severance of statutory from common law grounds of review: T Adams, 'Ultra Vires Revisited' [2018] *PL* 31. It is not possible, as he wishes, to separate matters of 'structure' from those of 'justification' (ibid 43): a persuasive account fuses these issues. See Allan, 'Constitutionalism at Common Law' (n 28) 243–45.

INDEX

www.ingramcontent.com/pod-product-compliance
Ingram Content Group UK Ltd.
Pitfield, Milton Keynes, MK11 3LW, UK
UKHW020232290926
15470UKWH00002B/486

9 781509 970957